CEDU 쎄듀는 A **C**omprehensive **E**nglish e**DU**cation(종합적 영어교육)의 약자입니다.

저자

김기훈　現 ㈜쎄듀 대표이사
　　　　現 메가스터디 영어영역 대표강사
　　　　前 서울특별시 교육청 외국어 교육정책자문위원회 위원
　　저서　천일문 / 천일문 Training Book / 천일문 GRAMMAR
　　　　어법끝 / 어휘끝 / 첫단추 / 쎈쓰업 / 파워업 / 빈칸백서 / 오답백서
　　　　쎄듀 본영어 / 문법의 골든룰 101 / ALL씀 서술형 / 수능실감
　　　　거침없이 Writing / Grammar Q / Reading Q / Listening Q 등

쎄듀 영어교육연구센터
쎄듀 영어교육센터는 영어 콘텐츠에 대한 전문지식과 경험을 바탕으로
최고의 교육 콘텐츠를 만들고자 최선의 노력을 다하는 전문가 집단입니다.

마케팅　　콘텐츠 마케팅 사업본부
영업　　　문병구
제작　　　정승호
디자인　　DOTS · 윤혜영
전산 편집　김미선
삽화　　　플러스툰
영문교열　엄태원

쎄듀 빠르게 중학영어듣기 모의고사 20회

3

Structure & Features
구성 및 특징

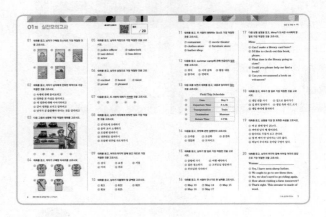

실전모의고사 20회

가장 최신의 출제 경향을 반영한 실전모의고사 20회를 수록했습니다. 〈시도교육청 주관 영어듣기능력평가〉에 비해 지문의 길이가 10~20% 길고, 난이도가 다소 높은 것이 특징입니다. 특히 18회~20회는 20~30% 정도 긴 지문과 높은 난이도의 문제들로 구성하여, 학생들이 고1 이상 수준의 듣기 문제를 경험할 수 있도록 했습니다.

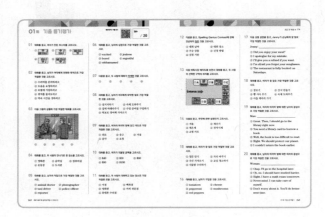

기출 듣기평가 5회

2013년부터 2015년까지 실시된 〈시도교육청 주관 영어듣기능력평가〉의 기출 문제를 총 5회분 수록했습니다. 시험 직전에 최종 점검을 하는 목적으로 문제를 풀어보시기 바랍니다.

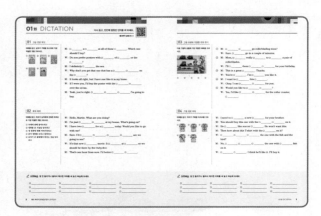

DICTATION

문제 풀이에 중요한 단서가 되는 명사, 동사, 형용사 등의 핵심 어휘와, 어휘 실력 향상에 도움이 되는 동사구, 전명구 등을 위주로 딕테이션 연습을 할 수 있도록 구성했습니다. 잘 안 들리거나 모르는 단어는 박스에 체크한 뒤 페이지 하단의 어휘복습 코너에 적어 놓고 복습하세요. 아울러, 문장과 문장 사이에 일정한 간격을 두어, 학생들이 단어를 직접 써볼 수 있도록 마련했습니다.

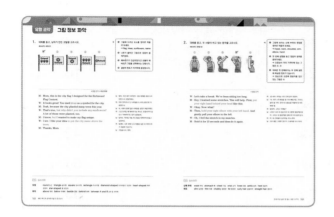

문제 유형 공략 및 필수 표현 익히기

〈시도교육청 주관 영어듣기능력평가〉 기출 문제를 면밀히 분석하여 총 18개의 유형으로 분류하고 문제 공략법을 소개했습니다. 또한 유형별 주요표현과 필수어휘 등도 함께 수록했으므로 시험을 보기 전에 꼭 확인해 보세요.

다양한 교사용 부가자료 및 학습 지원

쎄듀 홈페이지에 들어오시면 다양한 교사용 부가자료가 준비되어 있습니다.

- Q&A 게시판
- 본문 스크립트
- 본문 수록 어휘
- 모의고사 음원
- 딕테이션 음원
- 문항 단위 음원

Contents
목차

**실전모의고사
20회**

실전모의고사 1회   **6**

실전모의고사 2회   **18**

실전모의고사 3회   **30**

실전모의고사 4회   **42**

실전모의고사 5회   **54**

실전모의고사 6회   **66**

실전모의고사 7회   **78**

실전모의고사 8회   **90**

실전모의고사 9회   **102**

실전모의고사 10회   **114**

실전모의고사 11회   **126**

실전모의고사 12회   **138**

실전모의고사 13회   **150**

실전모의고사 14회   **162**

실전모의고사 15회   **174**

실전모의고사 16회   **186**

실전모의고사 17회   **198**

고난도 실전모의고사 18회   **210**

고난도 실전모의고사 19회   **226**

고난도 실전모의고사 20회   **244**

기출 듣기평가
5회

기출 듣기평가 1회	**262**
기출 듣기평가 2회	**274**
기출 듣기평가 3회	**286**
기출 듣기평가 4회	**298**
기출 듣기평가 5회	**310**

문제 유형
공략 및
필수 표현 익히기

그림 정보 파악	**322**
목적 파악	**324**
그림 상황에 적절한 대화 찾기	**326**
심정 추론	**327**
직업·관계 추론	**328**
장소 추론	**330**
의도 파악	**331**
부탁 파악	**332**
할 일 파악	**333**
숫자 정보 파악	**334**
특정 정보 파악	**335**
미언급 파악	**336**
도표·실용문 파악	**337**
속담 추론	**338**
화제 추론	**340**
어색한 대화 찾기	**341**
상황에 적절한 말 찾기	**342**
알맞은 응답 찾기	**343**

◀) MP3 실전 01

점수 / 20

01 대화를 듣고, 남자가 구매할 포스터로 가장 적절한 것을 고르시오.

02 대화를 듣고, 여자가 남자에게 전화한 목적으로 가장 적절한 것을 고르시오.

① 숙제에 관해 물어보려고
② 영화를 본 사실을 알리려고
③ 새 영화에 대해 이야기하려고
④ 같이 영화를 보자고 말하려고
⑤ 남자가 곧 출발해야 한다는 것을 알리려고

03 다음 그림의 상황에 가장 적절한 대화를 고르시오.

① ② ③ ④ ⑤

04 대화를 듣고, 여자가 구매할 티셔츠를 고르시오.

05 대화를 듣고, 남자의 직업으로 가장 적절한 것을 고르시오.

① police officer ② salesclerk
③ taxi driver ④ bus driver
⑤ actor

06 대화를 듣고, 남자의 심정으로 가장 적절한 것을 고르시오.

① excited ② bored ③ tired
④ proud ⑤ pleased

07 다음을 듣고, 두 사람의 대화가 <u>어색한</u> 것을 고르시오.

① ② ③ ④ ⑤

08 대화를 듣고, 남자가 여자에게 부탁한 일로 가장 적절한 것을 고르시오.

① 콘서트에 초대하기
② 음악 교사 소개하기
③ 트럼펫 빌려주기
④ 전화번호 알려주기
⑤ 트럼펫 연주법 가르쳐주기

09 대화를 듣고, 여자의 마지막 말에 담긴 의도로 가장 적절한 것을 고르시오.

① 감사 ② 요청 ③ 거절
④ 이의 ⑤ 위로

10 대화를 듣고, 남자가 지불해야 할 금액을 고르시오.

① $21 ② $22 ③ $23
④ $24 ⑤ $25

11 대화를 듣고, 두 사람이 대화하는 장소로 가장 적절한 곳을 고르시오.

① restaurant ② movie theater
③ clothing store ④ furniture store
⑤ barber shop

12 다음을 듣고, summer camp에 관해 언급되지 <u>않은</u> 것을 고르시오.

① 위치 ② 시작 날짜 ③ 활동 내용
④ 참가비 ⑤ 연락처

13 다음 표를 보면서 대화를 듣고, 내용과 일치하지 <u>않는</u> 것을 고르시오.

Field Trip Schedule

①	Date	May 9
②	Departure Time	8 A.M.
③	Transportation	Train
④	Destination	Museum
⑤	Return Time	6 P.M.

14 다음을 듣고, 무엇에 관한 설명인지 고르시오.

① 조각품 ② 초상화 ③ 풍경화
④ 정물화 ⑤ 모자이크

15 대화를 듣고, 남자가 할 일로 가장 적절한 것을 고르시오.

① 공항에 가기 ② 여행 예약하기
③ 집안 청소하기 ④ 조부모님 방문하기
⑤ 부모님과 식사하기

16 대화를 듣고, 두 사람이 만나기로 한 날짜를 고르시오.

① May 13 ② May 14 ③ May 15
④ May 16 ⑤ May 17

17 다음 상황 설명을 듣고, Mina가 도서관 사서에게 할 말로 가장 적절한 것을 고르시오.

Mina: _____

① Can I make a library card here?
② I'd like to check out this book, please.
③ What time is the library going to close?
④ Could you please help me find a book?
⑤ Can you recommend a book on volcanoes?

18 대화를 듣고, 여자가 할 일로 가장 적절한 것을 고르시오.

① 생일 선물 사기 ② 집으로 돌아가기
③ 집 위치 알려주기 ④ 생일 축하 카드 쓰기
⑤ 생일 파티에 참석하기

19 대화를 듣고, 상황을 가장 잘 표현한 속담을 고르시오.

① 비 온 뒤에 땅이 굳는다.
② 까마귀 날자 배 떨어진다.
③ 돌다리도 두들겨 보고 건너라.
④ 열 번 찍어 안 넘어가는 나무 없다.
⑤ 하늘이 무너져도 솟아날 구멍이 있다.

20 대화를 듣고, 남자의 마지막 말에 이어질 여자의 응답으로 가장 적절한 것을 고르시오.

Woman: _____

① Yes, I have seen sheep before.
② We ought to go to see them then.
③ No, we don't need to go riding again.
④ How about visiting a farm tomorrow?
⑤ That's right. This sweater is made of wool.

01회 DICTATION

01 그림 정보 파악

대화를 듣고, 남자가 구매할 포스터로 가장
적절한 것을 고르시오.

① ② ③ ④ ⑤

M : □ _____ a □ _____ at all of these □ _____. Which one
should I buy?

W : Do you prefer posters with □ _____ of □ _____ or the
□ _____?

M : I definitely □ _____ the sea.

W : Why don't you get that one that has a □ _____ □ _____ on
the □ _____?

M : It looks all right, but I have one like it in my home.

W : If I were you, I'd buy the poster with the □ _____ □ _____
over the ocean.

M : Yeah, you're right. □ _____ □ _____ □ _____ I'm going to
buy.

02 목적 파악

대화를 듣고, 여자가 남자에게 전화한 목적으
로 가장 적절한 것을 고르시오.

① 숙제에 관해 물어보려고
② 영화를 본 사실을 알리려고
③ 새 영화에 대해 이야기하려고
④ 같이 영화를 보자고 말하려고
⑤ 남자가 곧 출발해야 한다는 것을 알리
   려고

W : Hello, Martin. What are you doing?

M : I'm just □ _____ □ _____ at my house. What's going on?

W : I have two □ _____ for a □ _____ today. Would you like to go
with me?

M : Sure. I'd □ _____ □ _____. □ _____ □ _____ are we
going to see?

W : It's that new □ _____ movie. It □ _____ at □ _____, so we
should be there by five forty-five.

M : That's one hour from now. I'd better □ _____ □ _____.

✎ **어휘복습** 잘 안 들리거나 몰라서 체크한 어휘를 써 놓고 복습해 보세요.

□ _____   □ _____   □ _____   □ _____

□ _____   □ _____   □ _____   □ _____

□ _____   □ _____   □ _____   □ _____

다음 그림의 상황에 가장 적절한 대화를 고르시오.

① ② ③ ④ ⑤

① M : □ _____ □ _____ go rollerblading soon?

　 W : Sure. □ _____ go in a couple of minutes.

② M : Mom, □ _____ really □ _____ to □ _____ a pair of
　　　 rollerblades.

　 W : I'll □ _____ them □ _____ □ _____ for your birthday.

③ M : This is a great □ _____. Thanks.

　 W : You're □ _____. I'm □ _____ you like it.

④ M : I want to □ _____ this □ _____.

　 W : Okay. I can □ _____ □ _____ for you.

⑤ M : Would you like to □ _____ □ _____?

　 W : Yes, I'd like □ _____ □ _____ for the roller coaster,
　　　 □ _____.

대화를 듣고, 여자가 구매할 티셔츠를 고르시오.

① 　② 　③

④ 　⑤

W : I need to □ _____ a new □ _____ for your brother.

M : You should buy this one with the □ _____ □ _____ on it.

W : He □ _____ like soccer □ _____. He won't want this.

M : Then how about this T-shirt with the □ _____ on it?

W : □ _____ □ _____ □ _____ the one with the fish and the
　　 bird?

M : No, □ _____ □ _____ □ _____ the one with □ _____ fish
　　 on it.

W : □ _____ □ _____. I think he'll like it. I'll buy it.

✎ 어휘복습 잘 안 들리거나 몰라서 체크한 어휘를 써 놓고 복습해 보세요.

□ _____　□ _____　□ _____　□ _____

□ _____　□ _____　□ _____　□ _____

□ _____　□ _____　□ _____　□ _____

05 직업 추론

대화를 듣고, 남자의 직업으로 가장 적절한 것을 고르시오.

① police officer ② salesclerk
③ taxi driver ④ bus driver
⑤ actor

W : Good afternoon.

M : Hello. □ _____ are you □ _____ today?

W : Can you □ _____ □ _____ to the Greenville □ _____ □ _____?

M : Sure, but □ _____ is really □ _____ right now. It might □ _____ a □ _____.

W : □ _____ □ _____ will it take?

M : About forty minutes. Or I can □ _____ a □ _____, which will probably take only thirty minutes.

W : Take the shortcut, please. I need to get to the □ _____ □ _____ there □ _____.

06 심정 추론

대화를 듣고, 남자의 심정으로 가장 적절한 것을 고르시오.

① excited ② bored
③ tired ④ proud
⑤ pleased

W : Minsu, □ _____ are you □ _____ out here in the sun?

M : I'm □ _____ □ _____ □ _____ in the park.

W : I thought you came here for a □ _____. □ _____ are you □ _____ here?

M : I'm doing □ _____ □ _____. So many people come here and just □ _____ their □ _____ on the □ _____.

W : It's □ _____ that you're □ _____ □ _____. Can I help you?

M : That would be great. It's nice to □ _____ that □ _____ □ _____, too.

✏ **어휘복습** 잘 안 들리거나 몰라서 체크한 어휘를 써 놓고 복습해 보세요.

□ _____ □ _____ □ _____ □ _____

□ _____ □ _____ □ _____ □ _____

□ _____ □ _____ □ _____ □ _____

07 어색한 대화 찾기

다음을 듣고, 두 사람의 대화가 <u>어색한</u> 것을 고르시오.

①   ②   ③   ④   ⑤

① W : □ _____ □ _____ is this book?

    M : It □ _____ ten dollars and fifty cents.

② W : Are we going the □ _____ □ _____?

    M : I think so. I just □ _____ the map.

③ W : □ _____ were you □ _____ □ _____ the meeting today?

    M : I □ _____ □ _____ him yet.

④ W : □ _____ □ _____ take the train or the bus?

    M : □ _____ of them is fine with me.

⑤ W : There's something □ _____ □ _____ my tooth.

    M : □ _____ □ _____ visit the dentist then.

08 부탁 파악

대화를 듣고, 남자가 여자에게 부탁한 일로 가장 적절한 것을 고르시오.

① 콘서트에 초대하기
② 음악 교사 소개하기
③ 트럼펫 빌려주기
④ 전화번호 알려주기
⑤ 트럼펫 연주법 가르쳐주기

M : Tina, how do you enjoy □ _____ in the school □ _____?

W : It's a lot of □ _____. We're □ _____ our first □ _____ soon.

M : That's good to hear. I'll □ _____ □ _____.

W : Why don't you □ _____ the band? I know you love music.

M : I do, but I can't □ _____ an □ _____.

W : You should learn the □ _____. I know a really good teacher.

M : Can you □ _____ him to me?

W : Sure. I'll give him your □ _____ □ _____ today.

✎ **어휘복습** 잘 안 들리거나 몰라서 체크한 어휘를 써 놓고 복습해 보세요.

□ _____   □ _____   □ _____   □ _____

□ _____   □ _____   □ _____   □ _____

□ _____   □ _____   □ _____   □ _____

09 의도 파악

대화를 듣고, 여자의 마지막 말에 담긴 의도로 가장 적절한 것을 고르시오.

① 감사   ② 요청   ③ 거절
④ 이의   ⑤ 위로

W : Did you go to the □ _____ last □ _____?
M : I did. My parents, sister, and I all went.
W : □ _____ the □ _____ my □ _____. We went there on Friday night.
M : We □ _____ a really □ _____ □ _____. How about you?
W : □ _____, I □ _____ the □ _____. I felt □ _____ for the □ _____.

10 숫자 정보 파악

대화를 듣고, 남자가 지불해야 할 금액을 고르시오.

① $21   ② $22   ③ $23
④ $24   ⑤ $25

W : Good evening. How may I help you?
M : I'd like to get □ _____ □ _____ for □ _____ to the □ _____.
W : Tickets cost □ _____ dollars for □ _____ and □ _____ dollars for □ _____.
M : Okay. I'll take □ _____ tickets for adults and □ _____ for a child.
W : If you have a □ _____ □ _____, you can □ _____ one dollar on □ _____ ticket.
M : Excellent. Here's my card.

✎ **어휘복습** 잘 안 들리거나 몰라서 체크한 어휘를 써 놓고 복습해 보세요.

□ _____   □ _____   □ _____   □ _____
□ _____   □ _____   □ _____   □ _____
□ _____   □ _____   □ _____   □ _____

대화를 듣고, 두 사람이 대화하는 장소로 가장 적절한 곳을 고르시오.

① restaurant ② movie theater
③ clothing store ④ furniture store
⑤ barber shop

M : Good afternoon. I'm here for my four o'clock □ _____.
W : Hello, Mr. Stephens. □ _____ a □ _____ in this chair, please.
M : Thank you very much.
W : □ _____ would you like your □ _____ □ _____ this time?
M : Just □ _____ a little off the □ _____ and the □ _____.
   Please do it like you did the □ _____ □ _____.
W : That won't be a problem.
M : If it's possible, could you work quickly, please? I have dinner
   □ _____ at five.

다음을 듣고, summer camp에 관해 언급되지 않은 것을 고르시오.

① 위치 ② 시작 날짜
③ 활동 내용 ④ 참가비
⑤ 연락처

M : This summer, □ _____ □ _____ sending your children to
   □ _____ □ _____ ? □ _____ Bear Lake, children
   □ _____ eight to fifteen can spend two weeks at the
   □ _____. Each day, they'll □ _____ □ _____ such as
   swimming, sports, hiking, and horseback riding. We'll
   □ _____ food and cabins □ _____ them. The □ _____
   is only five hundred dollars per student. □ _____ four oh four,
   six seven four eight □ _____ □ _____ □ _____.

✎ **어휘복습** 잘 안 들리거나 몰라서 체크한 어휘를 써 놓고 복습해 보세요.

□ _____ □ _____ □ _____ □ _____
□ _____ □ _____ □ _____ □ _____
□ _____ □ _____ □ _____ □ _____

13 도표·실용문 파악

다음 표를 보면서 대화를 듣고, 내용과 일치하지 <u>않는</u> 것을 고르시오.

Field Trip Schedule

	Date	May 9
①	Date	May 9
②	Departure Time	8 A.M.
③	Transportation	Train
④	Destination	Museum
⑤	Return Time	6 P.M.

W : George, □ _____ are we going on our class □ _____ □ _____ to the □ _____? Is it May tenth?

M : No, we're going on □ _____, □ _____ □ _____.

W : Oh, that's right. Are we □ _____ the □ _____ or a □ _____?

M : The bus will □ _____ □ _____ school at □ _____ in the morning.

W : And □ _____ will we □ _____ □ _____?

M : We'll be there the □ _____ day. So we'll □ _____ back at school □ _____ □ _____.

W : I □ _____ □ _____ until we leave. We're going to have lots of fun.

14 화제 추론

다음을 듣고, 무엇에 관한 설명인지 고르시오.

① 조각품
② 초상화
③ 풍경화
④ 정물화
⑤ 모자이크

W : This is a special type of □ _____ that □ _____ □ _____ the □ _____ of a person. To make it, an □ _____ has a person visit his studio. Then, the □ _____ □ _____ a certain □ _____ and remains in that pose for a long time. □ _____ the person is □ _____, the artist □ _____ a □ _____ of that person.

✏ **어휘복습** 잘 안 들리거나 몰라서 체크한 어휘를 써 놓고 복습해 보세요.

□ _____ □ _____ □ _____ □ _____

□ _____ □ _____ □ _____ □ _____

□ _____ □ _____ □ _____ □ _____

15 할 일 파악

대화를 듣고, 남자가 할 일로 가장 적절한 것을 고르시오.

① 공항에 가기
② 여행 예약하기
③ 집안 청소하기
④ 조부모님 방문하기
⑤ 부모님과 식사하기

W : You look excited, Ted. What's going on?
M : My dad told me my □ _____ are □ _____ tonight.
W : That's great. You haven't seen them □ _____ a □ _____, have you?
M : It's been two years since they visited. We're □ _____ to the □ _____ to □ _____ them □ _____ in an hour.
W : □ _____ □ _____ will they □ _____ here?
M : They'll stay with us for □ _____ □ _____.

16 특정 정보 파악

대화를 듣고, 두 사람이 만나기로 한 날짜를 고르시오.

① May 13　　② May 14
③ May 15　　④ May 16
⑤ May 17

M : Julie, we need to □ _____ □ _____ to □ _____ our summer □ _____ to Europe.
W : You're right. □ _____ do you □ _____ □ _____? How about □ _____ □ _____?
M : □ _____, but I have □ _____ □ _____ on that day. But May □ _____ is □ _____ for me.
W : Hmm... □ _____ □ _____ my □ _____, I have a math club meeting □ _____ □ _____ □ _____.
M : □ _____ □ _____ the day after that? The □ _____?
W : I believe that I have time on that day. □ _____ □ _____ at □ _____ o'clock then.
M : Great. See you then.

✎ **어휘복습** 잘 안 들리거나 몰라서 체크한 어휘를 써 놓고 복습해 보세요.

□ _____　　□ _____　　□ _____　　□ _____
□ _____　　□ _____　　□ _____　　□ _____
□ _____　　□ _____　　□ _____　　□ _____

17 상황에 적절한 말 찾기

다음 상황 설명을 듣고, Mina가 도서관 사서에게 할 말로 가장 적절한 것을 고르시오.

Mina: _____

① Can I make a library card here?
② I'd like to check out this book, please.
③ What time is the library going to close?
④ Could you please help me find a book?
⑤ Can you recommend a book on volcanoes?

W : Mina went to the public □ _____ to find a book for her □ _____ □ _____. She □ _____ □ _____ some □ _____ on □ _____ on the computer. There was one □ _____, so she went to the □ _____. □ _____, she couldn't find the book anywhere. She decided to □ _____ the □ _____ about this □ _____. In this situation, what would Mina most likely say to the librarian?

Mina: _____

18 할 일 파악

대화를 듣고, 여자가 할 일로 가장 적절한 것을 고르시오.

① 생일 선물 사기
② 집으로 돌아가기
③ 집 위치 알려주기
④ 생일 축하 카드 쓰기
⑤ 생일 파티에 참석하기

M : I can't wait to go to Brian's birthday party.
W : Oh, no. I □ _____ □ _____ about his □ _____.
M : Did you buy a □ _____ for him?
W : Yes, I got a card and a present, but □ _____ at my □ _____. I'll have to □ _____ □ _____ □ _____.
M : Do you know where Brian's house is?
W : Yes, I do. He □ _____ a couple of blocks □ _____ from me.

✏️ 어휘복습 잘 안 들리거나 몰라서 체크한 어휘를 써 놓고 복습해 보세요.

□ _____   □ _____   □ _____   □ _____
□ _____   □ _____   □ _____   □ _____
□ _____   □ _____   □ _____   □ _____

16 쎄듀 빠르게 중학영어듣기 모의고사

19 속담 추론

대화를 듣고, 상황을 가장 잘 표현한 속담을 고르시오.

① 비 온 뒤에 땅이 굳는다.
② 까마귀 날자 배 떨어진다.
③ 돌다리도 두들겨 보고 건너라.
④ 열 번 찍어 안 넘어가는 나무 없다.
⑤ 하늘이 무너져도 솟아날 구멍이 있다.

M : There are so many things to □ _____ □ _____ at this
   □ _____. What are you going to buy?
W : I'm definitely going to get that □ _____ with the □ _____
   □ _____ on it.
M : Do you know □ _____ □ _____ it?
W : It □ _____ □ _____. I love how pretty it looks.
M : But it has □ _____ in it, and you're □ _____ □ _____ them.
W : Oh, right. Thanks for telling me that. I □ _____ □ _____ buy
   □ _____ □ _____.

20 알맞은 응답 찾기

대화를 듣고, 남자의 마지막 말에 이어질 여자의 응답으로 가장 적절한 것을 고르시오.

Woman: _____

① Yes, I have seen sheep before.
② We ought to go to see them then.
③ No, we don't need to go riding again.
④ How about visiting a farm tomorrow?
⑤ That's right. This sweater is made of wool.

W : □ _____ □ _____ taking me to your uncle's □ _____.
   I'm having a good time here.
M : I'm glad to hear that you're □ _____ □ _____.
W : I was □ _____ that I would □ _____ being □ _____
   □ _____.
M : But you liked □ _____ the □ _____, didn't you?
W : I sure did. That was so much fun.
M : My uncle also has some □ _____ in the □ _____.
W : _____

✎ **어휘복습** 잘 안 들리거나 몰라서 체크한 어휘를 써 놓고 복습해 보세요.

□ _____ □ _____ □ _____ □ _____
□ _____ □ _____ □ _____ □ _____
□ _____ □ _____ □ _____

01 대화를 듣고, 여자가 내일 입을 셔츠를 고르시오.

① ② ③ ④ ⑤

02 대화를 듣고, 남자가 옷 가게를 방문한 목적으로 가장 적절한 것을 고르시오.

① 양말을 사려고
② 환불을 요청하려고
③ 불만을 접수하려고
④ 상품을 교환하려고
⑤ 사은품을 문의하려고

03 다음 그림의 상황에 가장 적절한 대화를 고르시오.

① ② ③ ④ ⑤

04 대화를 듣고, 여자가 구매할 여행 가방을 고르시오.

① ② ③ ④ ⑤

05 대화를 듣고, 남자의 직업으로 가장 적절한 것을 고르시오.

① firefighter　　② tour guide
③ police officer　④ store manager
⑤ lawyer

06 대화를 듣고, 여자의 심정으로 가장 적절한 것을 고르시오.

① depressed　　② angry
③ satisfied　　④ excited
⑤ regretful

07 다음을 듣고, 두 사람의 대화가 어색한 것을 고르시오.

① ② ③ ④ ⑤

08 대화를 듣고, 남자가 여자에게 부탁한 일로 가장 적절한 것을 고르시오.

① 오류 수정하기　② 원고 작성하기
③ 정보 검색하기　④ 대신 발표하기
⑤ 보고서 출력하기

09 대화를 듣고, 남자의 마지막 말에 담긴 의도로 가장 적절한 것을 고르시오.

① 격려　　② 꾸중　　③ 초대
④ 제안　　⑤ 감사

10 대화를 듣고, 여자가 지불할 금액을 고르시오.

① $25　　② $45　　③ $50
④ $55　　⑤ $100

11 대화를 듣고, 두 사람이 대화하고 있는 장소로 가장 적절한 곳을 고르시오.

① used-car market
② car rental
③ car dealership
④ car repair shop
⑤ driver's education classroom

12 다음을 듣고, Sam's Sports Center에 관해 언급 되지 <u>않은</u> 것을 고르시오.

① 개관 연도   ② 이용 시간
③ 프로그램 종류   ④ 이용 요금
⑤ 회원 가입 방법

13 다음 지도를 보면서 대화를 듣고, 두 사람이 있는 곳 을 고르시오.

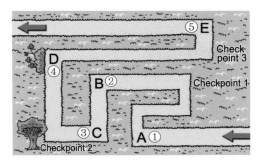

14 다음을 듣고, 무엇에 관한 설명인지 고르시오.

① 피아노   ② 가야금
③ 트럼펫   ④ 플루트
⑤ 바이올린

15 대화를 듣고, 남자가 대화 직후에 할 일로 가장 적절 한 것을 고르시오.

① 저녁 먹기   ② 숙제 끝내기
③ 방 청소하기   ④ 집안일 돕기
⑤ TV 프로그램 보기

16 대화를 듣고, 두 사람이 모이기로 한 날짜를 고르시 오.

① 5월 14일   ② 5월 15일   ③ 5월 16일
④ 5월 23일   ⑤ 5월 24일

17 다음 상황 설명을 듣고, 엄마가 Peter에게 할 말로 가장 적절한 것을 고르시오.

Mother: _____

① I'm sorry I didn't call you.
② Is basketball your favorite sport?
③ How long was the basketball game?
④ It's okay. You will win the next game.
⑤ Where have you been? I was worried about you!

18 대화를 듣고, 여자가 할 일로 가장 적절한 것을 고르 시오.

① 직원 보내기
② 컴퓨터 다시 켜기
③ 비밀번호 알려주기
④ 바이러스 검사하기
⑤ 서비스 센터 방문하기

19 대화를 듣고, 상황을 가장 잘 표현한 속담을 고르시오.

① 그 아버지에 그 아들이다.
② 남의 떡이 더 커 보인다.
③ 자꾸 연습하면 아주 잘하게 된다.
④ 닭 쫓던 개 지붕 쳐다보듯 한다.
⑤ 사공이 많으면 배가 산으로 간다.

20 대화를 듣고, 여자의 마지막 말에 대한 남자의 응답으 로 가장 적절한 것을 고르시오.

Man: _____

① Awesome! I want to buy a Gold pass.
② How long are the lines for the rides?
③ The restaurant is far from here.
④ How do I get to the amusement park?
⑤ I want to get a refund on my ticket.

◀》 **MP3 실전 02-1**

01 그림 정보 파악

대화를 듣고, 여자가 내일 입을 셔츠를 고르시오.

① ② ③
④ ⑤

M : Jane, what are you doing in your room?
W : I'm looking for a □ _____ □ _____ □ _____ tomorrow.
M : I see. □ _____ □ _____ this shirt with the heart and star?
W : It's okay, but I want to wear □ _____ □ _____.
M : Okay. Well, □ _____ one with a heart and a ribbon. Do you want to wear this one?
W : Not really. I think I like this one □ _____ a □ _____ □ _____ a □ _____.
M : I agree, this shirt □ _____ very □ _____ □ _____ you.
W : Okay, then I'll □ _____ □ _____ this one.

02 목적 파악

대화를 듣고, 남자가 옷 가게를 방문한 목적으로 가장 적절한 것을 고르시오.

① 양말을 사려고
② 환불을 요청하려고
③ 불만을 접수하려고
④ 상품을 교환하려고
⑤ 사은품을 문의하려고

W : How may I help you?
M : I □ _____ this □ _____ yesterday, but it □ _____ □ _____ me.
W : Would you like to □ _____ it for a different □ _____?
M : No, I would like to □ _____ a □ _____.
W : Okay, but you can get a □ _____ □ _____ of □ _____ if you buy one of our new summer shirts.
M : No, thank you.

✎ **어휘복습** 잘 안 들리거나 몰라서 체크한 어휘를 써 놓고 복습해 보세요.

□ _____ □ _____ □ _____ □ _____
□ _____ □ _____ □ _____ □ _____
□ _____ □ _____ □ _____ □ _____

03 그림 상황에 적절한 대화 찾기

다음 그림의 상황에 가장 적절한 대화를 고르시오.

① ② ③ ④ ⑤

① W : Dad, I'm hungry. What are we eating □ _____ □ _____ ?

M : I'm going to □ _____ spaghetti and garlic bread.

② W : Sir, this □ _____ □ _____ I □ _____ .

M : I'm so sorry. I will □ _____ it for you right away.

③ W : What dish would you □ _____ ?

M : The vegetable soup, lobster, and beef spaghetti are tonight's □ _____ .

④ W : James, have you □ _____ the dinner □ _____ ?

M : Yes. Now I'm washing the dishes.

⑤ W : Sir, do you know □ _____ restaurant □ _____ pasta?

M : Yes, □ _____ the □ _____ Italian restaurants in this building.

04 그림 정보 파악

대화를 듣고, 여자가 구매할 여행 가방을 고르시오.

①   ②   ③

④   ⑤

M : How may I help you?

W : I'm looking for a □ _____ to □ _____ on my □ _____ .

M : Let's see. How about this □ _____ , □ _____ one? It is one of our □ _____ □ _____ .

W : It's alright, but I would like something that is □ _____ to □ _____ .

M : Well, that small □ _____ one with a □ _____ and pockets is □ _____ and □ _____ .

W : How much is it? I don't want to □ _____ too much □ _____ on a suitcase.

M : It's □ _____ □ _____ for a hundred and forty dollars.

W : Okay, that one is perfect.

✎ **어휘복습** 잘 안 들리거나 몰라서 체크한 어휘를 써 놓고 복습해 보세요.

□ _____ □ _____ □ _____ □ _____

□ _____ □ _____ □ _____ □ _____

□ _____ □ _____ □ _____ □ _____

05 직업 추론

대화를 듣고, 남자의 직업으로 가장 적절한 것을 고르시오.

① firefighter
② tour guide
③ police officer
④ store manager
⑤ lawyer

M : What can I help you with, ma'am?

W : I've □ _____ my □ _____. I think someone □ _____ it. Please help me!

M : When and where did you □ _____ it?

W : In the □ _____ □ _____ not far □ _____ this □ _____ □ _____, about an hour ago.

M : What does it □ _____ □ _____?

W : It is square, red, and has a golden lock on it.

M : Okay, we will □ _____ □ _____ □ _____ it right away. Please □ _____ □ _____ your name and phone number.

W : Here you go. Please call me □ _____ □ _____ □ _____ you find it.

06 심정 추론

대화를 듣고, 여자의 심정으로 가장 적절한 것을 고르시오.

① depressed
② angry
③ satisfied
④ excited
⑤ regretful

M : Hey, your computer looks nice!

W : Thanks. I liked it □ _____ □ _____, □ _____ now I'm □ _____ □ _____ the color.

M : Then why don't you go to the store and □ _____ it?

W : I can't. I've □ _____ □ _____ it for over a month.

M : Oh, then I guess you just have to keep using it.

W : Yeah, I □ _____ I □ _____ just □ _____ the pink one.

✎ **어휘복습** 잘 안 들리거나 몰라서 체크한 어휘를 써 놓고 복습해 보세요.

□ _____   □ _____   □ _____   □ _____

□ _____   □ _____   □ _____   □ _____

□ _____   □ _____   □ _____   □ _____

다음을 듣고, 두 사람의 대화가 <u>어색한</u> 것을 고르시오.

①   ②   ③   ④   ⑤

① M : How do I □ _____ □ _____ the city police station?

   W : Go straight for three blocks, and you will see it □ _____ the □ _____.

② M : May I help you?

   W : Yes, I would like to □ _____ two □ _____ for tonight's show.

③ M : Hey, can I □ _____ a □ _____ for today's class?

   W : □ _____, here you go.

④ M : □ _____ □ _____ any good Chinese restaurants □ _____ □ _____?

   W : Yeah, I really like Chinese food, too.

⑤ M : What are you doing □ _____?

   W : I'm going to watch a movie.

대화를 듣고, 남자가 여자에게 부탁한 일로 가장 적절한 것을 고르시오.

① 오류 수정하기
② 원고 작성하기
③ 정보 검색하기
④ 대신 발표하기
⑤ 보고서 출력하기

W : Hey, John. What are you up to?

M : I'm □ _____ □ _____ a group presentation.

W : □ _____ is it □ _____?

M : It's about □ _____ □ _____.

W : That sounds interesting. Do you need any help?

M : Well, I wrote a □ _____, but I don't think I □ _____ it □ _____. Can you read it and □ _____ any □ _____?

W : Sure, I can do that. □ _____ do you need it □ _____?

M : I need it □ _____ the □ _____ □ _____ this week. Thank you so much!

✎ **어휘복습** 잘 안 들리거나 몰라서 체크한 어휘를 써 놓고 복습해 보세요.

□ _____   □ _____   □ _____   □ _____

□ _____   □ _____   □ _____   □ _____

□ _____   □ _____   □ _____   □ _____

09 의도 파악

대화를 듣고, 남자의 마지막 말에 담긴 의도로 가장 적절한 것을 고르시오.

① 격려　　② 꾸중　　③ 초대
④ 제안　　⑤ 감사

M : Ms. Stanley, I □ _____ my art □ _____ last night!

W : Wow, I'm very □ _____ □ _____ you, Jason! Your hard work □ _____ □ _____.

M : I □ _____ have been able to finish it □ _____ your □ _____.

W : I appreciate your saying that. I know how much □ _____ you □ _____ □ _____ this project.

M : I'm very □ _____ with it.

W : That's great! □ _____ □ _____ on your next project.

M : I can □ _____ □ _____ you □ _____ for all you have done for me.

10 숫자 정보 파악

대화를 듣고, 여자가 지불할 금액을 고르시오.

① $25　　② $45　　③ $50
④ $55　　⑤ $100

W : □ _____ □ _____ is this yellow bag?

M : It's one of our □ _____ □ _____, so it's fifty dollars.

W : That is too □ _____.

M : Hmm… Then how about this red one? It's only □ _____ dollars.

W : It looks nice. Do you have the □ _____ □ _____ in purple?

M : Yes. If you buy two bags in this design, you □ _____ a □ _____ - dollar □ _____ on the □ _____ price.

W : That's great! Then I'll take □ _____ □ _____ □ _____ and one in purple.

M : Okay.

✏ **어휘복습** 잘 안 들리거나 몰라서 체크한 어휘를 써 놓고 복습해 보세요.

□ _____　　□ _____　　□ _____　　□ _____

□ _____　　□ _____　　□ _____　　□ _____

□ _____　　□ _____　　□ _____　　□ _____

11 장소 추론

대화를 듣고, 두 사람이 대화하고 있는 장소로 가장 적절한 곳을 고르시오.

① used-car market
② car rental
③ car dealership
④ car repair shop
⑤ driver's education classroom

M : How can I help you?

W : My □ _____ horn □ _____ □ _____ . There must be □ _____ □ _____ with it.

M : Okay. Have you had this □ _____ □ _____ ?

W : No, this is the □ _____ □ _____ .

M : Please □ _____ □ _____ this □ _____ and we will try to help you.

W : Okay. □ _____ □ _____ will it take?

M : Probably about an hour □ _____ □ _____ . You can wait here or come back at three P.M.

12 미언급 파악

다음을 듣고, Sam's Sports Center에 관해 언급되지 <u>않은</u> 것을 고르시오.

① 개관 연도
② 이용 시간
③ 프로그램 종류
④ 이용 요금
⑤ 회원 가입 방법

M : Sam's Sports Center, which □ _____ □ _____ October two thousand ten, is now the biggest fitness complex in the city. It is □ _____ □ _____ nine A.M. to eleven P.M. Monday □ _____ Friday, and ten A.M. to eight P.M. on Saturday and Sunday. We □ _____ a □ _____ of sports □ _____ , such as swimming, aerobics, basketball, yoga, and golf for fifty dollars □ _____ □ _____ . Come and have a great time!

✎ **어휘복습** 잘 안 들리거나 몰라서 체크한 어휘를 써 놓고 복습해 보세요.

□ _____   □ _____   □ _____   □ _____

□ _____   □ _____   □ _____   □ _____

□ _____   □ _____   □ _____   □ _____

13 그림 정보 파악

다음 지도를 보면서 대화를 듣고, 두 사람이 있는 곳을 고르시오.

M : How long has it been since we □ _____ this □ _____? It feels like we've been here all day.

W : I really want to □ _____ □ _____ □ _____ here. Let's look at the map to □ _____ □ _____ □ _____ we are.

M : Okay. I'm sure we □ _____ the □ _____ checkpoint a little while ago.

W : How about the □ _____ □ _____?

M : We passed that tree a few minutes ago. So, we need to □ _____ □ _____ □ _____ here, in □ _____ of the flowers.

W : Are you sure? I don't want to □ _____ □ _____ in here.

M : Trust me! After we take a right, we will see the □ _____ checkpoint.

14 화제 추론

다음을 듣고, 무엇에 관한 설명인지 고르시오.

① 피아노　　② 가야금
③ 트럼펫　　④ 플루트
⑤ 바이올린

W : This is a □ _____ □ _____ that people play. It has □ _____ □ _____, and it is normally □ _____ □ _____ □ _____. You □ _____ this instrument □ _____ your □ _____ and play it with a bow. The □ _____ makes music when it □ _____ the strings. People who play this instrument are normally part of an orchestra.

✎ **어휘복습** 잘 안 들리거나 몰라서 체크한 어휘를 써 놓고 복습해 보세요.

□ _____　　□ _____　　□ _____　　□ _____

□ _____　　□ _____　　□ _____　　□ _____

□ _____　　□ _____　　□ _____　　□ _____

15 할 일 파악

대화를 듣고, 남자가 대화 직후에 할 일로 가장 적절한 것을 고르시오.

① 저녁 먹기
② 숙제 끝내기
③ 방 청소하기
④ 집안일 돕기
⑤ TV 프로그램 보기

W : Nick, are you watching TV again?

M : Mom, I will go to my room □ _____ this □ _____ is □ _____.

W : Did you □ _____ your □ _____? You told me you had a lot to □ _____ □ _____.

M : No, I was going to □ _____ it □ _____ with my friend.

W : Well, I think you □ _____ □ _____ your □ _____ □ _____. □ _____ you can watch TV.

M : The show will be over □ _____ □ _____ □ _____ I finish, □ _____ okay.

16 특정 정보 파악

대화를 듣고, 두 사람이 모이기로 한 날짜를 고르시오.

① 5월 14일　　② 5월 15일
③ 5월 16일　　④ 5월 23일
⑤ 5월 24일

M : Helen, the school club □ _____ □ _____ on May twenty third.

W : Yes, I know. We need to □ _____ a □ _____ this week to □ _____ for it.

M : That sounds good. How about May □ _____?

W : □ _____, I have math □ _____ that day.

M : Okay, then why don't we go on May □ _____?

W : I think □ _____ □ _____ □ _____. Let's meet early so we can □ _____ the topic □ _____ □ _____.

M : Okay. I will see you then.

✎ **어휘복습** 잘 안 들리거나 몰라서 체크한 어휘를 써 놓고 복습해 보세요.

□ _____　　□ _____　　□ _____　　□ _____

□ _____　　□ _____　　□ _____　　□ _____

□ _____　　□ _____　　□ _____　　□ _____

17 상황에 적절한 말 찾기

다음 상황 설명을 듣고, 엄마가 Peter에게 할 말로 가장 적절한 것을 고르시오.

Mother: _____

① I'm sorry I didn't call you.
② Is basketball your favorite sport?
③ How long was the basketball game?
④ It's okay. You will win the next game.
⑤ Where have you been? I was worried about you!

W : Peter usually comes home □ _____ three P.M. Today, Peter and his friends □ _____ a basketball game □ _____ □ _____. His team □ _____, and the game finished around six P.M, which was □ _____ □ _____ he □ _____. Peter didn't call his mother to tell her he □ _____ □ _____ □ _____ and he □ _____ □ _____ □ _____ her phone calls □ _____. She got very □ _____. What would Peter's mother most likely say to Peter when he comes home?

Mother: _____

18 할 일 파악

대화를 듣고, 여자가 할 일로 가장 적절한 것을 고르시오.

① 직원 보내기
② 컴퓨터 다시 켜기
③ 비밀번호 알려주기
④ 바이러스 검사하기
⑤ 서비스 센터 방문하기

W : Hello, what can I do for you?
M : I'm □ _____ because I can't □ _____ □ _____ my online game □ _____.
W : Did you check your □ _____ and password?
M : Yes. I checked it □ _____. An error keeps □ _____ □ _____.
W : Hmm… Have you checked your □ _____ □ _____?
M : Yes, I have. But, it's still □ _____ □ _____.
W : Okay. I will □ _____ □ _____ to □ _____ it out for you soon.
M : Thank you so much.

✎ **어휘복습** 잘 안 들리거나 몰라서 체크한 어휘를 써 놓고 복습해 보세요.

□ _____   □ _____   □ _____   □ _____

□ _____   □ _____   □ _____   □ _____

□ _____   □ _____   □ _____   □ _____

19 속담 추론

대화를 듣고, 상황을 가장 잘 표현한 속담을
고르시오.

① 그 아버지에 그 아들이다.
② 남의 떡이 더 커 보인다.
③ 자꾸 연습하면 아주 잘하게 된다.
④ 닭 쫓던 개 지붕 쳐다보듯 한다.
⑤ 사공이 많으면 배가 산으로 간다.

W : I'm so □ _____ . Ice skating is so much □ _____ □ _____
　　I thought.
M : What are you having the most □ _____ □ _____ ?
W : Well, I □ _____ □ _____ every time I try to skate
　　□ _____ or turn a corner.
M : It's □ _____ your □ _____ □ _____ of lessons! Don't get
　　□ _____ . All famous skaters started out just like you.
W : You're right. Do you think I'll □ _____ □ _____ if I practice
　　every day?
M : Of course! The only way to □ _____ and □ _____ skills is to
　　□ _____ □ _____ .

20 알맞은 응답 찾기

대화를 듣고, 여자의 마지막 말에 대한 남자
의 응답으로 가장 적절한 것을 고르시오.

Man: _____

① Awesome! I want to buy a Gold
　 pass.
② How long are the lines for the
　 rides?
③ The restaurant is far from here.
④ How do I get to the amusement
　 park?
⑤ I want to get a refund on my ticket.

M : Hello, I would like to buy an □ _____ □ _____ to the
　　amusement park.
W : Okay, would you like to □ _____ □ _____ □ _____
　　a Silver or Gold pass?
M : What is the □ _____ ?
W : The Silver pass is □ _____ dollars a □ _____ . The Gold pass
　　is one □ _____ dollars a year. With the Gold pass, you don't
　　have to □ _____ □ _____ □ _____ for the □ _____ .
M : Great. Is that all?
W : As a Gold member you also get a □ _____ □ _____ .
M : _____

✎ **어휘복습** 잘 안 들리거나 몰라서 체크한 어휘를 써 놓고 복습해 보세요.

□ _____　　□ _____　　□ _____　　□ _____

□ _____　　□ _____　　□ _____　　□ _____

□ _____　　□ _____　　□ _____　　□ _____

01 대화를 듣고, 여자가 구매할 그림책을 고르시오.

① ② ③

④ ⑤

02 대화를 듣고, 여자가 남자에게 전화한 목적으로 가장 적절한 것을 고르시오.

① 생일 파티 계획을 의논하려고
② 수영장이 언제 여는지 물어보려고
③ 생일 파티를 할 식당을 예약하려고
④ 동물원이 언제 닫는지 물어보려고
⑤ 수영장에 몇 명이 오는지 물어보려고

03 다음 그림의 상황에 가장 적절한 대화를 고르시오.

①　　②　　③　　④　　⑤

04 대화를 듣고, 두 사람이 구매할 컵케이크를 고르시오.

① ② ③

④ ⑤

05 대화를 듣고, 남자의 직업으로 가장 적절한 것을 고르시오.

① tour guide ② salesperson
③ travel agent ④ flight attendant
⑤ plane technician

06 대화를 듣고, 여자의 심정으로 가장 적절한 것을 고르시오.

① annoyed ② excited ③ calm
④ jealous ⑤ satisfied

07 다음을 듣고, 두 사람의 대화가 어색한 것을 고르시오.

①　　②　　③　　④　　⑤

08 대화를 듣고, 남자가 여자에게 부탁한 일로 가장 적절한 것을 고르시오.

① 자리 맡기 ② 음료수 사기
③ 마중 나오기 ④ 티켓 예매하기
⑤ 차로 태워다 주기

09 대화를 듣고, 여자의 마지막 말에 담긴 의도로 가장 적절한 것을 고르시오.

① 감사 ② 동의 ③ 제안
④ 요청 ⑤ 불평

10 대화를 듣고, 남자가 지불해야 할 금액을 고르시오.

① $30 ② $40 ③ $45
④ $50 ⑤ $60

11 대화를 듣고, 두 사람이 대화하고 있는 장소로 가장 적절한 곳을 고르시오.

① aquarium   ② movie theater

③ beach   ④ mountains

⑤ museum

12 다음을 듣고, Great Square Museum에 관해 언급되지 <u>않은</u> 것을 고르시오.

① 개관 날짜   ② 관람 시간

③ 입장료   ④ 위치

⑤ 입장권 구매 방법

13 다음 표를 보면서 대화를 듣고, 내용과 일치하지 <u>않는</u> 것을 고르시오.

Dog for Sale

①	Breed of dog	Poodle
②	Boy/Girl	Girl
③	Color	Brown
④	Age	6 Months
⑤	Price	$200

14 다음을 듣고, 무엇에 관한 설명인지 고르시오.

① 구명조끼   ② 낙하산   ③ 튜브

④ 잠수함   ⑤ 구급차

15 대화를 듣고, 남자가 대화 직후에 할 일로 가장 적절한 것을 고르시오.

① 부엌에 가기   ② 안방에 가기

③ 딸을 기다리기   ④ 부엌 청소하기

⑤ 열쇠 복사하기

16 대화를 듣고, 회의를 하기로 한 날짜를 고르시오.

① 9월 4일   ② 9월 6일   ③ 9월 7일

④ 9월 8일   ⑤ 9월 9일

17 다음 상황 설명을 듣고, Rob이 Tina에게 할 말로 가장 적절한 것을 고르시오.

Rob: _____

① How much are the tickets?

② Have you seen a musical before?

③ I would like to buy two tickets.

④ Would you rather do something else?

⑤ Do you mind if we go eat something before the show?

18 대화를 듣고, 남자가 할 일로 가장 적절한 것을 고르시오.

① 역사 숙제하기

② 서점에 전화하기

③ 역사책 검색하기

④ 도서관에 전화하기

⑤ 서점에서 책 구매하기

19 대화를 듣고, 상황을 가장 잘 표현한 속담을 고르시오.

① 백지장도 맞들면 낫다.

② 아니 땐 굴뚝에 연기 나랴.

③ 일찍 일어나는 새가 벌레를 잡는다.

④ 하늘이 무너져도 솟아날 구멍이 있다.

⑤ 어떤 이의 약이 다른 이에겐 독이 된다.

20 대화를 듣고, 여자의 마지막 말에 대한 남자의 응답으로 가장 적절한 것을 고르시오.

Man: _____

① It will cost you about $100.

② Have you replaced it before?

③ We can't replace your camera lens.

④ Because that's how our policy works.

⑤ Would you like to apply for insurance now?

다시 듣고, 빈칸에 알맞은 단어를 써 보세요.

◀)) **MP3 실전 03-1**

01 그림 정보 파악

대화를 듣고, 여자가 구매할 그림책을 고르시오.

① ② ③ ④ ⑤

M : Hello. Can I help you with something?

W : Yes. I'd like to buy a coloring □ _____ □ _____ my □ _____.

M : Okay. Would you like this one □ _____ □ _____? It's a very □ _____ □ _____.

W : It seems alright, □ _____ do you have any with □ _____?

M : We sure do. Here's one with □ _____. What do you think of it?

W : It's nice, □ _____ I □ _____ □ _____ a coloring book with □ _____ □ _____.

M : Okay. We have this one with □ _____ and □ _____. She'll love it. I'm sure of it!

02 목적 파악

대화를 듣고, 여자가 남자에게 전화한 목적으로 가장 적절한 것을 고르시오.

① 생일 파티 계획을 의논하려고
② 수영장이 언제 여는지 물어보려고
③ 생일 파티를 할 식당을 예약하려고
④ 동물원이 언제 닫는지 물어보려고
⑤ 수영장에 몇 명이 오는지 물어보려고

M : Hi, Mom.

W : Jack, have you □ _____ what you want to do □ _____ your □ _____?

M : Hmm… I'm not sure. I can't decide. Do you □ _____ any □ _____?

W : □ _____ □ _____ going to the □ _____ □ _____? Or the zoo?

M : That sounds great! I'll tell my friends that we're □ _____ □ _____ the □ _____ for my birthday party.

W : Let me know □ _____ □ _____ people are □ _____. I have to buy tickets.

✎ **어휘복습** 잘 안 들리거나 몰라서 체크한 어휘를 써 놓고 복습해 보세요.

□ _____   □ _____   □ _____   □ _____

□ _____   □ _____   □ _____   □ _____

□ _____   □ _____   □ _____

03 그림 상황에 적절한 대화 찾기

다음 그림의 상황에 가장 적절한 대화를 고르시오.

① ② ③ ④ ⑤

① W : Isaac, can you □ _____ the □ _____?

　　M : I □ _____ can. Let me get a washcloth.

② W : Could you □ _____ □ _____ the volume?

　　M : But my favorite TV □ _____ is □ _____!

③ W : I like your sofa. It's very □ _____.

　　M : Thanks! I bought it last month.

④ W : It's really □ _____ □ _____.

　　M : It sure is. Should we □ _____ □ _____ a □ _____?

⑤ W : Isaac, would you □ _____ the □ _____ for me?

　　M : Yes, I can do that.

04 그림 정보 파악

대화를 듣고, 두 사람이 구매할 컵케이크를 고르시오.

① ② ③

④ ⑤

W : Chris, look at these cupcakes! They all have real □ _____ on them!

M : They all look delicious. Do you want to □ _____ □ _____ for our □ _____?

W : Absolutely! I □ _____ that the strawberry and banana ones are □ _____ □ _____.

M : Really? I would □ _____ the cupcake with the orange or kiwi □ _____ □ _____.

W : Well, let's □ _____ □ _____ today, and we can buy a kiwi cupcake tomorrow.

M : Okay, that □ _____ □ _____ □ _____.

✏️ **어휘복습** 잘 안 들리거나 몰라서 체크한 어휘를 써 놓고 복습해 보세요.

□ _____　□ _____　□ _____　□ _____

□ _____　□ _____　□ _____　□ _____

□ _____　□ _____　□ _____　□ _____

05 직업 추론

대화를 듣고, 남자의 직업으로 가장 적절한 것을 고르시오.

① tour guide
② salesperson
③ travel agent
④ flight attendant
⑤ plane technician

M : Hello, what can I do for you today?

W : Hi. I would like to □ _____ a □ _____ □ _____.

M : Okay. □ _____ are you planning to □ _____?

W : I'm going to Greece for a □ _____ □ _____ with my friends.

M : Great! Do you know □ _____ you want to □ _____?

W : Yes, □ _____ August fourteenth □ _____ August twentieth would be great. I hope there are tickets □ _____!

M : You're a □ _____ woman. There is one □ _____ package □ _____ for nine hundred dollars.

W : Wonderful! It's a good thing I called early.

06 심정 추론

대화를 듣고, 여자의 심정으로 가장 적절한 것을 고르시오.

① annoyed   ② excited
③ calm   ④ jealous
⑤ satisfied

M : Hey, Sandra, what are you doing? You seem busy.

W : I'm □ _____ the □ _____ because my dog □ _____ a □ _____.

M : Oh no! What did he do?

W : He □ _____ □ _____ my new sofa cushions that my mom bought me!

M : That sounds like a □ _____. Are you okay?

W : No, I'm so □ _____. I can't □ _____ him □ _____ even for one hour!

M : Yeah, □ _____ can be a □ _____ sometimes.

W : Tell me about it!

✎ **어휘복습** 잘 안 들리거나 몰라서 체크한 어휘를 써 놓고 복습해 보세요.

□ _____   □ _____   □ _____   □ _____

□ _____   □ _____   □ _____   □ _____

□ _____   □ _____   □ _____   □ _____

다음을 듣고, 두 사람의 대화가 <u>어색한</u> 것을 고르시오.

①   ②   ③   ④   ⑤

①   M : They're building a balcony □ _____ □ _____ □ _____ the café.

     W : Ice coffee would be great. Thanks!

②   M : It's □ _____ □ _____ snow this weekend.

     W : Cool! Let's go make a □ _____ .

③   M : Are you □ _____ □ _____ ?

     W : No, I don't think I can go to school today.

④   M : Are you □ _____ on Friday?

     W : I sure am. Let's □ _____ □ _____ together.

⑤   M : Can you □ _____ me a □ _____ ?

     W : Of course, anything for you! What is it?

---

08 부탁 파악

대화를 듣고, 남자가 여자에게 부탁한 일로 가장 적절한 것을 고르시오.

① 자리 맡기
② 음료수 사기
③ 마중 나오기
④ 티켓 예매하기
⑤ 차로 태워다 주기

W : Hello, this is Susan □ _____ .

M : Hey, Susan! This is Don. Are you at the □ _____ □ _____ already?

W : Yes, I just □ _____ □ _____ . Where are you?

M : I'm on my way. Can you □ _____ some □ _____ ? I'm really □ _____ .

W : Yeah, □ _____ □ _____ . Do you need □ _____ □ _____ ?

M : No, that's all. Thanks so much! By the way, I'll be there □ _____ □ _____ □ _____ .

✏️ **어휘복습** 잘 안 들리거나 몰라서 체크한 어휘를 써 놓고 복습해 보세요.

□ _____   □ _____   □ _____   □ _____

□ _____   □ _____   □ _____   □ _____

□ _____   □ _____   □ _____   □ _____

09 의도 파악

대화를 듣고, 여자의 마지막 말에 담긴 의도로 가장 적절한 것을 고르시오.

① 감사 　② 동의 　③ 제안
④ 요청 　⑤ 불평

W : Michael, are you □ _____ □ _____ move into your new house?

M : No, not yet. I'm □ _____ some □ _____.

W : Oh no, what's the □ _____?

M : I'm trying to □ _____ all the □ _____ into my car, but they won't □ _____. I have □ _____ □ _____ cargo.

W : There's a much easier way. □ _____ □ _____ a moving van service.

10 숫자 정보 파악

대화를 듣고, 남자가 지불해야 할 금액을 고르시오.

① $30 　② $40 　③ $45
④ $50 　⑤ $60

W : Good morning! Welcome to Sherry Flowers!

M : Hello. I'd like to □ _____ some □ _____. How much are they?

W : □ _____ dollars for □ _____ □ _____. But if you buy two, you can get the □ _____ one for □ _____ □ _____.

M : Okay! I would like one dozen □ _____ roses and one dozen □ _____ roses.

W : I'll □ _____ them □ _____ for you right away.

M : Thank you. Here's my credit card.

✎ **어휘복습** 잘 안 들리거나 몰라서 체크한 어휘를 써 놓고 복습해 보세요.

□ _____ 　□ _____ 　□ _____ 　□ _____

□ _____ 　□ _____ 　□ _____ 　□ _____

□ _____ 　□ _____ 　□ _____ 　□ _____

11 장소 추론

대화를 듣고, 두 사람이 대화하고 있는 장소로 가장 적절한 곳을 고르시오.

① aquarium   ② movie theater
③ beach   ④ mountains
⑤ museum

M : I'm so glad we came here for our □ _____ □ _____.

W : I agree. Look at that! There are so □ _____ □ _____ of □ _____ here!

M : The children are going to □ _____ seeing the □ _____.

W : Definitely. I can already see □ _____ □ _____ they are!

M : There's going to be a □ _____ □ _____ in one hour.

W : Wonderful! If we go now, we can get □ _____ □ _____.

M : Good point. Let's take the children there □ _____.

12 미언급 파악

다음을 듣고, Great Square Museum에 관해 언급되지 <u>않은</u> 것을 고르시오.

① 개관 날짜   ② 관람 시간
③ 입장료   ④ 위치
⑤ 입장권 구매 방법

W : Ladies and gentlemen. I'm pleased to announce the □ _____ □ _____ of the Great Square □ _____. It will be open to the public □ _____ □ _____ October twentieth. The museum has □ _____ exhibition □ _____. It will be □ _____ □ _____ through □ _____ from nine thirty A.M. to five thirty P.M., and □ _____ and □ _____ from ten A.M. to four P.M. □ _____ □ _____ are fifteen dollars □ _____ □ _____ and five dollars □ _____ □ _____. □ _____ nine three oh, one two three four to □ _____ □ _____ now.

✎ **어휘복습** 잘 안 들리거나 몰라서 체크한 어휘를 써 놓고 복습해 보세요.

□ _____   □ _____   □ _____   □ _____

□ _____   □ _____   □ _____   □ _____

□ _____   □ _____   □ _____   □ _____

13 도표·실용문 파악

다음 표를 보면서 대화를 듣고, 내용과 일치하지 <u>않는</u> 것을 고르시오.

Dog for Sale

	Breed of dog	Poodle
①		
②	Boy/Girl	Girl
③	Color	Brown
④	Age	6 Months
⑤	Price	$200

W : Henry, we need to □ _____ our □ _____. We don't have the time to □ _____ □ _____ □ _____ her.

M : Okay, we can □ _____ an □ _____ in the newspaper.

W : Can you help me with this □ _____?

M : Sure! Ruby is a □ _____ poodle.

W : Right. Do you remember □ _____ □ _____ □ _____ is?

M : I would say she is about □ _____ □ _____ □ _____.

W : Yeah. □ _____ □ _____ do you think we can □ _____ □ _____ her?

M : I think between two hundred dollars and three hundred dollars is a □ _____ □ _____.

W : People might think three hundred dollars is too expensive. Let's □ _____ □ _____ two hundred dollars.

14 화제 추론

다음을 듣고, 무엇에 관한 설명인지 고르시오.

① 구명조끼　　② 낙하산
③ 튜브　　　　④ 잠수함
⑤ 구급차

M : This is a □ _____ precaution for people who are □ _____ □ _____ of □ _____, such as a swimming pool, lake, or ocean. It is normally □ _____ □ _____ a □ _____, and has buckles on the front. Also, you can find these on □ _____ □ _____. Even if you fall into the water, you don't have to worry because you will □ _____ when you wear this.

✏️ **어휘복습** 잘 안 들리거나 몰라서 체크한 어휘를 써 놓고 복습해 보세요.

□ _____　　□ _____　　□ _____　　□ _____

□ _____　　□ _____　　□ _____　　□ _____

15 할 일 파악

대화를 듣고, 남자가 대화 직후에 할 일로 가장 적절한 것을 고르시오.

① 부엌에 가기
② 안방에 가기
③ 딸을 기다리기
④ 부엌 청소하기
⑤ 열쇠 복사하기

M : Katie, when are you □ _____ □ _____ from school?

W : Maybe □ _____ a few □ _____, Dad. Why?

M : I have to go to the department store right now, but I can't find the □ _____ □ _____.

W : Did you □ _____ the living room?

M : Yes, but they aren't there. □ _____ did you □ _____ them □ _____ you □ _____ them last night?

W : Let me think. Oh! I remember. I □ _____ them □ _____ the □ _____ □ _____.

M : Alright. Please □ _____ them □ _____ in my room next time.

16 특정 정보 파악

대화를 듣고, 회의를 하기로 한 날짜를 고르시오.

① 9월 4일   ② 9월 6일
③ 9월 7일   ④ 9월 8일
⑤ 9월 9일

W : Mr. Wright, when should we □ _____ our □ _____?

M : I'm thinking □ _____ September fourth □ _____ ninth.

W : Hmm… September fourth is □ _____ □ _____ and September ninth is too □ _____. Does the seventh or eighth □ _____ □ _____ you?

M : I □ _____ have a meeting □ _____ for the seventh at nine A.M.

W : Alright. Then, I guess I'll see you □ _____ □ _____ □ _____ your meeting on the □ _____.

M : Okay, that will work for me.

✎ **어휘복습** 잘 안 들리거나 몰라서 체크한 어휘를 써 놓고 복습해 보세요.

□ _____   □ _____   □ _____   □ _____

□ _____   □ _____   □ _____   □ _____

□ _____   □ _____   □ _____   □ _____

17 상황에 적절한 말 찾기

다음 상황 설명을 듣고, Rob이 Tina에게 할 말로 가장 적절한 것을 고르시오.

Rob: _____

① How much are the tickets?
② Have you seen a musical before?
③ I would like to buy two tickets.
④ Would you rather do something else?
⑤ Do you mind if we go eat something before the show?

W : Rob took his friend Tina to □ _____ a popular □ _____ in town. However, he didn't □ _____ a □ _____. It is his □ _____ to □ _____ □ _____, but the closest show time is all □ _____ □ _____. The next □ _____ is in two hours. So, Rob decides to ask Tina if she'd be okay with going to □ _____ □ _____ □ _____ □ _____ the musical. In this situation, what would Rob most likely say to Tina?

Rob: _____

18 할 일 파악

대화를 듣고, 남자가 할 일로 가장 적절한 것을 고르시오.

① 역사 숙제하기
② 서점에 전화하기
③ 역사책 검색하기
④ 도서관에 전화하기
⑤ 서점에서 책 구매하기

M : Mom, can we go to the □ _____?
W : Okay. Do you □ _____ □ _____ for school?
M : Yes, I have to □ _____ □ _____ books for my history class.
W : There will □ _____ be a lot of history books at the □ _____. Did you □ _____ □ _____ they have the book you need?
M : No, I didn't think of that. That's a good idea, Mom.
W : It's □ _____ □ _____ □ _____ today. □ _____ □ _____ does the library □ _____?
M : I'll □ _____ them and □ _____ right now.

✎ **어휘복습** 잘 안 들리거나 몰라서 체크한 어휘를 써 놓고 복습해 보세요.

□ _____   □ _____   □ _____   □ _____
□ _____   □ _____   □ _____   □ _____
□ _____

19 속담 추론

대화를 듣고, 상황을 가장 잘 표현한 속담을 고르시오.

① 백지장도 맞들면 낫다.
② 아니 땐 굴뚝에 연기 나랴.
③ 일찍 일어나는 새가 벌레를 잡는다.
④ 하늘이 무너져도 솟아날 구멍이 있다.
⑤ 어떤 이의 약이 다른 이에겐 독이 된다.

M : Betty, what are you doing up so □ _____ in the □ _____?
　　Aren't you □ _____?
W : No, not really. I'm □ _____ □ _____ waking up at this time.
　　It's so □ _____!
M : I don't understand you. What do you do at this hour?
W : I eat, exercise, study, and □ _____ myself □ _____ the
　　□ _____.
M : I see. What □ _____ come from that?
W : I get □ _____. More importantly, my □ _____ □ _____.
M : Hmm… Maybe I should try □ _____ □ _____ □ _____ too.
W : I promise you that you □ _____ □ _____ it!

20 알맞은 응답 찾기

대화를 듣고, 여자의 마지막 말에 대한 남자의 응답으로 가장 적절한 것을 고르시오.

Man: _____

① It will cost you about $100.
② Have you replaced it before?
③ We can't replace your camera lens.
④ Because that's how our policy works.
⑤ Would you like to apply for insurance now?

M : Is there a □ _____ □ _____ your camera, ma'am?
W : Yes. I need to □ _____ my lens □ _____. It's □ _____.
M : How did it break?
W : I □ _____ it on the side of the road while I was trying to
　　□ _____ a □ _____.
M : I see. Do you have □ _____?
W : No, I didn't □ _____ □ _____ it when I bought it.
M : Then I'm afraid you have to pay an □ _____ □ _____ to
　　□ _____ it □ _____.
W : □ _____ is that?
M : _____

✏ **어휘복습** 잘 안 들리거나 몰라서 체크한 어휘를 써 놓고 복습해 보세요.

□ _____　　□ _____　　□ _____　　□ _____
□ _____　　□ _____　　□ _____　　□ _____
□ _____　　□ _____　　□ _____　　□ _____

01 대화를 듣고, 여자가 만든 깃발을 고르시오.

02 대화를 듣고, 남자가 여자에게 전화한 목적으로 가장 적절한 것을 고르시오.

① 축구장이 다 찼다는 것을 알려주려고
② 축구장이 닫혔다는 것을 알려주려고
③ 축구장의 개장 시간을 물어보려고
④ 여자의 도착 시간을 물어보려고
⑤ 여자의 주말 계획을 물어보려고

03 다음 그림의 상황에 가장 적절한 대화를 고르시오.

① ② ③ ④ ⑤

04 대화를 듣고, 두 사람이 구매할 시계를 고르시오.

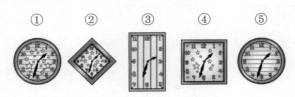

05 대화를 듣고, 여자의 직업으로 가장 적절한 것을 고르시오.

① athlete ② nurse ③ doctor
④ reporter ⑤ pharmacist

06 대화를 듣고, 남자의 심정으로 가장 적절한 것을 고르시오.

① relieved ② jealous
③ regretful ④ relaxed
⑤ angry

07 다음을 듣고, 두 사람의 대화가 <u>어색한</u> 것을 고르시오.

① ② ③ ④ ⑤

08 대화를 듣고, 여자가 남자에게 부탁한 일로 가장 적절한 것을 고르시오.

① 기차표 환불하기
② 기차 좌석 변경하기
③ 기차 좌석 예약하기
④ 기차표 요금 할인해주기
⑤ 기차 출발 시간 변경하기

09 대화를 듣고, 남자의 마지막 말에 담긴 의도로 가장 적절한 것을 고르시오.

① 제안 ② 사과 ③ 감사
④ 허락 ⑤ 거절

10 대화를 듣고, 여자가 지불할 금액을 고르시오.

① $40 ② $60 ③ $80
④ $100 ⑤ $120

11 대화를 듣고, 두 사람이 대화하고 있는 장소로 가장 적절한 곳을 고르시오.

① library ② school
③ bookstore ④ furniture store
⑤ clothing store

12 다음을 듣고, Rock & Roll Climbing Center에 관해 언급되지 <u>않은</u> 것을 고르시오.

① 위치　　　　　　② 운영 시간
③ 회원 할인율　　　④ 개업 연도
⑤ 회원 가입 방법

13 다음 배치도를 보면서 대화를 듣고, 두 사람이 선택한 구역의 위치를 고르시오.

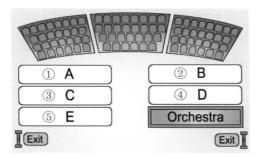

14 다음을 듣고, 무엇에 관한 설명인지 고르시오.

① 수레　　　② 썰매　　　③ 자전거
④ 자동차　　⑤ 오토바이

15 대화를 듣고, 남자가 대화 직후에 할 일로 가장 적절한 것을 고르시오.

① 치과 가기　　　　② 아내 깨우기
③ 알람 맞추기　　　④ 치과 예약하기
⑤ 치과 예약 취소하기

16 대화를 듣고, 두 사람이 뉴욕에 도착할 날짜를 고르시오.

① December 19
② December 20
③ December 21
④ December 22
⑤ December 24

17 다음 상황 설명을 듣고, Ms. Stewart가 Brittany에게 할 말로 가장 적절한 것을 고르시오.

Ms. Stewart: _____

① Do you live around here?
② Can you work on weekends?
③ Is math your favorite subject?
④ Have you taught math before?
⑤ I need to hire a new English teacher.

18 대화를 듣고, 남자가 대화 직후에 할 일로 가장 적절한 것을 고르시오.

① 우산 찾기　　　　② 휴대폰 찾기
③ 가방 가져오기　　④ 졸업식 참석하기
⑤ 일기 예보 확인하기

19 대화를 듣고, 상황을 가장 잘 표현한 속담을 고르시오.

① 소 잃고 외양간 고친다.
② 믿는 도끼에 발등 찍힌다.
③ 높이 나는 새가 멀리 본다.
④ 하룻강아지 범 무서운 줄 모른다.
⑤ 낮말은 새가 듣고 밤말은 쥐가 듣는다.

20 대화를 듣고, 여자의 마지막 말에 대한 남자의 응답으로 가장 적절한 것을 고르시오.

Man: _____

① I had a terrible time. Let's go home right now.
② How many scoops of ice cream would you like?
③ Parents can never worry too much for their children.
④ There's a new ballet studio that's opening down the street.
⑤ The ballet studio isn't far from here. We can probably walk there.

01 그림 정보 파악

대화를 듣고, 여자가 만든 깃발을 고르시오.

① ② ③
④ ⑤

W : Dad, this is my □ _____ for the school's flag □ _____
□ _____.

M : It looks great! I see you □ _____ a □ _____ on the flag.

W : Yeah. My teacher □ _____ me to □ _____ a □ _____ for
the school, so I used a rainbow.

M : Good job. But □ _____ □ _____ □ _____ include any
unicorns? You love unicorns.

W : I know, but they are too □ _____ □ _____ □ _____.

M : I see. I like your idea to put the □ _____ □ _____ the
□ _____ □ _____ the rainbow.

W : Thanks, Dad.

02 목적 파악

대화를 듣고, 남자가 여자에게 전화한 목적으로 가장 적절한 것을 고르시오.

① 축구장이 다 찼다는 것을 알려주려고
② 축구장이 닫혔다는 것을 알려주려고
③ 축구장의 개장 시간을 물어보려고
④ 여자의 도착 시간을 물어보려고
⑤ 여자의 주말 계획을 물어보려고

M : Jennifer, I'm at the soccer field. I have □ _____ □ _____ for
you.

W : Don't tell me there are □ _____ □ _____ fields □ _____!

M : Sorry, there are people playing on all the fields. It doesn't
□ _____ □ _____ they're going to leave □ _____
□ _____ □ _____.

W : Oh no! □ _____ □ _____ we can't play soccer today! That's
so □ _____.

M : I know. I □ _____ □ _____ □ _____ a field for us.

W : It's alright. We can always go back and play tomorrow.

M : Sounds good. I'll be □ _____ □ _____ next time.

✏️ **어휘복습** 잘 안 들리거나 몰라서 체크한 어휘를 써 놓고 복습해 보세요.

□ _____   □ _____   □ _____   □ _____

□ _____   □ _____   □ _____   □ _____

□ _____   □ _____   □ _____   □ _____

03 그림 상황에 적절한 대화 찾기

다음 그림의 상황에 가장 적절한 대화를 고르시오.

① ② ③ ④ ⑤

① M : □ _____ □ _____ □ _____ to ride the merry-go-round?

　 W : □ _____! I want to □ _____ the white horse.

② M : □ _____ □ _____ have you been □ _____ in line?

　 W : About □ _____ □ _____ □ _____.

③ M : □ _____ □ _____ the rollercoaster over there.

　 W : Wow, it □ _____ really □ _____.

④ M : Would you like to □ _____ a □ _____?

　 W : □ _____ □ _____. After I eat all of my popcorn.

⑤ M : I'm sorry, but you're □ _____ □ _____ □ _____ to ride the bumper cars.

　 W : Oh, no! I can't believe it.

04 그림 정보 파악

대화를 듣고, 두 사람이 구매할 시계를 고르시오.

① ② ③

④ ⑤

W : Wow, there are so many clocks we can □ _____ □ _____.

M : You're right. It's □ _____ to □ _____ one for Nathan. I hope we find one that he'll like.

W : What do you think about this □ _____ one with □ _____?

M : It looks fancy, but I don't think he'll like the stripes. I think he'll □ _____ this □ _____ one with stars.

W : That looks nice too, but the □ _____ one □ _____ □ _____ seems best. I'm sure he'll be □ _____ □ _____ it.

M : Yeah, you're □ _____ □ _____. Let's buy that one.

✎ **어휘복습** 잘 안 들리거나 몰라서 체크한 어휘를 써 놓고 복습해 보세요.

□ _____ □ _____ □ _____ □ _____

□ _____ □ _____ □ _____ □ _____

□ _____ □ _____ □ _____ □ _____

05 직업 추론

대화를 듣고, 여자의 직업으로 가장 적절한 것을 고르시오.

① athlete   ② nurse
③ doctor   ④ reporter
⑤ pharmacist

W : Robert, ☐ _____ are you ☐ _____ today?
M : I'm doing ☐ _____ ☐ _____ ☐ _____ than when I first came here. That's ☐ _____ ☐ _____.
W : I'm really happy that your ☐ _____ is ☐ _____.
M : Me too, I've stayed in the hospital ☐ _____ ☐ _____. I ☐ _____ ☐ _____ to go home.
W : You can ☐ _____ the ☐ _____ today, but please ☐ _____ ☐ _____ you come for a ☐ _____ next Thursday.
M : Sure, I'll call to ☐ _____ an ☐ _____.
W : The ☐ _____ will give you your ☐ _____ soon. Take it ☐ _____ ☐ _____ ☐ _____ ☐ _____ and look after yourself.
M : Okay, thank you!

06 심정 추론

대화를 듣고, 남자의 심정으로 가장 적절한 것을 고르시오.

① relieved   ② jealous
③ regretful   ④ relaxed
⑤ angry

M : Honey, ☐ _____ you ☐ _____ my black ☐ _____?
W : Yeah, I ☐ _____ them ☐ _____ the ☐ _____ ☐ _____ because you asked me to.
M : Already? I should have ☐ _____ everything ☐ _____ ☐ _____ the ☐ _____.
W : What was ☐ _____?
M : A ☐ _____ with my new manager's ☐ _____ ☐ _____ on it.
W : Oh, I was wondering ☐ _____ that ☐ _____ of ☐ _____ was. I took it out of your pants ☐ _____ sending them to be ☐ _____.
M : Did you really? Thank you so much! A ☐ _____ ☐ _____ was just lifted ☐ _____ my ☐ _____.
W : No problem. ☐ _____ ☐ _____ to ☐ _____ it yourself next time.

✎ **어휘복습** 잘 안 들리거나 몰라서 체크한 어휘를 써 놓고 복습해 보세요.

☐ _____   ☐ _____   ☐ _____   ☐ _____

☐ _____   ☐ _____   ☐ _____   ☐ _____

☐ _____   ☐ _____   ☐ _____   ☐ _____

다음을 듣고, 두 사람의 대화가 <u>어색한</u> 것을 고르시오.

① ② ③ ④ ⑤

① M : I'll be □ _____ at the □ _____ around six P.M.

　　W : Alright, I'll be there to □ _____ you □ _____.

② M : □ _____ □ _____ will it take to get there □ _____

　　　 □ _____?

　　W : Go straight and there will be a bus station □ _____

　　　 □ _____ □ _____.

③ M : Mary, my wife is □ _____ with a son.

　　W : That's wonderful. Congratulations!

④ M : I'm wondering if you could □ _____ me the □ _____

　　　 □ _____ □ _____.

　　W : Of course. I'll send it as soon as possible.

⑤ M : Would you □ _____ □ _____ with me on Saturday?

　　W : I would □ _____ □ _____.

08 부탁 파악

대화를 듣고, 여자가 남자에게 부탁한 일로 가장 적절한 것을 고르시오.

① 기차표 환불하기
② 기차 좌석 변경하기
③ 기차 좌석 예약하기
④ 기차표 요금 할인해주기
⑤ 기차 출발 시간 변경하기

W : Excuse me, sir.

M : Yes, can I help you with something?

W : I □ _____ a □ _____ □ _____ to Central Plaza a few

　　days ago. Could you tell me if it is a □ _____ or □ _____

　　□ _____?

M : Sure. What is your seat number?

W : It's twelve B.

M : It □ _____ □ _____ that is an aisle seat.

W : Oh, can I □ _____ it □ _____ a window seat?

M : I'll see what I can do. It might be □ _____.

✎ **어휘복습** 잘 안 들리거나 몰라서 체크한 어휘를 써 놓고 복습해 보세요.

□ _____　□ _____　□ _____　□ _____

□ _____　□ _____　□ _____　□ _____

□ _____　□ _____　□ _____　□ _____

09 의도 파악

대화를 듣고, 남자의 마지막 말에 담긴 의도로 가장 적절한 것을 고르시오.

① 제안   ② 사과   ③ 감사
④ 허락   ⑤ 거절

M : Honey, there's □ _____ □ _____ □ _____ in the refrigerator. We had better do something about that.

W : I know. We need to go □ _____ □ _____ and buy some fruit, cereal, bread, and yogurt □ _____ □ _____.

M : I agree. When should we go? I'm actually □ _____ □ _____ □ _____ right □ _____.

W : □ _____ □ _____. I'm in the middle of cleaning. How about □ _____ □ _____ □ _____?

M : I'd □ _____ □ _____, □ _____ my friend is coming over then.

10 숫자 정보 파악

대화를 듣고, 여자가 지불할 금액을 고르시오.

① $40   ② $60   ③ $80
④ $100   ⑤ $120

M : Did you enjoy your □ _____ here □ _____ the Shining Star Hotel?

W : Yeah. I □ _____ □ _____ □ _____ my hotel room, and the room service was great.

M : I'm glad. You stayed □ _____ □ _____ □ _____, so your □ _____ is one hundred and twenty dollars.

W : There must be □ _____ □ _____. I only stayed for two nights.

M : Let me check. Oh, you're right. I □ _____ a □ _____. I'm so sorry.

W : It's okay.

M : You □ _____ □ _____ □ _____ pay for the □ _____ night, which makes your total □ _____ dollars less.

W : Okay, here is my credit card.

✎ **어휘복습** 잘 안 들리거나 몰라서 체크한 어휘를 써 놓고 복습해 보세요.

□ _____   □ _____   □ _____   □ _____

□ _____   □ _____   □ _____   □ _____

□ _____   □ _____   □ _____   □ _____

11 장소 추론

대화를 듣고, 두 사람이 대화하고 있는 장소로 가장 적절한 곳을 고르시오.

① library
② school
③ bookstore
④ furniture store
⑤ clothing store

W : Good afternoon, can I help you?

M : I'm looking for the book *The Yellowtail*. □ _____ can I □ _____ it?

W : Right this way. It's □ _____ □ _____ our □ _____ □ _____.

M : Yeah, all my friends are talking about it.

W : Do you see the □ _____ □ _____ over there? It's on the □ _____ □ _____.

M : I □ _____ your help.

W : Of course. I'll be at the counter if you need me.

12 미언급 파악

다음을 듣고, Rock & Roll Climbing Center에 관해 언급되지 않은 것을 고르시오.

① 위치
② 운영 시간
③ 회원 할인율
④ 개업 연도
⑤ 회원 가입 방법

W : Are you an active person? Are you □ _____ □ _____ playing the same sport every day? Then □ _____ □ _____ Rock & Roll Climbing Center on thirty-fourth Street now! We're □ _____ every day □ _____ ten A.M. □ _____ ten P.M., □ _____ □ _____ holidays. If you □ _____ a □ _____ now, we will □ _____ you a twenty-percent □ _____. To □ _____ □ _____, please □ _____ our □ _____ at rocknrollclimbers dot com or □ _____ us □ _____ nine four one, four nine four one.

✏ **어휘복습** 잘 안 들리거나 몰라서 체크한 어휘를 써 놓고 복습해 보세요.

□ _____   □ _____   □ _____   □ _____

□ _____   □ _____   □ _____   □ _____

□ _____   □ _____   □ _____   □ _____

13 그림 정보 파악

다음 배치도를 보면서 대화를 듣고, 두 사람이 선택한 구역의 위치를 고르시오.

M : Ms. Green, can you help me □ _____ a □ _____ for my band at the school music festival? Here's the map.

W : Okay, let me see. How about section E? It's □ _____ □ _____ the □ _____ sections.

M : No, that section is □ _____ □ _____ to the exit. I want my band to be □ _____ the □ _____.

W : Well, sections A and B are □ _____ □ _____. Is section D close enough?

M : I'd like it if my band wasn't □ _____ □ _____ □ _____ the orchestra.

W : All right. Then we have □ _____ □ _____ section □ _____ to choose from.

M : That seems like the □ _____ □ _____. Thank you.

14 화제 추론

다음을 듣고, 무엇에 관한 설명인지 고르시오.

① 수레   ② 썰매
③ 자전거   ④ 자동차
⑤ 오토바이

M : This is a type of □ _____ that people use every day. It runs on □ _____ □ _____. You can drive this by stepping on two pedals. One of the pedals is used to □ _____ □ _____. And □ _____ □ _____ one is used to □ _____ □ _____ or stop. You need a □ _____ □ _____ □ _____ this. And if you drive above the □ _____ □ _____, you have to □ _____ a □ _____.

✎ **어휘복습** 잘 안 들리거나 몰라서 체크한 어휘를 써 놓고 복습해 보세요.

□ _____   □ _____   □ _____   □ _____

□ _____   □ _____   □ _____   □ _____

□ _____   □ _____   □ _____   □ _____

15 할 일 파악

대화를 듣고, 남자가 대화 직후에 할 일로 가장 적절한 것을 고르시오.

① 치과 가기
② 아내 깨우기
③ 알람 맞추기
④ 치과 예약하기
⑤ 치과 예약 취소하기

W : Brian, are you □ _____ □ _____?

M : Oh, Lily. I just □ _____ □ _____. What time is it?

W : It's already one thirty P.M!

M : What? You've got to be □ _____ me. Why didn't you wake me up?

W : What's the problem?

M : I had a □ _____ □ _____ scheduled for one P.M. I'm □ _____ thirty minutes □ _____!

W : Really? Then you'd □ _____ □ _____ now.

M : Okay. I'll call you later. I'm definitely setting an alarm □ _____ □ _____ □ _____.

16 특정 정보 파악

대화를 듣고, 두 사람이 뉴욕에 도착할 날짜를 고르시오.

① December 19
② December 20
③ December 21
④ December 22
⑤ December 24

W : Dad, we've been □ _____ for our flight for □ _____ □ _____ □ _____. What is going on?

M : They just made an □ _____ that it will be □ _____ for two days □ _____ □ _____ the □ _____.

W : That's going to □ _____ our □ _____. Then when are we getting to New York?

M : Well, we □ _____ □ _____ □ _____ land on December □ _____, but now I guess we'll arrive □ _____ □ _____ □ _____.

W : Then we should call Uncle Tom to tell him about the changes.

M : Yeah, we also have to book a □ _____ □ _____ □ _____.

W : Don't worry about that. I'll □ _____ □ _____ □ _____ it.

✏️ **어휘복습** 잘 안 들리거나 몰라서 체크한 어휘를 써 놓고 복습해 보세요.

□ _____   □ _____   □ _____   □ _____
□ _____   □ _____   □ _____   □ _____
□ _____   □ _____   □ _____   □ _____

17 상황에 적절한 말 찾기

다음 상황 설명을 듣고, Ms. Stewart가 Brittany에게 할 말로 가장 적절한 것을 고르시오.

Ms. Stewart: _____

① Do you live around here?
② Can you work on weekends?
③ Is math your favorite subject?
④ Have you taught math before?
⑤ I need to hire a new English teacher.

W : Ms. Stewart is the principal at Merry Road Middle School. She needs to ☐ _____ a ☐ _____ math ☐ _____. One day, Brittany comes to ☐ _____ ☐ _____ the position. Ms. Stewart wants to ☐ _____ ☐ _____ that Brittany is ☐ _____ ☐ _____ the ☐ _____. She wants to know Brittany's ☐ _____ teaching ☐ _____. What would Ms. Stewart most likely say to Brittany?
Ms. Stewart: _____

18 할 일 파악

대화를 듣고, 남자가 대화 직후에 할 일로 가장 적절한 것을 고르시오.

① 우산 찾기
② 휴대폰 찾기
③ 가방 가져오기
④ 졸업식 참석하기
⑤ 일기 예보 확인하기

M : Honey, are you ☐ _____ ☐ _____? We're going to be ☐ _____ ☐ _____ the graduation.
W : ☐ _____ a ☐ _____! I can't find my cellphone. You know I can't leave the house without it.
M : Cellphone? I ☐ _____ you ☐ _____ it ☐ _____ your purse.
W : Oh, right! Let's go. Wait! I need to ☐ _____ my ☐ _____.
M : Why do you need your umbrella? It's sunny outside.
W : The weather forecast said that it will ☐ _____ ☐ _____ ☐ _____.
M : Are you sure about that? Let me ☐ _____ it ☐ _____ ☐ _____.

✏️ **어휘복습** 잘 안 들리거나 몰라서 체크한 어휘를 써 놓고 복습해 보세요.

☐ _____ ☐ _____ ☐ _____ ☐ _____
☐ _____ ☐ _____ ☐ _____ ☐ _____
☐ _____ ☐ _____ ☐ _____ ☐ _____

대화를 듣고, 상황을 가장 잘 표현한 속담을 고르시오.

① 소 잃고 외양간 고친다.
② 믿는 도끼에 발등 찍힌다.
③ 높이 나는 새가 멀리 본다.
④ 하룻강아지 범 무서운 줄 모른다.
⑤ 낮말은 새가 듣고 밤말은 쥐가 듣는다.

W : Henry, did you hear that Stacey □ _____ □ _____ □ _____ Shawn?

M : No, I haven't. But I don't think we should talk about it.

W : Why not? It's the □ _____ talked about □ _____ at school □ _____ □ _____.

M : Because it's not nice to □ _____ □ _____ other people. Plus, you never know who □ _____ □ _____ □ _____.

W : Relax. There's □ _____ □ _____ except for me and you.

M : Still, I was taught to be careful of what I say anytime and anywhere.

W : Okay, fine. I'll be □ _____ □ _____ □ _____ □ _____ about it.

대화를 듣고, 여자의 마지막 말에 대한 남자의 응답으로 가장 적절한 것을 고르시오.

Man: _____

① I had a terrible time. Let's go home right now.
② How many scoops of ice cream would you like?
③ Parents can never worry too much for their children.
④ There's a new ballet studio that's opening down the street.
⑤ The ballet studio isn't far from here. We can probably walk there.

M : Nancy, are you □ _____ □ _____ go to your □ _____ ballet □ _____?

W : Yes, I am. I □ _____ □ _____ everything I need.

M : You look so excited. What are you □ _____ □ _____ □ _____ the most?

W : Hmm… I want to learn how to □ _____ and □ _____ □ _____ my □ _____. That will probably be the □ _____ □ _____ □ _____ of class.

M : Okay, but □ _____ □ _____ □ _____! Make sure you don hurt yourself.

W : Dad, you □ _____ □ _____ □ _____. I'll be fine.

M : _____

✎ **어휘복습** 잘 안 들리거나 몰라서 체크한 어휘를 써 놓고 복습해 보세요.

□ _____   □ _____   □ _____   □ _____
□ _____   □ _____   □ _____   □ _____
□ _____   □ _____   □ _____   □ _____

01 대화를 듣고, 두 사람이 하고 있는 동작을 고르시오.

02 대화를 듣고, 남자가 여자에게 전화한 목적으로 가장 적절한 것을 고르시오.

① 식당을 추천하려고
② 책 대출을 부탁하려고
③ 책 반납을 부탁하려고
④ 요리책을 추천하려고
⑤ 함께 식사하자고 하려고

03 다음 그림의 상황에 가장 적절한 대화를 고르시오.

①　②　③　④　⑤

04 대화를 듣고, 두 사람이 만나기로 한 요일을 고르시오.

① Monday
② Tuesday
③ Thursday
④ Friday
⑤ Saturday

05 대화를 듣고, 두 사람이 대화하고 있는 장소로 가장 적절한 곳을 고르시오.

① museum
② classroom
③ movie theater
④ toy store
⑤ park

06 대화를 듣고, 여자의 심정으로 가장 적절한 것을 고르시오.

① grateful
② frustrated
③ happy
④ satisfied
⑤ scared

07 다음을 듣고, 두 사람의 대화가 <u>어색한</u> 것을 고르시오.

①　②　③　④　⑤

08 대화를 듣고, 여자가 남자에게 부탁한 일로 가장 적절한 것을 고르시오.

① 표 예매하기
② 영화 검색하기
③ 저녁 사기
④ 팝콘 사기
⑤ 좌석 바꾸기

09 대화를 듣고, 여자의 마지막 말에 담긴 의도로 가장 적절한 것을 고르시오.

① 거절
② 충고
③ 요청
④ 제안
⑤ 감사

10 대화를 듣고, 여자가 지불해야 할 금액을 고르시오.

① $30
② $80
③ $100
④ $160
⑤ $240

11 대화를 듣고, 두 사람의 관계로 가장 적절한 것을 고르시오.

① 식당 종업원 – 손님
② 호텔 직원 – 투숙객
③ 택시 기사 – 승객
④ 엄마 – 아들
⑤ 관광 안내원 – 관광객

12 다음을 듣고, North Valley English Camp에 관해 언급되지 <u>않은</u> 것을 고르시오.

① 운영 시간　② 위치　③ 시설
④ 프로그램　⑤ 요금

13 다음 백화점 주차 안내도를 보면서 대화를 듣고, 두 사람이 주차할 구역을 고르시오.

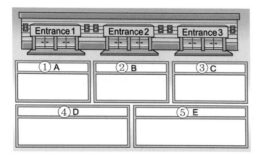

14 다음을 듣고, 무엇에 관한 설명인지 고르시오.

① 야구　② 농구　③ 배구
④ 축구　⑤ 핸드볼

15 대화를 듣고, 남자가 오늘 할 일로 가장 적절한 것을 고르시오.

① 강아지 사기　② 강아지 팔기
③ 블로그 만들기　④ 여자의 집에 가기
⑤ 강아지 사진 배포하기

16 대화를 듣고, 두 사람이 구매할 물건을 고르시오.

① shoes　② water
③ backpack　④ shirt
⑤ bandage

17 다음 상황 설명을 듣고, John이 엄마에게 할 말로 가장 적절한 것을 고르시오.

John: Mom, _____

① how much is the lamp?
② do you like my new lamp?
③ where should I put the lamp?
④ can you help me make food for the guests?
⑤ could you help me clean the house?

18 대화를 듣고, 남자가 할 일로 가장 적절한 것을 고르시오.

① 화분에 물주기　② 화장실 청소하기
③ 청소기 돌리기　④ 식사 준비하기
⑤ 쓰레기 갖다 버리기

[19-20] 대화를 듣고, 여자의 마지막 말에 대한 남자의 응답으로 가장 적절한 것을 고르시오.

19 Man: _____

① Well, I can go to the store with you.
② That's not necessary. I don't use that TV anyway.
③ I need to stop by the bank before we go.
④ The electronics store is open now.
⑤ I will call the store and ask when they close.

20 Man: _____

① Thanks for the ride home.
② No, I built a new house for my cat.
③ Yes, how long has it been since you moved here?
④ Yeah. I hope someone calls me tell me that they found my cat.
⑤ I'll call you the next time I'm in t

01 그림 정보 파악

대화를 듣고, 두 사람이 하고 있는 동작을 고르시오.

① ② ③
④ ⑤

W : Can we take a break? My □ _____ are □ _____.

M : Okay, let's stretch. □ _____ □ _____ your □ _____ and □ _____ your left □ _____ □ _____ your □ _____.

W : Okay. Now what?

M : □ _____ your left □ _____ with □ _____ hands and □ _____ it □ _____ you.

W : Oh, this feels so good!

M : □ _____ it for five seconds and do it on the right side too.

02 목적 파악

대화를 듣고, 남자가 여자에게 전화한 목적으로 가장 적절한 것을 고르시오.

① 식당을 추천하려고
② 책 대출을 부탁하려고
③ 책 반납을 부탁하려고
④ 요리책을 추천하려고
⑤ 함께 식사하자고 하려고

M : Hey, Jean. This is Steven. Are you busy?

W : Hi, not really. I'm just □ _____ □ _____ □ _____ □ _____ the school □ _____. Did you need something?

M : Yes, actually. Could you □ _____ □ _____ a □ _____?
I need to go the library, but I don't think I'll be able to today.

W : Sure. □ _____ □ _____ do you need?

M : Well, I was □ _____ □ _____ making dinner for my parents.
Can you □ _____ □ _____ a □ _____ for me?

W : I can do that. What type of food are you going to make?

M : I was thinking lasagna and salad, so an Italian cuisine book would be perfect.

✎ **어휘복습** 잘 안 들리거나 몰라서 체크한 어휘를 써 놓고 복습해 보세요.

□ _____   □ _____   □ _____   □ _____

□ _____   □ _____   □ _____   □ _____

□ _____   □ _____   □ _____   □ _____

03 그림 상황에 적절한 대화 찾기

다음 그림의 상황에 가장 적절한 대화를 고르시오.

① ② ③ ④ ⑤

① W : □ _____ □ _____ are the shoes in the □ _____ □ _____?

   M : They are □ _____ □ _____ □ _____ forty-five dollars.

② W : Do you have these shoes □ _____ a □ _____ □ _____?

   M : No, ma'am.

③ W : These shoes are too big. Could you show me □ _____ □ _____?

   M : Sure. □ _____ me □ _____ them for you.

④ W : I □ _____ my shoes. What should I do?

   M : I'll help you □ _____ □ _____ them.

⑤ W : How long will it take to □ _____ my shoes □ _____?

   M : It'll take about two hours.

04 특정 정보 파악

대화를 듣고, 두 사람이 만나기로 한 요일을 고르시오.

① Monday   ② Tuesday
③ Thursday   ④ Friday
⑤ Saturday

W : Hey, Marvin! What's up?

M : Hello, Mary. I'm at home □ _____ a □ _____.

W : That sounds like so much fun! Are you going to □ _____ it □ _____ soon?

M : Yeah, I'm probably going on □ _____ □ _____ □ _____. Do you want to go with me?

W : Oh, man! I □ _____ go on Tuesday because I □ _____ □ _____ □ _____ at my part-time job.

M : That's fine. We can go on Friday, then.

W : Great! Let's hope □ _____ □ _____ a good □ _____ to fly the kite that day.

✎ **어휘복습** 잘 안 들리거나 몰라서 체크한 어휘를 써 놓고 복습해 보세요.

□ _____ □ _____ □ _____ □ _____

□ _____ □ _____ □ _____ □ _____

□ _____ □ _____ □ _____ □ _____

05 장소 추론

대화를 듣고, 두 사람이 대화하고 있는 장소로 가장 적절한 곳을 고르시오.

① museum   ② classroom
③ movie theater   ④ toy store
⑤ park

W : Dad, look at all the dinosaurs! There are so many □ _____ □ _____!

M : I'm glad you're having a good time. □ _____ □ _____ to □ _____, but tell me □ _____ you're going first.

W : Alright. Let's □ _____ □ _____ there to see the □ _____ dinosaurs.

M : Okay. If you □ _____ this button you can □ _____ the □ _____ they make.

W : This is amazing! I only saw dinosaurs in books, but seeing them in this exhibit is □ _____ □ _____ □ _____! Can we come again?

M : Of course, we can come back □ _____ you want.

W : You're the best, Dad.

06 심정 추론

대화를 듣고, 여자의 심정으로 가장 적절한 것을 고르시오.

① grateful   ② frustrated
③ happy   ④ satisfied
⑤ scared

M : Janice, why didn't you □ _____ □ _____ your □ _____?

W : What do you mean? I □ _____ it □ _____ you last Monday.

M : I didn't □ _____ an email from you. Which □ _____ did you send it to?

W : Let me see, g-a-r-y-nine-one-two at cedubook dot com.

M : Oh, I see what the □ _____ is. I'm afraid you □ _____ my email address □ _____. It is h-a-r-y-nine-one-five at cedubook dot com.

W : That's terrible! How could I have done such a thing? Can I send it to you today?

M : No, I'm sorry. The □ _____ was yesterday, and I □ _____ □ _____ □ _____ □ _____ for you.

✎ **어휘복습** 잘 안 들리거나 몰라서 체크한 어휘를 써 놓고 복습해 보세요.

□ _____   □ _____   □ _____   □ _____

□ _____   □ _____   □ _____   □ _____

□ _____   □ _____   □ _____   □ _____

다음을 듣고, 두 사람의 대화가 어색한 것을
고르시오.

① ② ③ ④ ⑤

① M : I was □ _____ □ _____ the photo exhibit.

   W : You're right. I □ _____ the □ _____ way.

② M : How □ _____ □ _____ is the bank □ _____ □ _____?

   W : It's a five-minute □ _____ □ _____.

③ M : How would you like to □ _____?

   W : □ _____ cash.

④ M : I □ _____ some tomatoes to put in my salad.

   W : Did you □ _____ your potato salad?

⑤ M : □ _____ you □ _____ □ _____ today?

   W : Absolutely not. It's too hot.

대화를 듣고, 여자가 남자에게 부탁한 일로
가장 적절한 것을 고르시오.

① 표 예매하기　　② 영화 검색하기
③ 저녁 사기　　　④ 팝콘 사기
⑤ 좌석 바꾸기

M : Jess, □ _____ you □ _____ the □ _____ *The Girl in Red*?

W : No, I want to watch it, though.

M : Are you free to go see it □ _____ □ _____?

W : That'd be great, but I □ _____ □ _____ there are □ _____ □ _____, since it's the most popular play right now.

M : I can □ _____ the □ _____ right now. Hmm… There aren't any seats left near the □ _____, so we'll have to sit in the □ _____. Is that okay?

W : Yeah, I don't □ _____ at all □ _____ we sit. Can you □ _____ the tickets? I'll □ _____ you □ _____ after the play.

M : Of course. I'll see you soon!

✎ **어휘복습** 잘 안 들리거나 몰라서 체크한 어휘를 써 놓고 복습해 보세요.

□ _____　　□ _____　　□ _____　　□ _____

□ _____　　□ _____　　□ _____　　□ _____

□ _____　　□ _____　　□ _____

09 의도 파악

대화를 듣고, 여자의 마지막 말에 담긴 의도로 가장 적절한 것을 고르시오.

① 거절　② 충고　③ 요청
④ 제안　⑤ 감사

M : Irene, I have a wedding □ _____ □ _____ for you.

W : That's so sweet of you! What is it?

M : It's a surprise! □ _____ your eyes and □ _____ me into the kitchen.

W : When can I open my eyes? I'm so □ _____ to □ _____ □ _____ you bought for me.

M : You can open your eyes now.

W : Oh my goodness! It's a □ _____ refrigerator! How did you know I needed this?

M : Well, our old one □ _____ □ _____ because it was so old. I thought you might like a new one.

W : Thank you. You're such a □ _____ person. I couldn't ask for a better gift.

10 숫자 정보 파악

대화를 듣고, 여자가 지불해야 할 금액을 고르시오.

① $30　② $80　③ $100
④ $160　⑤ $240

M : How was dinner, ma'am?

W : It was delicious, thank you. How much do I □ _____ you?

M : You had the chicken salad, mushroom soup, onion rings, and beef lasagna. So your □ _____ is □ _____ □ _____ □ _____ dollars.

W : Oh, I have a □ _____ □ _____ □ _____ coupon. Can I use this now?

M : Yes, you □ _____ □ _____ it on today's meal. With the discount, your total is □ _____ dollars. Would you like to pay with cash or credit card?

W : Cash, please. Here is a one-hundred dollar bill.

✏️ **어휘복습** 잘 안 들리거나 몰라서 체크한 어휘를 써 놓고 복습해 보세요.

□ _____　□ _____　□ _____　□ _____

□ _____　□ _____　□ _____　□ _____

□ _____　□ _____　□ _____　□ _____

대화를 듣고, 두 사람의 관계로 가장 적절한 것을 고르시오.

① 식당 종업원 – 손님
② 호텔 직원 – 투숙객
③ 택시 기사 – 승객
④ 엄마 – 아들
⑤ 관광 안내원 – 관광객

M : Excuse me. Can you give me a □ _____ call for six thirty tomorrow morning? I have an important □ _____ to go to.

W : Absolutely. What is your □ _____ □ _____?

M : It's room eleven oh four.

W : Alright, will that be all?

M : Oh, I almost □ _____. I would also like □ _____ □ _____ □ _____ breakfast at seven.

W : No problem. I'll □ _____ it □ _____ for you.

다음을 듣고, North Valley English Camp 에 관해 언급되지 <u>않은</u> 것을 고르시오.

① 운영 시간   ② 위치
③ 시설   ④ 프로그램
⑤ 요금

M : Are you looking for □ _____ □ _____ to do over the summer? Our North Valley English Camp first □ _____ □ _____ two thousand ten. Our □ _____ are □ _____ □ _____ Seattle. We provide dormitories, classrooms, □ _____ □ _____ □ _____ computer labs. The □ _____ □ _____ □ _____ fun lessons, team work, games, and outdoor activities. You can enjoy the camp □ _____ only □ _____ dollars! To □ _____ □ _____, please call our office □ _____ nine three one, two four one, two nine one two.

✎ **어휘복습** 잘 안 들리거나 몰라서 체크한 어휘를 써 놓고 복습해 보세요.

□ _____   □ _____   □ _____   □ _____

□ _____   □ _____   □ _____   □ _____

□ _____   □ _____   □ _____   □ _____

13 그림 정보 파악

다음 백화점 주차 안내도를 보면서 대화를 듣고, 두 사람이 주차할 구역을 고르시오.

W : Rex, where should we □ _____ at the shopping center?

M : Hmm… Sections D and E would be □ _____ since they are too □ _____ □ _____ the □ _____.

W : You're right. Then let's park in Section A.

M : There are □ _____ more □ _____ spots □ _____ in that section.

W : Okay then, what about the section in front of Entrance two? There are more □ _____ □ _____ there.

M : But all of our favorite stores are □ _____ □ _____ Entrance □ _____.

W : Well then, let's park in front of that entrance.

14 화제 추론

다음을 듣고, 무엇에 관한 설명인지 고르시오.

① 야구 ② 농구 ③ 배구
④ 축구 ⑤ 핸드볼

M : This is a popular □ _____ sport using a □ _____. The ball is white with red stitches. This sport is usually played outdoors. The □ _____ is shaped like a □ _____. Some players stand □ _____ □ _____ one, two, three, and home base. There are players who □ _____ the ball, and players who □ _____ the ball with a □ _____. Players □ _____ by running to home base safely.

✎ **어휘복습** 잘 안 들리거나 몰라서 체크한 어휘를 써 놓고 복습해 보세요.

□ _____   □ _____   □ _____   □ _____

□ _____   □ _____   □ _____   □ _____

□ _____   □ _____   □ _____   □ _____

15 할 일 파악

대화를 듣고, 남자가 오늘 할 일로 가장 적절한 것을 고르시오.

① 강아지 사기
② 강아지 팔기
③ 블로그 만들기
④ 여자의 집에 가기
⑤ 강아지 사진 배포하기

M : Laura, what are you doing here?

W : I'm □ _____ □ _____ of my dog's □ _____ on my blog.

M : Oh, I didn't know you had a blog. Your dog had puppies? I would love to see the pictures.

W : Here, you can see them now. I just □ _____ □ _____ them.

M : They are so cute! □ _____ □ _____ any □ _____ you could give me one?

W : I'll □ _____ □ _____ □ _____ one □ _____ □ _____ □ _____ you promise to take good care of it.

M : I promise! □ _____ do I have to go to see the puppies?

W : □ _____ □ _____ my house later today.

16 특정 정보 파악

대화를 듣고, 두 사람이 구매할 물건을 고르시오.

① shoes   ② water
③ backpack   ④ shirt
⑤ bandage

W : Robert, I think I □ _____ my □ _____ while I was hiking.

M : Here, give me your arm. I'll take a look at it.

W : I probably □ _____ □ _____ by a tree branch or □ _____ it on a rock.

M : Goodness, you're □ _____! Do you have a □ _____?

W : No, I □ _____ have □ _____ in my backpack.

M : Hmm… We can □ _____ □ _____ after we clean the □ _____ with water.

W : Okay. There should be a □ _____ around here.

✎ **어휘복습** 잘 안 들리거나 몰라서 체크한 어휘를 써 놓고 복습해 보세요.

□ _____   □ _____   □ _____   □ _____

□ _____   □ _____   □ _____   □ _____

□ _____   □ _____   □ _____   □ _____

17 상황에 적절한 말 찾기

다음 상황 설명을 듣고, John이 엄마에게 할 말로 가장 적절한 것을 고르시오.

John: Mom, _____

① how much is the lamp?
② do you like my new lamp?
③ where should I put the lamp?
④ can you help me make food for the guests?
⑤ could you help me clean the house?

M : John bought a new ☐ _____ to ☐ _____ his apartment. He is expecting ☐ _____ to come over in an hour. However, he's ☐ _____ ☐ _____ ☐ _____ ☐ _____ ☐ _____ the lamp. So he decides to ask his mom about it. In this situation, what would John most likely say to his mom?

John: Mom, _____

18 할 일 파악

대화를 듣고, 남자가 할 일로 가장 적절한 것을 고르시오.

① 화분에 물주기
② 화장실 청소하기
③ 청소기 돌리기
④ 식사 준비하기
⑤ 쓰레기 갖다 버리기

W : Honey, I'm busy washing the dishes. Can you ☐ _____ the bedroom?

M : I vacuumed the house this morning. Did you forget ☐ _____?

W : Oh yeah, I forgot. I've just been so busy lately that I can't ☐ _____ ☐ _____.

M : I understand. If you need, I can ☐ _____ you ☐ _____ some other ☐ _____.

W : Actually, there is one more thing. I just ☐ _____ that I ☐ _____ ☐ _____ the ☐ _____ for three days.

M : I'll do it right away.

✎ **어휘복습** 잘 안 들리거나 몰라서 체크한 어휘를 써 놓고 복습해 보세요.

☐ _____   ☐ _____   ☐ _____   ☐ _____
☐ _____   ☐ _____   ☐ _____   ☐ _____
☐ _____   ☐ _____   ☐ _____   ☐ _____

대화를 듣고, 여자의 마지막 말에 대한 남자의 응답으로 가장 적절한 것을 고르시오.

Man: _____

① Well, I can go to the store with you.
② That's not necessary. I don't use that TV anyway.
③ I need to stop by the bank before we go.
④ The electronics store is open now.
⑤ I will call the store and ask when they close.

M : Hey Vicky. I'm going to the □ _____ □ _____ tomorrow. You can □ _____ □ _____ if you'd like.
W : Yeah, I'd like that. I have to buy a □ _____ TV anyway.
M : What kind of TV do you want? I actually have an □ _____ □ _____ in my apartment.
W : Oh, really? Well, I'm not looking for anything □ _____ □ _____.
M : Then I'll □ _____ my TV □ _____ your house in the morning. If you like it, I'll □ _____ you □ _____ for free.
W : □ _____ □ _____? That's too □ _____ of you. Let me buy it from you for fifty dollars.
M : _____

대화를 듣고, 여자의 마지막 말에 대한 남자의 응답으로 가장 적절한 것을 고르시오.

Man: _____

① Thanks for the ride home.
② No, I built a new house for my cat.
③ Yes, how long has it been since you moved here?
④ Yeah. I hope someone calls me telling me that they found my cat.
⑤ I'll call you the next time I'm in town.

W : Hi, Louie. You look so down, what's wrong?
M : Hey, Julie. I'm □ _____ about my □ _____. I □ _____ the door □ _____ for five minutes and she □ _____.
W : Oh no! How long has she been □ _____?
M : For a few hours now. I should □ _____ □ _____ and start looking for her.
W : It's really □ _____ outside. You'll probably have a □ _____ □ _____ of finding her in the morning.
M : □ _____ □ _____ something happens to her before then?
W : Nothing's going to happen. She □ _____ a □ _____ □ _____ with □ _____ phone number and □ _____, right?
M : _____

✎ **어휘복습** 잘 안 들리거나 몰라서 체크한 어휘를 써 놓고 복습해 보세요.

□ _____   □ _____   □ _____   □ _____
□ _____   □ _____   □ _____   □ _____
□ _____   □ _____   □ _____

점수 / 20

01 대화를 듣고, 남자가 마실 음료를 고르시오.

02 대화를 듣고, 남자가 여자에게 전화한 목적으로 가장 적절한 것을 고르시오.

① 물건을 돌려주려고
② 주소를 물어보려고
③ 약속 장소를 바꾸려고
④ 상품에 대해 불평하려고
⑤ 버스 노선을 물어보려고

03 다음 그림의 상황에 가장 적절한 대화를 고르시오.

①　　②　　③　　④　　⑤

04 대화를 듣고, 두 사람이 말하고 있는 표지판을 고르시오.

① No Cooking
② No Campfires
③ No Cars
④ No Smoking
⑤ No Fishing

05 대화를 듣고, 여자의 직업으로 가장 적절한 것을 고르시오.

① hotel employee
② taxi driver
③ tour guide
④ bus driver
⑤ immigration officer

06 대화를 듣고, 여자의 심정으로 가장 적절한 것을 고르시오.

① nervous　② upset　③ surprised
④ dreadful　⑤ excited

07 다음을 듣고, 두 사람의 대화가 <u>어색한</u> 것을 고르시오.

①　　②　　③　　④　　⑤

08 대화를 듣고, 여자가 남자에게 부탁한 일로 가장 적절한 것을 고르시오.

① 식사 함께 하기
② 새로운 식단 짜기
③ 자전거 함께 타기
④ 체육관에 함께 가기
⑤ 자전거 타는 법 가르쳐주기

09 대화를 듣고, 남자의 마지막 말에 담긴 의도로 가장 적절한 것을 고르시오.

① 요청　　② 거절　　③ 위로
④ 제안　　⑤ 허락

10 다음 표를 보면서 대화를 듣고, 남자가 지불할 금액을 고르시오.

shirt	$10	pants	$10
sweater	$12	hat	$8
jacket	$15	sunglasses	$5
blouse	$10	shoes	$15

① $40　　② $45　　③ $50
④ $55　　⑤ $60

11 대화를 듣고, 두 사람이 대화하고 있는 장소로 가장 적절한 곳을 고르시오.

① daycare center　　② art gallery
③ school　　　　　　④ stadium
⑤ wedding hall

12 다음을 듣고, Trim History Museum에 관해 언급되지 <u>않은</u> 것을 고르시오.

① 전시 제목　　② 개장 시간　　③ 위치
④ 입장료　　　　⑤ 전시 기간

13 다음 표를 보면서 대화를 듣고, 내용과 일치하지 <u>않는</u> 것을 고르시오.

All-star Marathon

①	Date	March 12th
②	Time	1 P.M.
③	Location	Franklin Street Bridge
④	How to sign up	here or online
⑤	Fee	free

14 다음을 듣고, 무엇에 대한 설명인지 고르시오.

① 자연 재해 종류　　　② 태풍 이동 경로
③ 여름 휴가철 준비물　④ 장마 대처 방법
⑤ 여름 휴양지 추천

15 대화를 듣고, 두 사람이 대화 직후에 할 일로 가장 적절한 것을 고르시오.

① 병문안 가기　　② 안부 전화하기
③ 파티 준비하기　④ 생일 선물 사기
⑤ 생일파티에 가기

16 대화를 듣고, 두 사람이 만날 요일과 시각을 고르시오.

① 화요일 6시　　② 수요일 6시
③ 수요일 8시　　④ 목요일 6시
⑤ 목요일 8시

17 다음 상황 설명을 듣고, Danny가 Derick에게 할 말로 가장 적절한 것을 고르시오.

Danny: _____

① I'm hungry. Let's go to the food court.
② Hey, do you want to go to the waterpark?
③ This line is too long. Let's go ride something else.
④ Hurry up, Derick! I've been waiting for you for two hours!
⑤ Derick, I'll go get the sunblock. Just wait in line until I come back.

18 대화를 듣고, 여자가 할 일로 가장 적절한 것을 고르시오.

① 사진 찍기　　② 호텔 찾기
③ 택시 잡기　　④ 지도 살피기
⑤ 카메라 사기

19 대화를 듣고, 상황을 가장 잘 표현한 속담을 고르시오.

① Habit is second nature.
② First come, first served.
③ Honesty is the best policy.
④ The early bird catches the worm.
⑤ Where there is smoke, there is fire.

20 대화를 듣고, 여자의 마지막 말에 이어질 남자의 응답으로 가장 적절한 것을 고르시오.

Man: _____

① I put them in the freezer.
② They are in the kitchen sink.
③ What is your favorite vegetable?
④ I bought them from a greenhouse.
⑤ Have you planted vegetables before?

다시 듣고, 빈칸에 알맞은 단어를 써 보세요.

◀)) MP3 실전 06-1

01 그림 정보 파악

대화를 듣고, 남자가 마실 음료를 고르시오.

① ② ③
④ ⑤

W : What would you like to drink, sir?

M : I □ _____ □ _____ iced coffee in the □ _____, but I think I'll □ _____ □ _____ without caffeine today.

W : Okay, then how about some fruit juice? There is □ _____ □ _____ □ _____ fruit you can □ _____ □ _____.

M : Fruit juice? That sounds □ _____ □ _____ for my □ _____.

W : Then how is some □ _____ with one of our special muffins?

M : That sounds delicious.

02 목적 파악

대화를 듣고, 남자가 여자에게 전화한 목적으로 가장 적절한 것을 고르시오.

① 물건을 돌려주려고
② 주소를 물어보려고
③ 약속 장소를 바꾸려고
④ 상품에 대해 불평하려고
⑤ 버스 노선을 물어보려고

M : Hello, may I speak to Megan Redd?

W : This is □ _____. Who is □ _____?

M : My name is Robert. I □ _____ a □ _____ on the □ _____. Your name and phone number were on the back of it.

W : Oh, my! I am so □ _____ that you called! You are a life saver!

M : I'm □ _____ I could □ _____. □ _____ can I □ _____ it back to you?

W : Where are you right now? I'll go □ _____ it □ _____.

✏ **어휘복습** 잘 안 들리거나 몰라서 체크한 어휘를 써 놓고 복습해 보세요.

□ _____ □ _____ □ _____ □ _____
□ _____ □ _____ □ _____ □ _____
□ _____ □ _____ □ _____ □ _____

03 그림 상황에 적절한 대화 찾기

다음 그림의 상황에 가장 적절한 대화를 고르시오.

① ② ③ ④ ⑤

① W : Did you □ _____ your homework?

　　M : No, I will do it □ _____ I clean my room.

② W : What are you doing? You □ _____ □ _____.

　　M : I'm □ _____ □ _____ my science project.

③ W : What are you doing □ _____ □ _____ □ _____?
Get ready for school!

　　M : I'm so □ _____. I want to □ _____ all day.

④ W : What are you going to do this □ _____?

　　M : I'm going to my friend's house to □ _____ my □ _____.

⑤ W : What would you like to eat □ _____ □ _____?

　　M : Eggs and toast, please.

04 그림 정보 파악

대화를 듣고, 두 사람이 말하고 있는 표지판을 고르시오.

① No Cooking　② No Campfires　③ No Cars

④ No Smoking　⑤ No Fishing

M : Excuse me, ma'am? You can't □ _____ a □ _____ here.

W : Really? Why not?

M : We have □ _____ here. Didn't you see the □ _____
□ _____ in front of that tree?

W : What signs? I didn't see any □ _____ the □ _____ here.

M : Okay, let's □ _____ □ _____ there and □ _____ the signs.

W : I see, no □ _____, no □ _____, no □ _____, no
□ _____ …

M : Yes, and how about the □ _____ sign?

W : It says "□ _____ □ _____." Sorry, I will □ _____ the fire
□ _____ right now. Thanks for telling me.

M : My pleasure.

✎ **어휘복습** 잘 안 들리거나 몰라서 체크한 어휘를 써 놓고 복습해 보세요.

□ _____　□ _____　□ _____　□ _____

□ _____　□ _____　□ _____　□ _____

□ _____　□ _____　□ _____　□ _____

05 직업 추론

대화를 듣고, 여자의 직업으로 가장 적절한 것을 고르시오.

① hotel employee ② taxi driver
③ tour guide ④ bus driver
⑤ immigration officer

W : Good afternoon, sir. Where are you □ _____ today?
M : I want to □ _____ □ _____ Middle Town Square, please.
W : Are you talking about the place near Morris Lane?
M : Yeah, that's right. □ _____ □ _____ will it □ _____ to get there?
W : I think we can get there □ _____ □ _____ □ _____ or less.
M : Oh no, that's going to be problem. I need to get there in fifteen minutes.
W : Are you □ _____ □ _____ □ _____ to get to your □ _____?
M : Yes, my friend is waiting for me there and I'm already □ _____ □ _____ □ _____.
W : Okay, I'll take Highway eighty-nine since there is □ _____ □ _____ there.
M : Wonderful.

06 심정 추론

대화를 듣고, 여자의 심정으로 가장 적절한 것을 고르시오.

① nervous ② upset
③ surprised ④ dreadful
⑤ excited

M : How were □ _____ for the volleyball team today?
W : Awesome! I have a □ _____ □ _____ about it.
M : You seem □ _____. Tell me about what happened.
W : My team □ _____ a practice game □ _____ seven points. Can you guess who □ _____ the □ _____ points?
M : Let me think. Was it you?
W : That's right! The volleyball coach told me that I am a great player.
M : That's wonderful! I think we'll be □ _____ some □ _____ □ _____ soon.

✎ **어휘복습** 잘 안 들리거나 몰라서 체크한 어휘를 써 놓고 복습해 보세요.

□ _____ □ _____ □ _____ □ _____
□ _____ □ _____ □ _____ □ _____
□ _____ □ _____ □ _____ □ _____

다음을 듣고, 두 사람의 대화가 <u>어색한</u> 것을
고르시오.

①　　②　　③　　④　　⑤

① W : Can I □ _____ you □ _____? I'm busy right now.

　 M : All the phone □ _____ were □ _____ so I couldn't
　　　 □ _____ □ _____.

② W : I like this coat. May I □ _____ it?

　 M : Yes, but I need it □ _____ □ _____ Wednesday.

③ W : You're great! Have you been □ _____ □ _____?

　 M : Yeah, I go □ _____ □ _____ with my family.

④ W : What are you going to □ _____?

　 M : □ _____ □ _____ □ _____ cereal and some fruit.

⑤ W : □ _____ was the ski resort?

　 M : It was □ _____! Everyone had a great time.

대화를 듣고, 여자가 남자에게 부탁한 일로
가장 적절한 것을 고르시오.

① 식사 함께 하기
② 새로운 식단 짜기
③ 자전거 함께 타기
④ 체육관에 함께 가기
⑤ 자전거 타는 법 가르쳐주기

W : I think I'm □ _____ □ _____. What do you think I should do?

M : □ _____ your □ _____ around the neighborhood will
　　 □ _____.

W : That's a great idea. Do you have any other tips?

M : You have to □ _____ your □ _____ to lose weight.

W : How can I do that?

M : Eat □ _____ □ _____ and stay away from junk food.

W : Sounds great, but I have never □ _____ my □ _____. Can you
　　 help me do that?

M : Yes, I can do that.

✎ **어휘복습** 잘 안 들리거나 몰라서 체크한 어휘를 써 놓고 복습해 보세요.

□ _____ 　 □ _____ 　 □ _____ 　 □ _____

□ _____ 　 □ _____ 　 □ _____ 　 □ _____

□ _____ 　 □ _____ 　 □ _____ 　 □ _____

09 의도 파악

대화를 듣고, 남자의 마지막 말에 담긴 의도로 가장 적절한 것을 고르시오.

① 요청   ② 거절   ③ 위로
④ 제안   ⑤ 허락

W : Where are you going, Kirk?
M : I'm going to my friend's house. We're □ _____ □ _____ study for final exams.
W : Do you □ _____ study □ _____ someone else?
M : Yeah, □ _____ □ _____ the time I study with a friend who is taking the same class.
W : Isn't it □ _____ for you □ _____ □ _____?
M : No, not at all. We solve problems together and □ _____ each other □ _____.
W : Oh, really? I always thought it was best to just study alone.
M : You □ _____ □ _____ studying with a friend next time.
   I □ _____, it's □ _____ it!

10 숫자 정보 파악

다음 표를 보면서 대화를 듣고, 남자가 지불할 금액을 고르시오.

shirt	$10	pants	$10
sweater	$12	hat	$8
jacket	$15	sunglasses	$5
blouse	$10	shoes	$15

① $40   ② $45   ③ $50
④ $55   ⑤ $60

W : Good morning! Are you looking for anything □ _____ □ _____?
M : Yes, where can I find the □ _____ □ _____?
W : □ _____, sweaters, jackets, and □ _____ on this rack are on sale.
M : Is anything else on sale?
W : Yes, the pants, hats, □ _____, and shoes are on those shelves.
M : Thank you. How much is it for □ _____ □ _____?
W : You can find a □ _____ □ _____ on each item, and the price on the tag is the sale price.
M : Okay, I got it. I will buy □ _____ shirts, □ _____ blouses, and □ _____ □ _____ □ _____ sunglasses.

✎ **어휘복습** 잘 안 들리거나 몰라서 체크한 어휘를 써 놓고 복습해 보세요.

□ _____   □ _____   □ _____   □ _____
□ _____   □ _____   □ _____   □ _____
□ _____   □ _____   □ _____   □ _____

11 장소 추론

대화를 듣고, 두 사람이 대화하고 있는 장소로 가장 적절한 곳을 고르시오.

① daycare center　② art gallery
③ school　④ stadium
⑤ wedding hall

M : Hello, Carly! Congratulations.

W : Nick! ☐ _____ you so much for ☐ _____.

M : I wouldn't miss it! You make such a ☐ _____ ☐ _____.

W : Thank you for the ☐ _____. Did you come alone?

M : No, I'm here with my fiancée, Jennifer.

W : Really? That's great! When do you plan on ☐ _____ ☐ _____?

M : Actually, I'm getting married next year. I'll be sure to ☐ _____ you.

W : Well, congratulations to you too!

12 미언급 파악

다음을 듣고, Trim History Museum에 관해 언급되지 않은 것을 고르시오.

① 전시 제목　② 개장 시간
③ 위치　④ 입장료
⑤ 전시 기간

W : Welcome to the Trim History Museum. We are pleased to announce our ☐ _____ ☐ _____, *The Lost Empire.* Come to explore the history of Rome and Egypt! It will be ☐ _____ ☐ _____ on February thirteenth. We are open ☐ _____ A.M. ☐ _____ ☐ _____ P.M. ☐ _____ ☐ _____, even on national holidays. ☐ _____ ☐ _____ are ten dollars for adults, and children under three years old can enjoy the museum for free. The exhibition will only be ☐ _____ ☐ _____ February twenty seventh, so book your tickets now at trimhistory dot org.

✎ **어휘복습** 잘 안 들리거나 몰라서 체크한 어휘를 써 놓고 복습해 보세요.

☐ _____　☐ _____　☐ _____　☐ _____
☐ _____　☐ _____　☐ _____　☐ _____
☐ _____　☐ _____　☐ _____　☐ _____

13 도표·실용문 파악

다음 표를 보면서 대화를 듣고, 내용과 일치하지 <u>않는</u> 것을 고르시오.

All-star Marathon

①	Date	March 12th
②	Time	1 P.M.
③	Location	Franklin Street Bridge
④	How to sign up	here or online
⑤	Fee	free

M : This is Ohio Marathon. What can I do for you?

W : I want to know about this year's All-star Marathon.

M : Okay, well, it takes place on Sunday, □ _____ □ _____, at □ _____.

W : Can you tell me where the □ _____ □ _____ is?

M : The race starts □ _____ the Franklin Street □ _____.

W : Great. How can I participate?

M : You can fill out this form □ _____ or you can sign up on our □ _____.

W : Is there a registration □ _____ for the race?

M : □ _____, ma'am.

14 화제 추론

다음을 듣고, 무엇에 대한 설명인지 고르시오.

① 자연 재해 종류
② 태풍 이동 경로
③ 여름 휴가철 준비물
④ 장마 대처 방법
⑤ 여름 휴양지 추천

M : It is □ _____ season, so the National Weather Channel is telling you how to □ _____ □ _____ from the □ _____. Even though it is sunny right now, the □ _____ can □ _____ □ _____. Please make sure you always □ _____ an □ _____ with you. Also, wearing rain boots and a raincoat will help you □ _____ □ _____. If it is raining heavily, please □ _____ □ _____. If you are outside when it starts to rain, find □ _____ or go to a □ _____ □ _____.

✎ **어휘복습** 잘 안 들리거나 몰라서 체크한 어휘를 써 놓고 복습해 보세요.

□ _____   □ _____   □ _____   □ _____

□ _____   □ _____   □ _____   □ _____

□ _____   □ _____   □ _____   □ _____

15 할 일 파악

대화를 듣고, 두 사람이 대화 직후에 할 일로 가장 적절한 것을 고르시오.

① 병문안 가기
② 안부 전화하기
③ 파티 준비하기
④ 생일 선물 사기
⑤ 생일파티에 가기

M : Do you remember that it's Stacy's birthday party this Saturday?

W : Yeah, but Lori □ _____ earlier □ _____ she won't □ _____ □ _____ □ _____ □ _____ us.

M : Is something the matter?

W : She has to □ _____ □ _____ □ _____ for a few days.

M : Oh, no! What happened to her?

W : I think she □ _____ a bad □ _____ from the freezing weather.

M : I'm sorry to hear that. Should we visit her after school?

W : Lori told me □ _____ □ _____ □ _____ because we could catch the cold □ _____ her.

M : I see. I think we should □ _____ □ _____ □ _____ her to see how she's doing.

W : Awesome idea!

16 특정 정보 파악

대화를 듣고, 두 사람이 만날 요일과 시각을 고르시오.

① 화요일 6시　　② 수요일 6시
③ 수요일 8시　　④ 목요일 6시
⑤ 목요일 8시

M : Hey, the weather is nice these days.

W : I know. The weather is supposed to be □ _____ □ _____ □ _____. It will be □ _____ to go to the □ _____.

M : Why don't we go □ _____ □ _____ this week?

W : That sounds like fun. When is the □ _____ □ _____ and □ _____ for you?

M : Well, I'll be free on □ _____ at □ _____ A.M.

W : I can't go that day because I have a meeting scheduled □ _____ □ _____ □ _____ □ _____.

M : So □ _____ □ _____ □ _____ we can't go running together this week?

W : No, I think I'll be able to move my meeting to Wednesday at eight A.M.

M : Okay. Then, I'll see you soon!

✏ **어휘복습** 잘 안 들리거나 몰라서 체크한 어휘를 써 놓고 복습해 보세요.

□ _____　□ _____　□ _____　□ _____

□ _____　□ _____　□ _____　□ _____

□ _____　□ _____　□ _____　□ _____

17 상황에 적절한 말 찾기

다음 상황 설명을 듣고, Danny가 Derick에게 할 말로 가장 적절한 것을 고르시오.

Danny: _____

① I'm hungry. Let's go to the food court.
② Hey, do you want to go to the waterpark?
③ This line is too long. Let's go ride something else.
④ Hurry up, Derick! I've been waiting for you for two hours!
⑤ Derick, I'll go get the sunblock. Just wait in line until I come back.

18 할 일 파악

대화를 듣고, 여자가 할 일로 가장 적절한 것을 고르시오.

① 사진 찍기   ② 호텔 찾기
③ 택시 잡기   ④ 지도 살피기
⑤ 카메라 사기

W : Danny went to the waterpark □ _____ his □ _____ □ _____, Derick. They were □ _____ □ _____ □ _____ for a ride. Derick □ _____ Danny □ _____ some □ _____, but it was in the locker room. They had been standing in line for two hours already. It would be a □ _____ to stand in line □ _____ □ _____ □ _____. So, Danny decided to □ _____ □ _____ while Derick waited in line for him. In this situation, what would Danny most likely say to Derick?

Danny: _____

M : I can't believe we're actually in France!
W : I know, I □ _____ □ _____ I'm in a □ _____.
M : Is this your □ _____ □ _____ coming here?
W : Yeah, I've □ _____ to □ _____ □ _____ in Europe, but it's my first time visiting France. How about you?
M : Me too. This is actually my first time in a European country. I've □ _____ □ _____ to tour here.
W : I see. Hey! Isn't that the □ _____ we saw in the □ _____ □ _____ □ _____? It looks really cool.
M : Do you want me to take your picture?
W : I would □ _____ that. Thank you. I'll □ _____ a □ _____ for you too.

✎ **어휘복습** 잘 안 들리거나 몰라서 체크한 어휘를 써 놓고 복습해 보세요.

□ _____ □ _____ □ _____ □ _____
□ _____ □ _____ □ _____ □ _____
□ _____ □ _____ □ _____ □ _____

19 속담 추론

대화를 듣고, 상황을 가장 잘 표현한 속담을 고르시오.

① Habit is second nature.
② First come, first served.
③ Honesty is the best policy.
④ The early bird catches the worm.
⑤ Where there is smoke, there is fire.

W : Harry, please sit down. I need to □ _____ □ _____ you.
M : Did I do something wrong, Ms. Thompson?
W : It's about your history report. Did you □ _____ □ _____ □ _____?
M : Actually, my parents □ _____ □ _____ write it.
W : I thought so. I □ _____ □ _____ a middle school student did it □ _____.
M : I'm sorry, Ms. Thompson.
W : □ _____ you for □ _____ □ _____ the □ _____. In the future, try to write your reports on your own.

20 알맞은 응답 찾기

대화를 듣고, 여자의 마지막 말에 이어질 남자의 응답으로 가장 적절한 것을 고르시오.

Man: _____

① I put them in the freezer.
② They are in the kitchen sink.
③ What is your favorite vegetable?
④ I bought them from a greenhouse.
⑤ Have you planted vegetables before?

W : Rob, what are you up to?
M : I'm □ _____ □ _____ in my new vegetable garden.
W : What □ _____ □ _____ seeds do you have?
M : Well, right now I have tomato, lettuce, and peppers. I plan on buying some more tomorrow.
W : Interesting. □ _____ □ _____ will it □ _____ for them to □ _____?
M : It's my first time gardening, so I'm not sure. It'll □ _____ take □ _____ □ _____ weeks.
W : □ _____ did you □ _____ the seeds?
M : _____

✏️ **어휘복습** 잘 안 들리거나 몰라서 체크한 어휘를 써 놓고 복습해 보세요.

□ _____ □ _____ □ _____ □ _____
□ _____ □ _____ □ _____ □ _____
□ _____ □ _____ □ _____ □ _____

01 대화를 듣고, 남자가 만들 피자를 고르시오.

①   ②   ③

④   ⑤

02 대화를 듣고, 남자가 여자에게 전화한 목적으로 가장 적절한 것을 고르시오.

① 약속 시간을 정하려고
② 식료품을 사오라고 말하려고
③ 놀이방에 전화하라고 말하려고
④ 약속 시간에 늦는다고 말하려고
⑤ 여동생을 데려오라고 말하려고

03 다음 그림 상황에 가장 적절한 대화를 고르시오.

① ② ③ ④ ⑤

04 대화를 듣고, 두 사람이 구매할 모자를 고르시오.

①   ②   ③

④   ⑤

05 대화를 듣고, 여자의 직업으로 가장 적절한 것을 고르시오.

① veterinarian   ② teacher
③ dentist   ④ lawyer
⑤ pet shop owner

06 대화를 듣고, 남자의 심정으로 가장 적절한 것을 고르시오.

① angry   ② indifferent
③ regretful   ④ disappointed
⑤ embarrassed

07 다음을 듣고, 두 사람의 대화가 <u>어색한</u> 것을 고르시오.

①   ②   ③   ④   ⑤

08 대화를 듣고, 여자가 남자에게 부탁한 일로 가장 적절한 것을 고르시오.

① 숙제 도와주기   ② 숙제 제출하기
③ 프린터 고치기   ④ 보고서 출력하기
⑤ 서비스 센터에 전화하기

09 대화를 듣고, 여자의 마지막 말에 담긴 의도로 가장 적절한 것을 고르시오.

① 동의   ② 격려   ③ 거절
④ 칭찬   ⑤ 요청

10 대화를 듣고, 남자가 지불할 금액을 고르시오.

① $30   ② $40   ③ $50
④ $60   ⑤ $100

11 대화를 듣고, 두 사람이 대화하고 있는 장소로 가장 적절한 곳을 고르시오.

① ski resort   ② movie theater
③ waterpark   ④ swimming pool
⑤ restaurant

12 다음을 듣고, Witches and Princesses에 관해 언급되지 <u>않은</u> 것을 고르시오.

① 일일 진행 횟수   ② 등장인물
③ 시작 시각   ④ 진행 장소
⑤ 진행 시간

13 다음 표를 보면서 대화를 듣고, 내용과 일치하지 <u>않는</u> 것을 고르시오.

Time	8/31	9/1
9 P.M.	① Dragon Warrior	③ Magician's Fury
10 P.M.	The Man in White	④ Dragon Warrior
11 P.M.	② Magician's Fury	⑤ The Man in White

14 다음을 듣고, 무엇에 관한 설명인지 고르시오.

① 스승의 날   ② 광복절   ③ 새해 첫날
④ 어버이날   ⑤ 크리스마스

15 대화를 듣고, 남자가 대화 직후에 할 일로 가장 적절한 것을 고르시오.

① 페인트 사기   ② 서랍장 보기
③ 전구 사기   ④ 차 문 잠그기
⑤ 드라이버 사기

16 대화를 듣고, 콘서트가 시작하는 시각을 고르시오.

① 5:00   ② 5:30   ③ 6:00
④ 6:30   ⑤ 7:00

17 다음 상황 설명을 듣고, Ted가 Helen에게 할 말로 가장 적절한 것을 고르시오.

Ted: _____

① I think we should take one car to school and go together.
② I can't drive to school today, my car is in the repair shop.
③ The water is so polluted here. Let's go to another beach.
④ When you take out the trash, make sure you recycle.
⑤ Shall we walk to class together?

18 대화를 듣고, 남자가 할 일로 가장 적절한 것을 고르시오.

① 오븐 예열하기   ② 오븐에 쿠키 믹스 넣기
③ 쿠키 믹스 사기   ④ 냉장고에서 달걀 꺼내기
⑤ 쿠키 믹스를 쿠키판 위에 올리기

19 대화를 듣고, 상황을 가장 잘 표현한 속담을 고르시오.

① Like father, like son.
② The more, the better.
③ Out of sight, out of mind.
④ Honesty is the best policy.
⑤ Two heads are better than one.

20 대화를 듣고, 여자의 마지막 말에 이어질 남자의 응답으로 가장 적절한 것을 고르시오.

Man: _____

① Can you turn on some music?
② The bus stop is too far from here.
③ Sorry, we are all out of food today.
④ Have you done volunteer work before?
⑤ I volunteer every weekend from 2 P.M. to 4 P.M.

01 그림 정보 파악

대화를 듣고, 남자가 만들 피자를 고르시오.

① ② ③
④ ⑤

W : Welcome to Harry's Pizzeria! Today you will be able to
□ _____ your □ _____ □ _____ pizza.

M : I'm so excited to □ _____ □ _____. Where do I begin?

W : Well, all you have to do is □ _____ the □ _____ of the pizza
you want, and □ _____ the toppings on the □ _____.

M : I'm having a hard time □ _____. Do you have any □ _____?

W : I think you should make a □ _____ pizza, or a □ _____ pizza.

M : Hmm, but those shapes are too □ _____. I want to make one
with a □ _____ shape.

W : Okay then, we have □ _____, star, and □ _____ pizzas too.

M : I've □ _____ □ _____ a pizza shaped like a □ _____ before.
I think I'll go with that one.

W : That's a good choice. Now, let's put the □ _____ on top and put
it in the □ _____!

02 목적 파악

대화를 듣고, 남자가 여자에게 전화한 목적으
로 가장 적절한 것을 고르시오.

① 약속 시간을 정하려고
② 식료품을 사오라고 말하려고
③ 놀이방에 전화하라고 말하려고
④ 약속 시간에 늦는다고 말하려고
⑤ 여동생을 데려오라고 말하려고

M : Hey Sherry, this is Dad. Where are you right now?

W : I'm □ _____ □ _____ □ _____ to meet some friends. Why?

M : I don't mean to □ _____ you, but can I □ _____ a □ _____?

W : Of course, what is it?

M : I'm supposed to □ _____ □ _____ your sister from
□ _____ at six P.M., but I don't think I'll be able to because I
have to □ _____ □ _____ nine P.M.

W : So, do you need me to go and pick her up?

M : Right. □ _____ □ _____ do that for me?

W : Yeah, I'll □ _____ my friends and say I'm going to be
□ _____.

✏ 어휘복습 잘 안 들리거나 몰라서 체크한 어휘를 써 놓고 복습해 보세요.

□ _____ □ _____ □ _____ □ _____
□ _____ □ _____ □ _____ □ _____
□ _____ □ _____ □ _____ □ _____

다음 그림 상황에 가장 적절한 대화를 고르시오.

① ② ③ ④ ⑤

① M : Is there □ _____ □ _____ you need?

   W : Yes, I would like a box of pencils.

② M : Hey, can I use your □ _____?

   W : Here you are. □ _____ □ _____ next time.

③ M : What was our homework □ _____?

   W : We have to write a □ _____ □ _____.

④ M : Excuse me, could I □ _____ a pencil?

   W : Yeah, sure. Just make sure to □ _____ it □ _____ to me.

⑤ M : Do you know □ _____ this word □ _____?

   W : I'm not sure. □ _____ it □ _____ in the □ _____.

대화를 듣고, 두 사람이 구매할 모자를 고르시오.

① ② ③

④ ⑤

W : Which □ _____ should we □ _____ for our singing club □ _____?

M : I like this one with the microphone on it.

W : I do too, □ _____ I want a more □ _____ design.

M : Then what do you think about this one with the □ _____ □ _____?

W : Hmm, it's okay. But I like the design with the □ _____ □ _____.

M : Then □ _____ □ _____ we get the one with the guitar and music notes?

W : Yeah, that □ _____ □ _____. I hope the other □ _____ □ _____ will like the design we □ _____, too.

✏️ **어휘복습** 잘 안 들리거나 몰라서 체크한 어휘를 써 놓고 복습해 보세요.

□ _____   □ _____   □ _____   □ _____

□ _____   □ _____   □ _____   □ _____

□ _____   □ _____   □ _____   □ _____

05 직업 추론

대화를 듣고, 여자의 직업으로 가장 적절한 것을 고르시오.

① veterinarian   ② teacher
③ dentist   ④ lawyer
⑤ pet shop owner

W : Hello, □ _____ □ _____ you □ _____? Is your □ _____ □ _____ □ _____ well?
M : Yeah, he seems □ _____. He won't eat anything and keeps □ _____ these □ _____ □ _____.
W : Okay, let's take an X-ray and □ _____ him □ _____ right away.
M : Is my cat going to be okay?
W : I'll □ _____ □ _____ I can to help him □ _____ □ _____.
M : Thank you. □ _____ □ _____ will the □ _____ take?
W : I think your cat will have to □ _____ here □ _____. Please come back tomorrow.

06 심정 추론

대화를 듣고, 남자의 심정으로 가장 적절한 것을 고르시오.

① angry   ② indifferent
③ regretful   ④ disappointed
⑤ embarrassed

W : Hello, may I help you?
M : My name is Richard Owen and I □ _____ a □ _____ for a □ _____.
W : Just a minute, please. I will check it for you. There □ _____ be a □ _____ for □ _____. You are □ _____ □ _____ our □ _____.
M : That □ _____ □ _____. I'm sure I made a reservation. Could you please □ _____ it □ _____?
W : I'm sorry, sir. Are you sure you □ _____ a □ _____ at Paradise Hotel?
M : Oh, this isn't Paradise Falls Hotel?
W : No sir, that hotel is □ _____ the □ _____.
M : Oh, dear. I'm so sorry!

✏️ **어휘복습** 잘 안 들리거나 몰라서 체크한 어휘를 써 놓고 복습해 보세요.

□ _____   □ _____   □ _____   □ _____

□ _____   □ _____   □ _____   □ _____

□ _____   □ _____   □ _____   □ _____

다음을 듣고, 두 사람의 대화가 <u>어색한</u> 것을 고르시오.

① ② ③ ④ ⑤

① W : □ _____ do you □ _____ your new □ _____?

　 M : It's good. I'm still getting □ _____ □ _____ it.

② W : I hope it doesn't □ _____ today.

　 M : Me too. I didn't □ _____ an □ _____.

③ W : Do you want □ _____ to □ _____?

　 M : Yeah, orange juice please.

④ W : Wow, look at all the sea □ _____!

　 M : I've been □ _____ with my dad □ _____ □ _____.

⑤ W : Did you □ _____ the □ _____?

　 M : Oh, I forgot. I'll □ _____ right □ _____.

대화를 듣고, 여자가 남자에게 부탁한 일로 가장 적절한 것을 고르시오.

① 숙제 도와주기
② 숙제 제출하기
③ 프린터 고치기
④ 보고서 출력하기
⑤ 서비스 센터에 전화하기

M : Hello? This is Steve.

W : Steve! It's me, Lauren.

M : Hey, what's up?

W : I was □ _____ □ _____ you could come over and □ _____ my □ _____.

M : Is it □ _____ again? What's □ _____ with it?

W : I have no idea. I tried printing my report □ _____ the □ _____ keeps getting □ _____.

M : I see. Did you □ _____ □ _____ the □ _____ □ _____ center?

W : Yeah, but the □ _____ is □ _____. My call isn't □ _____ □ _____.

M : Okay then. I'll be over in a few minutes.

✎ **어휘복습** 잘 안 들리거나 몰라서 체크한 어휘를 써 놓고 복습해 보세요.

□ _____　□ _____　□ _____　□ _____

□ _____　□ _____　□ _____　□ _____

□ _____　□ _____　□ _____　□ _____

09 의도 파악

대화를 듣고, 여자의 마지막 말에 담긴 의도로 가장 적절한 것을 고르시오.

① 동의　　② 격려　　③ 거절
④ 칭찬　　⑤ 요청

M : Janice, □ _____ are you □ _____ for the triathlon?

W : I run, swim, and □ _____ at the fitness center every day.

M : Do you think you're □ _____?

W : Who □ _____? I'm doing my best, so □ _____ there'll be □ _____ □ _____. How about you?

M : I can't say. I □ _____ been able to □ _____ a lot □ _____. I've been so □ _____ with work.

W : I understand, but try to □ _____ □ _____ a □ _____ □ _____. It'll □ _____ you □ _____ □ _____.

M : I'll try that out, thanks!

W : Anytime. I'm sure you'll do great. Stay strong! You can do it!

10 숫자 정보 파악

대화를 듣고, 남자가 지불할 금액을 고르시오.

① $30　　② $40　　③ $50
④ $60　　⑤ $100

W : Good evening. May I help you with something?

M : □ _____ □ _____ are these puzzles?

W : It □ _____ □ _____ how many pieces they have.

M : How much are the fifty-□ _____ and one hundred-□ _____ puzzles?

W : The □ _____-piece puzzles are □ _____ dollars □ _____, and the one □ _____-piece puzzles are □ _____ dollars □ _____.

M : Okay, can you □ _____ me a □ _____?

W : I'm afraid not.

M : All right, I will take □ _____ fifty-piece puzzles and □ _____ one hundred-piece puzzle.

✎ **어휘복습** 잘 안 들리거나 몰라서 체크한 어휘를 써 놓고 복습해 보세요.

□ _____　　□ _____　　□ _____　　□ _____

□ _____　　□ _____　　□ _____　　□ _____

□ _____　　□ _____　　□ _____　　□ _____

11 장소 추론

대화를 듣고, 두 사람이 대화하고 있는 장소로 가장 적절한 곳을 고르시오.

① ski resort
② movie theater
③ waterpark
④ swimming pool
⑤ restaurant

W : May I see your □ _____ ticket, please?

M : Here it is. Oh, is this the lift to the □ _____ □ _____?

W : No, this lift □ _____ you □ _____ the □ _____ slope.

M : Good thing I asked, because I'm a beginner. By the way, what time does the □ _____ □ _____ start?

W : Normally, lessons □ _____ at □ _____ P.M. in front of the ski □ _____ shop.

M : Thank you! I should head there soon.

12 미언급 파악

다음을 듣고, Witches and Princesses에 관해 언급되지 않은 것을 고르시오.

① 일일 진행 횟수　　② 등장인물
③ 시작 시각　　　　④ 진행 장소
⑤ 진행 시간

W : Welcome to Fantasy Adventure, the land of imagination! We would like to □ _____ our new special □ _____, *Witches and Princesses*. The parade will □ _____ □ _____ □ _____ a day, at one P.M., three P.M., and five P.M. every day, □ _____ holidays. The parade will □ _____ at the West entrance, and □ _____ at the South entrance. Each parade will □ _____ □ _____ about □ _____ minutes. There is □ _____ □ _____ □ _____ to watch the parade. Come and enjoy our new show! Thank you and have a great time!

✎ **어휘복습** 잘 안 들리거나 몰라서 체크한 어휘를 써 놓고 복습해 보세요.

□ _____　□ _____　□ _____　□ _____

□ _____　□ _____　□ _____　□ _____

□ _____　□ _____　□ _____　□ _____

13 도표·실용문 파악

다음 표를 보면서 대화를 듣고, 내용과 일치하지 <u>않는</u> 것을 고르시오.

Time	8/31	9/1
9 P.M.	① Dragon Warrior	③ Magician's Fury
10 P.M.	The Man in White	④ Dragon Warrior
11 P.M.	② Magician's Fury	⑤ The Man in White

M : Sandra, let's go □ _____ a □ _____.

W : Good idea. Let me □ _____ □ _____ the movie □ _____.
There is *Dragon Warrior*, *The Man in White*, and *Magician's Fury*.

M : What are the times for *Dragon Warrior*?

W : Today is □ _____ □ _____ □ _____, so… nine P.M.

M : How about *Magician's Fury*?

W : □ _____ P.M.

M : What times do they □ _____ □ _____?

W : *Magician's Fury* at □ _____ P.M. and *Dragon Warrior* at
□ _____ □ _____ □ _____ P.M.

14 화제 추론

다음을 듣고, 무엇에 관한 설명인지 고르시오.

① 스승의 날   ② 광복절
③ 새해 첫날   ④ 어버이날
⑤ 크리스마스

M : This is one of the biggest □ _____. This holiday is □ _____ in
□ _____, and people normally celebrate for two days.
People buy □ _____ to □ _____ with lights, and □ _____
□ _____ for their friends and family. Some children take
pictures with □ _____ □ _____ and sing □ _____ together.
Most of the time, family members □ _____ □ _____ and
enjoy a delicious meal. This holiday is even □ _____ □ _____
when it □ _____.

✎ **어휘복습** 잘 안 들리거나 몰라서 체크한 어휘를 써 놓고 복습해 보세요.

□ _____   □ _____   □ _____   □ _____

□ _____   □ _____   □ _____   □ _____

□ _____   □ _____   □ _____   □ _____

15 할 일 파악

대화를 듣고, 남자가 대화 직후에 할 일로 가장 적절한 것을 고르시오.

① 페인트 사기
② 서랍장 보기
③ 전구 사기
④ 차 문 잠그기
⑤ 드라이버 사기

W : Honey, are you □ _____ home?

M : Yes, I am. Do you need something?

W : Yeah, the □ _____ in the bathroom isn't □ _____ □ _____.

M : I think you should □ _____ the □ _____ □ _____.

W : I just did. I think we need to □ _____ it.

M : Are there any □ _____ ones in the □ _____?

W : Let me see. No, can you □ _____ □ _____ before you come home?

M : Okay.

16 숫자 정보 파악

대화를 듣고, 콘서트가 시작하는 시각을 고르시오.

① 5:00   ② 5:30   ③ 6:00
④ 6:30   ⑤ 7:00

M : We need to leave the house right now.

W : Why are you □ _____ such a □ _____? There's still an □ _____ □ _____ before the □ _____ starts.

M : I want to get there □ _____ so we can □ _____ some □ _____.

W : Don't worry, it's only □ _____ P.M.! It only □ _____ □ _____ minutes to get there.

M : But there's □ _____ □ _____ at this time. Can we just leave now?

W : I'm not □ _____ to go □ _____. If you're so worried, we can take □ _____ ninety. There's never traffic there.

M : Fine, then let's leave in □ _____ minutes.

✎ **어휘복습** 잘 안 들리거나 몰라서 체크한 어휘를 써 놓고 복습해 보세요.

□ _____   □ _____   □ _____   □ _____

□ _____   □ _____   □ _____   □ _____

□ _____   □ _____   □ _____   □ _____

17 상황에 적절한 말 찾기

다음 상황 설명을 듣고, Ted가 Helen에게 할 말로 가장 적절한 것을 고르시오.

Ted: _____

① I think we should take one car to school and go together.
② I can't drive to school today, my car is in the repair shop.
③ The water is so polluted here. Let's go to another beach.
④ When you take out the trash, make sure you recycle.
⑤ Shall we walk to class together?

W : Ted and Helen □ _____ □ _____ school every day. In class, Ted learned about the □ _____. His teacher explained how □ _____ are □ _____ □ _____ the □ _____. All the students talked about ways to □ _____ □ _____ □ _____. Ted decided to □ _____ to Helen □ _____ it. Since Helen □ _____ □ _____ □ _____ to Ted, Ted asks Helen if they should drive to school together. In this situation, what would Ted most likely say to Helen?

Ted: _____

18 할 일 파악

대화를 듣고, 남자가 할 일로 가장 적절한 것을 고르시오.

① 오븐 예열하기
② 오븐에 쿠키 믹스 넣기
③ 쿠키 믹스 사기
④ 냉장고에서 달걀 꺼내기
⑤ 쿠키 믹스를 쿠키판 위에 올리기

M : I didn't know □ _____ □ _____ was this □ _____.
W : What do you mean? It's easy!
M : Could you □ _____ me □ _____ it?
W : First, □ _____ □ _____ the □ _____ and turn the □ _____ □ _____.
M : I just did.
W : Then, take the cookie mix, water, and eggs and □ _____ them □ _____ □ _____.
M : Mix all of those □ _____ together? Alright, I'm done.
W : Next, □ _____ the mix □ _____ a cookie □ _____.
M : Okay, is there anything else I need to do?
W : Lastly, □ _____ it in the □ _____.

✏️ **어휘복습** 잘 안 들리거나 몰라서 체크한 어휘를 써 놓고 복습해 보세요.

□ _____ □ _____ □ _____ □ _____
□ _____ □ _____ □ _____ □ _____
□ _____ □ _____ □ _____ □ _____

19 속담 추론

대화를 듣고, 상황을 가장 잘 표현한 속담을
고르시오.

① Like father, like son.
② The more, the better.
③ Out of sight, out of mind.
④ Honesty is the best policy.
⑤ Two heads are better than one.

W : I'm so □ _____ Leslie is □ _____ to New York next week.
M : I □ _____ the □ _____ □ _____ you do.
W : Do you think she will □ _____ □ _____ □ _____?
M : I'm not sure. She's going to be busy □ _____ □ _____ □ _____ a new city.
W : You're right. She'll have new friends □ _____ □ _____ □ _____.
M : Probably. We can't □ _____ her though.
W : Why do you say that?
M : Because, we're so □ _____ □ _____ from her. We can't □ _____ her □ _____.
W : That's sad, but true.

20 알맞은 응답 찾기

대화를 듣고, 여자의 마지막 말에 이어질 남
자의 응답으로 가장 적절한 것을 고르시오.

Man: _____

① Can you turn on some music?
② The bus stop is too far from here.
③ Sorry, we are all out of food today.
④ Have you done volunteer work
before?
⑤ I volunteer every weekend from
2 P.M. to 4 P.M.

M : □ _____ do you do in your □ _____ □ _____?
W : □ _____ □ _____. I read or listen to music.
M : Would you like to □ _____ □ _____ with me?
W : That sounds interesting. Where?
M : At the □ _____ □ _____ on Merry Road.
W : That's wonderful! What do you do there?
M : I □ _____ □ _____ food, water, and blankets.
W : I'd love to □ _____ □ _____. □ _____ do you □ _____?
M : _____

✎ **어휘복습** 잘 안 들리거나 몰라서 체크한 어휘를 써 놓고 복습해 보세요.

□ _____ □ _____ □ _____ □ _____

□ _____ □ _____ □ _____ □ _____

□ _____ □ _____ □ _____ □ _____

01 대화를 듣고, 남자가 원하는 물고기를 고르시오.

02 대화를 듣고, 남자가 여자에게 전화한 목적으로 가장 적절한 것을 고르시오.

① 길을 물어보려고   ② 열쇠를 구하려고
③ 아파트를 팔려고   ④ 신분증을 만들려고
⑤ 카드 분실 신고를 하려고

03 다음 그림의 상황에 가장 적절한 대화를 고르시오.

①   ②   ③   ④   ⑤

04 대화를 듣고, 남자가 구매할 물건을 고르시오.

05 대화를 듣고, 남자의 직업으로 가장 적절한 것을 고르시오.

① doctor   ② vet   ③ lawyer
④ mechanic   ⑤ dentist

06 대화를 듣고, 여자의 심정으로 가장 적절한 것을 고르시오.

① satisfied   ② frightened
③ relaxed   ④ disappointed
⑤ joyful

07 다음을 듣고, 두 사람의 대화가 <u>어색한</u> 것을 고르시오.

①   ②   ③   ④   ⑤

08 대화를 듣고, 남자가 여자에게 부탁한 일로 가장 적절한 것을 고르시오.

① 소포 보관하기   ② 소포 부치기
③ 편지 부치기   ④ 우체국 가기
⑤ 상품 주문하기

09 대화를 듣고, 남자의 마지막 말에 담긴 의도로 가장 적절한 것을 고르시오.

① 위로   ② 요청   ③ 거절
④ 동의   ⑤ 조언

10 대화를 듣고, 남자가 지불할 금액을 고르시오.

① $10   ② $15   ③ $30
④ $35   ⑤ $40

11 대화를 듣고, 두 사람이 대화하고 있는 장소로 가장 적절한 곳을 고르시오.

① clothing store   ② dry cleaner's
③ flower shop   ④ post office
⑤ meeting room

12 다음을 듣고, Trudy's Fruit Farm에 관해 언급되지 않은 것을 고르시오.

① 개장 연도   ② 프로그램   ③ 입장료
④ 위치   ⑤ 연락처

13 다음 표를 보면서 대화를 듣고, 내용과 일치하지 않는 것을 고르시오.

Ultimate Band Contest

	Name of the Band	Where
①	Crazy Peppers	Merlin Street
②	Loud and Proud	Cradle Road
③	The Hungry Fighters	Cradle Road
④	Whipping Scream	Yorkshire Lane
⑤	Ultra Sound	Yorkshire Lane

14 다음을 듣고, 무엇에 관한 설명인지 고르시오.

① game player   ② remote control
③ cellphone   ④ digital camera
⑤ keyboard

15 대화를 듣고, 남자가 대화 직후에 할 일로 가장 적절한 것을 고르시오.

① 쇼핑하기   ② 신발 버리기
③ 새 신발 사기   ④ 신발 수선 맡기기
⑤ 자동차 수리 맡기기

16 대화를 듣고, 두 사람이 학회에 참석할 날짜를 고르시오.

① July 13   ② July 14   ③ July 15
④ July 16   ⑤ July 17

17 다음 상황을 듣고, Joseph이 Judy에게 할 말로 가장 적절한 것을 고르시오.

Joseph: _____

① Tell him you'll buy him some more.
② What's your favorite type of candy?
③ How could you do something like that?
④ I'm busy right now. Can I call you back?
⑤ I would prefer chocolate over candy any day.

18 대화를 듣고, 여자가 할 일로 가장 적절한 것을 고르시오.

① 전화하기   ② 회사 가기
③ 점심 먹기   ④ 약속 취소하기
⑤ 약속 시간 바꾸기

19 대화를 듣고, 상황을 가장 잘 표현한 속담을 고르시오.

① Like father, like son.
② Two heads are better than one.
③ Even if the sky falls down, there is a way out.
④ One man's medicine is another man's poison.
⑤ A journey of a thousand miles begins with a single step.

20 대화를 듣고, 남자의 마지막 말에 이어질 여자의 응답으로 가장 적절한 것을 고르시오.

Woman: _____

① I ordered a new electric guitar.
② How do I audition for the band?
③ That's terrific! You are so generous.
④ There's a music store down the street.
⑤ The band will perform on Sunday at noon.

01 그림 정보 파악

대화를 듣고, 남자가 원하는 물고기를 고르시오.

W : Welcome to Pet's Mart. Which fish are you □ _____
□ _____?

M : I □ _____ a fish in a book yesterday that I □ _____ □ _____.

W : Can you tell me about it?

M : I remember it had □ _____ □ _____ its □ _____.

W : Maybe this flat one is what you're □ _____ □ _____.

M : Not quite. The fish I want was □ _____.

W : Then, how about this one with large eyes?

M : Nope, the fish had □ _____ □ _____. I think it's this one over here.

02 목적 파악

대화를 듣고, 남자가 여자에게 전화한 목적으로 가장 적절한 것을 고르시오.

① 길을 물어보려고
② 열쇠를 구하려고
③ 아파트를 팔려고
④ 신분증을 만들려고
⑤ 카드 분실 신고를 하려고

W : Hello, this is Lane Housing.

M : Hi, my name is Jonathan. I'm □ _____ □ _____ □ _____
about how to get a □ _____ apartment □ _____.

W : Okay, what exactly is the problem?

M : Well, I □ _____ the key to my apartment and I was
□ _____ you could send □ _____ to □ _____ me.

W : Alright, what is your apartment number?

M : Three one two B.

W : Do you have an ID card with you? I need to □ _____ your
□ _____ and □ _____ them with your ID card □ _____.

M : Yes, I do.

W : Okay, I'll be there soon. Please show it to me when I get there.

✏ **어휘복습** 잘 안 들리거나 몰라서 체크한 어휘를 써 놓고 복습해 보세요.

□ _____ □ _____ □ _____ □ _____

□ _____ □ _____ □ _____ □ _____

□ _____ □ _____ □ _____ □ _____

03 그림 상황에 적절한 대화 찾기

다음 그림의 상황에 가장 적절한 대화를 고르시오.

① ② ③ ④ ⑤

① W : The neighbors are □ _____ □ _____ today.

M : That's □ _____! I can't wait.

② W : I □ _____ pizza and breadsticks.

M : Sounds like a perfect □ _____.

③ W : There's someone □ _____ the □ _____ for you.

M : Thanks, I've been □ _____ □ _____ that □ _____.

④ W : I'm on my way to the □ _____.

M : Don't forget to bring your □ _____ □ _____!

⑤ W : Do you have any □ _____ coupons?

M : No, I don't.

04 그림 정보 파악

대화를 듣고, 남자가 구매할 물건을 고르시오.

① ② ③

④ ⑤

M : I'm looking for □ _____ □ _____ □ _____ during the winter season.

W : We have these scarves. They are our □ _____ items.

M : I already have a lot of scarves. Is there □ _____ □ _____?

W : Okay then, would you like to □ _____ some gloves?

M : Let me □ _____ □ _____ □ _____. What styles of gloves do you have?

W : There are these leather ones, and these polka dot ones.

M : Hmm, □ _____ □ _____ □ _____ are my type. I don't think I'll be buying gloves today. I like that □ _____ □ _____ □ _____.

W : Yes, this jacket is very popular nowadays. You can □ _____ □ _____ the checked one □ _____ the plain one with no pattern on it.

M : I'll take the one □ _____ the □ _____ □ _____.

✎ **어휘복습** 잘 안 들리거나 몰라서 체크한 어휘를 써 놓고 복습해 보세요.

□ _____ □ _____ □ _____ □ _____

□ _____ □ _____ □ _____ □ _____

□ _____ □ _____ □ _____ □ _____

05 직업 추론

대화를 듣고, 남자의 직업으로 가장 적절한 것을 고르시오.

① doctor   ② vet
③ lawyer   ④ mechanic
⑤ dentist

M : Please take a seat on this chair. What seems to be the problem?

W : Every time I try to eat something, my □ _____ □ _____.

M : Okay, I'm going to take a look. I need you to □ _____ your □ _____ □ _____.

W : Alright, will this be □ _____?

M : No, not really. I'm just going to look at the □ _____ □ _____ your □ _____. I promise it will be over before you know it.

W : Well, that's a □ _____. So, what's wrong with my teeth?

M : I'm afraid you have some □ _____ near the back of your mouth.

W : Cavities? That's terrible! How many □ _____ □ _____ do I have?

M : You have three, and they need to □ _____ □ _____ □ _____ as soon as possible.

06 심정 추론

대화를 듣고, 여자의 심정으로 가장 적절한 것을 고르시오.

① satisfied   ② frightened
③ relaxed   ④ disappointed
⑤ joyful

W : Owen, it's getting late. These woods are □ _____ □ _____ and darker.

M : I know. I think I just □ _____ something □ _____ those trees.

W : What? What do you think it is?

M : I have □ _____ □ _____. Maybe a □ _____? Or a □ _____?

W : Don't say that! You're □ _____ me.

M : Is it just me, or is it getting cold out here?

W : I'm getting cold too. Let's □ _____ □ _____ of here. Do you know □ _____ □ _____ to go?

M : No, it's so dark. I □ _____ □ _____ what's in front of me.

✎ **어휘복습** 잘 안 들리거나 몰라서 체크한 어휘를 써 놓고 복습해 보세요.

□ _____   □ _____   □ _____   □ _____

□ _____   □ _____   □ _____   □ _____

□ _____   □ _____   □ _____   □ _____

07 어색한 대화 찾기

다음을 듣고, 두 사람의 대화가 <u>어색한</u> 것을 고르시오.

①   ②   ③   ④   ⑤

① W: I wonder if □ _____ is □ _____.
    M: I don't think so. The lights are □ _____ □ _____.

② W: □ _____ □ _____ you're not late for the recital.
    M: I've learned ballet □ _____ □ _____ □ _____.

③ W: What is your home □ _____?
    M: I □ _____ □ _____ ninety-one thirty-eight Wicker Lane.

④ W: What are you doing for □ _____?
    M: I'm going to a □ _____ □ _____.

⑤ W: Did you □ _____ a lot of □ _____?
    M: Yeah, the trees were □ _____ □ _____ them!

08 부탁 파악

대화를 듣고, 남자가 여자에게 부탁한 일로 가장 적절한 것을 고르시오.

① 소포 보관하기   ② 소포 부치기
③ 편지 부치기   ④ 우체국 가기
⑤ 상품 주문하기

M: Hey, Heather.

W: Hi, Daniel, what are you up to?

M: Nothing much. I was just □ _____ if you could □ _____ me.

W: Sure, what is it?

M: Well, I'm □ _____ a package in the mail today, but I won't get home □ _____ □ _____.

W: Okay, so what do you want me to do?

M: Can you □ _____ the □ _____ for me until I get there?

W: That's □ _____ a □ _____. Call me when you get home and I'll □ _____ the package □ _____ you.

✏ **어휘복습** 잘 안 들리거나 몰라서 체크한 어휘를 써 놓고 복습해 보세요.

□ _____   □ _____   □ _____   □ _____

□ _____   □ _____   □ _____   □ _____

□ _____   □ _____   □ _____   □ _____

09 의도 파악

대화를 듣고, 남자의 마지막 말에 담긴 의도
로 가장 적절한 것을 고르시오.

① 위로　　② 요청　　③ 거절
④ 동의　　⑤ 조언

M : I heard there is a new restaurant in town.

W : ☐ _____ ☐ _____ ☐ _____ the Italian restaurant on Main Street?

M : Yes, that's the one. Have you ☐ _____ ☐ _____ ☐ _____?

W : No, but it's already ☐ _____ ☐ _____ its steak and salad.

M : I see. I ☐ _____ ☐ _____ it's ☐ _____ ☐ _____ Sir Jack's Bistro's steak.

W : Yeah, they have delicious steak. But, ☐ _____ ☐ _____ ☐ _____, nothing can beat Sir Jack's Bistro's seafood pasta.

M : Oh, yeah. I ☐ _____ exactly ☐ _____ ☐ _____ way.

10 숫자 정보 파악

대화를 듣고, 남자가 지불할 금액을 고르시오.

① $10　　② $15　　③ $30
④ $35　　⑤ $40

M : Excuse me, how much does it ☐ _____ to go ☐ _____?

W : It is ☐ _____ dollars ☐ _____ ☐ _____.

M : I see. I would like to play ☐ _____ games.

W : Very well. Do you need to ☐ _____ ☐ _____?

M : I would like that. My size is nine.

W : That will cost you an ☐ _____ ☐ _____ dollars.

M : That's fine.

✏ **어휘복습** 잘 안 들리거나 몰라서 체크한 어휘를 써 놓고 복습해 보세요.

☐ _____　　☐ _____　　☐ _____　　☐ _____

☐ _____　　☐ _____　　☐ _____　　☐ _____

☐ _____　　☐ _____　　☐ _____　　☐ _____

11 장소 추론

대화를 듣고, 두 사람이 대화하고 있는 장소로 가장 적절한 곳을 고르시오.

① clothing store ② dry cleaner's
③ flower shop ④ post office
⑤ meeting room

W : Hello, how can I help you?

M : I would like to □ _____ some clothes.

W : How many items of □ _____ need to be done?

M : Two □ _____ and a pair of □ _____.

W : Alright. They'll be □ _____ □ _____ tomorrow morning.

M : Can I have them □ _____ to my house?

W : Yes, it is □ _____ if you pay an extra fee.

12 미언급 파악

다음을 듣고, Trudy's Fruit Farm에 관해 언급되지 않은 것을 고르시오.

① 개장 연도 ② 프로그램
③ 입장료 ④ 위치
⑤ 연락처

M : Ladies and gentlemen, boys and girls! We invite you to Trudy's Fruit Farm! We recently □ _____ □ _____ twenty fourteen and we have a □ _____ of fruits you can □ _____ □ _____. There are apples, □ _____, □ _____, and watermelon. □ _____ is three dollars for children and five dollars for adults. We are □ _____ □ _____ forty-five Middletown Street. We are open □ _____ □ _____ □ _____ from ten A.M. to six P.M. One more thing! □ _____ September seventh, you can enjoy our farm □ _____ □ _____. Call us at nine three one, two one nine two for more questions.

✏ **어휘복습** 잘 안 들리거나 몰라서 체크한 어휘를 써 놓고 복습해 보세요.

□ _____ □ _____ □ _____ □ _____

□ _____ □ _____ □ _____ □ _____

□ _____ □ _____ □ _____ □ _____

13 도표·실용문 파악

다음 표를 보면서 대화를 듣고, 내용과 일치하지 <u>않는</u> 것을 고르시오.

Ultimate Band Contest

Name of the Band	Where
① Crazy Peppers	Merlin Street
② Loud and Proud	Cradle Road
③ The Hungry Fighters	Cradle Road
④ Whipping Scream	Yorkshire Lane
⑤ Ultra Sound	Yorkshire Lane

W : I'm so excited for this year's Ultimate Band Contest!

M : Who are you □ _____ □ _____ □ _____ □ _____ the most?

W : I like Crazy Peppers and Loud and Proud. I'm □ _____ that they will be □ _____ □ _____ Cradle Road. I can □ _____ □ _____.

M : The Hungry Fighters will be performing there too. I □ _____ don't really like their music, though.

W : Yeah, me neither. Which teams are your □ _____?

M : Well, I really like Whipping Scream and Ultra Sound.

W : Oh, I've □ _____ □ _____ them before. Where are they playing?

W : They'll be at Yorkshire Lane, which is □ _____ because I live □ _____ the □ _____ □ _____.

M : I see. I'm glad we will be able to enjoy this event.

14 화제 추론

다음을 듣고, 무엇에 관한 설명인지 고르시오.

① game player
② remote control
③ cellphone
④ digital camera
⑤ keyboard

M : Almost □ _____ □ _____ this item and □ _____ it around with them □ _____ □ _____. It is an electronic □ _____ and people use it for a variety of reasons. People can use it to □ _____ phone □ _____ or □ _____ □ _____ messages to their friends and family. Also, they can □ _____ □ _____ and browse the □ _____ with this item. People can also □ _____ □ _____ and □ _____ them on this device. What is this item?

✎ **어휘복습** 잘 안 들리거나 몰라서 체크한 어휘를 써 놓고 복습해 보세요.

□ _____ □ _____ □ _____ □ _____

□ _____ □ _____ □ _____ □ _____

□ _____ □ _____ □ _____ □ _____

15 할 일 파악

대화를 듣고, 남자가 대화 직후에 할 일로 가장 적절한 것을 고르시오.

① 쇼핑하기
② 신발 버리기
③ 새 신발 사기
④ 신발 수선 맡기기
⑤ 자동차 수리 맡기기

W : Honey, I think you need to go buy a new pair of shoes.

M : I only ☐ _____ them ☐ _____ ☐ _____ ☐ _____!

W : They look like you've ☐ _____ them ☐ _____ ☐ _____.

M : But, I don't want to ☐ _____ ☐ _____ ☐ _____ them yet. They are the ☐ _____ ☐ _____ pair I own.

W : Then ☐ _____ them to the shoe ☐ _____ shop.

M : Where is the ☐ _____ one from here?

W : There should be one in Brick Square Mall.

M : Okay, I should go there now.

16 특정 정보 파악

대화를 듣고, 두 사람이 학회에 참석할 날짜를 고르시오.

① July 13
② July 14
③ July 15
④ July 16
⑤ July 17

W : Wesley, I'm going to a ☐ _____ next week.

M : ☐ _____ ☐ _____ ☐ _____ conference are you talking about?

W : It's for ☐ _____ ☐ _____ in business. You should go too.

M : It sounds interesting. When is it?

W : They ☐ _____ ☐ _____ on July ☐ _____, July sixteenth, and July seventeenth.

M : I can't go on the sixteenth and seventeenth. I'm going on a trip.

W : That's fine. Then let's go the ☐ _____ ☐ _____.

✎ **어휘복습** 잘 안 들리거나 몰라서 체크한 어휘를 써 놓고 복습해 보세요.

☐ _____   ☐ _____   ☐ _____   ☐ _____

☐ _____   ☐ _____   ☐ _____   ☐ _____

☐ _____   ☐ _____   ☐ _____   ☐ _____

17 상황에 적절한 말 찾기

다음 상황을 듣고, Joseph가 Judy에게 할 말로 가장 적절한 것을 고르시오.

Joseph: _____

① Tell him you'll buy him some more.
② What's your favorite type of candy?
③ How could you do something like that?
④ I'm busy right now. Can I call you back?
⑤ I would prefer chocolate over candy any day.

M : Judy and her brother □ _____ □ _____ ten pieces of candy for helping their mom clean the house. Judy □ _____ □ _____ of her candy □ _____ □ _____ □ _____ she □ _____ them. □ _____ □ _____ □ _____ □ _____, her brother put them in a jar to □ _____ □ _____. Judy went into his room and ate all of his candy. Judy □ _____ doing this, and she is □ _____ to tell her brother what happened. So, Judy calls her friend, Joseph. After listening to her story, Joseph tells Judy to □ _____ her brother the □ _____, and then offer to □ _____ him a new □ _____ □ _____ □ _____. In this situation, what would Joseph most likely say to Judy?

Joseph: _____

18 할 일 파악

대화를 듣고, 여자가 할 일로 가장 적절한 것을 고르시오.

① 전화하기
② 회사 가기
③ 점심 먹기
④ 약속 취소하기
⑤ 약속 시간 바꾸기

M : You look upset. What's wrong, Hillary?
W : I □ _____ □ _____ a big □ _____ with my boyfriend.
M : Oh, that's too bad. What happened?
W : We were supposed to meet, but he □ _____ □ _____ me.
M : I see. What was the □ _____ □ _____ cancelling on you?
W : He said his company □ _____ □ _____ him in □ _____ □ _____.
M : Well, in that situation, he probably didn't have a choice.
W : Do you really think so? I'll □ _____ □ _____ to talk about it □ _____ □ _____.

✎ **어휘복습** 잘 안 들리거나 몰라서 체크한 어휘를 써 놓고 복습해 보세요.

□ _____   □ _____   □ _____   □ _____
□ _____   □ _____   □ _____   □ _____
□ _____   □ _____   □ _____   □ _____

19 속담 추론

대화를 듣고, 상황을 가장 잘 표현한 속담을 고르시오.

① Like father, like son.
② Two heads are better than one.
③ Even if the sky falls down, there is a way out.
④ One man's medicine is another man's poison.
⑤ A journey of a thousand miles begins with a single step.

W : Josh, may I ask what you're doing?
M : I'm working on a □ _____ for the school □ _____.
W : That's wonderful! Are you a □ _____ □ _____?
M : Actually, I'm not. I try, but I'm not □ _____ any □ _____. I don't know what to do.
W : Then why don't you □ _____ a beginner's □ _____ □ _____? There are two classes every week in Room three three one.
M : Do you think that will □ _____?
W : Of course! You just have to take it □ _____ step □ _____ □ _____ □ _____.
M : You're right. Thanks for the advice!

20 알맞은 응답 찾기

대화를 듣고, 남자의 마지막 말에 이어질 여자의 응답으로 가장 적절한 것을 고르시오.

Woman: _____

① I ordered a new electric guitar.
② How do I audition for the band?
③ That's terrific! You are so generous.
④ There's a music store down the street.
⑤ The band will perform on Sunday at noon.

W : Do you know □ _____ □ _____ □ _____ any □ _____?
M : Hmm, □ _____ □ _____ □ _____. I can play piano, guitar, and the drums.
W : Wow! You're so □ _____.
M : I just play □ _____ □ _____. How about you?
W : I want to learn, but I don't have the time.
M : Really? When you're not busy, I □ _____ □ _____ you.
W : _____

✎ **어휘복습** 잘 안 들리거나 몰라서 체크한 어휘를 써 놓고 복습해 보세요.

□ _____ □ _____ □ _____ □ _____
□ _____ □ _____ □ _____ □ _____
□ _____ □ _____ □ _____ □ _____

01 대화를 듣고, 남자가 구매할 필통을 고르시오.

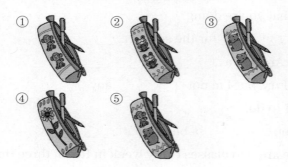

① ② ③ ④ ⑤

02 대화를 듣고, 남자가 여자에게 전화한 목적으로 가장 적절한 것을 고르시오.

① 책을 빌리려고
② 파티에 초대하려고
③ 프로젝트를 논의하려고
④ 숙제에 관해 물어보려고
⑤ 여동생을 돌봐달라고 부탁하려고

03 다음 그림의 상황에 가장 적절한 대화를 고르시오.

① ② ③ ④ ⑤

04 대화를 듣고, 남자가 만들 호박을 고르시오.

① ② ③ ④ ⑤

05 대화를 듣고, 남자의 직업으로 가장 적절한 것을 고르시오.

① tour guide
② bank teller
③ doctor
④ sales clerk
⑤ flight attendant

06 대화를 듣고, 여자의 심정으로 가장 적절한 것을 고르시오.

① annoyed
② proud
③ excited
④ nervous
⑤ surprised

07 다음을 듣고, 두 사람의 대화가 어색한 것을 고르시오.

① ② ③ ④ ⑤

08 대화를 듣고, 여자가 남자에게 부탁한 일로 가장 적절한 것을 고르시오.

① 귀걸이 사주기
② 7시에 깨워주기
③ 세탁소에 같이 가기
④ 귀 뚫으러 같이 가기
⑤ 세탁소에서 옷 찾아오기

09 대화를 듣고, 남자의 마지막 말에 담긴 의도로 가장 적절한 것을 고르시오.

① 제안
② 요청
③ 불평
④ 설득
⑤ 충고

10 대화를 듣고, 남자가 지불할 금액을 고르시오.

① $8
② $10
③ $13
④ $15
⑤ $18

11 대화를 듣고, 두 사람이 대화하고 있는 장소로 가장 적절한 곳을 고르시오.

① bank
② police station
③ hotel
④ classroom
⑤ restaurant

12 다음을 듣고, 화재 사건에 관해 언급되지 <u>않은</u> 것을 고르시오.

① 화재 발생 시각   ② 화재 지속 시간
③ 인명 피해 현황   ④ 화재 발생 지점
⑤ 주변 교통 상황

13 다음 표를 보면서 대화를 듣고, 두 사람이 선택할 프로그램을 고르시오.

Fitness Programs at Lolly Gym

	Program	Location/Time
①	Yoga	Room 101 12:00 P.M.
②	Cycling	Room 102 12:30 P.M.
③	Aerobics	Room 103 1:30 P.M.
④	Ballet	Room 103 12:00 P.M.
⑤	Basketball	Room 105 4:00 P.M.

14 다음을 듣고, 무엇에 관한 설명인지 고르시오.

① 연   ② 팽이
③ 줄다리기   ④ 종이 비행기
⑤ 세발 자전거

15 대화를 듣고, 남자가 대화 직후에 할 일로 가장 적절한 것을 고르시오.

① 자물쇠 사기
② 사물함 옮기기
③ 컴퓨터실에 가기
④ 컴퓨터 비밀번호 바꾸기
⑤ 사물함 비밀번호 바꾸기

16 대화를 듣고, 두 사람이 만나기로 한 요일과 시각을 고르시오.

① 월요일 3:00   ② 월요일 3:30
③ 화요일 3:00   ④ 수요일 3:00
⑤ 수요일 3:30

17 다음 상황을 듣고, Beatrice가 Justin에게 할 말로 가장 적절한 것을 고르시오.

Beatrice: _____

① Can I borrow your library card?
② I'm so excited that we are partners!
③ The books at the library are all checked out.
④ The boxes need to be moved to the storage room.
⑤ I'm upset with you. You need to help me with this assignment!

18 대화를 듣고, 남자가 주말에 할 일로 가장 적절한 것을 고르시오.

① 산에 가기   ② 여동생 돌보기
③ 수영 배우기   ④ 바닷가에 가기
⑤ 여동생 데리러 가기

19 대화를 듣고, 상황을 가장 잘 표현한 속담을 고르시오.

① Like father, like son.
② The more, the better.
③ All's well that ends well.
④ As you sow, so you reap.
⑤ Out of sight, out of mind.

20 대화를 듣고, 여자의 마지막 말에 이어질 남자의 응답으로 가장 적절한 것을 고르시오.

Man: _____

① I'll be on the lookout for your keys.
② I'll keep my fingers crossed for you.
③ There's a vending machine over there.
④ There's a hospital across the street from here.
⑤ Check out the clothing store on West Boulevard.

01 그림 정보 파악

대화를 듣고, 남자가 구매할 필통을 고르시오.

① ② ③

④ ⑤

W : Hey, Mark. □ _____ are you going to □ _____?

M : I need a new □ _____ □ _____ for school.

W : Here's one with □ _____ on it. Would you want this one?

M : No, I □ _____ these ones with the □ _____ or □ _____.

W : I see. Are those your □ _____ animals?

M : □ _____ □ _____, but there isn't much to □ _____ □ _____ here.

W : You're right. Do you want to go to a □ _____ □ _____?

M : That's okay. I think I'll just □ _____ the □ _____ with frogs.

W : Alright, if that's what you want.

02 목적 파악

대화를 듣고, 남자가 여자에게 전화한 목적으로 가장 적절한 것을 고르시오.

① 책을 빌리려고
② 파티에 초대하려고
③ 프로젝트를 논의하려고
④ 숙제에 관해 물어보려고
⑤ 여동생을 돌봐달라고 부탁하려고

M : Hello, Donna? This is Frank.

W : Hey, what are you □ _____ □ _____?

M : I'm □ _____ □ _____ to go to a party with my friend. Can you □ _____ something □ _____ □ _____?

W : Yeah, what is it?

M : If you're not busy, I need you to □ _____ my younger □ _____ □ _____ I'm □ _____.

W : Okay, I can do that. Do you need me to go □ _____ □ _____ now?

M : Yes, I'll be □ _____ the house □ _____ □ _____.
I'll be back in about two hours.

W : Alright! I'll be there soon.

✏ **어휘복습** 잘 안 들리거나 몰라서 체크한 어휘를 써 놓고 복습해 보세요.

□ _____ □ _____ □ _____ □ _____

□ _____ □ _____ □ _____ □ _____

□ _____ □ _____ □ _____ □ _____

03 그림 상황에 적절한 대화 찾기

다음 그림의 상황에 가장 적절한 대화를 고르시오.

① ② ③ ④ ⑤

① W : □ _____ is the nearest □ _____ □ _____?

　　M : It's a ten minute walk □ _____ □ _____.

② W : There are so many people □ _____ the □ _____.

　　M : Yeah, it's □ _____ □ _____ every day during □ _____ □ _____.

③ W : Is this the □ _____ □ _____ Lincoln Lane?

　　M : Yes. It is three □ _____ □ _____.

④ W : Thank you for □ _____ me your □ _____.

　　M : No problem. I'm □ _____ □ _____ the train soon anyway.

⑤ W : I hope there are □ _____ □ _____ on the train.

　　M : Me too. I'm □ _____ □ _____ □ _____ on the way home.

04 그림 정보 파악

대화를 듣고, 남자가 만들 호박을 고르시오.

① 　② 　③

④ 　⑤

M : Do you like my □ _____? I'm going to □ _____ it for Halloween and put it on my front porch.

W : Yeah, it □ _____ □ _____. Do you know how you're going to carve it?

M : I'm thinking of giving it a □ _____ □ _____ and □ _____ □ _____.

W : Hmm, I think it'll □ _____ □ _____ with an □ _____ □ _____ triangular nose and a □ _____.

M : □ _____ for the idea, □ _____ I think I □ _____ the triangular nose and scary eyes. I'm going to □ _____ a □ _____ on it too.

W : Well, it's your pumpkin, so it's □ _____ □ _____ you. Maybe I should carve □ _____ □ _____ pumpkin.

M : Yes, you □ _____ should. It'll be a lot of □ _____.

W : Okay, I should go to the pumpkin patch and buy one □ _____ □ _____.

✏ **어휘복습** 잘 안 들리거나 몰라서 체크한 어휘를 써 놓고 복습해 보세요.

□ _____　□ _____　□ _____　□ _____

□ _____　□ _____　□ _____　□ _____

□ _____　□ _____　□ _____　□ _____

05 직업 추론

대화를 듣고, 남자의 직업으로 가장 적절한 것을 고르시오.

① tour guide   ② bank teller
③ doctor   ④ sales clerk
⑤ flight attendant

M : Next customer □ _____ □ _____, please.
W : Hello. I would like to □ _____ these □ _____.
M : Sure, □ _____ would you □ _____ the cash? Also, I need to see your □ _____ □ _____.
W : Okay, □ _____ □ _____ □ _____. I would like it in twenty-dollar □ _____, please.
M : Alright. Please □ _____ □ _____ this □ _____ and □ _____ at the □ _____ of the page.
W : All done. Is there □ _____ □ _____ I need to do?
M : No, you're □ _____ □ _____. Here's your two thousand dollars in cash. Thank you for □ _____ our □ _____ today.

06 심정 추론

대화를 듣고, 여자의 심정으로 가장 적절한 것을 고르시오.

① annoyed   ② proud
③ excited   ④ nervous
⑤ surprised

M : You □ _____ so □ _____, Kristin.
W : I couldn't □ _____ □ _____ □ _____ last night!
M : Why, what's the □ _____?
W : I have a □ _____ □ _____ today for a company I really want to □ _____ □ _____. I spent all night □ _____ for it.
M : I see. □ _____ □ _____ of □ _____ does the company do?
W : It's an □ _____ company, and I □ _____ □ _____ the □ _____ □ _____ position. I hope I can stay calm and say everything I prepared.
M : That □ _____ □ _____ a great □ _____. I'm sure you'll do fine, since you practiced a lot for it.
W : I hope so. Well, I'd better □ _____ □ _____ to the company now.
M : Okay. Be □ _____ and □ _____ your □ _____.

✎ **어휘복습** 잘 안 들리거나 몰라서 체크한 어휘를 써 놓고 복습해 보세요.

□ _____   □ _____   □ _____   □ _____
□ _____   □ _____   □ _____   □ _____
□ _____   □ _____   □ _____   □ _____

다음을 듣고, 두 사람의 대화가 <u>어색한</u> 것을 고르시오.

①   ②   ③   ④   ⑤

① M : I can't get this □ _____ out of my □ _____.
   W : Take them to the □ _____ □ _____.
② M : □ _____ do you want for □ _____?
   W : A piece of red velvet □ _____.
③ M : My pen ran □ _____ □ _____ □ _____.
   W : You can □ _____ □ _____ for the day.
④ M : I □ _____ □ _____ we won the game!
   W : The □ _____ □ _____ in ten minutes.
⑤ M : The weather is □ _____ □ _____ and colder.
   W : I know. Make sure you □ _____ a □ _____!

대화를 듣고, 여자가 남자에게 부탁한 일로 가장 적절한 것을 고르시오.

① 귀걸이 사주기
② 7시에 깨워주기
③ 세탁소에 같이 가기
④ 귀 뚫으러 같이 가기
⑤ 세탁소에서 옷 찾아오기

W : Oh my goodness, I'm freaking out! The □ _____ is □ _____.
M : What's wrong? I've □ _____ □ _____ you this □ _____ before. Are you okay?
W : No, I'm about to go □ _____ my □ _____ □ _____.
M : Don't worry! I got □ _____ pierced last month and it didn't □ _____ at all.
W : If you have time, please □ _____ □ _____ me.
M : Actually, I'm □ _____ until seven P.M. but my mom asked me to □ _____ □ _____ her □ _____ from the dry cleaner's.
W : We'll be back □ _____ □ _____, I'm sure. The ear piercing shop is □ _____ □ _____.
M : Okay then, let's go.

✎ **어휘복습** 잘 안 들리거나 몰라서 체크한 어휘를 써 놓고 복습해 보세요.

□ _____   □ _____   □ _____   □ _____
□ _____   □ _____   □ _____   □ _____
□ _____   □ _____   □ _____   □ _____

09 의도 파악

대화를 듣고, 남자의 마지막 말에 담긴 의도로 가장 적절한 것을 고르시오.

① 제안   ② 요청   ③ 불평
④ 설득   ⑤ 충고

M : Are you □ _____ □ _____ for your test?

W : Yes, professor. but I think I □ _____ more □ _____ to □ _____ .

M : There was a lot to learn this □ _____ , right?

W : Seriously, there is too much □ _____ to □ _____ and so □ _____ □ _____ !

M : Sorry. I □ _____ I □ _____ □ _____ something about it.

W : Can you □ _____ the test □ _____ □ _____ □ _____ □ _____ ?

M : No, I can't. □ _____ □ _____ I □ _____ some hints □ _____ ? It may help you.

10 숫자 정보 파악

대화를 듣고, 남자가 지불할 금액을 고르시오.

① $8   ② $10   ③ $13
④ $15   ⑤ $18

W : Good afternoon, what can I help you with?

M : I □ _____ □ _____ some pizza and breadsticks.

W : □ _____ □ _____ pepperoni, cheese, and vegetable pizza.

M : □ _____ □ _____ is it for one □ _____ ?

W : It's □ _____ dollars each for pepperoni, □ _____ dollars each for cheese, and □ _____ dollars each for vegetable.

M : And □ _____ □ _____ the breadsticks?

W : □ _____ dollars, but □ _____ you buy two pieces of pizza, you can □ _____ the breadsticks □ _____ □ _____ .

M : Okay then, I'll have one pepperoni and one cheese pizza with breadsticks.

✎ **어휘복습** 잘 안 들리거나 몰라서 체크한 어휘를 써 놓고 복습해 보세요.

□ _____   □ _____   □ _____   □ _____
□ _____   □ _____   □ _____   □ _____
□ _____   □ _____   □ _____   □ _____

11 장소 추론

대화를 듣고, 두 사람이 대화하고 있는 장소로 가장 적절한 곳을 고르시오.

① bank
② police station
③ hotel
④ classroom
⑤ restaurant

M : Hello, ma'am. □ _____ □ _____ you here?

W : I would like to □ _____ a missing person □ _____.

M : □ _____ is □ _____?

W : My son. He didn't come home last night.

M : Oh no! □ _____ and □ _____ did you last see him?

W : I saw him □ _____ □ _____, at □ _____. He left saying he was going to school. Please find him, □ _____.

M : I'll □ _____ my □ _____. Please □ _____ your □ _____ □ _____ and your son's □ _____. Do you have a □ _____ of him?

W : Yes, here you go. I hope to □ _____ □ _____ you □ _____.

12 미언급 파악

다음을 듣고, 화재 사건에 관해 언급되지 <u>않</u>은 것을 고르시오.

① 화재 발생 시각
② 화재 지속 시간
③ 인명 피해 현황
④ 화재 발생 지점
⑤ 주변 교통 상황

M : Leyman's Factory □ _____ □ _____ due to a □ _____. The fire □ _____ around one P.M. and □ _____ for about two hours. A person living nearby □ _____ the fire and □ _____ nine one one. The police say that □ _____ people have been □ _____ and are □ _____ at the □ _____. The □ _____ has also been badly □ _____. The □ _____ of the □ _____ is still □ _____. Please be □ _____ that there is □ _____ □ _____ in the area. This is Miley Kent, live for GSC eight o'clock news.

✎ **어휘복습** 잘 안 들리거나 몰라서 체크한 어휘를 써 놓고 복습해 보세요.

□ _____   □ _____   □ _____   □ _____

□ _____   □ _____   □ _____   □ _____

□ _____   □ _____   □ _____   □ _____

13 도표·실용문 파악

다음 표를 보면서 대화를 듣고, 두 사람이 선택할 프로그램을 고르시오.

Fitness Programs at Lolly Gym

	Program	Location/Time
①	Yoga	Room 101 12:00 P.M.
②	Cycling	Room 102 12:30 P.M.
③	Aerobics	Room 103 1:30 P.M.
④	Ballet	Room 103 12:00 P.M.
⑤	Basketball	Room 105 4:00 P.M.

M : What □ _____ do you want to □ _____ □ _____?

W : They all seem like a good □ _____. How about yoga or ballet?

M : I'm not □ _____ enough. Plus, I won't get to the □ _____ until one P.M.

W : Oh. Then, that only leaves us two □ _____.

M : Hmm, should we go □ _____ some □ _____?

W : No, I've played basketball too often the past few weeks. I want to □ _____ □ _____ □ _____.

M : Then □ _____ do the □ _____ program in Room one oh three.

W : Okay! That works for me.

14 화제 추론

다음을 듣고, 무엇에 관한 설명인지 고르시오.

① 연　　　　　② 팽이
③ 줄다리기　　④ 종이 비행기
⑤ 세발 자전거

W : Most people have □ _____ enjoyed □ _____ one of these at least once. People fly this on beaches, rivers, and parks. They □ _____ □ _____ many shapes, sizes, and colors. They are made of □ _____ or □ _____. Normally, they have a □ _____ □ _____ and are □ _____ to a long □ _____. All you need is some □ _____ to fly it.

✎ **어휘복습** 잘 안 들리거나 몰라서 체크한 어휘를 써 놓고 복습해 보세요.

□ _____　□ _____　□ _____　□ _____

□ _____　□ _____　□ _____　□ _____

□ _____　□ _____　□ _____　□ _____

15 할 일 파악

대화를 듣고, 남자가 대화 직후에 할 일로 가장 적절한 것을 고르시오.

① 자물쇠 사기
② 사물함 옮기기
③ 컴퓨터실에 가기
④ 컴퓨터 비밀번호 바꾸기
⑤ 사물함 비밀번호 바꾸기

W : Ken, where's your □ _____ ?

M : It's right □ _____ the □ _____ from here. How about you?

W : Mine is in front of the □ _____ □ _____ . I just got finished □ _____ my □ _____ .

M : Why did you do that?

W : Well, it's just to be □ _____ . If someone already knows my password, they □ _____ □ _____ my things.

M : Good point. I □ _____ □ _____ □ _____ that. I should go change my password too.

W : Yeah. It's best to change it □ _____ □ _____ once every □ _____ . Let me know if you need any help.

16 특정 정보 파악

대화를 듣고, 두 사람이 만나기로 한 요일과 시각을 고르시오.

① 월요일 3:00   ② 월요일 3:30
③ 화요일 3:00   ④ 수요일 3:00
⑤ 수요일 3:30

M : Beth, this plate is awesome. I really □ _____ the □ _____ on it.

W : Thanks! I actually □ _____ it □ _____ at a □ _____ class. I've been going to the class for over a year now.

M : Pottery class? That □ _____ like so much □ _____ ! Can I □ _____ you □ _____ □ _____ ?

W : Of course! There are two classes a week, one on □ _____ and the other on □ _____ .

M : I can't go to the Monday class because I do □ _____ work that day. □ _____ □ _____ is the class on Wednesday?

W : That class starts at □ _____ □ _____ P.M. Let's meet □ _____ □ _____ □ _____ and go together.

M : That □ _____ □ _____ . I'll see you then.

✎ **어휘복습** 잘 안 들리거나 몰라서 체크한 어휘를 써 놓고 복습해 보세요.

□ _____   □ _____   □ _____   □ _____
□ _____   □ _____   □ _____   □ _____
□ _____   □ _____   □ _____   □ _____

17 상황에 적절한 말 찾기

다음 상황을 듣고, Beatrice가 Justin에게 할 말로 가장 적절한 것을 고르시오.

Beatrice: _____

① Can I borrow your library card?
② I'm so excited that we are partners!
③ The books at the library are all checked out.
④ The boxes need to be moved to the storage room.
⑤ I'm upset with you. You need to help me with this assignment!

W: Beatrice and Justin are □ _____ for a team □ _____ . They were □ _____ □ _____ work on the project together. However, Justin is not □ _____ Beatrice □ _____ □ _____ . He doesn't □ _____ her □ _____ □ _____ or read her emails. Beatrice is □ _____ □ _____ doing all the work □ _____ □ _____ . So, she went to her teacher □ _____ some □ _____ . Her teacher told her to be □ _____ and □ _____ to Justin □ _____ the □ _____ . In this situation, what would Beatrice most likely say to Justin?

Beatrice: _____

18 할 일 파악

대화를 듣고, 남자가 주말에 할 일로 가장 적절한 것을 고르시오.

① 산에 가기   ② 여동생 돌보기
③ 수영 배우기   ④ 바닷가에 가기
⑤ 여동생 데리러 가기

W: What are your □ _____ for the □ _____ ?
M: I □ _____ have any □ _____ . I'm still thinking about it. What about you?
W: You should □ _____ □ _____ the □ _____ ! It's near here, plus the □ _____ is really □ _____ . I'm going to the □ _____ behind the school.
M: I was actually □ _____ □ _____ going to the beach. My sister likes it there too. Maybe I should □ _____ her □ _____ .
W: Yeah, you should do that. I went last month and had a lot of fun.
M: Cool! Then I'll go this weekend to □ _____ and build a □ _____ □ _____ .
W: Alright, have a good time!

✏ **어휘복습** 잘 안 들리거나 몰라서 체크한 어휘를 써 놓고 복습해 보세요.

□ _____   □ _____   □ _____   □ _____
□ _____   □ _____   □ _____   □ _____
□ _____   □ _____   □ _____   □ _____

19 속담 추론

대화를 듣고, 상황을 가장 잘 표현한 속담을 고르시오.

① Like father, like son.
② The more, the better.
③ All's well that ends well.
④ As you sow, so you reap.
⑤ Out of sight, out of mind.

M : Grandma, □ _____ was Dad □ _____ when he was my age?
W : Hmm… That was a □ _____ □ _____ □ _____.
M : Was he □ _____? I bet he liked □ _____ □ _____ just like me.
W : Yeah, he told a lot of jokes. He also □ _____ in front of people and □ _____ animals.
M : Haha, I do all of those things with my friends too! I think we have □ _____ □ _____ □ _____ music as well.
W : That's right. You are like a □ _____ □ _____ of him.
M : I'll □ _____ that as a □ _____.

20 알맞은 응답 찾기

대화를 듣고, 여자의 마지막 말에 이어질 남자의 응답으로 가장 적절한 것을 고르시오.

Man: _____

① I'll be on the lookout for your keys.
② I'll keep my fingers crossed for you.
③ There's a vending machine over there.
④ There's a hospital across the street from here.
⑤ Check out the clothing store on West Boulevard.

M : You □ _____ so □ _____ today. Is there □ _____ □ _____?
W : I went to the □ _____. My □ _____ might be □ _____.
M : That's terrible! □ _____ □ _____ have you been □ _____?
W : It has been twenty weeks. I'm so □ _____. □ _____ □ _____ something bad happens to him?
M : That's not going to happen. Think □ _____.
W : I'm trying. The □ _____ □ _____ come out tomorrow.
M : _____

✎ **어휘복습** 잘 안 들리거나 몰라서 체크한 어휘를 써 놓고 복습해 보세요.

□ _____   □ _____   □ _____   □ _____

□ _____   □ _____   □ _____   □ _____

□ _____   □ _____   □ _____   □ _____

■)) MP3 실전 10

점수
/ 20

01 대화를 듣고, 남자가 먹을 음식을 고르시오.

① ② ③

④ ⑤

02 대화를 듣고, 여자가 남자에게 전화한 목적으로 가장 적절한 것을 고르시오.

① 창고 정리를 부탁하려고
② 식탁 정리를 부탁하려고
③ 식탁보를 찾는 것을 부탁하려고
④ 새 식탁보를 사오라고 부탁하려고
⑤ 손님 마중 나가는 것을 부탁하려고

03 다음 그림의 상황에 가장 적절한 대화를 고르시오.

① ② ③ ④ ⑤

04 대화를 듣고, 여자가 구매할 신발을 고르시오.

① ② ③

④ ⑤

05 대화를 듣고, 남자의 직업으로 가장 적절한 것을 고르시오.

① dentist   ② magician
③ singer   ④ doctor
⑤ police officer

06 대화를 듣고, 여자의 심정으로 가장 적절한 것을 고르시오.

① worried   ② jealous   ③ bored
④ excited   ⑤ proud

07 다음을 듣고, 두 사람의 대화가 어색한 것을 고르시오.

① ② ③ ④ ⑤

08 대화를 듣고, 여자가 남자에게 부탁한 일로 가장 적절한 것을 고르시오.

① 가구 고르기   ② 선반 고치기
③ 숙제 같이 하기   ④ 책상 정리 돕기
⑤ 가구점에 데려가기

09 대화를 듣고, 여자의 마지막 말에 담긴 의도로 가장 적절한 것을 고르시오.

① 동의   ② 거절   ③ 요청
④ 제안   ⑤ 설득

10 대화를 듣고, 남자가 지불할 금액을 고르시오.

① $8   ② $10   ③ $14
④ $16   ⑤ $20

11 대화를 듣고, 두 사람이 대화하고 있는 장소로 가장 적절한 곳을 고르시오.

① café   ② baseball field
③ classroom   ④ fitness center
⑤ football stadium

12 다음을 듣고, The Lost Safari에 관해 언급되지 <u>않</u>은 것을 고르시오.

① 개장 시기 ② 투어 횟수
③ 동물의 종류 ④ 안전상의 유의사항
⑤ 입장료

13 다음을 듣고, 표와 일치하지 <u>않는</u> 것을 고르시오.

Eugene's Class Schedule

Class No.	Day / Time
Biology 101	Mon., Wed. / 12:00 P.M.
Reading 201	Mon., Tue. / 1:30 P.M.
History 201	Thur. / 1:00 P.M.
Math 401	Fri. / 11:00 A.M.
Writing 302	Fri. / 12:30 P.M.

① ② ③ ④ ⑤

14 다음을 듣고, 무엇에 관한 설명인지 고르시오.

① 육상 ② 권투 ③ 하키
④ 야구 ⑤ 테니스

15 대화를 듣고, 남자가 대화 직후에 할 일로 가장 적절한 것을 고르시오.

① 병원에 가기 ② 자전거 타기
③ 서점에 가기 ④ 스파 예약하기
⑤ 헬스클럽 등록하기

16 대화를 듣고, 두 사람이 만나기로 한 요일을 고르시오.

① 월요일 ② 화요일 ③ 수요일
④ 토요일 ⑤ 일요일

17 다음 상황 설명을 듣고, Sarah가 점원에게 할 말로 가장 적절한 것을 고르시오.

Sarah: _____

① The zipper on my jacket is broken.
② I would like to buy a new one.
③ I would like the receipt in the bag, please.
④ Is there a car repair shop in this neighborhood?
⑤ Can I get my purse fixed somewhere around here?

18 대화를 듣고, 남자가 할 일로 가장 적절한 것을 고르시오.

① 책 읽기 ② 연 날리기
③ 열기구 타기 ④ 축제 방문하기
⑤ 무서운 쇼 보기

19 대화를 듣고, 상황을 가장 잘 표현한 속담을 고르시오.

① Kill two birds with one stone.
② Two heads are better than one.
③ All roads lead to Rome.
④ Strike while the iron is hot.
⑤ Where there is a will, there is a way.

20 대화를 듣고, 여자의 마지막 말에 이어질 남자의 응답으로 가장 적절한 것을 고르시오.

Man: _____

① What time is your driver's license test?
② Don't be upset. You'll pass the test next time.
③ Good luck on your test! You'll pass, don't worry.
④ Look at all this traffic. Let's take a different route.
⑤ I don't think you're ready to do that yet.

01 그림 정보 파악

대화를 듣고, 남자가 먹을 음식을 고르시오.

① ② ③ ④ ⑤

M : Do you know what's for □ _____ today?
W : No, let's look at the cafeteria □ _____ on the □ _____
□ _____.
M : Let's see. We can □ _____ □ _____ five different □ _____.
W : Hmm, I think I'm going to □ _____ the □ _____ sandwich.
How about you?
M : I can't choose □ _____ the salad □ _____ the French fries.
W : I thought fried □ _____ was your □ _____. Why don't you
just get that one?
M : It is, but I ate fried chicken for dinner yesterday. I think I'll
□ _____ □ _____ the salad with French dressing.
W : Okay, if that's what you want!

02 목적 파악

대화를 듣고, 여자가 남자에게 전화한 목적으로 가장 적절한 것을 고르시오.

① 창고 정리를 부탁하려고
② 식탁 정리를 부탁하려고
③ 식탁보를 찾는 것을 부탁하려고
④ 새 식탁보를 사오라고 부탁하려고
⑤ 손님 마중 나가는 것을 부탁하려고

M : Honey, did you call? Sorry I □ _____ it. I was in the
□ _____ of a □ _____.
W : Yeah. Do you remember I told you we're having □ _____
□ _____ for □ _____ today?
M : Oh, I □ _____ □ _____. Thanks for □ _____ me. What
about it?
W : I'm □ _____ the □ _____, but I can't find the new
□ _____ we bought.
M : Hmm, did you □ _____ the □ _____ □ _____?
W : Yes. I just did, but □ _____ □ _____. I need you to come find
it for me.
M : Alright. If I leave now, I'll get home in about □ _____
□ _____ □ _____.
W : Okay. □ _____ □ _____.

✏ **어휘복습** 잘 안 들리거나 몰라서 체크한 어휘를 써 놓고 복습해 보세요.

□ _____   □ _____   □ _____   □ _____
□ _____   □ _____   □ _____   □ _____
□ _____   □ _____   □ _____

다음 그림의 상황에 가장 적절한 대화를 고르시오.

①   ②   ③   ④   ⑤

① W : □ _____ □ _____ has it been □ _____ you started to □ _____?

M : I □ _____ □ _____ about three months ago.

② W : Wow, look at that skateboard! It has a □ _____ □ _____ on it.

M : Yeah, it's □ _____ really □ _____.

③ W : Can I □ _____ your ice skates? □ _____ are at the repair shop.

M : Sure, but I □ _____ them □ _____ by tomorrow morning.

④ W : Excuse me, where is the □ _____ for the □ _____ □ _____?

M : It's over there □ _____ the □ _____ □ _____.

⑤ W : Could you tell me □ _____ □ _____ □ _____ to the skateboard shop?

M : Sure. Walk □ _____ for two blocks and □ _____ a □ _____.

대화를 듣고, 여자가 구매할 신발을 고르시오.

M : Why did you want to meet me at the □ _____?

W : I □ _____ □ _____ □ _____ which pair of sandals to get.

M : Okay, these □ _____ with □ _____ and no heels look good on you.

W : Do you think so? But I □ _____ shoes with □ _____ □ _____.

M : Then go with the high heels with zippers or □ _____.

W : □ _____ □ _____ do you think is □ _____ for the □ _____ season?

M : I □ _____ □ _____ the one with □ _____. They seem to be a better □ _____ □ _____ you.

W : Then, I'll buy those. Thanks a lot!

✏ **어휘복습** 잘 안 들리거나 몰라서 체크한 어휘를 써 놓고 복습해 보세요.

□ _____ □ _____ □ _____ □ _____

□ _____ □ _____ □ _____ □ _____

□ _____ □ _____ □ _____ □ _____

05 직업 추론

대화를 듣고, 남자의 직업으로 가장 적절한 것을 고르시오.

① dentist
② magician
③ singer
④ doctor
⑤ police officer

W : Sir, □ _____ □ _____ □ _____ here? Why are there so many people?

M : I'm going to □ _____ □ _____ a □ _____. I'll be □ _____ on this stage in five minutes.

W : Wow! □ _____ □ _____ there's a crowd. What kind of □ _____ is it?

M : I'll be □ _____ a few □ _____ with this deck of □ _____.

W : That sounds awesome. What else will you do?

M : Well, I'm going to □ _____ a □ _____ out of my □ _____ and do some coin tricks.

W : Really? I'm going to have to see that to believe it.

M : You'll be impressed. Please take a seat, the □ _____ □ _____ will start now.

06 심정 추론

대화를 듣고, 여자의 심정으로 가장 적절한 것을 고르시오.

① worried
② jealous
③ bored
④ excited
⑤ proud

W : We're finally college students! I □ _____ □ _____ for school to start.

M : You're so happy to be here, aren't you?

W : Are you □ _____ me? This is the □ _____ □ _____ of my □ _____.

M : Why? This is the start of a lot of studying and □ _____ □ _____.

W : But there's so □ _____ □ _____ that college has □ _____ □ _____!

M : Give me an □ _____.

W : You can meet a lot of new people, □ _____ a □ _____, and □ _____ □ _____ □ _____.

M : We'll □ _____ □ _____ you think the same way next month.

✎ **어휘복습** 잘 안 들리거나 몰라서 체크한 어휘를 써 놓고 복습해 보세요.

□ _____   □ _____   □ _____   □ _____

□ _____   □ _____   □ _____   □ _____

□ _____   □ _____   □ _____   □ _____

다음을 듣고, 두 사람의 대화가 <u>어색한</u> 것을 고르시오.

① ② ③ ④ ⑤

① W : Is your dog in the □ _____?
   M : No, I □ _____ him □ _____ because my mom was □ _____.
② W : □ _____ is the art □ _____ going to be □ _____?
   M : □ _____ on Loft Street.
③ W : What time does your plane □ _____ □ _____?
   M : I □ _____ at the □ _____ on Tuesday at nine P.M.
④ W : The □ _____ looks really □ _____.
   M : It just □ _____ □ _____ of the □ _____ five minutes ago.
⑤ W : Are you going to the □ _____ tomorrow?
   M : I don't think so. I have □ _____ □ _____.

대화를 듣고, 여자가 남자에게 부탁한 일로 가장 적절한 것을 고르시오.

① 가구 고르기
② 선반 고치기
③ 숙제 같이 하기
④ 책상 정리 돕기
⑤ 가구점에 데려가기

M : You are probably the messiest person I know.
W : I admit that. I □ _____ □ _____ it! I'm a busy person.
M : Buy some □ _____ and □ _____ to store everything.
W : I've tried that, but my desk just □ _____ □ _____ all over again.
M : Hmm, why don't I □ _____ you □ _____ □ _____ to keep your desk □ _____?
W : Can't you just □ _____ to my □ _____ someday and □ _____ me □ _____ it?
M : Fine. I'll □ _____ □ _____ next week when I have time.
W : Perfect. Thanks so much!

✎ **어휘복습** 잘 안 들리거나 몰라서 체크한 어휘를 써 놓고 복습해 보세요.

□ _____ □ _____ □ _____ □ _____
□ _____ □ _____ □ _____ □ _____
□ _____ □ _____ □ _____ □ _____

09 의도 파악

대화를 듣고, 여자의 마지막 말에 담긴 의도
로 가장 적절한 것을 고르시오.

① 동의   ② 거절   ③ 요청
④ 제안   ⑤ 설득

M : Honey, I can't sleep because of all the □ _____ that is coming
    from □ _____ □ _____.
W : You can □ _____ □ _____ □ _____. What do you think
    they're doing this □ _____ □ _____ □ _____?
M : Who knows? I think they're □ _____ a □ _____. I see a lot of
    cars parked in their driveway.
W : Another party? This is the third time this week! I've □ _____
    □ _____. We need to □ _____ □ _____ about it.
M : What do you □ _____ we do?
W : Should we go talk to them about it?
M : That would be a □ _____ of □ _____. I would prefer
    □ _____ the □ _____ and □ _____ a □ _____.
W : You're right. □ _____ they'll □ _____ □ _____ after that.

10 숫자 정보 파악

대화를 듣고, 남자가 지불할 금액을 고르시오.

① $8   ② $10   ③ $14
④ $16   ⑤ $20

W : Hi, what are you looking for?
M : I need to buy some writing □ _____ and a notepad.
W : The pens, pencils, and highlighters are □ _____ this □ _____,
    and the notepads are □ _____ the □ _____ □ _____ the store.
M : How much does □ _____ □ _____?
W : The pens □ _____ pencils are □ _____ dollars □ _____,
    the highlighters are □ _____ dollars each, and the notepad is
    □ _____ dollars.
M : Okay. I'll buy a pencil, a pen, a highlighter, and a notepad.

✎ **어휘복습** 잘 안 들리거나 몰라서 체크한 어휘를 써 놓고 복습해 보세요.

□ _____	□ _____	□ _____	□ _____
□ _____	□ _____	□ _____	□ _____
□ _____	□ _____	□ _____	□ _____

대화를 듣고, 두 사람이 대화하고 있는 장소로 가장 적절한 곳을 고르시오.

① café   ② baseball field
③ classroom   ④ fitness center
⑤ football stadium

M : Laura, which team are you □ _____ □ _____?

W : The Hawks, of course! They're the best □ _____ □ _____ ever!

M : Oh please. No team will ever be □ _____ □ _____ The Bears.

W : Nonsense! Let's □ _____ a □ _____. If your team loses, you have to □ _____ me □ _____. If my team loses, I'll buy you coffee.

M : That's fine with me! I'm □ _____ that The Bears will □ _____ this □ _____.

W : Oh, look! The Hawks just □ _____ a □ _____.

M : No! That means the score is already thirty-six to eighteen!

W : That's right. I'm □ _____ □ _____ you're going to □ _____ □ _____ buying me coffee.

다음을 듣고, The Lost Safari에 관해 언급되지 않은 것을 고르시오.

① 개장 시기
② 투어 횟수
③ 동물의 종류
④ 안전상의 유의사항
⑤ 입장료

W : To all visitors: First of all, we would like to welcome you all to our □ _____. This announcement is to □ _____ our □ _____ □ _____ through The Lost Safari. You can □ _____ this tour □ _____ on November thirtieth. You will be □ _____ to □ _____ tigers, lions, bears, zebras, and many more animals □ _____ □ _____! You will also have the opportunity to □ _____ the □ _____ while on the bus. □ _____ your □ _____, we ask that you □ _____ on the □ _____, and please □ _____ your hands and feet □ _____ the metal railings. □ _____ is □ _____ for □ _____ and □ _____ dollars for □ _____.

✎ **어휘복습** 잘 안 들리거나 몰라서 체크한 어휘를 써 놓고 복습해 보세요.

□ _____   □ _____   □ _____   □ _____

□ _____   □ _____   □ _____   □ _____

□ _____   □ _____   □ _____   □ _____

13 도표·실용문 파악

다음을 듣고, 표와 일치하지 <u>않는</u> 것을 고르시오.

Eugene's Class Schedule

Class No.	Day / Time
Biology 101	Mon., Wed. / 12:00 P.M.
Reading 201	Mon., Tue. / 1:30 P.M.
History 201	Thur. / 1:00 P.M.
Math 401	Fri. / 11:00 A.M.
Writing 302	Fri. / 12:30 P.M.

①   ②   ③   ④   ⑤

① Biology one oh one is Eugene's □ _____ □ _____ on
□ _____ .

② After the Reading two oh one class, Eugene is □ _____
□ _____ classes on □ _____ .

③ Eugene's one P.M. class on □ _____ is the □ _____ four oh
one class.

④ Eugene has to go to the □ _____ two oh one class □ _____
□ _____ .

⑤ On □ _____ , Eugene will learn how to write □ _____ and
□ _____ □ _____ .

14 화제 추론

다음을 듣고, 무엇에 관한 설명인지 고르시오.

① 육상   ② 권투   ③ 하키
④ 야구   ⑤ 테니스

M : To □ _____ this □ _____ , you need at least □ _____
□ _____ . It is played on a □ _____ with a □ _____ secured
in the □ _____ of it. The net is fixed on the ground and is about
□ _____ □ _____ . One person stands □ _____ □ _____
□ _____ of the court, and the other person stands on the
□ _____ side. You use a □ _____ to hit a small □ _____
ball. One person □ _____ the ball, and the other person
□ _____ the ball. If the ball hits the net and doesn't □ _____
it □ _____ , the other player □ _____ the □ _____ .

✎ **어휘복습** 잘 안 들리거나 몰라서 체크한 어휘를 써 놓고 복습해 보세요.

□ _____   □ _____   □ _____   □ _____

□ _____   □ _____   □ _____   □ _____

□ _____   □ _____   □ _____   □ _____

15 할 일 파악

대화를 듣고, 남자가 대화 직후에 할 일로 가장 적절한 것을 고르시오.

① 병원에 가기
② 자전거 타기
③ 서점에 가기
④ 스파 예약하기
⑤ 헬스클럽 등록하기

M : I'm so □ _____ . All this _____ □ _____ is wearing me out.

W : Are you getting □ _____ □ _____ in your back again?

M : I sure am. I □ _____ □ _____ in my □ _____ during the day, too.

W : There's a □ _____ in the □ _____ . I think you should go.

M : Oh, really? Have you □ _____ □ _____ □ _____ ?

W : Yeah, I go once a month to get a □ _____ and □ _____ □ _____ .

M : It's □ _____ just thinking about it. I'll go □ _____ □ _____ to get one.

W : Great. But □ _____ □ _____ you call and □ _____ a □ _____ . They're usually □ _____ □ _____ .

M : Yes, □ _____ □ _____ . Thanks.

16 특정 정보 파악

대화를 듣고, 두 사람이 만나기로 한 요일을 고르시오.

① 월요일   ② 화요일
③ 수요일   ④ 토요일
⑤ 일요일

M : What are you doing for Independence Day?

W : I have □ _____ □ _____ , yet. Do you □ _____ any □ _____ ?

M : I heard there's going to be □ _____ by the lake on □ _____ and □ _____ .

W : Oh, really? The last time I saw fireworks was three years ago! □ _____ □ _____ do they □ _____ ?

M : It starts at □ _____ P.M. on Wednesday and □ _____ P.M. on Saturday.

W : Hmm, I'm going on a □ _____ □ _____ □ _____ the □ _____ , so I can't go on Saturday.

M : That's fine. I'll see you at the □ _____ fireworks □ _____ then.

W : Alright! I'll □ _____ □ _____ to it.

✎ **어휘복습** 잘 안 들리거나 몰라서 체크한 어휘를 써 놓고 복습해 보세요.

□ _____   □ _____   □ _____   □ _____

□ _____   □ _____   □ _____   □ _____

□ _____   □ _____   □ _____   □ _____

17 상황에 적절한 말 찾기

다음 상황 설명을 듣고, Sarah가 점원에게 할 말로 가장 적절한 것을 고르시오.

Sarah: _____

① The zipper on my jacket is broken.
② I would like to buy a new one.
③ I would like the receipt in the bag, please.
④ Is there a car repair shop in this neighborhood?
⑤ Can I get my purse fixed somewhere around here?

M : Sarah bought a ☐ _____ from a ☐ _____ ☐ _____ last Tuesday. The ☐ _____ on her purse ☐ _____ a week later. Today, she took it to the store to ask them to ☐ _____ the item ☐ _____ a new one. But Sarah didn't have her ☐ _____, so the store could not help her. Sarah did not know ☐ _____ ☐ _____ ☐ _____. So she decided to ☐ _____ the store worker if there is a purse ☐ _____ ☐ _____ in the ☐ _____. In this situation, what would Sarah most likely say to the worker?
Sarah: _____

18 할 일 파악

대화를 듣고, 남자가 할 일로 가장 적절한 것을 고르시오.

① 책 읽기
② 연 날리기
③ 열기구 타기
④ 축제 방문하기
⑤ 무서운 쇼 보기

M : I'm going to Turkey with my sister ☐ _____ ☐ _____. Can you ☐ _____ any ☐ _____ ☐ _____?
W : ☐ _____ ☐ _____ ☐ _____ ☐ _____, I would definitely check out the ☐ _____.
M : I ☐ _____ have that on my ☐ _____. Is there ☐ _____ ☐ _____ I should go?
W : Hmm, when I was there, I personally enjoyed riding a ☐ _____ ☐ _____ ☐ _____.
M : Hot air balloon? That ☐ _____ ☐ _____ to me. How was it?
W : It wasn't scary at all. I rode it, and it was the ☐ _____ ☐ _____ of my ☐ _____!
M : ☐ _____ ☐ _____ ☐ _____, I'll have to ride it while I'm there.
W : Good thinking. You're going to have a blast!

✏️ **어휘복습** 잘 안 들리거나 몰라서 체크한 어휘를 써 놓고 복습해 보세요.

☐ _____   ☐ _____   ☐ _____   ☐ _____

☐ _____   ☐ _____   ☐ _____   ☐ _____

☐ _____   ☐ _____   ☐ _____   ☐ _____

19 속담 추론

대화를 듣고, 상황을 가장 잘 표현한 속담을 고르시오.

① Kill two birds with one stone.
② Two heads are better than one.
③ All roads lead to Rome.
④ Strike while the iron is hot.
⑤ Where there is a will, there is a way.

W : My children drew all over the □ _____ □ _____ in the dining room.
M : Oh □ _____ □ _____. What are you going to do about it?
W : As of now, I'm □ _____ □ _____. Has this □ _____ to you □ _____?
M : No, but I □ _____ □ _____ □ _____ on what you should do.
W : What's your idea?
M : □ _____ □ _____ □ _____ change your wallpaper? That way you can □ _____ the house and □ _____ □ _____ the mess at the □ _____ □ _____.
W : Hmm, now that I think about it, the wallpaper was a bit □ _____. Plus, new wallpaper will □ _____ the □ _____ look □ _____, too! I think there will be a lot of □ _____ from changing it. Thanks for the idea!
M : I'm glad I could □ _____ you □ _____.

20 알맞은 응답 찾기

대화를 듣고, 여자의 마지막 말에 이어질 남자의 응답으로 가장 적절한 것을 고르시오.

Man : _____

① What time is your driver's license test?
② Don't be upset. You'll pass the test next time.
③ Good luck on your test! You'll pass, don't worry.
④ Look at all this traffic. Let's take a different route.
⑤ I don't think you're ready to do that yet.

W : Dad, I have to □ _____ driving before my □ _____ □ _____ □ _____ on Saturday.
M : Would you like me to help you? We can use my car if you want.
W : That would be great. □ _____ should we □ _____ to practice?
M : I think the □ _____ □ _____ □ _____ on Grover Lane will be a good place to start.
W : Yeah, I agree. After I try parking a few times, can we □ _____ □ _____ on the □ _____?
M : _____

✎ **어휘복습** 잘 안 들리거나 몰라서 체크한 어휘를 써 놓고 복습해 보세요.

□ _____ □ _____ □ _____ □ _____

□ _____ □ _____ □ _____ □ _____

□ _____ □ _____ □ _____ □ _____

01 대화를 듣고, 여자가 입어 볼 블라우스를 고르시오.

①   ②   ③

④   ⑤

02 대화를 듣고, 남자가 여자에게 전화한 목적으로 가장 적절한 것을 고르시오.

① 수업을 변경하려고
② 선생님과 약속을 잡으려고
③ 화학 수업에 대해 물어보려고
④ 역사 수업에 대해 물어보려고
⑤ 수업 신청 방법에 대해 물어보려고

03 다음 그림의 상황에 가장 적절한 대화를 고르시오.

① ② ③ ④ ⑤

04 대화를 듣고, 여자가 구매할 꽃병을 고르시오.

①   ②   ③

④   ⑤

05 대화를 듣고, 두 사람의 관계로 가장 적절한 것을 고르시오.

① 감독 – 축구선수
② 감독 – 야구선수
③ 교사 – 학생
④ 관광객 – 여행가이드
⑤ 점원 – 고객

06 대화를 듣고, 남자의 심정으로 가장 적절한 것을 고르시오.

① joyful   ② upset
③ relaxed   ④ excited
⑤ surprised

07 다음을 듣고, 두 사람의 대화가 <u>어색한</u> 것을 고르시오.

①   ②   ③   ④   ⑤

08 대화를 듣고, 여자가 남자에게 부탁한 일로 가장 적절한 것을 고르시오.

① 창문 청소하기   ② 커튼 교체하기
③ 거실 청소하기   ④ 세탁기에 커튼 넣기
⑤ 새로운 커튼 구매하기

09 대화를 듣고, 남자의 마지막 말에 담긴 의도로 가장 적절한 것을 고르시오.

① 제안   ② 요청   ③ 충고
④ 거절   ⑤ 감사

10 대화를 듣고, 여자가 지불해야 할 금액을 고르시오.

① $50   ② $70   ③ $100
④ $120   ⑤ $140

11 대화를 듣고, 두 사람이 대화하고 있는 장소로 가장 적절한 곳을 고르시오.

① playground　　② classroom
③ doctor's office　　④ bedroom
⑤ daycare center

12 다음을 듣고, Spring Mint Singing Contest에 관해 언급되지 <u>않은</u> 것을 고르시오.

① 대회 날짜　　② 오디션 장소
③ 등록 인원 수　　④ 최종 공연자 수
⑤ 오디션 날짜

13 다음 표를 보면서 대화를 듣고, 내용과 일치하지 <u>않는</u> 것을 고르시오.

Moby's Ski Resort Fees

①	Ski Rental	$10 per hour
②	Snowboard Rental	$20 per hour
③	Sled Rental	$15 per hour
④	Lift Ticket	$10 for all day use
⑤	Glove Rental	$5 for all day use

14 다음을 듣고, 무엇에 관한 설명인지 고르시오.

① 서핑 선수　② 어부　③ 안전요원
④ 수영 선수　⑤ 선생님

15 대화를 듣고, 두 사람이 대화 직후에 할 일로 가장 적절한 것을 고르시오.

① 병원 가기　② 치과 가기　③ 약국 가기
④ 잠자기　⑤ 영화 보기

16 대화를 듣고, 산악 자전거 여행 신청 마감 날짜를 고르시오.

① November 10　　② November 11
③ November 12　　④ November 13
⑤ November 14

17 다음 상황 설명을 듣고, Joe가 Samantha에게 할 말로 가장 적절한 것을 고르시오.

Joe: _____

① My bike will be fixed by next Monday.
② Thank you for letting me borrow your bike.
③ How much does it cost to get my bike fixed?
④ How much is the bicycle in the display window?
⑤ I'm so sorry about what happened. Can you forgive me?

18 대화를 듣고, 두 사람이 일요일에 할 일로 가장 적절한 것을 고르시오.

① 쇼핑하기　② 낚시하기　③ 보트 타기
④ 생선 사기　⑤ 생선 먹기

19 대화를 듣고, 상황을 가장 잘 표현한 속담을 고르시오.

① Like father, like son.
② Two heads are better than one.
③ Kill two birds with one stone.
④ Even if the sky falls, there is a way out.
⑤ All work and no play makes Jack a dull boy.

20 대화를 듣고, 남자의 마지막 말에 대한 여자의 응답으로 가장 적절한 것을 고르시오.

Woman: _____

① I'm hungry. Let's grab something to eat.
② I need to buy some dog food before we leave.
③ The graduation ceremony will take place at 12 P.M.
④ How long will it take to get to the graduation ceremony?
⑤ Our dog will probably be starving by the time we get back.

01 그림 정보 파악

대화를 듣고, 여자가 입어 볼 블라우스를 고르시오.

① ② ③ ④ ⑤

M : Good morning, welcome to Bloom's Clothing. Can I help you?
W : I'm □ _____ □ _____ a □ _____ to wear to my piano recital.
M : Okay. We have this one □ _____ □ _____, and we also have this one with □ _____ on it.
W : They look too □ _____. I would like a □ _____ □ _____ better.
M : Well then, □ _____ □ _____ this one with □ _____ on the □ _____?
W : I'd □ _____ a blouse without buttons. Are there any with □ _____?
M : Yes, there are. This one has a pocket on the front. Would you like to □ _____ it □ _____?
W : Okay. I will try on this blouse in □ _____ □ _____. Where are the □ _____ □ _____?
M : They are □ _____ □ _____ at the back of the store.

02 목적 파악

대화를 듣고, 남자가 여자에게 전화한 목적으로 가장 적절한 것을 고르시오.

① 수업을 변경하려고
② 선생님과 약속을 잡으려고
③ 화학 수업에 대해 물어보려고
④ 역사 수업에 대해 물어보려고
⑤ 수업 신청 방법에 대해 물어보려고

M : Hey, Danielle, this is Jared calling.
W : Hi! It's been a long time □ _____ we've □ _____. How have you been?
M : I've been terrific, thanks for asking. I'm calling to □ _____ you about Mr. Rogers' □ _____ □ _____.
W : Sure! What would you like to know about it?
M : Well, I'm planning on □ _____ it this □ _____. But I wanted to know □ _____ □ _____ the class is.
W : Hmm… It □ _____ □ _____ how hard you study. You have to take three □ _____ and do a lot of □ _____, too.
M : Wow! That sounds like a lot of work. I'm not sure I can □ _____ it.
W : You should definitely think about it before □ _____ □ _____.
M : Alright, thanks for the advice!

✎ **어휘복습** 잘 안 들리거나 몰라서 체크한 어휘를 써 놓고 복습해 보세요.

□ _____   □ _____   □ _____   □ _____
□ _____   □ _____   □ _____   □ _____
□ _____   □ _____   □ _____   □ _____

03 그림 상황에 적절한 대화 찾기

다음 그림의 상황에 가장 적절한 대화를 고르시오.

① ② ③ ④ ⑤

① M : I would like a ☐ _____ of ☐ _____ , please.

W : Here you are. Be ☐ _____ not to ☐ _____ it. It's very hot.

② M : Can I get you ☐ _____ to ☐ _____ ?

W : No, ☐ _____ ☐ _____ . Thank you for the thought.

③ M : The ☐ _____ is so ☐ _____ ! My drink is melting.

W : Here, you should put some ☐ _____ ☐ _____ in it.

④ M : Are you ready to ☐ _____ ☐ _____ ?

W : Just a minute. Let me ☐ _____ my water ☐ _____ .

⑤ M : ☐ _____ do you want to ☐ _____ ?

W : ☐ _____ ☐ _____ pizza for dinner today.

04 그림 정보 파악

대화를 듣고, 여자가 구매할 꽃병을 고르시오.

① ② ③

④ ⑤

M : Hello, ma'am. Are you looking for anything ☐ _____ ☐ _____ ?

W : Yes, I need to buy a new ☐ _____ ☐ _____ . My husband ☐ _____ my old one and it ☐ _____ into ☐ _____ .

M : I'm sorry to hear that. Would you be ☐ _____ ☐ _____ this ☐ _____ , ☐ _____ vase?

W : No, I won't be able to ☐ _____ a lot of flowers in it. I normally put an ☐ _____ bouquet in the vase ☐ _____ ☐ _____ ☐ _____ .

M : I see. This ☐ _____ , ☐ _____ vase may be ☐ _____ for you.

W : It seems nice, but I think this ☐ _____ , ☐ _____ one with the ☐ _____ ☐ _____ is the one I want.

M : Sure, this vase is one of our ☐ _____ ☐ _____ items. Would you like me to ☐ _____ it ☐ _____ for you?

W : Yes, that would be wonderful. I wouldn't want it to break ☐ _____ ☐ _____ ☐ _____ back home.

M : Here you go. Have a nice day!

✎ **어휘복습** 잘 안 들리거나 몰라서 체크한 어휘를 써 놓고 복습해 보세요.

☐ _____   ☐ _____   ☐ _____   ☐ _____

☐ _____   ☐ _____   ☐ _____   ☐ _____

☐ _____   ☐ _____   ☐ _____   ☐ _____

05 관계 추론

대화를 듣고, 두 사람의 관계로 가장 적절한 것을 고르시오.

① 감독 – 축구선수
② 감독 – 야구선수
③ 교사 – 학생
④ 관광객 – 여행가이드
⑤ 점원 – 고객

M : Michelle, you need to work on _____ the _____ to other_____ on the _____.
W : I'm □ _____, but I don't seem to □ _____. For me, passing the ball is the □ _____ □ _____ of □ _____ □ _____.
M : I understand. Every player has a □ _____ □ _____.
W : I'll □ _____ every day for a few hours. Hopefully I'll □ _____ □ _____ at it.
M : If you want, I can □ _____ □ _____. We can pass the ball to each other.
W : That would be great! Can we □ _____ the □ _____ right now?
M : I think there are other teams who will be using the field today.
W : I'll □ _____ you here □ _____ □ _____.
M : Alright, I'll see you then.

06 심정 추론

대화를 듣고, 남자의 심정으로 가장 적절한 것을 고르시오.

① joyful   ② upset
③ relaxed   ④ excited
⑤ surprised

M : Oh my goodness, this is □ _____!
W : What's the □ _____? Did something □ _____ to your □ _____?
M : Yeah, look at this! I have a □ _____ □ _____, and I need to be at an □ _____ in an hour.
W : Is there □ _____ I can do to □ _____?
M : Yes. Can you call the □ _____ □ _____ □ _____ and ask if they can □ _____ a □ _____ over here?
W : Sure, I'll do that. Do you think they can □ _____ your tire □ _____ □ _____?
M : I hope they can. I'm so □ _____ □ _____. □ _____ are all these bad things □ _____ to me? Last week my side mirror broke, and now I have a flat tire.
W : Cheer up!

✎ **어휘복습** 잘 안 들리거나 몰라서 체크한 어휘를 써 놓고 복습해 보세요.

□ _____   □ _____   □ _____   □ _____
□ _____   □ _____   □ _____   □ _____
□ _____   □ _____   □ _____   □ _____

다음을 듣고, 두 사람의 대화가 <u>어색한</u> 것을 고르시오.

①   ②   ③   ④   ⑤

① M : I would like to □ _____ □ _____ this □ _____.

    W : Sure. May I see your □ _____ □ _____?

② M : There are so many □ _____ here.

    W : Yeah, how are we going to □ _____ one?

③ M : □ _____ are you □ _____ on TV?

    W : I'm watching a □ _____ □ _____.

④ M : □ _____ is our homework assignment □ _____?

    W : We have to turn it in □ _____ □ _____.

⑤ M : Can you plug in the □ _____ □ _____ for me?

    W : The □ _____ is already turned on.

---

08 부탁 파악

대화를 듣고, 여자가 남자에게 부탁한 일로 가장 적절한 것을 고르시오.

① 창문 청소하기
② 커튼 교체하기
③ 거실 청소하기
④ 세탁기에 커튼 넣기
⑤ 새로운 커튼 구매하기

W : Honey, what are you doing?

M : I'm □ _____ a □ _____ in the bedroom. What's up?

W : Can you come to the living room □ _____ □ _____ □ _____?

M : Yeah, sure. Do you need something?

W : Yes. I can't □ _____ the □ _____ of the □ _____ because I'm too short. Can you □ _____ the □ _____ □ _____ these new ones?

M : Of course. But I think the □ _____ need to be □ _____ first. They're so □ _____!

W : You're right. I'll clean the windows before you change the curtains.

M : Okay, that sounds like a good plan. □ _____ should I □ _____ □ _____ the old curtains?

W : You can give them to me. I'll put them in the □ _____ □ _____.

✏️ **어휘복습** 잘 안 들리거나 몰라서 체크한 어휘를 써 놓고 복습해 보세요.

□ _____   □ _____   □ _____   □ _____

□ _____   □ _____   □ _____   □ _____

□ _____   □ _____   □ _____   □ _____

09 의도 파악

대화를 듣고, 남자의 마지막 말에 담긴 의도로 가장 적절한 것을 고르시오.

① 제안　　② 요청　　③ 충고
④ 거절　　⑤ 감사

M : Hey, Linda. I didn't think I'd see you at the □ _____ □ _____. □ _____ a nice □ _____!

W : I know! Are you here to □ _____ a □ _____?

M : Yes, I am. How about you? □ _____ are you going to do □ _____ your □ _____?

W : I haven't decided yet. Maybe I'll □ _____ a □ _____ and □ _____ it. What do you think?

M : Well, I □ _____ □ _____ you with □ _____ hair. You □ _____ □ _____ with □ _____ hair.

W : Really? Then maybe I should get it cut and dye it.

M : That seems like a good idea. Do you have any □ _____ □ _____ □ _____?

W : I was thinking either □ _____ □ _____ or □ _____ brown.

M : Hmm… □ _____ □ _____ □ _____ try dying your hair □ _____?

10 숫자 정보 파악

대화를 듣고, 여자가 지불해야 할 금액을 고르시오.

① $50　　② $70　　③ $100
④ $120　　⑤ $140

M : Ma'am, may I help you find something?

W : Yes, please. □ _____ are Vitamin Ultra and Vitamin Plus?

M : They are □ _____ □ _____ □ _____. Would you like a bottle of each?

W : Yeah. □ _____ □ _____ is it for each □ _____?

M : Vitamin Ultra costs □ _____ dollars each, and Vitamin Plus costs □ _____ dollars each.

W : Okay. I have this buy-one-get-one-free □ _____. Can I use it?

M : Of course. But in that case, you have to □ _____ for the □ _____ that □ _____ □ _____.

W : So, if I buy Vitamin Plus, I get Vitamin Ultra □ _____ □ _____, correct?

M : Yes, ma'am. Your □ _____ is seventy dollars.

W : Wait a minute. I □ _____ my □ _____. I would just like to purchase Vitamin Ultra today. I'll come back next time to buy Vitamin Plus.

✎ **어휘복습** 잘 안 들리거나 몰라서 체크한 어휘를 써 놓고 복습해 보세요.

□ _____　　□ _____　　□ _____　　□ _____

□ _____　　□ _____　　□ _____　　□ _____

□ _____　　□ _____　　□ _____　　□ _____

대화를 듣고, 두 사람이 대화하고 있는 장소로 가장 적절한 곳을 고르시오.

① playground　　② classroom
③ doctor's office　　④ bedroom
⑤ daycare center

W : Sir, I would like to □ _____ to you □ _____ your □ _____.
M : Sure. Should I be □ _____ □ _____ her?
W : Well, she's □ _____ a □ _____ □ _____ getting used to the people here. She cries every time you leave her here.
M : Oh, I □ _____ □ _____ □ _____. Does she □ _____ □ _____ □ _____ the other children?
W : She normally □ _____ □ _____ □ _____. We're starting to think that this isn't the best place for her to stay.
M : I see, but there is □ _____ □ _____ □ _____ □ _____. My wife and I both work during the day, and there's □ _____ to □ _____ □ _____ her.
W : Okay. Let's talk about this more when you come to □ _____ her □ _____.
M : Alright. I'll be here around six P.M.

다음을 듣고, Spring Mint Singing Contest에 관해 언급되지 않은 것을 고르시오.

① 대회 날짜
② 오디션 장소
③ 등록 인원 수
④ 최종 공연자 수
⑤ 오디션 날짜

W : To all of you who signed up to □ _____ □ _____ the Spring Mint □ _____ □ _____ on □ _____ □ _____, we would like to □ _____ an □ _____. There have been over one □ _____ people who □ _____ □ _____ for our contest. However, we only have □ _____ □ _____ □ _____ people. In order to choose our final □ _____, we will be □ _____ □ _____ on September □ _____ and September □ _____. In order to □ _____ □ _____ an audition □ _____, please □ _____ or □ _____ □ _____ two one oh, two three nine one.

✎ 어휘복습 잘 안 들리거나 몰라서 체크한 어휘를 써 놓고 복습해 보세요.

□ _____　□ _____　□ _____　□ _____
□ _____　□ _____　□ _____　□ _____
□ _____　□ _____　□ _____　□ _____

13 도표·실용문 파악

다음 표를 보면서 대화를 듣고, 내용과 일치하지 <u>않는</u> 것을 고르시오.

Moby's Ski Resort Fees

①	Ski Rental	$10 per hour
②	Snowboard Rental	$20 per hour
③	Sled Rental	$15 per hour
④	Lift Ticket	$10 for all day use
⑤	Glove Rental	$5 for all day use

① At Moby's Ski Resort, you can ☐ _____ ☐ _____ for ☐ _____ dollars an ☐ _____ .

② It costs ☐ _____ dollars per hour to rent a ☐ _____ .

③ Do you want to ride a ☐ _____ ? Rent one for ☐ _____ dollars an hour.

④ You can purchase a ☐ _____ ☐ _____ at the resort for ☐ _____ dollars per hour.

⑤ If you forgot to bring your ☐ _____ , don't worry. You can rent some for ☐ _____ dollars and use them ☐ _____ ☐ _____ .

14 화제 추론

다음을 듣고, 무엇에 관한 설명인지 고르시오.

① 서핑 선수   ② 어부
③ 안전요원   ④ 수영 선수
⑤ 선생님

M : People with this job ☐ _____ at ☐ _____ ☐ _____ , ☐ _____ ☐ _____ , ☐ _____ , and ☐ _____ . They are trained to help people who can't swim or are in ☐ _____ ☐ _____ ☐ _____ . If you're in trouble, they will ☐ _____ ☐ _____ the ☐ _____ to save you. They are great ☐ _____ . Most of the time, they have a ☐ _____ around their ☐ _____ , and ☐ _____ ☐ _____ people are ☐ _____ in the water.

✎ **어휘복습** 잘 안 들리거나 몰라서 체크한 어휘를 써 놓고 복습해 보세요.

☐ _____	☐ _____	☐ _____	☐ _____
☐ _____	☐ _____	☐ _____	☐ _____
☐ _____	☐ _____	☐ _____	☐ _____

15 할 일 파악

대화를 듣고, 두 사람이 대화 직후에 할 일로 가장 적절한 것을 고르시오.

① 병원 가기　② 치과 가기
③ 약국 가기　④ 잠자기
⑤ 영화 보기

M : Mom, my □ _____ □ _____. I think I have a □ _____, too.

W : Oh no! □ _____ □ _____ has this been going on?

M : I'm not sure, maybe a few hours. Now I'm starting to □ _____.

W : Why didn't you □ _____ me □ _____?

M : I didn't want you to worry. Plus, I'm □ _____ □ _____ □ _____ □ _____.

W : Still, you should have □ _____ me □ _____. Let me □ _____ you some □ _____.

M : I already □ _____ □ _____, but it's not □ _____ any □ _____.

W : Well then, I need to □ _____ you to a □ _____. I'll get my car keys.

16 특정 정보 파악

대화를 듣고, 산악 자전거 여행 신청 마감 날짜를 고르시오.

① November 10
② November 11
③ November 12
④ November 13
⑤ November 14

M : Sandy, are you □ _____ on the mountain □ _____ □ _____ on November fourteenth?

W : Yeah, I am. Didn't you say you were going, too?

M : You're right, but I haven't □ _____ □ _____ yet.

W : Why haven't you? You □ _____ be □ _____ to go if all the □ _____ are □ _____. Only twenty people can go this year.

M : Oh, I didn't know that! Do you know □ _____ the □ _____ to sign up is?

W : Wait a minute. I □ _____ it □ _____ on my □ _____. You have to sign up □ _____ November □ _____.

M : November twelfth? That's □ _____! I should □ _____ and sign up now.

W : Good idea. I hope there's a spot left for you.

✎ **어휘복습** 잘 안 들리거나 몰라서 체크한 어휘를 써 놓고 복습해 보세요.

□ _____　□ _____　□ _____　□ _____

□ _____　□ _____　□ _____　□ _____

□ _____　□ _____　□ _____　□ _____

17 상황에 적절한 말 찾기

다음 상황 설명을 듣고, Joe가 Samantha 에게 할 말로 가장 적절한 것을 고르시오.

Joe:_____

① My bike will be fixed by next Monday.
② Thank you for letting me borrow your bike.
③ How much does it cost to get my bike fixed?
④ How much is the bicycle in the display window?
⑤ I'm so sorry about what happened. Can you forgive me?

M : Joe ☐ _____ his ☐ _____ everywhere he goes. But on his way home from school, the ☐ _____ ☐ _____. So, Joe asked Samantha if he could ☐ _____ her bicycle until his gets ☐ _____. She ☐ _____ him ☐ _____ it right away. However, while he was riding it, the brakes ☐ _____ ☐ _____. He was ☐ _____ ☐ _____ what Samantha would say. He decided to tell her what happened and ☐ _____. In this situation, what would Joe most likely say to Samantha?

Joe: _____

18 할 일 파악

대화를 듣고, 두 사람이 일요일에 할 일로 가장 적절한 것을 고르시오.

① 쇼핑하기
② 낚시하기
③ 보트 타기
④ 생선 사기
⑤ 생선 먹기

M : Hannah, do you have ☐ _____ for the ☐ _____?
W : No. I was supposed to ☐ _____ ☐ _____ with my friend, but that got ☐ _____.
M : Oh, I see. Then will you go ☐ _____ with me on Sunday? My dad is ☐ _____ me ☐ _____ on his ☐ _____, and he said I could ☐ _____ a ☐ _____.
W : I've never been fishing before, but that ☐ _____ ☐ _____!
M : I can teach you ☐ _____ ☐ _____ ☐ _____. It's actually really ☐ _____.
W : Alright! I'll ☐ _____ ☐ _____ ☐ _____ it. I like learning new things.
M : Okay, I'll see you on Sunday.

✎ **어휘복습** 잘 안 들리거나 몰라서 체크한 어휘를 써 놓고 복습해 보세요.

☐ _____   ☐ _____   ☐ _____   ☐ _____

☐ _____   ☐ _____   ☐ _____   ☐ _____

☐ _____   ☐ _____   ☐ _____   ☐ _____

19 속담 추론

대화를 듣고, 상황을 가장 잘 표현한 속담을 고르시오.

① Like father, like son.
② Two heads are better than one.
③ Kill two birds with one stone.
④ Even if the sky falls, there is a way out.
⑤ All work and no play makes Jack a dull boy.

M : You've been □ _____ □ _____ that □ _____ □ _____ for over two hours.
W : I know. I'm □ _____ and □ _____ of it. I'm about to □ _____ □ _____.
M : Let me □ _____ □ _____ □ _____. I might be able to help you.
W : Here you are. I'm telling you, this problem is □ _____ to □ _____!
M : Hmm… Give me a minute. You're right, this is really hard. I think I can solve □ _____ □ _____ □ _____ of the problem, but I don't know the □ _____ part.
W : Oh, really? I can solve the first part. I was □ _____ □ _____ □ _____ the last part.
M : Then □ _____ try solving it □ _____. If we □ _____ □ _____ □ _____, I'm sure we can do it.
W : That's a great idea.
M : Yes! We finally solved it! It □ _____ have been □ _____ □ _____ you.

20 알맞은 응답 찾기

대화를 듣고, 남자의 마지막 말에 대한 여자의 응답으로 가장 적절한 것을 고르시오.

Woman : _____

① I'm hungry. Let's grab something to eat.
② I need to buy some dog food before we leave.
③ The graduation ceremony will take place at 12 P.M.
④ How long will it take to get to the graduation ceremony?
⑤ Our dog will probably be starving by the time we get back.

W : Hey, Peter. Did you □ _____ the □ _____ before we left home?
M : Oh no. I □ _____ □ _____. What should we do?
W : □ _____ □ _____ you forget? I asked you three times!
M : I'm sorry. Should we □ _____ □ _____ home?
W : It's □ _____ □ _____ now. We'll be late for the □ _____ □ _____.
M : Okay then. Let's drive home □ _____ □ _____ □ _____ it's over.
W : _____

✏ **어휘복습** 잘 안 들리거나 몰라서 체크한 어휘를 써 놓고 복습해 보세요.

□ _____   □ _____   □ _____   □ _____
□ _____   □ _____   □ _____   □ _____
□ _____   □ _____   □ _____   □ _____

01 대화를 듣고, 여자가 입을 의상을 고르시오.

①   ②   ③

④   ⑤

02 대화를 듣고, 남자가 여자에게 전화한 목적으로 가장 적절한 것을 고르시오.

① 과제에 대해 물어보려고
② 태양계에 대해 토론하려고
③ 태양계에 대한 책을 빌리려고
④ 보고서 제출 기한을 물어보려고
⑤ 보고서를 함께 작성하자고 말하려고

03 다음 그림의 상황에 가장 적절한 대화를 고르시오.

①   ②   ③   ④   ⑤

04 대화를 듣고, 경찰이 찾고 있는 여자를 고르시오.

①   ②   ③

④   ⑤

05 대화를 듣고, 남자의 직업으로 가장 적절한 것을 고르시오.

① 육상선수   ② 복싱선수
③ 헬스 트레이너   ④ 보컬 트레이너
⑤ 체육 교사

06 대화를 듣고, 남자의 심정으로 가장 적절한 것을 고르시오.

① hopeless   ② nervous
③ satisfied   ④ disappointed
⑤ angry

07 다음을 듣고, 두 사람의 대화가 <u>어색한</u> 것을 고르시오.

①   ②   ③   ④   ⑤

08 대화를 듣고, 여자가 남자에게 부탁한 일로 가장 적절한 것을 고르시오.

① 리모컨 고치기   ② 텔레비전 옮기기
③ 새 건전지 사기   ④ 식료품점에 가기
⑤ 새 텔레비전 사기

09 대화를 듣고, 여자의 마지막 말에 담긴 의도로 가장 적절한 것을 고르시오.

① 거절   ② 동의   ③ 제안
④ 요청   ⑤ 충고

10 대화를 듣고, 여자가 지불해야 할 금액을 고르시오.

① $25   ② $30   ③ $40
④ $50   ⑤ $70

11 대화를 듣고, 두 사람이 대화하고 있는 장소로 가장 적절한 곳을 고르시오.

① airport   ② hotel
③ post office   ④ police station
⑤ department store

12 다음을 듣고, Stevie Wonder에 관해 언급되지 <u>않은</u> 것을 고르시오.

① 생년월일
② 수상 횟수
③ 앨범 판매량
④ 노래 제목
⑤ 연주하는 악기

13 다음 표를 보면서 대화를 듣고, 내용과 일치하지 <u>않는</u> 것을 고르시오.

Live Music at Riverside Restaurant

	Performers	Day
①	Jazz Trio	Tuesday
②	Classical Breeze	Wednesday
③	Rock Stars	Monday
④	Ballad Kings	Thursday
⑤	Dance Fever	Friday

14 다음을 듣고, 무엇에 관한 설명인지 고르시오.

① 호루라기
② 전화번호부
③ 운전면허증
④ 애완동물 집
⑤ 애완동물용 목걸이

15 대화를 듣고, 여자가 겨울 방학에 할 일로 가장 적절한 것을 고르시오.

① 목도리 뜨기
② 스웨터 뜨기
③ 스키 배우기
④ 뜨개질 배우기
⑤ 조부모님 방문하기

16 대화를 듣고, 두 사람이 만나기로 한 시각을 고르시오.

① 4:00
② 4:30
③ 5:00
④ 5:30
⑤ 6:00

17 다음 상황 설명을 듣고, Jessica가 여자에게 할 말로 가장 적절한 것을 고르시오.

Jessica: _____

① Where do I go to check in my bags?
② Hello, ma'am. May I help you find your seat?
③ Excuse me. Could I book an aisle seat please?
④ The flight will take off shortly. Please stay in your seats.
⑤ Excuse me, ma'am. Would you please change seats with me?

18 대화를 듣고, 두 사람이 할 일로 가장 적절한 것을 고르시오.

① 사막에 가기
② 디저트 먹기
③ 길 물어보기
④ 주유소에 가기
⑤ 자동차 고치기

19 대화를 듣고, 상황을 가장 잘 표현한 속담을 고르시오.

① Better late than never.
② Bad news travels quickly.
③ Out of sight, out of mind.
④ Kill two birds with one stone.
⑤ Hope for the best, but prepare for the worst.

20 대화를 듣고, 여자의 마지막 말에 대한 남자의 응답으로 가장 적절한 것을 고르시오.

Man: _____

① Yes. I paid for the running shoes already.
② How much are the white running shoes?
③ The phone number is on the back of the card.
④ What is the name of the online shopping mall?
⑤ No. I'm going to check the website to see when they open.

다시 듣고, 빈칸에 알맞은 단어를 써 보세요.

◀)) MP3 실전 12-1

01 그림 정보 파악

대화를 듣고, 여자가 입을 의상을 고르시오.

① ② ③
④ ⑤

M : Welcome to Wicked Costumes! May I help you?

W : Yes. I need to buy a □ _____ to wear to my friend's □ _____.

M : That sounds like fun! Would you be □ _____ □ _____ this □ _____ costume? Or this □ _____ costume?

W : They are great, but I would □ _____ the bumble □ _____ or □ _____ costumes.

M : Okay. There is only one more princess costume left, and it's □ _____ □ _____ for □ _____ dollars.

W : Really? That's a good price for a costume. I'll take it.

M : Alright. Would you like to buy a □ _____ for an □ _____ □ _____ dollars?

W : Hmm… Yes, please.

02 목적 파악

대화를 듣고, 남자가 여자에게 전화한 목적으로 가장 적절한 것을 고르시오.

① 과제에 대해 물어보려고
② 태양계에 대해 토론하려고
③ 태양계에 대한 책을 빌리려고
④ 보고서 제출 기한을 물어보려고
⑤ 보고서를 함께 작성하자고 말하려고

M : Hello, Megan? It's me, George.

W : Hey, George! □ _____ □ _____?

M : I'm calling to ask about our □ _____ □ _____.

W : Sure. What do you need to know?

M : Well, I □ _____ □ _____ in class when the teacher told us □ _____ to □ _____ in the report. Could you tell me what she said?

W : Yeah, no problem. We have to write □ _____ the □ _____ in the □ _____ □ _____.

M : I see. Thanks a lot. Have you □ _____ your report?

W : No, I'm actually □ _____ □ _____ □ _____ □ _____ writing it right now.

✎ 어휘복습 잘 안 들리거나 몰라서 체크한 어휘를 써 놓고 복습해 보세요.

□ _____   □ _____   □ _____   □ _____
□ _____   □ _____   □ _____   □ _____
□ _____   □ _____   □ _____   □ _____

03 그림 상황에 적절한 대화 찾기

다음 그림의 상황에 가장 적절한 대화를 고르시오.

① ② ③ ④ ⑤

① M : Would you like to □ _____ to the aquarium □ _____ me?

W : □ _____, when is a good time for you?

② M : Hey, look! Do you see those □ _____ in the □ _____?

W : Oh, wow! I've □ _____ seen dolphins this close □ _____!

③ M : □ _____ □ _____ is it to the dolphin show?

W : It's □ _____ □ _____. If you keep walking straight, you'll see it □ _____ your □ _____.

④ M : I'm □ _____ to the □ _____ to see dolphins tomorrow.

W : Sounds like fun! □ _____ □ _____ I could go, too.

⑤ M : Be careful not to □ _____ □ _____ the □ _____.

W : □ _____ □ _____ I'm a good swimmer.

04 그림 정보 파악

대화를 듣고, 경찰이 찾고 있는 여자를 고르시오.

① ② ③
④ ⑤

M : Good afternoon, ma'am. I am □ _____ Samuels. Could I □ _____ □ _____ you for a moment?

W : Yes, sir. Is there a □ _____?

M : Well, I'm trying to □ _____ a □ _____ who lives around here. She □ _____ a □ _____ and □ _____ □ _____.

W : Oh, that's □ _____! What can I do to help?

M : I'm going to □ _____ her to you. Can you tell me if you've seen her in this café?

W : Alright, I'll do my best to help you. □ _____ does she □ _____ □ _____?

M : She has □ _____, □ _____ □ _____ and wears □ _____. She was last seen wearing a □ _____ □ _____.

W : Hmm… I'm sorry. I haven't seen anyone like that.

✎ **어휘복습** 잘 안 들리거나 몰라서 체크한 어휘를 써 놓고 복습해 보세요.

□ _____   □ _____   □ _____   □ _____
□ _____   □ _____   □ _____   □ _____
□ _____   □ _____   □ _____   □ _____

05 직업 추론

대화를 듣고, 남자의 직업으로 가장 적절한 것을 고르시오.

① 육상선수　　② 복싱선수
③ 헬스 트레이너　④ 보컬 트레이너
⑤ 체육 교사

M : You're □ _____ □ _____, Helen! You have five more □ _____ left.
W : Don't you think I've □ _____ □ _____? I'm so □ _____ already.
M : Come on, you can do it! After push-ups you have to □ _____ some □ _____, too.
W : Are you kidding me? This is the □ _____ day of □ _____ □ _____.
M : I know, but this is the □ _____ □ _____ you're going to □ _____ □ _____.
W : Alright, fine. What do you have planned for me after sit-ups?
M : I'm going to teach you how to use this □ _____ □ _____.

06 심정 추론

대화를 듣고, 남자의 심정으로 가장 적절한 것을 고르시오.

① hopeless　　② nervous
③ satisfied　　④ disappointed
⑤ angry

M : I've only gotten □ _____ □ _____ of □ _____ during the past two days.
W : What? □ _____ □ _____. Why couldn't you sleep?
M : I have to □ _____ this history □ _____ □ _____ the □ _____ of this □ _____. But it's □ _____ me □ _____.
W : Hmm… How much do you have left to do?
M : I still have to □ _____ a □ _____, □ _____ some □ _____, and prepare for a □ _____.
W : Oh, □ _____ □ _____! That sounds like a lot of work. □ _____ □ _____ is that going to □ _____?
M : I □ _____ □ _____ □ _____, but I feel like I'm □ _____ going to □ _____ this □ _____.

✎ **어휘복습** 잘 안 들리거나 몰라서 체크한 어휘를 써 놓고 복습해 보세요.

□ _____　□ _____　□ _____　□ _____
□ _____　□ _____　□ _____　□ _____
□ _____　□ _____　□ _____　□ _____

다음을 듣고, 두 사람의 대화가 <u>어색한</u> 것을 고르시오.

①   ②   ③   ④   ⑤

① M : □ _____ □ _____ people are coming over for dinner?
    W : I'm expecting □ _____ □ _____ guests.
② M : I really like your new computer. □ _____ did you
        □ _____ it?
    W : I bought it at the □ _____ □ _____ □ _____.
③ M : Our □ _____ is not □ _____ her □ _____ right now.
    W : Okay, do you know □ _____ she'll be □ _____?
④ M : I can't believe it's □ _____ □ _____!
    W : I know! Let's go □ _____ a □ _____.
⑤ M : I'm at the □ _____ store. Do you need anything?
    W : Yes, could you buy some ice cream?

08 부탁 파악

대화를 듣고, 여자가 남자에게 부탁한 일로 가장 적절한 것을 고르시오.

① 리모컨 고치기
② 텔레비전 옮기기
③ 새 건전지 사기
④ 식료품점에 가기
⑤ 새 텔레비전 사기

W : Honey, the □ _____ □ _____ is □ _____. The buttons aren't working.
M : Are you sure? It was □ _____ a □ _____ □ _____. Let me see it.
W : Here you go.
M : Hmm… I think the □ _____ □ _____ □ _____. We need to □ _____ them.
W : Well, I don't think we have any □ _____ ones at home.
M : You're right. □ _____ are □ _____ in the □ _____. What should we do?
W : Why don't you □ _____ to the □ _____ and □ _____ □ _____?
M : Okay, I'll go right now.

✎ **어휘복습** 잘 안 들리거나 몰라서 체크한 어휘를 써 놓고 복습해 보세요.

□ _____   □ _____   □ _____   □ _____

□ _____   □ _____   □ _____   □ _____

□ _____   □ _____   □ _____   □ _____

09 의도 파악

대화를 듣고, 여자의 마지막 말에 담긴 의도로 가장 적절한 것을 고르시오.

① 거절 ② 동의 ③ 제안
④ 요청 ⑤ 충고

W : Hello, □ _____ □ _____ Amanda.
M : Hey, Amanda! It's me, Josh.
W : Hi, Josh! How's it going?
M : Everything is fine with me, thanks for asking! □ _____ □ _____ just □ _____ □ _____ you could pick me up from the train station.
W : Of course. □ _____ does your □ _____ □ _____?
M : I get there at □ _____ P.M. this □ _____. Are you busy that day?
W : Saturday? □ _____ □ _____ I can't □ _____ you □ _____ that day because I have □ _____ □ _____ with my parents.
M : Oh, □ _____ □ _____. Then you can't meet me at the train station, right?
W : Yeah, I'm so sorry. □ _____ □ _____ we meet on Sunday or Monday?

10 숫자 정보 파악

대화를 듣고, 여자가 지불해야 할 금액을 고르시오.

① $25 ② $30 ③ $40
④ $50 ⑤ $70

M : Excuse me, ma'am. Can I help you find something?
W : Yeah, that would be great. I'm looking for a □ _____ for my mother.
M : Okay. □ _____ □ _____ we have the □ _____ candles. And on this shelf we have some □ _____-scented candles.
W : □ _____ □ _____ are the orange and rose candles?
M : The fruit-scented candles are □ _____ dollars each, and the flower-scented candles are □ _____ dollars each.
W : I see. I'll take one □ _____-scented candle and one □ _____-scented candle, please. Also, I would like to □ _____ this □ _____-dollar □ _____ on my purchase.
M : Alright. Then you just have to □ _____ □ _____ the □ _____ □ _____ dollars. Do you need anything else today?
W : Yes. I would like to get the candles □ _____.
M : I can do that, but it will □ _____ you an □ _____ □ _____ dollars.
W : That's fine. Thank you so much.

✎ **어휘복습** 잘 안 들리거나 몰라서 체크한 어휘를 써 놓고 복습해 보세요.

□ _____ □ _____ □ _____ □ _____
□ _____ □ _____ □ _____ □ _____
□ _____ □ _____ □ _____ □ _____

11 장소 추론

대화를 듣고, 두 사람이 대화하고 있는 장소로 가장 적절한 곳을 고르시오.

① airport
② hotel
③ post office
④ police station
⑤ department store

W : Sir, can I help you with something?

M : Yes, please. □ _____ are the □ _____? I need to □ _____ a □ _____ to my friend in Australia.

W : The boxes are on the third □ _____ □ _____ □ _____.

M : Oh, thank you. Also, where can I find the □ _____ □ _____?

W : The tape is on the table □ _____ □ _____ □ _____. Please □ _____ □ _____ you write your □ _____ and the address of the □ _____ clearly on top of the box.

M : Alright. What do I do after that?

W : You have to □ _____ □ _____ □ _____ and pay the □ _____ □ _____.

M : Okay. I □ _____ your help!

12 미언급 파악

다음을 듣고, Stevie Wonder에 관해 언급되지 <u>않은</u> 것을 고르시오.

① 생년월일   ② 수상 횟수
③ 앨범 판매량   ④ 노래 제목
⑤ 연주하는 악기

M : Have you □ _____ □ _____ Stevie Wonder? He is probably one of the most □ _____ □ _____ □ _____. Some people say that he is a □ _____. He was □ _____ □ _____ May thirteenth, nineteen fifty, and became blind when he was young. □ _____ □ _____ he is blind, his □ _____ for □ _____ is very □ _____. He □ _____ over twenty-five □ _____ and □ _____ over one hundred million □ _____. He has many □ _____ □ _____, such as "Isn't She Lovely," "I Just Called to Say I Love You," and "You Are the Sunshine of My Life."

✎ **어휘복습** 잘 안 들리거나 몰라서 체크한 어휘를 써 놓고 복습해 보세요.

□ _____   □ _____   □ _____   □ _____
□ _____   □ _____   □ _____   □ _____
□ _____   □ _____   □ _____   □ _____

13 도표·실용문 파악

다음 표를 보면서 대화를 듣고, 내용과 일치하지 <u>않는</u> 것을 고르시오.

Live Music at Riverside Restaurant

	Performers	Day
①	Jazz Trio	Tuesday
②	Classical Breeze	Wednesday
③	Rock Stars	Monday
④	Ballad Kings	Thursday
⑤	Dance Fever	Friday

M : Nora, Riverside Restaurant has □ _____ □ _____ □ _____ during dinner time this week.

W : Yeah, I know. Jazz Trio will be □ _____ on □ _____ □ _____. I would like to see them. Do you like □ _____ □ _____?

M : No, not really. I enjoy □ _____ and □ _____ music more, so I would rather go on □ _____ to see Classical Breeze or on □ _____ to see the Rock Stars.

W : Hmm… Listening to Classical Breeze □ _____ □ _____ to □ _____ and the Rock Stars are too □ _____ for me. □ _____ do you □ _____ of the Ballad Kings?

M : I like their music, but I'm going on a □ _____ □ _____ on □ _____.

W : I guess we can't go this week, then. Both the Ballad Kings and Dance Fever are performing on Thursday.

14 화제 추론

다음을 듣고, 무엇에 관한 설명인지 고르시오.

① 호루라기
② 전화번호부
③ 운전면허증
④ 애완동물 집
⑤ 애완동물용 목걸이

W : This item can be □ _____ on the □ _____ of most house □ _____. It has the pet's □ _____ on it. Sometimes it has the owner's □ _____ □ _____ and □ _____ on it, too. Even if you lose your pet, someone will be able to □ _____ you □ _____ □ _____ at the □ _____ on this. You can □ _____ a □ _____ to this item when you □ _____ your pet □ _____ a □ _____.

✎ **어휘복습** 잘 안 들리거나 몰라서 체크한 어휘를 써 놓고 복습해 보세요.

□ _____   □ _____   □ _____   □ _____

□ _____   □ _____   □ _____   □ _____

□ _____   □ _____   □ _____   □ _____

15 할 일 파악

대화를 듣고, 여자가 겨울 방학에 할 일로 가장 적절한 것을 고르시오.

① 목도리 뜨기
② 스웨터 뜨기
③ 스키 배우기
④ 뜨개질 배우기
⑤ 조부모님 방문하기

M : Hey, Jenna. Are you doing anything special □ _____ □ _____?

W : Yes, I am. I'm going to □ _____ a □ _____ since the □ _____ is going to be □ _____.

M : That's so cool! I didn't know you knew □ _____ □ _____ knit.

W : Yeah, I've been knitting □ _____ about □ _____ □ _____ now. What are you going to do during the winter?

M : I'm going to learn □ _____ □ _____ □ _____ and □ _____ my grandparents' house. I haven't seen them □ _____ □ _____ □ _____.

W : It sounds like you'll □ _____ a □ _____ □ _____. I'll see you after □ _____.

M : Okay, I hope you enjoy making your scarf.

W : Thank you!

16 숫자 정보 파악

대화를 듣고, 두 사람이 만나기로 한 시각을 고르시오.

① 4:00   ② 4:30   ③ 5:00
④ 5:30   ⑤ 6:00

M : What are you doing tomorrow □ _____ □ _____?

W : I have to go to my □ _____ □ _____ at □ _____.

M : □ _____ □ _____ does your lesson □ _____? I was hoping to go eat ice cream with you.

W : It's normally □ _____ by □ _____, but it □ _____ □ _____ □ _____. What time did you want to meet?

M : I was thinking around □ _____ □ _____. Is that okay with you?

W : Hmm… Can we meet □ _____ □ _____ □ _____? I don't want you to wait for me if my lesson ends □ _____ □ _____ □ _____.

M : Okay, that's fine. I'll see you then.

✎ **어휘복습** 잘 안 들리거나 몰라서 체크한 어휘를 써 놓고 복습해 보세요.

□ _____   □ _____   □ _____   □ _____

□ _____   □ _____   □ _____   □ _____

□ _____   □ _____   □ _____   □ _____

17 상황에 적절한 말 찾기

다음 상황 설명을 듣고, Jessica가 여자에게 할 말로 가장 적절한 것을 고르시오.

Jessica: _____

① Where do I go to check in my bags?
② Hello, ma'am. May I help you find your seat?
③ Excuse me. Could I book an aisle seat please?
④ The flight will take off shortly. Please stay in your seats.
⑤ Excuse me, ma'am. Would you please change seats with me?

W : Jessica is going to □ _____ her best □ _____ in Taiwan. She □ _____ □ _____ her bags and passes the □ _____ □ _____. After a while, she □ _____ □ _____ the □ _____ and heads to her seat. When she gets there, she realizes that she □ _____ a □ _____ □ _____ instead of an □ _____ seat □ _____ □ _____. When she □ _____ □ _____ her, she sees a woman sitting in an aisle seat. Jessica wants to ask her if they can □ _____ seats. In this situation, what would Jessica most likely say to the woman?

Jessica: _____

18 할 일 파악

대화를 듣고, 두 사람이 할 일로 가장 적절한 것을 고르시오.

① 사막에 가기
② 디저트 먹기
③ 길 물어보기
④ 주유소에 가기
⑤ 자동차 고치기

M : Honey, we have one □ _____ □ _____ to go until we □ _____ □ _____ Las Vegas.

W : One hundred miles? That seems like a □ _____ □ _____ □ _____ □ _____.

M : We'll get there □ _____ □ _____ you □ _____. Oh, look. We're almost □ _____. □ _____ □ _____.

W : You're right. □ _____ □ _____ if there's a □ _____ □ _____ around here.

M : Yeah, the roads □ _____ so □ _____.

W : That □ _____ □ _____ the next gas station is ten miles away. Do we have □ _____ gas to get there?

M : Yes, I'm □ _____ □ _____ we do.

W : Okay, let's □ _____ □ _____ and get there.

✎ **어휘복습** 잘 안 들리거나 몰라서 체크한 어휘를 써 놓고 복습해 보세요.

□ _____   □ _____   □ _____   □ _____
□ _____   □ _____   □ _____   □ _____
□ _____   □ _____   □ _____   □ _____

대화를 듣고, 상황을 가장 잘 표현한 속담을 고르시오.

① Better late than never.
② Bad news travels quickly.
③ Out of sight, out of mind.
④ Kill two birds with one stone.
⑤ Hope for the best, but prepare for the worst.

W : Did you see the □ _____ □ _____ for □ _____?
There's a chance of □ _____.
M : Yeah, I saw it this morning. But look at □ _____ □ _____ it is □ _____! I don't think it's going to rain.
W : But □ _____ □ _____ it does? That means our □ _____ to go camping will be □ _____.
M : If you're that □ _____, we can think of □ _____ □ _____ to do, □ _____ □ _____ □ _____.
W : Okay. If there are thunderstorms, we should go □ _____ a □ _____.
M : Alright, we can do that. I really hope the weather stays nice.
W : Me too.

대화를 듣고, 여자의 마지막 말에 대한 남자의 응답으로 가장 적절한 것을 고르시오.

Man: _____

① Yes. I paid for the running shoes already.
② How much are the white running shoes?
③ The phone number is on the back of the card.
④ What is the name of the online shopping mall?
⑤ No. I'm going to check the website to see when they open.

M : I □ _____ some running □ _____ from an online □ _____ □ _____ two weeks ago, but I still haven't gotten them.
W : Hmm… Did you □ _____ the □ _____ □ _____ Center?
M : Yeah. I called them, but □ _____ □ _____ □ _____.
W : Maybe something □ _____ □ _____ with your □ _____.
M : I have □ _____ □ _____. I'll try calling them again tomorrow morning.
W : Okay. Do you know their □ _____ □ _____?
M : _____

✏️ **어휘복습** 잘 안 들리거나 몰라서 체크한 어휘를 써 놓고 복습해 보세요.

□ _____ □ _____ □ _____ □ _____
□ _____ □ _____ □ _____ □ _____
□ _____ □ _____ □ _____ □ _____

01 대화를 듣고, 남자가 좋아하는 무당벌레를 고르시오.

02 대화를 듣고, 여자가 남자에게 전화한 목적으로 가장 적절한 것을 고르시오.

① 조사를 부탁하려고
② 도서 대출을 부탁하려고
③ 보고서 작성을 부탁하려고
④ 발표 원고 작성을 부탁하려고
⑤ 지구온난화에 대해 토론하려고

03 다음 그림의 상황에 가장 적절한 대화를 고르시오.

① ② ③ ④ ⑤

04 대화를 듣고, 여자가 구매할 개를 고르시오.

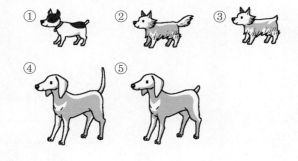

05 대화를 듣고, 남자의 직업으로 가장 적절한 것을 고르시오.

① news reporter   ② firefighter
③ lawyer   ④ doctor
⑤ taxi driver

06 대화를 듣고, 여자의 심정의 변화로 가장 적절한 것을 고르시오.

① angry – relieved
② happy – embarrassed
③ excited – disappointed
④ nervous – satisfied
⑤ upset – proud

07 다음을 듣고, 두 사람의 대화가 <u>어색한</u> 것을 고르시오.

① ② ③ ④ ⑤

08 대화를 듣고, 여자가 남자에게 부탁한 일로 가장 적절한 것을 고르시오.

① 공원 가기   ② 야채 사기
③ 집 청소하기   ④ 식물에 물 주기
⑤ 나무와 꽃 사기

09 대화를 듣고, 남자의 마지막 말에 담긴 의도로 가장 적절한 것을 고르시오.

① 제안   ② 요청   ③ 거절
④ 동의   ⑤ 감사

10 대화를 듣고, 소풍에 필요한 샌드위치의 총 개수를 고르시오.

① 4   ② 5   ③ 6   ④ 10   ⑤ 20

11 대화를 듣고, 두 사람이 대화하고 있는 장소로 가장 적절한 곳을 고르시오.

① grocery store   ② bakery
③ ice cream shop   ④ cookie store
⑤ restaurant

12 다음을 듣고, 현장 학습에 관해 언급되지 <u>않은</u> 것을 고르시오.

① 박물관 위치　　　② 박물관 입장료
③ 이용할 교통 수단　④ 출발 장소
⑤ 출발 시간

13 다음 표를 보면서 대화를 듣고, 내용과 일치하지 <u>않는</u> 것을 고르시오.

Bobby's Schedule for the Week

	Day	To Do
①	Mon.	Family Trip
②	Tue.	Family Trip
③	Wed.	Doctor's Appointment
④	Thur.	Piano Lesson
⑤	Fri.	Piano Lesson

14 다음을 듣고, 무엇에 관한 설명인지 고르시오.

① 유람선　　② 비행기
③ 헬리콥터　④ 요트
⑤ 화물차

15 대화를 듣고, 여자가 대화 직후에 할 일로 가장 적절한 것을 고르시오.

① 병원에 가기　　② 학교에 가기
③ 친구 초대하기　④ 수업 내용 물어보기
⑤ 선생님에게 전화하기

16 대화를 듣고, 두 사람이 만나기로 한 요일과 시각을 고르시오.

① 화요일 오후 1시 30분
② 화요일 오후 2시
③ 목요일 오후 12시
④ 목요일 오후 1시 30분
⑤ 목요일 오후 2시

17 다음 상황 설명을 듣고, 아빠가 Min에게 할 말로 가장 적절한 것을 고르시오.

Father: _____

① Keep up the good work!
② I found a $5 bill on the street.
③ How much do you get for allowance every month?
④ There is a $20 admission fee to go to the amusement park.
⑤ Don't waste your money. You need to learn how to save it.

18 대화를 듣고, 두 사람이 대화 직후에 할 일로 가장 적절한 것을 고르시오.

① 조깅하기　　② 저녁 먹기
③ 차 마시기　　④ 친구 만나기
⑤ 식료품점 가기

19 대화를 듣고, 상황을 가장 잘 표현한 속담을 고르시오.

① Look before you leap.
② There's no place like home.
③ You can't always get what you want.
④ A picture is worth a thousand words.
⑤ A journey of a thousand miles begins with one step.

20 대화를 듣고, 남자의 마지막 말에 대한 여자의 응답으로 가장 적절한 것을 고르시오.

Woman: _____

① Sorry, but I can't go with you.
② The TV show starts at 9:00 P.M.
③ The movie theater is walking distance from here.
④ It starts at 7:00 P.M. I'll see you in front of the theater.
⑤ I don't think there will be tickets left. It's a popular movie.

01 그림 정보 파악

대화를 듣고, 남자가 좋아하는 무당벌레를 고르시오.

① ② ③ ④ ⑤

M : Mom, □ _____ □ _____ all these ladybugs! There are five of them on this □ _____.

W : Wow, that's so cool! They all have a □ _____ □ _____ of □ _____ on them.

M : Yeah, □ _____ □ _____ this one. This one doesn't have any spots on it. I can □ _____ its □ _____, though.

W : You're right. I've □ _____ □ _____ a ladybug without spots □ _____. Hey, there are ladybugs with two spots and four spots □ _____ □ _____.

M : Hmm… I can't see their wings. I think they're □ _____. I □ _____ this one with □ _____ spots □ _____ □ _____. I can see its wings, too!

W : Well, I think I like this one with three spots the best.

M : You can see the wings on this one, too. But it's not □ _____ □ _____ the one with five spots.

02 목적 파악

대화를 듣고, 여자가 남자에게 전화한 목적으로 가장 적절한 것을 고르시오.

① 조사를 부탁하려고
② 도서 대출을 부탁하려고
③ 보고서 작성을 부탁하려고
④ 발표 원고 작성을 부탁하려고
⑤ 지구온난화에 대해 토론하려고

M : Hello, this is Bob.

W : Bob! It's me, Nora.

M : Oh, hey! What's up? I heard you've been really □ _____ □ _____.

W : Yeah, I've been □ _____ a lot of □ _____ □ _____ for my □ _____. I'm actually calling to ask if you could help me with it.

M : Sure, what do you need me to do?

W : Well, my presentation is about □ _____ □ _____, but I'm □ _____ □ _____ finding □ _____ on it.

M : So, do you want me to □ _____ some □ _____ on global warming?

W : Yes, please. I really □ _____ your help!

M : It's not a problem. I'll let you know □ _____ I □ _____ on the □ _____.

✏️ **어휘복습** 잘 안 들리거나 몰라서 체크한 어휘를 써 놓고 복습해 보세요.

□ _____ □ _____ □ _____ □ _____

□ _____ □ _____ □ _____ □ _____

□ _____ □ _____ □ _____ □ _____

03 그림 상황에 적절한 대화 찾기

다음 그림의 상황에 가장 적절한 대화를 고르시오.

① ② ③ ④ ⑤

① W : □ _____ can I find the lemons?

　 M : They are □ _____ □ _____ in the fruit section.

② W : □ _____ do I □ _____ □ _____ the marketplace?

　 M : □ _____ □ _____ for two blocks and then turn left.

③ W : What □ _____ do you □ _____ for the summer?

　 M : Hmm… I think □ _____ are □ _____ fit for hot weather.

④ W : □ _____ you □ _____ some watermelon?

　 M : No thanks. I □ _____ strawberries.

⑤ W : Is there □ _____ to □ _____ in the □ _____?

　 M : I'm not sure. There should be a watermelon in there □ _____.

04 그림 정보 파악

대화를 듣고, 여자가 구매할 개를 고르시오.

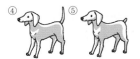

M : Welcome to Stevie's □ _____ □ _____. What can I help you with today?

W : Hello. I'm □ _____ □ _____ buying a □ _____.
　 Can you help me choose one?

M : Sure, no problem. □ _____ □ _____ of dog are you □ _____ □ _____?

W : Well, I would □ _____ a □ _____ dog with □ _____ □ _____.

M : Okay. Here is one that you might like. What do you think?

W : It's alright, but its □ _____ is □ _____ □ _____.
　 I □ _____ a dog with a □ _____ tail.

M : I'm sorry, but we don't have any small, long furred dogs with short tails.

W : Oh, then I'll just take the one with a long tail. Thank you.

✎ **어휘복습** 잘 안 들리거나 몰라서 체크한 어휘를 써 놓고 복습해 보세요.

□ _____　　□ _____　　□ _____　　□ _____

□ _____　　□ _____　　□ _____　　□ _____

□ _____　　□ _____　　□ _____　　□ _____

05 직업 추론

대화를 듣고, 남자의 직업으로 가장 적절한 것을 고르시오.

① news reporter   ② firefighter
③ lawyer   ④ doctor
⑤ taxi driver

M : Hello, this is □ _____ four five one on Linden Street. What is your □ _____?

W : I □ _____ □ _____ coming □ _____ my neighbor's house. I think it's □ _____ □ _____!

M : Ma'am, please stay calm. What is your neighbor's □ _____?

W : Okay, it is thirty-nine ten Heathen Lane. How long will it take you to get here?

M : We will get there □ _____ □ _____ □ _____ we can.

W : Alright, is there anything I can do □ _____ you get here?

M : No, ma'am, it is □ _____. Please □ _____ □ _____ □ _____ the fire.

W : Yes, sir.

06 심정 추론

대화를 듣고, 여자의 심정의 변화로 가장 적절한 것을 고르시오.

① angry – relieved
② happy – embarrassed
③ excited – disappointed
④ nervous – satisfied
⑤ upset – proud

M : Hey, Ashley! What are you up to?

W : I'm □ _____ □ _____ to go to the □ _____ with my friends. I've been □ _____ □ _____ □ _____ it for days!

M : Hmm… It's kind of □ _____ outside. Look at the trees swaying! I □ _____ that there's a □ _____ □ _____ soon.

W : Are you □ _____? I can't believe it! The □ _____ □ _____ said that the storm wouldn't be coming □ _____ □ _____.

M : Look! It's □ _____ to □ _____ right now. I don't think you can go to the beach.

W : Oh, my goodness. This is □ _____! I thought we were going to □ _____ so much □ _____ today!

M : I'm sorry to hear that. □ _____ □ _____! You can always go □ _____ □ _____ □ _____.

W : You're right, but I'm just upset that things □ _____ □ _____ □ _____ □ _____.

✎ **어휘복습** 잘 안 들리거나 몰라서 체크한 어휘를 써 놓고 복습해 보세요.

□ _____   □ _____   □ _____   □ _____

□ _____   □ _____   □ _____   □ _____

□ _____   □ _____   □ _____   □ _____

다음을 듣고, 두 사람의 대화가 어색한 것을 고르시오.

① ② ③ ④ ⑤

① M : Do you know □ _____ the coffee mugs are?

　 W : Yeah, they are in the □ _____ □ _____.

② M : What are the bank's □ _____ □ _____?

　 W : You can □ _____ a □ _____ □ _____ today.

③ M : I think I'll be □ _____ □ _____ □ _____. I'm sorry.

　 W : It's okay. □ _____ □ _____ will it take you to get here?

④ M : □ _____ are you doing this □ _____?

　 W : I'm □ _____ □ _____ with my family.

⑤ M : Can you help me write my □ _____ □ _____?

　 W : □ _____. I'll be over to help you □ _____ □ _____ minutes.

대화를 듣고, 여자가 남자에게 부탁한 일로 가장 적절한 것을 고르시오.

① 공원 가기　　② 야채 사기
③ 집 청소하기　④ 식물에 물 주기
⑤ 나무와 꽃 사기

W : Honey, I think we should □ _____ some □ _____ in the □ _____.

M : Yeah, I was thinking the same thing. Our backyard □ _____ so □ _____.

W : What □ _____ of trees should we plant? I think flowers would look pretty, too.

M : I agree. Should we □ _____ □ _____ some now? There's a □ _____ □ _____ on Sherry Road.

W : Hmm… I would love to. But I'm busy cleaning the house right now. Can you go and □ _____ some □ _____ □ _____?

M : Sure, no problem.

✎ **어휘복습** 잘 안 들리거나 몰라서 체크한 어휘를 써 놓고 복습해 보세요.

□ _____　　□ _____　　□ _____　　□ _____

□ _____　　□ _____　　□ _____　　□ _____

□ _____　　　　　　　　　　□ _____

09 의도 파악

대화를 듣고, 남자의 마지막 말에 담긴 의도로 가장 적절한 것을 고르시오.

① 제안 ② 요청 ③ 거절
④ 동의 ⑤ 감사

M : Helen, what is your □ _____ □ _____ so far?
W : Well, I like all of them, but I □ _____ Mr. Clark's □ _____ class □ _____ □ _____! How about you?
M : Mr. Clark's class is my favorite, too! He is such a fun teacher.
W : You're right. I always □ _____ a □ _____ □ _____ in his class. Oh, did you hear? He promised to buy us pizza after class tomorrow!
M : Really? That's □ _____! It's □ _____ □ _____ □ _____ everyone likes him.
W : Yeah, it is □ _____ □ _____ class □ _____!
M : You can say that again.

10 숫자 정보 파악

대화를 듣고, 소풍에 필요한 샌드위치의 총 개수를 고르시오.

① 4 ② 5 ③ 6 ④ 10 ⑤ 20

M : Hey, Julia. Are you almost done □ _____ the □ _____?
W : No, □ _____ □ _____. I'm not sure if I made enough. Do you know □ _____ □ _____ people are □ _____ to the picnic?
M : I think about □ _____ people will be there. How many have you made □ _____ □ _____?
W : Well, I've made □ _____ □ _____ sandwiches, and five □ _____ sandwiches.
M : Oh, you're □ _____ □ _____! Should I help you make □ _____ □ _____?
W : Yes, please. □ _____ □ _____ of sandwich should we make?
M : Hmm… How about □ _____ □ _____ sandwiches and six □ _____ sandwiches?
W : That sounds great.

✎ **어휘복습** 잘 안 들리거나 몰라서 체크한 어휘를 써 놓고 복습해 보세요.

□ _____   □ _____   □ _____   □ _____
□ _____   □ _____   □ _____   □ _____
□ _____   □ _____   □ _____   □ _____

11 장소 추론

대화를 듣고, 두 사람이 대화하고 있는 장소로 가장 적절한 곳을 고르시오.

① grocery store　② bakery
③ ice cream shop　④ cookie store
⑤ restaurant

M : Excuse me, ma'am.

W : Hello, may I help you with something?

M : Yes. □ _____ □ _____ of these has □ _____ inside it?

W : □ _____ of the □ _____ on this table has cream in it.

M : Oh, okay. They look really fresh! Did they just □ _____
□ _____ □ _____ the □ _____?

W : Yes, they did. We □ _____ new bread □ _____ □ _____
minutes.

M : I see. Could I also get a loaf of □ _____ □ _____ □ _____
and a piece of □ _____?

W : Alright. Would you like the loaf of bread □ _____?

M : That would be great. Thank you so much.

12 미언급 파악

다음을 듣고, 현장 학습에 관해 언급되지 <u>않</u>은 것을 고르시오.

① 박물관 위치
② 박물관 입장료
③ 이용할 교통 수단
④ 출발 장소
⑤ 출발 시간

W : Good morning, students. I would like to □ _____ an
□ _____ about the □ _____ □ _____ we will be going on
□ _____ □ _____. As you all know, we will be going to the
Lawrence National Art Museum on □ _____ □ _____. Before
we go, you must □ _____ □ _____ a □ _____ and ask your
parents to □ _____ it. You must □ _____ □ _____ this form
□ _____ February □ _____. Also, make sure to □ _____
□ _____ dollars to □ _____ the □ _____. Lastly, please
remember that the □ _____ will □ _____ from school
□ _____ □ _____ A.M., so do not be late.

✎ **어휘복습** 잘 안 들리거나 몰라서 체크한 어휘를 써 놓고 복습해 보세요.

□ _____　□ _____　□ _____　□ _____

□ _____　□ _____　□ _____　□ _____

□ _____　□ _____　□ _____　□ _____

13 도표·실용문 파악

다음 표를 보면서 대화를 듣고, 내용과 일치하지 <u>않는</u> 것을 고르시오.

Bobby's Schedule for the Week

	Day	To Do
①	Mon.	Family Trip
②	Tue.	Family Trip
③	Wed.	Doctor's Appointment
④	Thur.	Piano Lesson
⑤	Fri.	Piano Lesson

W : Good afternoon, Bobby. Can I do something for you?

M : Ms. Jackson, I have to ☐ _____ my ☐ _____ ☐ _____ for another day this week. I'm going on a ☐ _____ ☐ _____ on ☐ _____.

W : Okay, that's fine. ☐ _____ you come on ☐ _____ or ☐ _____?

M : I ☐ _____ ☐ _____ from the trip on Tuesday night, and I have a ☐ _____ ☐ _____ on Wednesday.

W : Hmm… Do you have ☐ _____ ☐ _____ on ☐ _____ and ☐ _____?

M : No, I don't have any plans. I can come on ☐ _____ ☐ _____ those days.

W : Oh, ☐ _____, I have ☐ _____ ☐ _____ coming on Friday. I think we will have to have our lesson on Thursday.

M : Okay, that works for me. When will we start ☐ _____ for the piano ☐ _____?

W : ☐ _____ ☐ _____ ☐ _____, we can begin on Thursday when you come for your lesson.

M : Alright, that sounds great. I'll see you then!

14 화제 추론

다음을 듣고, 무엇에 관한 설명인지 고르시오.

① 유람선　　② 비행기
③ 헬리콥터　　④ 요트
⑤ 화물차

M : This is a ☐ _____ of ☐ _____. Sometimes, ☐ _____ ☐ _____ ride this to get a view of the city, and ☐ _____ ride this to quickly go from one place to another. It can also be used to ☐ _____ the ☐ _____ of a beautiful ☐ _____. ☐ _____ an ☐ _____, you can only fit a few people in this. This can be found in the sky, and it ☐ _____ a ☐ _____ ☐ _____ as it ☐ _____ by. On the ☐ _____ ☐ _____ of some tall buildings and hospitals, there is ☐ _____ ☐ _____ especially for this ☐ _____ ☐ _____.

✎ **어휘복습** 잘 안 들리거나 몰라서 체크한 어휘를 써 놓고 복습해 보세요.

☐ _____　☐ _____　☐ _____　☐ _____

☐ _____　☐ _____　☐ _____　☐ _____

☐ _____　☐ _____　☐ _____　☐ _____

대화를 듣고, 여자가 대화 직후에 할 일로 가
장 적절한 것을 고르시오.

① 병원에 가기
② 학교에 가기
③ 친구 초대하기
④ 수업 내용 물어보기
⑤ 선생님에게 전화하기

M : Karen, you've already □ _____ three days of □ _____.
W : I know, Dad. But I'm still □ _____ □ _____ □ _____.
M : Okay. But I'm starting to □ _____ □ _____ your □ _____.
W : Yeah, I don't know □ _____ □ _____ □ _____. I don't even
    know what we learned in class.
M : Hmm… Why don't you □ _____ your □ _____ and
    □ _____ them what you missed?
W : That's a good idea, Dad. I'll □ _____ □ _____ them now.
M : Alright. I also hope your teacher will let you □ _____
    □ _____ your □ _____ □ _____.
W : Me too. I just want to □ _____ □ _____ soon. Being sick is
    really not helping.

대화를 듣고, 두 사람이 만나기로 한 요일과
시각을 고르시오.

① 화요일 오후 1시 30분
② 화요일 오후 2시
③ 목요일 오후 12시
④ 목요일 오후 1시 30분
⑤ 목요일 오후 2시

M : Kristy, □ _____ should we □ _____ to plan our trip to Busan?
W : I'm □ _____ □ _____ week on □ _____, □ _____, and
    □ _____. How about you?
M : Okay, during the week I □ _____ □ _____ on □ _____,
    Thursdays, and □ _____.
W : Well then, □ _____ □ _____ there's only one day that we can
    meet.
M : Yeah, you're right. □ _____ □ _____ works for you? I'm free
    all day, so it's □ _____ □ _____ □ _____.
W : Hmm… I have lunch plans at twelve P.M., but that will be over
    around one thirty P.M. Should we meet □ _____ □ _____ P.M.?
M : Sure, I'll see you then!

✏ **어휘복습** 잘 안 들리거나 몰라서 체크한 어휘를 써 놓고 복습해 보세요.

□ _____   □ _____   □ _____   □ _____

□ _____   □ _____   □ _____   □ _____

□ _____   □ _____   □ _____   □ _____

17 상황에 적절한 말 찾기

다음 상황 설명을 듣고, 아빠가 Min에게 할 말로 가장 적절한 것을 고르시오.

Father: _____

① Keep up the good work!
② I found a $5 bill on the street.
③ How much do you get for allowance every month?
④ There is a $20 admission fee to go to the amusement park.
⑤ Don't waste your money. You need to learn how to save it.

W : Every month, Min's father gives Min □ _____ dollars □ _____ □ _____. However, Min □ _____ □ _____ of his □ _____ in a week and □ _____ his father □ _____ □ _____. Min's father was □ _____ with Min, but decided to □ _____ him an □ _____ □ _____ dollars. But Min used all of this money in two days. Min's father asked Min □ _____ he was □ _____ all of his money. Min's father □ _____ □ _____ that Min was □ _____ things that he didn't need. Min's father decided that it was time to □ _____ Min □ _____ □ _____. In this situation, what would his father most likely say to Min?

Father: _____

18 할 일 파악

대화를 듣고, 두 사람이 대화 직후에 할 일로 가장 적절한 것을 고르시오.

① 조깅하기 ② 저녁 먹기
③ 차 마시기 ④ 친구 만나기
⑤ 식료품점 가기

W : Harry, is that you?
M : Martha! Wow, □ _____ □ _____ □ _____ □ _____!
  How have you been?
W : I've been wonderful, thanks for asking! You □ _____ □ _____!
M : Thank you! □ _____ □ _____ □ _____ □ _____?
  I thought you moved to the west side of town.
W : I did, but I had □ _____ to □ _____ a □ _____ who lives in this □ _____. I was about to go home when I saw you.
M : I see. Would you like to □ _____ □ _____ to my □ _____ for some □ _____?
W : Yes, that'd be great!
M : Oh, actually, I just remembered I □ _____ □ _____ □ _____ tea bags. Can we □ _____ □ _____ the □ _____ to buy some?
W : Yeah, of course!

✎ **어휘복습** 잘 안 들리거나 몰라서 체크한 어휘를 써 놓고 복습해 보세요.

□ _____ □ _____ □ _____ □ _____

□ _____ □ _____ □ _____ □ _____

□ _____ □ _____ □ _____ □ _____

19 속담 추론

대화를 듣고, 상황을 가장 잘 표현한 속담을 고르시오.

① Look before you leap.
② There's no place like home.
③ You can't always get what you want.
④ A picture is worth a thousand words.
⑤ A journey of a thousand miles begins with one step.

M : Hey, look at this □ _____. What do you think it means?

W : Hmm… I don't know. I wonder □ _____ the □ _____ was □ _____ when he took it.

M : Maybe he was trying to □ _____ his □ _____ through it.

W : Yeah, I think the photographer was trying to express □ _____ or □ _____.

M : I agree, since the man in the photo is □ _____ on the □ _____ □ _____ □ _____.

W : You're right. I guess there are □ _____ □ _____ that □ _____ □ _____ □ _____.

20 알맞은 응답 찾기

대화를 듣고, 남자의 마지막 말에 대한 여자의 응답으로 가장 적절한 것을 고르시오.

Woman: _____

① Sorry, but I can't go with you.
② The TV show starts at 9:00 P.M.
③ The movie theater is walking distance from here.
④ It starts at 7:00 P.M. I'll see you in front of the theater.
⑤ I don't think there will be tickets left. It's a popular movie.

M : □ _____ □ _____ of □ _____ do you enjoy watching?

W : I normally watch □ _____ or □ _____ movies. How about you?

M : I like □ _____ movies and □ _____ movies.

W : I see. Have you heard of the new action movie called *Hawk Fighter*?

M : Yeah! All my friends □ _____ it. It must be a good movie.

W : Well, I actually have □ _____ to go see it □ _____ at Regal Movies. Do you want to □ _____ □ _____ □ _____?

M : Of course I do! But do you know □ _____ □ _____ away Regal Movies is? □ _____ □ _____ how long it'll take to get there.

W : _____

✎ **어휘복습** 잘 안 들리거나 몰라서 체크한 어휘를 써 놓고 복습해 보세요.

□ _____ □ _____ □ _____ □ _____
□ _____ □ _____ □ _____ □ _____
□ _____ □ _____ □ _____ □ _____

01 대화를 듣고, 두 사람이 사용할 열쇠를 고르시오.

02 대화를 듣고, 남자가 여자에게 전화한 목적으로 가장 적절한 것을 고르시오.

① 책 제목을 알려주려고
② 연체료를 내라고 말하려고
③ 책을 빌려달라고 부탁하려고
④ 독후감 쓰는 데 도움을 요청하려고
⑤ 책이 도서관에 들어온 것을 알려주려고

03 다음 그림의 상황에 가장 적절한 대화를 고르시오.

① ② ③ ④ ⑤

04 대화를 듣고, 두 사람이 말하고 있는 그림을 고르시오.

05 대화를 듣고, 여자의 직업으로 가장 적절한 것을 고르시오.

① doctor　　② dentist　　③ nurse
④ vet　　　　⑤ pharmacist

06 대화를 듣고, 여자의 심정으로 가장 적절한 것을 고르시오.

① upset　　　　　② excited
③ thankful　　　　④ surprised
⑤ satisfied

07 다음을 듣고, 두 사람의 대화가 <u>어색한</u> 것을 고르시오.

①　　②　　③　　④　　⑤

08 대화를 듣고, 여자가 남자에게 부탁한 일로 가장 적절한 것을 고르시오.

① 공구 빌려주기　　② 타이어 사오기
③ 트렁크 확인하기　④ 타이어 교체하기
⑤ 정비소에 전화하기

09 대화를 듣고, 여자의 마지막 말의 의도로 가장 적절한 것을 고르시오.

① 요청　　② 거절　　③ 동의
④ 제안　　⑤ 감사

10 대화를 듣고, 남자가 지불해야 할 금액을 고르시오.

① $10　　② $20　　③ $30
④ $40　　⑤ $60

11 대화를 듣고, 두 사람이 대화하고 있는 장소로 가장 적절한 곳을 고르시오.

① café　　　　　② restaurant
③ clothing store　④ dry cleaner's
⑤ stationery store

12 다음을 듣고, *Puppets and Kings*에 관해 언급되지 <u>않은</u> 것을 고르시오.

① 공연 장소   ② 시작 날짜
③ 공연 횟수   ④ 공연 시간
⑤ 입장료

13 다음을 듣고, Jean의 집으로 가는 경로와 일치하지 <u>않는</u> 것을 고르시오.

Directions to Jean's House

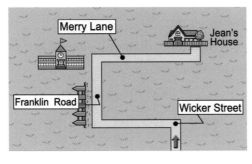

①   ②   ③   ④   ⑤

14 다음을 듣고, 무엇에 관한 설명인지 고르시오.

① 경찰차   ② 구급차   ③ 소방차
④ 화물선   ⑤ 헬리콥터

15 대화를 듣고, 남자가 대화 직후에 할 일로 가장 적절한 것을 고르시오.

① 전화하기   ② 편지 보내기
③ 우체국에 가기   ④ 이메일 보내기
⑤ 상담 예약하기

16 대화를 듣고, 여자가 결혼하게 될 날짜를 고르시오.

① April 14   ② April 21   ③ April 22
④ April 23   ⑤ April 28

17 다음 상황 설명을 듣고, James가 엄마에게 할 말로 가장 적절한 것을 고르시오.

James: _____

① I'm going to keep drinking coffee.
② I need some medicine for my headache.
③ There's no more soda in the refrigerator.
④ I can't sleep early today. I have a lot of homework to do.
⑤ I'm going to drink water instead of coffee from now on.

18 대화를 듣고, 두 사람이 할 일로 가장 적절한 것을 고르시오.

① 집에 가기   ② 농구하기
③ 볼링 치기   ④ 컴퓨터실에 가기
⑤ 비디오 게임하기

19 대화를 듣고, 남자의 충고를 가장 잘 표현한 속담을 고르시오.

① Bad news travels quickly.
② Two heads are better than one.
③ The early bird catches the worm.
④ You can't always get what you want.
⑤ Heaven helps those who help themselves.

20 대화를 듣고, 여자의 마지막 말에 대한 남자의 응답으로 가장 적절한 것을 고르시오.

Man: _____

① Do you want to play baseball with me?
② I'm already at the baseball stadium.
③ Thanks for saying that. I feel a lot better now.
④ I can't go to the baseball game today. I have other plans.
⑤ I'm going to be late for lunch. Would you mind waiting for me?

14회 DICTATION

다시 듣고, 빈칸에 알맞은 단어를 써 보세요.

◀》 MP3 실전 14-1

01 그림 정보 파악

대화를 듣고, 두 사람이 사용할 열쇠를 고르시오.

W : Honey, there are so many □ _____ here. Do you know □ _____ □ _____ opens the □ _____ box?

M : I don't know. Let's try this □ _____, □ _____ key. It might □ _____ the □ _____.

W : I □ _____ □ _____ that one and this □ _____, □ _____ key. But, both don't work.

M : Well, then □ _____ □ _____ this long, □ _____ key?

W : No, that's the key to the □ _____ □ _____. Hey, isn't this short, circular one the key to your □ _____ □ _____?

M : Oh, you're right. □ _____ this long, diamond-shaped key must be the one that opens the jewelry box.

W : Yes! It's □ _____ □ _____. Thanks for your help.

M : Sure, no problem.

02 목적 파악

대화를 듣고, 남자가 여자에게 전화한 목적으로 가장 적절한 것을 고르시오.

① 책 제목을 알려주려고
② 연체료를 내라고 말하려고
③ 책을 빌려달라고 부탁하려고
④ 독후감 쓰는 데 도움을 요청하려고
⑤ 책이 도서관에 들어온 것을 알려주려고

W : Hello, □ _____ □ _____ Amanda.

M : My name is Jason, □ _____ □ _____ Hickory □ _____.

W : Yes, □ _____ □ _____ □ _____ why you're calling?

M : I'm calling to tell you that you have to □ _____ a □ _____ □ _____ for two books, *The Fortune Teller* and *The Black Cat*.

W : A late fee? I □ _____ those books from the library □ _____ □ _____.

M : Actually, you were □ _____ □ _____ □ _____ them two weeks ago.

W : Oh my goodness! Has it been □ _____ □ _____ already?

M : I'm □ _____ □ _____. Please □ _____ □ _____ to return the books and pay the fee.

W : Alright, I will. Thank you for □ _____ me □ _____.

✎ **어휘복습** 잘 안 들리거나 몰라서 체크한 어휘를 써 놓고 복습해 보세요.

□ _____ □ _____ □ _____ □ _____

□ _____ □ _____ □ _____ □ _____

□ _____ □ _____ □ _____ □ _____

03 그림 상황에 적절한 대화 찾기

다음 그림의 상황에 가장 적절한 대화를 고르시오.

① ② ③ ④ ⑤

① W : □ _____ □ _____ to your arm?

   M : I □ _____ it while playing soccer.

② W : Dad, I think my □ _____ is □ _____.

   M : Oh, no! Let's go to the □ _____.

③ W : Dad, □ _____ is that woman □ _____?

   M : She's □ _____ □ _____ □ _____ to buy ice cream.

④ W : Dad, what is that woman □ _____?

   M : Oh, she's □ _____ a □ _____. She must have broken her leg.

⑤ W : Look! The people in the park are skateboarding.

   M : That □ _____ like □ _____. Do you want to □ _____?

04 그림 정보 파악

대화를 듣고, 두 사람이 말하고 있는 그림을 고르시오.

① ② ③

④ ⑤

W : I like all of Sarah Mitchell's □ _____. She is such a □ _____ □ _____.

M : I agree. I like this painting □ _____ □ _____. Look at how she drew the □ _____ in the □ _____.

W : They're beautiful! I like the □ _____, too. They □ _____ so □ _____.

M : I know. Do you see how she painted the □ _____? This painting must have □ _____ her □ _____ to finish.

W : Yeah, you're right.

M : Well, thank you for bringing me to this □ _____ □ _____. I think I'm a fan of Sarah Mitchell now.

W : I'm glad to hear that! I □ _____ a □ _____ □ _____, too.

M : Let's □ _____ □ _____ next time!

✎ **어휘복습** 잘 안 들리거나 몰라서 체크한 어휘를 써 놓고 복습해 보세요.

□ _____ □ _____ □ _____ □ _____

□ _____ □ _____ □ _____ □ _____

□ _____ □ _____ □ _____ □ _____

05 직업 추론

대화를 듣고, 여자의 직업으로 가장 적절한 것을 고르시오.

① doctor　　② dentist
③ nurse　　④ vet
⑤ pharmacist

W : Mr. Joseph Lance?

M : Yes, ma'am.

W : Here's your □ _____ for today. □ _____ one □ _____ after you eat lunch and dinner. Also, I will be back later to □ _____ you some □ _____.

M : Okay. I □ _____ □ _____ this morning that I might be able to □ _____ the □ _____ today. Is that true?

W : Well, the □ _____ has to come see if you're □ _____ □ _____ to go home.

M : Okay, □ _____ will the doctor be □ _____ to □ _____ me?

W : He'll be here □ _____ □ _____. Let me know if there's anything else you need.

M : I will. Thank you, ma'am.

06 심정 추론

대화를 듣고, 여자의 심정으로 가장 적절한 것을 고르시오.

① upset　　② excited
③ thankful　　④ surprised
⑤ satisfied

M : You look □ _____. Is there □ _____ □ _____?

W : Yeah, I □ _____ really □ _____ on my □ _____ test. This is the worst grade I've ever gotten!

M : Oh no, did you not □ _____ for the □ _____?

W : I studied all night for it! □ _____ □ _____ I'm so □ _____.

M : It's okay. I'm sure you'll □ _____ □ _____ next time.

W : Yeah, I □ _____ □ _____. This □ _____ just □ _____ my day. I guess I'll just have to study even harder for the next test.

✎ **어휘복습** 잘 안 들리거나 몰라서 체크한 어휘를 써 놓고 복습해 보세요.

□ _____　　□ _____　　□ _____　　□ _____

□ _____　　□ _____　　□ _____　　□ _____

□ _____　　□ _____　　□ _____　　□ _____

다음을 듣고, 두 사람의 대화가 <u>어색한</u> 것을 고르시오.

①   ②   ③   ④   ⑤

① M : What are we □ _____ for □ _____?

    W : I'm making □ _____ noodle □ _____.

② M : □ _____ is the meeting □ _____ □ _____?

    W : It's going to be in Room three ou five.

③ M : Are you □ _____ □ _____ the first day of school?

    W : The □ _____ □ _____ of school is August thirty first.

④ M : □ _____ do you do in your □ _____ □ _____?

    W : I usually □ _____ my □ _____ or take naps.

⑤ M : Listen! My □ _____ □ _____ is on the radio.

    W : I really like this song, too.

대화를 듣고, 여자가 남자에게 부탁한 일로 가장 적절한 것을 고르시오.

① 공구 빌려주기
② 타이어 사오기
③ 트렁크 확인하기
④ 타이어 교체하기
⑤ 정비소에 전화하기

M : Grace, what's the □ _____ with your □ _____?

W : Well, I □ _____ □ _____ some □ _____ on the side of the road, and now I have a □ _____ □ _____! I don't know what to do.

M : Oh no, that's □ _____! Do you have an □ _____ □ _____ in your car?

W : Yeah, there should be one in the □ _____. Do you know □ _____ to □ _____ tires?

M : Yes. I □ _____ last year when I worked at a □ _____ □ _____ □ _____.

W : That's great! Then could you □ _____ me □ _____ it?

M : □ _____ □ _____, I can do that. Do you have any □ _____ with you?

W : I sure do. They're in the trunk, too.

M : Okay then, let's □ _____ □ _____.

✎ **어휘복습** 잘 안 들리거나 몰라서 체크한 어휘를 써 놓고 복습해 보세요.

□ _____   □ _____   □ _____   □ _____

□ _____   □ _____   □ _____   □ _____

□ _____   □ _____   □ _____   □ _____

09 의도 파악

대화를 듣고, 여자의 마지막 말의 의도로 가장 적절한 것을 고르시오.

① 요청 ② 거절 ③ 동의
④ 제안 ⑤ 감사

W : Hey Victor, □ _____ are you going?

M : I'm on my way to □ _____ my □ _____ □ _____.
This is the third time this month.

W : Why? What's wrong with it?

M : Well, I □ _____ it and the □ _____ cracked. I have to
□ _____ it □ _____.

W : I'm sorry to hear that. It must be □ _____ to get it fixed.

M : Yeah, it is. I've □ _____ so much □ _____ on my phone
□ _____.

W : Hmm… Why don't you buy a □ _____ for your phone and
□ _____ □ _____ □ _____ phone □ _____?

M : Oh, those are really □ _____ □ _____!

10 숫자 정보 파악

대화를 듣고, 남자가 지불해야 할 금액을 고르시오.

① $10 ② $20 ③ $30
④ $40 ⑤ $60

W : Good morning, welcome to Splash Water Park. What can I do for you?

M : I would like to □ _____ four □ _____, please.

W : Okay, □ _____ □ _____ □ _____ and □ _____ are you buying tickets for?

M : I need tickets for two adults and two children.

W : Alright, your □ _____ is □ _____ dollars.

M : Oh, can I use this □ _____-dollar □ _____ □ _____?
I would also like to use the □ _____ □ _____.

W : Yes, you can use it. With the coupon your total is thirty dollars, and to use the locker room, you have to □ _____ an □ _____
□ _____ dollars.

M : That's fine. Here's the money.

✎ **어휘복습** 잘 안 들리거나 몰라서 체크한 어휘를 써 놓고 복습해 보세요.

□ _____ □ _____ □ _____ □ _____

□ _____ □ _____ □ _____ □ _____

□ _____ □ _____ □ _____ □ _____

11 장소 추론

대화를 듣고, 두 사람이 대화하고 있는 장소로 가장 적절한 곳을 고르시오.

① café
② restaurant
③ clothing store
④ dry cleaner's
⑤ stationery store

W : Hello, sir. Can I help you?

M : Yes, I bought this □ _____ two days ago, and I would like to □ _____ □ _____ □ _____ because the □ _____ is □ _____.

W : Okay, do you have the □ _____?

M : Yes, here you are.

W : Please wait a minute while I □ _____ □ _____ □ _____ □ _____ the shirt. Sir, I'm afraid you can't get a refund on this □ _____.

M : Why not?

W : Because the □ _____ □ _____ is not on it, and it has a □ _____ □ _____ the □ _____.

M : I thought I just needed to bring the receipt.

W : I'm sorry, sir. That's our □ _____ □ _____. If the item is □ _____, you can't get a refund.

M : Oh, okay.

12 미언급 파악

다음을 듣고, *Puppets and Kings*에 관해 언급되지 <u>않은</u> 것을 고르시오.

① 공연 장소
② 시작 날짜
③ 공연 횟수
④ 공연 시간
⑤ 입장료

W : It's that time of the year again! Are you ready for the □ _____ □ _____ □ _____? We invite you to □ _____ □ _____ our new puppet □ _____, *Puppets and Kings*, which opens on □ _____ □ _____. There will be four shows a day, at □ _____ P.M., □ _____ P.M., □ _____ P.M., and □ _____ P.M. To see the show, you must pay a □ _____ □ _____. Also, you can □ _____ □ _____ □ _____ puppet at the Create-A-Puppet booth □ _____ the □ _____. Lastly, there will be a □ _____ □ _____ full of puppets from all over the world. Don't forget to □ _____ a □ _____ in the □ _____ □ _____!

✏️ **어휘복습** 잘 안 들리거나 몰라서 체크한 어휘를 써 놓고 복습해 보세요.

□ _____ □ _____ □ _____ □ _____

□ _____ □ _____ □ _____ □ _____

□ _____ □ _____ □ _____ □ _____

13 그림 정보 파악

다음을 듣고, Jean의 집으로 가는 경로와 일치하지 <u>않는</u> 것을 고르시오.

Directions to Jean's House

① ① ② ③ ④ ⑤

① □ _____ a □ _____ □ _____ at Wicker Street, and go □ _____ until you see a □ _____.

② When you see the fence, take a □ _____ turn onto Franklin Road.

③ □ _____ □ _____ Franklin Road until you □ _____ the school.

④ □ _____ □ _____ □ _____ you pass the school, take a left turn onto Merry Lane.

⑤ □ _____ □ _____ straight, and you will see Jean's house.

14 화제 추론

다음을 듣고, 무엇에 관한 설명인지 고르시오.

① 경찰차   ② 구급차
③ 소방차   ④ 화물선
⑤ 헬리콥터

M : This is used to □ _____ people to the □ _____ quickly during □ _____ situations. It is normally a □ _____ □ _____, and it has a □ _____ on top of it. The siren rings to □ _____ □ _____ □ _____ that there is a □ _____ □ _____ in it. When drivers hear the siren, they □ _____ to the □ _____ of the □ _____ so that it can □ _____ □ _____. Inside this vehicle, there is □ _____ □ _____. Paramedics, people who take care of the □ _____ inside the vehicle, also ride in the vehicle.

✎ 어휘복습 잘 안 들리거나 몰라서 체크한 어휘를 써 놓고 복습해 보세요.

□ _____   □ _____   □ _____   □ _____

□ _____   □ _____   □ _____   □ _____

□ _____   □ _____   □ _____   □ _____

15 할 일 파악

대화를 듣고, 남자가 대화 직후에 할 일로 가장 적절한 것을 고르시오.

① 전화하기
② 편지 보내기
③ 우체국에 가기
④ 이메일 보내기
⑤ 상담 예약하기

W : Hello, may I help you with something?
M : Yes, please. I'm □ _____ □ _____ Ms. Williams, my guidance counselor.
W : She □ _____ □ _____ to attend a conference two days ago.
M : Oh, I need to □ _____ □ _____ her as soon as possible. Do you know □ _____ she will be □ _____?
W : Yes, she will be in her office □ _____ next □ _____. Is there anything I can help you with until she comes back?
M : Hmm… Is there any way I can □ _____ her □ _____ she's □ _____?
W : Actually, I can □ _____ you her □ _____ □ _____. Maybe you can send her an email.
M : That would be wonderful! Thank you very much.
W : No problem.

16 특정 정보 파악

대화를 듣고, 여자가 결혼하게 될 날짜를 고르시오.

① April 14   ② April 21
③ April 22   ④ April 23
⑤ April 28

M : This is Queen Wedding Hall. May I help you?
W : Yes, I would like to □ _____ a □ _____ for my □ _____ this month.
M : Okay, we have □ _____ □ _____, April □ _____ □ _____, and April □ _____ □ _____ open. Will you be interested in any of those dates?
W : Well, I have to go □ _____ at wedding □ _____ on April fourteenth.
M : Oh, then □ _____ □ _____ the twenty first and twenty eighth?
W : Hmm… The wedding □ _____ I □ _____ won't be finished until April twenty second, so April twenty first □ _____ □ _____ □ _____.
M : Alright. Then should I □ _____ the wedding hall for you on the twenty eighth?
W : □ _____, □ _____, I think that will be the best date.

✎ **어휘복습** 잘 안 들리거나 몰라서 체크한 어휘를 써 놓고 복습해 보세요.

□ _____   □ _____   □ _____   □ _____

□ _____   □ _____   □ _____   □ _____

□ _____   □ _____   □ _____   □ _____

17 상황에 적절한 말 찾기

다음 상황 설명을 듣고, James가 엄마에게 할 말로 가장 적절한 것을 고르시오.

James: _____

① I'm going to keep drinking coffee.
② I need some medicine for my headache.
③ There's no more soda in the refrigerator.
④ I can't sleep early today. I have a lot of homework to do.
⑤ I'm going to drink water instead of coffee from now on.

M : James ☐ _____ ☐ _____ cups of ☐ _____ every day. On days that he doesn't drink coffee, he drinks ☐ _____ or ☐ _____. James' mother knows that too much caffeine is ☐ _____ ☐ _____ James' ☐ _____. She tried talking to him about it, but he wouldn't listen. One day, James ☐ _____ ☐ _____ a ☐ _____ and can't sleep. He ends up ☐ _____ ☐ _____ all night. The next morning, he tells his mother what happened. She tells him that it's because of all the caffeine he drinks. James ☐ _____ to ☐ _____ drinking coffee, tea, and soda, and start ☐ _____ ☐ _____ ☐ _____ his ☐ _____.
In this situation, what would James most likely say to his mother?
James : _____

18 할 일 파악

대화를 듣고, 두 사람이 할 일로 가장 적절한 것을 고르시오.

① 집에 가기
② 농구하기
③ 볼링 치기
④ 컴퓨터실에 가기
⑤ 비디오 게임하기

W : What should we do ☐ _____ ☐ _____ today?
M : I haven't thought about it yet. Do you want to go ☐ _____ ☐ _____ ☐ _____?
W : Aren't you ☐ _____ ☐ _____ video games? You play with your friends every day!
M : You're right. Then let's do ☐ _____ ☐ _____. Do you have any ideas?
W : Hmm… I haven't been ☐ _____ in a long time.
M : Bowling? I've never gone bowling before.
W : It's easy! All you have to do is ☐ _____ the ☐ _____ and ☐ _____ ☐ _____ the ☐ _____.
M : Alright. You can teach me when we get to the bowling ☐ _____.
W : Okay! I'm excited. This should be fun!

✎ **어휘복습** 잘 안 들리거나 몰라서 체크한 어휘를 써 놓고 복습해 보세요.

☐ _____ ☐ _____ ☐ _____ ☐ _____
☐ _____ ☐ _____ ☐ _____ ☐ _____
☐ _____ ☐ _____ ☐ _____ ☐ _____

19 속담 추론

대화를 듣고, 남자의 충고를 가장 잘 표현한 속담을 고르시오.

① Bad news travels quickly.
② Two heads are better than one.
③ The early bird catches the worm.
④ You can't always get what you want.
⑤ Heaven helps those who help themselves.

W : Dad, can we please go to the □ _____ □ _____?
M : Sure, Nina.
W : Wow! There are so many □ _____ here. Isn't this one pretty?
M : It looks really □ _____ □ _____ the one I bought you last week.
W : But, Dad! I really like this one! Can you buy it for me?
M : No, Nina. You □ _____ have a lot of □ _____ at home. You don't even wear all of them.
W : Dad, if you buy me this blouse, I □ _____ I'll never □ _____ □ _____ one again.
M : That's what you said □ _____ □ _____ □ _____ I bought you one. My answer is no, Nina.
W : Okay, Dad. I'll just wear the ones I have at home.

20 알맞은 응답 찾기

대화를 듣고, 여자의 마지막 말에 대한 남자의 응답으로 가장 적절한 것을 고르시오.

Man: _____

① Do you want to play baseball with me?
② I'm already at the baseball stadium.
③ Thanks for saying that. I feel a lot better now.
④ I can't go to the baseball game today. I have other plans.
⑤ I'm going to be late for lunch. Would you mind waiting for me?

W : Why do you □ _____ so □ _____, Jim?
M : My baseball team □ _____ the □ _____ last night and I think it's my □ _____.
W : Why do you say that? I'm sure you □ _____ □ _____ □ _____.
M : Well, my teammate □ _____ the □ _____ to me, but I □ _____ it. So the □ _____ □ _____ □ _____ the game.
W : I see. But everyone □ _____ □ _____. Even famous players make mistakes sometimes. You can win your next game.
M : Do you really think so?
W : Yes, I sure do. I'll be at your next game to □ _____ □ _____ you.
M : _____

🖊 **어휘복습** 잘 안 들리거나 몰라서 체크한 어휘를 써 놓고 복습해 보세요.

□ _____ □ _____ □ _____ □ _____
□ _____ □ _____ □ _____ □ _____
□ _____ □ _____ □ _____ □ _____

점수 / 20

01 대화를 듣고, 두 사람이 구매할 물건을 고르시오.

①   ②   ③

④   ⑤

02 대화를 듣고, 남자가 여자에게 전화한 목적으로 가장 적절한 것을 고르시오.

① 전기공사를 예약하려고
② 전기회사에 취직하려고
③ 운영 시간을 물어보려고
④ 요금에 대해 문의하려고
⑤ 전기 절약 방법을 배우려고

03 다음 그림의 상황에 가장 적절한 대화를 고르시오.

① ② ③ ④ ⑤

04 대화를 듣고, 여자가 구매할 귀걸이를 고르시오.

①   ②   ③

④   ⑤

05 대화를 듣고, 두 사람의 관계로 가장 적절한 것을 고르시오.

① doctor – patient
② teacher – student
③ mailman – resident
④ customer service staff – customer
⑤ furniture salesman – furniture designer

06 대화를 듣고, 여자의 심정으로 가장 적절한 것을 고르시오.

① anxious   ② bored   ③ surprised
④ excited   ⑤ jealous

07 다음을 듣고, 두 사람의 대화가 <u>어색한</u> 것을 고르시오.

①   ②   ③   ④   ⑤

08 대화를 듣고, 여자가 남자에게 부탁한 일로 가장 적절한 것을 고르시오.

① 탁자 고르기   ② 선반 청소하기
③ 침실 청소하기   ④ 가구 옮기기
⑤ 의자 고치기

09 대화를 듣고, 남자의 마지막 말에 담긴 의도로 가장 적절한 것을 고르시오.

① 충고   ② 제안   ③ 확인
④ 감사   ⑤ 초대

10 대화를 듣고, 남자가 지불할 금액을 고르시오.

Jolly Food Stand Prices

Hamburger	$5
Hot Dog	$4 ($2 extra for cheese sauce)
French Fries	$3
Soda	$2

① $5   ② $8   ③ $9
④ $10   ⑤ $11

11 대화를 듣고, 두 사람이 대화하고 있는 장소로 가장 적절한 곳을 고르시오.

① airport   ② bus station
③ travel agency   ④ subway station
⑤ department store

12 대화를 듣고, Cary의 생일파티에 관해 언급되지 <u>않은</u> 것을 고르시오.

① 요일   ② 인원 수   ③ 시간
④ 장소   ⑤ 준비물

13 표를 보면서 다음을 듣고, 내용과 일치하지 <u>않는</u> 것을 고르시오.

Why Do You Use Your Cellphone?

■ ① phone call 13%
■ ② Internet 25%
■ ③ application 20%
■ ④ text message 30%
■ ⑤ pictures 12%

14 다음을 듣고, 무엇에 관한 설명인지 고르시오.

① dolphin   ② shark   ③ seal
④ shrimp   ⑤ sea turtle

15 대화를 듣고, 두 사람이 할 일로 가장 적절한 것을 고르시오.

① 산에서 걷기   ② 산에서 점심 먹기
③ 공원에서 산책하기   ④ 헬스클럽에 등록하기
⑤ 헬스클럽에서 운동하기

16 대화를 듣고, 두 사람이 오늘 보기로 한 것을 고르시오.

① sports game   ② news program
③ cooking show   ④ comedy show
⑤ movie

17 다음 설명을 듣고, Peter가 엄마에게 할 말로 가장 적절한 것을 고르시오.

Peter: _____

① But Mom, I don't want to study!
② How much are these video games?
③ I'm going to do my homework with my friend.
④ I'll do my homework and play less video games.
⑤ I'm going to play video games after school today.

18 대화를 듣고, 여자가 대화 직후에 할 일로 가장 적절한 것을 고르시오.

① 걷기   ② 버스 타기
③ 지하철 타기   ④ 택시 부르기
⑤ 기차 표 사기

19 대화를 듣고, 상황을 가장 잘 표현한 속담을 고르시오.

① The walls have ears.
② Look before you leap.
③ Kill two birds with one stone.
④ Don't judge a book by its cover.
⑤ Even if the sky falls, there is a way out.

20 대화를 듣고, 남자의 마지막 말에 대한 여자의 응답으로 가장 적절한 것을 고르시오.

Woman: _____

① What's your favorite holiday?
② It is too cold to go outside these days.
③ The flowers in the park haven't bloomed yet.
④ What kinds of outdoor activities do you do in your free time?
⑤ Oh, I don't really like fall. What do you like the most about it?

01 그림 정보 파악

대화를 듣고, 두 사람이 구매할 물건을 고르시오.

① ② ③
④ ⑤

W : Hey, Michael. Did you hear that Betty □ _____ □ _____ □ _____ a baby girl?

M : Yes! I bet she's □ _____ □ _____ baby □ _____! We should go visit her and the baby.

W : Yeah, but let's □ _____ a □ _____ for the baby □ _____ we go.

M : Okay. Should we buy a □ _____? Betty can use it □ _____ □ _____ the baby.

W : No, she □ _____ □ _____ has one. How about a □ _____?

M : The baby is □ _____ young □ _____ play with a doll. Let's get □ _____ □ _____.

W : Hmm… I don't think diapers would make a good gift. We should buy a □ _____. It'll □ _____ the baby □ _____.

M : Alright, that sounds like a □ _____ □ _____.

02 목적 파악

대화를 듣고, 남자가 여자에게 전화한 목적으로 가장 적절한 것을 고르시오.

① 전기공사를 예약하려고
② 전기회사에 취직하려고
③ 운영 시간을 물어보려고
④ 요금에 대해 문의하려고
⑤ 전기 절약 방법을 배우려고

W : This is Eugene, at Bolt Electricity. What can I help you with today?

M : Hi. My name is Patrick Ford. I'm calling □ _____ □ _____ about my □ _____ □ _____ for this month.

W : Yes, sir. What □ _____ □ _____ be the □ _____?

M : Well, I □ _____ □ _____ two hundred dollars, and I would like to know why. My bill is □ _____ one hundred dollars.

W : Please wait a minute. I will check that for you. I see what the problem is. We charged you □ _____ ⊡ _____ □ _____.

M : Oh, okay. So my bill is one hundred dollars, □ _____?

W : Yes, sir.

✎ **어휘복습** 잘 안 들리거나 몰라서 체크한 어휘를 써 놓고 복습해 보세요.

□ _____   □ _____   □ _____   □ _____
□ _____   □ _____   □ _____   □ _____
□ _____   □ _____   □ _____   □ _____

03 그림 상황에 적절한 대화 찾기

다음 그림의 상황에 가장 적절한 대화를 고르시오.

① ② ③ ④ ⑤

① M : Honey, did you □ _____ my car □ _____?

W : Yes, they are □ _____ the kitchen □ _____.

② M : You □ _____ so □ _____, honey.

W : I am. There are a lot of □ _____ □ _____ □ _____.

③ M : □ _____ are you □ _____ in the □ _____?

W : I'm □ _____ the □ _____. It's so dirty.

④ M : When will you be □ _____ doing the □ _____?

W : I'm not sure. Maybe □ _____ □ _____.

⑤ M : Honey, I □ _____ something □ _____.

W : Oh my goodness! I □ _____ all the cookies!

04 그림 정보 파악

대화를 듣고, 여자가 구매할 귀걸이를 고르시오.

① ② ③ ④ ⑤

M : Welcome to Rita's Jewels. Are you looking for something □ _____ □ _____?

W : Yes, I want to buy some earrings that would □ _____ □ _____ □ _____ the necklace I am wearing right now.

M : Alright. I think these long, star-shaped earrings would look good on you.

W : They look nice, but I □ _____ □ _____ earrings. How much are these cat-shaped ones?

M : Those are one hundred dollars.

W : That's □ _____ □ _____ for me. How about these □ _____ earrings? And these cross-shaped earrings?

M : The leaf-shaped earrings are fifty dollars and the cross-shaped ones are forty-five dollars.

W : Hmm… I think the leaf-shaped earrings will □ _____ □ _____ □ _____ my necklace.

✎ **어휘복습** 잘 안 들리거나 몰라서 체크한 어휘를 써 놓고 복습해 보세요.

□ _____   □ _____   □ _____   □ _____

□ _____   □ _____   □ _____   □ _____

□ _____   □ _____   □ _____   □ _____

05 관계 추론

대화를 듣고, 두 사람의 관계로 가장 적절한
것을 고르시오.

① doctor – patient
② teacher – student
③ mailman – resident
④ customer service staff – customer
⑤ furniture salesman – furniture
　designer

W : Hello, this is Susan, at Sunray Pots & Pans. What can I do for you?
M : Well, I □ _____ two sets of pots from the store □ _____
　□ _____, and I was told I would □ _____ a frying pan in
　the mail □ _____ □ _____ because I bought two sets. But I
　haven't gotten it yet.
W : Alright, please □ _____ □ _____ I □ _____ it for you. Okay,
　I see what's wrong. I'm sorry, but we are all □ _____ □ _____
　frying pans.
M : So, does that □ _____ I won't be □ _____ one?
W : I'm □ _____ □ _____. Would you like us to send you a
　□ _____ □ _____ □ _____ instead?
M : □ _____, that'll be fine. Thank you.

06 심정 추론

대화를 듣고, 여자의 심정으로 가장 적절한
것을 고르시오.

① anxious　　② bored
③ surprised　④ excited
⑤ jealous

W : Dad, I've □ _____ a huge □ _____. What do I do?
M : Why, Gina? What's the □ _____?
W : Well, I □ _____ □ _____ the □ _____ and was walking
　home, and then I □ _____ that I □ _____ my bag on the train!
　This is the □ _____ □ _____ of my life.
M : Oh, no! You should have been □ _____ □ _____. What was in
　the bag?
W : I □ _____ my jacket, my sunglasses, my camera, and my laptop
　computer □ _____ □ _____!
M : Oh my goodness, that is a lot of things you lost. Let's try
　□ _____ the train □ _____.
W : Okay, do you think they can help?
M : I hope they can. If there's a □ _____ □ _____ □ _____
　Center in the station, then you might be able to find your bag.

✏ **어휘복습** 잘 안 들리거나 몰라서 체크한 어휘를 써 놓고 복습해 보세요.

□ _____　□ _____　□ _____　□ _____
□ _____　□ _____　□ _____　□ _____
□ _____　□ _____　□ _____　□ _____

07 어색한 대화 찾기

다음을 듣고, 두 사람의 대화가 <u>어색한</u> 것을 고르시오.

①   ②   ③   ④   ⑤

① M : Do you know □ _____ the train will □ _____?
   W : It'll be here □ _____ □ _____ minutes.

② M : □ _____ can I □ _____ the salad dressing?
   W : I don't like □ _____ dressing □ _____ my salad.

③ M : □ _____ □ _____ have you been □ _____ the piano?
   W : It's been about □ _____ □ _____.

④ M : Is the café □ _____ today?
   W : No, they don't open □ _____ □ _____.

⑤ M : What □ _____ are you □ _____?
   W : I'm reading *Under the Sea*. You □ _____ □ _____ it, too.

08 부탁 파악

대화를 듣고, 여자가 남자에게 부탁한 일로 가장 적절한 것을 고르시오.

① 탁자 고르기
② 선반 청소하기
③ 침실 청소하기
④ 가구 옮기기
⑤ 의자 고치기

W : Hello, my name is Anna. I just □ _____ in □ _____ □ _____.
M : It's nice to meet you, Anna. My name is Hank. You look like you
   □ _____ a □ _____ □ _____ the □ _____.
W : Yeah, you're right. I can't move my □ _____ and □ _____
   because they're too □ _____. Could you help me?
M : Sure. □ _____ do you need me to □ _____ this table?
W : I would like it □ _____ the □ _____, please.
M : Alright. □ _____ □ _____ the shelf? Should I put it in the
   □ _____?
W : Yes, that would be great. Thank you so much for your help!
M : No problem. □ _____ me □ _____ if you need help with
   anything else.

✎ **어휘복습** 잘 안 들리거나 몰라서 체크한 어휘를 써 놓고 복습해 보세요.

□ _____   □ _____   □ _____   □ _____

□ _____   □ _____   □ _____   □ _____

□ _____   □ _____   □ _____

09 의도 파악

대화를 듣고, 남자의 마지막 말에 담긴 의도
로 가장 적절한 것을 고르시오.

① 충고   ② 제안   ③ 확인
④ 감사   ⑤ 초대

W : Hey, Robert. Can I □ _____ you a □ _____ ?
M : Sure, anything for you, Melanie. What is it?
W : I'm flying in to West End Airport this Thursday, and I was
    □ _____ you could come □ _____ □ _____ □ _____ .
M : Yeah, I can do that. □ _____ □ _____ does your □ _____
    □ _____ ?
W : It's □ _____ □ _____ □ _____ at five P.M., but I need to go
    to the □ _____ □ _____ . You can come by five thirty.
M : Okay, and let me know □ _____ your plane □ _____
    □ _____ .
W : I will. Don't worry.
M : Alright. So □ _____ to be □ _____ , you're arriving on
    Thursday, □ _____ ?

10 숫자 정보 파악

대화를 듣고, 남자가 지불할 금액을 고르시오.

Jolly Food Stand Prices

Hamburger	$5
Hot Dog	$4 ($2 extra for cheese sauce)
French Fries	$3
Soda	$2

① $5   ② $8   ③ $9
④ $10   ⑤ $11

W : Hello, sir! What can I get for you?
M : I would like one □ _____ and one □ _____ □ _____ with
    □ _____ □ _____ , please.
W : Okay. Is there □ _____ □ _____ you would like to
    □ _____ ?
M : Yes. I would □ _____ like some □ _____ □ _____ .
W : Alright. Can I get you □ _____ □ _____ □ _____ with that?
M : No, I already have a bottle of water with me.
W : Okay. Do you have □ _____ □ _____ with you today?
M : Yes, I have this □ _____-dollar-□ _____ coupon. Can I use it
    now?
W : Yes, of course you can.

✎ **어휘복습** 잘 안 들리거나 몰라서 체크한 어휘를 써 놓고 복습해 보세요.

□ _____   □ _____   □ _____   □ _____
□ _____   □ _____   □ _____   □ _____
□ _____   □ _____   □ _____   □ _____

11 장소 추론

대화를 듣고, 두 사람이 대화하고 있는 장소로 가장 적절한 곳을 고르시오.

① airport
② bus station
③ travel agency
④ subway station
⑤ department store

M : Excuse me, ma'am.

W : Yes, can I help you?

M : I need to get to Huckleberry Station, but I don't know □ _____ □ _____ □ _____ there from here. Could you □ _____ me □ _____ ?

W : Sure, I can do that. The trains here only go to stations on □ _____ □ _____, and Huckleberry Station is on line □ _____. So you have to □ _____ the □ _____ to Crane Station □ _____, and □ _____ □ _____ □ _____ line seven.

M : Oh, okay. □ _____ □ _____ □ _____ is Crane Station from here?

W : I'm not sure, but I think it is about □ _____ □ _____ □ _____ stops □ _____.

M : Hmm… Alright. Once I transfer to line seven, how many stops do I have to go to get to Huckleberry Station?

W : There are only two stops □ _____ Crane Station □ _____ Huckleberry Station.

M : Okay, that's great! Thank you so much.

12 미언급 파악

대화를 듣고, Cary의 생일파티에 관해 언급되지 <u>않은</u> 것을 고르시오.

① 요일　　　　② 인원 수
③ 시간　　　　④ 장소
⑤ 준비물

W : John, are you going to Cary's birthday party □ _____ □ _____ ?

M : Yes, I am. How about you? I heard it's going to be a lot of fun.

W : I'm going, too. □ _____ □ _____ does it start again? I lost the invitation.

M : The party □ _____ □ _____ □ _____ P.M.

W : Oh, okay. □ _____ is she □ _____ her party?

M : I think it's at a □ _____ □ _____. The invitation said to □ _____ a □ _____.

W : That sounds like fun! I wonder if there's going to be music and balloons.

M : I'm sure there will be. She said there's going to be a lot of food, too.

W : That's great! I'm □ _____ □ _____ □ _____ □ _____ to her party.

M : Me too! I'll see you on Tuesday then.

✎ **어휘복습** 잘 안 들리거나 몰라서 체크한 어휘를 써 놓고 복습해 보세요.

□ _____　□ _____　□ _____　□ _____

□ _____　□ _____　□ _____　□ _____

□ _____　□ _____　□ _____　□ _____

13 도표 · 실용문 파악

표를 보면서 다음을 듣고, 내용과 일치하지 <u>않는</u> 것을 고르시오.

Why Do You Use Your Cellphone?

- ■ ① phone call 13%
- ■ ② Internet 25%
- ■ ③ application 20%
- ■ ④ text message 30%
- ■ ⑤ pictures 12%

M : Good morning, everyone. My research team and I □ _____ a □ _____ □ _____ cellphone use. We asked a thousand people □ _____ they □ _____ □ _____ their □ _____, and here are the results. □ _____ percent of them said they make □ _____ □ _____ and □ _____ percent said they use the □ _____ the most. Also, twenty-five percent replied that they use phone □ _____ □ _____ □ _____, and □ _____ percent said they use their phone to send □ _____ □ _____. The last twelve percent like to □ _____ □ _____ with their cellphone. Thank you all for listening. I will be happy to answer any questions.

14 화제 추론

다음을 듣고, 무엇에 관한 설명인지 고르시오.

① dolphin ② shark
③ seal ④ shrimp
⑤ sea turtle

W : This is an animal that □ _____ in the □ _____. It can be very small in size, and it can also be very big in size, □ _____ □ _____ what □ _____ it is. It is □ _____, and has a □ _____ □ _____ on its □ _____. When people see its fin in the water, they □ _____ □ _____. Because unlike a dolphin, this animal can □ _____ □ _____. It eats other fish and has very □ _____ □ _____.

✎ **어휘복습** 잘 안 들리거나 몰라서 체크한 어휘를 써 놓고 복습해 보세요.

- □ _____
- □ _____
- □ _____
- □ _____
- □ _____
- □ _____
- □ _____
- □ _____
- □ _____
- □ _____
- □ _____
- □ _____

15 할 일 파악

대화를 듣고, 두 사람이 할 일로 가장 적절한 것을 고르시오.

① 산에서 걷기
② 산에서 점심 먹기
③ 공원에서 산책하기
④ 헬스클럽에 등록하기
⑤ 헬스클럽에서 운동하기

W : Hey, Dan. What are we doing □ _____ □ _____?
M : I don't know. Did you □ _____ to do □ _____ □ _____?
W : Well, I haven't exercised in a long time, and I was □ _____ if we could □ _____ □ _____.
M : Hiking sounds great, but I would □ _____ go to the □ _____.
W : Hmm… You □ _____ at the gym on Thompson Street, right?
M : Yes, that's the one.
W : They □ _____ on the first and third Sundays of □ _____ □ _____, so I don't think you can go today.
M : Oh, really? I didn't know that. Thanks for telling me.
W : Yeah, □ _____ □ _____. So, do you want to go to the □ _____ with me?
M : Sure, let's go.

16 특정 정보 파악

대화를 듣고, 두 사람이 오늘 보기로 한 것을 고르시오.

① sports game
② news program
③ cooking show
④ comedy show
⑤ movie

W : Honey, what TV □ _____ do you want to watch □ _____?
M : Hmm… How about a □ _____ show or a □ _____ game?
W : I've watched too many cooking shows □ _____, and I'm □ _____ □ _____ □ _____ sports. How about we watch a □ _____ show or a □ _____ program □ _____?
M : Well, I don't □ _____ □ _____ watching the news today. Let's watch the comedy show. Do you know what □ _____ and □ _____ it's supposed to □ _____ □ _____?
W : Actually, I'm not sure. Why don't you □ _____ the TV program □ _____?
M : Okay, let's see. It says comedian Ted Baker will be doing a comedy show at six P.M.
W : Oh, we can't watch it if it starts □ _____ □ _____ □ _____. We won't be home from work □ _____ □ _____ P.M.
M : Yeah, you're right. Then do you want to □ _____ a □ _____ tonight?
W : That □ _____ □ _____ □ _____. We can watch the comedy show next time.

✎ **어휘복습** 잘 안 들리거나 몰라서 체크한 어휘를 써 놓고 복습해 보세요.

□ _____ □ _____ □ _____ □ _____
□ _____ □ _____ □ _____ □ _____
□ _____ □ _____ □ _____ □ _____

17 상황에 적절한 말 찾기

다음 설명을 듣고, Peter가 엄마에게 할 말로 가장 적절한 것을 고르시오.

Peter: _____

① But Mom, I don't want to study!
② How much are these video games?
③ I'm going to do my homework with my friend.
④ I'll do my homework and play less video games.
⑤ I'm going to play video games after school today.

18 할 일 파악

대화를 듣고, 여자가 대화 직후에 할 일로 가장 적절한 것을 고르시오.

① 걷기
② 버스 타기
③ 지하철 타기
④ 택시 부르기
⑤ 기차 표 사기

M : Peter □ _____ playing □ _____ □ _____ with his friends. But □ _____, he's been □ _____ way □ _____ □ _____ □ _____ playing games. He doesn't do his homework, and he doesn't want to go to school. Peter's mom □ _____ him that if he doesn't do his schoolwork, she's going to □ _____ □ _____ all of his video games. After hearing this, Peter □ _____ to □ _____ □ _____ and just play video games □ _____ his □ _____ □ _____. In this situation, what would Peter most likely say to his mom?

Peter : _____

W : Excuse me, sir. Could you tell me where I can □ _____ □ _____ number two seven three?

M : Yeah, sure. There's a bus station right down the street. But there are □ _____ □ _____ □ _____ at this time. The last bus was at eleven P.M.

W : Oh, no! Then where is the □ _____ □ _____ station?

M : I'm afraid you can't take the subway this □ _____ □ _____ □ _____, □ _____.

W : I'm in big trouble, then. □ _____ □ _____ I □ _____ □ _____ get home?

M : Well, the □ _____ □ _____ you can go home now is to □ _____ a □ _____.

W : I see. Do you know the □ _____ □ _____ for the taxi □ _____?

M : Yes, it's three nine one, two nine three oh.

W : Thank you so much! You are a lifesaver.

✎ **어휘복습** 잘 안 들리거나 몰라서 체크한 어휘를 써 놓고 복습해 보세요.

□ _____ □ _____ □ _____ □ _____

□ _____ □ _____ □ _____ □ _____

□ _____ □ _____ □ _____ □ _____

19 속담 추론

대화를 듣고, 상황을 가장 잘 표현한 속담을 고르시오.

① The walls have ears.
② Look before you leap.
③ Kill two birds with one stone.
④ Don't judge a book by its cover.
⑤ Even if the sky falls, there is a way out.

W : There are so many people □ _____ in the □ _____ today.
M : Yeah, I know! Look at that man □ _____ □ _____.
He □ _____ so □ _____! How is he going to □ _____ the
□ _____?
W : Yeah, he's really □ _____, with □ _____ □ _____. But you
never know. He could be a good □ _____.
M : I don't think so. He'll □ _____ □ _____ in the □ _____ of
the race.
W : I guess we'll □ _____ □ _____ when the race is over. I think
the race is over. I wonder who won the race. Let's go find out.
M : I can't believe it! The man we saw earlier □ _____ □ _____
□ _____! He definitely didn't □ _____ □ _____ someone
who □ _____ □ _____.

20 알맞은 응답 찾기

대화를 듣고, 남자의 마지막 말에 대한 여자의 응답으로 가장 적절한 것을 고르시오.

Woman: _____

① What's your favorite holiday?
② It is too cold to go outside these days.
③ The flowers in the park haven't bloomed yet.
④ What kinds of outdoor activities do you do in your free time?
⑤ Oh, I don't really like fall. What do you like the most about it?

M : Linda, what's your □ _____ □ _____ of the □ _____?
W : Hmm… That's a hard question. I think I like □ _____ the
□ _____.
M : Can you tell me why?
W : Well, first of all, the □ _____ is really □ _____. It's not too hot
and it's not too cold. It's □ _____ weather to do □ _____
□ _____.
M : Okay, what else do you like about it?
W : It's the time of the year when all the □ _____ □ _____ and
the □ _____ is □ _____. It makes me feel happy.
M : I see. I like spring too, but my favorite season is fall.
W : _____

✎ **어휘복습** 잘 안 들리거나 몰라서 체크한 어휘를 써 놓고 복습해 보세요.

□ _____   □ _____   □ _____   □ _____

□ _____   □ _____   □ _____   □ _____

□ _____   □ _____   □ _____   □ _____

01 대화를 듣고, 여자가 먹을 샐러드를 고르시오.

①   ②   ③

④   ⑤

02 대화를 듣고, 여자가 남자에게 전화한 목적으로 가장 적절한 것을 고르시오.

① 예약을 취소하려고
② 예약을 변경하려고
③ 영수증을 요청하려고
④ 음식 배달을 요청하려고
⑤ 식당 메뉴를 물어보려고

03 다음 그림의 상황에 가장 적절한 대화를 고르시오.

① ② ③ ④ ⑤

04 대화를 듣고, 여자가 원하는 벽지를 고르시오.

①   ②   ③

④   ⑤

05 대화를 듣고, 두 사람의 관계로 가장 적절한 것을 고르시오.

① 음악 교사 – 학생
② 영화감독 – 배우
③ 화가 – 큐레이터
④ 작가 – 독자
⑤ 가수 – 팬

06 대화를 듣고, 남자의 심정으로 가장 적절한 것을 고르시오.

① bored
② excited
③ disappointed
④ jealous
⑤ relieved

07 다음을 듣고, 두 사람의 대화가 <u>어색한</u> 것을 고르시오.

① ② ③ ④ ⑤

08 대화를 듣고, 남자가 여자에게 부탁한 일로 가장 적절한 것을 고르시오.

① 설거지하기
② 셔츠 사주기
③ 셔츠 다리기
④ 세탁소에 전화하기
⑤ 세탁소에서 셔츠 찾아오기

09 대화를 듣고, 남자의 마지막 말에 담긴 의도로 가장 적절한 것을 고르시오.

① 충고
② 칭찬
③ 제안
④ 요청
⑤ 거절

10 대화를 듣고, 여자가 지불해야 할 금액을 고르시오.

① $5
② $10
③ $15
④ $20
⑤ $25

11 대화를 듣고, 두 사람이 대화하고 있는 장소로 가장 적절한 곳을 고르시오.

① hospital
② classroom
③ bookstore
④ museum
⑤ electronics store

12 다음을 듣고, Championship Boxing Match에 관해 언급되지 <u>않은</u> 것을 고르시오.

① 참가 선수 ② 날짜
③ 장소 ④ 좌석 가격
⑤ 입장권 구입 방법

13 다음을 듣고, 표와 일치하지 <u>않는</u> 것을 고르시오.

Weekly Weather Forecast

Day	Weather
Mon.	Cloudy, Gentle Breeze
Tue.	Sunny
Wed.	Cloudy, Rain
Thur.	Heavy Rain, Strong Wind
Fri.	Snowstorm
Sat.	Snowstorm
Sun.	Snowstorm

①   ②   ③   ④   ⑤

14 다음을 듣고, 무엇에 관한 설명인지 고르시오.

① 안경 ② 립스틱 ③ 마스크
④ 귀걸이 ⑤ 콘택트렌즈

15 대화를 듣고, 남자가 대화 직후에 할 일로 가장 적절한 것을 고르시오.

① 새 지갑 사기 ② 주문 취소하기
③ 은행에 전화하기 ④ 지갑 돌려주기
⑤ 새 신용카드 만들기

16 대화를 듣고, 두 사람이 만나기로 한 장소를 고르시오.

① library ② bookstore
③ restaurant ④ coffee shop
⑤ the man's house

17 다음 상황 설명을 듣고, Kate가 George에게 할 말로 가장 적절한 것을 고르시오.

Kate: _____

① I'm so happy that you're my friend.
② I'm so disappointed with the movie.
③ I don't like how you left me for a new friend.
④ Can you tell me the name of your new friend?
⑤ I would like to go see a movie with you this weekend.

18 대화를 듣고, 여자가 대화 직후에 할 일로 가장 적절한 것을 고르시오.

① 교과서 사기 ② 시험 공부하기
③ 이메일 계정 만들기 ④ 친구에게 전화하기
⑤ 선생님에게 이메일 보내기

19 대화를 듣고, 상황을 가장 잘 표현한 속담을 고르시오.

① Like father, like son.
② Every rule has its exception.
③ If it's not broken, don't fix it.
④ Even Homer sometimes nods.
⑤ Actions speak louder than words.

20 대화를 듣고, 여자의 마지막 말에 대한 남자의 응답으로 가장 적절한 것을 고르시오.

Man: _____

① I don't have any plans for Sunday.
② Okay. I can't wait to see everyone!
③ I don't want to eat anything right now.
④ I'm a busy person. I always have plans over the weekend.
⑤ I'm going to be late. I'll meet you guys at the camping grounds.

다시 듣고, 빈칸에 알맞은 단어를 써 보세요.

◀ MP3 실전 16-1

01 그림 정보 파악

대화를 듣고, 여자가 먹을 샐러드를 고르시오.

① ② ③
④ ⑤

M : Good morning! Welcome to Green Spoon! □ _____ would you □ _____ □ _____ your □ _____ today? We have tomatoes, olives, cucumbers, eggs, and onions.

W : I would like some □ _____ and □ _____ in it, please.

M : Okay. Do you want any cucumbers or eggs with that?

W : Hmm… Yes, □ _____ some □ _____. I really □ _____ □ _____ □ _____ in my food.

M : Alright, □ _____ □ _____ your salad.

W : Oh, I □ _____ □ _____ told you earlier, □ _____ could you □ _____ some □ _____ in my salad too?

M : Sure, that's not a problem. But if you add onions to your salad, you will have to □ _____ □ _____. Is that okay?

W : Okay, here's the money. Thank you!

02 목적 파악

대화를 듣고, 여자가 남자에게 전화한 목적으로 가장 적절한 것을 고르시오.

① 예약을 취소하려고
② 예약을 변경하려고
③ 영수증을 요청하려고
④ 음식 배달을 요청하려고
⑤ 식당 메뉴를 물어보려고

M : Hello, this is Octagon Seafood Buffet.

W : Yes, hello. My name is Tiffany Kings, and I □ _____ a □ _____ □ _____ □ _____ people □ _____ □ _____ P.M.

M : That's right. You are □ _____ □ _____ □ _____. What can I help you with?

W : I would like to □ _____ some □ _____ □ _____ my reservation. Will that be □ _____?

M : Well, it □ _____ □ _____ what changes you would like to make.

W : Okay. □ _____ people will be there □ _____ □ _____ □ _____, and I would like to □ _____ at □ _____ P.M. instead of □ _____ P.M.

M : I'm sorry, but our □ _____ for seven are all □ _____. But there is □ _____ table □ _____ for □ _____ □ _____. Would you like to come then?

W : Yes, that will work. Thank you so much!

✎ **어휘복습** 잘 안 들리거나 몰라서 체크한 어휘를 써 놓고 복습해 보세요.

□ _____ □ _____ □ _____ □ _____
□ _____ □ _____ □ _____ □ _____
□ _____ □ _____ □ _____ □ _____

다음 그림의 상황에 가장 적절한 대화를 고르시오.

① ② ③ ④ ⑤

① W : Did you □ _____ all the □ _____ ?

M : Yeah. They're already in the car.

② W : □ _____ □ _____ boxes do we □ _____ ?

M : We'll probably need □ _____ □ _____ ten of them.

③ W : Do you □ _____ a □ _____ with that?

M : Yes, please. Can you □ _____ □ _____ take this box down?

④ W : □ _____ did you put my □ _____ ?

M : It should be □ _____ top of □ _____ □ _____ .

⑤ W : □ _____ did you □ _____ the □ _____ without asking me?

M : I'm □ _____ . I thought it was addressed to me.

대화를 듣고, 여자가 원하는 벽지를 고르시오.

① ② ③
④ ⑤

M : Molly, do you like our new house? You get to □ _____ this □ _____ all □ _____ □ _____ .

W : I'm happy that I have □ _____ □ _____ room, but I liked the old room better. It was □ _____ and had □ _____ □ _____ .

M : We can □ _____ your new room with wallpaper, too! Do you want some with □ _____ ? Or □ _____ □ _____ cars?

W : Hmm… I don't really like □ _____ . And since I had ballerinas in the old room, I want something □ _____ □ _____ □ _____ .

M : Alright. Do you □ _____ anything □ _____ □ _____ ?

W : Well, how about wallpaper with □ _____ or □ _____ on it?

M : Those all sound great. I think butterflies would be the □ _____ □ _____ .

W : Yeah, I agree.

✎ **어휘복습** 잘 안 들리거나 몰라서 체크한 어휘를 써 놓고 복습해 보세요.

□ _____ □ _____ □ _____ □ _____
□ _____ □ _____ □ _____ □ _____
□ _____ □ _____ □ _____ □ _____

05 관계 추론

대화를 듣고, 두 사람의 관계로 가장 적절한 것을 고르시오.

① 음악 교사 — 학생
② 영화감독 — 배우
③ 화가 — 큐레이터
④ 작가 — 독자
⑤ 가수 — 팬

M : Oh, my goodness! I □_____ □_____ I'm finally getting to meet you! Could you □_____ this □_____ for me?

W : Sure, I can do that. What's your name?

M : My name is Jason Hurley. Wow, this is so □_____!

W : □_____ □_____ □_____, Jason.

M : Thank you so much! I □_____ you a lot. I really □_____ your □_____ "Love Melody" and "Dance Tonight."

W : I appreciate that very much.

M : Oh, one last thing. □_____ is your next □_____ □_____ □_____? I've been □_____ for it □_____ □_____ □_____!

W : I'm □_____ □_____ it now. It should be out by next month.

06 심정 추론

대화를 듣고, 남자의 심정으로 가장 적절한 것을 고르시오.

① bored   ② excited
③ disappointed   ④ jealous
⑤ relieved

M : Wow, Susie. What a nice computer! □_____ did you □_____ it?

W : Thank you! My dad □_____ it for me last week □_____ a □_____ □_____.

M : That's so awesome! Did you get a □_____ and □_____ cover for it, too?

W : Yeah. The case is □_____ □_____ □_____ and the keyboard cover is white.

M : Cool! You're so lucky. I wish I had a computer like this! I've □_____ my computer for □_____ □_____ □_____ so it's in □_____ □_____.

W : □_____ □_____ □_____ ask your parents to buy you one?

M : I □_____ tried asking them, □_____ they said to use it for at least □_____ □_____ □_____.

W : Oh, I see. Then I guess you just have to wait until next year.

M : Yeah, I □_____ □_____ to get a nice computer like you.

✎ **어휘복습** 잘 안 들리거나 몰라서 체크한 어휘를 써 놓고 복습해 보세요.

□ _____   □ _____   □ _____   □ _____

□ _____   □ _____   □ _____   □ _____

□ _____   □ _____   □ _____   □ _____

11 장소 추론

대화를 듣고, 두 사람이 대화하고 있는 장소로 가장 적절한 곳을 고르시오.

① hospital
② classroom
③ bookstore
④ museum
⑤ electronics store

M : Mrs. Albright, can you tell me what the □ _____ □ _____ is? I was □ _____ yesterday.

W : Sure. You have to □ _____ a □ _____ on □ _____ and □ _____.

M : I see. □ _____ □ _____ do I have to □ _____ in the □ _____?

W : Well, □ _____ some □ _____ on the □ _____ □ _____, and □ _____ □ _____ the different types of bones and muscles.

M : Hmm… Okay. □ _____ can I find □ _____ about the □ _____?

W : I'm sure there are plenty of □ _____ in the □ _____ you can use. Also, you can use our □ _____ □ _____.

M : Oh, alright. □ _____ is the □ _____ for the assignment?

W : You have to □ _____ it □ _____ before our next class, so October first.

M : Okay! Thanks a lot!

12 미언급 파악

다음을 듣고, Championship Boxing Match에 관해 언급되지 <u>않은</u> 것을 고르시오.

① 참가 선수
② 날짜
③ 장소
④ 좌석 가격
⑤ 입장권 구입 방법

M : Ladies and gentlemen! Are you □ _____ □ _____ the biggest □ _____ of the year? That's right! Anderson and Hartfield will be □ _____ against each other this □ _____, □ _____ □ _____ at Horizon □ _____! The match will □ _____ at □ _____ P.M. so make sure you're here □ _____ □ _____! Front row seats are □ _____ □ _____ □ _____ and all other seats are □ _____ dollars. Please remember that children □ _____ □ _____ years old will □ _____ be □ _____ to enter. Come out and have a great time!

✏️ **어휘복습** 잘 안 들리거나 몰라서 체크한 어휘를 써 놓고 복습해 보세요.

□ _____ □ _____ □ _____ □ _____

□ _____ □ _____ □ _____ □ _____

□ _____ □ _____ □ _____ □ _____

13 도표·실용문 파악

다음을 듣고, 표와 일치하지 <u>않는</u> 것을 고르시오.

Weekly Weather Forecast

Day	Weather
Mon.	Cloudy, Gentle Breeze
Tue.	Sunny
Wed.	Cloudy, Rain
Thur.	Heavy Rain, Strong Wind
Fri.	Snowstorm
Sat.	Snowstorm
Sun.	Snowstorm

①   ②   ③   ④   ⑤

① On □ _____, there will be a gentle □ _____, and it may be a little □ _____, but it will not rain.

② On □ _____, the clouds will clear, and the □ _____ will □ _____ □ _____. Enjoy a day outdoors!

③ □ _____ on □ _____, the clouds will □ _____ □ _____, and it will □ _____. Make sure to □ _____ your □ _____.

④ On □ _____, there will be a lot of □ _____, with □ _____ □ _____, so be prepared before you go outside.

⑤ We advise you to □ _____ □ _____ over the □ _____, because there will be □ _____ on □ _____, □ _____, and □ _____.

14 화제 추론

다음을 듣고, 무엇에 관한 설명인지 고르시오.

① 안경   ② 립스틱
③ 마스크   ④ 귀걸이
⑤ 콘택트렌즈

W : This is a very commonly used item. You can see people □ _____ this everywhere you go. People who □ _____ □ _____ □ _____ □ _____ wear these on their nose and ears. The □ _____ is normally □ _____ or □ _____ and it helps people see □ _____ that are □ _____ □ _____. It is hard for people to see once they □ _____ this □ _____ their face. When the lens gets dirty, people □ _____ it with a soft □ _____. Also, there are many different □ _____ and □ _____ of this item, so you can □ _____ one that fits you the best.

✎ **어휘복습** 잘 안 들리거나 몰라서 체크한 어휘를 써 놓고 복습해 보세요.

□ _____   □ _____   □ _____   □ _____

□ _____   □ _____   □ _____   □ _____

□ _____   □ _____   □ _____   □ _____

15 할 일 파악

대화를 듣고, 남자가 대화 직후에 할 일로 가장 적절한 것을 고르시오.

① 새 지갑 사기
② 주문 취소하기
③ 은행에 전화하기
④ 지갑 돌려주기
⑤ 새 신용카드 만들기

M : Honey, I think I □ _____ my □ _____ . My □ _____ □ _____ was in it, too.

W : What? □ _____ did you lose it?

M : I don't know. I □ _____ □ _____ it in my □ _____ , but when I checked, it wasn't there. What should I do?

W : I'm not sure. □ _____ □ _____ somebody finds your wallet and uses your credit card?

M : That would be □ _____ ! Do you know □ _____ I can □ _____ my credit card?

W : No, I've □ _____ □ _____ this problem □ _____ . Should we □ _____ □ _____ the □ _____ ?

M : Hmm… Would the bank be able to help?

W : I think so. If they can cancel your card, □ _____ will be □ _____ □ _____ use it.

M : Oh, you're right! That's a really good idea. I'll call them now.

16 특정 정보 파악

대화를 듣고, 두 사람이 만나기로 한 장소를 고르시오.

① library   ② bookstore
③ restaurant   ④ coffee shop
⑤ the man's house

W : Wesley, □ _____ do you want to meet to □ _____ for our □ _____ ?

M : How about the □ _____ □ _____ on Rose Street? It's a new place that □ _____ □ _____ .

W : I □ _____ □ _____ we should meet at the coffee shop. There are too many people there, and it's □ _____ □ _____ □ _____ . The library might be better.

M : Well, we have to be very □ _____ in the □ _____ . It'll be □ _____ to □ _____ to each other.

W : Yeah, I guess you're right. Then where should we meet?

M : Let's see… Do you want to □ _____ □ _____ to my □ _____ ?

W : Okay, I □ _____ □ _____ . Are you sure that'll be okay with you?

M : I'm sure. □ _____ is □ _____ during the day and we can talk □ _____ □ _____ □ _____ we want.

W : Alright, that sounds perfect. I'll see you later!

✎ **어휘복습** 잘 안 들리거나 몰라서 체크한 어휘를 써 놓고 복습해 보세요.

□ _____   □ _____   □ _____   □ _____

□ _____   □ _____   □ _____   □ _____

□ _____   □ _____   □ _____   □ _____

17 상황에 적절한 말 찾기

다음 상황 설명을 듣고, Kate가 George에게 할 말로 가장 적절한 것을 고르시오.

Kate: _____

① I'm so happy that you're my friend.
② I'm so disappointed with the movie.
③ I don't like how you left me for a new friend.
④ Can you tell me the name of your new friend?
⑤ I would like to go see a movie with you this weekend.

M : Kate and George have been □ _____ □ _____ since elementary school. They □ _____ everything □ _____ and even □ _____ □ _____ □ _____ to each other. One day, George meets a new friend. George □ _____ to □ _____ more and more □ _____ □ _____ his new friend □ _____ □ _____ Kate. Over the weekend, Kate sees George and his new friend □ _____ □ _____ the □ _____ together. Kate thinks that George □ _____ □ _____ wants to □ _____ □ _____ her. She decides to □ _____ him □ _____ she □ _____.

In this situation, what would Kate most likely say to George?
Kate: _____

18 할 일 파악

대화를 듣고, 여자가 대화 직후에 할 일로 가장 적절한 것을 고르시오.

① 교과서 사기
② 시험 공부하기
③ 이메일 계정 만들기
④ 친구에게 전화하기
⑤ 선생님에게 이메일 보내기

M : Hi, Hannah. How did you do on the □ _____ □ _____?
W : I got a D on it. But there must be □ _____ □ _____. I knew every problem on the test.
M : That's strange. Are you sure you wrote down the □ _____ □ _____?
W : Yes, I'm sure. I even □ _____ the right answers in my □ _____.
M : Then maybe Mr. Owen □ _____ a □ _____ when he was □ _____ your test.
W : Yeah, you might be right. □ _____ do you think I □ _____ □ _____?
M : Well, □ _____ him an □ _____ and ask him about your grade.
W : □ _____, I'll do that now. Do you know his email □ _____?
M : It's o-w-e-n at bmail dot com.
W : Thank you so much! I hope this works out well.

✎ **어휘복습** 잘 안 들리거나 몰라서 체크한 어휘를 써 놓고 복습해 보세요.

□ _____   □ _____   □ _____   □ _____

□ _____   □ _____   □ _____   □ _____

□ _____   □ _____   □ _____   □ _____

19 속담 추론

대화를 듣고, 상황을 가장 잘 표현한 속담을 고르시오.

① Like father, like son.
② Every rule has its exception.
③ If it's not broken, don't fix it.
④ Even Homer sometimes nods.
⑤ Actions speak louder than words.

M : Nancy, are you eating ice cream again? I thought you were □ _____ □ _____ □ _____!

W : I was going to start today, but these ice cream cones were □ _____ □ _____! I had to buy some. I'll □ _____ my diet □ _____.

M : You've been saying that for the past few months, Nancy.

W : I know, but I □ _____ □ _____, and it's □ _____ for me to □ _____ □ _____.

M : Well, you'll never □ _____ □ _____ if you □ _____ the □ _____ □ _____ and don't exercise.

W : Yeah, you're right. Will you □ _____ me □ _____ □ _____?

M : Yes, I can help you. But □ _____ □ _____ □ _____ that you'll go on a diet. You □ _____ □ _____ □ _____ □ _____ that you're trying.

W : I'll start tomorrow, I promise! I'll show you □ _____ my □ _____.

20 알맞은 응답 찾기

대화를 듣고, 여자의 마지막 말에 대한 남자의 응답으로 가장 적절한 것을 고르시오.

Man: _____

① I don't have any plans for Sunday.
② Okay. I can't wait to see everyone!
③ I don't want to eat anything right now.
④ I'm a busy person. I always have plans over the weekend.
⑤ I'm going to be late. I'll meet you guys at the camping grounds.

W : David, do you have any □ _____ for the □ _____?

M : Yes, I do. I'm □ _____ □ _____ with my friends □ _____ □ _____. Why do you ask, Mom?

W : Well, I □ _____ your grandparents, aunts, uncles, and cousins over □ _____ □ _____ on Saturday. That's the only day everyone can come.

M : You invited them on Saturday? Hmm… Then I'll □ _____ □ _____ my □ _____ and go camping on □ _____ □ _____.

W : Oh, that'll be perfect! Thank you so much for doing that.

M : It's □ _____ a □ _____. □ _____ are they going to □ _____ □ _____?

W : Your grandparents will □ _____ □ _____ □ _____ □ _____, and everyone else will be here by seven thirty.

M : _____

✎ **어휘복습** 잘 안 들리거나 몰라서 체크한 어휘를 써 놓고 복습해 보세요.

□ _____   □ _____   □ _____   □ _____

□ _____   □ _____   □ _____   □ _____

□ _____   □ _____   □ _____   □ _____

01 대화를 듣고, 여자가 구매할 인형을 고르시오.

① ② ③ ④ ⑤

02 대화를 듣고, 남자가 여자에게 전화한 목적으로 가장 적절한 것을 고르시오.

① TV를 사려고
② TV를 고치려고
③ 케이블 상품을 신청하려고
④ 케이블 상품을 취소하려고
⑤ 케이블 상품을 변경하려고

03 다음 그림의 상황에 가장 적절한 대화를 고르시오.

① ② ③ ④ ⑤

04 대화를 듣고, 남자가 가장 좋아하는 음식을 고르시오.

① pasta   ② pizza
③ hamburger   ④ French fries
⑤ fried chicken

05 대화를 듣고, 여자의 직업으로 가장 적절한 것을 고르시오.

① teacher   ② tour guide
③ bus driver   ④ flight attendant
⑤ travel agent

06 대화를 듣고, 남자의 심정으로 가장 적절한 것을 고르시오.

① angry   ② excited   ③ lonely
④ relieved   ⑤ disappointed

07 다음을 듣고, 두 사람의 대화가 <u>어색한</u> 것을 고르시오.

①   ②   ③   ④   ⑤

08 대화를 듣고, 여자가 남자에게 부탁한 일로 가장 적절한 것을 고르시오.

① 알람시계 사주기   ② 알람시계 고쳐주기
③ 함께 등교하기   ④ 아침식사 사주기
⑤ 전화로 깨워주기

09 대화를 듣고, 여자의 마지막 말에 담긴 의도로 가장 적절한 것을 고르시오.

① 제안   ② 요청   ③ 거절
④ 격려   ⑤ 동의

10 다음 표를 보면서 대화를 듣고, 여자가 지불할 금액을 고르시오.

Coffee / Tea	Dessert
Ice Latte $5	Chocolate Cake $3
Ice Mocha $6	Cheesecake $4
Hot Chocolate $4	Blueberry Muffin $3
Green Tea $4	Doughnut $3

① $17   ② $18   ③ $19
④ $20   ⑤ $21

11 대화를 듣고, 두 사람이 대화하고 있는 장소로 가장 적절한 곳을 고르시오.

① park ② repair shop
③ bicycle shop ④ electronics store
⑤ department store

12 다음을 듣고, Peabody Circus에 관해 언급되지 <u>않</u>은 것을 고르시오.

① 개장일 ② 위치 ③ 공연 시간
④ 폐장일 ⑤ 입장료

13 다음을 듣고, 표와 일치하지 <u>않는</u> 것을 고르시오.

Dormitory Shuttle Bus Times

12:00 P.M., 12:20 P.M., 12:40 P.M.
1:00 P.M., 1:15 P.M., 1:30 P.M.
2:00 P.M., 2:20 P.M., 2:40 P.M.
4:00 P.M., 4:15 P.M., 4:35 P.M.
5:00 P.M., 5:15 P.M., 5:30 P.M.

① ② ③ ④ ⑤

14 다음을 듣고, 무엇에 관한 설명인지 고르시오.

① banana ② mango
③ pineapple ④ lemon
⑤ kiwi

15 대화를 듣고, 남자가 할 일로 가장 적절한 것을 고르시오.

① 문구점 가기 ② 계산기 고치기
③ 계산기 빌리기 ④ 수학 숙제 제출하기
⑤ 과학 프로젝트 진행하기

16 대화를 듣고, 두 사람이 만날 요일을 고르시오.

① Monday ② Tuesday
③ Wednesday ④ Friday
⑤ Saturday

17 다음 상황 설명을 듣고, Danielle이 Jane에게 할 말로 가장 적절한 것을 고르시오.

Danielle: _____

① I couldn't find my cellphone.
② Let's grab lunch on Thursday.
③ The restaurant doesn't open on weekends.
④ I waited 3 hours for you! Why didn't you come to meet me?
⑤ I'll call you back in 30 minutes. I'm in the middle of eating lunch.

18 대화를 듣고, 여자가 대화 직후에 할 일로 가장 적절한 것을 고르시오.

① 옷 사기 ② 공항 가기
③ 은행 가기 ④ 짐 꾸리기
⑤ 은행에 전화하기

19 대화를 듣고, 상황을 가장 잘 표현한 속담을 고르시오.

① Better late than never.
② Too many cooks spoil the broth.
③ The early bird catches the worm.
④ All good things must come to an end.
⑤ Heaven helps those who help themselves.

20 대화를 듣고, 여자의 마지막 말에 대한 남자의 응답으로 가장 적절한 것을 고르시오.

Man: _____

① How long have you been dancing?
② I'll meet you in front of the student hall on Thursday.
③ What's your favorite type of dance? Mine is ballet and jazz.
④ Alright. Can you write my name down on the list? I want to try out.
⑤ There is a dance performance in the student hall on Wednesday.

01 그림 정보 파악

대화를 듣고, 여자가 구매할 인형을 고르시오.

① ② ③
④ ⑤

M : Ruth, do you know which □ _____ □ _____ you want yet?
W : No, I like all of them, Dad! It's □ _____ □ _____ □ _____ one.
M : Okay, then let me help you. How do you like this □ _____ doll wearing a long □ _____?
W : It's alright, but I □ _____ a doll with a □ _____ □ _____ her □ _____ like this one with the short dress and short hair.
M : Hmm… □ _____ □ _____ with long hair and a short dress. She has a crown on her head, too. Do you want this one?
W : No. I like this one with the □ _____ □ _____ and □ _____ □ _____ □ _____ □ _____.
M : Alright, then. □ _____ □ _____ □ _____ this is the one you want?
W : Yes, Dad. I'm □ _____!

02 목적 파악

대화를 듣고, 남자가 여자에게 전화한 목적으로 가장 적절한 것을 고르시오.

① TV를 사려고
② TV를 고치려고
③ 케이블 상품을 신청하려고
④ 케이블 상품을 취소하려고
⑤ 케이블 상품을 변경하려고

W : Hello, Time-Warp Cable here. How can I help you?
M : I would like to get □ _____ □ _____ my □ _____, please.
W : Okay. You can □ _____ □ _____ three □ _____. Package A gives you one hundred □ _____. If you sign up for Package B, you get one hundred fifty channels. And Package C provides two hundred channels.
M : Hmm… I think I will □ _____ □ _____ □ _____ Package B. Can you □ _____ □ _____ to my house to □ _____ it □ _____ for me?
W : Yes, sir. If you tell me □ _____ □ _____, I will □ _____ a □ _____ over by ten o'clock tomorrow morning.
M : Alright, forty-four thirty-one Allenwood Road. Oh, and how do I □ _____ □ _____ the □ _____ cable □ _____?
W : A □ _____ will be □ _____ to your home address at the end of each month.
M : Okay, that sounds good. Thank you!

✎ **어휘복습** 잘 안 들리거나 몰라서 체크한 어휘를 써 놓고 복습해 보세요.

□ _____ □ _____ □ _____ □ _____

□ _____ □ _____ □ _____ □ _____

□ _____ □ _____ □ _____ □ _____

03 그림 상황에 적절한 대화 찾기

다음 그림의 상황에 가장 적절한 대화를 고르시오.

① ② ③ ④ ⑤

① W : □ _____ a □ _____ at all those flowers in the park!
   M : Wow! They're so beautiful!
② W : □ _____ □ _____ would you like today?
   M : I would like a □ _____ □ _____ □ _____, please.
③ W : I need to buy a □ _____ for my □ _____.
   M : □ _____ □ _____ □ _____ buy her a necklace?
④ W : You □ _____ really □ _____ today.
   M : I know. I only □ _____ for □ _____ □ _____ last night.
⑤ W : □ _____ □ _____ □ _____ some flowers for your
       mother's birthday?
   M : □ _____ □ _____. She doesn't really like flowers.

04 특정 정보 파악

대화를 듣고, 남자가 가장 좋아하는 음식을 고르시오.

① pasta   ② pizza
③ hamburger   ④ French fries
⑤ fried chicken

W : Jeff, what food do you □ _____ eating □ _____ □ _____?
M : □ _____ what it is. If you □ _____ it □ _____,
    I'll □ _____ you □ _____.
W : Okay! Is it a type of □ _____ □ _____, like pasta?
M : No. I don't really like Italian food. I'll □ _____ you a □ _____.
    You normally □ _____ this □ _____ a type of □ _____ food
    and □ _____.
W : Oh! I think I'm starting to □ _____ it □ _____. The fried food
    is □ _____ □ _____, right?
M : Yes! You □ _____ that part □ _____. So what do you eat with
    French fries and soda?
W : Hmm… I'm □ _____ □ _____ this is it. It has □ _____,
    □ _____, and □ _____ in it, right? And you use your hands to
    eat it.
M : Yeah! You figured it out! Let's go eat dinner now.

✎ **어휘복습** 잘 안 들리거나 몰라서 체크한 어휘를 써 놓고 복습해 보세요.

□ _____   □ _____   □ _____   □ _____
□ _____   □ _____   □ _____   □ _____
□ _____   □ _____   □ _____   □ _____

05 직업 추론

대화를 듣고, 여자의 직업으로 가장 적절한 것을 고르시오.

① teacher
② tour guide
③ bus driver
④ flight attendant
⑤ travel agent

W : □ _____ □ _____ flight three oh one, sir. May I help you?

M : Yes, could you □ _____ me □ _____ my □ _____? It's thirty-two A.

W : Of course, it's right □ _____ □ _____. Is there anything else I can do for you?

M : Actually, yes. I would like an □ _____ □ _____, please. It gets □ _____ □ _____ the □ _____.

W : Okay, I will get it for you □ _____ □ _____.

M : Alright. One last thing, □ _____ is this seatbelt sign □ _____?

W : When the □ _____ is □ _____ □ _____, you must □ _____ □ _____ your □ _____ and stay in your seat. When the sign is □ _____ □ _____, you can get up and walk around.

M : Oh, I see. Thank you for your help!

06 심정 추론

대화를 듣고, 남자의 심정으로 가장 적절한 것을 고르시오.

① angry   ② excited
③ lonely   ④ relieved
⑤ disappointed

W : Steve, you □ _____ so □ _____ today. Are you okay?

M : No, not really. I really □ _____ my □ _____. I haven't seen them in □ _____ □ _____ □ _____.

W : I understand. I □ _____ the □ _____ □ _____ when I first started my □ _____ here as an □ _____ □ _____.

M : I want to □ _____ □ _____ to my □ _____ right now. I feel so □ _____ living in a different country.

W : I'm sure you'll be okay. Have you □ _____ any □ _____ □ _____ yet?

M : No, □ _____ wants to □ _____ to me. I feel like I □ _____ □ _____ □ _____. I miss my friends back home.

W : Well, there are only four weeks left until the semester is over. □ _____ □ _____ there!

M : Okay, I'll try. Thank you!

✎ **어휘복습** 잘 안 들리거나 몰라서 체크한 어휘를 써 놓고 복습해 보세요.

□ _____   □ _____   □ _____   □ _____
□ _____   □ _____   □ _____   □ _____
□ _____   □ _____   □ _____   □ _____

07 어색한 대화 찾기

다음을 듣고, 두 사람의 대화가 <u>어색한</u> 것을 고르시오.

①   ②   ③   ④   ⑤

① M : □ _____ □ _____ people are going to the □ _____ game?

    W : The game is □ _____ □ _____ □ _____ at six thirty P.M.

② M : □ _____ do you want to eat for □ _____?

    W : I □ _____ □ _____ toast or a ham sandwich.

③ M : Is □ _____ □ _____ A □ _____ today?

    W : No, the □ _____ team will be □ _____ it.

④ M : Are you □ _____ □ _____ □ _____ □ _____ yet?

    W : Yes. I'll be there □ _____ □ _____ □ _____.

⑤ M : □ _____ is the □ _____ □ _____?

    W : It's □ _____ the □ _____ across the street.

08 부탁 파악

대화를 듣고, 여자가 남자에게 부탁한 일로 가장 적절한 것을 고르시오.

① 알람시계 사주기
② 알람시계 고쳐주기
③ 함께 등교하기
④ 아침식사 사주기
⑤ 전화로 깨워주기

M : Hey, Sophie. □ _____ were you □ _____ to □ _____ today?

W : I □ _____ to □ _____ an □ _____ before going to sleep. This isn't the first time I've been late.

M : If you keep coming to class late, Mr. Hoover is going to □ _____ □ _____ □ _____ your □ _____ □ _____.

W : Yeah, I know. But I □ _____ a □ _____ □ _____. What should I do?

M : Hmm… I don't know. I never □ _____ □ _____ □ _____ □ _____ in the morning.

W : I see. Then could you call me every morning? □ _____ □ _____ even if I forget to set an alarm, I can □ _____ □ _____ □ _____ □ _____.

M : Sure, I can do that for you. I normally □ _____ □ _____ □ _____ □ _____. Is that a good time?

W : Yes! That works for me. Thank you!

□ _____   □ _____   □ _____   □ _____

□ _____   □ _____   □ _____   □ _____

□ _____   □ _____   □ _____   □ _____

09 의도 파악

대화를 듣고, 여자의 마지막 말에 담긴 의도로 가장 적절한 것을 고르시오.

① 제안   ② 요청   ③ 거절
④ 격려   ⑤ 동의

W : What's up, Brad? You □ _____ □ _____ for something.
M : Well, I'm excited and □ _____ at the same time. I'm □ _____ □ _____ a □ _____ with this girl that I really like.
W : Good for you! Have you decided □ _____ you're going □ _____ □ _____? It's important to □ _____ a □ _____ □ _____.
M : Yeah, I know. I have an outfit planned out, but I don't know if I should wear it. Can you tell me □ _____ □ _____ □ _____?
W : Sure, I can do that.
M : Okay, I was going to wear these □ _____ □ _____ and denim □ _____.
W : Hmm… □ _____ □ _____ you wear this white shirt □ _____? It □ _____ □ _____ on you.

10 숫자 정보 파악

다음 표를 보면서 대화를 듣고, 여자가 지불할 금액을 고르시오.

Coffee / Tea	Dessert
Ice Latte $5	Chocolate Cake $3
Ice Mocha $6	Cheesecake $4
Hot Chocolate $4	Blueberry Muffin $3
Green Tea $4	Doughnut $3

① $17   ② $18   ③ $19
④ $20   ⑤ $21

W : □ _____ so □ _____ for □ _____ me on my □ _____!
M : It's no problem. I can help you □ _____ □ _____ □ _____.
W : To thank you, I would like to □ _____ you some □ _____ and □ _____. What would you like?
M : Oh, that's so thoughtful of you. I'll have the □ _____ □ _____ and □ _____ □ _____.
W : Okay. Are you sure that's all you want? You can □ _____ □ _____ dessert if you'd like.
M : Really? Well then, I'll have the □ _____ □ _____, too. What are you going to order?
W : I think I'll get a cup of □ _____ □ _____ and □ _____.
M : Okay! I □ _____ you doing this.

✎ **어휘복습** 잘 안 들리거나 몰라서 체크한 어휘를 써 놓고 복습해 보세요.

□ _____   □ _____   □ _____   □ _____

□ _____   □ _____   □ _____   □ _____

□ _____   □ _____   □ _____   □ _____

11 장소 추론

대화를 듣고, 두 사람이 대화하고 있는 장소로 가장 적절한 곳을 고르시오.

① park
② repair shop
③ bicycle shop
④ electronics store
⑤ department store

W : Good afternoon, welcome to Speedy Bicycles. Can I help you?

M : Yes, I □ _____ this □ _____ a few months ago, and the □ _____ doesn't seem to □ _____.

W : Okay, but there isn't anything we can do for you here. You'll have to take your bicycle to the □ _____ □ _____ □ _____ □ _____ □ _____.

M : Oh, alright. Would you happen to know □ _____ □ _____ it will □ _____ to □ _____ my brakes?

W : It will cost you □ _____ one □ _____ dollars.

M : What? That's so expensive! I might as well □ _____ a □ _____ □ _____.

W : I know, it does □ _____ □ _____ □ _____. Would you be □ _____ □ _____ buying a □ _____ bicycle?

M : Yes. I'll take a look around. Thank you.

12 미언급 파악

다음을 듣고, Peabody Circus에 관해 언급되지 <u>않은</u> 것을 고르시오.

① 개장일   ② 위치
③ 공연 시간   ④ 폐장일
⑤ 입장료

M : Ladies and Gentlemen! We are pleased to announce the □ _____ □ _____ of Peabody □ _____! We will □ _____ our gates on □ _____, □ _____ □ _____ at □ _____ A.M. We are □ _____ on Seventh Avenue. There will be □ _____ that draw pictures, □ _____ that jump through fire, □ _____ doing tricks, and so □ _____ □ _____! There will be □ _____ □ _____ every day, at one P.M., two thirty P.M., and five P.M. □ _____ is □ _____ for □ _____ and □ _____ dollars for □ _____. Come out and have the time of your life!

✎ **어휘복습** 잘 안 들리거나 몰라서 체크한 어휘를 써 놓고 복습해 보세요.

□ _____   □ _____   □ _____   □ _____

□ _____   □ _____   □ _____   □ _____

□ _____   □ _____   □ _____   □ _____

13 도표·실용문 파악

다음을 듣고, 표와 일치하지 <u>않는</u> 것을 고르시오.

Dormitory Shuttle Bus Times

12:00 P.M., 12:20 P.M., 12:40 P.M.
1:00 P.M., 1:15 P.M., 1:30 P.M.
2:00 P.M., 2:20 P.M., 2:40 P.M.
4:00 P.M., 4:15 P.M., 4:35 P.M.
5:00 P.M., 5:15 P.M., 5:30 P.M.

①   ②   ③   ④   ⑤

① Students who want to go to the □ _____ can □ _____ the □ _____ bus □ _____ □ _____ .

② The shuttle bus runs □ _____ □ _____ □ _____ from □ _____ P.M. to one □ _____ P.M.

③ Students who wait for the shuttle bus at □ _____ □ _____ P.M. will have to □ _____ for □ _____ □ _____ until it comes.

④ The shuttle bus □ _____ □ _____ □ _____ □ _____ P.M., four □ _____ P.M., and four □ _____ P.M.

⑤ If you do not ride the shuttle bus □ _____ □ _____ □ _____ P.M., you will have to □ _____ to the dormitory.

14 화제 추론

다음을 듣고, 무엇에 관한 설명인지 고르시오.

① banana   ② mango
③ pineapple   ④ lemon
⑤ kiwi

W : This is a type of □ _____ that □ _____ on □ _____ . It is □ _____ with □ _____ □ _____ . The □ _____ of this fruit □ _____ many □ _____ on it, so you must be careful not to poke yourself. You have to □ _____ the □ _____ before eating it. This fruit is □ _____ and □ _____ at the same time. This fruit grows in places where there is □ _____ □ _____ . You can buy it at a □ _____ or □ _____ □ _____ .

✎ **어휘복습** 잘 안 들리거나 몰라서 체크한 어휘를 써 놓고 복습해 보세요.

□ _____   □ _____   □ _____   □ _____
□ _____   □ _____   □ _____   □ _____
□ _____   □ _____   □ _____   □ _____

15 할 일 파악

대화를 듣고, 남자가 할 일로 가장 적절한 것을 고르시오.

① 문구점 가기
② 계산기 고치기
③ 계산기 빌리기
④ 수학 숙제 제출하기
⑤ 과학 프로젝트 진행하기

W : Aaron, have you □ _____ your □ _____ □ _____?
M : No, Mom. I □ _____ □ _____ I can do it today.
W : □ _____ □ _____?
M : I can't □ _____ any of the □ _____ because there's
   □ _____ □ _____ with my □ _____.
W : Let me see it. I see what the problem is. The □ _____ and
   □ _____ □ _____ on your calculator aren't □ _____.
M : Oh, I see. How am I going to finish my □ _____ with a
   □ _____ calculator?
W : Hmm… Can you □ _____ □ _____ from a friend tomorrow?
M : I think so. I'll □ _____ □ _____ from my math class if I can
   □ _____ □ _____.

16 특정 정보 파악

대화를 듣고, 두 사람이 만날 요일을 고르시오.

① Monday   ② Tuesday
③ Wednesday   ④ Friday
⑤ Saturday

W : Wow, John! I didn't know you could □ _____ so □ _____!
   □ _____ □ _____ have you been swimming?
M : Thanks for the □ _____. I've been swimming □ _____ about
   □ _____ □ _____.
W : That's a long time. □ _____ □ _____ you're so good!
   I □ _____ I could swim well, too.
M : If you want, I can teach you □ _____ □ _____ swim.
   It's □ _____ □ _____ □ _____ □ _____, I promise.
W : I would love that! □ _____ do you want to □ _____?
   I'm □ _____ every day this week □ _____ □ _____
   □ _____ and □ _____.
M : Okay, I can do Monday and Friday. You can □ _____ □ _____
   those two days.
W : Hmm… I think □ _____ would be □ _____. That way I can
   □ _____ over the □ _____.
M : Alright, I'll see you then!

✎ **어휘복습** 잘 안 들리거나 몰라서 체크한 어휘를 써 놓고 복습해 보세요.

□ _____   □ _____   □ _____   □ _____
□ _____   □ _____   □ _____   □ _____
□ _____   □ _____   □ _____   □ _____

17 상황에 적절한 말 찾기

다음 상황 설명을 듣고, Danielle이 Jane에게 할 말로 가장 적절한 것을 고르시오.

Danielle: _____

① I couldn't find my cellphone.
② Let's grab lunch on Thursday.
③ The restaurant doesn't open on weekends.
④ I waited 3 hours for you! Why didn't you come to meet me?
⑤ I'll call you back in 30 minutes. I'm in the middle of eating lunch.

W : Danielle and Jane made plans to □ _____ each other □ _____ □ _____ on □ _____. Danielle got to the □ _____ first, so she □ _____ for Jane □ _____ □ _____. However, Jane □ _____ □ _____ □ _____. She didn't even call Danielle to tell her that she wouldn't be coming. Danielle □ _____ very □ _____ □ _____ Jane and decided to □ _____ her. But Jane did not □ _____ her □ _____. The next day, when Danielle sees Jane at school, what would Danielle most likely say to Jane?

Danielle: _____

18 할 일 파악

대화를 듣고, 여자가 대화 직후에 할 일로 가장 적절한 것을 고르시오.

① 옷 사기
② 공항 가기
③ 은행 가기
④ 짐 꾸리기
⑤ 은행에 전화하기

M : Are you □ _____ □ _____ □ _____ going on your □ _____ to Hong Kong?
W : Yes, I am. By this time tomorrow, I'll be □ _____ the □ _____ □ _____!
M : Did you □ _____ □ _____ to see if you □ _____ □ _____?
W : Of course I did! My bags are all □ _____ □ _____ □ _____. I just need to □ _____ to the □ _____.
M : You didn't □ _____ your □ _____, yet?
W : No, I was going to go □ _____ □ _____. Is there a problem?
M : Well, the bank □ _____ □ _____ today because it's a □ _____ □ _____ tomorrow.
W : Oh, my goodness! I □ _____ □ _____! I'd better go now.

✏️ **어휘복습** 잘 안 들리거나 몰라서 체크한 어휘를 써 놓고 복습해 보세요.

□ _____ □ _____ □ _____ □ _____
□ _____ □ _____ □ _____ □ _____
□ _____ □ _____ □ _____ □ _____

19 속담 추론

대화를 듣고, 상황을 가장 잘 표현한 속담을 고르시오.

① Better late than never.
② Too many cooks spoil the broth.
③ The early bird catches the worm.
④ All good things must come to an end.
⑤ Heaven helps those who help themselves.

W : Robert, what did you do over □ _____ □ _____?
M : I □ _____ a few □ _____, went □ _____ in the □ _____, and visited my cousins. What did you do?
W : That's awesome! I □ _____ to the □ _____ with my friends and □ _____ how to □ _____ a □ _____.
M : It seems like you had a great summer! □ _____ □ _____ □ _____ that we start school again tomorrow?
W : No, I can't! It □ _____ □ _____ summer vacation □ _____ □ _____, but it's □ _____ □ _____!
M : I □ _____ □ _____ with you □ _____. I'm □ _____ □ _____ for the □ _____ □ _____ of school.
W : I'm not ready, either. I wish we could turn back time and go on vacation again.
M : I guess we'll just have to look forward to the last day of school.

20 알맞은 응답 찾기

대화를 듣고, 여자의 마지막 말에 대한 남자의 응답으로 가장 적절한 것을 고르시오.

Man : _____

① How long have you been dancing?
② I'll meet you in front of the student hall on Thursday.
③ What's your favorite type of dance? Mine is ballet and jazz.
④ Alright. Can you write my name down on the list? I want to try out.
⑤ There is a dance performance in the student hall on Wednesday.

W : Hello, would you like to □ _____ □ _____ for our school □ _____ □ _____?
M : Hmm… I'm not sure. □ _____ □ _____ □ _____ dance team is it?
W : Well, we do □ _____ □ _____ □ _____ dance, from ballet and jazz to tap dancing and hip-hop! Are you □ _____ □ _____ any of those genres?
M : Yes, I really like hip-hop dance. □ _____ do you □ _____ □ _____?
W : Auditions are this Wednesday and Thursday in the □ _____ □ _____.
M : Okay. □ _____ do I need to □ _____ for the audition?
W : You have to □ _____ □ _____ two □ _____. One of the songs we will decide for you, and the other song is your choice.
M : _____

✏ **어휘복습** 잘 안 들리거나 몰라서 체크한 어휘를 써 놓고 복습해 보세요.

□ _____ □ _____ □ _____ □ _____

□ _____ □ _____ □ _____ □ _____

□ _____ □ _____ □ _____ □ _____

◀))MP3 실전 18

점수 / 20

01 대화를 듣고, 남자가 설명하는 곳을 고르시오.

①   ②   ③

④   ⑤

02 대화를 듣고, 남자가 여자에게 전화한 목적으로 가장 적절한 것을 고르시오.

① 책을 빌리려고
② 노트북을 빌리려고
③ 노트북을 돌려주려고
④ 도서관의 위치를 물어보려고
⑤ 보고서 작성을 도와달라고 부탁하려고

03 다음 그림의 상황에 가장 적절한 대화를 고르시오.

①   ②   ③   ④   ⑤

04 대화를 듣고, 두 사람이 만나게 될 시각을 고르시오.

① 5:00   ② 6:00   ③ 7:00
④ 7:30   ⑤ 8:00

05 대화를 듣고, 여자의 직업으로 가장 적절한 것을 고르시오.

① 축구 감독   ② 축구 선수
③ 옷 가게 직원   ④ 신발 가게 직원
⑤ 신발 디자이너

06 대화를 듣고, 여자의 심정으로 가장 적절한 것을 고르시오.

① relieved   ② angry   ③ scared
④ excited   ⑤ disappointed

07 다음을 듣고, 두 사람의 대화가 <u>어색한</u> 것을 고르시오.

①   ②   ③   ④   ⑤

08 대화를 듣고, 여자가 남자에게 부탁한 일로 가장 적절한 것을 고르시오.

① 같이 공부하기   ② 대신 필기하기
③ 시험문제 알려주기   ④ 병원에 데려다 주기
⑤ 학교까지 태워 주기

09 대화를 듣고, 남자의 마지막 말에 담긴 의도로 가장 적절한 것을 고르시오.

① 조언   ② 요청   ③ 동의
④ 감사   ⑤ 후회

10 대화를 듣고, 여자가 지불해야 할 금액을 고르시오.

① $27   ② $28   ③ $30
④ $54   ⑤ $60

11 대화를 듣고, 두 사람이 대화하고 있는 장소로 가장 적절한 곳을 고르시오.

① department store   ② parking lot
③ car repair shop   ④ travel agency
⑤ used-car market

12 다음을 듣고, 사진전에 관해 언급되지 <u>않은</u> 것을 고르시오.

① 날짜 ② 참여 작가 ③ 위치
④ 입장료 ⑤ 시간

13 다음 표를 보면서 대화를 듣고, 내용과 일치하지 <u>않는</u> 것을 고르시오.

Wright Baseball Stadium

	Section	Fee	
		Adult	Child
①	Section A	$50	$30
②	Section B	$40	$25
③	Section C	$30	$15
④	Section D	$20	$5
⑤	Section E	$10	Free

14 다음을 듣고, 무엇에 관한 설명인지 고르시오.

① 수영 ② 아이스하키
③ 럭비 ④ 스키
⑤ 피겨스케이팅

15 대화를 듣고, 여자가 할 일로 가장 적절한 것을 고르시오.

① 시리얼 먹기 ② 할인쿠폰 받기
③ 쇼핑 목록 적기 ④ 식료품점에 가기
⑤ 시리얼 한 박스 사기

16 대화를 듣고, 두 사람이 영화를 보기로 한 시각을 고르시오.

① 5:00 ② 5:30 ③ 6:30
④ 9:30 ⑤ 10:00

17 다음 상황 설명을 듣고, 아빠가 Sarah에게 할 말로 가장 적절한 것을 고르시오.

Dad: _____

① Call me when you have time.
② I want to change my phone plan.
③ If you don't get a text message from me by 2, give me a call.
④ What have you been doing on your phone? The bill is so expensive!
⑤ How much is the phone plan for 400 texts and 100 minutes of phone calls?

18 대화를 듣고, 두 사람이 대화 직후에 할 일로 가장 적절한 것을 고르시오.

① 격파 연습하기 ② 태권도 등록하기
③ 범죄자 신고하기 ④ 태권도복 고르기
⑤ 태권도 대회 참가하기

19 대화를 듣고, 상황을 가장 잘 표현한 속담을 고르시오.

① All roads lead to Rome.
② A stitch in time saves nine.
③ All that glitters is not gold.
④ When in Rome, do as the Romans do.
⑤ A journey of a thousand miles starts with a single step.

20 대화를 듣고, 남자의 마지막 말에 대한 여자의 응답으로 가장 적절한 것을 고르시오.

Woman: _____

① Can you clean the tables, please?
② Why don't you call the café and ask them what time they open?
③ I'm driving to the café now, but I think I'll be about 5 minutes late.
④ I'm sure you'll be fine. Be a responsible person and work hard.
⑤ Do you see the traffic light in front of Café Rose? Take a left turn there.

다시 듣고, 빈칸에 알맞은 단어를 써 보세요.

◀)) MP3 실전 18-1

01 그림 정보 파악

대화를 듣고, 남자가 설명하는 곳을 고르시오.

① ② ③
④ ⑤

W : Hey, Mark. If you could □ _____ to □ _____ in the world,
□ _____ would you go?

M : Hmm… There are a lot of places I would like to go to, but there is
one □ _____ □ _____ I really want to visit.

W : Oh, and where is that?

M : You should try □ _____ it! I'll give you a hint. It's □ _____
□ _____ □ _____.

W : Are you kidding me? There are probably hundreds of things to see
in Egypt. Can you give me □ _____ □ _____?

M : Okay. It is □ _____ □ _____ a □ _____, and it has a big
□ _____ □ _____ □ _____ □ _____ of it.

W : I think I can guess it right if you give me one last hint.

M : Alright. The purpose of this place was to □ _____ □ _____.
Plus, it is a □ _____ of Egypt.

W : Oh! I think I □ _____ □ _____ where you're talking about.
I would like to go there sometime, too!

✎ 어휘복습 잘 안 들리거나 몰라서 체크한 어휘를 써 놓고 복습해 보세요.

□ _____ □ _____ □ _____ □ _____
□ _____ □ _____ □ _____ □ _____
□ _____ □ _____ □ _____ □ _____

대화를 듣고, 남자가 여자에게 전화한 목적으로 가장 적절한 것을 고르시오.

① 책을 빌리려고
② 노트북을 빌리려고
③ 노트북을 돌려주려고
④ 도서관의 위치를 물어보려고
⑤ 보고서 작성을 도와달라고 부탁하려고

M : Hey, Anna! This is Brad from your Writing one oh one class.

W : Oh, hey Brad! What's up?

M : Well, I have to □ _____ a □ _____ □ _____, but my □ _____ suddenly □ _____ □ _____. I was wondering if I could □ _____ □ _____.

W : Sure, you can. But I □ _____ it □ _____ by tomorrow night. I have to use it for an □ _____ as well.

M : Yeah, that's not a problem. I'll □ _____ □ _____ writing my paper □ _____.

W : Okay then. □ _____ do you want to □ _____ me?

M : I'm in the Central □ _____ right now. Are you □ _____?

W : Actually, yes. Plus, I □ _____ my laptop □ _____ □ _____ so I can give it to you right now.

M : Alright! I'll meet you □ _____ □ _____ □ _____ the □ _____ in a few minutes.

03 그림 상황에 적절한 대화 찾기

다음 그림의 상황에 가장 적절한 대화를 고르시오.

① ② ③ ④ ⑤

① M : Do you want to go □ _____ a □ _____?
　 W : No, I would rather have a □ _____ □ _____.

② M : What did you do □ _____ □ _____ □ _____?
　 W : I □ _____ □ _____ with my family.

③ M : Wow, that's a really □ _____ snowman. I like its black hat.
　 W : Thanks! Your igloo is □ _____, too!

④ M : Look at the □ _____! They're so pretty!
　 W : Wow! They all □ _____ □ _____.

⑤ M : □ _____ □ _____ snowmen did you make?
　 W : I made □ _____ yesterday and □ _____ today.

✎ **어휘복습** 잘 안 들리거나 몰라서 체크한 어휘를 써 놓고 복습해 보세요.

□ _____　　□ _____　　□ _____　　□ _____
□ _____　　□ _____　　□ _____　　□ _____
□ _____　　□ _____　　□ _____　　□ _____

04 숫자 정보 파악

대화를 듣고, 두 사람이 만나게 될 시각을 고르시오.

① 5:00　　② 6:00　　③ 7:00
④ 7:30　　⑤ 8:00

W : Justin, did you □ _____ □ _____ the Rock Festival this Saturday?

M : Yes, of course. Everybody's been talking about it. I'm glad it's going to be at the □ _____ in front of Harrison □ _____. I □ _____ right □ _____ □ _____ it.

W : Oh, really? Well then, do you want to □ _____ □ _____? I can meet you □ _____ □ _____ □ _____ the □ _____ station.

M : I would love to go with you. □ _____ □ _____ do you think you'll □ _____ □ _____ Harrison Station?

W : Well, I'm not sure yet. I can ride the □ _____ P.M., □ _____ P.M., or □ _____ P.M. train, and it will □ _____ me □ _____ □ _____ to get there.

M : Hmm… Then you should □ _____ the □ _____ P.M. □ _____ since the festival □ _____ at □ _____ □ _____ P.M.

W : Okay, that □ _____ □ _____! I'll call you when I get on the six P.M. train.

M : Alright. I'll see you when you get to Harrison Station!

✎ **어휘복습** 잘 안 들리거나 몰라서 체크한 어휘를 써 놓고 복습해 보세요.

□ _____　　□ _____　　□ _____　　□ _____

□ _____　　□ _____　　□ _____　　□ _____

□ _____　　□ _____　　□ _____　　□ _____

대화를 듣고, 여자의 직업으로 가장 적절한
것을 고르시오.

① 축구 감독　　　② 축구 선수
③ 옷 가게 직원　　④ 신발 가게 직원
⑤ 신발 디자이너

W : Good afternoon! Welcome to Bruner's! Are you looking for
    something □ _____ □ _____?
M : Yes, I'm □ _____ □ _____ the model, Starlight Z. Do you have
    it here?
W : Of course, it's □ _____ this □ _____. It must be a □ _____
    □ _____. There have been a lot of people here asking for it.
    Would you like to □ _____ some □ _____?
M : I would like that, thank you. My □ _____ is two seventy.
W : Please wait a minute while I go to the □ _____ □ _____ to get
    it for you. Here you go. How does it □ _____?
M : Hmm… I think it's □ _____ □ _____. That's strange because
    I always wear size two seventy.
W : Actually, this model □ _____ □ _____ □ _____ than
    normal □ _____ □ _____. You may need to try it on in a
    □ _____ size.
M : I see. Then, could you bring me a smaller size?
W : Sure, I can do that. I'll □ _____ □ _____ □ _____.

06 심정 추론

대화를 듣고, 여자의 심정으로 가장 적절한 것을 고르시오.

① relieved   ② angry
③ scared   ④ excited
⑤ disappointed

M : Brittany, you □ _____ so □ _____ . Is something the matter?
W : Today has been such a long day! I had to go to so □ _____ □ _____ and □ _____ a lot of □ _____ □ _____ .
M : Why? □ _____ have you been □ _____ all day?
W : Well, in the □ _____ I had to □ _____ □ _____ some □ _____ at the dry cleaner's. Then, I □ _____ □ _____ some □ _____ at the coffee shop to prepare for a presentation. And now, I just □ _____ □ _____ □ _____ finishing a ten page research paper for my history class.
M : Wow, you did all that □ _____ □ _____ □ _____ ? □ _____ □ _____ you look so tired.
W : Yeah, but I'm so glad that I got everything done. Now I can □ _____ □ _____ and □ _____ some □ _____ .
M : That's a good idea. Will you be □ _____ □ _____ , too?
W : No, thank goodness. I didn't make any plans because I wanted to □ _____ □ _____ and □ _____ .

07 어색한 대화 찾기

다음을 듣고, 두 사람의 대화가 <u>어색한</u> 것을 고르시오.

①   ②   ③   ④   ⑤

① M : When's the last time you □ _____ the □ _____ ?
    W : I cleaned it a few days ago.
② M : Can you □ _____ this □ _____ back on the □ _____ over there?
    W : You have to □ _____ □ _____ this □ _____ to make a library card.
③ M : Excuse me, ma'am. The □ _____ starts □ _____ □ _____ .
    W : Oh, I'm sorry. I didn't see the line.
④ M : □ _____ was this □ _____ □ _____ ?
    W : Hmm… I'm not sure. □ _____ a few years ago.
⑤ M : □ _____ are there so □ _____ □ _____ here?
    W : They're here □ _____ □ _____ the street □ _____ .

✎ **어휘복습** 잘 안 들리거나 몰라서 체크한 어휘를 써 놓고 복습해 보세요.

□ _____   □ _____   □ _____   □ _____
□ _____   □ _____   □ _____   □ _____
□ _____   □ _____   □ _____   □ _____

대화를 듣고, 여자가 남자에게 부탁한 일로
가장 적절한 것을 고르시오.

① 같이 공부하기
② 대신 필기하기
③ 시험문제 알려주기
④ 병원에 데려다 주기
⑤ 학교까지 태워 주기

W : Hey, Kurt. Are you going to □ _____ □ _____ □ _____
tomorrow?

M : Yeah, I'll be here. How about you?

W : I'm going to be □ _____ because I have a □ _____ □ _____.

M : Oh, tomorrow isn't a good day to □ _____ class. Ms. Levine said
that we will be □ _____ important □ _____ that will be
□ _____ □ _____ □ _____.

W : Yes, I know. I'm □ _____ because I'm going to miss □ _____
she will be □ _____ during class.

M : Yeah, I would be worried too □ _____ I □ _____ □ _____.
Is there anything I can do to help?

W : Would you mind □ _____ □ _____ during class for me? I'll
□ _____ a □ _____ and give them back to you.

M : Sure, I can do that. I'll give them to you after school.

W : Thank you so much! You're a □ _____!

✎ **어휘복습** 잘 안 들리거나 몰라서 체크한 어휘를 써 놓고 복습해 보세요.

□ _____   □ _____   □ _____   □ _____

□ _____   □ _____   □ _____   □ _____

□ _____   □ _____   □ _____   □ _____

09 의도 파악

대화를 듣고, 남자의 마지막 말에 담긴 의도
로 가장 적절한 것을 고르시오.

① 조언　　② 요청　　③ 동의
④ 감사　　⑤ 후회

W : Steve, can I ask your □ _____ about something?

M : Yes, of course you can. What's on your □ _____?

W : Well, I □ _____ for a □ _____ at two companies and
□ _____ an □ _____ with both of them. I found out today
that □ _____ □ _____ the companies want me to □ _____
□ _____ them.

M : Wow, that's great! So, what's the □ _____?

W : I □ _____ □ _____ which company to work for! Both have
□ _____ □ _____ and □ _____ things about them.

M : Well, you should □ _____ □ _____ a few things. First, which
one is □ _____ □ _____ your house?

W : One company is an □ _____ □ _____ from my house, and the
second company is □ _____ □ _____ away.

M : Alright. Then which one □ _____ you □ _____?

W : I think both companies are willing to □ _____ me the
□ _____ □ _____.

M : Okay. Then think about which company you'll □ _____
□ _____ for more.

✎ **어휘복습** 잘 안 들리거나 몰라서 체크한 어휘를 써 놓고 복습해 보세요.

□ _____　　□ _____　　□ _____　　□ _____

□ _____　　□ _____　　□ _____　　□ _____

□ _____　　□ _____　　□ _____　　□ _____

10 숫자 정보 파악

대화를 듣고, 여자가 지불해야 할 금액을 고르시오.

① $27　　② $28　　③ $30
④ $54　　⑤ $60

M : Welcome to Seven Flags □ _____ □ _____ ! May I help you?

W : Yes, I would like to □ _____ □ _____ □ _____ □ _____ people. One adult, one senior, and one child. □ _____ □ _____ is the □ _____ □ _____ ?

M : Well, admission is normally □ _____ dollars for □ _____ , □ _____ dollars for □ _____ , and □ _____ dollars for □ _____ . But for this week only, you can get a □ _____ □ _____ □ _____ on admission fees.

W : Wow, that's great! I also have this □ _____ □ _____ off □ _____ . Can I use it today?

M : I'm sorry, but we are □ _____ □ _____ people use other coupons □ _____ we are already □ _____ them a □ _____ .

W : Oh, alright. I guess I'll □ _____ it the □ _____ □ _____ I come.

M : Yes, but □ _____ that you can't use the coupon during this week.

W : Okay. How much is my □ _____ ?

✏ **어휘복습** 잘 안 들리거나 몰라서 체크한 어휘를 써 놓고 복습해 보세요.

□ _____　　□ _____　　□ _____　　□ _____

□ _____　　□ _____　　□ _____　　□ _____

□ _____　　□ _____　　□ _____　　□ _____

11 장소 추론

대화를 듣고, 두 사람이 대화하고 있는 장소로 가장 적절한 곳을 고르시오.

① department store ② parking lot
③ car repair shop ④ travel agency
⑤ used-car market

W : Excuse me, sir. I'm visiting the Elite □ _____ □ _____.
Should I go this way?
M : Hello, ma'am. I'm □ _____ □ _____ if there are any
□ _____ □ _____. Let me check for you. Actually, there is one
spot left, □ _____ I □ _____ □ _____ your car will be able
to □ _____ because the □ _____ is very □ _____.
W : Hmm… Okay. Are there any other parking lots □ _____
□ _____ □ _____?
M : Yes, □ _____ □ _____ on Bridget Lane and one on Georgetown
Street. But the one on Bridget Lane is pretty □ _____ □ _____
the department store, so you'll have to □ _____ □ _____
□ _____ □ _____.
W : Alright. So do you □ _____ that I park on Georgetown Street?
M : Yes. That one is only a □ _____ □ _____ □ _____ from the
department store.
W : Oh, that's great! I guess I'll park there, then. Thanks for your help!
M : No problem. Have a great day!

12 미언급 파악

다음을 듣고, 사진전에 관해 언급되지 않은 것을 고르시오.

① 날짜 ② 참여 작가 ③ 위치
④ 입장료 ⑤ 시간

M : Are you interested in □ _____ □ _____? Would you like to see
the works of famous □ _____? Then Flash Gallery is the perfect
place for you! □ _____ on □ _____ □ _____, our gallery
will be opening an exhibit of Jane Truman and Michael Stewart's
photos! As you may already know, both of these □ _____ are
known for □ _____ beautiful □ _____ □ _____. There is
□ _____ □ _____ □ _____, and you may come any time
□ _____ □ _____ A.M. and □ _____ P.M. Please hurry and
□ _____ □ _____ □ _____ this great opportunity! The
exhibit will only be open □ _____ May □ _____ □ _____.

✎ **어휘복습** 잘 안 들리거나 몰라서 체크한 어휘를 써 놓고 복습해 보세요.

□ _____ □ _____ □ _____ □ _____
□ _____ □ _____ □ _____ □ _____
□ _____ □ _____ □ _____ □ _____

13 도표·실용문 파악

다음 표를 보면서 대화를 듣고, 내용과 일치하지 <u>않는</u> 것을 고르시오.

Wright Baseball Stadium

	Section	Fee	
		Adult	Child
①	Section A	$50	$30
②	Section B	$40	$25
③	Section C	$30	$15
④	Section D	$20	$5
⑤	Section E	$10	Free

W : Good evening, sir. Would you like to □ _____ □ _____ for tonight's game?

M : Yes, I would like to buy some for myself and my son. □ _____ □ _____ are □ _____ in Sections B and C?

W : The seats in □ _____ B are □ _____ dollars for □ _____ and twenty-five dollars for □ _____, and those in Section C cost □ _____ dollars □ _____ □ _____ Section B for both adults and children.

M : Hmm… Okay. What's the □ _____ □ _____ Sections A and E?

W : Well, Section A is the area □ _____ to the □ _____ □ _____, and it is fifty dollars for adults and thirty dollars for children. Section E is the area □ _____ from the field, and it is □ _____ dollars for adults and □ _____ dollars for children.

M : Oh, alright. □ _____ section would you □ _____?

W : I think you should sit in D.

M : Why do you say that?

W : Well, Sections C and D are the □ _____ □ _____ □ _____ the field. But Section D costs ten dollars less than Section C. Plus, you might be able to □ _____ a □ _____ □ _____ in Section D.

M : My son would love that! I'll get two tickets for Section D, please.

✏ **어휘복습** 잘 안 들리거나 몰라서 체크한 어휘를 써 놓고 복습해 보세요.

□ _____   □ _____   □ _____   □ _____

□ _____   □ _____   □ _____   □ _____

□ _____   □ _____   □ _____   □ _____

14 화제 추론

다음을 듣고, 무엇에 관한 설명인지 고르시오.

① 수영 ② 아이스하키 ③ 럭비
④ 스키 ⑤ 피겨스케이팅

M : This is a type of sport that is played □ _____ □ _____. You have to □ _____ □ _____ □ _____ in order to play. Players are mostly men, and they tend to be □ _____ and □ _____ each other. They □ _____ big, □ _____ □ _____ and □ _____ so they don't get hurt. You play the game by □ _____ and □ _____ a black puck with a □ _____ □ _____. The team that hits the puck past the □ _____ □ _____ and □ _____ the □ _____ gets a point.

15 할 일 파악

대화를 듣고, 여자가 할 일로 가장 적절한 것을 고르시오.

① 시리얼 먹기
② 할인쿠폰 받기
③ 쇼핑 목록 적기
④ 식료품점에 가기
⑤ 시리얼 한 박스 사기

W : Greg! Look at all those □ _____ □ _____! Why did you buy so much?

M : There is a □ _____ □ _____ □ _____ at Horizon Foods right now! I went to buy a box of cereal, and □ _____ □ _____ □ _____ all of this.

W : What? I didn't know that there was a sale! What did you buy?

M : Well, everything in the store is □ _____ □ _____ □ _____, so I basically □ _____ everything I could find.

W : Everything in the store is thirty percent off? That's a □ _____ □ _____! There must be □ _____ □ _____ on the shelves by now.

M : Actually, the sale started □ _____ □ _____ □ _____ □ _____. If you go now, there'll probably be a lot of □ _____ left.

W : Hmm… Then I should □ _____ □ _____ there now. I needed to □ _____ grocery □ _____ anyway. Thanks for letting me know!

M : Don't mention it.

✎ **어휘복습** 잘 안 들리거나 몰라서 체크한 어휘를 써 놓고 복습해 보세요.

□ _____ □ _____ □ _____ □ _____

□ _____ □ _____ □ _____ □ _____

□ _____ □ _____ □ _____ □ _____

16 숫자 정보 파악

대화를 듣고, 두 사람이 영화를 보기로 한 시각을 고르시오.

① 5:00　　② 5:30　　③ 6:30
④ 9:30　　⑤ 10:00

W : Hi, Ted. Are you □ _____ tomorrow □ _____ □ _____ ?
M : No, I don't have □ _____ □ _____ . Why do you ask?
W : Well, I have □ _____ □ _____ for *True Mystery*, but I can't find anyone to □ _____ □ _____ . Would you be □ _____ ?
M : How did you know I wanted to watch that? I'd love to go with you!
W : I'm so glad to hear that! We can use the tickets for □ _____ of the □ _____ □ _____ , so you can □ _____ □ _____ . There are showings at five P.M., six thirty P.M., and ten P.M.
M : Hmm… Would you mind going to the □ _____ □ _____ ?
W : Actually, my parents told me to □ _____ □ _____ □ _____ nine thirty, so I think we should watch the movie at □ _____ □ _____ □ _____ □ _____ .
M : Hmm… Okay then. □ _____ watch the □ _____ showing of the movie.

17 상황에 적절한 말 찾기

다음 상황 설명을 듣고, 아빠가 Sarah에게 할 말로 가장 적절한 것을 고르시오.

Dad : _____

① Call me when you have time.
② I want to change my phone plan.
③ If you don't get a text message from me by 2, give me a call.
④ What have you been doing on your phone? The bill is so expensive!
⑤ How much is the phone plan for 400 texts and 100 minutes of phone calls?

W : Sarah likes □ _____ to her friends □ _____ □ _____ □ _____ . Ever since school started, she has been using her phone □ _____ □ _____ □ _____ . Her □ _____ □ _____ includes four hundred □ _____ □ _____ and one hundred minutes of phone □ _____ , but she sent over one thousand text messages and talked on the phone for three hundred minutes. When the phone □ _____ came in the mail, her □ _____ was □ _____ because the □ _____ was two hundred dollars. He couldn't □ _____ □ _____ the bill came out to be so much. So he decided to talk to Sarah about it and ask her □ _____ she's been using her phone □ _____ . In this situation, what would Sarah's Dad most likely say to Sarah?
Dad : _____

✎ **어휘복습** 잘 안 들리거나 몰라서 체크한 어휘를 써 놓고 복습해 보세요.

□ _____　　□ _____　　□ _____　　□ _____

□ _____　　□ _____　　□ _____　　□ _____

□ _____　　□ _____　　□ _____　　□ _____

18 할 일 파악

대화를 듣고, 두 사람이 대화 직후에 할 일로
가장 적절한 것을 고르시오.

① 격파 연습하기
② 태권도 등록하기
③ 범죄자 신고하기
④ 태권도복 고르기
⑤ 태권도 대회 참가하기

W : Ricky, I think I'm going to □ _____ □ _____ Taekwondo.
What do you think?

M : □ _____ all of a sudden? You were □ _____ □ _____
□ _____ that sport before.

W : Well, there are a lot of □ _____ going on □ _____. I just want
to □ _____ how to □ _____ □ _____.

M : That's actually a really good idea. Maybe I should learn □ _____
□ _____. It □ _____ □ _____ □ _____.

W : Yes, you □ _____ □ _____! We'll learn how to punch, kick,
and break wooden boards! Doesn't that sound exciting?

M : □ _____ □ _____ you mention it, I'm looking forward to it
more and more. Once we □ _____ the □ _____, we'll be able
to protect ourselves □ _____ □ _____.

W : Yeah, you're right. Thanks for offering to go with me. I □ _____
your □ _____.

M : It's no problem. Let's go □ _____ □ _____ □ _____ our
first class.

✎ **어휘복습** 잘 안 들리거나 몰라서 체크한 어휘를 써 놓고 복습해 보세요.

□ _____ □ _____ □ _____ □ _____
□ _____ □ _____ □ _____ □ _____
□ _____ □ _____ □ _____ □ _____

19 속담 추론

대화를 듣고, 상황을 가장 잘 표현한 속담을 고르시오.

① All roads lead to Rome.
② A stitch in time saves nine.
③ All that glitters is not gold.
④ When in Rome, do as the Romans do.
⑤ A journey of a thousand miles starts with a single step.

W : Jason, have you □ _____ □ _____ □ _____ living in Korea, yet?
M : No, not yet. Korea's □ _____ is so □ _____ □ _____ the culture in the United States.
W : Really? Can you □ _____ □ _____ an □ _____?
M : Well, I saw someone from my class and I wanted to □ _____ □ _____, so I □ _____ my □ _____ at her. But □ _____ □ _____ waving back, she □ _____ her □ _____ at me.
W : Oh, okay. In Korea, you bow heads to each other until you □ _____ □ _____. Once you become friends, then you wave to each other.
M : I see. It's so □ _____ □ _____ me because the culture is so □ _____.
W : I understand. But □ _____ you live here now, you have to get used to it.
M : Yeah, you're right.

20 알맞은 응답 찾기

대화를 듣고, 남자의 마지막 말에 대한 여자의 응답으로 가장 적절한 것을 고르시오.

Woman : _____

① Can you clean the tables, please?
② Why don't you call the café and ask them what time they open?
③ I'm driving to the café now, but I think I'll be about 5 minutes late.
④ I'm sure you'll be fine. Be a responsible person and work hard.
⑤ Do you see the traffic light in front of Café Rose? Take a left turn there.

M : Hey, Mom. I'm going to □ _____ □ _____ at Café Rose □ _____ □ _____.
W : Oh, really? I hope you know it's going to be □ _____ □ _____ □ _____ □ _____. I know because I used to work at a café too when I was your age.
M : □ _____ is □ _____ □ _____ about it? Don't you just ask people what they want to order and give them their drinks?
W : No, it's □ _____ □ _____ □ _____. You have to do other work too, like □ _____ the □ _____, □ _____ □ _____, and □ _____ □ _____ the □ _____. You also have to learn how to □ _____ □ _____.
M : Wow, I □ _____ □ _____ □ _____ I had to do all of that! Maybe I should □ _____ about this □ _____.
W : Well, didn't you already tell the café that you would start working tomorrow?
M : Yes, I did. But I don't know if I can □ _____ it.
W : _____

✎ **어휘복습** 잘 안 들리거나 몰라서 체크한 어휘를 써 놓고 복습해 보세요.

□ _____   □ _____   □ _____   □ _____

□ _____   □ _____   □ _____   □ _____

□ _____   □ _____   □ _____   □ _____

◀》 MP3 실전 19

점수 / 20

01 대화를 듣고, 여자가 구매할 모자를 고르시오.

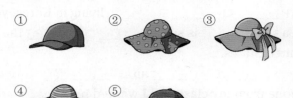

① ② ③
④ ⑤

02 대화를 듣고, 여자가 남자에게 전화한 목적으로 가장 적절한 것을 고르시오.

① 약속을 취소하려고
② 약속 장소를 변경하려고
③ 약속 시간을 변경하려고
④ 병원 진료일을 변경하려고
⑤ 병원 앞에서 만나자고 말하려고

03 다음 그림의 상황에 가장 적절한 대화를 고르시오.

① ② ③ ④ ⑤

04 대화를 듣고, 두 사람이 학회에 도착할 방법을 고르시오.

① car → on foot
② subway → bus
③ subway → on foot
④ subway → bus → on foot
⑤ bus → subway → on foot

05 대화를 듣고, 두 사람의 관계로 가장 적절한 것을 고르시오.

① 요리사 – 손님
② 선장 – 낚시꾼
③ 카페 주인 – 직원
④ 방송 프로듀서 – 진행자
⑤ 수산물 판매자 – 식당 직원

06 대화를 듣고, 남자의 심정으로 가장 적절한 것을 고르시오.

① angry   ② scared
③ curious   ④ jealous
⑤ relieved

07 다음을 듣고, 두 사람의 대화가 어색한 것을 고르시오.

①   ②   ③   ④   ⑤

08 대화를 듣고, 여자가 남자에게 부탁한 일로 가장 적절한 것을 고르시오.

① 약 사오기   ② 휴지 가져오기
③ 체온계 빌려주기   ④ 병원에 데려다 주기
⑤ 알레르기 예방법 검색하기

09 대화를 듣고, 남자의 마지막 말에 담긴 의도로 가장 적절한 것을 고르시오.

① compliment   ② gratitude
③ suggestion   ④ denial
⑤ request

10 대화를 듣고, 여자가 지불할 금액을 고르시오.

① $5   ② $10   ③ $15
④ $20   ⑤ $25

11 대화를 듣고, 두 사람이 대화하고 있는 장소로 가장 적절한 곳을 고르시오.

① parking lot　　　　② bank
③ subway station　　④ airport
⑤ electronics store

12 다음을 듣고, 언급되지 <u>않은</u> 것을 고르시오.

① 아파트의 이름　　② 아파트의 위치
③ 수리 시작 일자　　④ 수리 마감 일자
⑤ 관리실 연락처

13 표를 보면서 다음을 듣고, 내용과 일치하지 <u>않는</u> 것을 고르시오.

What Do You Need to Bake a Cake?

	Ingredients	Amount
①	Water	1 cup
②	Flour	1/2 cup
③	Sugar	3 tablespoons
④	Eggs	2 eggs
⑤	Butter	2 tablespoons

14 다음을 듣고, 무엇에 관한 설명인지 고르시오.

① viking　　　　　② roller coaster
③ bumper cars　　④ haunted house
⑤ merry-go-round

15 대화를 듣고, 여자가 대화 직후에 할 일로 가장 적절한 것을 고르시오.

① 외투 사기　　　② 불꽃놀이 하기
③ 호수 구경하기　④ 재킷 찾아보기
⑤ 일기예보 확인하기

16 대화를 듣고, 여자의 생일을 고르시오.

① January 4　　　② February 14
③ December 15　④ December 24
⑤ December 25

17 다음 상황 설명을 듣고, 상담교사가 Martha에게 할 말로 가장 적절한 것을 고르시오.

Counselor: _____

① Can we reschedule our meeting?
② I'll make sure I go to your graduation.
③ How many school clubs have you participated in?
④ 100 hours of volunteer service are required to apply to any college.
⑤ I think you should check out the different colleges online before deciding.

18 대화를 듣고, 남자가 할 일로 가장 적절한 것을 고르시오.

① 성금 모으기　　② 팔찌 만들기
③ 팔찌 주문하기　④ 아프리카에 성금 보내기
⑤ 친구들에게 이메일 보내기

19 대화를 듣고, 상황을 가장 잘 표현한 속담을 고르시오.

① Better late than never.
② No smoke without fire.
③ Many hands make light work.
④ Make hay while the sun shines.
⑤ Actions speak louder than words.

20 대화를 듣고, 남자의 마지막 말에 대한 여자의 응답으로 가장 적절한 것을 고르시오.

Woman: _____

① I'll meet you at the bus company.
② Thanks for coming with me to get my new phone.
③ I can never thank you enough for finding my phone for me.
④ Why didn't you tell me that you changed your phone number?
⑤ Okay! I'll call you as soon as I get it. Sorry for worrying you yesterday.

다시 듣고, 빈칸에 알맞은 단어를 써 보세요.

🔊 MP3 실전 19-1

01 그림 정보 파악

대화를 듣고, 여자가 구매할 모자를 고르시오.

① ② ③
④ ⑤

M : Good morning, ma'am. Can I help you find something?

W : Yes, please. I'm □ _____ □ _____ □ _____, and I need to □ _____ a □ _____ to wear. Do you have any □ _____?

M : I would recommend this □ _____ hat. It's □ _____ and you can wear it □ _____ □ _____.

W : Well, I already □ _____ a lot of baseball hats. Plus, I would like a hat with a □ _____ □ _____ to □ _____ my □ _____ from the □ _____.

M : Okay, how about this hat □ _____ □ _____ on it? Or this one with □ _____ on it? Both of them have wide brims.

W : I think both are great! But I think this hat with the □ _____ □ _____ is □ _____. It has a wide brim, too.

M : Yes, this hat is very □ _____ among women □ _____ the □ _____ □ _____. Would you like to □ _____ this one?

W : Yes please, that would be great. Thank you!

✏️ **어휘복습** 잘 안 들리거나 몰라서 체크한 어휘를 써 놓고 복습해 보세요.

□ _____ □ _____ □ _____ □ _____

□ _____ □ _____ □ _____ □ _____

□ _____ □ _____ □ _____ □ _____

02 목적 파악

대화를 듣고, 여자가 남자에게 전화한 목적으로 가장 적절한 것을 고르시오.

① 약속을 취소하려고
② 약속 장소를 변경하려고
③ 약속 시간을 변경하려고
④ 병원 진료일을 변경하려고
⑤ 병원 앞에서 만나자고 말하려고

M : Hello, this is Steven.

W : Hey, Steven, It's me, Sarah. I'm calling to ask you if we can
□ _____ our □ _____ □ _____ from four P.M. to five P.M.
I'm so □ _____ □ _____ the sudden □ _____.

M : Hmm… Moving the time isn't a problem, but may I □ _____
□ _____?

W : I'm at the □ _____ □ _____, and my □ _____ was at three,
but there are still a lot of □ _____ □ _____ □ _____ in
front of me. I think they're □ _____ □ _____.

M : Oh, alright. Are we still meeting at Garden Grove? □ _____
□ _____ □ _____, I can meet you closer to the doctor's office.

W : Thanks for the offer, but I can't ask you to do that. Let's just meet
at Garden Grove. I'll get there □ _____ □ _____ □ _____
I can.

M : Okay, then. Can you □ _____ me □ _____ □ _____ when
you leave the doctor's office?

W : Yes, of course I can. I'll □ _____ □ _____ □ _____! Thanks
for understanding.

✎ **어휘복습** 잘 안 들리거나 몰라서 체크한 어휘를 써 놓고 복습해 보세요.

□ _____ □ _____ □ _____ □ _____

□ _____ □ _____ □ _____ □ _____

□ _____ □ _____ □ _____ □ _____

03 그림 상황에 적절한 대화 찾기

다음 그림의 상황에 가장 적절한 대화를 고르시오.

① ② ③ ④ ⑤

① W : I'm □ _____ □ _____ □ _____ my □ _____ from washing these dishes.

M : Here, let me help you □ _____ this □ _____ □ _____.

② W : □ _____ did you □ _____ the clean plates and cups?

M : The □ _____ are in the □ _____ □ _____ and the □ _____ are in the □ _____ cabinet.

③ M : □ _____ □ _____ □ _____ □ _____ the dress I got you?

W : It's beautiful! I'm going to wear it every day.

④ W : Can you □ _____ □ _____ □ _____ these plates? They're too high up.

M : Sure, □ _____ □ _____ □ _____ do you need?

⑤ W : I'm □ _____ □ _____ to cook today. Let's □ _____ □ _____ for □ _____.

M : Okay, that's fine with me. What do you want to eat?

✎ **어휘복습** 잘 안 들리거나 몰라서 체크한 어휘를 써 놓고 복습해 보세요.

□ _____   □ _____   □ _____   □ _____
□ _____   □ _____   □ _____   □ _____
□ _____   □ _____   □ _____   □ _____

대화를 듣고, 두 사람이 학회에 도착할 방법을 고르시오.

① car → on foot
② subway → bus
③ subway → on foot
④ subway → bus → on foot
⑤ bus → subway → on foot

M : Janice, are you □ _____ □ _____ the □ _____ on Sunday?

W : Yes, I am. But it's really □ _____ □ _____ my □ _____.
I need to □ _____ □ _____ the □ _____ □ _____ to get there.

M : I see. We live near each other, so I can help you find the □ _____ □ _____.

W : Okay! I wonder if we can □ _____ there. You have a car, right?

M : Yeah, I do. But there's □ _____ going to be a lot of □ _____ during that time. Let's □ _____ the subway □ _____.

W : Alright. If we □ _____ the six P.M. □ _____, we can get to Newbury Station in one hour. Do you know □ _____ □ _____ Newbury Station is □ _____ the conference center?

M : I think it's a □ _____ □ _____ □ _____ from the station.

W : So it'll probably take us a little over an hour. I think that's the fastest way to get to the conference.

M : Yeah, I agree.

✎ **어휘복습** 잘 안 들리거나 몰라서 체크한 어휘를 써 놓고 복습해 보세요.

□ _____ □ _____ □ _____ □ _____

□ _____ □ _____ □ _____ □ _____

□ _____ □ _____ □ _____ □ _____

05 관계 추론

대화를 듣고, 두 사람의 관계로 가장 적절한
것을 고르시오.

① 요리사 – 손님
② 선장 – 낚시꾼
③ 카페 주인 – 직원
④ 방송 프로듀서 – 진행자
⑤ 수산물 판매자 – 식당 직원

M : Good afternoon, ma'am. How may I help you today?

W : Yes, hello. I □ _____ □ _____ □ _____ some shrimp, tuna, squid, and salmon.

M : Alright. The tuna and salmon are in the □ _____ □ _____ □ _____ □ _____. The shrimp are □ _____ □ _____ in these □ _____ □ _____, and the squid are in the tank to your □ _____.

W : I see. I would like a box of shrimp, fifteen of both the tuna and salmon, and five squid.

M : Okay! Are you cooking for a lot of people today? I'm asking because people □ _____ don't buy so much □ _____ □ _____ □ _____ □ _____.

W : Actually, I work at the □ _____ down the street. Our customers have been □ _____ □ _____ our special □ _____ menu, so we decided to make it a □ _____ □ _____.

M : Oh, that's great! I'll □ _____ everything □ _____ □ _____ you now.

W : Thank you! I'll be back next week for more.

✎ **어휘복습** 잘 안 들리거나 몰라서 체크한 어휘를 써 놓고 복습해 보세요.

□ _____   □ _____   □ _____   □ _____

□ _____   □ _____   □ _____   □ _____

□ _____   □ _____   □ _____   □ _____

06 심정 추론

대화를 듣고, 남자의 심정으로 가장 적절한 것을 고르시오.

① angry
② scared
③ curious
④ jealous
⑤ relieved

M : Mom, what is that animal □ _____ □ _____ □ _____ from the □ _____?

W : Tommy, that animal is called a bat. It hangs upside down when it's sleeping.

M : Oh, that's so cool! Why does it hang upside down? What does a bat eat? And why do bats live in dark places? I □ _____ □ _____ □ _____ □ _____!

W : Wow, there's so much that you □ _____ □ _____ □ _____! Well, I □ _____ □ _____ □ _____ they hang upside down or why they live in dark places. But I know that they eat sweet fruit like apples and oranges.

M : I see. Can we go □ _____ the □ _____ □ _____ some questions? I want to know more about bats.

W : Yeah, we can do that. Are there any □ _____ □ _____ that you're □ _____ □ _____?

M : I want to know about all of them, the polar bears, the giraffes, the alligators, and the elephants!

W : Okay then, let's go □ _____ and □ _____ □ _____ all those animals.

✎ **어휘복습** 잘 안 들리거나 몰라서 체크한 어휘를 써 놓고 복습해 보세요.

□ _____   □ _____   □ _____   □ _____

□ _____   □ _____   □ _____   □ _____

□ _____   □ _____   □ _____   □ _____

07 어색한 대화 찾기

다음을 듣고, 두 사람의 대화가 어색한 것을 고르시오.

①   ②   ③   ④   ⑤

① W : Dad, □ _____ the new bottle of □ _____ we just bought?

   M : I already □ _____ it □ _____ the □ _____ for you.

② W : Can you tell me □ _____ □ _____ jars are in the

          □ _____ □ _____ ?

   M : The jars are all □ _____ □ _____ and □ _____.

③ W : What are you doing on Monday night?

   M : I don't have plans yet, but I want to □ _____ □ _____.

④ W : Are you sure you □ _____ the □ _____ □ _____ ?

   M : Yes, I'm □ _____. I □ _____ □ _____, so don't worry.

⑤ W : Are you □ _____ □ _____ the □ _____ game next Friday?

   M : No, I'm □ _____ some □ _____ □ _____ my family

      that day.

08 부탁 파악

대화를 듣고, 여자가 남자에게 부탁한 일로 가장 적절한 것을 고르시오.

① 약 사오기
② 휴지 가져오기
③ 체온계 빌려주기
④ 병원에 데려다 주기
⑤ 알레르기 예방법 검색하기

M : Molly, what's wrong? You □ _____ so □ _____.

W : I feel terrible! Every time the □ _____ □ _____, I □ _____

   these □ _____. It's □ _____ me □ _____.

M : Oh, no! What happens when you get allergies? Do you get a

   □ _____ or a □ _____ □ _____ ?

W : I don't get a fever. My □ _____ □ _____ and then it gets really

   stuffy. Plus, my □ _____ □ _____ □ _____ and □ _____,

   too. I hate allergies so much!

M : Is there anything I can do to help you? Maybe you should

   □ _____ □ _____ the □ _____.

W : Well, I've been to the hospital many times, but it doesn't really

   help. I'd □ _____ just □ _____ □ _____ from the

   □ _____. Would you mind getting me some?

M : Okay, I'll go to the pharmacy right now. □ _____ □ _____ and

   □ _____ until I get back.

W : Thanks a lot. I □ _____ it.

✎ **어휘복습** 잘 안 들리거나 몰라서 체크한 어휘를 써 놓고 복습해 보세요.

□ _____   □ _____   □ _____   □ _____

□ _____   □ _____   □ _____   □ _____

□ _____   □ _____   □ _____   □ _____

대화를 듣고, 남자의 마지막 말에 담긴 의도
로 가장 적절한 것을 고르시오.

① compliment   ② gratitude
③ suggestion   ④ denial
⑤ request

M : Hey, Sophia. You □ _____ □ _____. What's the matter?

W : It's my grandmother's eightieth □ _____ on the weekend

    □ _____ our □ _____ □ _____ week. All of my □ _____

    are going to be there, and we will be □ _____ the □ _____

    □ _____ together.

M : Okay, what seems to be the problem?

W : If I go to her birthday □ _____, I won't have □ _____

    □ _____ to prepare □ _____ my □ _____. If I don't go,

    I feel like my □ _____ would be □ _____.

M : Hmm… That does sound like a □ _____ □ _____ to

    □ _____. Did you □ _____ □ _____ your parents and

    grandmother □ _____ the □ _____?

W : I told my parents, and they think I should go since it's a big

    □ _____ □ _____. I □ _____ □ _____ to my grandmother

    about it □ _____.

M : Well then, I think you should call your grandmother and

    □ _____ your □ _____. Maybe you can visit her after final

    exams. I think she'll □ _____ even if you can't be there.

10 숫자 정보 파악

대화를 듣고, 여자가 지불할 금액을 고르시오.

① $5   ② $10   ③ $15
④ $20   ⑤ $25

M : Hello, ma'am. Welcome to Sunnyside □ _____. What can I do for you today?

W : I would like to □ _____ □ _____ for myself and my two children.

M : Okay. □ _____ □ _____ are your children? The □ _____ □ _____ may □ _____ depending on their □ _____.

W : My □ _____ is □ _____ years old and my □ _____ is □ _____ years old. □ _____ □ _____ would the admission fee be?

M : Admission is □ _____ for children □ _____ the □ _____ of □ _____, and the fee for children □ _____ the ages of five and □ _____ is five dollars. Anyone over twelve, □ _____ □ _____, must pay □ _____ dollars to □ _____.

W : Oh, alright. Can I use this □ _____ entrance □ _____ for my daughter's admission?

M : Yes, you can. Is there anything else I can do for you?

W : No, □ _____ □ _____ □ _____ □ _____. Thank you. How much do I owe you?

✎ **어휘복습** 잘 안 들리거나 몰라서 체크한 어휘를 써 놓고 복습해 보세요.

□ _____   □ _____   □ _____   □ _____
□ _____   □ _____   □ _____   □ _____
□ _____   □ _____   □ _____   □ _____

11 장소 추론

대화를 듣고, 두 사람이 대화하고 있는 장소로 가장 적절한 곳을 고르시오.

① parking lot   ② bank
③ subway station   ④ airport
⑤ electronics store

M : Excuse me, ma'am. Is there anything I can help you with?

W : Actually, yes. I need to □ _____ more □ _____ □ _____ my □ _____ □ _____, but I don't know how. Could you □ _____ me □ _____ □ _____?

M : Absolutely! Do you see those □ _____ over there □ _____ □ _____ □ _____? Those are the subway card □ _____ □ _____.

W : Oh, I see. How do I use it?

M : First, □ _____ your subway card □ _____ the □ _____. Then, □ _____ the □ _____ of □ _____ you want to put in the card. Once you do that, □ _____ the dollar □ _____ □ _____ the machine. Wait a few seconds until the card finishes charging, and then you can take your card and go.

W : Alright! I thought it would be a lot harder than that. Oh, one more thing. Can I use a twenty-dollar bill with the machines?

M : No, □ _____ □ _____ □ _____. The machine only takes one-dollar, five-dollar, and ten-dollar bills.

W : Okay. Thank you so much for all of your help!

✎ **어휘복습** 잘 안 들리거나 몰라서 체크한 어휘를 써 놓고 복습해 보세요.

□ _____   □ _____   □ _____   □ _____

□ _____   □ _____   □ _____   □ _____

□ _____   □ _____   □ _____   □ _____

12 미연급 파악

다음을 듣고, 언급되지 <u>않은</u> 것을 고르시오.

① 아파트의 이름
② 아파트의 위치
③ 수리 시작 일자
④ 수리 마감 일자
⑤ 관리실 연락처

W : All residents of Spring View Apartments, we would like to
□ _____ □ _____ important □ _____. There have been
some □ _____ □ _____ our apartment □ _____, and they
need to be □ _____. The □ _____ work will □ _____ on
□ _____ □ _____ at □ _____ A.M. and □ _____ on April
□ _____ around □ _____ P.M. Please remember that during
this time, the elevators will not be □ _____. Please □ _____
the □ _____ until the elevators are ready to be used. We
□ _____ □ _____ the □ _____. If you have any further
questions, please □ _____ our □ _____ at four three two, two
one nine three.

13 도표·실용문 파악

표를 보면서 다음을 듣고, 내용과 일치하지
<u>않은</u> 것을 고르시오.

What Do You Need to Bake a Cake?

	Ingredients	Amount
①	Water	1 cup
②	Flour	1/2 cup
③	Sugar	3 tablespoons
④	Eggs	2 eggs
⑤	Butter	2 tablespoons

W : Welcome to Anne's □ _____ □ _____! Before we get started
on □ _____ the □ _____, we will □ _____ the □ _____.
Take a □ _____ and □ _____ it completely □ _____
□ _____. Now, □ _____ some □ _____ into another cup,
but only fill it □ _____. Next, you will need □ _____
□ _____ of □ _____. After that, take out □ _____
□ _____ from the refrigerator and □ _____ them □ _____.
Lastly, you will need to prepare two tablespoons of □ _____.
Once you have □ _____ all of the ingredients □ _____, we
will be able to start baking the cake!

✎ **어휘복습** 잘 안 들리거나 몰라서 체크한 어휘를 써 놓고 복습해 보세요.

□ _____ □ _____ □ _____ □ _____

□ _____ □ _____ □ _____ □ _____

□ _____ □ _____ □ _____ □ _____

14 화제 추론

다음을 듣고, 무엇에 관한 설명인지 고르시오.

① viking   ② roller coaster
③ bumper cars   ④ haunted house
⑤ merry-go-round

M : This can be found in an □ _____ □ _____. To □ _____ this, you have to be a certain height. Once you □ _____ □ _____ a □ _____, a □ _____ □ _____ is lowered to protect you from getting hurt. At the beginning, you are taken up a □ _____ □ _____, and then all of a sudden, it □ _____ □ _____ the hill at a □ _____ □ _____ □ _____. There are many of these hills, and sometimes there are even □ _____, where you go □ _____ □ _____ and □ _____. Some people enjoy riding this, and some people are afraid of riding it.

15 할 일 파악

대화를 듣고, 여자가 대화 직후에 할 일로 가장 적절한 것을 고르시오.

① 외투 사기
② 불꽃놀이 하기
③ 호수 구경하기
④ 재킷 찾아보기
⑤ 일기예보 확인하기

M : The □ _____ is so □ _____ lately. Don't you think so?
W : Yeah, you're right. I can't tell if it's still □ _____ or if it's □ _____. The □ _____ □ _____ so much during the day.
M : You can say that again. When I leave the house in the □ _____, it is super □ _____, and □ _____ the □ _____ it's really □ _____. But then at □ _____, it □ _____ □ _____ again!
W : I know what you mean. I don't know □ _____ □ _____ □ _____ nowadays. Oh, by the way, are you going to the □ _____ □ _____ this weekend?
M : Yes, I'm planning on going. How about you?
W : I'll be there, too. The festival is □ _____ the □ _____, so it'll □ _____ be even □ _____ at night, right?
M : I think so. You have to be □ _____ not to □ _____ a □ _____ during times like this. You should □ _____ □ _____ □ _____ and □ _____ a □ _____ just in case it gets cold.
W : That's a good idea. I'll □ _____ □ _____ a jacket when I get home. I'll see you this weekend then!
M : Alright, see you!

✎ **어휘복습** 잘 안 들리거나 몰라서 체크한 어휘를 써 놓고 복습해 보세요.

□ _____   □ _____   □ _____   □ _____
□ _____   □ _____   □ _____   □ _____
□ _____   □ _____   □ _____   □ _____

16 특정 정보 파악

대화를 듣고, 여자의 생일을 고르시오.

① January 4　　　② February 14
③ December 15　　④ December 24
⑤ December 25

M : Julie, □ _____ is your □ _____? I'm writing all my friends' birthdays in my □ _____.

W : Try to □ _____ it! □ _____ do you think I □ _____ □ _____?

M : Hmm… Were you born during the □ _____, □ _____, □ _____, or □ _____?

W : I was born □ _____ the winter. It normally □ _____ □ _____ □ _____ on my birthday.

M : So, □ _____ □ _____ your birthday is in December, January, or February, right? □ _____ me some □ _____ □ _____!

W : Well, an important □ _____ is in the □ _____ □ _____ as my birthday. People □ _____ it with their friends and family, □ _____ □ _____ to each other, and □ _____ a □ _____.

M : Oh, okay! □ _____ □ _____ □ _____ before or after this holiday is your birthday?

W : My birthday is □ _____ □ _____ □ _____ this holiday. Do you know when my birthday is now?

17 상황에 적절한 말 찾기

다음 상황 설명을 듣고, 상담교사가 Martha 에게 할 말로 가장 적절한 것을 고르시오.

Counselor: _____

① Can we reschedule our meeting?
② I'll make sure I go to your graduation.
③ How many school clubs have you participated in?
④ 100 hours of volunteer service are required to apply to any college.
⑤ I think you should check out the different colleges online before deciding.

W : Martha wants to go talk to her □ _____ □ _____ about □ _____ □ _____. She has a □ _____ □ _____ □ _____ that she's □ _____ in, but she can't decide □ _____ colleges to □ _____ □ _____ and which ones may want to □ _____ □ _____. Her □ _____ are pretty □ _____ and she has □ _____ in a lot of □ _____ □ _____. The next day, Martha and her guidance counselor □ _____ a □ _____. Martha asks her counselor to □ _____ some colleges that would □ _____ □ _____ □ _____ □ _____. Her counselor says that she should □ _____ □ _____ the college's □ _____ first and look at the □ _____ and the □ _____. That way, it will be easier to decide which one to go to. In this situation, what would her guidance counselor most likely say to Martha?

Counselor: _____

✎ **어휘복습** 잘 안 들리거나 몰라서 체크한 어휘를 써 놓고 복습해 보세요.

□ _____　　□ _____　　□ _____　　□ _____

□ _____　　□ _____　　□ _____　　□ _____

□ _____　　□ _____　　□ _____　　□ _____

18 할 일 파악

대화를 듣고, 남자가 할 일로 가장 적절한 것을 고르시오.

① 성금 모으기
② 팔찌 만들기
③ 팔찌 주문하기
④ 아프리카에 성금 보내기
⑤ 친구들에게 이메일 보내기

M : Megan, your □ _____ is so □ _____. □ _____ did you □ _____ it?

W : Thanks! It's actually a □ _____ bracelet. I □ _____ it □ _____ a few days ago.

M : A charity bracelet? What is that? I've □ _____ □ _____ of it □ _____.

W : Well, if you buy a bracelet, then that money goes to help people □ _____ □ _____ □ _____. For example, countries that □ _____ □ _____ a □ _____ or an □ _____. Or it could go to help □ _____ □ _____ or □ _____ □ _____ in places like Africa.

M : Wow! That is such a wonderful thing to do! Can you tell me the □ _____ where I can order one too?

W : Sure! It is www dot betweenworlds dot org. The color of the bracelet changes □ _____ □ _____ which country you want to help, so □ _____ □ _____ you □ _____ that □ _____.

M : Alright, I'll □ _____ □ _____ to do that. I'm so glad you told me about this! I think I'm going to tell my friends about it too.

W : I'm glad to hear that! It's nice to know that people are so □ _____ □ _____ □ _____ □ _____ □ _____.

✏️ **어휘복습** 잘 안 들리거나 몰라서 체크한 어휘를 써 놓고 복습해 보세요.

□ _____   □ _____   □ _____   □ _____
□ _____   □ _____   □ _____   □ _____
□ _____   □ _____   □ _____   □ _____

19 속담 추론

대화를 듣고, 상황을 가장 잘 표현한 속담을
고르시오.

① Better late than never.
② No smoke without fire.
③ Many hands make light work.
④ Make hay while the sun shines.
⑤ Actions speak louder than words.

M : Hey, Cassandra, what are you doing? You look so busy.

W : I'm writing my □_____ □_____ for history class. □_____ aren't you □_____ □_____ yours? Have you finished already?

M : No, I haven't even started yet. It's □_____ □_____ □_____, so I still have a lot of time to do it.

W : What are you talking about? The □_____ is due □_____! We have to □_____ it □_____ before class starts.

M : What? Please tell me you're □_____! I thought it was due next week.

W : Well, it was. But Mr. Groves □_____ the due □_____. He □_____ everyone an □_____. Didn't you get it?

M : I don't □_____ my □_____ that □_____! Oh my goodness, what should I do? Even if I start on it now, I □_____ □_____ □_____ □_____ finish it by tomorrow.

W : Well, you'd □_____ □_____ working on it □_____! Even if you turn it in late, that's a lot □_____ □_____ □_____ turning it in □_____ □_____.

✎ **어휘복습** 잘 안 들리거나 몰라서 체크한 어휘를 써 놓고 복습해 보세요.

□_____ □_____ □_____ □_____
□_____ □_____ □_____ □_____
□_____ □_____ □_____ □_____

20 알맞은 응답 찾기

대화를 듣고, 남자의 마지막 말에 대한 여자의 응답으로 가장 적절한 것을 고르시오.

Woman: _____

① I'll meet you at the bus company.
② Thanks for coming with me to get my new phone.
③ I can never thank you enough for finding my phone for me.
④ Why didn't you tell me that you changed your phone number?
⑤ Okay! I'll call you as soon as I get it. Sorry for worrying you yesterday.

M : Jane! Why didn't you □ _____ □ _____ your □ _____ yesterday? Do you have any idea □ _____ □ _____ I was?

W : I'm so sorry, Ben. I □ _____ my □ _____ on the □ _____ ride home. By the time I got off the bus and realized that I didn't have my phone, it was □ _____ □ _____.

M : I see. I'm □ _____ that you're □ _____. What are you going to do about your phone?

W : I don't know. I □ _____ the □ _____ □ _____, but they said it would be □ _____ to □ _____ since there are so many buses in the city.

M : Oh, I'm sorry to hear that. Then □ _____ do you □ _____ □ _____ □ _____?

W : I guess I'll just have to □ _____ a □ _____ □ _____. There's □ _____ I can □ _____ □ _____ my old cellphone now.

M : Okay, □ _____ □ _____ when you get your new phone so I can □ _____ your new □ _____ □ _____.

W : _____

✎ **어휘복습** 잘 안 들리거나 몰라서 체크한 어휘를 써 놓고 복습해 보세요.

□ _____ □ _____ □ _____ □ _____
□ _____ □ _____ □ _____ □ _____
□ _____ □ _____ □ _____ □ _____

01 대화를 듣고, 사진 속 여자의 모습을 고르시오.

① ② ③ ④ ⑤

02 대화를 듣고, 여자가 남자에게 전화한 목적으로 가장 적절한 것을 고르시오.

① 요리를 부탁하려고
② 장 보기를 부탁하려고
③ 피자 주문을 부탁하려고
④ 식사 주문을 부탁하려고
⑤ 쿠폰 찾기를 부탁하려고

03 다음 그림의 상황에 가장 적절한 대화를 고르시오.

① ② ③ ④ ⑤

04 대화를 듣고, 교통체증이 예상되는 때를 고르시오.

① 금요일 오전과 일요일 오전
② 금요일 밤과 토요일 오전
③ 토요일 오전과 일요일 오전
④ 토요일 오전과 일요일 밤
⑤ 토요일 밤과 일요일 오전

05 대화를 듣고, 두 사람의 관계로 가장 적절한 것을 고르시오.

① 교사 – 학생   ② 엄마 – 아들
③ 카페 주인 – 고객   ④ 카페 주인 – 종업원
⑤ 고객센터 직원 – 고객

06 대화를 듣고, 여자의 심정으로 가장 적절한 것을 고르시오.

① thankful   ② anxious   ③ relieved
④ surprised   ⑤ embarrassed

07 다음을 듣고, 두 사람의 대화가 어색한 것을 고르시오.

① ② ③ ④ ⑤

08 대화를 듣고, 여자가 남자에게 부탁한 일로 가장 적절한 것을 고르시오.

① 자동차 빌려 주기   ② 치과 예약 변경하기
③ 치과에 태워다 주기   ④ 치과에 데리러 오기
⑤ 자동차 정비소에 가기

09 다음을 듣고, 여자의 전화 메시지의 의도로 가장 적절한 것을 고르시오.

① 축하   ② 요청   ③ 거절
④ 감사   ⑤ 충고

10 대화를 듣고, 여자가 지불해야 할 금액을 고르시오.

① $80   ② $100   ③ $120
④ $140   ⑤ $150

11 대화를 듣고, 두 사람이 대화하고 있는 장소로 가장 적절한 곳을 고르시오.

① train station   ② travel agency
③ fitness center   ④ airport
⑤ department store

12 다음을 듣고, Dolphin Show에 관해 언급되지 않은 것을 고르시오.

① 개막일   ② 시간
③ 공연장 위치   ④ 단체 관람 혜택
⑤ 입장료

13 다음 표를 보면서 대화를 듣고, 내용과 일치하지 <u>않는</u> 것을 고르시오.

Apartment Prices at Windsor Housing

	Bedroom & Bathroom	Price per Month
①	1 Bedroom, 1 Bathroom	$100
②	2 Bedrooms, 1 Bathroom	$175
③	3 Bedrooms, 2 Bathrooms	$250
④	4 Bedrooms, 3 Bathrooms	$325
⑤	4 Bedrooms, 4 Bathrooms	$375

14 다음을 듣고, 무엇에 관한 설명인지 고르시오.

① 깃발   ② 사이렌   ③ 신호등
④ 전봇대   ⑤ 감시 카메라

15 대화를 듣고, 두 사람이 대화 직후에 할 일로 가장 적절한 것을 고르시오.

① 편지 보내기   ② 개 목걸이 사기
③ 동물 병원에 가기   ④ 개에게 먹이 주기
⑤ 개 주인을 찾아가기

16 대화를 듣고, 피아노 연주회가 시작하는 시각을 고르시오.

① 6:30   ② 7:00   ③ 7:15
④ 7:30   ⑤ 8:00

17 다음 상황 설명을 듣고, Anna가 Jenna에게 할 말로 가장 적절한 것을 고르시오.

Anna: _____

① I think I lost my phone charger.
② Is there an electrical outlet here?
③ Did you break my phone charger?
④ You should buy me a new charger since you broke mine.
⑤ Could I have my charger back now? I need to use it, too.

18 대화를 듣고, 여자가 할 일로 가장 적절한 것을 고르시오.

① 회원권 취소하기
② 신분증 발급받기
③ 1개월 회원권 등록하기
④ 3개월 회원권 등록하기
⑤ 다른 헬스클럽 찾아보기

19 대화를 듣고, 여자의 마지막 말에 대한 남자의 응답으로 가장 적절한 것을 고르시오.

Man: _____

① Do you know how I can make a library card?
② If you check out books today, they will be due in 2 weeks.
③ Well, you can always go to the library to check out a book.
④ I think you would enjoy reading this fantasy book, *Wings of Fire*.
⑤ The science fiction and mystery books are on the 3rd floor of the library.

20 대화를 듣고, 남자의 마지막 말에 대한 여자의 응답으로 가장 적절한 것을 고르시오.

Woman: _____

① Why didn't you pick up your phone? I called you 5 times.
② I drove here early so I could see the sunrise in the morning.
③ I think I'm going to be late to the beach. I'll be there in 20 minutes.
④ The store is down the street. You have to walk for about 10 minutes.
⑤ I make a list of things to do so I don't forget. You should try it, too.

01 그림 정보 파악

대화를 듣고, 사진 속 여자의 모습을 고르시오.

① ② ③

④ ⑤

W : Hey, Mark! What are you up to these days? I haven't seen you in a long time. I heard you □ _____ a □ _____!

M : Hi, Susie! Yeah, we've been □ _____ for six months now. How have you been?

W : I've been great! It's nice to hear that you're dating! Can you tell me about her? □ _____ did you □ _____?

M : Well, she has a □ _____ □ _____ and we □ _____ a lot □ _____ □ _____. I met her at a book club last year.

W : Oh, I see. That's great! □ _____ does she □ _____ □ _____?

M : She has □ _____, □ _____ □ _____ and she □ _____ □ _____ □ _____. She likes wearing □ _____, and she likes □ _____. Here, let me show you a □ _____.

W : She looks □ _____ □ _____ your □ _____! □ _____ she's not wearing a hat in this picture. I think you guys make a great couple!

M : Thanks for saying that!

✏ **어휘복습** 잘 안 들리거나 몰라서 체크한 어휘를 써 놓고 복습해 보세요.

□ _____   □ _____   □ _____   □ _____

□ _____   □ _____   □ _____   □ _____

□ _____   □ _____   □ _____   □ _____

02 목적 파악

대화를 듣고, 여자가 남자에게 전화한 목적으로 가장 적절한 것을 고르시오.

① 요리를 부탁하려고
② 장 보기를 부탁하려고
③ 피자 주문을 부탁하려고
④ 식사 주문을 부탁하려고
⑤ 쿠폰 찾기를 부탁하려고

W : Hello? Ross, this is Mom calling.

M : Hey, Mom. What's up?

W : I'm □ _____ □ _____ □ _____ if you can □ _____ some □ _____ before your dad and I get home from work. I was □ _____ □ _____ □ _____ □ _____ tonight, but I'm so □ _____.

M : Yeah, I can do that for you. □ _____ do you want me to order?

W : Well, we had pizza last night, so □ _____ □ _____ some □ _____ □ _____? Is there anything that you'd like to eat?

M : Fried chicken sounds good to me. I'll order some from Ultra Chicken. Didn't we get a □ _____ drink □ _____ the last time we ordered?

W : Yeah, it should be in the □ _____ □ _____ □ _____ the kitchen □ _____. Oh, and can you ask them for some □ _____ □ _____?

M : Alright. I'll □ _____ □ _____ to ask them when I order.

✎ **어휘복습** 잘 안 들리거나 몰라서 체크한 어휘를 써 놓고 복습해 보세요.

□ _____   □ _____   □ _____   □ _____

□ _____   □ _____   □ _____   □ _____

□ _____   □ _____   □ _____   □ _____

03 그림 상황에 적절한 대화 찾기

다음 그림의 상황에 가장 적절한 대화를 고르시오.

① ② ③ ④ ⑤

① W : Here's your coffee, sir. Please be careful □ _____ □ _____ □ _____ it.

M : Thank you, I'll be □ _____.

② W : Excuse me, sir. There is a spill on the floor.

M : I'm sorry about that, ma'am. I'll □ _____ it □ _____ □ _____ right away.

③ W : The □ _____ are all □ _____ up. What should we do?

M : I'm sure they'll □ _____ □ _____ □ _____ □ _____ once we □ _____ them.

④ W : Can you get me a □ _____ □ _____ □ _____? I'm so thirsty.

M : Yeah, sure. Do you want □ _____ □ _____ □ _____?

⑤ W : Are you done □ _____ the □ _____? There was □ _____ □ _____.

M : Yes, I just got finished. Everything's clean now.

✎ **어휘복습** 잘 안 들리거나 몰라서 체크한 어휘를 써 놓고 복습해 보세요.

□ _____ □ _____ □ _____ □ _____

□ _____ □ _____ □ _____ □ _____

□ _____ □ _____ □ _____ □ _____

04 특정 정보 파악

대화를 듣고, 교통체증이 예상되는 때를 고르시오.

① 금요일 오전과 일요일 오전
② 금요일 밤과 토요일 오전
③ 토요일 오전과 일요일 오전
④ 토요일 오전과 일요일 밤
⑤ 토요일 밤과 일요일 오전

W : Are you ready for our □ _____ □ _____ the □ _____?
I hope the □ _____ isn't □ _____ □ _____ or □ _____
during the weekend.

M : Yeah, I'm so excited! I'm sure the weather will be fine. I think
we should □ _____ the □ _____ □ _____ before leaving
tomorrow morning.

W : Okay, let me □ _____ it □ _____. Oh, no! It says there's going
to be □ _____ □ _____ over the weekend!

M : It must be because it's □ _____ □ _____ for everybody. Wait,
but it says that there will be heavy traffic □ _____ □ _____
□ _____ and □ _____ □ _____.

W : Oh, then that means we won't be stuck in traffic □ _____ we're
□ _____ on □ _____ □ _____ and □ _____ □ _____
on □ _____ □ _____!

M : That's □ _____ □ _____ □ _____! I was so □ _____ we
wouldn't be able to go on our hiking trip.

W : Me too! Now all we have to do is □ _____ our □ _____
□ _____ and put everything in the car.

M : Alright! I already packed our hiking clothes, shoes, backpacks,
tent, two flashlights, and two water bottles. □ _____
□ _____ should we □ _____?

W : I think we should bring some □ _____ to eat □ _____
□ _____ □ _____ up the □ _____.

M : Oh, yeah! That's a good idea.

✎ **어휘복습** 잘 안 들리거나 몰라서 체크한 어휘를 써 놓고 복습해 보세요.

□ _____   □ _____   □ _____   □ _____
□ _____   □ _____   □ _____   □ _____
□ _____   □ _____   □ _____   □ _____

05 관계 추론

대화를 듣고, 두 사람의 관계로 가장 적절한 것을 고르시오.

① 교사 – 학생
② 엄마 – 아들
③ 카페 주인 – 고객
④ 카페 주인 – 종업원
⑤ 고객센터 직원 – 고객

W : Richard, please take a seat. I need to □ _____ □ _____ you.

M : Yes, ma'am. Is there a problem?

W : I'm afraid so. You have been □ _____ □ _____ □ _____ every day for the past week. If you can't □ _____ to the café □ _____ □ _____, I'm going to have to □ _____ you.

M : I'm sorry about that, ma'am. I'll □ _____ □ _____ to get here on time □ _____ □ _____ □ _____.

W : There are still a few more things I need to talk to you about. First, customers have been □ _____ □ _____ your □ _____ □ _____ when □ _____ drink □ _____. You need to smile and □ _____ them □ _____ □ _____.

M : I □ _____. I'll □ _____ □ _____ next time. What else did you want to speak to me about?

W : When you're working during □ _____ □ _____, you have to □ _____ □ _____ the □ _____ every day. If you don't, it starts to rot and smell.

M : Alright. I promise that I'll get here on time, be nice to customers, and take out the garbage every day. Thank you for □ _____ □ _____ □ _____.

✏️ **어휘복습** 잘 안 들리거나 몰라서 체크한 어휘를 써 놓고 복습해 보세요.

□ _____ □ _____ □ _____ □ _____

□ _____ □ _____ □ _____ □ _____

□ _____ □ _____ □ _____ □ _____

06 심정 추론

대화를 듣고, 여자의 심정으로 가장 적절한 것을 고르시오.

① thankful　　② anxious
③ relieved　　④ surprised
⑤ embarrassed

W : Hey dad, did anything come for me in the mail today?

M : No, □ _____ □ _____ □ _____ □ _____ □ _____.
Why? Are you □ _____ a □ _____?

W : Yes, I ordered a □ _____ for my □ _____ □ _____ on
Friday, and I was supposed to □ _____ it □ _____ the
□ _____ yesterday. But it's still not here.

M : Did you □ _____ the clothing □ _____? Maybe there was an
□ _____ □ _____ with the □ _____.

W : Yeah, I called this morning, but □ _____ □ _____ the
□ _____. □ _____ □ _____ the dress doesn't come before
Friday? I won't have anything to wear to my graduation!

M : I'm sure it'll get here by then. There are still □ _____ □ _____
□ _____, so don't worry too much.

W : I hope you're right. I just want it to □ _____ □ _____
□ _____ so I can stop thinking about it.

M : I understand. I'll □ _____ □ _____ □ _____ if the package
gets here tomorrow.

✏ **어휘복습** 잘 안 들리거나 몰라서 체크한 어휘를 써 놓고 복습해 보세요.

□ _____　　□ _____　　□ _____　　□ _____

□ _____　　□ _____　　□ _____　　□ _____

□ _____　　□ _____　　□ _____　　□ _____

07 어색한 대화 찾기

다음을 듣고, 두 사람의 대화가 어색한 것을 고르시오.

①   ②   ③   ④   ⑤

① W : When are you going to ☐ _____ the ☐ _____ to me?

   M : The ☐ _____ ☐ _____ is open every day from ten A.M. to five P.M.

② W : Have you been to the ☐ _____ ☐ _____ down the street?

   M : Yes, but it ☐ _____ ☐ _____ ☐ _____. I ☐ _____ the one on Central Avenue.

③ W : ☐ _____ ☐ _____ ☐ _____ are you inviting to your birthday party?

   M : I'm not sure yet, but I'm thinking ☐ _____ ☐ _____ people.

④ W : ☐ _____ much ☐ _____ do we have to ☐ _____ ☐ _____ ☐ _____?

   M : There are three people in front of you, so it'll be about twenty minutes.

⑤ W : Can I ☐ _____ you ☐ _____ ☐ _____ today? I have to talk to you.

   M : Of course, but ☐ _____ ☐ _____ you call ☐ _____ ☐ _____ P.M.

✏️ **어휘복습** 잘 안 들리거나 몰라서 체크한 어휘를 써 놓고 복습해 보세요.

☐ _____ ☐ _____ ☐ _____ ☐ _____

☐ _____ ☐ _____ ☐ _____ ☐ _____

☐ _____ ☐ _____ ☐ _____ ☐ _____

대화를 듣고, 여자가 남자에게 부탁한 일로
가장 적절한 것을 고르시오.

① 자동차 빌려 주기
② 치과 예약 변경하기
③ 치과에 태워다 주기
④ 치과에 데리러 오기
⑤ 자동차 정비소에 가기

W : Jonathan, are you busy right now?

M : No, not really. Do you need something?

W : Yeah, I need you to □ _____ □ _____ □ _____ □ _____.
I have to go to my □ _____ □ _____ at one P.M., but my
□ _____ □ _____ □ _____ yesterday and it's in the repair
shop. So, I was wondering if you could □ _____ me □ _____
□ _____ there.

M : I would □ _____ □ _____, □ _____ my sister is using my
car for the day. She's not getting back until three P.M. Can you
□ _____ your appointment?

W : Oh, I see. Let me □ _____ them and □ _____ □ _____ I can
go at a later time. Okay, they said that I could come □ _____
□ _____ P.M. □ _____ □ _____ □ _____ P.M.

M : That's great! Then I can give you a ride there after my sister gets
home.

W : Alright, that □ _____ □ _____! Thank you so much, Jonathan.

M : It's not a problem. I'll □ _____ you □ _____ □ _____ once
my sister gets back.

✎ **어휘복습** 잘 안 들리거나 몰라서 체크한 어휘를 써 놓고 복습해 보세요.

□ _____   □ _____   □ _____   □ _____

□ _____   □ _____   □ _____   □ _____

□ _____   □ _____   □ _____   □ _____

09 의도 파악

다음을 듣고, 여자의 전화 메시지의 의도로
가장 적절한 것을 고르시오.

① 축하　② 요청　③ 거절
④ 감사　⑤ 충고

W : Hi Elizabeth! This is Jessica. I wanted to □ _____ to you
□ _____ □ _____, but I guess you're □ _____ preparing
for the □ _____. I just got your □ _____ in the mail today and I
plan on □ _____ the □ _____ □ _____ of work to be there.
I just want to tell you □ _____ □ _____ □ _____ □ _____
for you! I can't believe you and John are finally □ _____
□ _____! I've known you two for over seven years now, and I
knew you guys would get married someday. I □ _____ □ _____
□ _____ for you and I hope your life will be □ _____
□ _____ □ _____. I'll see you at the wedding □ _____!

10 숫자 정보 파악

대화를 듣고, 여자가 지불해야 할 금액을 고
르시오.

① $80　② $100　③ $120
④ $140　⑤ $150

M : Good afternoon, welcome to Gretchen Hair & Spa. What can I do
for you today?
W : Hello, I would like to □ _____ my □ _____ □ _____. Also,
I would like to □ _____ a □ _____, please.
M : Alright, what would you like to do to your hair? And what kind of
massage would you like?
W : I want to □ _____ □ _____ □ _____, □ _____, and
□ _____. After doing my hair, I would like to get a □ _____
□ _____. □ _____ □ _____ would it □ _____ me to do
all of that?
M : Getting a □ _____ □ _____ □ _____ dollars, and a
□ _____ □ _____ costs □ _____ dollars. □ _____
□ _____ how much hair you want to get cut off, the □ _____
for getting a perm and dyeing your hair □ _____.
W : Oh, □ _____ □ _____ I get my hair cut to □ _____
□ _____? How much would that be?
M : Shoulder length hair costs □ _____ dollars to □ _____ and
□ _____ dollars to □ _____. If that's okay with you, we will
□ _____ □ _____.
W : Okay, that sounds great.

✎ **어휘복습** 잘 안 들리거나 몰라서 체크한 어휘를 써 놓고 복습해 보세요.

□ _____　□ _____　□ _____　□ _____

□ _____　□ _____　□ _____　□ _____

□ _____　□ _____　□ _____　□ _____

11 장소 추론

대화를 듣고, 두 사람이 대화하고 있는 장소로 가장 적절한 곳을 고르시오.

① train station   ② travel agency
③ fitness center   ④ airport
⑤ department store

W : Good morning, sir. What may I do for you today?

M : I □ _____ a plane □ _____ online, and I would like to confirm my flight and check in.

W : Okay, could I see your □ _____ and □ _____ □ _____, please?

M : Here you go. I would also like to □ _____ □ _____ these two □ _____.

W : Alright. We have to □ _____ them first. Both of your suitcases weigh □ _____ □ _____ each. You can only check in bags that are □ _____ □ _____ □ _____ pounds.

M : Oh no! Is there anything I can do?

W : Well, I think it'll be a good idea to □ _____ some □ _____ □ _____ of the suitcases to □ _____ them □ _____. After you do that, we can weigh the suitcases again.

M : Alright then, I'll try to do that right now. Thank you.

12 미언급 파악

다음을 듣고, Dolphin Show에 관해 언급되지 않은 것을 고르시오.

① 개막일   ② 시간
③ 공연장 위치   ④ 단체 관람 혜택
⑤ 입장료

W : Hello, ladies and gentlemen, boys and girls! Today, □ _____ □ _____, is the □ _____ □ _____ of our new □ _____ □ _____! There will be □ _____ shows every day at □ _____ P.M., □ _____ P.M., □ _____ □ _____ P.M., and □ _____ P.M. The shows will □ _____ □ _____ □ _____ Splash Theater, which is in Section A of the □ _____. For □ _____ □ _____ paid the □ _____ □ _____ to enter the aquarium, there is no extra fee for the show. However, for people who only want to watch the dolphin show, there is a □ _____ □ _____ □ _____ dollars. Come and watch dolphins jump, flip in the air, dance, and do other cool tricks!

✎ **어휘복습** 잘 안 들리거나 몰라서 체크한 어휘를 써 놓고 복습해 보세요.

□ _____   □ _____   □ _____   □ _____

□ _____   □ _____   □ _____   □ _____

□ _____   □ _____   □ _____   □ _____

13 도표·실용문 파악

다음 표를 보면서 대화를 듣고, 내용과 일치하지 <u>않는</u> 것을 고르시오.

Apartment Prices at Windsor Housing

	Bedroom & Bathroom	Price per Month
①	1 Bedroom, 1 Bathroom	$100
②	2 Bedrooms, 1 Bathroom	$175
③	3 Bedrooms, 2 Bathrooms	$250
④	4 Bedrooms, 3 Bathrooms	$325
⑤	4 Bedrooms, 4 Bathrooms	$375

W : Hello, sir. May I help you □ _____ □ _____ an □ _____?

M : Yes, that would be great! Could you tell me about my □ _____? □ _____ □ _____ is it for each apartment □ _____?

W : Alright. We have apartments with □ _____ □ _____ and □ _____ □ _____ at □ _____ □ _____ □ _____ per month. We also have some with two bedrooms and one bathroom for one hundred □ _____ dollars a month. Also, there are apartments with three bedrooms and two bathrooms at □ _____ □ _____ □ _____ dollars a month or four bedrooms and three bathrooms at □ _____ □ _____ □ _____ dollars a month. The apartments that are three hundred □ _____ dollars a month have four bedrooms and four bathrooms.

M : I see. Then □ _____ apartment would you □ _____ for me?

W : Will you be living □ _____ □ _____, or will you be living with a □ _____ or a □ _____ □ _____?

M : I plan on living here with my younger sister, but my parents will be visiting often.

W : Okay, then. □ _____ □ _____ an apartment with two bedrooms and one bathroom?

M : That sounds okay, but I would □ _____ the apartment with □ _____ □ _____ and □ _____ □ _____. That way my parents can use the extra room when they visit.

W : Sure, if that's what you want. That'll be two hundred twenty-five dollars a month. Would you like to sign a contract now?

M : Yes, please. That would be great!

✎ **어휘복습** 잘 안 들리거나 몰라서 체크한 어휘를 써 놓고 복습해 보세요.

□ _____ □ _____ □ _____ □ _____

□ _____ □ _____ □ _____ □ _____

□ _____ □ _____ □ _____ □ _____

14 화제 추론

다음을 듣고, 무엇에 관한 설명인지 고르시오.

① 깃발　　② 사이렌　　③ 신호등
④ 전봇대　　⑤ 감시 카메라

M : This can be found on all □ _____ . It is used to □ _____ □ _____ □ _____ and allows people to □ _____ □ _____ while □ _____ . It has □ _____ □ _____ on it; □ _____ means to go, □ _____ means to slow down, and □ _____ means to stop. There are also □ _____ to □ _____ □ _____ and □ _____ □ _____ . People who drive must be □ _____ □ _____ these colors at all times. Normally, this is located □ _____ □ _____ the □ _____ and hangs from a metal pole. Sometimes there are □ _____ □ _____ □ _____ next to it to catch people who do not follow traffic rules.

15 할 일 파악

대화를 듣고, 두 사람이 대화 직후에 할 일로 가장 적절한 것을 고르시오.

① 편지 보내기
② 개 목걸이 사기
③ 동물 병원에 가기
④ 개에게 먹이 주기
⑤ 개 주인을 찾아가기

W : Honey! What is that on the side of the street?
M : I think it's a □ _____ ! I □ _____ what it's doing there. It's not □ _____ with all these cars □ _____ □ _____ .
W : I think it might be □ _____ ! It has a □ _____ □ _____ its □ _____ . Do you think we can find the owner's □ _____ □ _____ or □ _____ on it?
M : I think so. Seventy-three eighty-one West Lane, three eight one, one nine two one. I'll try calling now, let's hope that someone answers. Nobody's □ _____ □ _____ the □ _____ . What should we do?
W : Well, West Lane is really □ _____ □ _____ our □ _____ , isn't it? Why don't we just □ _____ the dog □ _____ its □ _____ ?
M : We can do that, if that's what you want to do. West Lane is just a □ _____ □ _____ □ _____ from our house.
W : Then let's □ _____ □ _____ there as soon as we can. Its owner must be so □ _____ about it!
M : Okay. We can try calling again □ _____ □ _____ □ _____ □ _____ .

✎ **어휘복습** 잘 안 들리거나 몰라서 체크한 어휘를 써 놓고 복습해 보세요.

□ _____　　□ _____　　□ _____　　□ _____

□ _____　　□ _____　　□ _____　　□ _____

□ _____　　□ _____　　□ _____　　□ _____

16 숫자 정보 파악

대화를 듣고, 피아노 연주회가 시작하는 시각을 고르시오.

① 6:30   ② 7:00   ③ 7:15
④ 7:30   ⑤ 8:00

W : Dad, you haven't forgotten about my □ _____ □ _____ on □ _____, right?

M : Of course not! I'll get there □ _____ □ _____ □ _____ I can.

W : Well, do you know □ _____ □ _____ you will be □ _____ to the recital hall?

M : I plan on □ _____ my □ _____ at □ _____ P.M., so I'll probably get there □ _____ □ _____ □ _____ at the latest.

W : Seven thirty? That's thirty minutes after the recital starts! □ _____ □ _____ you □ _____ my □ _____?

M : Don't worry! You'll be the fifteenth person to perform, so I'm sure I'll □ _____ □ _____ □ _____ □ _____ to watch you play.

W : Okay. I'll be looking for you in the □ _____, Dad. I'll be really □ _____ if you're not there.

M : Okay, sweetheart. I'll be there, I promise!

17 상황에 적절한 말 찾기

다음 상황 설명을 듣고, Anna가 Jenna에게 할 말로 가장 적절한 것을 고르시오.

Anna : _____

① I think I lost my phone charger.
② Is there an electrical outlet here?
③ Did you break my phone charger?
④ You should buy me a new charger since you broke mine.
⑤ Could I have my charger back now? I need to use it, too.

M : Anna's friend Jenna lost her □ _____ □ _____ while using it in the □ _____ last week. So, Jenna asked Anna if she could □ _____ her phone charger because they □ _____ the □ _____ □ _____ of □ _____. Anna let Jenna use it, thinking that she would □ _____ it □ _____ the next day. However, Jenna didn't □ _____ it □ _____. Anna couldn't □ _____ □ _____ □ _____ phone for a whole week. Jenna kept using Anna's charger □ _____ □ _____ it was □ _____ □ _____. She didn't even think of buying a new one for herself. Anna wanted to talk to Jenna about this situation. In this situation, what would Anna most likely have said to Jenna?

Anna : _____

✎ **어휘복습** 잘 안 들리거나 몰라서 체크한 어휘를 써 놓고 복습해 보세요.

□ _____   □ _____   □ _____   □ _____

□ _____   □ _____   □ _____   □ _____

□ _____   □ _____   □ _____   □ _____

대화를 듣고, 여자가 할 일로 가장 적절한 것을 고르시오.

① 회원권 취소하기
② 신분증 발급받기
③ 1개월 회원권 등록하기
④ 3개월 회원권 등록하기
⑤ 다른 헬스클럽 찾아보기

M : Good evening, ma'am. May I help you?

W : Yes. I got a □ _____ □ _____ earlier today saying that my □ _____ center □ _____ has □ _____. I would like to □ _____ □ _____ □ _____ another month, please.

M : Of course. I need your □ _____ □ _____, □ _____ □ _____, and your □ _____ card.

W : Alright, my name is Heather Morris, my phone number is two nine one, three four eight eight, and here is my ID card.

M : Please wait a moment while I □ _____ for you □ _____ our □ _____. Okay, I see that you have signed up for our monthly membership plan □ _____ □ _____ □ _____ □ _____ □ _____. Would you be interested in signing up for □ _____ months □ _____ □ _____ □ _____?

W : Hmm… How much is the □ _____ □ _____ □ _____ a one-month and a three-month membership?

M : Well, a three-month membership is only □ _____ dollars □ _____. So in my opinion, it would be a better choice.

W : Oh! I didn't know that! Then I □ _____ □ _____ to sign up for the □ _____ membership, please.

✎ **어휘복습** 잘 안 들리거나 몰라서 체크한 어휘를 써 놓고 복습해 보세요.

□ _____ □ _____ □ _____ □ _____
□ _____ □ _____ □ _____ □ _____
□ _____ □ _____ □ _____ □ _____

19 알맞은 응답 찾기

대화를 듣고, 여자의 마지막 말에 대한 남자의 응답으로 가장 적절한 것을 고르시오.

Man:_____

① Do you know how I can make a library card?
② If you check out books today, they will be due in 2 weeks.
③ Well, you can always go to the library to check out a book.
④ I think you would enjoy reading this fantasy book, *Wings of Fire*.
⑤ The science fiction and mystery books are on the 3rd floor of the library.

W : Greg, thanks so much for inviting me to your house! It looks like you spent a lot of time decorating it. It looks so nice!

M : Thanks for the compliment! Yeah, it □ _____ me □ _____ two months to □ _____ all of the □ _____. I even made a small □ _____ in my bedroom!

W : Wow! That sounds □ _____! Can you show it to me? I'd love to see your library.

M : Yes, of course! Follow me. Here it is! I □ _____ all the books □ _____ □ _____. All the fiction books are on the top shelf, the □ _____ □ _____ books are on the second shelf, the □ _____ books are on the third shelf, and so on.

W : Oh, my goodness! You have so many books here! It makes me want to sit down and start reading.

M : Well, you're welcome to □ _____ them □ _____ □ _____ □ _____! Just □ _____ to □ _____ them after you're done reading them.

W : That would be awesome! Then, can you □ _____ a book for me?

M : _____

✎ **어휘복습** 잘 안 들리거나 몰라서 체크한 어휘를 써 놓고 복습해 보세요.

□ _____   □ _____   □ _____   □ _____

□ _____   □ _____   □ _____   □ _____

□ _____   □ _____   □ _____   □ _____

20 알맞은 응답 찾기

대화를 듣고, 남자의 마지막 말에 대한 여자의 응답으로 가장 적절한 것을 고르시오.

Woman: _____

① Why didn't you pick up your phone? I called you 5 times.
② I drove here early so I could see the sunrise in the morning.
③ I think I'm going to be late to the beach. I'll be there in 20 minutes.
④ The store is down the street. You have to walk for about 10 minutes.
⑤ I make a list of things to do so I don't forget. You should try it, too.

W : Henry, did you □ _____ □ _____ □ _____ before coming out to the beach?

M : No, I □ _____ □ _____! What should I do?

W : I knew you'd forget. Here, I □ _____ □ _____ in my backpack □ _____ □ _____ □ _____.

M : What would I do without you? Thanks so much!

W : No problem. Did you bring the □ _____ and □ _____ to make □ _____ □ _____? How about the □ _____ □ _____?

M : Oh, my goodness! I forgot about those too! I don't know □ _____ □ _____ □ _____ □ _____ today. Should we go to the store and buy some?

W : I thought you'd forget that, too. Don't worry, I □ _____ some □ _____ before you got here.

M : You are amazing. I would be so □ _____ □ _____ □ _____. How do you remember everything so well?

W : _____

✏ **어휘복습** 잘 안 들리거나 몰라서 체크한 어휘를 써 놓고 복습해 보세요.

□ _____   □ _____   □ _____   □ _____

□ _____   □ _____   □ _____   □ _____

□ _____   □ _____   □ _____   □ _____

01 대화를 듣고, 여자가 만든 포스터를 고르시오.

①   ②   ③

④   ⑤

02 대화를 듣고, 남자가 여자에게 전화한 목적으로 가장 적절한 것을 고르시오.

① 수리비를 문의하려고
② 도움을 요청하려고
③ 보험에 가입하려고
④ 위치를 물어보려고
⑤ 약속 시간을 정하려고

03 다음 그림의 상황에 가장 적절한 대화를 고르시오.

① ② ③ ④ ⑤

04 대화를 듣고, 두 사람이 만나기로 한 장소를 고르시오.

① 영화관　　② 음악실　　③ 컴퓨터실
④ 운동장　　⑤ 도서관

05 대화를 듣고, 남자의 직업으로 가장 적절한 것을 고르시오.

① animal doctor　② photographer
③ taxi driver　④ police officer
⑤ reporter

06 대화를 듣고, 남자의 심정으로 가장 적절한 것을 고르시오.

① excited　　② jealous
③ bored　　④ regretful
⑤ embarrassed

07 다음을 듣고, 두 사람의 대화가 <u>어색한</u> 것을 고르시오.

① ② ③ ④ ⑤

08 대화를 듣고, 남자가 여자에게 부탁한 일로 가장 적절한 것을 고르시오.

① 설거지하기　　② 숙제 도와주기
③ 집에 바래다주기　④ 수업 준비물 구입하기
⑤ 학교로 영어책 가져오기

09 대화를 듣고, 여자의 마지막 말에 담긴 의도로 가장 적절한 것을 고르시오.

① 위로　　② 충고　　③ 거절
④ 감사　　⑤ 요청

10 대화를 듣고, 여자가 지불할 금액을 고르시오.

① $40　　② $50　　③ $60
④ $90　　⑤ $100

11 대화를 듣고, 두 사람이 대화하고 있는 장소로 가장 적절한 곳을 고르시오.

① 서점　　　　② 백화점
③ 영화관　　　④ 커피 전문점
⑤ 휴대폰 수리점

12 다음을 듣고, Spelling Genius Contest에 관해 언급되지 <u>않은</u> 것을 고르시오.

① 대회 날짜   ② 대회 장소
③ 우승 상품   ④ 신청 방법
⑤ 신청 기한

13 다음 벼룩시장 배치도를 보면서 대화를 듣고, 두 사람이 선택한 구역의 위치를 고르시오.

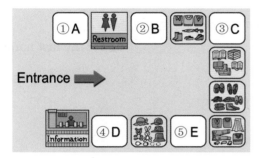

14 다음을 듣고, 무엇에 관한 설명인지 고르시오.

① 저울   ② 계산기
③ 체온계   ④ 전자시계
⑤ 쇼핑 카트

15 대화를 듣고, 여자가 할 일로 가장 적절한 것을 고르시오.

① 창문 닫기   ② 자리 바꾸기
③ 우산 가져오기   ④ 교실 청소하기
⑤ 사물함 수리하기

16 대화를 듣고, 남자가 구입할 것을 고르시오.

① tomatoes   ② cheese
③ pepperoni   ④ mushrooms
⑤ red peppers

17 다음 상황 설명을 듣고, Jenny가 손님에게 할 말로 가장 적절한 것을 고르시오.

Jenny: _____

① Did you enjoy your meal?
② I apologize for my mistake.
③ I'll give you a refund if you want.
④ I'm afraid you forgot your sunglasses.
⑤ The restaurant is fully booked on Saturdays.

18 대화를 듣고, 여자가 할 일로 가장 적절한 것을 고르시오.

① 장보기   ② 간식 만들기
③ 빵 사다 주기   ④ 숙제 도와주기
⑤ 아들 데리러 가기

19 대화를 듣고, 여자의 마지막 말에 대한 남자의 응답으로 가장 적절한 것을 고르시오.

Man: _____

① Great. Then, I should go to the library right now.
② You need a library card to borrow a book.
③ Well, the book is too difficult to read.
④ Right. We should protect our planet.
⑤ I couldn't return the book earlier.

20 대화를 듣고, 남자의 마지막 말에 대한 여자의 응답으로 가장 적절한 것을 고르시오.

Woman: _____

① Okay. I'll go to the hospital later.
② Oh, no. I should have studied harder.
③ Right. I have a math exam tomorrow.
④ Never mind. I can take care of myself.
⑤ Don't worry about it. You'll do better next time.

01 그림 정보 파악

대화를 듣고, 여자가 만든 포스터를 고르시오.

① 88 KIM ② KIM ③ 88 KIM
④ KIM ⑤ 88 KIM

W : Joe, look! This is the □ _____ I made for my □ _____
□ _____ □ _____ .

M : It looks cool! You used his □ _____ □ _____ , eighty-eight.

W : Yeah. I also □ _____ his □ _____ □ _____ , KIM, on the
poster.

M : □ _____ □ _____ . Then, why did you use a baseball
□ _____ □ _____ ?

W : You know, he's known as a great □ _____ .

M : I see. And you put a □ _____ □ _____ under the last name,
KIM.

W : Yes. I'm a □ _____ □ _____ .

02 전화 목적 파악

대화를 듣고, 남자가 여자에게 전화한 목적으로 가장 적절한 것을 고르시오.

① 수리비를 문의하려고
② 도움을 요청하려고
③ 보험에 가입하려고
④ 위치를 물어보려고
⑤ 약속 시간을 정하려고

W : Hello. This is ABC □ _____ Company. May I help you?

M : Hello. This is Ray Wilson. My □ _____ □ _____ □ _____ at
seven oh two Main Street. Could you □ _____ □ _____ to
□ _____ ?

W : Okay, but have you tried □ _____ your car?

M : Yes, I did. But it didn't □ _____ .

W : I see. Someone should be there in about □ _____ □ _____
□ _____ .

M : Thank you so much.

✎ **어휘복습** 잘 안 들리거나 몰라서 체크한 어휘를 써 놓고 복습해 보세요.

□ _____   □ _____   □ _____   □ _____
□ _____   □ _____   □ _____   □ _____
□ _____   □ _____   □ _____   □ _____

03 그림 상황에 적절한 대화 찾기

다음 그림의 상황에 가장 적절한 대화를 고르시오.

① ② ③ ④ ⑤

① M : The escalator is □ _____ □ _____ □ _____.

　 W : Let's □ _____ the □ _____.

② M : Sorry. This elevator is □ _____.

　 W : Okay. I'll take the □ _____ □ _____.

③ M : Excuse me. Where is the elevator?

　 W : Go □ _____ □ _____ □ _____. You'll see it.

④ M : □ _____ □ _____ are you going to?

　 W : I'm □ _____ □ _____ on the tenth floor. Thank you.

⑤ M : □ _____ may I □ _____ you?

　 W : Hi. Can I □ _____ a □ _____ on these?

04 특정 정보 파악

대화를 듣고, 두 사람이 만나기로 한 장소를 고르시오.

① 영화관　　　　② 음악실
③ 컴퓨터실　　　④ 운동장
⑤ 도서관

M : Hi, Sarah. □ _____ your video project □ _____?

W : Well, I'm □ _____ a □ _____ □ _____ the movie software program. I □ _____ □ _____ □ _____ to add music to my video clip.

M : Oh, I can □ _____ you □ _____ □ _____.

W : Great! If you're □ _____ this afternoon, can we □ _____ at the □ _____ □ _____ and work on it?

M : □ _____ □ _____. Let's meet there at two o'clock!

W : Thanks! See you then.

✎ **어휘복습** 잘 안 들리거나 몰라서 체크한 어휘를 써 놓고 복습해 보세요.

□ _____　　□ _____　　□ _____　　□ _____

□ _____　　□ _____　　□ _____　　□ _____

□ _____　　□ _____　　□ _____　　□ _____

05 직업 추론

대화를 듣고, 남자의 직업으로 가장 적절한 것을 고르시오.

① animal doctor ② photographer
③ taxi driver ④ police officer
⑤ reporter

M : How can I help you?

W : My □ _____ got away from me and was □ _____ □ _____ a □ _____. I should have been holding her more tightly.

M : All right. □ _____ □ _____ □ _____. Oh, it doesn't seem □ _____ □ _____, but she needs to get an X-ray.

W : Okay. Do you think she'll □ _____ □ _____?

M : Well, I have to see her X-ray first and then I can tell you about it.

W : Oh, I see.

06 심정 추론

대화를 듣고, 남자의 심정으로 가장 적절한 것을 고르시오.

① excited ② jealous
③ bored ④ regretful
⑤ embarrassed

W : Minsu, I have some □ _____ □ _____ for you.

M : Big news? Can I ask you what it is?

W : You've been □ _____ to the □ _____ □ _____ program you □ _____ for last month. This is really good for you, Minsu!

M : Really? I □ _____ □ _____ it!

W : In addition, they □ _____ a lot of interesting □ _____ □ _____ for the volunteers.

M : That's wonderful. I □ _____ □ _____! Thank you so much!

✎ **어휘복습** 잘 안 들리거나 몰라서 체크한 어휘를 써 놓고 복습해 보세요.

□ _____ □ _____ □ _____ □ _____

□ _____ □ _____ □ _____ □ _____

□ _____ □ _____ □ _____ □ _____

다음을 듣고, 두 사람의 대화가 <u>어색한</u> 것을
고르시오.

① ② ③ ④ ⑤

① M : What would you like to □ _____ □ _____ □ _____?

W : I'm □ _____ that □ _____. I'm going to □ _____ lunch today.

② M : Could you □ _____ me □ _____ □ _____ to school?

W : Yes. I can □ _____ to school □ _____ □ _____.

③ M : Eating breakfast is □ _____ □ _____ good health.

W : You can say that □ _____.

④ M : □ _____ is your □ _____?

W : I like □ _____ and □ _____.

⑤ M : □ _____ □ _____ will it take to □ _____ my □ _____?

W : It should be □ _____ within about three days.

대화를 듣고, 남자가 여자에게 부탁한 일로
가장 적절한 것을 고르시오.

① 설거지하기
② 숙제 도와주기
③ 집에 바래다주기
④ 수업 준비물 구입하기
⑤ 학교로 영어책 가져오기

W : Hello, Kevin.

M : Hi, Tiffany. I think I □ _____ my English □ _____ in your □ _____ when I came over to study.

W : □ _____ □ _____. I was just about to call you. Should I □ _____ it to □ _____ □ _____ later?

M : You □ _____ □ _____ □ _____ do that. Could you just bring it to □ _____ □ _____?

W : No problem. See you tomorrow.

✎ **어휘복습** 잘 안 들리거나 몰라서 체크한 어휘를 써 놓고 복습해 보세요.

□ _____   □ _____   □ _____   □ _____

□ _____   □ _____   □ _____   □ _____

□ _____   □ _____   □ _____   □ _____

09 의도 파악

대화를 듣고, 여자의 마지막 말에 담긴 의도로 가장 적절한 것을 고르시오.

① 위로　② 충고　③ 거절
④ 감사　⑤ 요청

W : Michael, what are you doing?

M : Hey, Kate. I'm □ _____ □ _____ for the □ _____ round-trip □ _____ to the Grand Canyon.

W : Wow! □ _____ are you planning to □ _____?

M : During the second week of □ _____. My □ _____ □ _____ starts then.

W : Oh, I envy you. □ _____ □ _____ I could go, too.

M : Really? If you want to go, we can □ _____ □ _____.

W : I'd like to, □ _____ I have to work □ _____ at the school □ _____ during the break.

10 숫자 정보 파악

대화를 듣고, 여자가 지불할 금액을 고르시오.

① $40　② $50　③ $60
④ $90　⑤ $100

W : Excuse me, I'd like to □ _____ a sports □ _____.

M : How about this one? It's □ _____ dollars.

W : Yes, I like it. I also need a pair of □ _____ □ _____. Do you have any?

M : Over here. These are our □ _____ □ _____. They're □ _____ dollars.

W : I like the □ _____, but I'm afraid I can't □ _____ them both. I'll □ _____ □ _____ the sports uniform for now.

M : Okay. Here you are.

✎ **어휘복습** 잘 안 들리거나 몰라서 체크한 어휘를 써 놓고 복습해 보세요.

□ _____　□ _____　□ _____　□ _____

□ _____　□ _____　□ _____　□ _____

□ _____　□ _____　□ _____　□ _____

11 장소 추론

대화를 듣고, 두 사람이 대화하고 있는 장소로 가장 적절한 곳을 고르시오.

① 서점
② 백화점
③ 영화관
④ 커피 전문점
⑤ 휴대폰 수리점

M : Hello, may I help you?

W : Yes. I □ _____ my □ _____ on the floor, and its □ _____ got □ _____.

M : That's too bad. You have to □ _____ it □ _____ a new one. It'll □ _____ about one hundred dollars.

W : Okay. □ _____ □ _____ does it □ _____ to get it fixed?

M : It □ _____ □ _____ about two hours. □ _____ □ _____ □ _____ have a coffee in the lobby and read a magazine □ _____ □ _____?

W : Thanks, but I think I'll □ _____ □ _____ and come back later.

12 미언급 파악

다음을 듣고, Spelling Genius Contest에 관해 언급되지 <u>않은</u> 것을 고르시오.

① 대회 날짜
② 대회 장소
③ 우승 상품
④ 신청 방법
⑤ 신청 기한

M : Good morning. This is your English teacher, Mr. Han speaking. Are you interested in □ _____ □ _____ your □ _____ □ _____? I'm □ _____ you to □ _____ this year's Spelling Genius Contest! It'll be held on □ _____ □ _____. The □ _____ will get a □ _____ and a fifty-dollar □ _____ □ _____. To sign up, please □ _____ the □ _____ form from our school □ _____, and □ _____ it □ _____ to my office □ _____ Friday, April twentieth. Thank you!

✏ **어휘복습** 잘 안 들리거나 몰라서 체크한 어휘를 써 놓고 복습해 보세요.

□ _____   □ _____   □ _____   □ _____
□ _____   □ _____   □ _____   □ _____
□ _____   □ _____   □ _____   □ _____

13 그림 정보 파악

다음 벼룩시장 배치도를 보면서 대화를 듣고, 두 사람이 선택한 구역의 위치를 고르시오.

W : Look, Jason. There are ☐ _____ sections ☐ _____ for the monthly ☐ _____ ☐ _____. ☐ _____ ☐ _____ would be best for us?

M : The sections ☐ _____ ☐ _____ the ☐ _____ are not good. I don't like the ☐ _____.

W : You're right. Then, what about section C?

M : It's too ☐ _____ ☐ _____ the ☐ _____.

W : Well, we have two ☐ _____ now. Which section do you think is ☐ _____?

M : I think the section right next to the ☐ _____ ☐ _____ is better because there'll be more people ☐ _____ ☐ _____.

W : Good! Let's ☐ _____ that section ☐ _____.

14 화제 추론

다음을 듣고, 무엇에 관한 설명인지 고르시오.

① 저울   ② 계산기
③ 체온계   ④ 전자시계
⑤ 쇼핑 카트

W : This is a ☐ _____ that is used in many different places. For example, you can see it in bakeries, grocery stores, seafood markets, or even in factories. It is a ☐ _____ for ☐ _____ the ☐ _____ of an ☐ _____. To do so, you usually ☐ _____ an ☐ _____ on ☐ _____ of it. It was made of two ☐ _____ ☐ _____ in the old days, but ☐ _____ ones are more popular now.

✎ **어휘복습** 잘 안 들리거나 몰라서 체크한 어휘를 써 놓고 복습해 보세요.

☐ _____ ☐ _____ ☐ _____ ☐ _____

☐ _____ ☐ _____ ☐ _____ ☐ _____

☐ _____ ☐ _____ ☐ _____ ☐ _____

대화를 듣고, 여자의 마지막 말에 대한 남자의 응답으로 가장 적절한 것을 고르시오.

Man:_____

① Great. Then, I should go to the library right now.
② You need a library card to borrow a book.
③ Well, the book is too difficult to read.
④ Right. We should protect our planet.
⑤ I couldn't return the book earlier.

M : Have you done your □ _____ □ _____ the green house effect?
W : Almost. How about you?
M : I □ _____ even started □ _____. I don't know how to □ _____ the □ _____.
W : Did you □ _____ the school □ _____?
M : Yeah. I went there □ _____, but people had already □ _____ □ _____ all the □ _____ on that □ _____.
W : □ _____, I checked out two books on Monday, but I □ _____ them this □ _____.
M : _____

대화를 듣고, 남자의 마지막 말에 대한 여자의 응답으로 가장 적절한 것을 고르시오.

Woman: _____

① Okay. I'll go to the hospital later.
② Oh, no. I should have studied harder.
③ Right. I have a math exam tomorrow.
④ Never mind. I can take care of myself.
⑤ Don't worry about it. You'll do better next time.

W : Hey, Mike. □ _____ □ _____? Are you okay?
M : Yeah. I just didn't do □ _____ on the □ _____ □ _____.
W : I can't believe it. You always get □ _____ □ _____ in math.
M : Maybe before, but this time I □ _____ so □ _____ foolish □ _____.
W : Don't feel bad. This kind of thing □ _____ to □ _____.
M : Well, I don't know. I don't feel □ _____ □ _____ □ _____.
W : _____

✎ **어휘복습** 잘 안 들리거나 몰라서 체크한 어휘를 써 놓고 복습해 보세요.

□ _____ □ _____ □ _____ □ _____
□ _____ □ _____ □ _____ □ _____
□ _____ □ _____ □ _____ □ _____

01 대화를 듣고, 두 사람이 하고 있는 동작을 고르시오.

① ② ③ ④ ⑤

02 대화를 듣고, 남자가 여자에게 전화한 목적으로 가장 적절한 것을 고르시오.

① 여행 가이드를 추천하려고
② 책 반납을 요청하려고
③ 책 대출을 부탁하려고
④ 여행 일정을 변경하려고
⑤ 도서관 위치를 문의하려고

03 다음 그림의 상황에 가장 적절한 대화를 고르시오.

① ② ③ ④ ⑤

04 대화를 듣고, 두 사람이 만나기로 한 요일을 고르시오.

① Sunday ② Monday
③ Wednesday ④ Friday
⑤ Saturday

05 대화를 듣고, 두 사람이 대화하고 있는 장소로 가장 적절한 곳을 고르시오.

① bank ② toy store
③ playground ④ concert hall
⑤ animal hospital

06 대화를 듣고, 여자의 심정으로 가장 적절한 것을 고르시오.

① bored ② excited ③ satisfied
④ thankful ⑤ frustrated

07 다음을 듣고, 두 사람의 대화가 어색한 것을 고르시오.

① ② ③ ④ ⑤

08 대화를 듣고, 여자가 남자에게 부탁한 일로 가장 적절한 것을 고르시오.

① 팝콘 사오기 ② 상자 옮겨주기
③ 휴대폰 충전하기 ④ 영화표 예매하기
⑤ 동영상 내려 받기

09 대화를 듣고, 여자의 마지막 말에 담긴 의도로 가장 적절한 것을 고르시오.

① 감사 ② 충고 ③ 위로
④ 거절 ⑤ 요청

10 대화를 듣고, 여자가 지불할 금액을 고르시오.

① $15 ② $30 ③ $50
④ $60 ⑤ $90

11 대화를 듣고, 두 사람의 관계로 가장 적절한 것을 고르시오.

① 택시 기사 – 승객 ② 공항 직원 – 탑승객
③ 주유소 직원 – 고객 ④ 호텔 직원 – 투숙객
⑤ 식당 종업원 – 손님

12 다음을 듣고, Angel English Camp에 관해 언급되지 않은 것을 고르시오.

① 설립 연도 ② 시설 ③ 위치
④ 프로그램 ⑤ 참가 비용

13 다음 공항 주차 안내도를 보면서 대화를 듣고, 두 사람이 주차할 구역을 고르시오.

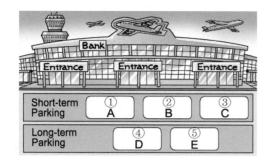

14 다음을 듣고, 무엇에 관한 설명인지 고르시오.

① 농구   ② 축구   ③ 배구
④ 야구   ⑤ 핸드볼

15 대화를 듣고, 남자가 할 일로 가장 적절한 것을 고르시오.

① 운동하기
② 공원 청소하기
③ 사진 나눠주기
④ 애완견 산책시키기
⑤ 동물 보호소 방문하기

16 대화를 듣고, 두 사람이 구입할 물건을 고르시오.

① screwdriver   ② glue   ③ tube
④ air pump   ⑤ water bottle

17 다음 상황 설명을 듣고, Sean이 엄마에게 할 말로 가장 적절한 것을 고르시오.

Sean: Mom, _____

① when is the job interview?
② how much did you pay for it?
③ could you buy me a new suit?
④ where is the department store?
⑤ does this suit look good on me?

18 대화를 듣고, 남자가 할 일로 가장 적절한 것을 고르시오.

① 전구 교체하기   ② 주방 정리하기
③ 욕실 청소하기   ④ 식사 준비하기
⑤ 쓰레기 버리기

19 대화를 듣고, 남자의 마지막 말에 대한 여자의 응답으로 가장 적절한 것을 고르시오.

Woman: _____

① I'd like to buy a birthday present for you.
② Online stores are available 24 hours a day.
③ Online prices are usually lower than offline prices.
④ It's easy to find part-time jobs on the Internet.
⑤ You should make sure the website is safe first.

20 대화를 듣고, 여자의 마지막 말에 대한 남자의 응답으로 가장 적절한 것을 고르시오.

Man: _____

① That's a good idea! I'll give it a try.
② Sure, I'll try to memorize the whole script.
③ Okay. I'll take notes during the presentation.
④ So, do you mean I should check the grammar?
⑤ Then, you need to practice English conversation.

02회 DICTATION

다시 듣고, 빈칸에 알맞은 단어를 써 보세요.

◀)) MP3 기출 02-1

01 그림 정보 파악

대화를 듣고, 두 사람이 하고 있는 동작을 고르시오.

① ② ③ ④ ⑤

W : Let's □ _____ a □ _____. We've been sitting too long.

M : Hey, I learned some □ _____. This will help. First,

□ _____ your □ _____ □ _____ □ _____ your

□ _____ like this.

W : Okay. Now what?

M : Then, □ _____ your □ _____ □ _____ with your

□ _____ □ _____. And □ _____ □ _____ your elbow

□ _____ the □ _____.

W : Oh, I feel the stretch in my □ _____.

M : □ _____ it for ten □ _____ and then do it again.

02 목적 파악

대화를 듣고, 남자가 여자에게 전화한 목적으로 가장 적절한 것을 고르시오.

① 여행 가이드를 추천하려고
② 책 반납을 요청하려고
③ 책 대출을 부탁하려고
④ 여행 일정을 변경하려고
⑤ 도서관 위치를 문의하려고

M : Hello, Mary. This is Brian. □ _____ are you?

W : Hi, Brian. I'm about to □ _____ the school □ _____.

M : Good. Can you □ _____ me a □ _____?

W : Sure. What is it?

M : I'm going to Jeju Island with my family next week. Can you

□ _____ □ _____ a Jeju □ _____ for me?

W : □ _____ □ _____. I'd be glad to.

✎ 어휘복습 잘 안 들리거나 몰라서 체크한 어휘를 써 놓고 복습해 보세요.

□ _____   □ _____   □ _____   □ _____

□ _____   □ _____   □ _____   □ _____

□ _____   □ _____   □ _____   □ _____

다음 그림의 상황에 가장 적절한 대화를 고르시오.

① ② ③ ④ ⑤

① W : □ _____ □ _____ will it take to get my bag fixed?

M : It'll □ _____ about a □ _____.

② W : I □ _____ you a new pair of □ _____ for your □ _____.

M : Really? □ _____ □ _____ so much.

③ W : I □ _____ my □ _____. □ _____ should I □ _____?

M : You should □ _____ □ _____ this □ _____ first.

④ W : □ _____ does the shoe-making class □ _____?

M : It □ _____ next □ _____.

⑤ W : These □ _____ feel so □ _____. Could you □ _____ me □ _____ pair?

M : Sure. □ _____ □ _____ go □ _____ them for you.

대화를 듣고, 두 사람이 만나기로 한 요일을 고르시오.

① Sunday   ② Monday
③ Wednesday   ④ Friday
⑤ Saturday

W : Hello, Justin! What's up?

M : Hi, Linda. I heard you're □ _____ □ _____ a new school next □ _____.

W : Yeah, that's true. I'll □ _____ □ _____.

M : Me, too. Why don't we □ _____ □ _____ together this □ _____?

W : □ _____, □ _____ I have to help my parents pack stuff during the weekend. □ _____ □ _____ on □ _____?

M : □ _____. I'll □ _____ □ _____ at the school cafeteria □ _____ □ _____.

✎ **어휘복습** 잘 안 들리거나 몰라서 체크한 어휘를 써 놓고 복습해 보세요.

□ _____ □ _____ □ _____ □ _____
□ _____ □ _____ □ _____ □ _____
□ _____ □ _____ □ _____ □ _____

05 장소 추론

대화를 듣고, 두 사람이 대화하고 있는 장소로 가장 적절한 곳을 고르시오.

① bank ② toy store
③ playground ④ concert hall
⑤ animal hospital

W : Dad, look! There's a ☐ _____.
M : Oh, it ☐ _____ so ☐ _____.
W : Yeah. It even ☐ _____ ☐ _____ a parrot. That's great.
M : It also has colorful ☐ _____ though they're ☐ _____
☐ _____ ☐ _____.
W : Dad, can you ☐ _____ me this one?
M : Okay. It's your birthday. If that's what you want, I'll buy it for you.
W : Thanks, Dad.

06 심정 추론

대화를 듣고, 여자의 심정으로 가장 적절한 것을 고르시오.

① bored ② excited
③ satisfied ④ thankful
⑤ frustrated

M : Sumi, why didn't you ☐ _____ ☐ _____ your ☐ _____?
W : What? I ☐ _____ it last Friday.
M : You just wrote your name and student number with
☐ _____ ☐ _____ ☐ _____.
W : Oh, I'm so ☐ _____. I didn't know that. Can I send the file this afternoon?
M : ☐ _____ ☐ _____ that's not possible. The deadline was last Friday.
W : Oh, no! I ☐ _____ ☐ _____ that I ☐ _____ such a big
☐ _____.

✎ **어휘복습** 잘 안 들리거나 몰라서 체크한 어휘를 써 놓고 복습해 보세요.

☐ _____ ☐ _____ ☐ _____ ☐ _____
☐ _____ ☐ _____ ☐ _____ ☐ _____
☐ _____ ☐ _____ ☐ _____ ☐ _____

다음을 듣고, 두 사람의 대화가 <u>어색한</u> 것을 고르시오.

①   ②   ③   ④   ⑤

① M : ☐ _____ would you like to ☐ _____?
    W : By ☐ _____ ☐ _____.

② M : I was ☐ _____ with the film.
    W : You were? I ☐ _____ the ☐ _____ way.

③ M : This ☐ _____ is too ☐ _____ for me.
    W : Would you like to ☐ _____ it for a ☐ _____ one?

④ M : ☐ _____ do you think we can ☐ _____ the ☐ _____?
    W : I ☐ _____ ☐ _____ ☐ _____ you like it or not.

⑤ M : You look so ☐ _____! Is that a new ☐ _____?
    W : Yes. It's a ☐ _____ ☐ _____ from my mom.

대화를 듣고, 여자가 남자에게 부탁한 일로 가장 적절한 것을 고르시오.

① 팝콘 사오기
② 상자 옮겨주기
③ 휴대폰 충전하기
④ 영화표 예매하기
⑤ 동영상 내려 받기

M : Helen, I've heard the ☐ _____, *The Man from Somewhere*, is a box-office ☐ _____. Have you seen it?

W : No, not yet.

M : Why don't we go ☐ _____ it ☐ _____ night?

W : I'd love to, ☐ _____ I ☐ _____ if there are ☐ _____ ☐ _____.

M : I can ☐ _____ for tickets with my ☐ _____ right now. Oh, there are ☐ _____ a few ☐ _____.

W : That's good. ☐ _____ you ☐ _____ them for us? Then, I'll buy some popcorn.

M : That sounds perfect.

✏ **어휘복습** 잘 안 들리거나 몰라서 체크한 어휘를 써 놓고 복습해 보세요.

☐ _____   ☐ _____   ☐ _____   ☐ _____

☐ _____   ☐ _____   ☐ _____   ☐ _____

☐ _____   ☐ _____   ☐ _____   ☐ _____

09 의도 파악

대화를 듣고, 여자의 마지막 말에 담긴 의도로 가장 적절한 것을 고르시오.

① 감사　② 충고　③ 위로
④ 거절　⑤ 요청

M : Honey, I □ _____ a special □ _____ for you. Please □ _____ your □ _____.
W : Okay. What is it?
M : Now □ _____ your □ _____ and look at this.
W : Wow! It's a new □ _____. Did you □ _____ it □ _____?
M : Of course! You're such a □ _____. I hope you like it.
W : Yeah, I □ _____ □ _____. There □ _____ be a □ _____ present for me.

10 숫자 정보 파악

대화를 듣고, 여자가 지불할 금액을 고르시오.

① $15　② $30　③ $50
④ $60　⑤ $90

M : Did you □ _____ your □ _____?
W : Yes, very much. Thank you. □ _____ □ _____ do I owe you?
M : You had the T-bone steak, French fries, and a salad. So your □ _____ is □ _____ □ _____.
W : That's with a □ _____ □ _____ □ _____, right?
M : Yes, the □ _____ □ _____ for the same meal is □ _____ dollars. This is the □ _____ of the □ _____ lunch special.
W : Thank you. It was □ _____. Here's my □ _____ □ _____.

✎ **어휘복습** 잘 안 들리거나 몰라서 체크한 어휘를 써 놓고 복습해 보세요.

□ _____　□ _____　□ _____　□ _____
□ _____　□ _____　□ _____　□ _____
□ _____　□ _____　□ _____　□ _____

대화를 듣고, 두 사람의 관계로 가장 적절한
것을 고르시오.

① 택시 기사 – 승객
② 공항 직원 – 탑승객
③ 주유소 직원 – 고객
④ 호텔 직원 – 투숙객
⑤ 식당 종업원 – 손님

M : Excuse me. Can you ☐ _____ me a ☐ _____ ☐ _____ for
    seven A.M.? I have a ☐ _____ to ☐ _____ tomorrow morning.
W : Sure. What's your ☐ _____ ☐ _____?
M : It's room nine oh two.
W : Okay! Is there ☐ _____ ☐ _____ I can ☐ _____ you with?
M : I'll need a ☐ _____ to the ☐ _____ at eight A.M.
W : No problem. I'll have one ready for you.

다음을 듣고, Angel English Camp에 관해
언급되지 <u>않은</u> 것을 고르시오.

① 설립 연도   ② 시설
③ 위치   ④ 프로그램
⑤ 참가 비용

M : Are you looking for an ☐ _____ ☐ _____? Our Angel
    English Camp was ☐ _____ in ☐ _____ ☐ _____.
    We ☐ _____ ☐ _____ dormitory ☐ _____ as well as high-
    tech computer labs to promote a quality ☐ _____ ☐ _____.
    The camp is ☐ _____ in Ottawa. Our ☐ _____ ☐ _____
    English conversation in the morning and sports activities in the
    afternoon. For ☐ _____ ☐ _____, visit our ☐ _____, www
    dot angelenglishcamp dot com.

✎ **어휘복습** 잘 안 들리거나 몰라서 체크한 어휘를 써 놓고 복습해 보세요.

☐ _____   ☐ _____   ☐ _____   ☐ _____
☐ _____   ☐ _____   ☐ _____   ☐ _____
☐ _____   ☐ _____   ☐ _____   ☐ _____

13 그림 정보 파악

다음 공항 주차 안내도를 보면서 대화를 듣고, 두 사람이 주차할 구역을 고르시오.

W: Honey, □ _____ should we □ _____ at the □ _____?
M: Hmm, the □ _____ parking is □ _____, isn't it?
W: Right, but it's too □ _____ □ _____ the □ _____.
M: □ _____, we can park in the □ _____ parking lot.
W: What about □ _____ A or B? We can □ _____ some
   □ _____ at the □ _____ before boarding.
M: But section C is □ _____ to our airline's □ _____. It would be
   □ _____ to □ _____ □ _____ first because we have a lot of
   □ _____.
W: I □ _____. Then let's park there.

14 화제 추론

다음을 듣고, 무엇에 관한 설명인지 고르시오.

① 농구 ② 축구 ③ 배구
④ 야구 ⑤ 핸드볼

W: This is a □ _____ □ _____ using a □ _____. You can play it
   both indoors and outdoors. The □ _____ is high
   □ _____ the □ _____. A □ _____ is attached to a
   □ _____ □ _____ on a board, and the bottom of the net is
   open. People □ _____ by □ _____ the □ _____ into the net.
   You don't need any other equipment to play. You can □ _____
   the ball □ _____ your □ _____, but not with your feet.

✎ **어휘복습** 잘 안 들리거나 몰라서 체크한 어휘를 써 놓고 복습해 보세요.

□ _____ □ _____ □ _____ □ _____
□ _____ □ _____ □ _____ □ _____
□ _____ □ _____ □ _____ □ _____

15 할 일 파악

대화를 듣고, 남자가 할 일로 가장 적절한 것을 고르시오.

① 운동하기
② 공원 청소하기
③ 사진 나눠주기
④ 애완견 산책시키기
⑤ 동물 보호소 방문하기

M : Hey, Vicky. □ _____ are you □ _____ here?

W : I'm handing out □ _____ of my □ _____ to people.

M : Why are you doing that?

W : I was walking him in the park yesterday, but he □ _____ □ _____ while I was □ _____ my □ _____ .

M : That's strange. Have you checked at any of the □ _____ □ _____ ?

W : Yes, but he's □ _____ to be □ _____ . Could you help me find my puppy?

M : Sure. No problem. □ _____ □ _____ some of the □ _____ , and I'll □ _____ them □ _____ to people.

16 특정 정보 파악

대화를 듣고, 두 사람이 구입할 물건을 고르시오.

① screwdriver   ② glue
③ tube   ④ air pump
⑤ water bottle

W : James, the front □ _____ of my □ _____ keeps going □ _____ . I took the □ _____ out of the tire, but I couldn't find the □ _____ .

M : Don't worry. Just put the tube in some water and you'll find it.

W : Like this? Wow! Now I can see the air □ _____ coming from the holes.

M : Let me see. Hmm, there are several holes, so you need to put in a □ _____ □ _____ .

W : But I don't have an □ _____ one.

M : Then we need to go out and □ _____ a new one.

W : Okay, let's go.

✎ **어휘복습** 잘 안 들리거나 몰라서 체크한 어휘를 써 놓고 복습해 보세요.

□ _____   □ _____   □ _____   □ _____

□ _____   □ _____   □ _____   □ _____

□ _____   □ _____   □ _____   □ _____

17 상황에 적절한 말 찾기

다음 상황 설명을 듣고, Sean이 엄마에게 할 말로 가장 적절한 것을 고르시오.

Sean: Mom, _____

① when is the job interview?
② how much did you pay for it?
③ could you buy me a new suit?
④ where is the department store?
⑤ does this suit look good on me?

M : Sean □ _____ a new □ _____ for his □ _____ □ _____ tomorrow. He wants to □ _____ □ _____ for the interview, but he's □ _____ □ _____ if he □ _____ □ _____ in his new clothes. So he decides to □ _____ his □ _____ □ _____ he □ _____ in his new suit. In this situation, what would Sean most likely say to his mom?
Sean : Mom, _____

18 할 일 파악

대화를 듣고, 남자가 할 일로 가장 적절한 것을 고르시오.

① 전구 교체하기　　② 주방 정리하기
③ 욕실 청소하기　　④ 식사 준비하기
⑤ 쓰레기 버리기

W : Honey, I'm busy cooking. Can you □ _____ the □ _____ □ _____ for me?
M : But isn't it □ _____ today? We're □ _____ to take it out on □ _____!
W : Oh, I forgot. You're right. I wish we could do that every day.
M : Is there □ _____ □ _____ I can □ _____ for you?
W : As a matter of fact, there is. We need to □ _____ the □ _____ □ _____ in the □ _____. It's out.
M : Okay. I'll do it right now.

✏️ **어휘복습** 잘 안 들리거나 몰라서 체크한 어휘를 써 놓고 복습해 보세요.

□ _____　　□ _____　　□ _____　　□ _____
□ _____　　□ _____　　□ _____　　□ _____
□ _____　　□ _____　　□ _____　　□ _____

19 알맞은 응답 찾기

대화를 듣고, 남자의 마지막 말에 대한 여자의 응답으로 가장 적절한 것을 고르시오.

Woman: _____

① I'd like to buy a birthday present for you.
② Online stores are available 24 hours a day.
③ Online prices are usually lower than offline prices.
④ It's easy to find part-time jobs on the Internet.
⑤ You should make sure the website is safe first.

W : Hey, Tommy. You told me your □ _____ □ _____ is this coming Sunday. Did you □ _____ a □ _____ for her?
M : Not yet. I wanted to get her a □ _____, but they were all so □ _____ at the □ _____ □ _____.
W : Oh, the problem is money, huh?
M : Yeah. I □ _____ some □ _____ while doing my part-time job, but it's □ _____ □ _____.
W : Then, □ _____ □ _____ you □ _____ for a hat □ _____?
M : □ _____ is it □ _____ to do that?
W : _____

20 알맞은 응답 찾기

대화를 듣고, 여자의 마지막 말에 대한 남자의 응답으로 가장 적절한 것을 고르시오.

Man: _____

① That's a good idea! I'll give it a try.
② Sure, I'll try to memorize the whole script.
③ Okay. I'll take notes during the presentation.
④ So, do you mean I should check the grammar?
⑤ Then, you need to practice English conversation.

W : Hey, Jin-su. What's the matter?
M : Hi, Susan. I'm □ _____ □ _____ my English □ _____ tomorrow.
W : Have you □ _____ □ _____ □ _____ you're going to □ _____?
M : Yes, I have. But I'm having □ _____ □ _____ it.
W : You don't have to memorize every word. Just □ _____ □ _____ the □ _____ □ _____.
M : What do you mean?
W : Just □ _____ down the key words on a □ _____ note □ _____. Then, you can □ _____ □ _____ them □ _____ the presentation.
M : _____

✎ **어휘복습** 잘 안 들리거나 몰라서 체크한 어휘를 써 놓고 복습해 보세요.

□ _____ □ _____ □ _____ □ _____
□ _____ □ _____ □ _____ □ _____
□ _____ □ _____ □ _____ □ _____

MP3 기출 03

점수 / 20

01 대화를 듣고, 남자가 만든 깃발을 고르시오.

① ② ③ ④ ⑤

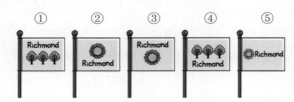

02 대화를 듣고, 남자가 여자에게 전화한 목적으로 가장 적절한 것을 고르시오.

① 제과점 영업 시간을 알아보려고
② 햄버거 가게 위치를 확인하려고
③ 원하는 햄버거 종류를 물어보려고
④ 참치 샌드위치 판매 여부를 문의하려고
⑤ 참치 샌드위치가 모두 팔렸음을 알려주려고

03 다음 그림의 상황에 가장 적절한 대화를 고르시오.

① ② ③ ④ ⑤

04 대화를 듣고, 두 사람이 구입할 시계를 고르시오.

① ② ③ ④ ⑤

05 대화를 듣고, 여자의 직업으로 가장 적절한 것을 고르시오.

① flight attendant ② doctor
③ shop manager ④ babysitter
⑤ teacher

06 대화를 듣고, 남자의 심정으로 가장 적절한 것을 고르시오.

① thankful ② relaxed
③ regretful ④ bored
⑤ indifferent

07 다음을 듣고, 두 사람의 대화가 어색한 것을 고르시오.

① ② ③ ④ ⑤

08 대화를 듣고, 여자가 남자에게 부탁한 일로 가장 적절한 것을 고르시오.

① 좌석 예매하기 ② 아들 데려오기
③ 아이의 부모 찾기 ④ 좌석 맞바꾸기
⑤ 기차 시간 변경하기

09 대화를 듣고, 남자의 마지막 말에 담긴 의도로 가장 적절한 것을 고르시오.

① 위로 ② 감사 ③ 거절
④ 충고 ⑤ 요청

10 대화를 듣고, 여자가 지불할 금액을 고르시오.

① $10 ② $20 ③ $30
④ $40 ⑤ $50

11 대화를 듣고, 두 사람이 대화하고 있는 장소로 가장 적절한 곳을 고르시오.

① bookstore ② library
③ school ④ travel agency
⑤ computer store

12 다음을 듣고, Cowboy Steak House에 관해 언급되지 <u>않은</u> 것을 고르시오.

① 개업 연도   ② 위치
③ 영업 시간   ④ 회원 할인율
⑤ 회원 가입 방법

13 다음 배치도를 보면서 대화를 듣고, 두 사람이 선택한 사진 동아리 구역의 위치를 고르시오.

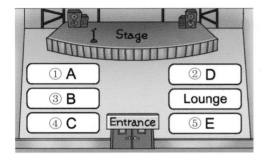

14 다음을 듣고, 무엇에 관한 설명인지 고르시오.

① 유모차   ② 스케이트보드
③ 오토바이   ④ 쇼핑 카트
⑤ 자전거

15 대화를 듣고, 남자가 할 일로 가장 적절한 것을 고르시오.

① 낮잠 자기   ② 산책하기
③ 교무실에 가기   ④ 점심 먹기
⑤ 영어 숙제하기

16 대화를 듣고, 두 사람이 여름휴가를 떠나기로 한 날짜를 고르시오.

① July 12   ② July 14   ③ July 17
④ July 20   ⑤ July 23

17 다음 상황 설명을 듣고, Ms. Brown이 Susan에게 할 말로 가장 적절한 것을 고르시오.

Ms. Brown: _____

① Right now our onion rings are on sale.
② We start serving dinner at 6:30 on weekends.
③ I can hire you if you can work on the weekends.
④ For your hard work, I'll give you a raise next week.
⑤ After you clean the tables, please take out the trash.

18 대화를 듣고, 남자가 할 일로 가장 적절한 것을 고르시오.

① 스카프 찾기   ② 소파 옮기기
③ 날씨 확인하기   ④ 장갑 가져오기
⑤ 콘서트 예매하기

19 대화를 듣고, 상황을 가장 잘 표현한 속담을 고르시오.

① 비 온 뒤에 땅이 굳는다.
② 돌다리도 두들겨 보고 건너라.
③ 가는 말이 고와야 오는 말이 곱다.
④ 하늘이 무너져도 솟아날 구멍이 있다.
⑤ 낮말은 새가 듣고 밤말은 쥐가 듣는다.

20 대화를 듣고, 여자의 마지막 말에 대한 남자의 응답으로 가장 적절한 것을 고르시오.

Man: _____

① Little by little, that's how great things get done.
② All right. I'll give you a ride to the piano concert.
③ Let's go to a shop for other musical instruments.
④ Above all, let's buy a brand-new grand piano first.
⑤ Your teacher will start organizing an orchestra.

01 그림 정보 파악

대화를 듣고, 남자가 만든 깃발을 고르시오.

① Richmond
② Richmond
③ Richmond
④ Richmond
⑤ Richmond

M : Mom, this is the city □ _____ I □ _____ for the Richmond Flag Contest.

W : It looks great! You used trees □ _____ □ _____ □ _____ for the city.

M : Yeah, because the city □ _____ many trees this year.

W : That's true, but why didn't you □ _____ any □ _____? A lot of those were planted, too.

M : I know, but I wanted to □ _____ my flag □ _____.

W : I see. I like your idea to □ _____ the city □ _____ □ _____ the trees.

M : Thanks, Mom.

02 목적 파악

대화를 듣고, 남자가 여자에게 전화한 목적으로 가장 적절한 것을 고르시오.

① 제과점 영업 시간을 알아보려고
② 햄버거 가게 위치를 확인하려고
③ 원하는 햄버거 종류를 물어보려고
④ 참치 샌드위치 판매 여부를 문의하려고
⑤ 참치 샌드위치가 모두 팔렸음을 알려주려고

M : Honey, I'm at the bakery. I have □ _____ □ _____ for you.

W : Don't tell me there are □ _____ tuna □ _____ □ _____!

M : Sorry. They're □ _____ □ _____.

W : Wow, they're really popular.

M : I □ _____ □ _____ □ _____ earlier.

W : It's okay. Please get me a cheeseburger at the Burger World next to the bakery.

M : Okay. I will.

✏️ **어휘복습** 잘 안 들리거나 몰라서 체크한 어휘를 써 놓고 복습해 보세요.

□ _____ □ _____ □ _____ □ _____

□ _____ □ _____ □ _____ □ _____

□ _____ □ _____ □ _____ □ _____

03 그림 상황에 적절한 대화 찾기

다음 그림의 상황에 가장 적절한 대화를 고르시오.

① ② ③ ④ ⑤

① M : Would you like to □ _____ a □ _____ ?

W : Not now. After I ride the bumper car.

② M : □ _____ □ _____ that monster car over there.

W : Oh, it □ _____ so □ _____ .

③ M : □ _____ □ _____ have you been □ _____ ?

W : About □ _____ an □ _____ .

④ M : Can I see your □ _____, please?

W : □ _____ you are.

⑤ M : I'm □ _____, □ _____ you're not tall enough to ride this.

W : Oh, no! I'm so □ _____ .

04 그림 정보 파악

대화를 듣고, 두 사람이 구입할 시계를 고르시오.

① ② ③

④ ⑤

W : Wow, there are so many clocks here. It's □ _____

□ _____ □ _____ one for Annie's birthday.

M : How about this round one?

W : Round clocks are so □ _____ . I think she'd like a □ _____ one.

M : Okay, then □ _____ □ _____ this square one with a cute monkey?

W : Well, that's nice, but she'd □ _____ one with a bear. Oh, look at this square one with two bears.

M : I think she'd really like that. Let's buy this one.

✎ **어휘복습** 잘 안 들리거나 몰라서 체크한 어휘를 써 놓고 복습해 보세요.

□ _____ □ _____ □ _____ □ _____

□ _____ □ _____ □ _____ □ _____

□ _____ □ _____ □ _____ □ _____

05 직업 추론

대화를 듣고, 여자의 직업으로 가장 적절한 것을 고르시오.

① flight attendant   ② doctor
③ shop manager   ④ babysitter
⑤ teacher

W : Sam, how are you feeling today?
M : I feel great. Thank you.
W : I'm really □ _____ that your □ _____ is □ _____.
M : Me too. I'm so □ _____ to finally □ _____ the □ _____.
W : Please □ _____ □ _____ you visit me next Friday to □ _____ your ankle □ _____.
M : Okay. I will.
W : My nurse will help you □ _____ your □ _____ □ _____ you □ _____.
M : Thank you.

06 심정 추론

대화를 듣고, 남자의 심정으로 가장 적절한 것을 고르시오.

① thankful   ② relaxed
③ regretful   ④ bored
⑤ indifferent

M : Mom, □ _____ you □ _____ my backpack?
W : Yes, it's □ _____ □ _____ in the washing machine. You □ _____ □ _____ □ _____ wash it.
M : Oh, no! I should □ _____ □ _____ my stuff □ _____ of my backpack.
W : What was inside?
M : There was a picture of me and my friends in the pocket.
W : That's too bad. Sorry to hear that.
M : Yeah. I should have been □ _____ □ _____.

✎ **어휘복습** 잘 안 들리거나 몰라서 체크한 어휘를 써 놓고 복습해 보세요.

□ _____   □ _____   □ _____   □ _____
□ _____   □ _____   □ _____   □ _____
□ _____   □ _____   □ _____   □ _____

07 어색한 대화 찾기

다음을 듣고, 두 사람의 대화가 <u>어색한</u> 것을 고르시오.

①   ②   ③   ④   ⑤

① M : □ _____ you □ _____ my □ _____ ?
    W : Yes. It's right □ _____ □ _____ .

② M : □ _____ □ _____ will it take to get there
        □ _____ □ _____ ?
    W : I haven't seen it □ _____ a □ _____ time.

③ M : I'm □ _____ □ _____ next month.
    W : □ _____ ! What is the exact date?

④ M : I'm wondering if you could □ _____ □ _____ the
        □ _____ again.
    W : Sure. I will send it □ _____ □ _____ □ _____
        □ _____ .

⑤ M : Would you □ _____ □ _____ with me this evening?
    W : That sounds □ _____ !

08 부탁 파악

대화를 듣고, 여자가 남자에게 부탁한 일로 가장 적절한 것을 고르시오.

① 좌석 예매하기
② 아들 데려오기
③ 아이의 부모 찾기
④ 좌석 맞바꾸기
⑤ 기차 시간 변경하기

W : Excuse me, Sir.
M : Yes?
W : My son and I aren't □ _____ □ _____ □ _____ each other
    on the train.
M : So do you □ _____ me □ _____ □ _____ seats with you?
W : Yes, please. My son isn't □ _____ not sitting next to me.
M : Okay. No problem. I know what young kids are like.
W : Thank you very much. I really □ _____ it.

✏️ **어휘복습** 잘 안 들리거나 몰라서 체크한 어휘를 써 놓고 복습해 보세요.

□ _____   □ _____   □ _____   □ _____

□ _____   □ _____   □ _____   □ _____

□ _____   □ _____   □ _____   □ _____

09 의도 파악

대화를 듣고, 남자의 마지막 말에 담긴 의도로 가장 적절한 것을 고르시오.

① 위로　② 감사　③ 거절
④ 충고　⑤ 요청

M : Julie, the Halloween party is next week.
W : I know. I need to □ _____ □ _____ for my □ _____.
M : Me too. □ _____ □ _____ □ _____ go to the shopping mall some time?
W : Great idea. How about now? Do you □ _____ □ _____?
M : I'd love to, but I have to □ _____ my mother □ _____ the □ _____ now.

10 숫자 정보 파악

대화를 듣고, 여자가 지불할 금액을 고르시오.

① $10　② $20　③ $30
④ $40　⑤ $50

M : Did you □ _____ your □ _____?
W : Yes. It was great.
M : Thank you. So you had □ _____ □ _____ □ _____ spaghetti and one chicken salad. Your □ _____ is forty dollars.
W : Oh, we didn't order a chicken salad.
M : □ _____ □ _____ □ _____. Oh, I'm sorry. I □ _____ a □ _____.
W : That's okay.
M : So you □ _____ have to □ _____ □ _____ the chicken salad, which is ten dollars.
W : All right. Here's my credit card.

✎ **어휘복습** 잘 안 들리거나 몰라서 체크한 어휘를 써 놓고 복습해 보세요.

□ _____　□ _____　□ _____　□ _____
□ _____　□ _____　□ _____　□ _____
□ _____　□ _____　□ _____　□ _____

대화를 듣고, 두 사람이 대화하고 있는 장소로 가장 적절한 곳을 고르시오.

① bookstore ② library
③ school ④ travel agency
⑤ computer store

W : Hello, how may I help you?
M : I'm □ _____ □ _____ the book *The American Tourist*. Can you □ _____ □ _____ □ _____ it?
W : Sure. That's a popular book these days.
M : Yeah. I'm buying it □ _____ a □ _____ for my □ _____ □ _____ □ _____ traveling.
W : How nice! It's □ _____ that □ _____ over there. Right next to the education section.
M : Thank you for your help.

다음을 듣고, Cowboy Steak House에 관해 언급되지 <u>않은</u> 것을 고르시오.

① 개업 연도 ② 위치
③ 영업 시간 ④ 회원 할인율
⑤ 회원 가입 방법

W : Do you like steak? Then □ _____ □ _____ □ _____ Cowboy Steak House. We're □ _____ □ _____ second Avenue. We're □ _____ every day □ _____ eleven a.m. □ _____ ten p.m., □ _____ Mondays. Customers □ _____ a Cowboy Steak House □ _____ will get a ten percent □ _____ for every meal they order. To □ _____ □ _____ to become a member, please □ _____ our □ _____ and □ _____ □ _____ a registration □ _____.

✎ **어휘복습** 잘 안 들리거나 몰라서 체크한 어휘를 써 놓고 복습해 보세요.

□ _____   □ _____   □ _____   □ _____
□ _____   □ _____   □ _____   □ _____
□ _____   □ _____   □ _____   □ _____

13 그림 정보 파악

다음 배치도를 보면서 대화를 듣고, 두 사람이 선택한 사진 동아리 구역의 위치를 고르시오.

M : Ms. White, here's a □ _____ of the sections for the school festival. □ _____ □ _____ do you think would be □ _____ □ _____ the photography club?

W : □ _____ □ _____ section B?

M : The science club has □ _____ been □ _____ that section.

W : Hmm... How about □ _____ the photography club □ _____ a section □ _____ □ _____ the □ _____?

M : Good idea! The lounge is □ _____ □ _____, which can □ _____ them □ _____ □ _____ postcards. □ _____ is □ _____, section D □ _____ E?

W : Why don't we give them the section □ _____ the □ _____?

M : Okay. Great.

14 화제 추론

다음을 듣고, 무엇에 관한 설명인지 고르시오.

① 유모차　　　② 스케이트보드
③ 오토바이　　④ 쇼핑 카트
⑤ 자전거

M : This is a vehicle which you □ _____ by □ _____ □ _____ it. Usually, it has □ _____ □ _____ attached to a frame, one behind the other. To □ _____ □ _____, you have to keep □ _____ two □ _____ with your □ _____. To change directions, you turn a bar that is connected to the front wheel. It is □ _____ □ _____ recreation, general fitness, or □ _____.

✎ **어휘복습** 잘 안 들리거나 몰라서 체크한 어휘를 써 놓고 복습해 보세요.

□ _____　□ _____　□ _____　□ _____

□ _____　□ _____　□ _____　□ _____

15 할 일 파악

대화를 듣고, 남자가 할 일로 가장 적절한 것을 고르시오.

① 낮잠 자기 ② 산책하기
③ 교무실에 가기 ④ 점심 먹기
⑤ 영어 숙제하기

W: Ted, wake up!

M: Oh, Jina. Is □ _____ time □ _____?

W: Not yet. Let's □ _____ □ _____ a □ _____.

M: Well, okay. Wait. □ _____ □ _____ is it?

W: It's one ten. Why?

M: Oh, no! My English teacher □ _____ □ _____ □ _____ □ _____ to the teachers' office □ _____ □ _____ o'clock.

W: Really? Then, hurry up.

M: Okay. See you later.

16 특정 정보 파악

대화를 듣고, 두 사람이 여름휴가를 떠나기로 한 날짜를 고르시오.

① July 12 ② July 14
③ July 17 ④ July 20
⑤ July 23

W: Dad, □ _____ are we □ _____ □ _____ our summer vacation □ _____?

M: Well, I □ _____ □ _____ yet. When does your summer school end?

W: July twelfth.

M: Hmm... I have a three-day □ _____ □ _____ from July fourteenth.

W: Then we can □ _____ □ _____ July seventeenth, right?

M: Yes, so let's □ _____ □ _____ July □ _____ and come back on July twenty third.

W: That's perfect. I'm so excited.

✎ **어휘복습** 잘 안 들리거나 몰라서 체크한 어휘를 써 놓고 복습해 보세요.

□ _____ □ _____ □ _____ □ _____

□ _____ □ _____ □ _____ □ _____

□ _____ □ _____ □ _____ □ _____

17 상황에 적절한 말 찾기

다음 상황 설명을 듣고, Ms. Brown이 Susan에게 할 말로 가장 적절한 것을 고르시오.

Ms. Brown: _____

① Right now our onion rings are on sale.
② We start serving dinner at 6:30 on weekends.
③ I can hire you if you can work on the weekends.
④ For your hard work, I'll give you a raise next week.
⑤ After you clean the tables, please take out the trash.

W : Ms. Brown □ _____ a fast food □ _____. She needs to □ _____ one more weekend part-time □ _____. One day Susan comes to the restaurant to □ _____ □ _____ the part-time □ _____. Ms. Brown wants to make sure that Susan can □ _____ □ _____ the □ _____. In this situation, what would Ms. Brown most likely say to Susan?
Ms. Brown : _____

18 할 일 파악

대화를 듣고, 남자가 할 일로 가장 적절한 것을 고르시오.

① 스카프 찾기   ② 소파 옮기기
③ 날씨 확인하기   ④ 장갑 가져오기
⑤ 콘서트 예매하기

M : Honey, please □ _____ □ _____ or we're going to be □ _____ □ _____ the □ _____.
W : Just a minute! I can't find my scarf.
M : Scarf? I saw it in the car.
W : Ah, right. Let's go. Wait! My □ _____! I need them. It's □ _____ □ _____.
M : I'll get them for you. □ _____ are □ _____?
W : They're □ _____ the □ _____. Thanks, Honey.
M : No problem.

✎ **어휘복습** 잘 안 들리거나 몰라서 체크한 어휘를 써 놓고 복습해 보세요.

□ _____   □ _____   □ _____   □ _____
□ _____   □ _____   □ _____   □ _____
□ _____   □ _____   □ _____   □ _____

19 속담 추론

대화를 듣고, 상황을 가장 잘 표현한 속담을 고르시오.

① 비 온 뒤에 땅이 굳는다.
② 돌다리도 두들겨 보고 건너라.
③ 가는 말이 고와야 오는 말이 곱다.
④ 하늘이 무너져도 솟아날 구멍이 있다.
⑤ 낮말은 새가 듣고 밤말은 쥐가 듣는다.

M : Judy, did you □ _____ □ _____ your bag for your trip?

W : Yes, I did.

M : Did you □ _____ your □ _____ □ _____ your bag?

W : Of course, I did. I even □ _____ a □ _____ □ _____ it.

M : Good. Make sure you □ _____ your flight □ _____ □ _____ you, too.

W : Come on, Dad. I already □ _____ everything.

M : Well, you can never be □ _____ □ _____ about whatever you do.

20 알맞은 응답 찾기

대화를 듣고, 여자의 마지막 말에 대한 남자의 응답으로 가장 적절한 것을 고르시오.

Man : _____

① Little by little, that's how great things get done.
② All right. I'll give you a ride to the piano concert.
③ Let's go to a shop for other musical instruments.
④ Above all, let's buy a brand-new grand piano first.
⑤ Your teacher will start organizing an orchestra.

M : Bella, you're going to be late for your piano lesson.

W : Dad, can I □ _____ today's □ _____?

M : □ _____? You really enjoy playing the piano.

W : I really □ _____ playing the □ _____ pieces □ _____ □ _____ □ _____.

M : I thought your □ _____ is □ _____ □ _____ a professional pianist.

W : That's true, but I don't think I need to □ _____ this much □ _____ □ _____.

M : _____

✎ **어휘복습** 잘 안 들리거나 몰라서 체크한 어휘를 써 놓고 복습해 보세요.

□ _____ □ _____ □ _____ □ _____

□ _____ □ _____ □ _____ □ _____

□ _____ □ _____ □ _____ □ _____

01 대화를 듣고, 여자가 구입할 마스크를 고르시오.

① ② ③ ④ ⑤

02 대화를 듣고, 남자가 여자에게 전화한 목적으로 가장 적절한 것을 고르시오.

① 기차표 예매를 부탁하려고
② 콘서트에 같이 갈 것을 제안하려고
③ 기다리게 한 것에 대해 사과하려고
④ 부산에서 돌아오는 날짜를 물어보려고
⑤ 할머니 생신 잔치에 갈 것인지를 확인하려고

03 다음 그림의 상황에 가장 적절한 대화를 고르시오.

① ② ③ ④ ⑤

04 대화를 듣고, 두 사람이 구입할 케이크를 고르시오.

05 대화를 듣고, 남자의 직업으로 가장 적절한 것을 고르시오.

① librarian   ② professor
③ police officer   ④ salesperson
⑤ science teacher

06 대화를 듣고, 여자의 심정으로 가장 적절한 것을 고르시오.

① bored   ② happy   ③ jealous
④ annoyed   ⑤ scared

07 다음을 듣고, 두 사람의 대화가 <u>어색한</u> 것을 고르시오.

① ② ③ ④ ⑤

08 대화를 듣고, 남자가 여자에게 부탁한 일로 가장 적절한 것을 고르시오.

① 표 예매하기   ② 간식 사오기
③ 대신 줄 서기   ④ 자리 맡아주기
⑤ 버스 노선 알려주기

09 대화를 듣고, 여자의 마지막 말에 담긴 의도로 가장 적절한 것을 고르시오.

① 요청   ② 동의   ③ 감사
④ 제안   ⑤ 거절

10 대화를 듣고, 남자가 지불할 금액을 고르시오.

① $30   ② $35   ③ $40
④ $60   ⑤ $70

11 대화를 듣고, 두 사람이 대화하고 있는 장소로 가장 적절한 곳을 고르시오.

① museum   ② parking lot
③ airport   ④ shopping mall
⑤ campsite

12 다음을 듣고, Central City Museum에 관해 언급 되지 <u>않은</u> 것을 고르시오.

① 개관 연도　　　　② 위치
③ 관람 시간　　　　④ 입장료
⑤ 단체 관람 혜택

13 다음 표를 보면서 대화를 듣고, 내용과 일치하지 <u>않는</u> 것을 고르시오.

Used Bicycle Information

①	Brand Name	Apollo
②	Wheel Size	12 inches
③	Color	Blue
④	Condition	Excellent
⑤	Price	$60

14 다음을 듣고, 무엇에 관한 설명인지 고르시오.

① 낙하산　　　　② 모형 비행기
③ 회전목마　　　　④ 화물차
⑤ 잠수함

15 대화를 듣고, 여자가 대화 직후에 할 일로 가장 적절 한 것을 고르시오.

① 책상 정리하기　　　　② 영화 검색하기
③ 안경 구입하기　　　　④ 휴대전화 가져오기
⑤ 엄마에게 전화하기

16 대화를 듣고, 회사 야유회를 가기로 한 날짜를 고르 시오.

① June 2　　② June 7　　③ June 9
④ June 10　　⑤ June 19

17 다음 상황 설명을 듣고, Chris가 Anna에게 할 말로 가장 적절한 것을 고르시오.

Chris: _____

① What's the special today?
② Can you recommend us a dish?
③ Do you like to cook Italian food?
④ How did you like your food here?
⑤ Are you okay with waiting for a table?

18 대화를 듣고, 남자가 할 일로 가장 적절한 것을 고르 시오.

① 선물 포장하기　　　② 사진 보여주기
③ 지갑 환불 받기　　　④ 엄마에게 전화하기
⑤ 가게 위치 알려주기

19 대화를 듣고, 상황을 가장 잘 표현한 속담을 고르시오.

① 까마귀 날자 배 떨어진다.
② 하룻강아지 범 무서운 줄 모른다.
③ 사공이 많으면 배가 산으로 간다.
④ 하늘은 스스로 돕는 자를 돕는다.
⑤ 일찍 일어나는 새가 벌레를 잡는다.

20 대화를 듣고, 여자의 마지막 말에 대한 남자의 응답으 로 가장 적절한 것을 고르시오.

Man: _____

① I'm sorry, but that's our policy.
② Actually, refunding takes longer.
③ Sure. People like to save money.
④ Well, would you like a larger size?
⑤ Right. This is a good place to shop.

다시 듣고, 빈칸에 알맞은 단어를 써 보세요.

◀)) MP3 기출 04-1

01 그림 정보 파악

대화를 듣고, 여자가 구입할 마스크를 고르시오.

① ② ③

④ ⑤

M : Hello. How may I help you?

W : Hi, I'd like to □ _____ a face □ _____ □ _____ my □ _____ .

M : Okay. □ _____ □ _____ this one with cars on it? It's □ _____ □ _____ boys.

W : It's nice, but do you have any with animals?

M : Yes, we do. How about this one with rabbits?

W : Not bad, but do you have any with □ _____ □ _____ □ _____ animal on it?

M : Yes. How about this □ _____ □ _____ □ _____ and □ _____ ?

W : Great! I'll take it!

02 목적 파악

대화를 듣고, 남자가 여자에게 전화한 목적으로 가장 적절한 것을 고르시오.

① 기차표 예매를 부탁하려고
② 콘서트에 같이 갈 것을 제안하려고
③ 기다리게 한 것에 대해 사과하려고
④ 부산에서 돌아오는 날짜를 물어보려고
⑤ 할머니 생신 잔치에 갈 것인지를 확인하려고

W : Hello, Dad.

M : Alice, I'm still □ _____ □ _____ your □ _____ .

W : Sorry it □ _____ so □ _____ . My answer is "Yes."

M : Great. I'm glad we'll □ _____ □ _____ □ _____ join the Grandma's birthday party together.

W : Me too. I □ _____ my friends □ _____ I can't go to the concert with them that day.

M : Good. Grandma will be so happy to see you. I'll □ _____ our train □ _____ □ _____ Busan.

✎ **어휘복습** 잘 안 들리거나 몰라서 체크한 어휘를 써 놓고 복습해 보세요.

□ _____   □ _____   □ _____   □ _____

□ _____   □ _____   □ _____   □ _____

□ _____   □ _____   □ _____   □ _____

다음 그림의 상황에 가장 적절한 대화를 고르시오.

① W : James, the □ _____ is so □ _____.

　　M : Okay. Let's □ _____ it then.

② W : Honey, would you □ _____ the curtain?

　　M : □ _____, I'll do that for you.

③ W : Oh, it's □ _____ outside!

　　M : I'll go get an □ _____ for you.

④ W : This is □ _____ a □ _____ curtain.

　　M : Thank you. I □ _____ it last month.

⑤ W : Do you know □ _____ □ _____ □ _____ a curtain?

　　M : I'm afraid I've □ _____ □ _____ that □ _____.

① 　 ② 　 ③ 　 ④ 　 ⑤

대화를 듣고, 두 사람이 구입할 케이크를 고르시오.

① 　 ② 　 ③

④ 　 ⑤

W : Honey, look at this □ _____. Isn't the □ _____ beautiful?

M : It's nice, but I'm □ _____ □ _____ □ _____ Mark will like it.

W : Then, how about this □ _____ □ _____ a □ _____?

M : It's good too, but I think Mark □ _____ □ _____ one with □ _____ □ _____.

W : Okay. Then we should □ _____ □ _____ the one with a polar bear □ _____ a penguin.

M : I think Mark would □ _____ the polar bear □ _____ the penguin.

W : I agree. Let's buy it.

✎ **어휘복습** 잘 안 들리거나 몰라서 체크한 어휘를 써 놓고 복습해 보세요.

□ _____　　□ _____　　□ _____　　□ _____

□ _____　　□ _____　　□ _____　　□ _____

□ _____　　□ _____　　□ _____　　□ _____

05 직업 추론

대화를 듣고, 남자의 직업으로 가장 적절한 것을 고르시오.

① librarian
② professor
③ police officer
④ salesperson
⑤ science teacher

W : Hello.
M : Hi. May I help you?
W : Yes. A week ago, I □ _____ □ _____ this book, and I'd like to □ _____ it one □ _____ □ _____. Is that possible?
M : Let me check. Yes, you can. There is □ _____ □ _____ on the □ _____ □ _____.
W : Great. And can you □ _____ □ _____ □ _____ the earth science books □ _____?
M : They're in section D, on the second floor.
W : Thank you.

06 심정 추론

대화를 듣고, 여자의 심정으로 가장 적절한 것을 고르시오.

① bored
② happy
③ jealous
④ annoyed
⑤ scared

M : Hi, Nancy. Looks like you're □ _____ □ _____ □ _____.
W : Yeah. I'm □ _____ my □ _____ □ _____ get my phone back.
M : Did you □ _____ it □ _____?
W : Yes, I did. I left it □ _____ a □ _____ last night.
M : Oh, my! Did you call your phone □ _____ you □ _____ that?
W : Yeah. The taxi driver □ _____ and said he'd □ _____ it □ _____ me. He's at the school gate now.
M : How nice! You're very lucky to □ _____ it □ _____.

✏ **어휘복습** 잘 안 들리거나 몰라서 체크한 어휘를 써 놓고 복습해 보세요.

□ _____ □ _____ □ _____ □ _____
□ _____ □ _____ □ _____ □ _____
□ _____ □ _____ □ _____ □ _____

07 어색한 대화 찾기

다음을 듣고, 두 사람의 대화가 <u>어색한</u> 것을 고르시오.

① ② ③ ④ ⑤

① M : Would you like □ _____ □ _____ □ _____?

　W : Just □ _____, please. Thank you.

② M : I □ _____ my watch yesterday.

　W : Oh, □ _____ to hear that.

③ M : □ _____ did you □ _____ last Monday?

　W : I □ _____ a □ _____ with my friend.

④ M : Ron is □ _____ today □ _____ he is □ _____.

　W : Right. He □ _____ □ _____ be a doctor.

⑤ M : Do you □ _____ □ _____ I sit here?

　W : □ _____. This seat is already □ _____.

08 부탁 파악

대화를 듣고, 남자가 여자에게 부탁한 일로 가장 적절한 것을 고르시오.

① 표 예매하기　　② 간식 사오기
③ 대신 줄 서기　　④ 자리 맡아주기
⑤ 버스 노선 알려주기

W : Hello.

M : Hi, Sue. Are you □ _____ □ _____ □ _____ to the baseball park?

W : Yes, I'm □ _____ the □ _____. Where are you?

M : I'm □ _____ □ _____ □ _____ to buy tickets.

W : Oh, really? I'll be there □ _____ □ _____ □ _____.

M : Okay. □ _____ □ _____ □ _____ some snacks? I skipped lunch. I'm really □ _____.

W : Sure, no problem. I'll buy some.

✎ **어휘복습** 잘 안 들리거나 몰라서 체크한 어휘를 써 놓고 복습해 보세요.

□ _____　　□ _____　　□ _____　　□ _____

□ _____　　□ _____　　□ _____　　□ _____

□ _____　　□ _____　　□ _____　　□ _____

09 의도 파악

대화를 듣고, 여자의 마지막 말에 담긴 의도
로 가장 적절한 것을 고르시오.

① 요청　　② 동의　　③ 감사
④ 제안　　⑤ 거절

W : Kevin, you look so happy in this picture!

M : Yes, I was. I had □ _____ □ _____ □ _____ during the
global camp. This French boy was my □ _____ □ _____
there.

W : He looks nice.

M : He is. He □ _____ me □ _____ □ _____ during the team
activities. I really □ _____ him.

W : □ _____ □ _____ □ _____ send this picture to him by
e-mail?

10 숫자 정보 파악

대화를 듣고, 남자가 지불할 금액을 고르시오.

① $30　　② $35　　③ $40
④ $60　　⑤ $70

W : Hello. Welcome to King Fishing.

M : Hi. I'd like to fish here with my son. □ _____ □ _____ is it?

W : □ _____ dollars □ _____ □ _____. How old is your son?

M : He's seven years old.

W : Then, his □ _____ is □ _____. Would you like to □ _____
fishing □ _____?

M : Yes. □ _____ chairs, please.

W : Okay. They're □ _____ dollars □ _____.

M : Great. Here's the money.

✎ **어휘복습** 잘 안 들리거나 몰라서 체크한 어휘를 써 놓고 복습해 보세요.

□ _____　□ _____　□ _____　□ _____

□ _____　□ _____　□ _____　□ _____

□ _____　□ _____　□ _____　□ _____

11 장소 추론

대화를 듣고, 두 사람이 대화하고 있는 장소로 가장 적절한 곳을 고르시오.

① museum ② parking lot
③ airport ④ shopping mall
⑤ campsite

M : Honey, this trip is going to be so □ _____.

W : □ _____. I'm so excited to be here.

M : What □ _____ □ _____!

W : For sure. Well, let's □ _____ □ _____ the □ _____ before it gets dark.

M : Okay. Let's □ _____ □ _____ the tent is not close to the □ _____ □ _____.

W : Good point. After we set up the tent, I'll □ _____ □ _____.

M : All right. Sounds great.

12 미언급 파악

다음을 듣고, Central City Museum에 관해 언급되지 <u>않은</u> 것을 고르시오.

① 개관 연도 ② 위치
③ 관람 시간 ④ 입장료
⑤ 단체 관람 혜택

W : Hello, listeners. Have you ever visited Central City Museum? The museum □ _____ □ _____ □ _____ nineteen seventy-three. It is □ _____ next to the City Hall. It has five exhibition rooms and a gift shop. The museum is □ _____ daily from □ _____ a.m. □ _____ □ _____ p.m. □ _____ □ _____ are thirty dollars for adults and ten dollars for children. If you have any questions, please visit the Central City Museum website.

✎ **어휘복습** 잘 안 들리거나 몰라서 체크한 어휘를 써 놓고 복습해 보세요.

□ _____   □ _____   □ _____   □ _____

□ _____   □ _____   □ _____   □ _____

□ _____   □ _____   □ _____   □ _____

13 도표·실용문 파악

다음 표를 보면서 대화를 듣고, 내용과 일치하지 <u>않는</u> 것을 고르시오.

Used Bicycle Information

①	Brand Name	Apollo
②	Wheel Size	12 inches
③	Color	Blue
④	Condition	Excellent
⑤	Price	$60

W : Honey, I'd like to □ _____ Ben's □ _____ □ _____ on the Internet. Can you help me □ _____ □ _____ the □ _____?

M : Sure. The brand □ _____ is Apollo.

W : Okay.

M : And the wheel □ _____ is □ _____ inches.

W : All right.

M : And it's □ _____. What □ _____ do you think it's □ _____?

W : I'd say □ _____. Ben rarely rode it.

M : Hmm.... Then I think we can □ _____ □ _____ dollars for it.

14 화제 추론

다음을 듣고, 무엇에 관한 설명인지 고르시오.

① 낙하산   ② 모형 비행기
③ 회전목마   ④ 화물차
⑤ 잠수함

M : This is used to □ _____ □ _____ a person □ _____ □ _____ the □ _____. It enables a person to □ _____ □ _____ an aircraft and □ _____ □ _____ the ground safely. It □ _____ □ _____ a large piece of thin □ _____ □ _____ □ _____ a person's body □ _____ □ _____. It is mostly used in □ _____ situations or in the □ _____, but people also use it □ _____ □ _____.

✎ **어휘복습** 잘 안 들리거나 몰라서 체크한 어휘를 써 놓고 복습해 보세요.

□ _____   □ _____   □ _____   □ _____

□ _____   □ _____   □ _____   □ _____

□ _____   □ _____   □ _____   □ _____

15 할 일 파악

대화를 듣고, 여자가 대화 직후에 할 일로 가장 적절한 것을 고르시오.

① 책상 정리하기
② 영화 검색하기
③ 안경 구입하기
④ 휴대전화 가져오기
⑤ 엄마에게 전화하기

M : Kaylee, we're going to be late for the movie.

W : Sorry, Dad. I was □ _____ □ _____ my □ _____.

M : I've told you so many times to □ _____ them □ _____ the □ _____ □ _____.

W : I know, Dad. Sorry. Oh, wait. I □ _____ my □ _____ on my desk.

M : Come on. Mom's waiting for us outside.

W : Okay. I'll just □ _____ □ _____ □ _____ it.

16 특정 정보 파악

대화를 듣고, 회사 야유회를 가기로 한 날짜를 고르시오.

① June 2   ② June 7
③ June 9   ④ June 10
⑤ June 19

W : Jack, we should □ _____ □ _____ a □ _____ for our company picnic.

M : Okay, Jean. How about June □ _____ or June □ _____?

W : I think we need a couple □ _____ □ _____ than that □ _____ □ _____ for it. How about June □ _____?

M : We □ _____ have a weekly □ _____ □ _____ on that day at ten o'clock.

W : I'm sure we can □ _____ the meeting.

M : Okay, then let's go with your suggested date.

✎ **어휘복습** 잘 안 들리거나 몰라서 체크한 어휘를 써 놓고 복습해 보세요.

□ _____   □ _____   □ _____   □ _____

□ _____   □ _____   □ _____   □ _____

□ _____   □ _____   □ _____   □ _____

17 상황에 적절한 말 찾기

다음 상황 설명을 듣고, Chris가 Anna에게 할 말로 가장 적절한 것을 고르시오.

Chris: _____

① What's the special today?
② Can you recommend us a dish?
③ Do you like to cook Italian food?
④ How did you like your food here?
⑤ Are you okay with waiting for a table?

W: Chris □ _____ his friend Anna □ _____ his favorite Italian restaurant for dinner, but he didn't □ _____ a □ _____.
He □ _____ many □ _____ □ _____ to get a table.
The waiter is writing people's names on a waiting list. Chris □ _____ □ _____ to eat with Anna at this restaurant, so he □ _____ □ _____ □ _____ Anna if she doesn't □ _____ □ _____. In this situation, what would Chris most likely say to Anna?
Chris: _____

18 할 일 파악

대화를 듣고, 남자가 할 일로 가장 적절한 것을 고르시오.

① 선물 포장하기
② 사진 보여주기
③ 지갑 환불 받기
④ 엄마에게 전화하기
⑤ 가게 위치 알려주기

M: Mom, I've decided □ _____ □ _____ □ _____ Jenny for her birthday.
W: What did you □ _____ □ _____?
M: I think I'll get her a wallet.
W: Good idea. □ _____ □ _____ □ _____ wallet do you □ _____ □ _____ □ _____?
M: I saw a nice one at the mall. I □ _____ a □ _____ of it □ _____ my □ _____.
W: Did you? Can I □ _____ it?
M: □ _____. Wait a second.

✎ **어휘복습** 잘 안 들리거나 몰라서 체크한 어휘를 써 놓고 복습해 보세요.

□ _____ □ _____ □ _____ □ _____
□ _____ □ _____ □ _____ □ _____
□ _____ □ _____ □ _____ □ _____

19 속담 추론

대화를 듣고, 상황을 가장 잘 표현한 속담을 고르시오.

① 까마귀 날자 배 떨어진다.
② 하룻강아지 범 무서운 줄 모른다.
③ 사공이 많으면 배가 산으로 간다.
④ 하늘은 스스로 돕는 자를 돕는다.
⑤ 일찍 일어나는 새가 벌레를 잡는다.

M : Jane, how was the science ☐ _____ last weekend?

W : It was a ☐ _____. My team members couldn't ☐ _____
☐ _____.

M : What do you mean?

W : All of them ☐ _____ that their ideas were ☐ _____
☐ _____, and they wouldn't ☐ _____ ☐ _____ ☐ _____
else's ideas.

M : That's too bad. So you didn't ☐ _____ ☐ _____ in the
competition.

W : Actually, we didn't even ☐ _____ our project ☐ _____
the ☐ _____.

M : That was terrible.

20 알맞은 응답 찾기

대화를 듣고, 여자의 마지막 말에 대한 남자의 응답으로 가장 적절한 것을 고르시오.

Man: _____

① I'm sorry, but that's our policy.
② Actually, refunding takes longer.
③ Sure. People like to save money.
④ Well, would you like a larger size?
⑤ Right. This is a good place to shop.

M : How can I help you, Ma'am?

W : I'd like to ☐ _____ a ☐ _____ for this dress I bought here.
Here's the ☐ _____.

M : Hmm... Your receipt shows that you bought this item
☐ _____ ☐ _____ ☐ _____.

W : That's right. Is that a problem?

M : I'm afraid so. You can ☐ _____ get a refund for goods
☐ _____ ☐ _____ ☐ _____ from the ☐ _____
☐ _____ ☐ _____. It's clearly written on the receipt.

W : I don't understand. That's nonsense.

M : _____

✏️ **어휘복습** 잘 안 들리거나 몰라서 체크한 어휘를 써 놓고 복습해 보세요.

☐ _____ ☐ _____ ☐ _____ ☐ _____

☐ _____ ☐ _____ ☐ _____ ☐ _____

☐ _____ ☐ _____ ☐ _____ ☐ _____

01 대화를 듣고, 여자가 주문할 상자를 고르시오.

① ② ③ ④ ⑤

02 대화를 듣고, 남자가 음반 가게를 방문한 목적으로 가장 적절한 것을 고르시오.

① 상품 교환　　② 환불 요청　　③ 제품 구매
④ 앨범 홍보　　⑤ 사은품 문의

03 다음 그림의 상황에 가장 적절한 대화를 고르시오.

① ② ③ ④ ⑤

04 대화를 듣고, 남자가 구입할 의자를 고르시오.

① ② ③ ④ ⑤

05 대화를 듣고, 남자의 직업으로 가장 적절한 것을 고르시오.

① teacher　　　② reporter
③ police officer　　④ shop manager
⑤ tour guide

06 대화를 듣고, 여자의 심정으로 가장 적절한 것을 고르시오.

① bored　　② satisfied　　③ regretful
④ excited　　⑤ thankful

07 다음을 듣고, 두 사람의 대화가 <u>어색한</u> 것을 고르시오.

① ② ③ ④ ⑤

08 대화를 듣고, 남자가 여자에게 부탁한 일로 가장 적절한 것을 고르시오.

① 원고 교정하기　　　② 주제 추천하기
③ 함께 발표하기　　　④ 정보 수집하기
⑤ 보고서 작성하기

09 대화를 듣고, 남자의 마지막 말에 담긴 의도로 가장 적절한 것을 고르시오.

① 충고　　　② 거절　　　③ 제안
④ 요청　　　⑤ 감사

10 대화를 듣고, 남자가 지불할 금액을 고르시오.

① $50　　② $55　　③ $60
④ $75　　⑤ $80

11 대화를 듣고, 두 사람이 대화하고 있는 장소로 가장 적절한 곳을 고르시오.

① car rental　　　② car museum
③ driving school　　④ car repair shop
⑤ used-car market

12 다음을 듣고, Max Sports Center에 관해 언급되지 <u>않은</u> 것을 고르시오.

① 개관 연도
② 이용 가능 시간
③ 프로그램 이용 요금
④ 회원 가입 방법
⑤ 인기 프로그램

13 다음 관람 구역 배치도를 보면서 대화를 듣고, 남자가 예약할 좌석의 구역을 고르시오.

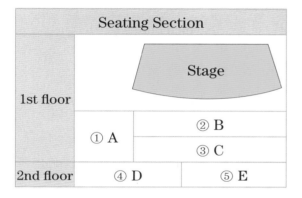

Seating Section		
	Stage	
1st floor		
	① A	② B
		③ C
2nd floor	④ D	⑤ E

14 다음을 듣고, 무엇에 관한 설명인지 고르시오.

① 커튼
② 천막
③ 파리채
④ 사다리
⑤ 방충망

15 대화를 듣고, 남자가 대화 직후에 할 일로 가장 적절한 것을 고르시오.

① 숙제 마무리하기
② 컴퓨터 게임하기
③ 앨범 정리하기
④ 블로그 꾸미기
⑤ 집안일 돕기

16 대화를 듣고, 동아리 회의를 하기로 한 날짜를 고르시오.

① May 15
② May 16
③ May 17
④ May 19
⑤ May 24

17 다음 상황 설명을 듣고, 엄마가 아들에게 할 말로 가장 적절한 것을 고르시오.

Mother: _____

① Have you ever played soccer before?
② My goodness! Where have you been?
③ Cheer up! You can beat them next time.
④ How many times did you win the game?
⑤ I'm sorry to have kept you waiting for me.

18 대화를 듣고, 여자가 할 일로 가장 적절한 것을 고르시오.

① 컴퓨터 재부팅하기
② 인터넷 선 연결하기
③ 홈페이지 주소 알려주기
④ 웹사이트 다시 접속하기
⑤ 컴퓨터 바이러스 검사하기

19 대화를 듣고, 상황을 가장 잘 표현한 속담을 고르시오.

① 쥐구멍에도 볕 들 날 있다.
② 하늘은 스스로 돕는 자를 돕는다.
③ 어떤 이의 약이 다른 이에겐 독이 된다.
④ 일찍 일어나는 새가 벌레를 잡아먹는다.
⑤ 열 번 찍어 안 넘어가는 나무 없다.

20 대화를 듣고, 여자의 마지막 말에 대한 남자의 응답으로 가장 적절한 것을 고르시오.

Man: _____

① Great! That sounds like the card that I want.
② Okay. I'll bring my library card right away.
③ Really? Have you already bought the DVDs?
④ Of course. You'll probably like this library.
⑤ Yes. I want to return these books.

01 그림 정보 파악

대화를 듣고, 여자가 주문할 상자를 고르시오.

① ② ③
④ ⑤

M : □ _____ are you doing □ _____ the □ _____, Julia?

W : I'm looking for a □ _____ □ _____ the □ _____ I made for my mom's birthday.

M : Let's see... I like this □ _____ box.

W : Hmm. Not bad, but isn't it □ _____ □ _____?

M : Well, then how about the heart-shaped one □ _____ □ _____? It looks fancy.

W : Oh, look! Here's a □ _____-shaped one □ _____ a □ _____.

M : Wow, that's pretty!

W : I think so, too. I'll order that one.

02 목적 파악

대화를 듣고, 남자가 음반 가게를 방문한 목적으로 가장 적절한 것을 고르시오.

① 상품 교환   ② 환불 요청
③ 제품 구매   ④ 앨범 홍보
⑤ 사은품 문의

W : What can I do for you?

M : I □ _____ this CD yesterday for my friend. But she □ _____ one □ _____!

W : Would you like to □ _____ □ _____ □ _____ a □ _____ CD?

M : I'd rather just □ _____ a □ _____.

W : Well, you can get a □ _____ □ _____ if you buy the new special album of JC Band.

M : No, thanks.

✏ **어휘복습** 잘 안 들리거나 몰라서 체크한 어휘를 써 놓고 복습해 보세요.

□ _____   □ _____   □ _____   □ _____
□ _____   □ _____   □ _____   □ _____
□ _____   □ _____   □ _____   □ _____

다음 그림의 상황에 가장 적절한 대화를 고르
시오.

① ② ③ ④ ⑤

① W : Dad, □ _____ for □ _____? I'm starving.

　M : We're □ _____ beef □ _____.

② W : Excuse me. This isn't □ _____ □ _____ □ _____.

　M : Oh, I'm sorry. □ _____ □ _____ □ _____ your order.

③ W : What's today's □ _____?

　M : Vegetable □ _____ □ _____ mushroom □ _____.

④ W : □ _____ □ _____ □ _____ cleaning the table, honey?

　M : Of course, I □ _____. And I'm washing the dishes now.

⑤ W : Do you □ _____ □ _____ the food court is in this
building?

　M : I'm □ _____ □ _____. It's my □ _____ □ _____ here.

대화를 듣고, 남자가 구입할 의자를 고르시오.

① ② ③

④ ⑤

M : I'm looking for a □ _____ for my □ _____.

W : How about this one □ _____ □ _____ □ _____? It's very
□ _____ □ _____ students.

M : Oh, my daughter is □ _____ □ _____ □ _____ old. I like
this square one.

W : But it □ _____ be □ _____ for five-year-olds because it
doesn't □ _____ a □ _____. How about this one?

M : Good. The □ _____ shape □ _____ □ _____. How much is
it?

W : It's thirty dollars.

M : Okay, I'll take it.

✎ **어휘복습** 잘 안 들리거나 몰라서 체크한 어휘를 써 놓고 복습해 보세요.

□ _____　□ _____　□ _____　□ _____

□ _____　□ _____　□ _____　□ _____

□ _____　□ _____　□ _____　□ _____

05 직업 추론

대화를 듣고, 남자의 직업으로 가장 적절한 것을 고르시오.

① teacher
② reporter
③ police officer
④ shop manager
⑤ tour guide

M : How may I help you, ma'am?

W : I've □ _____ my six-year-old □ _____. Please help me, □ _____.

M : □ _____ and □ _____ did you □ _____ □ _____ him?

W : □ _____ the street □ _____, not far from this police station, about □ _____ □ _____ □ _____.

M : What's his name?

W : Kevin Anderson. He's wearing a yellow T-shirt and jeans.

M : Okay, we'll □ _____ □ _____ right away. Write down your phone number here, please.

W : Thank you. Please find him.

06 심정 추론

대화를 듣고, 여자의 심정으로 가장 적절한 것을 고르시오.

① bored
② satisfied
③ regretful
④ excited
⑤ thankful

M : You □ _____ □ _____ □ _____ your □ _____.

W : Thanks. But they're □ _____ □ _____. I shouldn't have bought them.

M : Why don't you □ _____ them □ _____ a □ _____ □ _____?

W : I can't. I've □ _____ □ _____ them once.

M : Oh, I see. But they'll □ _____ if you □ _____ □ _____ them.

W : I doubt it. I □ _____ I □ _____ □ _____ them.

✎ **어휘복습** 잘 안 들리거나 몰라서 체크한 어휘를 써 놓고 복습해 보세요.

□ _____   □ _____   □ _____   □ _____

□ _____   □ _____   □ _____   □ _____

□ _____   □ _____   □ _____   □ _____

다음을 듣고, 두 사람의 대화가 어색한 것을 고르시오.

① ② ③ ④ ⑤

① M : □ _____ can I □ _____ □ _____ the city library?

W : Cross the road and □ _____ □ _____ number two six one.

② M : I'd like to □ _____ a □ _____ for the next show.

W : I'm sorry, sir. They're all □ _____ □ _____.

③ M : □ _____ are some of the □ _____ on this bus □ _____?

W : Oh, they're □ _____ □ _____ citizens.

④ M : □ _____ □ _____ any good Korean restaurants □ _____ □ _____?

W : Thank you, but I don't like fast food.

④ M : □ _____ □ _____ see a movie tonight.

W : I □ _____. I have to study for my math test.

대화를 듣고, 남자가 여자에게 부탁한 일로 가장 적절한 것을 고르시오.

① 원고 교정하기
② 주제 추천하기
③ 함께 발표하기
④ 정보 수집하기
⑤ 보고서 작성하기

W : Hi, Steve. You □ _____ □ _____ these days.

M : I'm □ _____ □ _____ a presentation in my Korean class.

W : □ _____ are you going to □ _____ □ _____?

M : I've decided to talk about □ _____ □ _____.

W : Did you □ _____ a □ _____?

M : I did, but it □ _____ □ _____ so □ _____ □ _____ to write it in Korean.

W : Do you need any help?

M : Yes. Would you □ _____ the script and □ _____ any □ _____?

W : Sure, no problem.

✏ **어휘복습** 잘 안 들리거나 몰라서 체크한 어휘를 써 놓고 복습해 보세요.

□ _____ □ _____ □ _____ □ _____
□ _____ □ _____ □ _____ □ _____
□ _____ □ _____ □ _____ □ _____

09 의도 파악

대화를 듣고, 남자의 마지막 말에 담긴 의도
로 가장 적절한 것을 고르시오.

① 충고　　② 거절　　③ 제안
④ 요청　　⑤ 감사

M : I □ _____ □ _____ my science project, Ms. Brown.
W : Great! I'm □ _____ □ _____ you, Tom.
M : I □ _____ □ _____ finished it □ _____ your □ _____.
W : I know □ _____ □ _____ you've been □ _____ on the
　　project.
M : I don't know how to □ _____ you □ _____ for your help.

10 숫자 정보 파악

대화를 듣고, 남자가 지불할 금액을 고르시오.

① $50　　② $55　　③ $60
④ $75　　⑤ $80

M : Excuse me. □ _____ □ _____ is that red shirt?
W : It's □ _____ dollars.
M : Hmm. It's too □ _____ for me.
W : How about this blue one? It's only □ _____ dollars.
M : I like the design. Do you have □ _____ □ _____ shirt
　　□ _____ □ _____ as well?
W : Yes. And if you □ _____ □ _____ in this design, you get
　　□ _____ dollars □ _____ of the total.
M : Great! Then I'll take one green and one blue.
W : Okay.

✎ **어휘복습** 잘 안 들리거나 몰라서 체크한 어휘를 써 놓고 복습해 보세요.

□ _____　□ _____　□ _____　□ _____
□ _____　□ _____　□ _____　□ _____
□ _____　□ _____　□ _____　□ _____

11 장소 추론

대화를 듣고, 두 사람이 대화하고 있는 장소로 가장 적절한 곳을 고르시오.

① car rental
② car museum
③ driving school
④ car repair shop
⑤ used-car market

W : How may I help you?

M : My car is making a □ _____ □ _____ .

W : Okay. Is it your □ _____ □ _____ here?

M : Yes, it is.

W : Then, would you please □ _____ □ _____ this □ _____ ?

M : Sure. How long will it take to □ _____ □ _____ □ _____ ?

W : Well, we have to take a look at it first.

12 미언급 파악

다음을 듣고, Max Sports Center에 관해 언급되지 않은 것을 고르시오.

① 개관 연도
② 이용 가능 시간
③ 프로그램 이용 요금
④ 회원 가입 방법
⑤ 인기 프로그램

M : The Max Sports Center, which □ _____ □ _____ June, two thousand two, is the first five-star □ _____ □ _____ in our city. It is open □ _____ □ _____ a day, □ _____ □ _____ a week for your convenience. We □ _____ a variety of programs □ _____ □ _____ □ _____ . Popular fitness programs like yoga, aerobics, and Taekwondo are offered throughout the year. □ _____ and □ _____ yourself!

✎ **어휘복습** 잘 안 들리거나 몰라서 체크한 어휘를 써 놓고 복습해 보세요.

□ _____ □ _____ □ _____ □ _____

□ _____ □ _____ □ _____ □ _____

□ _____ □ _____ □ _____ □ _____

13 도표·실용문 파악

다음 관람 구역 배치도를 보면서 대화를 듣고, 남자가 예약할 좌석의 구역을 고르시오.

Seating Section	
1st floor	Stage
	① A ② B
	③ C
2nd floor	④ D ⑤ E

M : □ _____ □ _____ do you think are the □ _____?

W : The seats in Section □ _____, of course.

M : But they're really □ _____. How about Section □ _____?

W : You can see □ _____ □ _____ □ _____ of the stage □ _____ □ _____.

M : Right, and the seats on the □ _____ □ _____ are □ _____ □ _____ from the stage.

W : I agree. We have □ _____ □ _____ option □ _____.

M : That's right. I'll □ _____ two □ _____ in that section.

14 화제 추론

다음을 듣고, 무엇에 관한 설명인지 고르시오.

① 커튼　　　　② 천막
③ 파리채　　　④ 사다리
⑤ 방충망

W : This is □ _____ □ _____ a frame of wood or metal and designed to □ _____ the opening of a □ _____. It is used to □ _____ □ _____ □ _____ □ _____. It is most useful in areas where there're □ _____ □ _____ □ _____ insects, especially □ _____. It also allows □ _____ □ _____ to □ _____ □ _____ a house.

✎ **어휘복습** 잘 안 들리거나 몰라서 체크한 어휘를 써 놓고 복습해 보세요.

□ _____　　□ _____　　□ _____　　□ _____

□ _____　　□ _____　　□ _____　　□ _____

□ _____　　□ _____　　□ _____

15 할 일 파악

대화를 듣고, 남자가 대화 직후에 할 일로 가장 적절한 것을 고르시오.

① 숙제 마무리하기
② 컴퓨터 게임하기
③ 앨범 정리하기
④ 블로그 꾸미기
⑤ 집안일 돕기

W : Mike, are you □ _____ computer □ _____ □ _____ ?
M : Mom, I'm just □ _____ □ _____ on my blog.
W : Did you □ _____ □ _____ of your □ _____ already?
M : Actually, I still have a little bit □ _____ □ _____ □ _____ .
W : Then I think you □ _____ finish your □ _____ □ _____ .
M : Okay, □ _____ □ _____ , Mom.

16 특정 정보 파악

대화를 듣고, 동아리 회의를 하기로 한 날짜를 고르시오.

① May 15 　　　② May 16
③ May 17 　　　④ May 19
⑤ May 24

M : Jenny, the school club festival is on May twenty fourth.
W : Yeah, I know. We need to □ _____ a □ _____ sometime this week so we can □ _____ □ _____ □ _____ .
M : Sure. Why don't we meet on May □ _____ ?
W : I don't think that's a good idea. We have two □ _____ classes on □ _____ □ _____
M : Right. What about May □ _____ ? It's Wednesday.
W : That's □ _____ the □ _____ day because we don't have any after-school classes on that day.
M : Okay. Let's meet on Wednesday.

✎ **어휘복습** 잘 안 들리거나 몰라서 체크한 어휘를 써 놓고 복습해 보세요.

□ _____　　□ _____　　□ _____　　□ _____

□ _____　　□ _____　　□ _____　　□ _____

□ _____　　□ _____　　□ _____　　□ _____

17 상황에 적절한 말 찾기

다음 상황 설명을 듣고, 엄마가 아들에게 할 말로 가장 적절한 것을 고르시오.

Mother: _____

① Have you ever played soccer before?
② My goodness! Where have you been?
③ Cheer up! You can beat them next time.
④ How many times did you win the game?
⑤ I'm sorry to have kept you waiting for me.

W : Chris □ _____ comes home □ _____ □ _____ p.m. Today, Chris and his friends □ _____ a □ _____ game. His team won, and the game □ _____ around □ _____ p.m. Chris □ _____ □ _____ his mother that he would be □ _____ today. His mother was □ _____ □ _____ him and getting □ _____.
In this situation, what would his mother most likely say to Chris when he came home?
Mother: _____

18 할 일 파악

대화를 듣고, 여자가 할 일로 가장 적절한 것을 고르시오.

① 컴퓨터 재부팅하기
② 인터넷 선 연결하기
③ 홈페이지 주소 알려주기
④ 웹사이트 다시 접속하기
⑤ 컴퓨터 바이러스 검사하기

M : Linda, I can't open this website. I don't know what's wrong with it.
W : Did you □ _____ the □ _____?
M : □ _____. And the Internet cable is □ _____.
W : Hmm. Have you □ _____ □ _____ □ _____ on your computer?
M : □ _____, I haven't. I just tried □ _____ it □ _____ and □ _____ again.
W : Well, you □ _____ □ _____ for viruses first. □ _____ □ _____ □ _____ that for you.
M : Thanks.

✎ **어휘복습** 잘 안 들리거나 몰라서 체크한 어휘를 써 놓고 복습해 보세요.

□ _____ □ _____ □ _____ □ _____
□ _____ □ _____ □ _____ □ _____
□ _____ □ _____ □ _____ □ _____

19 속담 추론

대화를 듣고, 상황을 가장 잘 표현한 속담을 고르시오.

① 쥐구멍에도 볕 들 날 있다.
② 하늘은 스스로 돕는 자를 돕는다.
③ 어떤 이의 약이 다른 이에겐 독이 된다.
④ 일찍 일어나는 새가 벌레를 잡아먹는다.
⑤ 열 번 찍어 안 넘어가는 나무 없다.

W : You □ _____ so □ _____. What's the matter?

M : I've been □ _____ to be a □ _____ □ _____ for weeks.

W : □ _____ did you □ _____ to do that?

M : I □ _____ this □ _____ called *Early Bird*. And I've been □ _____ □ _____ in it, but it □ _____ seem to □ _____ for me.

W : Well, then I don't think you're a morning person after all. That's why you feel tired these days.

M : Right. I'd □ _____ □ _____ □ _____ to my own style.

20 알맞은 응답 찾기

대화를 듣고, 여자의 마지막 말에 대한 남자의 응답으로 가장 적절한 것을 고르시오.

Man: _____

① Great! That sounds like the card that I want.
② Okay. I'll bring my library card right away.
③ Really? Have you already bought the DVDs?
④ Of course. You'll probably like this library.
⑤ Yes. I want to return these books.

M : Hi. I'd like to get a □ _____ □ _____.

W : Do you live in this area?

M : Yes, □ _____ □ _____ □ _____ this library.

W : Then you can get a Special Membership Card.

M : What □ _____ does it □ _____?

W : You can borrow □ _____ □ _____ □ _____ books □ _____ □ _____ □ _____.

M : Good. Is that all?

W : You can also check out our DVDs □ _____ □ _____ □ _____.

M : _____

✏️ **어휘복습** 잘 안 들리거나 몰라서 체크한 어휘를 써 놓고 복습해 보세요.

□ _____ □ _____ □ _____ □ _____

□ _____ □ _____ □ _____ □ _____

□ _____ □ _____ □ _____ □ _____

1. 대화를 듣고, 남자가 만든 깃발을 고르시오.

◀)) MP3 유형 01

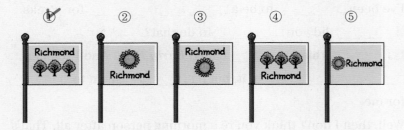

① ② ③ ④ ⑤

❶ 그림에 드러난 요소를 영어로 떠올려 보세요.
→ flag, trees, sunflowers, name

❷ 나무가 들어간 그림으로 정답이 좁혀지네요.

❸ 해바라기가 언급되었다고 섣불리 해바라기 그림을 선택해서는 안 됩니다.

❹ 결정적 힌트가 마지막에 등장합니다.

●정답 근거 ●오답 함정

M : Mom, this is the city flag I designed for the Richmond Flag Contest.

W : It looks great! You used trees as a symbol for the city.

M : Yeah, because the city planted many trees this year.

W : That's true, but why didn't you include any sunflowers? A lot of those were planted, too.

M : I know, but I wanted to make my flag unique.

W : I see. I like your idea to put the city name above the trees.

M : Thanks, Mom.

남 : 엄마, 이건 제가 리치먼드 깃발 대회를 위해 디자인한 도시 깃발이에요.

여 : 아주 멋지구나! 넌 나무들을 도시의 상징으로 이용했구나.

남 : 네, 시에서 올해 많은 나무들을 심었기 때문이에요.

여 : 그건 맞지만 왜 해바라기는 하나도 포함시키지 않았니? 해바라기도 많이 심었는데.

남 : 알아요, 하지만 저는 제 깃발을 독특하게 만들고 싶었어요.

여 : 알겠다. 나무 위에 도시 이름을 넣은 네 아이디어가 마음에 드는구나.

남 : 고맙습니다, 엄마.

📖 **필수어휘**

모양 round 둥근 모양 triangle 삼각형 square 정사각형 rectangle 직사각형 diamond-shaped 다이아몬드 모양의 heart-shaped 하트 모양의 star-shaped 별 모양의

위치 above 위에 below 아래에 beside 옆에 behind 뒤에 between A and B A와 B 사이에

2. 대화를 듣고, 두 사람이 하고 있는 동작을 고르시오.

🔊 **MP3 유형 02**

① ② ③ ④ ⑤

◀

❶ 그림에 보이는 신체 부위의 명칭을 영어로 떠올려 보세요.
→ head, neck, shoulder, arm, elbow, hand

❷ 첫 번째 설명을 듣고 정답의 범위를 좁혀가세요.
→ 오른손이 머리 가까이에 있는 그림은 ②, ④

❸ 대부분 첫 번째보다는 두 번째 설명에 확실한 힌트가 있습니다.
→ 왼손으로 오른쪽 팔꿈치를 잡고 있는 그림은 ④

●정답 근거

W : Let's take a break. We've been sitting too long.

M : Hey, I learned some stretches. This will help. First, put your right hand behind your head like this.

W : Okay. Now what?

M : Then, hold your right elbow with your left hand. And gently pull your elbow to the left.

W : Oh, I feel the stretch in my muscles.

M : Hold it for ten seconds and then do it again.

여 : 좀 쉬자. 우리는 너무 오래 앉아 있었어.

남 : 있잖아, 내가 스트레칭을 몇 가지 배웠거든. 이게 도움이 될 거야. 먼저 네 오른손을 이렇게 네 머리 뒤에 대.

여 : 알았어. 그리고 이제는?

남 : 그리고 나서 네 왼손으로 네 오른쪽 팔꿈치를 잡아. 그리고 네 팔꿈치를 왼쪽으로 부드럽게 당겨.

여 : 아, 내 근육들이 땅겨지는 게 느껴져.

남 : 10초 동안 그대로 있다가 그 동작을 다시 해 봐.

📖 **필수어휘**

신체 부위   waist 허리   stomach 배   chest 가슴   wrist 손목   knee 무릎   ankle 발목   heel 뒤꿈치
외모   slim 날씬한   thin 마른   chubby 통통한   fat 뚱뚱한   curly hair 곱슬머리   straight hair 생머리

1. 대화를 듣고, 남자가 여자에게 전화한 목적으로 가장 적절한 것을 고르시오. ◀ ♪ MP3 유형 03

① 기차표 예매를 부탁하려고
② 콘서트에 같이 갈 것을 제안하려고
③ 기다리게 한 것에 대해 사과하려고
④ 부산에서 돌아오는 날짜를 물어보려고
⑤ 할머니 생신 잔치에 갈 것인지를 확인하려고

> 목적을 파악하는 유형은 '전화' 상황이 주를 이루며 간혹 '방문' 상황도 등장합니다.
>
> ❶ 전화를 건 사람의 성별을 확인하세요. 남자의 목적을 물으면 남자의 목소리에, 여자의 목적을 물으면 여자의 목소리에 보다 귀를 기울여야 합니다.
>
> ❷ 두 사람의 관계가 바로 드러나네요.
> → Hello, Dad.
>
> ❸ 오답 함정이 선택지 곳곳에 포함되어 있으니 주의하세요.

● 정답 근거 ● 오답 함정

W : Hello, Dad.
M : Alice, I'm still waiting for your decision.
W : Sorry it took so long. **My answer is "Yes."**
M : Great. I'm glad we'll be able to join the Grandma's birthday party together.
W : Me too. I told my friends that I can't go to the concert with them that day.
M : Good. Grandma will be so happy to see you. I'll book our train tickets to Busan.

여 : 안녕하세요, 아빠.
남 : 앨리스, 난 너의 결정을 아직 기다리고 있단다.
여 : 너무 오래 걸려서 죄송해요. 제 대답은 "네"예요.
남 : 잘됐구나. 우리가 할머니 생신 잔치에 함께 갈 수 있어서 기쁘구나.
여 : 저도 그래요. 친구들에게 저는 그날 콘서트에 갈 수 없다고 말했어요.
남 : 좋아. 할머니께서 널 봐서 아주 기뻐하실 거야. 내가 부산행 기차표를 예매하마.

 주요 표현

부탁   **Would you** print out my homework for me? 제 숙제를 출력해 주시겠어요?
정보 요청   **Do you know** if there is a good restaurant near the museum? 박물관 근처에 좋은 식당이 있는지 아니?
약속   **What time** do you want to meet for dinner tomorrow? 내일 저녁식사를 위해 몇 시에 만나길 원하니?

2. 대화를 듣고, 남자가 음반 가게를 방문한 목적으로 가장 적절한 것을 고르시오. 🔊 MP3 유형 04

① 상품 교환　　② 환불 요청 ✓　　③ 제품 구매

④ 앨범 홍보　　⑤ 사은품 문의

▶

❶ 성별 확인!

❷ 지시문에 이미 대화 장소가 주어지기 때문에 대화를 이해하기 수월합니다.

❸ 여자가 제안하는 내용에 현혹되어 섣불리 답을 고르면 곤란해요! 남자의 대답을 꼭 확인하세요.

❹ I'd rather(차라리 ~하겠다)는 화자의 적극적인 의지를 드러냅니다. 이 문장에 정답이 있네요!

●정답 근거 ●오답 함정

W : What can I do for you?

M : I bought this CD yesterday for my friend. But she has one already!

W : Would you like to exchange it for a different CD?

M : I'd rather just get a refund.

W : Well, you can get a free gift if you buy the new special album of JC Band.

M : No, thanks.

여 : 무엇을 도와드릴까요?

남 : 제가 어제 친구를 주려고 이 CD를 샀는데요. 그런데 친구가 이미 이걸 갖고 있어요!

여 : 다른 CD로 교환하고 싶으신가요?

남 : 환불받는 게 좋겠어요.

여 : 음, JC밴드의 새로 나온 특별 앨범을 사면 사은품을 받을 수 있는데요.

남 : 고맙지만 됐어요.

 주요 표현

변경　I've decided to change my phone service to another company. 다른 회사로 전화 서비스를 바꾸기로 했어요.

초대　Can you come to my birthday party? 내 생일 파티에 올 수 있니?

그림 상황에 적절한 대화 찾기

다음 그림의 상황에 가장 적절한 대화를 고르시오. ◀》 MP3 유형 05 ◀

① ② ③ ④ ⑤✓

● 정답 근거 ● 오답 함정

① W : How long will it take to get my bag fixed?
　 M : It'll take about a week.

② W : I bought you a new pair of shoes for your birthday.
　 M : Really? Thank you so much.

③ W : I lost my bag. What should I do?
　 M : You should fill out this form first.

④ W : When does the shoe-making class start?
　 M : It begins next Monday.

⑤ W : These shoes feel so loose. Could you show me
　　 another pair?
　 M : Sure. Let me go get them for you.

❶ 그림을 보며 어떤 상황인지 파악하세요. 그림에서 강조되는 부분이 뭔지 확인하세요.
→ 신발 가게에서, 신발이 큰 것에 대해서 손님(여자)이 점원(남자)에게 말하는 상황

❷ 그림에서 눈에 띄는 shoes를 활용한 오답이 등장하므로 shoes만 듣고 답을 고르지 않도록 주의하세요.

① 여 : 제 가방을 고치는 데 얼마나 걸릴까요?
　 남 : 일주일 정도 걸릴 겁니다.

② 여 : 내가 네 생일 선물로 새 신발 한 켤레를 샀어.
　 남 : 그래? 정말 고마워.

③ 여 : 제 가방을 잃어버렸어요. 저는 어떻게 해야 하죠?
　 남 : 먼저 이 양식을 작성해 주십시오.

④ 여 : 신발 만들기 수업은 언제 시작하죠?
　 남 : 다음 주 월요일에 시작합니다.

⑤ 여 : 이 신발은 너무 헐겁게 느껴지네요. 다른 것을 보여주실 수 있나요?
　 남 : 물론이죠. 제가 가져다 드릴게요.

 오답 피하기

그림에 보이는 몇 개 단어를 이용한 그럴듯한 대화가 있어도, 그림에서 강조되는 상황과 맞는지를 꼭 확인하세요.

① W : James, the curtain is so dirty.
　 M : Okay. Let's wash it then.

② W : This is such a lovely curtain.
　 M : Thank you. I bought it last month.

③ W : Honey, **would you close the curtain**?
　 M : Sure, I'll do that for you.
→ 햇빛이 비쳐서 눈이 부신 여자의 상황이 담긴 대화

대화를 듣고, 남자의 심정으로 가장 적절한 것을 고르시오.

🔊 MP3 유형 06

① thankful ② relaxed
③ regretful ✓ ④ bored
⑤ indifferent

◀ ❶ 누구의 심정을 묻고 있는지 확인! 심정 추론 유형은 두 사람의 심정이 모두 드러나는 경우가 많기 때문에 대상을 정확히 구분해야 해요.

❷ 심정을 드러내는 직접적인 단어가 없더라도, 대화의 분위기 및 화자의 어조를 통해 심정을 추론해야 합니다.

❸ 'should have+과거분사'는 '~해야 했는데 (하지 못했다)'라는 의미로 후회의 심정을 나타냅니다.

●정답 근거

M : Mom, have you seen my backpack?
W : Yes, it's getting washed in the washing machine. You asked me to wash it.
M : Oh, no! I should have taken my stuff out of my backpack.
W : What was inside?
M : There was a picture of me and my friends in the pocket.
W : That's too bad. Sorry to hear that.
M : Yeah. I should have been more careful.

남 : 엄마, 제 책가방 보셨어요?
여 : 그래, 그건 세탁기로 세탁 중이야. 네가 세탁해 달라고 했잖니.
남 : 오, 이런! 제가 책가방에서 제 물건을 꺼내 놨어야 했는데요.
여 : 안에 뭐가 있었는데?
남 : 주머니에 저랑 제 친구가 나온 사진이 있었어요.
여 : 정말 안됐구나. 그 얘기를 듣게 돼서 유감이다.
남 : 네. 제가 좀 더 조심했어야죠.

💡 **주요 표현**

excited 즐거운	Good idea. It's going to be a great day! 좋은 생각이야! 멋진 날이 될 것 같아!
upset 화가 난	It's not the first time! It really drives me crazy. 이번이 처음이 아니잖아! 정말 미치겠다.
regretful 후회하는	I wish I hadn't bought the shoes. 난 그 신발을 사지 않았더라면 좋을 텐데.
	I should have listened to your advice. 내가 너의 충고를 들었어야 했어.
	I shouldn't have talked like that yesterday. 내가 어제 그렇게 말하지 말았어야 했어.
frustrated 좌절한	I can't believe that I made such a big mistake. 내가 그런 큰 실수를 저질렀다니 믿을 수 없어.
	I still don't understand the book I'm reading! I'd better give up. 내가 읽고 있는 책을 아직도 이해하지 못하겠어. 차라리 포기하는 게 낫겠어.
relieved 안도한	After three hours of searching, I finally got my phone back. 세 시간 동안 뒤진 끝에 드디어 내 휴대폰을 찾았다.

📖 **필수어휘**

proud 자랑스러운 relieved 안도한 satisfied 만족한 relaxed 느긋한 delighted 기쁜 touched 감동 받은 encouraged 용기를 얻은
enthusiastic 열정적인 depressed 우울한 anxious 불안한 frustrated 좌절한 disappointed 실망한 discouraged 낙담한
embarrassed 당황한 indifferent 무관심한 confused 혼란스러운

직업 · 관계 추론

1. 대화를 듣고, 여자의 직업으로 가장 적절한 것을 고르시오.

🔊 MP3 유형 07

① flight attendant　　☑ doctor
③ shop manager　　　④ babysitter
⑤ teacher

●정답 근거

W : Sam, how are you feeling today?
M : I feel great. Thank you.
W : I'm really happy that your ankle is better.
M : Me too. I'm so excited to finally leave the hospital.
W : Please make sure you visit me next Friday to check your ankle again.
M : Okay. I will.
W : My nurse will help you get your medicine before you leave.
M : Thank you.

> ❶ 성별을 확인하는 것이 중요! 엉뚱한 사람의 직업에 초점을 두지 않도록 하세요.
> ❷ 직업을 파악하는 문제는 상대방의 대사에 결정적인 힌트가 언급되기도 합니다.
> ❸ 직업을 가리키는 직접적인 단어는 없지만, 힌트가 여러 번에 걸쳐 주어집니다.
> ✪ 대화 장소와 두 사람의 관계까지 파악해 볼까요?
> → 장소: 병원　관계: 의사와 환자

여 : 샘, 너는 오늘 몸이 어떠니?
남 : 아주 좋아요. 고마워요.
여 : 네 발목이 나아졌다니 정말 기쁘다.
남 : 저도 그래요. 마침내 퇴원하게 되어 정말 신나요.
여 : 다음 주 금요일에 발목을 다시 확인하러 병원에 꼭 오거라.
남 : 알았어요. 그렇게 할게요.
여 : 내 간호사가 네가 가기 전에 약을 챙겨줄 거야.
남 : 고맙습니다.

2. 대화를 듣고, 두 사람의 관계로 가장 적절한 것을 고르시오.

🔊 MP3 유형 08

① 택시 기사 – 승객　　② 공항 직원 – 탑승객
③ 주유소 직원 – 고객　☑ 호텔 직원 – 투숙객
⑤ 식당 종업원 – 손님

●정답 근거　●오답 함정

M : Excuse me. Can you give me a wake-up call for seven A.M.? I have a plane to catch tomorrow morning.
W : Sure. What's your room number?
M : It's room nine oh two.
W : Okay! Is there anything else I can help you with?
M : I'll need a taxi to the airport at eight A.M.
W : No problem. I'll have one ready for you.

> ❶ 선택지를 훑어보세요. 제시된 관계에서 오갈 수 있는 대화를 빠르게 상상해봐도 좋습니다.
> ❷ 대화가 이루어지고 있는 장소가 어디인지를 파악하면 두 사람의 관계를 쉽게 찾을 수 있어요.
> → wake-up call은 호텔에서 해주는 서비스이고, room number를 묻는 걸 보니 호텔에서 이루어지는 대화로 추정 가능
> ✪ plane만 듣고 ②를 선택하거나, taxi만 듣고 ①을 선택하면 안돼요!

남 : 실례합니다. 오전 7시에 제게 모닝콜을 해주시겠어요? 내일 아침에 비행기를 타야 하거든요.
여 : 물론입니다. 객실 번호가 무엇인가요?
남 : 902호예요.
여 : 네! 제가 더 도와드릴 건 없을까요?
남 : 저는 오전 8시에 공항으로 가는 택시가 필요해요.
여 : 문제 없습니다. 손님을 위해 한 대 준비해 놓겠습니다.

주요 표현

doctor 의사
My surgery schedule has been changed. I have to operate at 3 p.m. tomorrow.
저의 수술 일정이 변경되었습니다. 내일 오후 3시에 수술을 해야 합니다.

clerk 점원
I'm sorry, but they're all sold out. How about these blue ones? Do you want us to order the green ones, then?
죄송하지만 그건 품절되었어요. 파란색은 어떠세요? 그렇다면 저희가 초록색을 주문해 드릴까요?

librarian 사서
You can keep the book five more days. There is no one on the waiting list.
그 책을 5일 동안 더 가지고 계셔도 됩니다. 대기자 명단에 아무도 없거든요.

banker 은행원
Would you like cash or traveler's checks? How much money do you want to exchange?
현금을 원하시나요, 아니면 여행자 수표를 원하시나요? 돈을 얼마나 환전하고 싶으세요?

news caster 뉴스진행자
It's my job to clearly deliver news and information to people.
제 업무는 뉴스와 정보를 사람들에게 명확히 전달하는 것입니다.

pilot 비행기 조종사
Good afternoon, ladies and gentlemen. I wish you had a pleasant flight with us.
안녕하십니까, 신사숙녀 여러분. 저희와 함께 즐거운 비행을 하셨기를 바랍니다.

coach (스포츠) 감독
I teach young players. It's hard to see my players get discouraged when they lose a game.
저는 어린 선수들을 지도합니다. 선수들이 경기에서 지고 낙담하는 모습을 볼 때가 힘들어요.

flight attendant 승무원
You're not allowed to use any electronic devices when the plane is taking off.
비행기가 이륙할 때는 전자기기를 사용할 수 없습니다.

pharmacist – patient 약사 – 환자

A : The doctor gave me this prescription. 의사 선생님께서 이 처방전을 주셨어요.
B : Okay. Let me go prepare your medicine. 알겠습니다. 제가 약을 준비해 드릴게요.

police officer – citizen 경찰관 – 시민

A : What did I do wrong? 제가 무엇을 잘못했나요?
B : You were speeding. All drivers are supposed to keep the speed less than 30 kilometers per hour in any safety zone.
과속을 하셨어요. 모든 운전자는 안전지역에서 시속 30킬로미터 이하의 속도를 유지해야 합니다.

taxi driver – passenger 택시 기사 – 승객

A : Well, we've arrived at the hotel. It'll be 20 dollars. 자, 호텔에 도착했습니다. 요금은 20달러입니다.
B : Here you go. Oh, could you help me get my baggage from the trunk? It's very heavy.
여기 있어요. 참, 트렁크에서 가방 꺼내는 것을 도와주시겠어요? 너무 무거워서요.

teacher – parent 교사 – 학부모

A : I'm afraid Brian has the flu. He's going to miss school for a few days. 브라이언이 독감에 걸렸어요. 며칠 동안 학교를 결석할 겁니다.
B : Oh, that's too bad. I'll email you the homework that he will do while at home.
아, 그거 정말 안됐네요. 집에 있는 동안 할 수 있도록 제가 숙제를 이메일로 보내겠습니다.

장소 추론

대화를 듣고, 두 사람이 대화하고 있는 장소로 가장 적절한 곳을 고르시오. ◀ MP3 유형 09

① bank
② toy store
③ playground
④ concert hall
⑤ animal hospital

❶ 처음부터 등장하는 함정에 속아서 ⑤를 선택하지 마세요! 좀 더 들어볼까요?

❷ 인내심을 갖고 듣다 보면 힌트가 나옵니다.
→ 플라스틱으로 만들어진 앵무새 장난감에 대해 얘기한다는 걸 알 수 있네요. 그렇다면 장소는 장난감 가게!

●정답 근거 ●오답 함정

W : Dad, look! There's a parrot.
M : Oh, it looks so real.
W : Yeah. It even sounds like a parrot. That's great.
M : It also has colorful feathers though they're made of plastic.
W : Dad, can you buy me this one?
M : Okay. It's your birthday. If that's what you want, I'll buy it for you.
W : Thanks, Dad.

여 : 아빠, 저것 봐요! 앵무새가 있어요.
남 : 아, 진짜같이 보이는구나.
여 : 네. 심지어 소리도 앵무새 같아요. 굉장해요.
남 : 그건 플라스틱으로 만들어졌지만 다양한 색깔의 깃털도 가지고 있네.
여 : 아빠, 저 이거 사주실 수 있어요?
남 : 그래. 네 생일이잖아. 그게 네가 원하는 거라면 사줄게.
여 : 고마워요, 아빠.

💡 **주요 표현**

bookstore 서점	Why don't you buy the book and read it at home? 그 책을 사서 집에서 읽는 게 어때?	
bakery 제과점	I was wondering if you could bake a cake that looks like a big castle. 거대한 성 모양의 케이크를 만들어 주실 수 있는지 궁금하네요.	
flower shop 꽃 가게	I think Janet likes lilies. How about buying ten lilies and five roses? 재닛은 백합을 좋아하는 것 같아. 백합 10송이와 장미 5송이를 사는 게 어때?	
hotel 호텔	Your room number is 206, and here is your key. 손님의 방은 206호이고요, 열쇠는 여기 있습니다.	
clothing store 옷 가게	What about this sweater, then? 그럼 이 스웨터는 어때?	
campsite 캠핑장	It's getting dark. Let's set up the tent. 날이 어두워지고 있어. 텐트를 치자.	
repair shop 수리점	My bike is making a funny noise. How long will it take to have it fixed? 제 자전거에서 이상한 소리가 나요. 고치는 데 얼마나 걸리나요?	
movie theater 영화관	I think the movie is about to start. 영화가 곧 시작할 것 같아.	
library 도서관	You can keep the book for two weeks. 당신은 그 책을 2주 동안 갖고 있을 수 있습니다.	
police station 경찰서	We'll do our best to find your bag and catch the thief. 저희는 당신의 가방을 찾고 절도범을 잡을 수 있도록 최선을 다하겠습니다.	

대화를 듣고, 여자의 마지막 말에 담긴 의도로 가장 적절한 것을 고르시오. ◀)) MP3 유형 10

① 감사　　　② 충고　　　③ 위로
④ 거절　　　⑤ 요청

❶ 먼저 누구의 의도를 파악해야 하는지 확인하세요! 여자의 의도라면 여자의 대사에, 남자의 의도라면 남자의 대사에 집중!

❷ 상대방을 honey라고 부르는 걸 보니 부부 사이의 대화군요.

❸ 선물을 주는 사람은 주로 "I hope you like it."이라고 말합니다.

❹ 여자의 마지막 대사는 긍정적인 말로 가득합니다. couldn't라는 부정형이 쓰였는데도 부정적인 의미가 아니라는 점에 주의하세요.
'I couldn't be happier.(이보다 더 행복할 수는 없어.)'처럼 not과 비교급을 함께 써서 긍정의 의미를 극대화시켰어요.

● 정답 근거

M : Honey, I have a special present for you. Please close your eyes.

W : Okay. What is it?

M : Now open your eyes and look at this.

W : Wow! It's a new bookshelf. Did you make it yourself?

M : Of course! You're such a bookworm. I hope you like it.

W : Yeah, I love it. There couldn't be a better present for me.

남 : 여보, 당신한테 줄 특별한 선물이 있어요. 눈을 감아 봐요.

여 : 알았어요. 그게 뭔데요?

남 : 이제 눈을 뜨고 이걸 봐요.

여 : 와! 새 책꽂이잖아요. 당신이 직접 만들었어요?

남 : 물론이죠! 당신은 대단한 책벌레잖아요. 당신 마음에 들었으면 좋겠어요.

여 : 아주 마음에 들어요. 저에게 이보다 더 좋은 선물은 없을 거예요.

💡 **주요 표현**

제안	**Why don't you** send this photo to him by e-mail?	이 사진을 그에게 이메일로 보내는 게 어때?
충고	**You'd better** drink enough water.	넌 물을 충분히 마시는 것이 좋겠어.
동의, 공감	That's a good idea.	좋은 생각이다.
	I **can't agree** with you **more**.	나도 전적으로 동의해.
	You can say that again.	네 말이 맞아.
거절	**I'd like to, but** I can't.	그렇게 하고 싶지만 못 해.
감사	I **couldn't have** finished it **without** your support.	당신의 지지 없이는 그것을 (성공적으로) 끝낼 수 없었을 겁니다.
	I don't know **how to thank you enough** for your help.	어떻게 해야 당신의 도움에 충분히 감사를 표할 수 있을지 모르겠어요.
사과	I **apologize for** keeping you waiting for so long.	오랫동안 기다리게 해서 죄송합니다.
위로	Think positive.	긍정적으로 생각하세요.
	There's a light at the end of the tunnel.	모든 터널의 끝에는 빛이 있다. (언젠가는 좋은 날이 올 것이다.)

유형 공략 | 부탁 파악

대화를 듣고, 여자가 남자에게 부탁한 일로 가장 적절한 것을 고르시오.

🔊 MP3 유형 11

① 팝콘 사오기 　　　　　② 상자 옮겨주기
③ 휴대폰 충전하기 　　　④ 영화표 예매하기
⑤ 동영상 내려 받기

◀

❶ 대화에서는 항상 성별을 확인하는 것을 잊지 마세요. 여자의 부탁이면 여자의 목소리에, 남자의 부탁이면 남자의 목소리에 귀를 기울이세요.

❷ Can you로 시작하는 문장에 정답이 있어요. 부탁할 때 쓰는 표현 Can[Could] you / Will[Would] you에 집중하세요.

★ 여자의 마지막 대사에는 두 가지 정보가 있어요.
　→ 남자에게 부탁한 일: 영화표 예매, 여자가 할 일: 팝콘 구매

●정답 근거 ●오답 함정

M : Helen, I've heard the movie, *The Man from Somewhere*, is a box-office hit. Have you seen it?
W : No, not yet.
M : Why don't we go see it Friday night?
W : I'd love to, but I wonder if there are tickets available.
M : I can check for tickets with my cellphone right now. Oh, there are still a few left.
W : That's good. Can you book them for us? Then, I'll buy some popcorn.
M : That sounds perfect.

남 : 헬렌, 난 '어딘가에서 온 사람'이라는 영화가 흥행하고 있다고 들었어. 넌 그 영화를 봤니?
여 : 아니, 아직이야.
남 : 우리 금요일 밤에 그걸 보러 가지 않을래?
여 : 나도 그러고 싶은데 표를 구할 수 있을지 모르겠네.
남 : 내가 지금 휴대폰으로 티켓을 확인할 수 있어. 아, 아직 몇 장 남아 있어.
여 : 좋은데. 네가 우리 표를 예매해 줄래? 그러면 내가 팝콘을 살게.
남 : 아주 좋은 생각이야.

💡 **주요 표현**

· **Will you** teach me, then? 그러면 네가 나를 가르쳐줄래?
· **Would you** read the script and correct any errors? 원고를 읽고 오류를 고쳐주시겠어요?
· **Can you** buy some snacks? 과자를 좀 사주겠니?
· **Could you** give me more information on how I could participate in the camp?
제게 캠프에 참가하는 방법에 대한 정보를 좀 더 주시겠어요?

A : My son and I aren't seated next to each other on the train.
제 아들하고 제가 기차에서 나란히 앉아 있지 않거든요.
B : So **do you want me to** change seats with you?
그러니까 저와 자리를 바꾸고 싶으시다는 거죠?
★ A가 부탁하는 상황이지만, 부탁의 내용은 오히려 B의 대사에 있다.

대화를 듣고, 대화 직후 남자가 가장 먼저 할 일을 고르시오.

🔊 MP3 유형 12

✓① 전화하기　　　　② 서점 가기
③ 인터넷하기　　　　④ 도서관 가기
⑤ 친구 만나기

❶ 성별 확인은 필수! 남자가 할 일이면 남자의 대사에, 여자가 할 일이면 여자의 대사에 집중하세요.

❷ Why don't we / Let's 등의 제안하는 표현이 등장하는군요. 게다가 Sure라는 긍정의 대답까지 나오지만, 좀 더 들어야 합니다.

❸ 앞서 언급된 인터넷 검색과 도서관 방문 역시 남자가 할 일에 포함되지만, 그보다 먼저 할 일은 '전화하기'입니다.

● 정답 근거 ● 오답 함정

W : Steve, are you busy now?
M : I'm just going out to meet some friends. What's up?
W : Do you remember what you said last week?
M : Umm... No, I don't. What was it?
W : You said you would help me with my report.
M : Oh, now I remember! So, what's your report about?
W : I'm thinking of writing about pollution and recycling.
M : Well, why don't we surf the Internet to get some information?
W : Sure, but first, let's go to the library before it closes to look through some magazines and newspapers.
M : Okay, wait a minute. I need to call my friends to tell them I can't come.

여 : 스티브, 너 지금 바쁘니?
남 : 난 친구들을 만나러 나가는 중이야. 무슨 일이니?
여 : 네가 지난주에 나한테 한 말 기억해?
남 : 음, 아니. 무슨 말이었더라?
여 : 내 보고서를 도와준다고 말했잖아.
남 : 아, 이제 기억난다! 그러니까, 무엇에 관한 보고서니?
여 : 나는 오염과 재활용에 대해 쓰려고 생각하고 있어.
남 : 음, 우리 인터넷을 검색해서 정보를 모으는 게 어떨까?
여 : 좋아. 하지만 먼저 도서관이 문을 닫기 전에 가서 잡지와 신문을 검토해 보자.
남 : 그래, 잠깐만 기다려. 친구들에게 전화해서 내가 못 간다고 말해야 하거든.

 주요 표현

본인이 할 일을 직접 말하는 경우
· **Let me** ask the driver where we are now. 우리가 지금 어디에 있는지 기사 아저씨께 여쭤볼게.
· **I have to** rush back to the restaurant. 나는 식당으로 급히 돌아가야 해.
· **I'll** wash the dishes. 내가 설거지를 할게.
· My teacher **told me to** come to the teachers' office by two o'clock. 선생님께서 내게 2시까지 교무실로 오라고 하셨어.

다른 사람이 제안/충고/부탁 등을 한 경우
· A : **Why don't you** take it to the service center? 그걸 서비스 센터로 가져가는 게 어때요?
　B : **I will.** 그렇게 할게요.
· A : **I think you should** finish your homework first. 나는 네가 숙제를 먼저 끝내야 한다고 생각해.
　B : **Okay,** I will. 알겠어요. 그럴게요.
· A : **Could you** help me find my puppy? 제 강아지를 찾는 걸 도와주시겠어요?
　B : **Sure.** No problem. 그럼요. 문제 없어요.
· A : **We need to** change the light bulb in the bathroom. 우리는 화장실의 전구를 교체해야 해요.
　B : **Okay.** I'll do it right now. 그래. 내가 지금 바로 할게.

숫자 정보 파악

1. 대화를 듣고, 남자가 지불할 금액을 고르시오. ◀⑩ MP3 유형 13

① $50　　② $55　　③ $60　　④ $75　　⑤ $80

●정답 근거

M : Excuse me. How much is that red shirt?
W : It's $50.
M : Hmm. It's too expensive for me.
W : How about this blue one? It's only $30.
M : I like the design. Do you have the same shirt in green as well?
W : Yes. And if you buy two in this design, you get $5 off of the total.
M : Great! Then I'll take one green and one blue.
W : Okay.

❶ 초반에는 물건의 가격이 제시돼요.
→ $50(red shirt), $30(blue shirt)

❷ 구매하는 개수 또는 할인 조건이 나와요.
→ 두 개 사면 총액에서 5달러 할인

❸ 최종적으로 구매를 결정하는 내용을 들은 후에 가격과 할인 조건을 반영해서 계산하세요.
→ $60($30 × 2) − $5 = $55

남 : 실례합니다. 저 빨간 셔츠는 얼마죠?
여 : 50달러입니다.
남 : 음. 제겐 너무 비싸네요.
여 : 이 파란 셔츠는 어떤가요? 겨우 30달러예요.
남 : 디자인은 마음에 드네요. 같은 셔츠로 초록색도 있나요?
여 : 네. 그리고 이 디자인으로 두 장을 사면 합계에서 5달러를 깎아드려요.
남 : 잘됐네요! 그럼 저는 초록색 한 장과 파란색 한 장을 살게요.
여 : 알겠습니다.

2. 대화를 듣고, 여자가 지불할 금액을 고르시오. ◀⑩ MP3 유형 14

① $10　　② $20　　③ $30　　④ $40　　⑤ $50

●정답 근거

M : Did you enjoy your meal?
W : Yes. It was great.
M : Thank you. So you had two dishes of spaghetti and one chicken salad. Your total is $40.
W : Oh, we didn't order a chicken salad.
M : Let me see. Oh, I'm sorry. I made a mistake.
W : That's okay.
M : So you don't have to pay for the chicken salad, which is $10.
W : All right. Here's my credit card.

❶ 초반에 총액이 먼저 나오기도 해요.
→ $40

❷ 계산을 실수했다는 변수가 나와요. 총액에서 얼마를 빼야 하는지 잘 들으세요.
→ $40 − $10 = $30

남 : 식사는 즐거우셨습니까?
여 : 네, 훌륭했어요.
남 : 감사합니다. 스파게티 두 접시와 치킨 샐러드 한 접시를 드셨네요. 총 40달러입니다.
여 : 아, 저희는 치킨 샐러드를 주문하지 않았어요.
남 : 확인해볼게요. 아, 죄송합니다. 제가 실수를 했네요.
여 : 괜찮아요.
남 : 그럼 10달러인 치킨 샐러드는 계산하실 필요가 없습니다.
여 : 알겠어요. 여기 제 신용카드요.

💡 **할인과 관련된 표현**

· We can **give you a one-dollar discount** for each ticket. 티켓 당 1달러를 할인해 드려요.
· In that case, you **get $5 off** of the total. 그 경우에는, 총액에서 5달러를 할인 받으시게 됩니다.
· That's **with a 50 percent discount**. 그건 50퍼센트 할인된 거예요.

특정 정보 파악

1. 대화를 듣고, 남자가 여자와 만나기로 한 날짜를 고르시오.

🔊 MP3 유형 15

① June 3　　② June 4　　③ June 5
④ June 6　　⑤ June 7

● 정답 근거 ● 오답 함정

M : Ms. Williams, I'd like to talk to you about my study plan.
W : Okay. When would be good for you? June 5?
M : I have a club meeting then. What about June 7?
W : Well, let me check my schedule. Sorry, I have a conference all day.
M : How about June 6?
W : I have a teachers' meeting at 3 o'clock, so I can see you at 4 that day.
M : Okay. I'll see you then.

❶ 지시문에서 어느 날짜를 찾아야 하는지 확인하세요.

❷ 초반에 여러 날짜가 언급되므로 최종적으로 의견이 수렴될 때까지 잘 들어야 해요.

❸ 'I can see you at 4 that day.'에서 시간인 'at 4'를 날짜로 착각하지 않도록 주의하세요.

남 : 윌리엄스 선생님, 제 공부 계획에 대해 말씀드리고 싶어요.
여 : 좋아. 언제가 너에게 좋니? 6월 5일?
남 : 그때는 동아리 모임이 있어요. 6월 7일은 어떤가요?
여 : 음, 내 일정을 확인해 볼게. 미안하지만, 하루 종일 회의가 있구나.
남 : 6월 6일은 어떠세요?
여 : 3시에 교사 회의가 있으니까, 그날 4시에 볼 수 있겠구나.
남 : 네. 그때 봬요.

2. 대화를 듣고, 두 사람이 만나기로 한 요일을 고르시오.

🔊 MP3 유형 16

① Sunday　　② Monday　　③ Wednesday
④ Friday　　⑤ Saturday

● 정답 근거 ● 오답 함정

W : Hello, Justin! What's up?
M : Hi, Linda. I heard you're transferring to a new school next Friday.
W : Yeah, that's true. I'll miss you.
M : Me, too. Why don't we have lunch together this Saturday?
W : Sorry, but I have to help my parents pack stuff during the weekend. What about on Monday?
M : Okay. I'll see you at the school cafeteria at noon.

❶ 지시문에서 무슨 요일을 찾아야 하는지 확인하세요.

❷ 두 개 이상의 요일이 언급되므로 어떤 요일인지 구분해서 들으세요.
→ next Friday: 전학 날짜

❸ 의견을 조율하는 과정을 거친 후 요일이 최종 결정되므로 끝까지 집중하세요!
→ Saturday: 남자의 제안 / Monday: 거절 후 여자의 제안에 대해 남자가 수락하여 최종 결정

여 : 안녕, 저스틴! 무슨 일이야?
남 : 안녕, 린다. 네가 다음 주 금요일에 새로운 학교로 전학 간다는 소리를 들었어.
여 : 응, 사실이야. 난 네가 그리울 거야.
남 : 나도 그래. 우리 이번 주 토요일에 점심을 같이 먹는 게 어떨까?
여 : 미안하지만 난 주말 동안에는 우리 부모님이 물건을 싸는 걸 도와야 해. 월요일은 어때?
남 : 좋아. 정오에 학교 식당에서 보자.

다음을 듣고, Max Sports Center에 관해 언급되지 <u>않은</u> 것을 고르시오. 🔊 MP3 유형 17

① 개관 연도　　　　② 이용 가능 시간
③ 프로그램 이용 요금　☑ 회원 가입 방법
⑤ 인기 프로그램

❶ 지시문에서 무엇에 관한 것인지 확인하세요.

❷ 선택지에서 어떤 내용이 나오는지 확인하세요.

❸ 선택지의 순서대로 담화가 진행되므로 들리는 선택지를 지워나가세요.
　→ 개관 연도
　　이용 가능 시간
　　이용 요금
　　인기 프로그램

● 정답 근거

M : The Max Sports Center, which opened in June, 2002, is the first five-star fitness facility in our city. It is open 24 hours a day, seven days a week for your convenience. We offer a variety of programs free of charge. Popular fitness programs like yoga, aerobics, and Taekwondo are offered throughout the year. Come and enjoy yourself!

2002년 6월에 개관한 맥스 스포츠센터는 우리 도시의 첫 번째 5성급 체력 단련 시설입니다. 그곳은 여러분의 편의를 위해 일주일 내내 하루 24시간 개방됩니다. 저희는 다양한 프로그램을 무료로 제공합니다. 요가, 에어로빅, 태권도와 같은 인기 피트니스 프로그램이 1년 내내 제공됩니다. 오셔서 마음껏 즐기세요!

다음 배치도를 보면서 대화를 듣고, 두 사람이 선택한 사진 동아리 구역의 위치를 고르시오. 🔊 MP3 유형 18

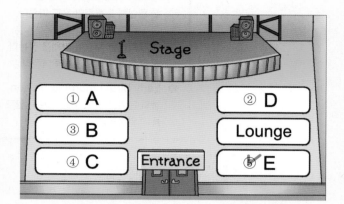

◀ ❶ 지시문을 보고 무엇을 들어야 할지 확인하세요.

❷ 배치도에서 위치의 기준이 되는 부분을 확인하세요.
→ Stage, Lounge, Entrance

❸ 두 사람이 결정하기 때문에 의견 조율 과정이 나와요. 상대방의 제안과 그에 대한 대답을 잘 들으세요.
→ Section B? → No (science club이 차지)
Section D or E (next to lounge)? → OK
Entrance에 가까운 쪽은? → E

●정답 근거 ●오답 함정

M : Ms. White, here's a map of the sections for the school festival. Which section do you think would be good for the photography club?

W : What about section B?

M : The science club has already been given that section.

W : Hmm... How about putting the photography club in a section next to the lounge?

M : Good idea! The lounge is always crowded, which can help them sell more postcards. Which is better, section D or E?

W : Why don't we give them the section near the entrance?

M : Okay. Great.

남 : 화이트 선생님, 여기 학교 축제 구역이 표시된 지도가 있습니다. 사진 동아리에게는 어느 구역이 좋은 것 같으세요?

여 : B구역은 어때요?

남 : 그 구역은 이미 과학 동아리에게 배정됐어요.

여 : 음, 사진 동아리를 라운지 옆의 구역에 배정하는 건 어때요?

남 : 좋은 생각이네요! 라운지는 항상 붐비는데, 그건 사진 동아리가 더 많은 엽서를 판매하는 것을 도울 수 있을 겁니다. D구역과 E구역 중에서 어디가 더 괜찮은가요?

여 : 그들에게 입구 근처에 있는 구역을 주는 건 어때요?

남 : 네. 좋습니다.

속담 추론

1. 대화를 듣고, 상황을 가장 잘 표현한 속담을 고르시오.

🔊 MP3 유형 19

① 쥐구멍에도 볕 들 날 있다.
② 하늘은 스스로 돕는 자를 돕는다.
✓③ 어떤 이의 약이 다른 이에겐 독이 된다.
④ 일찍 일어나는 새가 벌레를 잡아먹는다.
⑤ 열 번 찍어 안 넘어가는 나무 없다.

❶ 선택지의 속담의 의미를 파악한 후에 상황에 맞는 속담을 고르세요.
 ① 고생 속에서 좋은 날도 온다.
 ② 열심히 노력하면 운도 따른다.
 ③ 사람마다 다르다.
 ④ 부지런한 사람이 기회를 잡는다.
 ⑤ 포기하지 않으면 이루어진다.

❷ Early bird나 morning person 등의 단어만 듣고 ④를 고르지 않도록 주의하세요.

●정답 근거 ●오답 함정

W : You look so tired. What's the matter?
M : I've been trying to be a morning person for weeks.
W : Why did you decide to do that?
M : I read this book called *Early Bird*. And I've been following everything in it, but it doesn't seem to work for me.
W : Well, then I don't think you're a morning person after all. That's why you feel tired these days.
M : Right. I'd rather go back to my own style.

여 : 너 아주 피곤해 보여. 무슨 일이야?
남 : 나는 몇 주 동안 아침형 인간이 되려고 노력 중이야.
여 : 왜 그렇게 하기로 결정했어?
남 : '얼리 버드'라는 책을 내가 읽었거든. 그리고 거기에 있는 모든 걸 따라 하고 있는데 내게는 그게 효과가 있는 것 같지 않아.
여 : 음, 그렇다면 너는 결국 아침형 인간이 아닌 것 같아. 그게 요즘 네가 피곤함을 느끼는 이유지.
남 : 맞아. 나만의 스타일로 돌아가는 게 좋겠다.

💡 **기출 속담**

· Too many cooks spoil the broth. 사공이 많으면 배가 산으로 간다.
  (→ 여러 사람이 자기 주장만 내세우면 일이 제대로 되기 어렵다.)
· Many hands make light work. 백지장도 맞들면 낫다. (= Two heads are better than one.)
  (→ 아무리 쉬운 일이라도 함께 협력해서 하면 훨씬 더 쉽고 효과적이다.)
· Look before you leap. 돌다리도 두들겨 보고 건너라.
  (→ 비록 잘 아는 일이라도 세심한 주의를 기울여서 실수가 없도록 해야 한다.)

2. 대화를 듣고, 남자의 충고를 가장 잘 표현한 속담을 고르시오.

🔊 MP3 유형 20

① Walls have ears.
② Bad news travels fast.
③ Strike while the iron is hot. ✓
④ A bad workman blames his tools.
⑤ When in Rome, do as the Romans do.

> ✸ 속담 뜻을 몰라서 정답을 고르지 못할 수 있어요. 빈출 속담의 뜻을 알아두세요.
> ① 벽에도 귀가 있다. (말조심해라)
> ② 나쁜 소식은 빨리 퍼진다.
> ③ 쇠는 뜨거울 때 두드려라.
>   (기회를 놓치지 마라)
> ④ 서투른 목수가 연장을 탓한다.
> ⑤ 로마에 있을 때는 로마 사람들이 하는 대로 하라.

● 정답 근거

W : Bill, I've been offered a chance to go to France as an exchange student, but I can't decide.
M : Why not? You've always wanted to go abroad.
W : But I'm not sure I can live far away from my family.
M : Susan, an opportunity like this doesn't come every day.
W : Yeah, I know but...
M : If I were you, I would take it. This could be the best chance you'll ever have.
W : Maybe you're right.

여 : 빌, 내가 교환학생으로 프랑스에 갈 기회가 생겼는데, 결정을 못 하겠어.
남 : 왜 못하는데? 너는 항상 해외로 가고 싶어했잖아.
여 : 하지만 내가 가족이랑 멀리 떨어져서 살 수 있을지 잘 모르겠어.
남 : 수잔, 이런 기회는 매일 오지 않아.
여 : 응, 나도 알지만...
남 : 내가 너라면, 나는 그 기회를 잡을 거야. 이것은 네가 갖게 될 기회 중에서 최고일 수 있어.
여 : 네 말이 맞을지도 몰라.

💡 **출제 가능한 속담**

· Actions speak louder than words. 말보다 행동이 중요하다.
  (=Easier said than done. 행동하는 것보다 말하는 것이 쉽다.)
· Don't judge a book by its cover. 겉을 보고 속을 판단하지 마라.
· All that glitters is not gold. 반짝인다고 모두가 금은 아니다.
· A stitch in time saves nine. 제때의 한 땀은 나중의 아홉 땀을 덜어준다.
  (→ 문제를 즉각 처리하면 일이 훨씬 수월해진다.)
· Make hay while the sun shines. 해가 비추는 동안에 건초를 말려라.
  (→ 기회를 잡아라. = Strike while the iron is hot. 쇠뿔도 단김에 빼라.)
· No smoke without fire. 아니 땐 굴뚝에 연기 나랴. (→ 모든 일에는 그에 대한 이유가 있다.)
· All roads lead to Rome. 모든 길은 로마로 통한다. (→ 같은 목표에 도달하는 데는 많은 다른 방법이 있다.)

다음을 듣고, 무엇에 관한 설명인지 고르시오. 🔊 MP3 유형 21

① 낙하산 ✔　② 모형 비행기　③ 회전목마

④ 화물차　⑤ 잠수함

❶ 각각의 선택지를 읽으면서 쓰임새나 생김새를 떠올리세요.

❷ 대상의 쓰임새나 생김새를 듣고 종합하여 추론하세요.

●정답 근거

M : This is used to slow down a person falling through the air. It enables a person to jump from an aircraft and land on the ground safely. It consists of a large piece of thin cloth attached to a person's body by strings. It is mostly used in emergency situations or in the military, but people also use it for leisure.

이것은 사람이 공중으로 떨어지는 속도를 늦추는 데에 사용됩니다. 그것은 사람이 항공기에서 뛰어내려 땅 위에 안전하게 착지할 수 있게 합니다. 그것은 사람의 몸에 줄로 장착된 얇고 넓은 천 조각으로 이루어져있습니다. 그것은 주로 비상 사태나 군대에서 사용되지만 사람들은 그것을 여가를 위해 사용하기도 합니다.

다음을 듣고, 두 사람의 대화가 <u>어색한</u> 것을 고르시오. MP3 유형 22

①   ②   ③   ④   ⑤

> ⊛ 의문사 의문문, 일반 의문문뿐 아니라 평서문의 비중이 높아지는 추세예요. 평소에 빈출 문장들을 익혀두세요.

●정답 근거 ●오답 함정

① M : Have you seen my bag?
  W : Yes. It's right over there.

② M : How long will it take to get there by taxi?
  W : I haven't seen it for a long time.

③ M : I'm getting married next month.
  W : Congratulations! What is the exact date?

④ M : I'm wondering if you could send me the file again.
  W : Sure. I will send it as soon as possible.

⑤ M : Would you have dinner with me this evening?
  W : That sounds great!

① 남 : 제 가방을 보셨나요?
  여 : 네. 그건 저기 있어요.
② 남 : 거기까지 택시로 가는 데 얼마나 걸릴까?
  여 : 난 오랫동안 그걸 못 봤어.
③ 남 : 난 다음 달에 결혼해.
  여 : 축하해! 정확한 날짜가 언제야?
④ 남 : 당신이 제게 파일을 다시 보내주실 수 있는지 알고 싶어요.
  여 : 물론이죠. 가급적 빨리 보내드릴게요.
⑤ 남 : 오늘 저녁에 저와 함께 저녁식사 하실래요?
  여 : 좋아요!

💡 **기출 표현**

M : You're **not supposed to** bring pets to a bank. 은행에 애완동물을 데려와서는 안됩니다.
W : Sorry. I didn't know that. 죄송해요. 몰랐어요.

M : I **was disappointed with** the film. 나는 그 영화에 실망했어.
W : You were? I **felt the same way.** 그랬니? 나도 같은 느낌이었어.

W : I'm sure that **you must be** tired. 네가 피곤할 거라고 확신해.
M : Yes. I really need to get some sleep. 응. 난 정말 잠을 자야 해.

W : **How is** your science report **going**? 과학 보고서는 어떻게 돼가?
M : **So far so good.** Thanks for asking. 아직까지는 괜찮아. 물어봐 줘서 고마워.

M : How much does it cost to send this package? 이 소포를 보내는 데 얼마예요?
W : Well, **it depends on** how much it weighs. 음, 무게가 얼마나 나가느냐에 따라 달라요.

M : **Do you mind if** I sit here? 제가 여기에 앉아도 될까요?
W : Sorry. This seat **is already taken**. 죄송합니다. 이 자리는 이미 임자가 있어요.

다음 상황 설명을 듣고, 엄마가 아들에게 할 말로 가장 적절한 것을 고르시오. 🔊 MP3 유형 23

Mother : _____

① Have you ever played soccer before?
② My goodness! Where have you been?
③ Cheer up! You can beat them next time.
④ How many times did you win the game?
⑤ I'm sorry to have kept you waiting for me.

❶ 지시문에서 누가 누구에게 하는 말인지 확인하세요.

❷ 선택지를 빠르게 훑으면서 어떤 상황에서 쓸 수 있는 표현인지 파악하세요.

③ 오답 함정: 지문에서 나온 soccer game과 관련된 표현을 이용한 함정이 나올 수 있으며, ⑤는 아들이 엄마에게 할 말로 적절해요.

●정답 근거

W : Chris usually comes home before five p.m. Today, Chris and his friends played a soccer game. His team won, and the game finished around seven p.m. Chris didn't tell his mother that he would be late today. His mother was waiting for him and getting worried. In this situation, what would his mother most likely say to Chris when he came home?

크리스는 주로 오후 5시 전에 집으로 온다. 오늘, 크리스와 그의 친구들은 축구 경기를 했다. 그의 팀은 이겼고 게임은 오후 7시쯤 끝났다. 크리스는 오늘 늦을 거라고 엄마에게 말하지 않았다. 크리스의 엄마는 그를 기다리면서 걱정하고 있었다. 이 상황에서 크리스가 집에 왔을 때 엄마가 크리스에게 뭐라고 말하겠는가?

엄마 : _____

① 너는 전에 축구를 해본 적이 있니?
② 맙소사! 너 어디에 있었니?
③ 기운 내! 네가 다음엔 그들을 이길 거야.
④ 경기를 몇 번이나 이겼니?
⑤ 날 기다리게 해서 정말 미안하구나.

 기출 상황

상황 설명	상황에 적절한 말
So he decides to ask his mom how he looks in his new suit. 그래서 그는 새 정장을 입은 자신이 어떻게 보이는지 엄마에게 묻기로 결심한다.	Does this suit look good on me? 이 정장이 저에게 잘 어울리나요?
Ms. Brown wants to make sure that Susan can work on the weekends. 브라운 씨는 수잔이 주말에 일할 수 있는지 확인하고 싶어한다.	I can hire you if you can work on the weekends. 당신이 주말에 일할 수 있다면, 나는 당신을 고용할 수 있습니다.
So he decides to ask Anna if she doesn't mind waiting. 그래서 그는 애나가 기다리는 것이 괜찮은지 묻기로 결심한다.	Are you okay with waiting for a table? 테이블이 나기를 기다리는 게 괜찮아?
Tom wants to know if she's willing to babysit. 톰은 그녀가 아이를 봐줄 수 있는지 알고 싶어한다.	Are you interested in babysitting? 아이 보는 것에 관심이 있니?
She decides to ask the salesclerk where she can mail the postcard. 그녀는 어디에서 엽서를 보낼 수 있는지 점원에게 묻기로 결심한다.	Where is the nearest post office? 가장 가까운 우체국이 어디예요?

대화를 듣고, 남자의 마지막 말에 대한 여자의 응답으로 가장 적절한 것을 고르시오. ◀)) MP3 유형 24

Woman : _____

① I'd like to buy a birthday present for you.
② Online stores are available 24 hours a day.
③ Online prices are usually lower than offline prices.
④ It's easy to find part-time jobs on the Internet.
⑤ You should make sure the website is safe first.

❶ 지시문에서 누가 마지막 말을 하게 되는지 확인하세요.

❷ 선택지를 읽으면서 어떤 말에 대한 응답일지 생각하면서 들으세요.

❸ 주로 마지막 말만 들으면 풀 수 없게 구성하므로 대화의 흐름을 잘 따라가세요.
남자가 엄마의 생일 선물을 사려고 함.
↓
선물을 살 돈이 충분하지 않음.
(문제점)
↓
여자가 온라인 쇼핑을 권유.
(해결책)
↓
남자가 왜 온라인 쇼핑이 좋은지 물음.

❹ 들리는 몇 개의 단어로 오답을 구성하므로 주의하세요!

✦ 오답 함정: offline, birthday, part time 등 들리는 단어를 이용한 오답 선택지.

● 정답 근거

W : Hey, Tommy. You told me your mom's birthday is this coming Sunday. Did you buy a present for her?
M : Not yet. I wanted to get her a hat, but they were all so expensive at the department store.
W : Oh, the problem is money, huh?
M : Yeah. I saved some money while doing my part-time job, but it's not enough.
W : Then, why don't you shop for a hat online?
M : Why is it better to do that?
W : _____

여 : 토미야. 너희 엄마 생신이 이번 일요일이라고 했잖아? 엄마를 위한 선물은 샀니?
남 : 아직이야. 나는 엄마에게 모자를 사드리고 싶었는데, 백화점에 있는 모자는 죄다 너무 비싸.
여 : 아, 문제는 돈이네, 그렇지?
남 : 응. 내가 아르바이트를 하면서 돈을 좀 모았는데 그걸로는 충분하지가 않아.
여 : 그럼, 인터넷으로 모자를 사는 건 어때?
남 : 그렇게 하는 게 왜 더 좋은데?
여 : _____

① 난 너에게 생일 선물을 사주고 싶어.
② 인터넷 상점은 하루 24시간 이용할 수 있거든.
③ 보통 온라인 가격이 오프라인 가격보다 낮거든.
④ 인터넷에서는 아르바이트를 찾기 쉽거든.
⑤ 넌 그 웹사이트가 안전한지부터 확인해야 해.

1센치 영문법

쉽고 빠르게 한 달 안에 끝!

1센치 영문법

1cm English Grammar

1cm의 책 두께로 중등과 고등 영어의 틈을 메운다!
1회 완독으로 영문법이 한눈에 들어온다!
1권으로 꼭 알아야 할 핵심만 담았다!
1페이지 개념 정리로 쉽고 빠르게 넘어간다!

한 달 안에 끝!
영어 문법과 더 가까워지는 지름길!

- **01** 기초 영문법의 결정판!
- **02** 각종 커뮤니티에 올라온 수많은 영문법 질문을 분석!
- **03** 학생들이 어려워하는 영문법의 핵심을 쉽게 빠르게 정리!

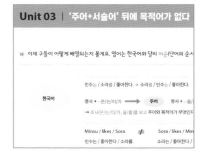

Warming Up!

어떤 개념을 배울지 그림으로 미리 보기!
도형으로 핵심 문법을 빠르게 파악!

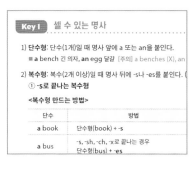

Key Points!

핵심 문법만 쉽고 간단하게!

실력 Up!

단계별 문제로 핵심 문법 익히기!
다양한 문제로 영문법 기초를 튼튼하게!

쎄듀북닷컴(www.cedubook.com)에서 부가 자료를 무료로 다운로드할 수 있습니다.

쎄듀

1 구문

판매 1위 '천일문' 콘텐츠를 활용하여 정확하고 다양한 구문 학습

(끊어읽기) (해석하기) (문장 구조 분석) (해설·해석 제공) (단어 스크램블링) (영작하기)

2 문법·서술형

쎄듀의 모든 문법 문항을 활용하여 내신까지 해결하는 정교한 문법 유형 제공

(객관식과 주관식의 결합) (문법 포인트별 학습) (보기를 활용한 집합 문항) (내신대비 서술형) (어법+서술형 문제)

3 어휘

초·중·고·공무원까지 방대한 어휘량을 제공하며 오프라인 TEST 인쇄도 가능

(영단어 카드 학습) (단어 ↔ 뜻 유형) (예문 활용 유형) (단어 매칭 게임)

4 선생님 보유 문항 이용

(Online Test) (OMR Test)

cafe.naver.com/cedulearnteacher

쎄듀런 학습 정보가 궁금하다면?

쎄듀런 Cafe

· 쎄듀런 사용법 안내 & 학습법 공유
· 공지 및 문의사항 QA
· 할인 쿠폰 증정 등 이벤트 진행

어법의 시작과 끝은 쎄듀다!

어법끝 START 2.0의
최신 개정판

어법끝
START

수능 · 고등 내신 어법의
기본 개념 익히기

1 대수능, 모의고사 27개년 기출문제 반영한 빈출 어법 포인트
2 단계적 학습으로 부담 없는 어법학습 가능
3 반복 학습을 도와주는 미니 암기북 추가 제공
4 고등 어법 입문자 추천

 출제량 40% 증가 | **내신 서술형 문항 추가** | **미니 암기북 추가 제공**

| 고등 어법 입문 (예비고1~고1) | 고등 내신 서술형 입문 (고1~고2) | 고등 어법 실전 적용 (고2) | 수능 어법 실전 마무리 (고3~고등 심화) |

어법끝 START · 실력다지기

| 수능 · 내신 어법 기본기 |

· 수능, 모의고사 최신 경향 반영
· 부담 없는 단계적 어법 학습
· 적용, 복습용 다양한 문제 유형 수록
· 실전 모의 15회분 제공

어법끝 서술형

| 서술형 빈출 유형 · 기준 학습 |

· 출제 포인트별 서술형 빈출 유형 수록
· 단계별 영작 문항 작성 가이드 제공
· 출제자 시각에서 출제 문장 예상하기 훈련
· 현직 교사 공동 저술로 내신 채점 기준 수록

어법끝 ESSENTIAL

| 고등 실전 어법의 완성 |

· 역대 기출의 출제 의도와 해결전략 제시
· 출제진의 함정 및 해결책 정리
· 누적 테스트, 실전모의고사로
실전 적용력 강화

어법끝 실전 모의고사

| 수능 어법의 실전 감각 향상 |

· 완벽한 기출 분석 및 대처법 소개
· TOP 5 빈출 어법 및 24개 기출 어법 정리
· 최신 경향에 꼭 맞춘 총 288문항

쎄듀 북닷컴(www.cedubook.com)에서 부가 자료를 무료로 다운로드할 수 있습니다.

쎄듀

빠르게

쎄듀
중학영어듣기
모의고사 20회

쎄듀 '빠르게' 중학영어듣기 모의고사 시리즈

정답 및 해설

3

실전 모의고사 20회
기출 듣기평가 5회
문제 유형 공략 및 필수 표현 익히기

QR코드 방식의 편리한 음원 재생
MP3 파일 무료 다운로드
모의고사, 딕테이션, 문항별 음원 제공

쎄듀 빠르게
중학영어듣기
모의고사 20회

정답 및 해설

3

01 ①	02 ④	03 ②	04 ③	05 ③
06 ⑤	07 ③	08 ②	09 ④	10 ②
11 ⑤	12 ②	13 ③	14 ②	15 ①
16 ④	17 ④	18 ②	19 ③	20 ②

01 ①

M: Take a look at all of these posters. Which one should I buy?
이 모든 포스터들을 좀 봐. 내가 뭘 사는 게 좋을까?

W: Do you prefer posters with scenery of mountains or the sea?
넌 산 또는 바다 풍경이 있는 포스터 중에 어떤 것을 더 좋아하니?

M: I definitely prefer the sea. 난 정말로 바다를 더 좋아해.

W: Why don't you get that one that has a ship sailing on the ocean?
바다를 항해하는 배가 있는 저 포스터를 사는 게 어때?

M: It looks all right, but I have one like it in my home.
좋아 보이긴 하는데, 우리 집에 저것과 비슷한 게 하나 있어.

W: If I were you, I'd buy the poster with the sun setting over the ocean.
내가 너라면 바다 위로 해가 지는 포스터를 사겠어.

M: Yeah, you're right. That's the one I'm going to buy.
그래, 네 말이 맞아. 저게 내가 사려는 거야.

어휘 take a look at ~을 한번 보다 poster (장식용) 포스터 prefer (~을 더) 좋아하다 scenery 풍경, 경치 definitely 분명히, 확실히 sail 항해하다 set (해나 달이) 지다 ocean 바다, 대양

02 ④

[Cellphone rings.] [휴대폰이 울린다.]

W: Hello, Martin. What are you doing?
여보세요, 마틴. 너 뭐 하고 있니?

M: I'm just hanging out at my house. What's going on?
그냥 우리 집에서 시간을 때우고 있어. 무슨 일인데?

W: I have two tickets for a movie today. Would you like to go with me?
나한테 오늘 영화 티켓이 두 장 있거든. 나랑 같이 갈래?

M: Sure. I'd love to. What film are we going to see?
물론이지. 가고 싶어. 우리는 어떤 영화를 보는 거야?

W: It's that new adventure movie. It starts at six, so we should be there by five forty-five. 새로 나온 모험 영화야.
6시에 시작하니까 5시 45분까지 거기 가야 해.

M: That's one hour from now. I'd better get ready.
앞으로 한 시간 후네. 나도 준비하는 게 좋겠어.

해설 전화의 전반적인 주제나 용건은 앞쪽에 나온다.

어휘 hang out 시간을 보내다 film 영화(= movie) adventure 모험 get ready 준비하다

03 ②

① M: Shall we go rollerblading soon?
우리 빨리 롤러블레이드를 타러 갈래요?

W: Sure. Let's go in a couple of minutes.
응. 2~3분 후에 가자.

② M: Mom, I'd really like to have a pair of rollerblades.
엄마, 저 정말로 롤러블레이드를 갖고 싶어요.

W: I'll buy them for you for your birthday.
네 생일에 내가 그걸 사줄게.

③ M: This is a great present. Thanks.
이건 정말 엄청난 선물이에요. 고마워요.

W: You're welcome. I'm glad you like it.
천만에. 네가 좋아한다니 나도 기쁘구나.

④ M: I want to buy this bike. 저는 이 자전거를 사고 싶어요.

W: Okay. I can get it for you. 알았다. 내가 사줄게.

⑤ M: Would you like to buy something?
무엇을 사고 싶으세요?

W: Yes, I'd like two tickets for the roller coaster, please. 네, 롤러코스터 티켓 두 장 주세요.

해설 상점에서 남자가 여자에게 롤러블레이드를 가리키며 사달라고 말하는 상황이다.

어휘 go rollerblading 롤러블레이드를 타러 가다 a couple of 둘의, 두어 개의 a pair of 한 쌍의, 한 켤레의 present 선물 roller coaster 롤러코스터

04 ③

W: I need to buy a new T-shirt for your brother.
난 네 남동생을 위해 새 티셔츠를 사야 한단다.

M: You should buy this one with the soccer ball on it.
축구공이 있는 이 티셔츠를 사는 게 좋겠어요.

W: He doesn't like soccer anymore. He won't want this.
그 애는 축구를 더 이상 좋아하지 않아. 이걸 원하지는 않을 거다.

M: Then how about this T-shirt with the fish on it?
그럼 물고기가 있는 이 티셔츠는 어때요?

W: Do you mean the one with the fish and the bird?
물고기와 새가 있는 것을 말하는 거니?

M: No, I'm talking about the one with three fish on it.
아니요, 물고기 세 마리가 있는 걸 말하는 거예요.

W: All right. I think he'll like it. I'll buy it.
알았다. 그 애가 좋아할 것 같구나. 저걸 살게.

해설 제안에 대해 동의가 이루어질 때까지 대화를 들어야 함정에 빠지지 않는다.

어휘 soccer ball 축구공 not ~ anymore 더 이상 ~않다

05 ③

W: Good afternoon. 안녕하세요.

M: Hello. Where are you going today?
안녕하세요. 오늘 어디로 가시죠?

W: Can you take me to the Greenville Department Store? 저를 그린빌 백화점에 데려다 주실 수 있나요?

M: Sure, but traffic is really heavy right now. It might take a while. 물론입니다. 하지만 지금은 교통량이 정말 많아요. 시간이 좀 걸릴 수도 있습니다.

W: How long will it take? 시간이 얼마나 걸릴까요?

M: About forty minutes. Or I can take a shortcut, which will probably take only thirty minutes. 약 40분이요. 아니면 제가 지름길로 갈 수도 있는데, 그러면 아마 30분밖에 안 걸릴 겁니다.

W: Take the shortcut, please. I need to get to the movie theater there quickly. 지름길로 가 주세요. 제가 거기 있는 영화관에 빨리 가야 하거든요.

어휘 take somebody to ~을 …로 데려가다 department store 백화점 traffic 교통(량) heavy 많은, 심한 take a while 시간이 좀 걸리다 take a shortcut 지름길로 가다 probably 아마도 quickly 빨리 salesclerk 점원, 판매원(= sales person)

06 ⑤

W: Minsu, what are you doing out here in the sun? 민수야, 해가 내리쬐는데 여기서 뭐 하고 있는 거니?

M: I'm picking up trash in the park. 난 공원에 있는 쓰레기를 줍고 있어.

W: I thought you came here for a picnic. Why are you working here? 난 네가 소풍 온 줄 알았어. 왜 여기서 일하고 있어?

M: I'm doing community service. So many people come here and just throw their trash on the ground. 나는 사회봉사 활동을 하고 있는 거야. 너무나 많은 사람들이 여기 와서 쓰레기를 그냥 바닥에 버리거든.

W: It's nice that you're cleaning up. Can I help you? 네가 청소를 하는 건 좋은 일이네. 내가 널 도와 줄까?

M: That would be great. It's nice to see that you care, too. 그러면 아주 좋지. 너도 신경 쓰는 걸 알게 되어 좋다.

해설 여자가 남자를 돕겠다고 하자, 남자는 great, 'It's nice to ~' 등의 표현으로 기쁨을 나타내고 있다.

어휘 pick up 줍다 trash 쓰레기 picnic 소풍 community service 사회[지역] 봉사 활동 throw trash 쓰레기를 버리다 ground 땅, 바닥 care 관심을 갖다, 돌보다 proud 자랑스러운 pleased 기쁜, 만족한

07 ③

① W: How much is this book? 이 책은 얼마인가요?
  M: It costs ten dollars and fifty cents. 그건 10달러 50센트입니다.

② W: Are we going the right way? 우리가 맞는 길로 가고 있는 거니?
  M: I think so. I just checked the map. 난 그렇게 생각해. 방금 지도를 확인했거든.

③ W: Why were you late for the meeting today? 넌 왜 오늘 회의에 늦었니?

M: I haven't met him yet. 난 아직 그를 만나지 못했어.

④ W: Should we take the train or the bus? 우리는 기차를 타야 할까, 버스를 타야 할까?
  M: Either of them is fine with me. 나한테는 둘 다 좋아.

⑤ W: There's something wrong with my tooth. 내 치아에 뭔가 문제가 있어.
  M: You'd better visit the dentist then. 그렇다면 치과의사를 찾아가 보는 게 좋겠군.

어휘 cost 비용이 들다; 비용 right 맞는, 올바른 check 확인하다 map 지도 late for ~에 늦다 take the train 기차를 이용하다 either of them 그것들 중 어느 한쪽 tooth 치아, 이빨 dentist 치과의사

08 ②

M: Tina, how do you enjoy playing in the school band? 티나, 너 학교 밴드에서 연주하는 거 즐거워?

W: It's a lot of fun. We're having our first concert soon. 정말 재미있어. 우리는 곧 첫 번째 콘서트를 갖게 될 거야.

M: That's good to hear. I'll definitely attend. 그 얘기를 들으니 좋네. 난 반드시 참석할게.

W: Why don't you join the band? I know you love music. 너도 밴드에 가입하는 게 어때? 난 네가 음악을 좋아하는 걸 알거든.

M: I do, but I can't play an instrument. 좋아하지만 난 악기를 연주하지 못해.

W: You should learn the trumpet. I know a really good teacher. 넌 트럼펫을 배워야 해. 내가 정말 좋은 선생님을 알고 있어.

M: Can you introduce him to me? 네가 그 분을 나에게 소개해 줄래?

W: Sure. I'll give him your phone number today. 물론이지. 내가 오늘 그 분께 네 전화번호를 드릴게.

어휘 band 밴드, 악단 have a concert 콘서트를 열다 definitely 분명히, 확실히 attend 참가하다, 참석하다 instrument 악기 introduce A to B A를 B에게 소개하다

09 ④

W: Did you go to the circus last weekend? 넌 지난 주말에 서커스에 갔었니?

M: I did. My parents, sister, and I all went. 갔어. 우리 부모님하고 여동생하고 나까지 모두 갔어.

W: So did my family. We went there on Friday night. 우리 가족도 마찬가지야. 우리는 금요일 밤에 거기에 갔어.

M: We had a really good time. How about you? 우리는 정말로 즐거운 시간을 보냈어. 넌 어땠니?

W: Actually, I felt the opposite. I felt sorry for the animals. 사실 난 그 반대의 기분을 느꼈어. 난 동물들이 불쌍하더라고.

해설 actually가 문장의 앞에 나오면 앞선 내용과는 대조적인 내용이 이어진다. 여자는 남자와 다른 의견을 말하고 있다.

어휘 go to the circus 서커스를 보러 가다   actually 사실은, 실제로   opposite 반대   feel sorry for ~을 애처롭게 생각하다

10 ②

W: Good evening. How may I help you?
안녕하세요. 무엇을 도와드릴까요?

M: I'd like to get three tickets for admission to the museum. 박물관 입장권 세 장을 사고 싶습니다.

W: Tickets cost ten dollars for adults and five dollars for children. 입장권은 성인은 10달러, 어린이는 5달러입니다.

M: Okay. I'll take two tickets for adults and one for a child. 네. 어른 두 장, 어린이 한 장을 살게요.

W: If you have a membership card, you can save one dollar on each ticket. 회원카드를 갖고 계시면 티켓 한 장마다 1달러를 아끼실 수 있어요.

M: Excellent. Here's my card. 아주 좋네요. 여기 제 카드요.

해설 10달러 티켓×2장 + 5달러 티켓×1장 = 25달러인데, 한 장당 1달러씩을 할인 받으면 22달러이다.

어휘 admission 입장   museum 박물관   adult 성인, 어른   membership card 회원카드   save 아끼다, 절약하다

11 ⑤

M: Good afternoon. I'm here for my four o'clock appointment. 안녕하세요. 저는 4시로 예약하고 왔습니다.

W: Hello, Mr. Stephens. Have a seat in this chair, please. 안녕하세요, 스티븐스 씨. 이 의자에 앉으세요.

M: Thank you very much. 고맙습니다.

W: How would you like your hair done this time?
이번에는 머리를 어떻게 해드릴까요?

M: Just cut a little off the top and the sides. Please do it like you did the last time. 윗머리와 옆머리를 조금만 깎아 주세요. 지난번에 했던 것처럼 해주시면 됩니다.

W: That won't be a problem. 그건 문제 없어요.

M: If it's possible, could you work quickly, please? I have dinner reservations at five.
가능하다면 빨리 해주시겠어요? 다섯 시에 저녁 약속이 있거든요.

어휘 appointment 약속, 예약   have a seat 앉다, 착석하다 do somebody's hair ~의 머리를 손질하다   side 옆면 reservation 예약   furniture 가구   barber shop 이발소

12 ②

M: This summer, how about sending your children to summer camp? At Bear Lake, children aged eight to fifteen can spend two weeks at the campground. Each day, they'll do activities such as swimming, sports, hiking, and horseback riding. We'll provide food and cabins for them. The price is only five hundred dollars per student. Call four oh four, six seven four eight for more information.

올 여름에는 여러분의 자녀를 여름 캠프에 보내는 게 어떨까요?

8살에서 15살 사이의 아이들은 베어 호수에 있는 캠핑장에서 2주를 보냅니다. 매일 그들은 수영, 스포츠, 하이킹, 그리고 승마와 같은 활동을 하게 됩니다. 저희는 아이들에게 음식과 오두막집을 제공합니다. 가격은 학생 한 명당 500달러에 불과합니다. 404-6748로 전화하셔서 보다 많은 정보를 얻으세요.

해설 'At Bear Lake'에 위치 정보가 나오며, 시작 날짜는 언급되지 않았고 캠프 기간이 2주라고 언급되었다.

어휘 aged (나이가) ~세[살]의   campground 캠핑장   activity 활동   hiking 하이킹, 도보여행   horseback riding 말 타기, 승마   provide 주다, 제공하다   cabin 오두막집   per ~당 information 정보

13 ③

현장 학습 일정	
① 날짜	5월 9일
② 출발 시각	오전 8시
③ 교통편	기차
④ 목적지	박물관
⑤ 돌아오는 시각	오후 6시

W: George, when are we going on our class field trip to the museum? Is it May tenth? 조지, 언제 우리 반이 박물관으로 현장 학습을 가지? 그게 5월 10일인가?

M: No, we're going on Thursday, May ninth.
아니, 우리는 5월 9일 목요일에 갈 거야.

W: Oh, that's right. Are we taking the bus or a train?
아, 맞다. 우리는 버스를 타게 되니, 기차를 타게 되니?

M: The bus will leave from school at eight in the morning. 버스가 오전 8시에 학교에서 출발할 거야.

W: And when will we get back? 그러면 우리는 언제 돌아오니?

M: We'll be there the entire day. So we'll arrive back at school at six. 우리는 하루 종일 그곳에 있을 거야. 그러니까 우리는 6시에 학교에 다시 오게 될 거야.

W: I can't wait until we leave. We're going to have lots of fun. 우리가 떠나는 날이 기다려지네. 우리는 정말 재미있는 시간을 보낼 거야.

어휘 field trip 견학, 현장 학습   get back 돌아오다   entire day 하루 종일   date 날짜   departure 출발   transportation 교통, 운송   destination 목적지   return 돌아옴, 돌아오다

14 ②

W: This is a special type of artwork that focuses on the face of a person. To make it, an artist has a person visit his studio. Then, the person makes a certain pose and remains in that pose for a long time. While the person is posing, the artist paints a picture of that person.

이것은 사람의 얼굴에 초점을 맞춘 특별한 종류의 예술품입니다. 이것을 만들기 위해 예술가는 한 사람을 화실로 초대합니다. 그런 다음 그 사람은 특정한 자세를 취하고 오랫동안 그 자세를 유지합니

다. 그 사람이 자세를 취하고 있는 동안 예술가는 그 사람의 그림을 그립니다.

어휘 type 종류　artwork 예술품　focus on ~에 초점을 맞추다, 집중하다　studio 화실　make a pose 포즈를 취하다　certain 특정한　remain 계속 ~이다, 남다　for a long time 오랫동안

15 ①

W: You look excited, Ted. What's going on?
　너 신나 보여, 테드. 무슨 일이야?
M: My dad told me my grandparents are visiting tonight. 우리 아빠가 나한테 우리 할아버지 할머니가 오늘 오신다고 말씀하셨거든.
W: That's great. You haven't seen them for a while, have you?
　굉장한 소식이네. 그분들을 오랫동안 못 뵀었잖아, 그렇지?
M: It's been two years since they visited. We're going to the airport to pick them up in an hour.
　그분들이 방문하신 지 2년이 됐어. 우리는 한 시간 후에 그분들을 모시러 공항에 갈 거야.
W: How long will they stay here?
　그분들은 여기서 얼마나 계시는 거야?
M: They'll stay with us for three weeks.
　그분들은 3주 동안 우리와 함께 계실 거야.

해설 남자의 대사 'We're going to ~'에 할 일이 나온다.

어휘 grandparents 조부모　for a while 잠시, 한동안　pick somebody up ~을 차에 태우러 가다　stay 머무르다

16 ④

M: Julie, we need to get together to discuss our summer trip to Europe.
　줄리, 우리는 우리의 유럽 여름 여행을 의논하기 위해 만나야 해.
W: You're right. When do you have time? How about May fourteenth?
　네 말이 맞아. 넌 언제 시간이 있니? 5월 14일은 어때?
M: Sorry, but I have soccer practice on that day. But May fifteenth is good for me.
　미안하지만 그 날은 축구 연습이 있어. 하지만 5월 15일은 괜찮아.
W: Hmm… According to my schedule, I have a math club meeting on that day.
　음, 내 일정에 따르면, 난 그날 수학 동아리 모임이 있어.
M: What about the day after that? The sixteenth?
　그 다음 날은 어때? 16일?
W: I believe that I have time on that day. Let's meet at three o'clock then.
　그 날은 시간이 될 것 같아. 그럼 3시에 만나자.
M: Great. See you then. 좋아. 그때 보자.

해설 상대방의 제안에 대해 동의가 이루어지는지 확인한다.

어휘 get together 만나다　soccer practice 축구 연습　according to ~에 따르면　schedule 일정, 스케줄　meeting 모임, 회의

17 ④

W: Mina went to the public library to find a book for her science report. She looked for some books on volcanoes on the computer. There was one available, so she went to the bookshelf. Unfortunately, she couldn't find the book anywhere. She decided to ask the librarian about this situation. In this situation, what would Mina most likely say to the librarian?
　미나는 그녀의 과학 보고서를 위한 책을 찾기 위해 공립 도서관에 갔다. 그녀는 컴퓨터로 화산에 관한 책을 몇 권 검색했다. 대출 가능한 책이 한 권 있었기 때문에 그녀는 책장으로 갔다. 하지만 그녀는 어디에서도 그 책을 찾을 수 없었다. 그녀는 이 상황에 대해 사서에게 물어보기로 결심했다. 이 상황에서 미나는 도서관 사서에게 뭐라고 말할 것 같은가?

Mina: Could you please help me find a book?
　제가 책을 찾는 것을 도와주시겠어요?

① Can I make a library card here?
　여기서 도서 대출 카드를 만들 수 있나요?
② I'd like to check out this book, please.
　이 책을 빌리고 싶어요.
③ What time is the library going to close?
　도서관이 몇 시에 문을 닫죠?
④ Could you please help me find a book?
　제가 책을 찾는 것을 도와주시겠어요?
⑤ Can you recommend a book on volcanoes?
　화산에 관한 책을 추천해 주시겠어요?

어휘 public library 공립 도서관　look for ~을 찾다　volcano 화산　available 이용할 수 있는, 구할 수 있는　bookshelf 책장　unfortunately 불행히도, 유감스럽게도　anywhere 어디에서도　librarian 도서관 사서　library card 도서 대출 카드　check out (책을) 대출하다　recommend 추천하다

18 ②

M: I can't wait to go to Brian's birthday party.
　난 브라이언의 생일 파티에 빨리 가고 싶어.
W: Oh, no. I completely forgot about his birthday.
　아, 안돼. 나는 그의 생일을 완전히 까먹고 있었어.
M: Did you buy a present for him?
　그에게 줄 생일 선물은 샀니?
W: Yes, I got a card and a present, but they're at my home. I'll have to go there first. 응, 카드하고 선물을 샀는데, 우리 집에 있어. 먼저 우리 집에 가야겠어.
M: Do you know where Brian's house is?
　넌 브라이언의 집이 어디 있는지 아니?
W: Yes, I do. He lives a couple of blocks away from me. 응, 알아. 그는 우리 집에서 두어 블록 떨어진 곳에 살아.

어휘 can't wait to 몹시 ~하고 싶다　completely 완전히　a couple of 둘의, 두어 개의　block 블록, 구역

19 ③

M: There are so many things to <u>choose from</u> at this <u>bakery</u>. What are you going to buy?
이 제과점에는 고를 수 있는 게 정말 많아. 넌 뭘 살 거니?

W: I'm definitely going to get that <u>cupcake</u> with the <u>chocolate icing</u> on it.
난 반드시 저 초콜릿 아이싱이 올려진 컵케이크를 살 거야.

M: Do you know <u>what's inside</u> it?
넌 그 안에 뭐가 들어 있는지 알아?

W: It <u>doesn't matter</u>. I love how pretty it looks.
상관없어. 모양이 예뻐서 좋거든.

M: But it has <u>peanuts</u> in it, and you're <u>allergic to</u> them.
하지만 그건 안에 땅콩이 들어 있어. 그리고 넌 땅콩 알레르기가 있잖아.

W: Oh, right. Thanks for telling me that. I <u>had better</u> buy <u>something else</u>.
아, 맞다. 나한테 그걸 말해줘서 고마워. 난 다른 걸 사는 게 좋겠어.

해설 '돌다리도 두들겨 보고 건너라.'는 어떤 일을 하기 전에 신중하게 확인하라는 뜻으로 쓰인다.

어휘 bakery 제과점 cupcake 컵케이크 icing (케이크에 장식용으로 쓰는) 당의, 설탕옷 inside 안에, 내부에 peanut 땅콩 allergic to ~에 대해 알레르기가 있는 had better ~하는 것이 좋겠다

20 ②

W: <u>Thanks for</u> taking me to your uncle's <u>farm</u>. I'm having a good time here. 너희 삼촌의 농장에 나를 데려와 줘서 고마워. 난 여기서 즐거운 시간을 보내고 있어.

M: I'm glad to hear that you're <u>enjoying yourself</u>.
난 네가 재미있게 지낸다는 얘기를 들으니 좋다.

W: I was <u>worried</u> that I would <u>hate</u> being <u>around animals</u>.
난 내가 동물들과 함께 있는 것을 싫어할까 봐 걱정했어.

M: But you liked <u>riding</u> the <u>horses</u>, didn't you?
하지만 넌 말 타는 걸 좋아했잖아, 그렇지 않니?

W: I sure did. That was so much fun.
분명히 좋아했지. 정말 재미있었어.

M: My uncle also has some <u>sheep</u> in the <u>field</u>.
우리 삼촌은 들판에 양도 몇 마리 키우셔.

W: We ought to go to see them then.
그럼 우리 양을 보러 가자.

① Yes, I have seen sheep before.
응, 난 전에 양을 본 적이 있어.

② We ought to go to see them then.
그럼 우리 양을 보러 가자.

③ No, we don't need to go riding again.
아니, 우린 또 다시 말을 탈 필요는 없어.

④ How about visiting a farm tomorrow?
내일 농장을 방문하는 게 어때?

⑤ That's right. This sweater is made of wool.
맞아. 이 스웨터는 양털로 만들어졌어.

어휘 farm 농장 have a good time 즐거운 시간을 보내다 (= enjoy oneself) sheep 양(복) sheep field 들판 ought to ~해야 한다 go riding 승마하러 가다 wool 양털, 울

본문 p.18-19

02회 실전모의고사

01 ④	02 ②	03 ③	04 ①	05 ③
06 ⑤	07 ④	08 ①	09 ⑤	10 ②
11 ④	12 ⑤	13 ④	14 ⑤	15 ②
16 ③	17 ⑤	18 ①	19 ③	20 ①

01 ④

M: Jane, what are you doing in your room?
제인, 네 방에서 뭐 하고 있니?

W: I'm looking for a <u>shirt to wear</u> tomorrow.
내일 입을 셔츠를 찾고 있어요.

M: I see. <u>How about</u> this shirt with the heart and star?
그렇구나. 하트와 별이 들어간 이 셔츠는 어떠니?

W: It's okay, but I want to wear <u>something else</u>.
괜찮지만, 저는 다른 걸 입고 싶어요.

M: Okay. Well, <u>here's</u> one with a heart and a ribbon. Do you want to wear this one? 좋아. 음, 하트와 리본이 들어간 게 여기 있다. 이걸 입고 싶니?

W: Not really. I think I like this one <u>with</u> a <u>bear wearing</u> a <u>ribbon</u>.
별로예요. 제 생각엔 리본을 단 곰이 들어간 이게 좋을 것 같아요.

M: I agree, this shirt <u>looks</u> very <u>nice on</u> you.
맞아, 이 셔츠가 너에게 참 잘 어울리네.

W: Okay, then I'll <u>go with</u> this one.
좋아요, 그럼 이걸 입을게요.

해설 남자가 제안을 여러 개 한다 해도 최종 결정을 하는 사람은 여자이다. 여자의 말인 'I think I like ~'에 정답이 등장한다.

어휘 look nice[good] on somebody ~에게 잘 어울리다

02 ②

W: How may I help you? 무엇을 도와드릴까요?

M: I <u>bought</u> this <u>shirt</u> yesterday, but it <u>doesn't fit</u> me.
제가 어제 이 셔츠를 샀는데, 저한테 사이즈가 맞지 않네요.

W: Would you like to <u>exchange</u> it for a different <u>size</u>?
다른 사이즈로 교환하길 원하세요?

M: No, I would like to <u>get</u> a <u>refund</u>.
아니요, 환불 받고 싶어요.

W: Okay, but you can get a <u>free pair</u> of <u>socks</u> if you buy one of our new summer shirts.
알겠어요, 하지만 저희 신상 여름 셔츠를 하나 구입하시면 무료 양말을 받을 수 있어요.

M: No, thank you. 괜찮습니다.

해설 남자의 대사인 'I would like to ~'에 방문 목적이 나온다.

어휘 fit (크기가) 꼭 맞다   exchange 교환하다   get a refund 환불 받다

03 ③

① W: Dad, I'm hungry. What are we eating for dinner?
아빠, 저 배고파요. 우린 저녁으로 뭘 먹을 거예요?

M: I'm going to make spaghetti and garlic bread.
내가 스파게티와 마늘 빵을 만들 거란다.

② W: Sir, this isn't what I ordered.
저기요, 이건 제가 주문한 것이 아니에요.

M: I'm so sorry. I will check it for you right away.
정말 죄송합니다. 지금 바로 손님의 주문을 확인하겠습니다.

③ W: What dish would you recommend?
어떤 음식을 추천하시겠어요?

M: The vegetable soup, lobster, and beef spaghetti are tonight's specials. 야채 수프, 바닷가재, 소고기 스파게티가 오늘 밤의 특선 요리입니다.

④ W: James, have you cleaned the dinner table?
제임스, 저녁 식사 테이블을 치웠니?

M: Yes. Now I'm washing the dishes.
네. 지금은 설거지를 하고 있어요.

⑤ W: Sir, do you know which restaurant serves pasta?
저기요, 어떤 식당이 파스타를 파는지 아세요?

M: Yes, try the two Italian restaurants in this building.
네, 이 건물에 있는 이탈리아 음식점 두 곳을 가보세요.

해설 웨이터가 손님에게 메뉴를 추천하는 그림에 적절한 대화는 ③이다. 식당에서 나올 만한 대화가 오답으로 등장하므로 주의한다.

어휘 garlic 마늘   recommend 추천하다   special 특별 상품   serve (식당 등에서 음식을) 제공하다

04 ①

M: How may I help you? 무엇을 도와드릴까요?

W: I'm looking for a suitcase to take on my trip.
저는 여행에 들고 갈 여행 가방을 찾고 있어요.

M: Let's see. How about this large, square one? It is one of our top products.
한번 보죠. 크고 정사각형 모양인 이 가방은 어떠세요? 저희 매장에서 가장 잘 나가는 상품 중 하나입니다.

W: It's alright, but I would like something that is easier to carry.
괜찮긴 한데, 저는 더 쉽게 들고 다닐 수 있는 것이 좋겠어요.

M: Well, that small rectangular one with a handle and pockets is portable and compact. 음, 손잡이와 주머니가 달린 작은 직사각형의 저 가방이 소형이라서 들고 다니기 편해요.

W: How much is it? I don't want to spend too much money on a suitcase. 그게 얼마예요? 전 여행 가방에 너무 많은 돈을 쓰고 싶지는 않거든요.

M: It's on sale for a hundred and forty dollars.
할인해서 140달러입니다.

W: Okay, that one is perfect. 좋아요. 완벽하군요.

해설 남자는 손잡이와 주머니가 달린 작은 직사각형의 여행 가방을 추천했고 여자는 그것을 골랐다.

어휘 suitcase 여행 가방   square 정사각형의; 정사각형   product 상품, 제품   easier 더 쉬운(easy-easier-easiest)   rectangular 직사각형의   handle 손잡이   pocket 주머니   portable 휴대하기 쉬운   compact 소형의   spend money on something ~에 돈을 쓰다

05 ③

M: What can I help you with, ma'am?
무엇을 도와드릴까요, 부인?

W: I've lost my wallet. I think someone stole it. Please help me! 제가 지갑을 잃어버렸어요. 누군가 훔쳐간 것 같아요. 저를 도와주세요!

M: When and where did you lose it?
언제 그리고 어디에서 그것을 잃어버렸죠?

W: In the subway station not far from this police station, about an hour ago.
이 경찰서에서 멀지 않은 지하철에서, 대략 한 시간 전에요.

M: What does it look like? 지갑은 어떻게 생겼죠?

W: It is square, red, and has a golden lock on it. 그건 정사각형에, 빨간색이고, 금색으로 된 자물쇠가 위에 있어요.

M: Okay, we will start looking for it right away. Please write down your name and phone number.
알겠습니다. 저희가 지금 바로 지갑을 찾기 시작할게요. 당신의 이름과 전화번호를 적어 주세요.

W: Here you go. Please call me as soon as you find it.
여기 있어요. 그걸 찾으면 바로 제게 전화 주세요.

해설 여자가 잃어버린 지갑을 남자에게 신고하고 있으므로 남자는 경찰이다.

어휘 lose 잃어버리다(lose-lost-lost)   steal 훔치다(steal-stole-stolen)   far from ~에서 먼   police station 경찰서   right away 즉각, 곧바로   as soon as ~하자마자

06 ⑤

M: Hey, your computer looks nice! 야, 네 컴퓨터 멋있다!

W: Thanks. I liked it at first, but now I'm tired of the color.
고마워. 처음에는 그게 마음에 들었는데, 요즘은 색깔이 질려.

M: Then why don't you go to the store and exchange it? 그럼 가게에 가서 교환하는 게 어때?

W: I can't. I've already used it for over a month.
그럴 수 없어. 벌써 한 달 넘게 그것을 사용했거든.

M: Oh, then I guess you just have to keep using it.
아, 그럼 이걸 계속 써야겠네.

W: Yeah, I wish I had just bought the pink one.
응, 그냥 핑크색을 살 걸 그랬어.

해설 여자의 마지막 말인 'I wish I had bought ~'에서 컴퓨터를 구입한 것을 후회하는 감정을 드러내고 있다.

어휘 be tired of ~에 싫증이 나다 exchange 교환하다 guess 추측하다 depressed 우울한 satisfied 만족하는 regretful 후회하는

07 ④

① M: How do I get to the city police station?
제가 시 경찰서에 어떻게 갈 수 있을까요?

W: Go straight for three blocks, and you will see it across the street.
세 블록을 곧장 가면, 길 건너편에 보일 거예요.

② M: May I help you? 도와드릴까요?

W: Yes, I would like to purchase two tickets for tonight's show. 네, 오늘 밤 공연 티켓 두 장을 사고 싶어요.

③ M: Hey, can I borrow a pencil for today's class?
얘, 내가 오늘 수업 동안에 연필을 빌려도 되니?

W: Sure, here you go. 물론이지, 여기 있어.

④ M: Are there any good Chinese restaurants around here? 이 근처에 괜찮은 중국집이 있나요?

W: Yeah, I really like Chinese food, too.
네, 저도 중식을 매우 좋아해요.

⑤ M: What are you doing tonight? 오늘 밤에 뭐 할 거니?

W: I'm going to watch a movie. 난 영화를 볼 거야.

해설 ④의 질문에서 정보를 물어봤으므로 아는지 모르는지를 답변하고, 안다면 구체적 정보를 제시하는 것이 자연스럽다.

어휘 across the street 길 건너에 purchase 구매하다(= buy) borrow 빌리다

08 ①

W: Hey, John. What are you up to?
이봐, 존. 너 뭐하고 있니?

M: I'm preparing for a group presentation.
조별 발표를 준비하고 있어.

W: What is it about? 뭐에 관한 발표인데?

M: It's about teenage bullying. 십 대 왕따에 관한 거야.

W: That sounds interesting. Do you need any help?
재미있겠다. 도움이 필요하니?

M: Well, I wrote a script, but I don't think I did it right. Can you read it and fix any mistakes?
음, 원고는 썼는데, 내 생각에 잘 쓴 것 같지는 않아. 네가 그것을 읽고 실수가 있다면 고쳐줄래?

W: Sure, I can do that. When do you need it by?
물론이지, 해줄 수 있어. 언제까지 필요해?

M: I need it by the end of this week. Thank you so much! 이번 주말까지 필요해. 정말 고마워!

어휘 prepare 준비하다 group presentation 조별 발표 teenage 십 대의 bullying 왕따 시키기, 괴롭히기 script 원고, 스크립트 fix 고치다 mistake 실수, 오류

09 ⑤

M: Ms. Stanley, I finished my art project last night!
스탠리 선생님, 저 어젯밤에 미술 프로젝트를 끝냈어요!

W: Wow, I'm very proud of you, Jason! Your hard work paid off.
와, 네가 정말 자랑스럽구나, 제이슨! 너의 노력이 결실을 맺었구나.

M: I wouldn't have been able to finish it without your help. 선생님의 도움이 없었다면, 그것을 끝낼 수 없었을 거예요.

W: I appreciate your saying that. I know how much effort you put into this project. 그렇게 말해주니 고맙구나. 나도 네가 이 프로젝트에 얼마나 많은 노력을 쏟았는지 안단다.

M: I'm very satisfied with it. 저는 그것에 매우 만족스러워요.

W: That's great! Good luck on your next project.
훌륭해! 다음 프로젝트에서도 행운을 빈다.

M: I can never thank you enough for all you have done for me. 저에게 해주신 모든 것에 뭐라고 감사의 말씀을 드려야 할지 모르겠어요.

해설 남자는 프로젝트를 도와준 선생께 감사하는 마음을 가지고 있다.

어휘 be proud of ~을 자랑스러워하다 pay off 결실을 맺다 appreciate 감사하다 put effort into ~에 노력을 쏟다 be satisfied with ~에 만족하다

10 ②

W: How much is this yellow bag?
이 노란색 가방은 얼마인가요?

M: It's one of our new items, so it's fifty dollars.
이건 저희 신상품 중에 하나라서 50달러예요.

W: That is too expensive. 너무 비싸네요.

M: Hmm… Then how about this red one? It's only twenty-five dollars.
음, 그럼 이 빨간색 가방은 어때요? 25달러밖에 하지 않아요.

W: It looks nice. Do you have the same bag in purple?
좋아 보이네요. 보라색으로 같은 가방이 있나요?

M: Yes. If you buy two bags in this design, you get a five-dollar discount on the total price.
네. 이 디자인으로 가방 두 개를 사시면, 총 금액에서 5달러를 할인 받게 됩니다.

W: That's great! Then I'll take one in red and one in purple. 좋아요! 그럼 빨간색 가방과 보라색 가방을 살게요.

M: Okay. 네.

해설 가방 단가가 나오고 할인 조건이 나오고 있다. 여자의 구매 결정까지 확인한 후 계산한다.

어휘 expensive 비싼 get a discount 할인을 받다 total price 총액

11 ④

M: How can I help you? 무엇을 도와드릴까요?

W: My car horn doesn't work. There must be something wrong with it.
제 차의 경적이 고장 났어요. 틀림없이 뭔가 문제가 있어요.

M: Okay. Have you had this problem before?
알겠습니다. 전에도 이런 문제를 겪어 보셨나요?

W: No, this is the first time. 아니요, 이번이 처음이에요.

M: Please fill out this form and we will try to help you.
이 양식을 작성하시면 저희가 손님을 돕기 위해 노력하겠습니다.

W: Okay. How long will it take? 알겠어요. 얼마나 걸리죠?

M: Probably about an hour or so. You can wait here or come back at three P.M. 아마도 한 시간 정도요. 여기에서 기다리셔도 되고 오후 3시에 돌아오셔도 됩니다.

해설 여자의 자동차의 경적이 고장 나서 온 곳이므로 정답은 자동차 수리점이다.

어휘 car horn 자동차 경적   fill out 작성하다   probably 아마도 or so ~정도, 쯤   used-car market 중고차 시장   car rental 자동차 대여점   car dealership 자동차 대리점   car repair shop 자동차 수리점   education 교육

12 ⑤

M: Sam's Sports Center, which opened in October two thousand ten, is now the biggest fitness complex in the city. It is open from nine A.M. to eleven P.M. Monday through Friday, and ten A.M. to eight P.M. on Saturday and Sunday. We offer a variety of sports programs, such as swimming, aerobics, basketball, yoga, and golf for fifty dollars a month. Come and have a great time!

2010년 10월에 개관한 샘 스포츠 센터는 현재 시에서 가장 큰 피트니스 복합 건물입니다. 월요일부터 금요일까지는 오전 9시부터 오후 11시까지, 토요일과 일요일에는 오전 10시부터 오후 8시까지 문을 엽니다. 저희는 수영, 에어로빅, 농구, 요가 그리고 골프와 같은 다양한 스포츠 프로그램을 한 달에 50달러에 제공해 드리고 있습니다. 오셔서 즐거운 시간을 보내세요!

어휘 complex 복합 건물, (건물) 단지   a variety of 다양한 such as ~와 같은   aerobics 에어로빅

13 ④

M: How long has it been since we entered this maze? It feels like we've been here all day.
우리가 이 미로에 들어온지 얼마나 됐지? 우리는 하루 종일 여기 있었던 것 같은 기분이 들어.

W: I really want to get out of here. Let's look at the map to figure out where we are. 난 정말로 여기에서 빠져나가고 싶어. 지도를 보고 우리가 어디에 있는지 알아보자.

M: Okay. I'm sure we passed the first checkpoint a little while ago.
응. 아까 첫 번째 체크포인트를 지난 것은 확실해.

W: How about the second checkpoint?
두 번째 체크포인트는?

M: We passed that tree a few minutes ago. So, we need to take a right here, in front of the flowers.
우리는 몇 분 전에 저 나무를 지났어. 그러니까 우리는 여기 꽃 앞에서 오른쪽으로 돌아야 해.

W: Are you sure? I don't want to get lost in here.
확실해? 난 여기서 길을 잃고 싶지 않아.

M: Trust me! After we take a right, we will see the third checkpoint.
날 믿어! 우회전한 후에, 우리는 세 번째 체크포인트를 보게 될 거야.

해설 남자의 말인 'here, in front of the flowers'에서 두 사람이 있는 곳이 꽃 앞이라는 것을 알 수 있다. 또한 두 번째 체크포인트를 지났고 우회전하면 세 번째 체크포인트가 보이는 곳이므로 정답은 D이다.

어휘 maze 미로   feel like ~한 느낌이 있다   get out of ~에서 나가다   figure out 알아내다, 생각해내다   get lost 길을 잃다 take a right 우회전하다(= turn right)

14 ⑤

W: This is a string instrument that people play. It has four strings, and it is normally made of wood. You put this instrument on your shoulder and play it with a bow. The bow makes music when it touches the strings. People who play this instrument are normally part of an orchestra.

이것은 사람들이 연주하는 현악기입니다. 4개의 현이 있고, 보통 나무로 만들어져요. 당신은 이 악기를 당신의 어깨에 올려놓고 활로 그것을 연주합니다. 활이 현에 닿으면 그것은 음악을 만듭니다. 이 악기를 연주하는 사람들은 보통은 오케스트라의 구성원입니다.

어휘 string instrument 현악기   string (악기의) 현, 줄 normally 보통   be made of ~으로 만들어지다   bow (바이올린 등의) 활   orchestra 오케스트라, 관현악단

15 ②

W: Nick, are you watching TV again?
닉, 넌 또 TV를 보고 있니?

M: Mom, I will go to my room after this show is over.
엄마, 이 프로그램이 끝나면 제 방에 들어갈게요.

W: Did you finish your homework? You told me you had a lot to get done.
넌 숙제를 끝냈니? 네가 나한테 해야 할 게 많다고 말했잖니.

M: No, I was going to do it later with my friend.
아니요, 이따가 친구랑 같이 숙제를 하려고 했어요.

W: Well, I think you should finish your homework first. Then you can watch TV. 음, 내 생각엔 네가 숙제를 먼저 끝내는 것이 좋을 것 같은데. 그런 후에 TV를 봐도 되잖아.

M: The show will be over by the time I finish, but okay.
제가 숙제를 끝낼 때쯤엔 프로그램이 끝날 것 같은데, 하지만 알겠어요.

해설 'I think you should ~'에 여자의 조언이 나오고, 남자의 마지막 말인 'but okay'에서 여자의 조언을 따르기로 한 것을 알 수 있다.

어휘 show (텔레비전 등의) 프로그램, 공연   get done 끝마치다 be over 끝나다   by the time ~무렵에

16 ③

M: Helen, the school club festival opens on May twenty third. 헬렌, 학교 동아리 축제가 5월 23일에 시작하잖아.

W: Yes, I know. We need to have a meeting this week to prepare for it.
응, 나도 알아. 우린 그걸 준비하려면 이번 주에 회의를 가져야 해.

M: That sounds good. How about May fourteenth?
그게 좋겠다. 5월 14일은 어때?

W: No, I have math tutoring that day.
안돼, 난 그날 수학 과외가 있어.

M: Okay, then why don't we go on May sixteenth?
응, 그럼 5월 16일로 하는 것은 어때?

W: I think that will work. Let's meet early so we can discuss the topic in detail. 내 생각엔 그게 좋을 것 같아.
일찍 만나서 그 주제에 대해서 자세히 논의해 보자.

M: Okay. I will see you then. 좋아. 그때 봐.

[해설] 5월 23일은 축제가 시작하는 날짜이고, 16일이 모이기로 한 날짜이다. 상대방의 제안에 동의가 이루어졌는지를 반드시 확인하자.

[어휘] prepare for ~을 준비하다   tutoring 과외   discuss 논의하다   topic 주제   in detail 자세하게

17 ⑤

W: Peter usually comes home before three P.M. Today, Peter and his friends played a basketball game after school. His team lost, and the game finished around six P.M, which was later than he expected. Peter didn't call his mother to tell her he would be late and he didn't pick up her phone calls either. She got very worried. What would Peter's mother most likely say to Peter when he comes home?

피터는 보통 오후 3시 전에 집에 온다. 오늘, 피터와 그의 친구들은 방과 후에 농구 시합을 했다. 그의 팀이 졌고, 경기는 오후 6시경에 끝났는데, 그것은 그의 예상보다 더 늦은 시각이었다. 피터는 그가 늦는다고 엄마에게 전화를 하지 않았고, 엄마의 전화를 받지도 않았다. 엄마는 매우 걱정되었다. 피터의 엄마는 피터가 집으로 돌아올 때 무슨 말을 할 것 같은가?

Mother: Where have you been? I was worried about you! 너 어디에 있었니? 널 걱정했잖아!

① I'm sorry I didn't call you. 전화를 드리지 못해서 죄송해요.
② Is basketball your favorite sport?
농구가 네가 좋아하는 운동이니?
③ How long was the basketball game?
농구 시합이 얼마나 오래 걸렸니?
④ It's okay. You will win the next game.
괜찮아. 너는 다음 시합에서 이길 거야.
⑤ Where have you been? I was worried about you!
너 어디에 있었니? 널 걱정했잖아!

[해설] 아무런 연락이 없는 상황에서는 ⑤와 같은 응답이 적절하다. ①은 Peter가 엄마에게 할 수 있는 말이다.

[어휘] expect 기대하다   pick up 전화를 받다   either (부정문에서) ~도, 역시

18 ①

[Telephone rings.] [전화벨이 울린다.]

W: Hello, what can I do for you?
안녕하세요, 무엇을 도와드릴까요?

M: I'm calling because I can't log into my online game account. 온라인 게임 계정에 접속이 안 돼서 전화 드렸습니다.

W: Did you check your username and password?
사용자 이름과 비밀번호를 확인하셨나요?

M: Yes. I checked it twice. An error keeps popping up.
네. 그걸 두 번 확인했어요. 오류가 계속 뜨네요.

W: Hmm… Have you checked your Internet connection?
음, 인터넷 연결은 확인하셨나요?

M: Yes, I have. But, it's still not working.
네, 했어요. 하지만, 여전히 되지 않아요.

W: Okay. I will send someone to check it out for you soon. 알겠습니다. 제가 그것을 점검해 줄 사람을 곧 보낼게요.

M: Thank you so much. 정말 감사합니다.

[해설] 여자의 마지막 대사인 'I will ~'에 할 일이 나온다. 여자는 문제를 점검해 줄 직원을 남자가 있는 곳으로 보낼 것이다.

[어휘] log into ~에 접속하다   account 계정   username 사용자명   password 비밀번호   error 오류   pop up (불쑥) 나타나다   Internet connection 인터넷 연결

19 ③

W: I'm so exhausted. Ice skating is so much harder than I thought.
난 너무 지쳤어. 스케이트를 타는 게 생각보다 많이 어렵네.

M: What are you having the most trouble with?
어떤 부분에서 가장 어려움을 겪니?

W: Well, I keep falling every time I try to skate backwards or turn a corner.
음, 뒤로 스케이트를 타거나 코너를 돌리고 할 때마다 계속 넘어져.

M: It's only your first day of lessons! Don't get discouraged. All famous skaters started out just like you. 겨우 수업 첫날이잖아! 좌절하지 마. 유명한 스케이트 선수들은 모두 너처럼 시작했다고.

W: You're right. Do you think I'll get better if I practice every day?
네 말이 맞아. 넌 내가 매일 연습하면 나아질 거라 생각하니?

M: Of course! The only way to improve and master skills is to practice hard.
물론이지! 기술을 향상시키고 숙달하는 유일한 방법은 열심히 연습하는 거야.

[어휘] keep -ing 계속 ~하다   every time ~할 때마다   backwards 뒤로, 거꾸로   turn a corner 코너를 돌다   discouraged 낙담한   start out 시작하다   get better 나아지다   improve 향상시키다, 향상되다   master 숙달하다

20 ①

M: Hello, I would like to buy an annual pass to the amusement park.
안녕하세요, 놀이공원 연간 회원권을 사고 싶은데요.

W: Okay, would you like to sign up for a Silver or Gold pass? 네, 실버와 골드 회원권 중에 어떤 걸로 신청하시겠어요?

M: What is the difference? 차이가 뭐예요?

W: The Silver pass is fifty dollars a year. The Gold pass is one hundred dollars a year. With the Gold pass, you don't have to wait in line for the rides.
실버 회원권은 1년에 50달러이고요. 골드 회원권은 1년에 100달러예요. 골드 회원권이 있으면 놀이기구를 이용할 때 줄을 설 필요가 없어요.

M: Great. Is that all? 좋네요. 그게 다예요?

W: As a Gold member you also get a free meal.
골드 회원이 되면, 무료로 식사도 하실 수 있어요.

M: Awesome! I want to buy a Gold pass.
굉장하네요! 저는 골드 회원권을 사고 싶어요.

① Awesome! I want to buy a Gold pass.
굉장하네요! 저는 골드 회원권을 사고 싶어요.

② How long are the lines for the rides?
놀이기구를 타는 줄은 얼마나 긴가요?

③ The restaurant is far from here.
식당은 여기에서 멀어요.

④ How do I get to the amusement park?
놀이공원까지 어떻게 가나요?

⑤ I want to get a refund on my ticket.
제 티켓에 대해 환불받고 싶어요.

해설 골드 회원권의 여러 장점을 듣고 난 후에 대한 응답으로는 ①이 가장 자연스럽다.

어휘 annual 연간의 pass 입장권, 회원권 sign up for ~을 신청하다 difference 차이 wait in line 줄을 서서 기다리다 ride 놀이기구 far from ~에서 먼 get a refund 환불받다

03회 실전모의고사
본문 p.30-31

01 ⑤	**02** ①	**03** ②	**04** ④	**05** ③
06 ①	**07** ①	**08** ②	**09** ③	**10** ③
11 ①	**12** ④	**13** ④	**14** ①	**15** ①
16 ④	**17** ⑤	**18** ④	**19** ③	**20** ④

01 ⑤

M: Hello. Can I help you with something?
안녕하세요. 제가 무엇을 도와드릴까요?

W: Yes. I'd like to buy a coloring book for my daughter.
네. 제 딸에게 줄 컬러링북을 사려고 해요.

M: Okay. Would you like this one with flowers? It's a very popular item.
네. 꽃 그림이 있는 이건 어때요? 굉장히 인기 있는 상품이에요.

W: It seems alright, but do you have any with animals?
괜찮아 보이지만, 동물 그림이 있는 것이 있나요?

M: We sure do. Here's one with birds. What do you think of it?
물론 있죠. 새 그림이 있는 것이 여기 있어요. 어떻게 생각하세요?

W: It's nice, but I would like a coloring book with more variety.
그것도 좋지만, 더 다양한 그림이 있는 컬러링북을 사고 싶어요.

M: Okay. We have this one with bears and turtles. She'll love it. I'm sure of it!
알겠습니다. 저희는 곰과 거북이 그림이 있는 컬러링북도 있답니다. 따님이 그걸 좋아할 겁니다. 확실해요.

어휘 coloring book 컬러링북(색칠공부를 할 수 있는 책) variety 다양성, 각양각색 excellent 훌륭한, 탁월한

02 ①

[Cellphone rings.] [휴대폰이 울린다.]

M: Hi, Mom. 여보세요, 엄마.

W: Jack, have you decided what you want to do for your birthday? 잭, 네 생일에 하고 싶은 것을 결정했니?

M: Hmm… I'm not sure. I can't decide. Do you have any ideas?
음, 아직 몰라요. 결정을 못 하겠어요. 생각한 게 있으세요?

W: How about going to the swimming pool? Or the zoo? 수영장에 가는 건 어떠니? 아니면 동물원?

M: That sounds great! I'll tell my friends that we're going to the zoo for my birthday party.
그거 좋겠네요! 제 생일 파티를 위해 동물원에 갈 거라고 제 친구들한테 말해야겠어요.

W: Let me know how many people are coming. I have to buy tickets.
친구들이 몇 명이나 오는지 내게 알려 주렴. 티켓을 사야 하거든.

해설 여자의 첫 대사인 'Have you decided ~?'에 전화를 건 목적이 나온다.

어휘 decide 결정하다 zoo 동물원

03 ②

① W: Isaac, can you clean the windows?
아이작, 창문 좀 청소해 주겠니?

M: I sure can. Let me get a washcloth.
물론 할 수 있어. 닦을 수건을 가져올게.

② W: Could you turn down the volume?
볼륨 좀 낮춰 줄래?

M: But my favorite TV show is on!
하지만 내가 좋아하는 TV 프로그램이 나오고 있다고!

③ W: I like your sofa. It's very comfortable.
난 네 소파가 마음에 들어. 정말 편하다.

M: Thanks! I bought it last month.
고마워! 난 그걸 지난달에 샀어.

④ W: It's really sunny outside. 밖이 매우 화창해.

M: It sure is. Should we go for a walk?
정말 그렇네. 우리 산책하러 갈래?

⑤ W: Isaac, would you close the curtain for me?
아이작, 커튼을 닫아주겠니?

M: Yes, I can do that. 응, 그렇게.

어휘 washcloth 수건, 마른 행주 turn down the volume 볼륨을 줄이다 comfortable 편한 go for a walk 산책하러 가다

04 ④

W: Chris, look at these cupcakes! They all have real fruit on them! 크리스, 이 컵케이크들을 봐! 컵케이크에 전부 생과일이 올려져 있네!

M: They all look delicious. Do you want to buy some for our picnic?
다 맛있어 보여. 소풍에 가져갈 컵케이크를 좀 살까?

W: Absolutely! I heard that the strawberry and banana ones are the best.
물론이지! 딸기랑 바나나 컵케이크가 최고라고 들었어.

M: Really? I would prefer the cupcake with the orange or kiwi on top.
정말? 난 오렌지나 키위가 올려진 컵케이크가 더 좋아.

W: Well, let's try strawberry today, and we can buy a kiwi cupcake tomorrow. 음, 오늘은 딸기 컵케이크를 먹어보자. 그리고 내일은 키위를 먹어보자.

M: Okay, that works for me. 알았어, 난 좋아.

해설 여자의 마지막 대사인 'Let's ~'에 제안이 나왔으므로 이에 대해 남자가 동의하는지 확인한다.

어휘 absolutely 물론이지(강한 동의를 나타냄), 전적으로 prefer (~을 더) 좋아하다, 선호하다

05 ③

[Telephone rings.] [전화벨이 울린다.]

M: Hello, what can I do for you today?
안녕하세요, 오늘은 무엇을 도와드릴까요?

W: Hi. I would like to reserve a plane ticket.
안녕하세요. 비행기 티켓을 예약하고 싶어요.

M: Okay. Where are you planning to go?
알겠습니다. 어디로 갈 계획이시죠?

W: I'm going to Greece for a backpacking trip with my friends. 그리스로 친구들과 배낭 여행을 가려고 해요.

M: Great! Do you know when you want to travel?
멋지네요! 언제 여행하고 싶은지 아시나요?

W: Yes, from August fourteenth to August twentieth would be great. I hope there are tickets left! 네, 8월 14일부터 20일까지가 좋겠네요. 티켓이 아직 남아 있길 바라요!

M: You're a lucky woman. There is one tour package available for nine hundred dollars. 손님은 운이 좋네요. 900달러에 구입 가능한 패키지 상품이 하나 있어요.

W: Wonderful! It's a good thing I called early.
완벽해요! 제가 일찍 전화하길 잘했네요.

해설 비행기 티켓을 예약하고, 패키지 상품을 소개하는 것으로 보아 남자는 여행사 직원이다.

어휘 reserve 예약하다 backpacking trip 배낭 여행 left 남은 available 이용할 수 있는, 구입할 수 있는 tour guide 여행 가이드 salesperson 판매원 travel agent 여행사 직원 flight attendant 승무원 technician 기술자

06 ①

M: Hey, Sandra, what are you doing? You seem busy.
이봐, 샌드라, 뭐하고 있어? 너 바빠 보여.

W: I'm cleaning the house because my dog made a mess. 우리 집 개가 어질러 놓아서 집을 청소하고 있어.

M: Oh no! What did he do? 이런! 개가 무슨 짓을 한 거야?

W: He ripped open my new sofa cushions that my mom bought me!
엄마가 나에게 사준 새 소파 쿠션을 찢어놓았어.

M: That sounds like a disaster. Are you okay?
듣기만 해도 끔찍하다. 넌 괜찮아?

W: No, I'm so frustrated. I can't leave him alone even for one hour! 아니, 난 너무 짜증이 나. 나는 개를 한 시간도 혼자 있게 둘 수 없어.

M: Yeah, pets can be a pain sometimes.
응, 애완동물은 때때로 골칫거리일 수 있어.

W: Tell me about it! 내 말이 그 말이야!

해설 여자의 말인 'I'm so frustrated.'에서 frustrated는 본인이 어떤 상황을 통제할 수 없어서 답답하고 짜증날 때 쓸 수 있으며, annoyed와 비슷한 감정의 형용사이다.

어휘 make a mess 어질러놓다 rip open (안에 내용물이 다 보일 정도로) 찢다 disaster 재난, 참사 frustrated 좌절한, 낙담한 leave somebody alone ~을 혼자 두다 pain 골칫거리 annoyed 짜증난 jealous 부러워하는, 질투하는

07 ①

① M: They're building a balcony in front of the café.
사람들이 카페 앞에 발코니를 만들고 있네.

W: Ice coffee would be great. Thanks!
아이스 커피가 좋겠어. 고마워!

② M: It's supposed to snow this weekend.
이번 주말에 눈이 온대.

W: Cool! Let's go make a snowman.
좋다! 눈사람 만들러 가자.

③ M: Are you feeling okay? 넌 몸이 괜찮니?

W: No, I don't think I can go to school today.
아니, 오늘은 학교에 갈 수 없을 것 같아.

④ M: Are you free on Friday? 너 금요일에 시간 있어?

W: I sure am. Let's grab lunch together.
물론 있지. 같이 점심 먹자.

⑤ M: Can you do me a favor? 내 부탁 좀 들어주겠니?

W: Of course, anything for you! What is it?
물론, 너라면 어떤 것이든! 뭔데?

해설 ①에서 건물 공사에 관한 내용을 말했으므로 커피 주문에 관한 응답은 부자연스럽다.

어휘 in front of ~ 앞에 be supposed to ~하기로 되어 있다 grab lunch 점심 먹다 do somebody a favor ~의 부탁을 들어주다

08 ②

[*Cellphone rings.*] [휴대폰이 울린다.]
W: Hello, this is Susan speaking. 여보세요, 수잔입니다.
M: Hey, Susan! This is Don. Are you at the baseball stadium already?
이봐, 수잔! 나 돈이야. 너 야구 경기장에 벌써 도착했니?
W: Yes, I just got here. Where are you?
응, 난 방금 여기에 도착했어. 넌 어디 있니?
M: I'm on my way. Can you buy some drinks? I'm really thirsty.
난 가는 길이야. 음료수 좀 사다 줄래? 난 정말 목이 말라.
W: Yeah, no problem. Do you need anything else?
응, 되고말고. 그것 말고 필요한 게 있니?
M: No, that's all. Thanks so much! By the way, I'll be there in ten minutes. 아니, 그게 다야. 정말 고마워! 그나저나, 난 10분 후에 거기 도착해.

해설 남자가 'Can you ~?'로 부탁의 내용을 말했다. thirsty도 힌트가 된다.

어휘 already 이미, 벌써 thirsty 목이 마른 by the way 그런데(화제를 바꿀 때)

09 ③

W: Michael, are you ready to move into your new house? 마이클, 새집으로 이사 갈 준비를 다 했니?
M: No, not yet. I'm having some trouble.
아니, 아직. 약간의 문제가 생겼어.
W: Oh no, what's the matter? 이런, 무슨 문제인데?
M: I'm trying to move all the boxes into my car, but they won't fit. I have too much cargo.
내 차에 모든 상자를 옮기려고 하는데, 다 들어가지 않을 것 같아. 나한테 짐이 너무 많거든.
W: There's a much easier way. Just call a moving van service. 훨씬 더 쉬운 방법이 있어. 이삿짐 트럭 회사에 전화해 봐.

해설 여자는 남자의 문제를 들은 후 해결책을 제안하고 있다.

어휘 move into ~로 이사 가다 fit (어느 장소에 들어가기에) 맞다 cargo (무거운) 짐, 화물 moving van 이삿짐 트럭 moving service 이삿짐 회사

10 ③

W: Good morning! Welcome to Sherry Flowers!
안녕하세요! 셰리 플라워스에 오신 것을 환영합니다!

M: Hello. I'd like to buy some roses. How much are they? 안녕하세요. 장미를 좀 사려고 하는데요. 얼마예요?
W: Thirty dollars for one dozen. But if you buy two, you can get the second one for half price.
12개짜리 한 다발이 30달러예요. 그런데 두 다발을 사시면, 두 번째 다발은 반값에 드려요.
M: Okay! I would like one dozen white roses and one dozen red roses.
좋아요! 백장미 한 다발과 빨간 장미 한 다발 주세요.
W: I'll wrap them up for you right away.
지금 바로 포장해 드릴게요.
M: Thank you. Here's my credit card.
감사합니다. 신용카드 여기 있어요.

해설 한 다발의 가격은 30달러, 두 번째 다발은 반값인 15달러이니 합계는 45달러이다.

어휘 dozen 12개짜리 한 묶음, 다스 for half price 반값으로 wrap up 포장하다

11 ①

M: I'm so glad we came here for our family trip.
우리가 가족여행으로 이곳에 오게 돼서 정말 좋네요.
W: I agree. Look at that! There are so many types of fish here! 저도 그래요. 저것 좀 봐요! 여기에는 정말 많은 종류의 물고기가 있네요!
M: The children are going to enjoy seeing the sharks.
애들이 상어를 보면 즐거워하겠어요.
W: Definitely. I can already see how excited they are!
당연하죠. 애들이 얼마나 신이 나 있는지 벌써 보이네요.
M: There's going to be a dolphin show in one hour.
한 시간 후에 돌고래 쇼가 있을 거예요.
W: Wonderful! If we go now, we can get good seats.
좋네요! 우리가 지금 가면, 좋은 자리를 얻을 수 있겠어요.
M: Good point. Let's take the children there quickly.
좋은 지적이에요. 애들을 데리고 저쪽으로 빨리 가요.

해설 fish, shark, dolphin 등이 힌트이다.

어휘 definitely 분명히, 틀림 없이 excited 신이 난, 들뜬 get a seat 자리를 잡다 aquarium 수족관

12 ④

W: Ladies and gentlemen. I'm pleased to announce the grand opening of the Great Square Museum. It will be open to the public starting on October twentieth. The museum has ten exhibition rooms. It will be open Monday through Friday from nine thirty A.M. to five thirty P.M., and Saturday and Sunday from ten A.M. to four P.M. Ticket prices are fifteen dollars for adults and five dollars for children. Call nine three oh, one two three four to purchase tickets now.

신사 숙녀 여러분. 그레이트 스퀘어 박물관의 개관을 알리게 되어

기쁩니다. 박물관은 10월 20일부터 일반에 개방될 것입니다. 박물관에는 10개의 전시실이 있습니다. 박물관은 요일일부터 금요일까지는 오전 9시 30분에서 오후 5시 30분까지, 토요일과 일요일에는 오전 10시부터 오후 4시까지 문을 엽니다. 티켓 가격은 성인이 15달러이고, 어린이는 5달러입니다. 지금 티켓을 구매하시려면 930-1234로 전화 주세요.

어휘 announce 알리다, 발표하다 grand opening 개장, 개관 exhibition 전시, 전시회 open to the public 대중에게 개방하다 purchase 구매하다

13 ④

| 개를 팝니다 |

①	개의 품종	푸들
②	수컷/암컷	암컷
③	색깔	갈색
④	나이	6개월
⑤	가격	200달러

W: Henry, we need to sell our dog. We don't have the time to take care of her.
헨리, 우리 개를 팔아야 하잖아. 우린 개를 돌볼 시간이 없으니까.

M: Okay, we can put an advertisement in the newspaper. 응, 우리는 신문에 광고를 낼 수 있어.

W: Can you help me with this form?
이 양식 작성 좀 도와줄래?

M: Sure! Ruby is a brown poodle.
물론! 루비는 갈색 푸들이야.

W: Right. Do you remember how old she is?
맞아. 넌 루비가 몇 살인지 기억하니?

M: I would say she is about one year old.
루비는 아마 한 살 정도 될 거야.

W: Yeah. How much do you think we can ask for her?
응. 넌 우리가 루비에 대해 얼마를 요구할 수 있다고 생각해?

M: I think between two hundred dollars and three hundred dollars is a reasonable price. 내 생각엔 200달러에서 300달러가 사이가 적당한 가격인 것 같아.

W: People might think three hundred dollars is too expensive. Let's go with two hundred dollars. 사람들은 300달러는 너무 비싸다고 생각할 거야. 200달러로 가자.

해설 동물도 사람과 마찬가지로 암컷은 she, 수컷은 he라고 부른다. 'Do you remember how old she is?'의 질문에 'one year old'라고 대답했으므로 12 months이다.

어휘 put an advertisement in ~에 광고를 내다 I would say 아마 ~이겠다 reasonable (가격이) 적정한, 타당한 breed (동물의) 품종

14 ①

M: This is a safety precaution for people who are near bodies of water, such as a swimming pool, lake, or ocean. It is normally shaped like a vest, and has buckles on the front. Also, you can find these on life boats. Even if you fall into the water, you don't have to worry because you will float when you wear this.

이것은 수영장, 호수나 바다와 같은 물가 근처에 있는 사람들을 위한 안전 예방책이에요. 이것은 일반적으로 조끼처럼 생겼고 앞에 버클이 있어요. 또한 인명 구조선에서 이것들을 볼 수 있지요. 여러분이 물에 빠진다 하더라도 이것을 입으면 물에 뜨기 때문에 걱정할 필요가 없어요.

어휘 safety precaution 안전 예방책 near 가까이에 body of water 물가, 수역 normally 보통, 일반적으로 vest 조끼 buckle 버클, 잠금장치 life boat 구조선 fall into ~에 빠지다 float (물에) 뜨다

15 ①

[Cellphone rings.] [휴대폰이 울린다.]

M: Katie, when are you getting home from school?
케이티, 학교에서 언제 집에 도착하니?

W: Maybe in a few hours, Dad. Why?
아마도 몇 시간 후에요, 아빠. 왜요?

M: I have to go to the department store right now, but I can't find the car keys.
내가 지금 백화점에 가야 하는데, 자동차 열쇠를 못 찾겠구나.

W: Did you check the living room?
거실 확인해 보셨어요?

M: Yes, but they aren't there. Where did you put them after you used them last night?
응, 그런데 거기에 없어. 지난밤에 네가 쓰고 나서 어디에 두었니?

W: Let me think. [pause] Oh! I remember. I put them on the kitchen table. 생각 좀 해볼게요. [잠시 후] 아! 기억나요. 제가 부엌 식탁 위에 그걸 놓았어요.

M: Alright. Please put them back in my room next time. 알겠어. 다음에는 아빠 방에 갖다 놓으렴.

해설 여자가 자동차 열쇠를 부엌 식탁에 두었다고 말했으므로 남자는 부엌에 가볼 것이다.

어휘 put something back ~을 제자리에 갖다 놓다

16 ④

W: Mr. Wright, when should we have our meeting?
라이트 씨, 우리가 언제 회의를 해야 할까요?

M: I'm thinking either September fourth or ninth.
전 9월 4일이나 9일 중에 하루를 생각하고 있었어요.

W: Hmm… September fourth is too soon and September ninth is too late. Does the seventh or eighth work for you? 음, 9월 4일은 너무 이르고 9월 9일은 너무 늦어요. 7일이나 8일은 괜찮아요?

M: I already have a meeting planned for the seventh at nine A.M. 저는 이미 7일 오전 9시에 회의가 잡혀 있어요.

W: Alright. Then, I guess I'll see you the day after your meeting on the seventh. 알겠어요. 그럼 우리는 7일에 있을 당신의 회의 다음 날에 당신을 만나야 할 것 같네요.

M: Okay, that will work for me.
알겠습니다. 그게 저한테도 좋아요.

해설 여자의 마지막 대사인 'I'll see you ~'에서 남자가 회의가 있는 7일의 다음 날에 보자고 했으므로 두 사람은 8일에 회의를 할 것이다.

어휘 either A or B A와 B 중 하나   planned 계획된
the day after 그 다음 날

17 ⑤

W: Rob took his friend Tina to watch a popular musical in town. However, he didn't make a reservation. It is his turn to buy tickets, but the closest show time is all sold out. The next showing is in two hours. So, Rob decides to ask Tina if she'd be okay with going to eat dinner before watching the musical. In this situation, what would Rob most likely say to Tina?

롭은 인기 있는 뮤지컬을 보기 위해 그의 친구인 티나를 시내에 데려갔다. 그러나, 그는 예약을 하지 않았다. 그가 티켓을 살 차례인데, 가장 가까운 공연 시간이 모두 매진되었다. 다음 공연이 2시간 후에 있다. 그래서 롭은 뮤지컬을 보기 전에 저녁을 먹는 것이 괜찮은지 티나에게 묻기로 결심한다. 이 상황에서 롭은 티나에게 뭐라고 말할 것 같은가?

Rob: Do you mind if we go eat something before the show? 공연 전에 뭔가를 먹으러 가는 게 괜찮니?

① How much are the tickets? 티켓이 얼마야?
② Have you seen a musical before?
   전에 뮤지컬을 본 적 있어?
③ I would like to buy two tickets.
   티켓 두 장을 사려고.
④ Would you rather do something else?
   차라리 다른 걸 할래?
⑤ Do you mind if we go eat something before the show? 공연 전에 뭔가를 먹으러 가는 게 괜찮니?

어휘 make a reservation 예약하다   turn 차례   sold out 매진된   would rather 차라리 ~하고 싶다, ~하겠다   something else 뭔가 다른 것

18 ④

M: Mom, can we go to the bookstore?
   엄마, 우리 서점에 갈 수 있어요?
W: Okay. Do you need books for school?
   그래. 학교에 필요한 책이라도 있니?
M: Yes, I have to buy some books for my history class.
   네, 전 역사 수업에 필요한 책 몇 권을 사야 해요.
W: There will probably be a lot of history books at the library. Did you check if they have the book you need? 아마도 도서관에 역사 책이 많을 것 같은데. 네가 필요한 책이 도서관에 있는지 확인해 봤니?
M: No, I didn't think of that. That's a good idea, Mom.
   아니요, 그걸 생각 못했네요. 좋은 생각이에요, 엄마.

W: It's a little late today. What time does the library close? 오늘은 좀 늦었구나. 도서관이 몇 시에 문을 닫니?
M: I'll call them and ask right now.
   지금 바로 도서관에 전화해서 물어볼게요.

해설 여자가 도서관이 몇 시에 닫는지 물어보자 남자는 'I'll call them ~'이라고 할 일을 말했다.

어휘 probably 아마도

19 ③

M: Betty, what are you doing up so early in the morning? Aren't you tired?
   베티, 너 아침 일찍 뭐하고 있니? 피곤하지 않니?
W: No, not really. I'm used to waking up at this time. It's so refreshing!
   아니, 전혀. 난 이 시간에 일어나는 게 익숙해. 정말 상쾌해!
M: I don't understand you. What do you do at this hour? 나는 널 이해할 수가 없어. 이 시간에 뭘 하는데?
W: I eat, exercise, study, and prepare myself for the day. 난 먹고, 운동하고, 공부하고, 하루를 준비하지.
M: I see. What benefits come from that?
   그렇구나. 그걸 하면 뭐가 좋아?
W: I get healthier. More importantly, my grades improve. 더 건강해지지. 더 중요한 건, 내 성적도 올라.
M: Hmm… Maybe I should try waking up early too.
   음, 어쩌면 나도 일찍 일어나려고 해봐야겠어.
W: I promise you that you won't regret it!
   난 네가 그걸 후회하지 않을 거라 장담해!

해설 부지런하면 좋은 결과를 얻는다는 의미를 가진 속담을 찾는다.

어휘 be used to -ing ~하는 것에 익숙하다   refreshing 상쾌한, 기운을 돋우는   benefit 이점, 혜택   more importantly (중요한 것을 덧붙여 말할 때) 더 중요한 건   regret 후회하다

20 ④

M: Is there a problem with your camera, ma'am?
   카메라에 무슨 문제가 있나요, 부인?
W: Yes. I need to get my lens replaced. It's broken.
   네. 렌즈를 교체해야 해요. 깨졌어요.
M: How did it break? 어쩌다가 깨졌죠?
W: I dropped it on the side of the road while I was trying to take a picture.
   제가 사진을 찍으려고 하다가 카메라를 도로변에 떨어뜨렸어요.
M: I see. Do you have insurance? 그렇군요. 보험은 있나요?
W: No, I didn't apply for it when I bought it.
   아뇨, 제가 그걸 샀을 때, 보험은 신청하지 않았어요.
M: Then I'm afraid you have to pay an extra fee to get it fixed. 그렇다면 죄송하지만 고객님은 카메라를 고치려면 추가 비용을 더 지불해야 합니다.
W: Why is that? 왜 그렇죠?
M: Because that's how our policy works.
   저희 회사 방침이 그렇기 때문이죠.

① It will cost you about a hundred dollars.
그건 100달러가 들 겁니다.

② Have you replaced it before?
전에 그것을 교체한 적이 있습니까?

③ We can't replace your camera lens.
저희는 고객님의 카메라 렌즈를 교체해드릴 수 없습니다.

④ Because that's how our policy works.
저희 회사 방침이 그렇기 때문이죠.

⑤ Would you like to apply for insurance now?
지금 보험에 가입하시겠습니까?

해설 여자가 추가 비용을 지불해야 하는 이유를 물었으니 'Because ~'로 설명하는 ④가 적절하다.

어휘 replace 교체하다 broken 깨진, 고장 난 drop 떨어뜨리다 on the side of the road 도로변에서 insurance 보험 apply for ~을 신청하다 extra fee 추가 요금 get something fixed ~을 고치다 policy 방침, 정책 work 작용하다, 영향을 미치다

04회 실전모의고사 본문 p.42~43

01 ③	02 ①	03 ②	04 ④	05 ③
06 ①	07 ②	08 ②	09 ⑤	10 ③
11 ③	12 ④	13 ③	14 ④	15 ①
16 ③	17 ④	18 ⑤	19 ⑤	20 ③

01 ③

W: Dad, this is my drawing for the school's flag design contest.
아빠, 이건 제가 학교의 깃발 디자인 대회에서 그린 거예요.

M: It looks great! I see you put a rainbow on the flag.
훌륭해 보인다! 네가 깃발에 무지개를 넣은 게 보이는구나.

W: Yeah. My teacher told me to include a symbol for the school, so I used a rainbow. 네. 선생님이 저에게 학교의 상징을 포함시키라고 해서, 저는 무지개를 활용했어요.

M: Good job. But why didn't you include any unicorns? You love unicorns. 잘했다. 그런데 유니콘은 왜 넣지 않았니? 너는 유니콘을 아주 좋아하잖아.

W: I know, but they are too hard to draw.
저도 알지만 유니콘은 그리기가 너무 어려워요.

M: I see. I like your idea to put the name of the school below the rainbow. 알겠다. 무지개 아래에 학교의 이름을 넣은 네 생각이 마음에 드는구나.

W: Thanks, Dad. 고마워요, 아빠.

어휘 include 포함하다 symbol 상징 below ~아래에

02 ①

[*Telephone rings.*] [전화벨이 울린다.]

M: Jennifer, I'm at the soccer field. I have bad news for you. 제니퍼, 나는 축구장에 있어. 네게 안 좋은 소식이 있어.

W: Don't tell me there are no empty fields left!
남은 경기장이 없다는 말은 하지 말아줘!

M: Sorry, there are people playing on all the fields. It doesn't look like they're going to leave any time soon. 유감스럽게도 사람들이 모든 경기장을 사용하고 있어. 그들이 곧 떠날 것 같지도 않아.

W: Oh no! That means we can't play soccer today! That's so disappointing. 안돼! 그건 우리가 오늘 축구를 할 수 없다는 의미잖아! 그건 정말 실망스럽다.

M: I know. I should have reserved a field for us.
나도 알아. 내가 우리가 쓸 경기장을 예약했어야 했는데.

W: It's alright. We can always go back and play tomorrow. 괜찮아. 우리는 내일이라도 언제든 돌아가서 경기할 수 있잖아.

M: Sounds good. I'll be more prepared next time.
그거 좋다. 내가 다음에는 준비를 더 잘할게.

해설 남자가 나쁜 소식이 있다고 하자 여자는 'Don't tell me ~'에서 듣고 싶지 않은 소식의 내용을 언급했다. 이어서 남자가 내용을 확인시켜준다. 대화 초반에 전화 목적이 분명히 드러난 것이다.

어휘 empty 비어 있는 look like ~할 것 같다, ~처럼 보이다 any time soon 곧, 가까운 시일 내에 disappointing 실망스러운 reserve 예약하다 prepared 준비가 된

03 ②

① M: Do you want to ride the merry-go-round?
너는 회전목마를 타고 싶어?

W: Yeah! I want to ride the white horse.
네! 저는 흰색 말을 타고 싶어요.

② M: How long have you been waiting in line?
얼마나 오래 줄을 서서 기다리고 있었나요?

W: About half an hour. 30분 정도요.

③ M: Look at the rollercoaster over there.
저기 롤러코스터를 봐.

W: Wow, it looks really scary.
우와, 정말 무서워 보여.

④ M: Would you like to take a picture?
너는 사진을 찍고 싶어?

W: Not now. After I eat all of my popcorn.
지금은 아니에요. 제 팝콘을 전부 먹은 후에요.

⑤ M: I'm sorry, but you're not tall enough to ride the bumper cars.
미안하지만, 손님은 범퍼카를 탈 수 있는 키가 되지 않네요.

W: Oh, no! I can't believe it. 아, 안돼요! 믿을 수가 없군요.

어휘 merry-go-round 회전목마 wait in line 줄을 서서 기다리다 scary 무서운 tall enough 키가 충분히 큰, 충분히 높은

04 ④

W: Wow, there are so many clocks we can choose from. 우와, 우리가 선택할 수 있는 시계가 아주 많이 있네.

M: You're right. It's difficult to pick one for Nathan. I hope we find one that he'll like.
네 말이 맞아. 네이선을 위해 하나를 고르기가 어렵네. 그가 좋아할 만한 걸 찾으면 좋겠는데.

W: What do you think about this rectangular one with stripes?
여기 줄무늬가 있는 직사각형 시계에 대해 어떻게 생각해?

M: It looks fancy, but I don't think he'll like the stripes. I think he'll prefer this diamond-shaped one with stars. 멋있어 보이긴 하는데 네이선이 줄무늬를 좋아할 것 같지 않아. 그는 별이 있는 이 다이아몬드 모양을 더 좋아할 거라 생각해.

W: That looks nice too, but the square one with stars seems best. I'm sure he'll be satisfied with it.
그것도 좋아 보이긴 하지만, 별이 있는 사각형 시계가 가장 좋아 보여. 나는 네이선이 이것에 만족할 거라고 확신해.

M: Yeah, you're probably right. Let's buy that one.
응, 아마도 네가 맞을 거야. 그걸 사자.

어휘 choose from ~에서 선택하다 pick 고르다, 뽑다 rectangular 직사각형의 with stripes 줄무늬가 있는 fancy 화려한, 고급의 prefer 선호하다 diamond-shaped 다이아몬드 모양의, 마름모꼴의 square 정사각형 모양의 be satisfied with ~에 만족하다 probably 아마

05 ③

W: Robert, how are you feeling today?
로버트, 오늘은 몸 상태가 어떠니?

M: I'm doing a lot better than when I first came here. That's for sure.
제가 이곳에 처음 왔을 때보다 훨씬 좋아졌어요. 그건 분명해요.

W: I'm really happy that your headache is gone.
네 두통이 사라졌다니 나는 정말 기쁘구나.

M: Me too, I've stayed in the hospital long enough. I can't wait to go home. 저도 마찬가지에요. 저는 병원에 충분히 오래 머물렀잖아요. 집에 가는 게 기다려져요.

W: You can leave the hospital today, but please make sure you come for a checkup next Thursday.
너는 오늘 퇴원할 수 있지만, 다음 주 목요일에 검사를 하러 오는 것을 명심하렴.

M: Sure, I'll call to make an appointment.
물론이죠, 제가 전화로 예약할게요.

W: The nurse will give you your medicine soon. Take it three times a day and look after yourself.
간호사가 네게 곧 약을 줄 거야. 그것을 하루에 세 번 먹고 네 몸을 스스로 잘 돌보렴.

M: Okay, thank you! 네, 고맙습니다!

해설 여자가 남자의 몸 상태, 두통 등을 언급하는 것으로 보아, 병원이나 약국에서 일하는 사람이란 것을 알 수 있다. 이어서 hospital, nurse 등의 힌트를 통해 여자가 의사라는 것이 확실해진다.

어휘 a lot better than ~보다 훨씬 좋은 headache 두통 gone 사라진 leave the hospital 퇴원하다 checkup 검사 make an appointment 예약하다, 약속하다 medicine 약 three times a day 하루에 세 번 look after ~을 돌보다

06 ①

M: Honey, have you seen my black pants?
여보, 내 검정 바지 본 적 있어요?

W: Yeah, I took them to the dry cleaner's because you asked me to.
네, 당신이 나한테 부탁한 대로 내가 그걸 세탁소에 맡겼어요.

M: Already? I should have taken everything out of the pockets. 벌써요? 내가 주머니에서 모든 걸 꺼냈어야 했는데.

W: What was inside? 안에 뭐가 있었어요?

M: A memo with my new manager's phone number on it. 새로 온 상사의 전화번호가 적힌 메모요.

W: Oh, I was wondering what that piece of paper was. I took it out of your pants before sending them to be cleaned. 아, 저는 그 종잇조각이 뭔지 궁금했어요. 제가 바지를 세탁 맡기기 전에 그걸 바지에서 꺼냈거든요.

M: Did you really? Thank you so much! A huge weight was just lifted off my shoulders. 당신이 정말 그랬어요? 정말 고마워요! 아주 무거운 짐이 내 어깨에서 내려진 기분이에요.

W: No problem. Be sure to check it yourself next time.
그럼요. 다음에는 당신이 꼭 확인하도록 하세요.

해설 'A huge weight was just lifted off my shoulders'는 우리말로는 '10년 묵은 체증이 내려갔다'는 의미로, 걱정거리나 어려운 일에서 벗어났다는 것을 의미한다.

어휘 Have you seen ~? ~을 본 적 있니? dry cleaner's 세탁소 take out of ~에서 꺼내다 a piece of paper 종이 한 장 weight (무거운 책임감 같은) 짐; 무게 lift 들어올리다 off one's shoulders 어깨에서 내려진 relieved 안도하는 jealous 질투하는 regretful 후회하는 relaxed 느긋한

07 ②

① M: I'll be arriving at the airport around six P.M.
나는 오후 6시쯤 공항에 도착할 거야.

W: Alright, I'll be there to pick you up.
알았어, 내가 널 데리러 그곳에 갈게.

② M: How long will it take to get there by bus?
거기에 가는 데 버스로 얼마나 걸리나요?

W: Go straight and there will be a bus station on your left. 직진하면 당신의 왼쪽에 버스 정류장이 있을 거예요.

③ M: Mary, my wife is pregnant with a son.
메리, 내 아내가 아들을 임신했어.

W: That's wonderful. Congratulations! 그거 멋지다. 축하해!

④ M: I'm wondering if you could send me the package by Tuesday.
당신이 제게 그 소포를 화요일까지 보내줄 수 있는지 궁금하군요.

W: Of course. I'll send it as soon as possible.
물론이죠. 제가 그걸 되도록 빨리 보낼게요.

⑤ M: Would you have dinner with me on Saturday?
저와 함께 토요일에 식사를 하시겠어요?

W: I would love to. 기꺼이 그럴게요.

해설 ②의 질문에서 'How long ~?'으로 소요 시간을 물었으므로 시간 정보를 포함하여 'It will take ~'로 답하는 게 자연스럽다.

어휘 pregnant with ~을 임신한 as soon as possible 되도록 빨리

08 ②

W: Excuse me, sir. 실례합니다, 선생님.

M: Yes, can I help you with something?
네, 제가 뭘 도와드릴까요?

W: I bought a train ticket to Central Plaza a few days ago. Could you tell me if it is a window or aisle seat? 제가 며칠 전에 센트럴 플라자로 가는 기차표를 샀거든요. 그게 창가 좌석인지 통로 좌석인지 알려주시겠어요?

M: Sure. What is your seat number?
물론이죠. 좌석 번호가 뭐가요?

W: It's twelve B. 12B입니다.

M: It looks like that is an aisle seat.
거긴 통로 좌석으로 보이는군요.

W: Oh, can I change it to a window seat?
아, 창가 좌석으로 바꿀 수 있을까요?

M: I'll see what I can do. It might be possible.
제가 뭘 할 수 있는지 알아볼게요. 아마 가능할 겁니다.

해설 여자의 마지막 대사인 'Can I change ~?'에 정답이 있다.

어휘 a few days ago 며칠 전에 aisle seat 통로 좌석 window seat 창가 좌석 possible 가능한

09 ⑤

M: Honey, there's nothing to eat in the refrigerator. We had better do something about that. 여보, 냉장고에 먹을 게 하나도 없어요. 우리 거기에 대해 뭐라도 해야죠.

W: I know. We need to go grocery shopping and buy some fruit, cereal, bread, and yogurt for breakfast.
알아요. 우리는 장을 보러 가서 아침에 먹을 과일, 시리얼, 빵, 그리고 요거트를 사야 해요.

M: I agree. When should we go? I'm actually free to go right now.
동의해요. 우리 언제 갈까요? 저는 사실 지금 시간이 있어요.

W: Not now. I'm in the middle of cleaning. How about in two hours?
지금은 안돼요. 저는 청소 중이거든요. 두 시간 뒤 어때요?

M: I'd love to, but my friend is coming over then.
저도 그러고 싶지만 그땐 제 친구가 올 거예요.

해설 'I'd love to, but ~'뒤에는 거절을 해야 하는 이유가 나온다.

어휘 refrigerator 냉장고 go grocery shopping 식료품을 사러 가다 in the middle of ~의 도중에 come over (집에) 들르다

10 ③

M: Did you enjoy your stay here at the Shining Star Hotel? 이곳 샤이닝 스타 호텔에서의 숙박이 즐거우셨나요?

W: Yeah. I was satisfied with my hotel room, and the room service was great.
네. 제 호텔 객실에 만족했고 룸 서비스도 좋았어요.

M: I'm glad. You stayed for three nights, so your total is one hundred and twenty dollars.
기쁘군요. 당신은 3일동안 머물렀으니 합계는 120달러입니다.

W: There must be something wrong. I only stayed for two nights.
뭔가 잘못된 것 같군요. 저는 이틀밖에 묵지 않았어요.

M: Let me check. [pause] Oh, you're right. I made a mistake. I'm so sorry. 제가 확인하겠습니다. [잠시 후] 아, 당신이 맞아요. 제가 실수를 했어요. 정말 죄송합니다.

W: It's okay. 괜찮아요.

M: You don't have to pay for the third night, which makes your total forty dollars less. 세 번째 날 요금은 지불하지 않아도 되니, 합계가 40달러 적어지네요.

W: Okay, here is my credit card. 네, 제 신용카드 여기 있어요.

해설 남자가 처음에 3박 요금인 120달러를 청구했으나 이것은 실수였고, 2박 요금은 거기에서 40달러가 적어진다고(40 dollars less) 말했다. $120 − $40 = $80

어휘 stay 머무름, 방문; 머무르다 be satisfied with ~에 만족하다 room service 룸 서비스(호텔에서 객실로 음식을 가져다 주는 것) less 더 적은; 더 적게

11 ③

W: Good afternoon, can I help you?
안녕하세요, 무엇을 도와드릴까요?

M: I'm looking for the book *The Yellowtail*. Where can I find it? 저는 '더 옐로우테일'이라는 책을 찾고 있어요. 그것을 어디에서 찾을 수 있죠?

W: Right this way. It's one of our best sellers.
바로 이쪽입니다. 베스트셀러 중 하나죠.

M: Yeah, all my friends are talking about it.
네, 제 친구들 모두 그 책에 대해 말해요.

W: Do you see the fiction section over there? It's on the second shelf.
저쪽에 소설 섹션이 보이시나요? 그것은 두 번째 칸에 있어요.

M: I appreciate your help. 도와주셔서 감사합니다.

W: Of course. I'll be at the counter if you need me.
당연하죠. 제가 필요할 때 저는 계산대에 있을 거예요.

해설 book, best seller, fiction 등은 서점이나 도서관에서 들을 수 있지만, 계산하는 곳인 counter가 있으므로 도서관이 아닌 서점임을 알 수 있다.

어휘 best seller 베스트셀러(매우 잘 팔리는 물품) fiction 소설 shelf 칸, 선반, 책꽂이 appreciate 고마워하다 counter 계산대, 판매대 furniture store 가구점

12 ④

W: Are you an active person? Are you tired of playing the same sport every day? Then come to Rock & Roll Climbing Center on thirty-fourth Street now! We're open every day from ten A.M. to ten P.M., except for holidays. If you make a membership now, we will give you a twenty-percent discount. To sign up, please visit our website at rocknrollclimbers dot com or call us at nine four one, four nine four one.

당신은 활동적인 사람인가요? 매일 똑같은 운동을 하는 게 지겨우신가요? 그렇다면 34번 가에 있는 로큰롤 클라이밍 센터로 지금 오세요! 저희는 공휴일을 제외한 매일 오전 10시부터 오후 10시까지 열립니다. 지금 회원이 되는 분들에게 저희가 20퍼센트 할인을 제공합니다. 가입하려면 저희의 웹사이트인 rocknrollclimbers.com 에 방문하거나 941-4941로 전화주세요.

어휘 active 활동적인   tired of ~에 싫증난   except for ~을 제외하고   membership 회원   sign up 가입하다, 등록하다

13 ③

M: Ms. Green, can you help me choose a spot for my band at the school music festival? Here's the map.
그린 선생님, 학교 음악 축제에서 저희 밴드의 위치를 고르는 걸 도와주시겠어요? 지도 여기 있어요.

W: Okay, let me see. How about section E? It's one of the available sections.
알겠어, 내가 볼게. E구역 어때? 그게 가능한 구역 중 하나구나.

M: No, that section is too close to the exit. I want my band to be near the audience.
아니요, 그 구역은 출구와 너무 가까워요. 저희 밴드가 관중과 가까우면 좋겠어요.

W: Well, sections A and B are already taken. Is section D close enough?
음, A와 B구역은 이미 배정되었구나. D구역은 충분히 가깝니?

M: I'd like it if my band wasn't right next to the orchestra.
저희 밴드가 오케스트라 바로 옆만 아니라면 좋겠는데요.

W: All right. Then we have only one section left to choose from.
알겠어. 그렇다면 우리가 선택할 구역이 하나만 남았구나.

M: That seems like the best option. Thank you.
그게 최선의 선택인 것 같아요. 감사합니다.

해설 그림에서 언급되는 장소를 제외시켜 나가면 한 군데가 남는다.

어휘 spot 장소, 위치   available 이용할 수 있는   audience 관중   best option 최선의 선택

14 ④

M: This is a type of transportation that people use every day. It runs on four wheels. You can drive this by stepping on two pedals. One of the pedals is used to speed up. And the other one is used to slow down or stop. You need a license to drive this. And if you drive above the speed limit, you have to pay a fine.

이것은 사람들이 매일 이용하는 교통수단의 한 종류입니다. 이것은 네 바퀴로 달립니다. 당신은 두 개의 페달을 밟아서 이것을 운전할 수 있습니다. 페달 하나는 가속하기 위해 사용됩니다. 다른 하나는 감속하거나 멈추기 위해 사용됩니다. 이것을 운전하기 위해 당신은 면허가 필요합니다. 그리고 만약 당신이 제한 속도를 넘어 운전하면, 벌금을 내야 합니다.

어휘 transportation 교통수단   wheel 바퀴   step on 밟다   speed up 속도를 올리다   slow down 속도를 늦추다   license 면허, 허가   above ~을 넘는, ~보다 위에   speed limit 제한 속도   pay a fine 벌금을 내다

15 ①

W: Brian, are you still sleeping?
브라이언, 너 아직도 자고 있니?

M: Oh, Lily. I just woke up. What time is it?
오, 릴리. 난 방금 깼어. 몇 시야?

W: It's already one thirty P.M! 벌써 오후 1시 30분이야!

M: What? You've got to be kidding me. Why didn't you wake me up? 뭐라고? 네가 농담하는 거겠지. 왜 나를 깨우지 않았어?

W: What's the problem? 무슨 문제야?

M: I had a dentist appointment scheduled for one P.M. I'm already thirty minutes late! 나는 오후 1시에 치과 진료를 예약했단 말이야. 나 벌써 30분 늦었어!

W: Really? Then you'd better leave now.
정말이야? 그렇다면 넌 당장 출발하는 게 좋겠다.

M: Okay. I'll call you later. I'm definitely setting an alarm from now on. 알았어. 내가 나중에 전화할게. 나는 이제부터 반드시 알람을 맞출 거야.

해설 여자의 마지막 대사 'Then you'd better ~'에 제안이 나오고, 남자는 Okay라고 했으므로 당장 할 일은 치과에 서둘러 가는 것이다.

어휘 wake up 깨다, 일어나다(wake-woke-woken)   dentist appointment 치과 예약   schedule for ~을 위해 스케줄을 잡다   definitely 분명히, 확실히   set an alarm 자명종 시계를 맞추다   from now on 이제부터

16 ③

W: Dad, we've been waiting for our flight for over three hours. What is going on? 아빠, 우리는 3시간이 넘도록 비행기를 기다리고 있어요. 일이 어떻게 되고 있는 거죠?

M: They just made an announcement that it will be delayed for two days because of the snowstorm.
그들이 방금 발표하기를 눈보라 때문에 비행이 이틀간 지연될 거라는구나.

W: That's going to affect our schedule. Then when are we getting to New York? 그건 저희 계획에 영향을 줄 거예요. 그러면 저희가 뉴욕에 언제 도착하죠?

19

M: Well, we <u>were</u> <u>supposed</u> <u>to</u> land on December <u>nineteenth</u>, but now I guess we'll arrive <u>two</u> <u>days</u> <u>later</u>. 음, 우리는 12월 19일에 도착하기로 돼 있었는데, 이제 이틀 후에 도착할 것 같구나.

W: Then we should call Uncle Tom to tell him about the changes. 그렇다면 톰 삼촌에게 전화해서 변경사항에 대해 말해줘야 해요.

M: Yeah, we also have to book a <u>place</u> <u>to</u> <u>stay</u>. 그래, 우리는 머물 장소 또한 예약해야 해.

W: Don't worry about that. I'll <u>take</u> <u>care</u> <u>of</u> it. 그건 걱정하지 마세요. 제가 해결할게요.

해설 원래 예정일인 19일보다 이틀 뒤인 21일에 도착할 것이다.

어휘 make an announcement 발표하다   delay 지연시키다, 미루다   snowstorm 눈보라   affect 영향을 주다   be supposed to ~하기로 되어 있다   land 도착하다, 착륙하다   book 예약하다; 책

17 ④

W: Ms. Stewart is the principal at Merry Road Middle School. She needs to <u>hire</u> a <u>new</u> math <u>teacher</u>. One day, Brittany comes to <u>apply</u> <u>for</u> the position. Ms. Stewart wants to <u>make</u> <u>sure</u> that Brittany is <u>right</u> <u>for</u> the job. She wants to know Brittany's <u>past</u> teaching <u>experience</u>. What would Ms. Stewart most likely say to Brittany?

스튜어트는 메리로드 중학교의 교장이다. 그녀는 새로운 수학 교사를 고용해야 한다. 어느 날, 브리트니가 그 자리에 지원하러 온다. 스튜어트는 브리트니가 그 업무에 적합한지 확인하고 싶어 한다. 그녀는 브리트니의 과거 강의 경험에 대해 알고 싶다. 스튜어트는 브리트니에게 뭐라고 말할까?

Ms. Stewart: Have you taught math before?
전에 수학을 가르친 적이 있나요?

① Do you live around here?
이 근처에 살고 있나요?

② Can you work on weekends?
주말에 근무할 수 있나요?

③ Is math your favorite subject?
수학이 당신이 좋아하는 과목인가요?

④ Have you taught math before?
전에 수학을 가르친 적이 있나요?

⑤ I need to hire a new English teacher.
저는 새로운 영어교사를 고용해야 해요.

해설 past teaching experience를 묻기에 가장 적절한 말은 'Have you taught ~?'이다.

어휘 principal 교장; 주요한   hire 고용하다   apply for ~에 지원하다   past 지난간, 과거의   experience 경험

18 ⑤

M: Honey, are you <u>ready</u> <u>yet</u>? We're going to be <u>late</u> <u>for</u> the graduation.
여보, 아직 준비가 안됐어요? 우리는 졸업식에 늦겠어요.

W: <u>Just</u> a <u>second</u>! I can't find my cellphone. You know I can't leave the house without it.
잠깐만요! 내 휴대폰을 찾을 수가 없군요. 내가 그거 없이는 집을 나설 수 없다는 거 당신도 알잖아요.

M: Cellphone? I <u>saw</u> you <u>put</u> <u>it</u> <u>in</u> your purse.
휴대폰이요? 나는 당신이 그걸 핸드백에 넣는 걸 봤어요.

W: Oh, right! Let's go. Wait! I need to <u>bring</u> my <u>umbrella</u>.
아, 맞네요! 갑시다. 잠깐만요! 내 우산을 가져와야겠어요.

M: Why do you need your umbrella? It's sunny outside. 당신은 우산이 왜 필요해요? 바깥은 화창해요.

W: The weather forecast said that it will <u>rain</u> <u>later</u> <u>today</u>. 일기예보에서 오늘 늦게 비가 올 거라고 했어요.

M: Are you sure about that? Let me <u>check</u> <u>it</u> <u>right</u> <u>now</u>. 그거 확실해요? 내가 지금 당장 확인할게요.

해설 여자가 일기예보를 말하자 남자는 자신이 직접 확인하겠다고 했다.

어휘 graduation 졸업식, 졸업   sure about ~에 대해 확신하는

19 ⑤

W: Henry, did you hear that Stacey <u>broke</u> <u>up</u> <u>with</u> Shawn? 헨리, 스테이시가 숀과 헤어졌다는 거 들었니?

M: No, I haven't. But I don't think we should talk about it. 아니, 못 들었어. 그런데 우리가 그거에 대해 얘기해선 안 될 것 같아.

W: Why not? It's the <u>most</u> talked about <u>topic</u> at school <u>these</u> <u>days</u>.
왜 안돼? 그게 요즘 학교에서 가장 많이 거론되는 이야깃거리잖아.

M: Because it's not nice to <u>gossip</u> <u>about</u> other people. Plus, you never know who <u>might</u> <u>be</u> <u>listening</u>.
다른 사람들에 대해 수군거리는 건 나쁘기 때문이야. 게다가, 누가 듣고 있을지도 모르잖아.

W: Relax. There's <u>nobody</u> <u>here</u> except for me and you.
진정해. 여기엔 너와 나를 제외하곤 아무도 없어.

M: Still, I was taught to be careful of what I say anytime and anywhere. 그래도, 나는 언제 어디서나 말을 조심하라고 배웠어.

W: Okay, fine. I'll be <u>careful</u> <u>not</u> <u>to</u> <u>talk</u> about it.
그래, 좋아. 거기에 대해 말하지 않도록 조심할게.

해설 남자는 남의 험담을 하는 것은 나쁜 일이며, 누가 듣고 있을 수 있기 때문에 조심해야 한다고 말했다. '낮말은 새가 듣고 밤말은 쥐가 듣는다'는 아무도 안 듣는 데서라도 말조심해야 한다는 의미이다.

어휘 break up with ~와 헤어지다   gossip 험담을 하다; 소문, 험담   except for ~을 제외하고는   still 그런데도   anytime and anywhere 언제 어디서나

20 ③

M: Nancy, are you <u>ready</u> <u>to</u> go to your <u>first</u> ballet <u>lesson</u>? 낸시, 너의 첫 번째 발레수업에 갈 준비 됐니?

W: Yes, I am. I finished packing everything I need.
네. 저는 필요한 것을 모두 챙겼어요.

M: You look so excited. What are you looking forward to the most?
너 아주 신나 보이는구나. 무엇이 가장 기대되니?

W: Hmm… I want to learn how to turn and stand on my toes. That will probably be the most fun part of class. 음, 저는 몸을 돌리고 발끝으로 서는 방법을 배우고 싶어요. 그게 아마 수업에서 가장 재미있는 부분일 거예요.

M: Okay, but take it easy! Make sure you don't hurt yourself. 그래, 하지만 살살 해! 다치지 않도록 꼭 명심하고.

W: Dad, you worry too much. I'll be fine.
아빠, 너무 걱정이 많으시네요. 전 괜찮을 거예요.

M: Parents can never worry too much for their children. 부모가 자식 걱정하는 데는 끝이 없단다.

① I had a terrible time. Let's go home right now.
난 끔찍한 시간을 보냈어. 지금 당장 집에 가자.

② How many scoops of ice cream would you like?
아이스크림을 몇 숟가락 원하시나요?

③ Parents can never worry too much for their children.
부모가 자식 걱정하는 데는 끝이 없단다.

④ There's a new ballet studio that's opening down the street. 길 아래에 새로 여는 발레교습소가 있어.

⑤ The ballet studio isn't far from here. We can probably walk there. 그 발레교습소는 여기에서 멀지 않아요. 우린 아마 거기까지 걸어갈 수 있을 거예요.

해설 여자가 마지막에 너무 걱정하지 말라고 했으므로 남자는 걱정과 관련된 답변을 할 것이다.

어휘 look forward to ~을 기대하다 stand on toes 발끝으로 서다 take it easy 쉬엄쉬엄 하다, 진정하다 make sure 반드시 ~하도록 하다 hurt oneself 다치다 scoop (음식을 덜 때 쓰는 국자처럼 생긴) 숟갈, 스쿠프

O5회 실전모의고사 본문 p.54-55

01 ④	02 ②	03 ⑤	04 ④	05 ①
06 ②	07 ④	08 ①	09 ⑤	10 ②
11 ②	12 ①	13 ③	14 ①	15 ④
16 ⑤	17 ③	18 ①	19 ②	20 ④

01 ④

W: Can we take a break? My legs are tired.
우리 잠깐 쉴까? 다리가 너무 피곤하네.

M: Okay, let's stretch. Lay on your back and bend your left leg towards your chest. 응, 스트레칭 하자. 너의 등을 대고 누워. 그리고 너의 왼쪽 다리를 가슴 쪽으로 굽혀봐.

W: Okay. Now what? 응. 이제 뭐하면 돼?

M: Grab your left knee with both hands and pull it towards you. 너의 왼쪽 무릎을 양손으로 잡고 네 쪽으로 무릎을 당겨봐

W: Oh, this feels so good! 오, 이거 시원하네!

M: Hold it for five seconds and do it on the right side too. 5초간 잡고 있어봐. 그리고 오른쪽도 그렇게 해봐.

어휘 lay 눕다 bend 굽히다, 구부리다 towards ~쪽으로, 향하여 chest 가슴 grab 잡다 knee 무릎

02 ②

[Telephone rings.] [전화벨이 울린다.]

M: Hey, Jean. This is Steven. Are you busy?
이봐, 진. 나 스티븐인데. 너 바쁘니?

W: Hi, not really. I'm just on my way to the school library. Did you need something? 안녕, 아니 별로. 난 학교 도서관에 가는 길이야. 뭐 필요한 게 있었니?

M: Yes, actually. Could you do me a favor? I need to go the library, but I don't think I'll be able to today. 응, 사실. 내 부탁을 들어 줄 수 있니? 난 도서관에 가야 하는데, 오늘은 갈 수 없을 것 같아.

W: Sure. What exactly do you need?
물론. 너 정확히 어떤 것이 필요하니?

M: Well, I was planning on making dinner for my parents. Can you check out a cookbook for me? 음, 난 부모님을 위해 저녁 식사를 준비할 계획이었거든. 날 위해 요리책 좀 대출해 줄래?

W: I can do that. What type of food are you going to make? 그럴게. 너 어떤 종류의 음식을 만들려고 하는데?

M: I was thinking lasagna and salad, so an Italian cuisine book would be perfect. 난 라자냐와 샐러드를 생각하고 있어서 이탈리아 요리 책이면 좋을 것 같아.

해설 남자의 대사 'Can you ~'에 전화한 목적이 나온다.

어휘 exactly 정확히 check out a book 책을 대출하다 cuisine 요리, 요리법

03 ⑤

① W: How much are the shoes in the display window?
진열장에 있는 신발은 얼마예요?

M: They are on sale for forty-five dollars.
그것들은 할인해서 45달러입니다.

② W: Do you have these shoes in a different color?
다른 색깔로 이 신발이 있나요?

M: No, ma'am. 없습니다, 손님.

③ W: These shoes are too big. Could you show me another size? 이 신발이 너무 크네요. 다른 사이즈를 보여주시겠어요?

M: Sure. Let me get them for you.
물론이죠. 제가 손님 사이즈로 가져올게요.

④ W: I lost my shoes. What should I do?
나 신발 잃어버렸어. 어떻게 하지?

M: I'll help you look for them. 내가 널 도와서 찾아볼게.

⑤ W: How long will it take to get my shoes fixed?
제 신발을 수선하는 데 얼마나 걸려요?

M: It'll take about two hours. 2시간 정도 걸릴 거예요.

어휘 display window 진열창 on sale 할인 중인, 판매 중인

04 ④

[Cellphone rings.] [휴대폰이 울린다.]

W: Hey, Marvin! What's up? 이봐, 마빈! 뭐해?

M: Hello, Mary. I'm at home making a kite.
안녕, 메리. 난 집에서 연을 만들고 있어.

W: That sounds like so much fun! Are you going to fly
it anytime soon? 무척 재미있겠다! 너 조만간 그걸 날릴 거야?

M: Yeah, I'm probably going on Tuesday or Friday. Do
you want to go with me? 응, 난 아마도 화요일이나 금요일
에 갈 거야. 나랑 같이 가길 원하니?

W: Oh, man! I can't go on Tuesday because I have to
work at my part-time job.
이런, 난 아르바이트를 해야 해서 화요일에는 갈 수가 없어.

M: That's fine. We can go on Friday, then.
괜찮아. 그럼 금요일에 가면 되지.

W: Great! Let's hope there'll be a good breeze to fly
the kite that day.
좋아! 우리 그날 연날리기에 딱 좋은 산들바람이 있길 바라보자.

어휘 anytime soon 곧 probably 아마도 part-time job
아르바이트 breeze 산들바람

05 ①

W: Dad, look at all the dinosaurs! There are so many
different kinds! 아빠, 공룡들을 보세요! 종류가 정말 많네요!

M: I'm glad you're having a good time. Feel free to
explore, but tell me where you're going first.
네가 재미있는 시간을 보내고 있어서 기분이 좋구나. 자유롭게 구경
하거라, 그런데 먼저 어디로 갈 건지는 이야기해 주고.

W: Alright. Let's go over there to see the flying
dinosaurs.
알겠어요. 우리 날아다니는 공룡을 보러 저기에 가봐요.

M: Okay. If you press this button you can hear the
sounds they make.
좋아. 네가 이 버튼을 누르면 공룡들이 내는 소리를 들을 수 있단다.

W: This is amazing! I only saw dinosaurs in books, but
seeing them in this exhibit is ten times better! Can
we come again?
이거 굉장한데요! 전 책에서만 공룡을 봤는데, 이렇게 전시되어 있
는 공룡들을 보니 10배 더 좋네요! 우리 다시 올 수 있죠?

M: Of course, we can come back whenever you want.
물론이란다, 네가 원하면 언제든 다시 오자꾸나.

W: You're the best, Dad. 아빠, 아빠가 최고예요.

어휘 dinosaur 공룡 feel free to 마음대로 ~하다 explore
탐험하다 press 누르다 ten times 10배 whenever ~할 때는
언제든지

06 ②

M: Janice, why didn't you hand in your application?
재니스, 넌 왜 지원서를 제출하지 않았니?

W: What do you mean? I emailed it to you last
Monday.
무슨 말이죠? 저 지난주 월요일에 그걸 이메일로 보냈어요.

M: I didn't receive an email from you. Which address
did you send it to?
난 너한테 온 이메일을 받지 못했는데. 어떤 메일 주소로 보냈니?

W: Let me see, g-a-r-y-nine-one-two at cedubook dot
com. 한번 볼게요. gary912@cedubook.com이요.

M: Oh, I see what the problem is. I'm afraid you got
my email address wrong. It is h-a-r-y-nine-one-five
at cedubook dot com.
아, 무슨 문제인지 알겠어. 미안하지만 네가 내 이메일 주소를 잘못
알고 있었구나. 그건 hary915@cedubook.com이거든.

W: That's terrible! How could I have done such a
thing? Can I send it to you today?
세상에 그럴 수가! 제가 어떻게 그런 짓을 했을까요? 제가 오늘 그
걸 보내도 될까요?

M: No, I'm sorry. The deadline was yesterday, and I
can't make an exception for you. 미안하지만 안 된단다.
마감일은 어제였고, 너한테만 예외를 둘 수가 없거든.

해설 지원서를 잘못된 이메일 주소로 보냈고, 마감일이 지나서 다시
제출할 수 없는 상황에서 여자는 좌절감을 느낄 것이다.

어휘 hand in 제출하다 application 지원서 receive 받다
get something wrong ~을 오해하다, 잘못 알다 deadline
마감일 make an exception 예외를 허락하다 grateful
감사하는 frustrated 좌절한 satisfied 만족한 scared 겁먹은

07 ④

① M: I was disappointed with the photo exhibit.
난 그 사진 전시회에 실망했어.

W: You're right. I felt the same way.
네 말이 맞아. 나도 같은 생각이야.

② M: How far away is the bank from here?
은행은 여기에서 얼마나 멀어요?

W: It's a five-minute car ride. 차를 타면 5분 거리예요.

③ M: How would you like to pay? 어떻게 계산하시겠어요?

W: By cash. 현금으로요.

④ M: I bought some tomatoes to put in my salad.
난 샐러드에 넣으려고 토마토를 좀 샀어.

W: Did you enjoy your potato salad?
넌 감자 샐러드를 맛있게 먹었니?

⑤ M: Have you been outside today?
오늘 밖에 나간 적 있니?

W: Absolutely not. It's too hot.
절대 아니죠. 너무 덥거든요.

어휘 disappointed with ~에 실망한 photo exhibit 사진
전시회 feel the same way 같은 기분을 느끼다

08 ①

M: Jess, have you seen the play *The Girl in Red*?
제스, 연극 '빨간 옷을 입은 소녀'를 본 적 있니?

W: No, I want to watch it, though. 아니, 보고 싶긴 했는데.

M: Are you free to go see it this weekend?
이번 주말에 그걸 보러 갈 시간이 되니?

W: That'd be great, but I wonder if there are tickets left, since it's the most popular play right now.
좋은데, 난 그게 요즘 가장 인기 있는 연극이라서 티켓이 남아 있을지 궁금하네.

M: I can check the website right now. [pause] Hmm… There aren't any seats left near the front, so we'll have to sit in the back. Is that okay?
지금 바로 웹사이트를 확인해 볼 수 있어. [잠시 후] 음, 앞쪽에는 빈 좌석이 없으니깐 우리는 뒤에 앉아야 할거야. 괜찮니?

W: Yeah, I don't mind at all where we sit. Can you buy the tickets? I'll serve you dinner after the play.
응, 난 우리가 어디에 앉든지 상관 없어. 네가 티켓 살래? 내가 공연 후에 저녁 살게.

M: Of course. I'll see you soon! 물론. 조만간 보자!

해설 여자의 마지막 대사 'Can you ~?'에 부탁하는 내용이 나온다.

어휘 left 남은   serve 대접하다

09 ⑤

M: Irene, I have a wedding anniversary present for you. 아이린, 내가 당신에게 줄 결혼 기념일 선물을 준비했어요.

W: That's so sweet of you! What is it?
당신 정말 사랑스럽네요! 뭐예요?

M: It's a surprise! Close your eyes and follow me into the kitchen. 깜짝 선물이에요! 눈을 감고 부엌으로 나를 따라와요.

W: When can I open my eyes? I'm so curious to see what you bought for me. 내가 언제 눈을 뜰 수 있죠?
난 당신이 날 위해 무엇을 샀는지 궁금해요.

M: You can open your eyes now. 지금 눈을 떠도 돼요.

W: Oh my goodness! It's a new refrigerator! How did you know I needed this? 어머나! 새 냉장고네요! 당신은 내가 이게 필요했단 걸 어떻게 알았죠?

M: Well, our old one kept breaking because it was so old. I thought you might like a new one. 음, 지금 쓰는 냉장고가 너무 오래돼서 계속 고장 났잖아요. 난 당신이 새 냉장고를 좋아할 줄 알았어요.

W: Thank you. You're such a thoughtful person. I couldn't ask for a better gift. 고마워요. 당신은 배려심 있는 사람이에요. 이보다 더 좋은 선물은 없을 거예요.

어휘 wedding anniversary 결혼 기념일   curious 궁금한
refrigerator 냉장고(= fridge)   thoughtful 배려심 있는

10 ②

M: How was dinner, ma'am? 손님, 저녁이 어떠셨나요?

W: It was delicious, thank you. How much do I owe you? 맛있었어요, 감사합니다. 제가 얼마를 내야 하죠?

M: You had the chicken salad, mushroom soup, onion rings, and beef lasagna. So your total is one hundred sixty dollars.
손님은 치킨 샐러드, 버섯 수프, 양파 튀김, 그리고 쇠고기 라자냐를 드셨습니다. 그래서 손님의 합계는 160달러입니다.

W: Oh, I have a fifty percent discount coupon. Can I use this now?
오, 저는 50퍼센트 할인 쿠폰이 있어요. 지금 이걸 써도 되나요?

M: Yes, you can use it on today's meal. With the discount, your total is eighty dollars. Would you like to pay with cash or credit card? 네, 오늘 식사에 그걸 사용할 수 있어요. 할인돼서, 손님의 합계는 80달러입니다. 현금이나 신용카드 중에 어떤 걸로 계산하시겠어요?

W: Cash, please. Here is a one-hundred dollar bill.
현금으로요. 여기 100달러 지폐요.

해설 총 합계인 160달러에서 50퍼센트 할인 쿠폰을 써서 80달러이다.

어휘 owe (물건의) 대금을 빚지고 있다   discount coupon 할인 쿠폰

11 ②

M: Excuse me. Can you give me a wake-up call for six thirty tomorrow morning? I have an important appointment to go to. 실례합니다. 내일 아침 6시 30분에 모닝콜을 해 주시겠어요? 제가 참석해야 할 중요한 약속이 있어요.

W: Absolutely. What is your room number?
물론이죠. 몇 호실이십니까?

M: It's room eleven oh four. 1104호예요.

W: Alright, will that be all? 알겠어요, 그게 전부입니까?

M: Oh, I almost forgot. I would also like room service for breakfast at seven.
오, 잊을 뻔 했네요. 7시에 아침 식사 룸서비스도 해주세요.

W: No problem. I'll have it ready for you.
알겠습니다. 준비해 드리겠습니다.

해설 wake-up call, room number, room service 등이 호텔 직원과 투숙객의 관계라는 것을 알려준다.

어휘 wake-up call 모닝콜   appointment 약속
room service 룸 서비스(호텔에서 객실로 음식을 날라다 주는 것)
have something ready ~을 준비시키다

12 ①

M: Are you looking for something exciting to do over the summer? Our North Valley English Camp first opened in two thousand ten. Our facilities are located in Seattle. We provide dormitories, classrooms, as well as computer labs. The program consists of fun lessons, team work, games, and outdoor activities. You can enjoy the camp for only fifty dollars! To sign up, please call our office at nine three one, two four one, two nine one two.

여름에 할 수 있는 흥미진진한 것을 찾고 계세요? 저희 노스 밸리 영어 캠프는 2010년에 처음 시작했습니다. 저희 시설은 시애틀에 있습니다. 저희는 기숙사, 교실뿐 아니라 컴퓨터실도 제공하고 있습니다. 프로그램은 재미있는 수업, 팀 활동, 게임, 야외 활동으로 구성되었습니다. 50달러에 캠프를 즐길 수 있어요! 등록하시려면 931-241-2912으로 전화주세요.

> 어휘 over the summer 여름 동안 facility 시설 located in ~에 위치한 provide 제공하다 dormitory 기숙사 as well as 게다가 computer labs 컴퓨터실 consist of ~로 구성되다 sign up 등록하다

13 ③

W: Rex, where should we park at the shopping center?
렉스, 우리가 쇼핑센터 어디에 주차해야 할까?

M: Hmm… Sections D and E would be inconvenient since they are too far from the entrances.
음, D랑 E구역은 입구랑 너무 떨어져 있어서 불편할거야.

W: You're right. Then let's park in Section A.
네 말이 맞아. 그럼 A구역에 주차하자.

M: There are no more empty spots left in that section.
그 구역에 빈 공간이 남아 있지 않아.

W: Okay then, what about the section in front of Entrance two? There are more available spots there. 그렇다면 좋아, 2번 입구 앞에 있는 구역은 어때? 거기엔 이용할 수 있는 자리가 더 많네.

M: But all of our favorite stores are closest to Entrance three.
그런데, 우리가 좋아하는 가게가 모두 3번 입구에 가장 가까워.

W: Well then, let's park in front of that entrance.
음 그럼, 그 입구 앞에 주차하자.

> 해설 남자의 마지막 대사에 3번 입구가 두 사람이 좋아하는 가게와 가깝다고 제안했고, 여자도 그 앞에 주차하는 것에 동의했다.

> 어휘 inconvenient 불편한 section 구역 entrance 입구 empty 빈 spot 공간 available 이용할 수 있는, 가능한

14 ①

M: This is a popular team sport using a ball. The ball is white with red stitches. This sport is usually played outdoors. The field is shaped like a diamond. Some players stand on bases one, two, three, and home base. There are players who throw the ball, and players who hit the ball with a bat. Players score by running to home base safely.

이것은 공을 사용하는 인기 있는 단체 경기입니다. 공은 하얗고 빨간색 바늘땀이 있죠. 이 경기는 주로 야외에서 합니다. 경기장은 다이아몬드처럼 생겼어요. 몇몇 선수들은 1루, 2루, 3루 베이스나 홈 베이스에 서 있어요. 공을 던지는 선수들이 있고, 야구방망이로 그 공을 치는 선수들이 있지요. 선수들은 뛰어서 홈 베이스에 아무 문제 없이 도착하면 득점합니다.

> 어휘 stitch 바늘땀 throw 던지다 score 득점하다; 점수 safely 아무 문제 없이, 안전하게

15 ④

M: Laura, what are you doing here?
로라, 여기에서 뭐 하고 있니?

W: I'm posting pictures of my dog's puppies on my blog. 난 내 블로그에 강아지 사진을 올리고 있어.

M: Oh, I didn't know you had a blog. Your dog had puppies? I would love to see the pictures.
아, 네가 블로그를 운영하는지 몰랐네. 네 개가 강아지를 낳았어? 나도 그 사진 보고 싶어.

W: Here, you can see them now. I just finished posting them.
여기, 지금 강아지들을 볼 수 있어. 내가 방금 그걸 다 올렸거든.

M: They are so cute! Is there any way you could give me one? 강아지들이 정말 귀엽다! 내가 한 마리 받을 수 있는 방법이 있니?

W: I'll let you take one as long as you promise to take good care of it. 난 네가 강아지를 잘 보살핀다는 약속을 한다면 한 마리 데려가는 걸 허락할게.

M: I promise! Where do I have to go to see the puppies? 약속할게! 강아지를 보러 어디로 가면 돼?

W: Come by my house later today.
오늘 이따가 우리 집으로 와.

> 해설 여자의 마지막 대사에서 남자의 할 일이 나온다.

> 어휘 post (웹사이트에 정보, 사진 등을) 올리다 as long as ~이기만 하면, ~하는 한은 promise 약속하다 take care of ~을 돌보다 come by (누구를 보러) 잠깐 들르다

16 ⑤

W: Robert, I think I hurt my arm while I was hiking.
로버트, 나 하이킹하다가 팔을 다친 것 같아.

M: Here, give me your arm. I'll take a look at it.
여기, 내게 팔을 줘봐. 내가 팔 좀 살펴볼게.

W: I probably got scratched by a tree branch or scraped it on a rock.
아마도 나뭇가지에 긁히거나 바위에 걸려서 까진 것 같아.

M: Goodness, you're bleeding! Do you have a bandage? 이런, 너 피가 나고 있어! 밴드 가지고 있니?

W: No, I don't have any in my backpack.
아니, 배낭에 아무것도 없어.

M: Hmm… We can buy some after we clean the wound with water. 음, 물에 상처를 씻은 후에 그걸 사도록 하자.

W: Okay. There should be a pharmacy around here.
알겠어. 여기 근처에 약국이 있을 거야.

> 해설 상처에 붙일 밴드가 없는 것을 알면 밴드를 살 것이다.

> 어휘 get scratched 긁히다 branch 나뭇가지 get scraped 까지다 bleeding 피 나는 bandage 밴드, 붕대 wound 상처 pharmacy 약국

17 ③

M: John bought a new lamp to decorate his apartment. He is expecting guests to come over in an hour. However, he's not sure where to put the lamp. So he decides to ask his mom about it. In this situation, what would John most likely say to his mom?

존은 그의 아파트를 장식하려고 새 램프를 샀다. 그는 손님들이 한 시간 후에 방문할 거라 기대하고 있다. 그러나 그는 램프를 어디에 두어야 할지 모른다. 그래서 그는 그걸 엄마께 여쭈어 보려고 결심한다. 이 상황에서 존은 엄마에게 뭐라고 말할 것 같은가?

John: Mom, where should I put the lamp?
엄마, 제가 램프를 어디에 두어야 할까요?

① how much is the lamp? 램프 얼마예요?
② do you like my new lamp? 제 새 램프가 마음에 드세요?
③ where should I put the lamp?
제가 램프를 어디에 두어야 할까요?
④ can you help me make food for the guests?
제가 손님께 드릴 음식 준비하는 걸 도와주실래요?
⑤ could you help me clean the house?
제가 집 청소하는 걸 도와주실래요?

해설 램프를 어디에 두어야 할지에 대해 묻는 ③이 적절하다.

어휘 decorate 장식하다 expect 기대하다 come over 들르다 decide 결정하다

18 ①

W: Honey, I'm busy washing the dishes. Can you vacuum the bedroom?
여보, 나 설거지하느라 바쁜데요. 침실에 청소기 돌려줄래요?

M: I vacuumed the house this morning. Did you forget already? 내가 오늘 아침에 청소기 돌렸어요. 당신 벌써 잊었어요?

W: Oh yeah, I forgot. I've just been so busy lately that I can't think straight.
아 네, 깜박했네요. 요즘 제가 바빠서 제대로 생각할 수가 없어요.

M: I understand. If you need, I can help you with some other housework.
이해해요. 당신이 필요하다면, 난 다른 집안일을 도울 수 있어요.

W: Actually, there is one more thing. I just remembered that I haven't watered the plants for three days.
사실, 한 가지 더 있어요. 제가 3일 동안 식물에 물을 주지 않은 게 방금 기억났어요.

M: I'll do it right away. 지금 바로 그걸 할게요.

해설 'there is one more thing' 뒤에 여자가 식물에 물을 주지 않았다고 간접적으로 부탁할 내용을 말하고 있다.

어휘 vacuum 진공청소기로 청소하다 forget 잊다(forget-forgot-forgotten) think straight 논리적으로 생각하다 water (화초 등에) 물을 주다; 물

19 ②

M: Hey Vicky. I'm going to the electronics store tomorrow. You can come along if you'd like.
이봐 비키, 난 내일 전자제품 매장에 가려고 해. 네가 원한다면 따라와도 돼.

W: Yeah, I'd like that. I have to buy a new TV anyway.
응, 그러고 싶어. 어차피 난 새 TV를 사야 하거든.

M: What kind of TV do you want? I actually have an extra one in my apartment.
어떤 종류의 TV를 원해? 사실 내 아파트에 남는 게 하나 있거든.

W: Oh, really? Well, I'm not looking for anything in particular. 아, 정말? 음, 난 특별히 찾는 것은 없어.

M: Then I'll bring my TV to your house in the morning. If you like it, I'll give you mine for free.
그럼 내가 아침에 너희 집으로 내 TV를 가져 갈게. 네가 맘에 들면, 내가 내 TV를 너에게 무료로 줄 수 있어.

W: For free? That's too generous of you. Let me buy it from you for fifty dollars. 무료로? 너 정말 마음이 넓구나. 내가 그걸 너한테 50달러에 사도록 할게.

M: That's not necessary. I don't use that TV anyway.
그럴 필요 없어. 어차피 난 그 TV를 쓰지도 않아.

① Well, I can go to the store with you.
음, 난 너랑 가게에 갈 수 있어.
② That's not necessary. I don't use that TV anyway.
그럴 필요 없어. 어차피 난 그 TV를 쓰지도 않아.
③ I need to stop by the bank before we go.
난 우리가 가기 전에 은행에 들러야 해.
④ The electronics store is open now.
전자제품 매장은 지금 문 열었어.
⑤ I will call the store and ask when they close.
난 가게에 전화해서 언제 가게를 닫는지 물어 볼 거야.

어휘 electronics store 전자제품 매장 come along 동행하다 anyway 어차피, 그래도 extra 추가의 in particular 특별히 for free 무료로 generous 관대한, 후한 necessary 필요한, 필수적인 stop by 들르다

20 ④

W: Hi, Louie. You look so down, what's wrong?
안녕, 루이. 너 너무 의기소침해 보여. 무슨 일 있니?

M: Hey, Julie. I'm worried about my cat. I left the door open for five minutes and she disappeared.
이봐, 줄리. 난 내 고양이가 걱정돼. 내가 5분 동안 문을 열어뒀는데 고양이가 사라졌어.

W: Oh no! How long has she been gone?
이런! 고양이가 사라진 지 얼마나 됐어?

M: For a few hours now. I should go outside and start looking for her. 지금까지 몇 시간 동안. 내가 밖에 나가서 찾기 시작하는 것이 좋겠어.

W: It's really dark outside. You'll probably have a better chance of finding her in the morning.
밖이 정말 어둡잖아. 넌 아마 아침에 고양이를 찾을 가능성이 더 많을 거야.

M: What if something happens to her before then?
그 전에 고양이에게 어떤 일이 생기면 어쩌지?

W: Nothing's going to happen. She has a collar on with your phone number and address, right?
아무런 일이 생기지 않을 거야. 고양이한테 네 전화번호랑 주소가 적힌 목걸이가 있지, 그렇지?

M: Yeah. I hope someone calls me telling me that they found my cat. 응. 난 누군가 내 고양이를 찾았다고 나에게 전화해서 말해주길 바라.

① Thanks for the ride home.
집까지 태워다 줘서 고맙다.

② No, I built a new house for my cat.
아니요, 고양이를 위해 새 집을 지었어요.

③ Yes, how long has it been since you moved here?
네, 여기에 이사 온 지 얼마나 되셨죠?

④ Yeah. I hope someone calls me telling me that they found my cat. 응. 난 누군가 내 고양이를 찾았다고 나에게 전화해서 말해주길 바라.

⑤ I'll call you the next time I'm in town.
다음에 내가 시내에 있을 때 너에게 전화할게.

해설 고양이에게 목걸이가 걸려 있는지에 관한 질문에 대답부터 한 뒤에 고양이를 찾기 바라는 심정을 덧붙여 말할 수 있다.

어휘 look down 의기소침하다, 내려다보다 leave something open ~을 열어두다 disappear 사라지다 have a better chance of ~할 가능성이 더 많다 What if ~면 어쩌지? collar (개 등의 목에 거는) 목걸이; (윗옷의) 칼라, 깃

06회 실전모의고사 본문 p.66~67

01 ④	02 ①	03 ③	04 ②	05 ②
06 ⑤	07 ①	08 ②	09 ④	10 ②
11 ⑤	12 ③	13 ②	14 ④	15 ②
16 ④	17 ⑤	18 ①	19 ③	20 ④

01 ④

W: What would you like to drink, sir?
무엇을 마시겠습니까, 손님?

M: I normally drink iced coffee in the morning, but I think I'll try something without caffeine today.
저는 보통 아침에는 아이스커피를 마시는데, 오늘은 카페인이 없는 것을 시도할 생각입니다.

W: Okay, then how about some fruit juice? There is a variety of fruit you can choose from.
좋아요, 그렇다면 과일 주스는 어떠세요? 선택할 수 있는 과일이 다양하게 있습니다.

M: Fruit juice? That sounds too sweet for my taste.
과일 주스요? 제 입맛에는 너무 달 것 같네요.

W: Then how is some milk with one of our special muffins? 그러면 저희의 특제 머핀 중 하나를 곁들여 우유를 드시는 건 어떠세요?

M: That sounds delicious. 그거 맛있겠군요.

해설 마지막에 여자가 우유를 제안하자 남자가 동의하는 의미를 비쳤다.

어휘 normally 보통, 일반적으로 caffeine 카페인 a variety of 여러 가지의 choose from ~에서 선택하다 taste 입맛, 맛, 취향

02 ①

[Cellphone rings.] [휴대폰이 울린다.]

M: Hello, may I speak to Megan Redd?
여보세요, 메건 레드와 통화할 수 있을까요?

W: This is she. Who is calling? 전데요. 누구시죠?

M: My name is Robert. I found a folder on the bus. Your name and phone number were on the back of it. 제 이름은 로버트예요. 제가 버스에서 폴더를 발견했어요. 당신의 이름과 전화번호가 뒤쪽에 있더군요.

W: Oh, my! I am so thankful that you called! You are a life saver!
오, 이런! 전화 주셔서 정말 감사합니다. 생명의 은인이시군요!

M: I'm glad I could help. How can I give it back to you? 도움이 되어 저도 기뻐요. 제가 어떻게 이걸 전해드릴까요?

W: Where are you right now? I'll go pick it up.
지금 어디에 계신가요? 제가 가지러 갈게요.

해설 두 사람은 모르는 사이이고, 여자가 잃어버린 물건을 남자가 발견한 상황임을 우선 파악한다. 남자의 대사 'How can I give it back to you?'에서 물건을 돌려주려고 전화했다는 걸 알 수 있다.

어휘 folder 폴더, 서류철 thankful 감사하는 life saver 궁지에서 벗어나게 해 주는 사람, 인명 구조원 give something back ~을 돌려주다 pick up ~을 찾아오다

03 ③

① W: Did you finish your homework? 너 숙제 다 했어?
M: No, I will do it after I clean my room.
아니요, 제 방을 청소한 뒤에 할 거예요.

② W: What are you doing? You look busy.
뭐 하고 있어? 너 바빠 보인다.
M: I'm working on my science project.
저는 과학 프로젝트를 준비하고 있어요.

③ W: What are you doing still in bed? Get ready for school! 아직도 침대에서 뭐 하는 거야? 학교 갈 준비하렴!
M: I'm so tired. I want to sleep all day.
저 너무 피곤해요. 종일 자고 싶어요.

④ W: What are you going to do this weekend?
이번 주말에 뭐 할 거니?
M: I'm going to my friend's house to do my homework.
제 친구 집에 가서 숙제를 할 거예요.

⑤ W: What would you like to eat for breakfast?
아침으로 무엇을 먹고 싶어?

M: Eggs and toast, please.
계란과 토스트 주세요.

04 ②

M: Excuse me, ma'am? You can't <u>have</u> a <u>campfire</u> here. 실례합니다, 부인? 여기에서 캠프파이어를 할 수 없습니다.

W: Really? Why not? 정말요? 왜 안 되죠?

M: We have <u>rules</u> here. Didn't you see the <u>signs hanging</u> in front of that tree? 저희는 이곳의 규칙이 있습니다. 저 나무 앞에 걸린 표지판을 보지 않으셨나요?

W: What signs? I didn't see any <u>on the way</u> here. 무슨 표지판이요? 전 여기 오는 길에 아무것도 못 봤어요.

M: Okay, let's <u>walk over</u> there and <u>check</u> the signs. 그렇군요, 저쪽으로 걸어가서 표지판을 확인합시다.

W: I see, no <u>fishing</u>, no <u>cooking</u>, no <u>smoking</u>, no <u>cars</u>… 알겠네요, 낚시 금지, 요리 금지, 금연, 자동차 금지…

M: Yes, and how about the <u>last</u> sign? 네, 그리고 마지막 표시요?

W: It says "<u>No Campfires</u>." Sorry, I will <u>put</u> the fire <u>out</u> right now. Thanks for telling me.
'캠프파이어 금지'라고 돼있네요. 죄송합니다, 제가 당장 불을 끌게요. 말씀해주셔서 고맙습니다.

M: My pleasure. 뭘요.

해설 캠프파이어를 하면 안 된다고 말하는 남자의 첫 대사부터 정답이 드러난다.

어휘 campfire 캠프파이어, 모닥불 rule 규칙 sign 표지판, 신호, 기호 hang 걸다, 걸리다 on the way ~하는 중에 put the fire out 불을 끄다(= put out the fire)

05 ②

W: Good afternoon, sir. Where are you <u>headed</u> today? 안녕하세요, 손님. 오늘은 어디로 가시나요?

M: I want to <u>go to</u> Middle Town Square, please. 미들타운 스퀘어로 가주세요.

W: Are you talking about the place near Morris Lane? 모리스 레인 근처에 있는 곳을 말씀하시는 건가요?

M: Yeah, that's right. <u>How long</u> will it <u>take</u> to get there? 네, 맞습니다. 거기까지 얼마나 걸릴까요?

W: I think we can get there <u>in thirty minutes</u> or less. 30분이나 그 이하로 도착할 것 같습니다.

M: Oh no, that's going to be problem. I need to get there in fifteen minutes. 오, 안돼요, 그거 문제겠군요. 저는 거기에 15분 안에 도착해야 해요.

W: Are you <u>in a hurry</u> to get to your <u>destination</u>? 목적지까지 서둘러 가시는 겁니까?

M: Yes, my friend is waiting for me there and I'm already <u>one hour late</u>. 네, 그곳에서 제 친구가 절 기다리고 있고, 전 벌써 한 시간이 늦었어요.

W: Okay, I'll take Highway eighty-nine since there is <u>no traffic</u> there.
네, 제가 교통체증이 없는 89번 고속도로를 탈게요.

M: Wonderful. 훌륭합니다.

해설 목적지, 소요 시간, 고속도로 이용 등의 힌트를 종합하여 정답을 찾는다.

어휘 be headed (for) ~로 향하다 less 더 적은; 더 적게 (little-less-least) in a hurry 서둘러, 급히 destination 목적지 highway 고속도로 traffic 교통량, 교통 hotel employee 호텔 직원 immigration officer 출입국 관리관

06 ⑤

M: How were <u>tryouts</u> for the volleyball team today? 오늘 배구팀 선발 시험은 어땠어?

W: Awesome! I have a <u>good feeling</u> about it. 대단했지! 나 좋은 예감이 들어.

M: You seem <u>confident</u>. Tell me about what happened. 너 자신 있는 것 같다. 무슨 일이 있었는지 말해봐.

W: My team <u>won</u> a practice game <u>by</u> seven points. Can you guess who <u>scored</u> the <u>most</u> points? 우리 팀이 연습 경기에서 7점 차이로 이겼어. 누가 가장 많은 점수를 냈는지 맞혀볼래?

M: Let me think. Was it you? 생각 좀 해보고. 너였어?

W: That's right! The volleyball coach told me that I am a great player. 맞아! 배구 감독님이 내게 훌륭한 선수라고 말했어.

M: That's wonderful! I think we'll be <u>hearing</u> some <u>good news</u> soon. 그거 멋진걸! 우리가 곧 좋은 소식을 들을 수 있을 거라 생각해.

해설 대화는 awesome, confident, great, wonderful 등 긍정적인 내용이 주를 이룬다.

어휘 tryout 선발 시험, 예선 confident 자신감 있는 score 득점을 올리다; 점수 nervous 불안해하는 dreadful 두려운

07 ①

① W: Can I <u>call</u> you <u>later</u>? I'm busy right now. 내가 나중에 전화해도 될까? 지금 바쁘거든.

M: All the phone <u>lines</u> were <u>busy</u> so I couldn't <u>get through</u>. 모든 전화가 통화 중이어서 전화연결을 할 수 없었어.

② W: I like this coat. May I <u>borrow</u> it? 이 코트 마음에 든다. 내가 빌려도 돼?

M: Yes, but I need it <u>back before</u> Wednesday. 응, 하지만 난 그걸 수요일 전에 돌려받아야 해.

③ W: You're great! Have you been <u>bowling before</u>? 너 잘한다! 전에도 볼링 친 적 있어?

M: Yeah, I go <u>every weekend</u> with my family. 응, 나는 가족과 주말마다 가.

④ W: What are you going to <u>buy</u>? 너는 뭘 살 거야?

M: <u>Two boxes of</u> cereal and some fruit. 시리얼 두 상자와 과일.

⑤ W: <u>How</u> was the ski resort? 스키 리조트 어땠어?

M: It was <u>amazing</u>! Everyone had a great time. 굉장했어! 모두가 좋은 시간을 보냈어.

어휘 The line is busy. 전화가 통화 중이다. get through (전화 등으로) 연락이 되다

08 ②

W: I think I'm gaining weight. What do you think I should do?
나 살 찌고 있는 것 같아. 내가 뭘 해야 한다고 생각하니?

M: Riding your bicycle around the neighborhood will help. 동네 주변에서 자전거를 타는 게 도움이 될 거야.

W: That's a great idea. Do you have any other tips?
좋은 생각이야. 다른 조언도 있니?

M: You have to change your diet to lose weight.
넌 체중을 줄이려면 식습관을 바꿔야 해.

W: How can I do that? 그건 어떻게 할 수 있어?

M: Eat healthy food and stay away from junk food.
건강에 좋은 음식을 먹고 정크푸드를 멀리 해.

W: Sounds great, but I have never planned my meals. Can you help me do that? 좋은 생각처럼 들리지만 나는 내 식단을 계획해본 적이 없어. 네가 그걸 도와주겠니?

M: Yes, I can do that. 응, 내가 할 수 있어.

해설 여자의 마지막 대사 'Sounds great, but ~' 이후에 부탁하는 이유와 내용이 언급된다.

어휘 gain weight 체중이 늘다 tip 조언, 정보 diet 식습관, 식단 stay away from ~을 멀리하다

09 ④

W: Where are you going, Kirk? 너 어디에 가니, 커크?

M: I'm going to my friend's house. We're supposed to study for final exams.
나는 친구 집에 가. 우리는 기말고사 공부를 하기로 했거든.

W: Do you always study with someone else?
너는 늘 다른 사람과 함께 공부하니?

M: Yeah, most of the time I study with a friend who is taking the same class.
응, 거의 나는 같은 수업을 듣는 친구와 함께 공부해.

W: Isn't it hard for you to concentrate?
너는 집중하기 어렵지 않니?

M: No, not at all. We solve problems together and help each other out.
아니, 전혀 그렇지 않아. 우린 문제를 함께 풀고 서로를 도와줘.

W: Oh, really? I always thought it was best to just study alone.
오, 그래? 나는 항상 혼자 공부하는 게 최고라고 생각했는데.

M: You should try studying with a friend next time. I promise, it's worth it! 다음엔 너도 친구와 함께 공부하도록 해봐. 약속하는데, 그럴만한 가치가 있어!

해설 'You should ~'는 제안할 때 자주 쓰는 표현이다.

어휘 be supposed to ~하기로 되어 있다 most of the time 대부분의 시간에 concentrate 집중하다 solve 풀다, 해결하다 help somebody out ~을 도와주다 each other 서로 promise 약속하다, 단언하다 worth 가치가 있는

10 ②

셔츠	10달러	바지	10달러
스웨터	12달러	모자	8달러
재킷	15달러	선글라스	5달러
블라우스	10달러	신발	15달러

W: Good morning! Are you looking for anything in particular? 안녕하세요! 특별히 찾는 물건이 있나요?

M: Yes, where can I find the sale items?
네, 할인 품목을 어디에서 찾을 수 있죠?

W: Shirts, sweaters, jackets, and blouses on this rack are on sale. 이 선반에 있는 셔츠, 스웨터, 재킷, 그리고 블라우스가 할인 중이에요.

M: Is anything else on sale? 다른 것도 할인 중인가요?

W: Yes, the pants, hats, sunglasses, and shoes are on those shelves.
네, 바지, 모자, 선글라스, 그리고 신발이 저 선반 위에 있어요.

M: Thank you. How much is it for each item?
감사합니다. 각각 얼마죠?

W: You can find a price tag on each item, and the price on the tag is the sale price. 각 물품마다 가격표가 보일 거예요, 그리고 붙어있는 가격이 할인된 가격이에요.

W: Okay, I got it. I will buy two shirts, two blouses, and one pair of sunglasses. 네, 알겠어요. 저는 셔츠 두 장, 블라우스 두 장, 그리고 선글라스 하나를 살게요.

해설 셔츠($10×2)＋블라우스($10×2)＋선글라스($5)＝$45

어휘 in particular 특별히 sale item 할인 품목 rack 선반 price tag 가격표 pair (옷, 신발 등의) 쌍, 켤레

11 ⑤

M: Hello, Carly! Congratulations. 안녕, 칼리! 축하해.

W: Nick! Thank you so much for coming.
닉! 와줘서 정말 고마워.

M: I wouldn't miss it! You make such a beautiful bride. 내가 놓칠 수 없지! 너 아주 아름다운 신부가 되었구나.

W: Thank you for the compliment. Did you come alone? 칭찬 고마워. 너 혼자 왔어?

M: No, I'm here with my fiancée, Jennifer.
아니, 나는 약혼녀 제니퍼와 함께 왔어.

W: Really? That's great! When do you plan on getting married? 정말이야? 잘됐다! 언제 결혼할 계획이야?

M: Actually, I'm getting married next year. I'll be sure to invite you.
사실, 나는 내년에 결혼할 거야. 물론 너를 초대할 거야.

W: Well, congratulations to you too! 그래, 너도 축하해!

해설 축하, 신부 등의 힌트를 통해 장소를 알아낼 수 있다.

어휘 bride 신부 compliment 칭찬, 찬사 fiancée 약혼녀(fiancé 약혼자) get married 결혼하다 daycare center 놀이방 art gallery 미술관 stadium 경기장 wedding hall 예식장

12 ③

W: Welcome to the Trim History Museum. We are pleased to announce our <u>new exhibition</u>, *The Lost Empire*. Come to explore the history of Rome and Egypt! It will be <u>open starting</u> on February thirteenth. We are open <u>ten A.M. to five P.M. every day</u>, even on national holidays. <u>Admission fees</u> are ten dollars for adults, and children under three years old can enjoy the museum for free. The exhibition will only be <u>open until</u> February twenty seventh, so book your tickets now at trimhistory dot org.

트림 역사박물관에 오신 것을 환영합니다. 저희의 새로운 전시회 '잃어버린 제국'을 알리게 되어 기쁩니다. 오셔서 로마와 이집트의 역사를 탐험하세요! 이 전시는 2월 13일에 시작합니다. 저희는 공휴일을 포함한 매일 오전 10시부터 오후 5시까지 개방합니다. 입장료는 성인 10달러이고, 3세 이하의 어린이는 박물관을 무료로 즐길 수 있습니다. 이 전시는 2월 27일까지만 진행되오니 trimhistory.org에서 지금 티켓을 예매하세요.

[어휘] announce 알리다, 발표하다   exhibition 전시회 explore 탐험하다   national holiday 국경일, 공휴일 admission fee 입장료   book 예약하다; 책

13 ②

| 올스타 마라톤 |

①	날짜	3월 12일
②	시간	오후 1시
③	위치	프랭클린 가 다리
④	참가 방법	현장 혹은 온라인
⑤	참가비	무료

M: This is Ohio Marathon. What can I do for you?
오하이오 마라톤입니다. 무엇을 도와드릴까요?

W: I want to know about this year's All-star Marathon.
저는 올해의 올스타 마라톤에 대해 알고 싶어요.

M: Okay, well, it takes place on Sunday, <u>March twelfth</u>, at <u>noon</u>. 네, 자, 그것은 3월 12일 일요일 정오에 개최됩니다.

W: Can you tell me where the <u>starting line</u> is?
출발선이 어디인지 알려주실래요?

M: The race starts <u>under</u> the Franklin Street <u>Bridge</u>.
경주는 프랭클린 거리 다리 밑에서 시작해요.

W: Great. How can I participate?
좋아요. 어떻게 참가할 수 있어요?

M: You can fill out this form <u>here</u> or you can sign up on our <u>website</u>. 여기에서 이 양식을 작성하거나 저희 웹사이트에서 신청할 수 있어요.

W: Is there a registration <u>fee</u> for the race?
경주 등록비용이 있나요?

M: <u>No</u>, ma'am. 아니요.

[해설] 마라톤 날짜와 시간이 한 문장에 언급되므로 집중하여 듣는다. noon은 정오, 즉 낮 12시이다.

[어휘] take place 개최되다   participate 참가하다   fill out 써넣다, 기입하다   sign up 등록하다   registration fee 등록비

14 ④

M: It is <u>monsoon</u> season, so the National Weather Channel is telling you how to <u>keep safe</u> from the <u>rainstorms</u>. Even though it is sunny right now, the <u>rain</u> can <u>fall suddenly</u>. Please make sure you always <u>carry</u> an <u>umbrella</u> with you. Also, wearing rain boots and a raincoat will help you <u>stay dry</u>. If it is raining heavily, please <u>stay indoors</u>. If you are outside when it starts to rain, find <u>shelter</u> or go to a <u>high place</u>.

장마철이어서 '전국날씨채널'은 여러분께 폭풍우로부터 안전하게 지내는 방법을 전해 드리겠습니다. 지금 당장은 화창할지라도 비가 갑자기 내릴 수 있습니다. 항상 우산을 갖고 다니도록 하세요. 또한 레인부츠를 신고 레인코트를 입는 게 여러분이 물에 젖지 않도록 도와줄 겁니다. 폭우가 쏟아지면 실내에 머무르세요. 만약 비가 내리기 시작하는데 밖에 있다면, 대피소를 찾거나 높은 장소로 가세요.

[해설] 장마철에는 우산, 레인부츠, 레인코트 등을 구비하고, 비가 오면 실내에 머무르거나 대피소 혹은 고지대를 찾아가라는 포괄하는 선택지를 찾는다.

[어휘] monsoon 장마   rainstorm 폭풍우   suddenly 갑자기 dry 건조한   indoors 실내에서   shelter 대피소, 보호소

15 ②

M: Do you remember that it's Stacy's birthday party this Saturday?
너 이번 주 토요일 스테이시의 생일파티 기억하고 있어?

W: Yeah, but Lori <u>called</u> earlier <u>saying</u> she won't <u>be able to join</u> us. 응, 그런데 로리가 이전에 전화해서 우리랑 같이 갈 수 없다고 말했어.

M: Is something the matter? 무슨 문제가 있대?

W: She has to <u>stay at home</u> for a few days.
며칠 동안 집에만 있어야 한대.

M: Oh, no! What happened to her?
오, 저런! 로리에게 무슨 일이 생겼지?

W: I think she <u>caught</u> a bad <u>cold</u> from the freezing weather.
매우 추운 날씨 때문에 그 애는 심한 감기에 걸린 것 같아.

M: I'm sorry to hear that. Should we visit her after school?
그 소식을 들어 유감이다. 우리 방과 후에 로리를 방문해야 할까?

W: Lori told me <u>not to come</u> because we could catch the cold <u>from</u> her.
우리가 로리에게 감기를 옮길 수 있다고 로리가 오지 말라고 했어.

M: I see. I think we should <u>at least call</u> her to see how she's doing. 그렇구나. 그 애가 어떻게 지내고 있는지 적어도 우리가 전화해야겠어.

W: Awesome idea! 멋진 생각이야!

어휘 for a few days 며칠 동안 freezing weather 매우 추운 날씨 at least 적어도, 최소한 awesome 멋진, 굉장한

16 ④

M: Hey, the weather is nice these days. 야, 요즘 날씨 좋다.

W: I know. The weather is supposed to be sunny all week. It will be perfect to go to the park.
알아. 한 주 내내 날씨가 화창할 거야. 공원에 가기에 완벽할 거야.

M: Why don't we go running together this week?
우리 이번 주에 달리기 하러 같이 가는 게 어때?

W: That sounds like fun. When is the best day and time for you? 재미있겠다. 언제, 몇 시가 괜찮아?

M: Well, I'll be free on Thursday at six A.M.
음, 나는 목요일 오전 6시에 한가할 거야.

W: I can't go that day because I have a meeting scheduled at the same time.
그때 같은 시간에 회의가 예정되어서 나는 그날은 못 가.

M: So does that mean we can't go running together this week? 그러면 우리가 이번 주에 함께 달리기를 하러 가지 못한다는 의미야?

W: No, I think I'll be able to move my meeting to Wednesday at eight A.M.
아니, 내가 회의를 수요일 오전 8시로 옮길 수 있을 것 같아.

M: Okay. Then, I'll see you soon! 그래. 그럼 조만간 보자!

해설 처음 언급된 약속시간은 주로 번복되는데, 이 대화에서는 처음에 언급된 시점이 결국 정답이다. 약속 시간을 변경하지 않고 여자의 회의 시간을 변경한 것에 주의한다.

어휘 scheduled 예정된 at the same time 동시에

17 ⑤

W: Danny went to the waterpark with his little brother, Derick. They were standing in line for a ride. Derick asked Danny for some sunblock, but it was in the locker room. They had been standing in line for two hours already. It would be a waste to stand in line all over again. So, Danny decided to go alone while Derick waited in line for him. In this situation, what would Danny most likely say to Derick?

대니는 그의 남동생 데릭과 함께 워터파크에 갔다. 그들은 놀이기구를 타려고 줄을 서 있었다. 데릭은 대니에게 선크림을 요구했는데 그것은 탈의실에 있었다. 그들은 벌써 두 시간 넘도록 줄을 서 있었다. 다시 줄을 서는 건 헛된 일일 것이다. 그래서 데릭이 줄을 서 있는 동안 대니가 혼자 가기로 결심했다. 이 상황에서 대니가 데릭에게 뭐라고 말할 것 같은가?

Danny: Derick, I'll go get the sunblock. Just wait in line until I come back. 데릭, 내가 선크림을 가져올게. 내가 돌아올 때까지 넌 줄을 서서 기다려.

① I'm hungry. Let's go to the food court.
나 배고파. 푸드코트에 가자.

② Hey, do you want to go to the waterpark?
야, 워터파크에 가고 싶어?

③ This line is too long. Let's go ride something else.
이 줄은 너무 길어. 다른 것을 타러 가자.

④ Hurry up, Derick! I've been waiting for you for two hours! 서둘러, 데릭! 내가 널 두 시간 동안 기다렸잖아!

⑤ Derick, I'll go get the sunblock. Just wait in line until I come back. 데릭, 내가 선크림을 가져올게. 내가 돌아올 때까지 넌 줄을 서서 기다려.

해설 선크림과 줄서기가 고민이니 그와 관련된 내용을 말할 것이다.

어휘 stand in line 줄을 서다 locker room 탈의실 waste 낭비, 허비; 쓰레기 all over again 또 다시 wait in line 줄을 서서 기다리다

18 ①

M: I can't believe we're actually in France!
우리가 정말 프랑스에 온 게 믿겨지지 않아!

W: I know, I feel like I'm in a dream.
알아, 나는 꿈 속에 있는 기분이야.

M: Is this your first time coming here?
너는 이번이 여기에 처음 온 거야?

W: Yeah, I've been to other countries in Europe, but it's my first time visiting France. How about you?
응, 나는 유럽의 다른 나라에는 가봤지만 프랑스에 온 건 처음이야. 너는?

M: Me too. This is actually my first time in a European country. I've always wanted to tour here.
나도 그래. 사실 이번이 유럽 국가에는 처음 온 거야. 나는 항상 이곳을 여행하고 싶었어.

W: I see. Hey! Isn't that the statue we saw in the tour guide book? It looks really cool. 그렇구나. 얘! 저거 우리가 여행 안내책에서 본 조각상 아니야? 정말 멋지다.

M: Do you want me to take your picture?
내가 사진 찍어 줄까?

W: I would appreciate that. Thank you. I'll take a picture for you too.
그러면 고맙겠어. 고마워. 나도 네 사진을 찍어줄게.

어휘 feel like ~한 느낌이다 statue 조각상 tour guide book 여행 안내서 appreciate 감사하다

19 ③

W: Harry, please sit down. I need to speak with you.
해리, 앉아보렴. 난 너와 이야기를 해야겠구나.

M: Did I do something wrong, Ms. Thompson?
제가 뭘 잘못했나요, 톰슨 선생님?

W: It's about your history report. Did you write it yourself? 네 역사 보고서에 관한 거야. 네가 스스로 쓴 거니?

M: Actually, my parents helped me write it.
사실은 저희 부모님께서 제가 쓰는 걸 도와주셨어요.

W: I thought so. I couldn't believe a middle school student did it alone. 나도 그렇게 생각했어. 중학생이 그걸 혼

자 했다고는 믿을 수 없었거든.

M: I'm sorry, Ms. Thompson. 죄송합니다, 톰슨 선생님.

W: Thank you for telling me the truth. In the future, try to write your reports on your own. 사실을 말해줘서 고맙구나. 다음부터는 네가 스스로 보고서를 쓰도록 노력하렴.

① Habit is second nature. 습관은 제2의 천성이다.

② First come, first served. 먼저 오면 먼저 대접 받는다(선착순).

③ Honesty is the best policy. 정직이 최상의 방책이다.

④ The early bird catches the worm. 일찍 일어나는 새가 벌레를 잡는다.

⑤ Where there is smoke, there is fire. 아니 땐 굴뚝에 연기 나랴.

해설 여자의 마지막 대사 'Thank you for telling me the truth.'가 가장 큰 힌트이다.

어휘 write oneself 스스로 쓰다 on one's own 혼자 힘으로 nature 본성; 자연 honesty 정직, 솔직함 policy 방침, 정책

20 ④

W: Rob, what are you up to? 롭, 뭐 하려는 거야?

M: I'm planting seeds in my new vegetable garden. 나의 새로운 채소밭에 씨앗을 심을 거야.

W: What types of seeds do you have? 어떤 종류의 씨앗을 갖고 있어?

M: Well, right now I have tomato, lettuce, and peppers. I plan on buying some more tomorrow. 음, 지금은 토마토, 상추, 그리고 고추가 있어. 내일 좀 더 살 계획이야.

W: Interesting. How long will it take for them to grow? 흥미롭다. 그것들이 자라는 데 얼마나 걸려?

M: It's my first time gardening, so I'm not sure. It'll probably take a few weeks. 재배하는 건 나도 처음이라 확실하지 않아. 아마도 몇 주 걸릴 거야.

W: Where did you get the seeds? 그 씨앗들을 어디에서 구했어?

M: I bought them from a greenhouse. 어떤 비닐하우스에서 샀어.

① I put them in the freezer. 내가 그걸 냉동실에서 넣었어.

② They are in the kitchen sink. 부엌 싱크대에 있어.

③ What is your favorite vegetable? 네가 좋아하는 채소가 뭐야?

④ I bought them from a greenhouse. 어떤 비닐하우스에서 샀어.

⑤ Have you planted vegetables before? 너는 전에 채소를 심어본 적 있어?

해설 대화의 소재인 씨앗, 채소 재배 등과 관련하여 'Where ~?'라는 의문문에 알맞은 답변을 한 것은 ④이다.

어휘 plant seeds 씨를 뿌리다 vegetable garden 채소밭 lettuce 상추 pepper 고추, 후추 probably 아마도 a few weeks 몇 주 kitchen sink 부엌 싱크대 greenhouse 온실, 비닐하우스

01 ②	02 ⑤	03 ④	04 ②	05 ①
06 ⑤	07 ④	08 ③	09 ②	10 ②
11 ①	12 ②	13 ⑤	14 ⑤	15 ③
16 ③	17 ①	18 ②	19 ③	20 ⑤

01 ②

W: Welcome to Harry's Pizzeria! Today you will be able to make your own personal pizza. 해리스 피제리아에 오신 것을 환영해요! 오늘은 손님만의 맞춤 피자를 만들 수 있습니다.

M: I'm so excited to get started. Where do I begin? 시작하게 되다니 굉장히 신나네요. 어디부터 시작하죠?

W: Well, all you have to do is choose the shape of the pizza you want, and put the toppings on the dough. 음, 손님이 해야 할 것은 손님이 원하는 피자 모양을 선택하고, 반죽 위에 토핑을 올리는 것뿐이에요.

M: I'm having a hard time deciding. Do you have any recommendations? 제가 결정하기가 힘드네요. 추천해 주시겠어요?

W: I think you should make a triangular pizza, or a circular pizza. 제 생각엔 세모 피자나 둥근 피자를 만드는 것이 좋을 것 같아요.

M: Hmm, but those shapes are too common. I want to make one with a unique shape. 음, 그런데 그런 모양들은 너무 흔하잖아요. 저는 좀 특이한 모양의 피자를 만들고 싶거든요.

W: Okay then, we have oval, star, and rectangular pizzas too. 좋아요 그럼, 저희는 타원형, 별 모양, 직사각형 피자도 있어요.

M: I've never seen a pizza shaped like a star before. I think I'll go with that one. 제가 전에는 별처럼 생긴 피자를 본 적이 없네요. 제 생각엔 그걸로 하는 게 좋겠어요.

W: That's a good choice. Now, let's put the ingredients on top and put it in the oven! 좋은 선택이네요. 이제, 재료를 위에 올리고 그걸 오븐에 넣으세요!

어휘 personal 개별적인, 개인의 choose 선택하다 topping (음식 위에 얹는) 토핑, 고명 dough 도우, 밀가루 반죽 have a hard time -ing ~하는 데 어려움을 겪다 recommendation 추천 triangular 삼각형의 circular 원형의, 둥근 common 흔한, 일반적인 unique 특이한 oval 타원형의 rectangular 직사각형의 shaped ~모양의 ingredient 재료

02 ⑤

[Cellphone rings.] [휴대폰이 울린다.]

M: Hey Sherry, this is Dad. Where are you right now? 얘 셰리야, 아빠다. 너 지금 어디에 있니?

W: I'm on my way to meet some friends. Why? 친구들을 만나러 가는 중이에요. 왜요?

저는 친구들을 만나러 가는 길이에요. 왜요?

M: I don't mean to bother you, but can I ask a favor?
널 귀찮게 하려는 건 아니지만, 부탁 좀 해도 되겠니?

W: Of course, what is it? 물론이죠, 뭔데요?

M: I'm supposed to pick up your sister from daycare at six P.M., but I don't think I'll be able to because I have to work until nine P.M.
내가 오후 6시에 어린이집에서 네 여동생을 데려와야 하는데, 내가 9시까지 일해야 해서 갈 수 없을 것 같구나.

W: So, do you need me to go and pick her up?
그래서, 제가 가서 동생을 데려오길 원하시나요?

M: Right. Could you do that for me?
그래. 나 대신 그렇게 해줄 수 있겠니?

W: Yeah, I'll call my friends and say I'm going to be late. 네, 친구들한테 전화해서 좀 늦는다고 말할게요.

해설 여자의 대사인 'do you need me to ~'에서 남자가 전화한 목적이 드러난다.

어휘 mean to ~할 속셈이다 bother 귀찮게 하다 be supposed to ~하기로 되어 있다 pick up somebody ~을 태우러 가다, 데리러 가다 daycare 어린이집, 놀이방

03 ④

① M: Is there anything else you need?
그 밖에 필요한 것이 있나요?

W: Yes, I would like a box of pencils.
네, 연필 한 상자 주세요.

② M: Hey, can I use your eraser?
얘, 내가 네 지우개를 써도 될까?

W: Here you are. Bring yours next time.
여기 있어. 다음엔 네 것을 가져와.

③ M: What was our homework assignment?
우리 숙제가 뭐였지?

W: We have to write a book report.
우린 독후감을 써야 해.

④ M: Excuse me, could I borrow a pencil?
미안하지만, 제가 연필을 빌릴 수 있을까요?

W: Yeah, sure. Just make sure to give it back to me.
네, 물론이죠. 다만 잊지 말고 저한테 그걸 돌려주세요.

⑤ M: Do you know what this word means?
넌 이 단어가 무슨 뜻인지 알아?

W: I'm not sure. Look it up in the dictionary.
모르겠어. 사전에서 찾아봐.

어휘 homework assignment 숙제(= homework, assignment) book report 독후감 make sure 꼭 ~해라 look something up ~을 찾아보다 dictionary 사전

04 ②

W: Which design should we choose for our singing club hats? 우리 노래 동아리 모자로 어떤 디자인을 골라야 할까?

M: I like this one with the microphone on it.

난 마이크가 그려진 이 모자가 마음에 들어.

W: I do too, but I want a more unique design.
나도 마음에 들긴 한데, 더 독특한 디자인을 원해.

M: Then what do you think about this one with the music notes? 그럼 음표들이 그려진 이건 어떻게 생각해?

W: Hmm, it's okay. But I like the design with the guitar better. 음, 괜찮아. 하지만 난 기타가 그려진 디자인이 더 좋아.

M: Then why don't we get the one with the guitar and music notes? 그렇다면, 우린 기타랑 음표가 그려진 모자를 사는 게 어때?

W: Yeah, that sounds great. I hope the other club members will like the design we chose, too.
응, 그거 좋다. 난 다른 동아리 회원들도 우리가 고른 디자인을 좋아하길 바라.

어휘 microphone 마이크 unique 독특한 note 음표 choose 선택하다(choose-chose-chosen)

05 ①

W: Hello, what brings you here? Is your cat not feeling well? 안녕하세요. 무슨 일로 오셨습니까? 손님의 고양이가 건강이 안 좋나요?

M: Yeah, he seems weak. He won't eat anything and keeps making these painful sounds.
네, 고양이가 쇠약해진 것 같아요. 아무것도 먹지 않으려 하고, 계속해서 이런 고통스러운 소리를 내요.

W: Okay, let's take an X-ray and give him medicine right away.
알겠습니다. 엑스레이를 찍고 바로 고양이에게 약을 주도록 하죠.

M: Is my cat going to be okay? 제 고양이가 괜찮겠죠?

W: I'll do everything I can to help him feel better.
고양이가 괜찮아지도록 제가 할 수 있는 것은 다 할게요.

M: Thank you. How long will the tests take?
고맙습니다. 검사는 얼마나 걸릴까요?

W: I think your cat will have to stay here overnight. Please come back tomorrow.
제 생각엔 손님의 고양이는 오늘 밤은 여기에 있어야 할 것 같아요. 내일 다시 오세요.

해설 남자가 아픈 고양이를 데리고 간 곳은 동물 병원이고, 여자는 동물을 치료하는 수의사일 것이다.

어휘 painful 고통스러운 take an X-ray 엑스레이를 찍다 medicine 약 overnight 하룻밤 동안 veterinarian 수의사(= vet, animal doctor) lawyer 변호사 pet shop 애완동물 가게 owner 주인

06 ⑤

W: Hello, may I help you? 안녕하세요. 무엇을 도와드릴까요?

M: My name is Richard Owen and I made a reservation for a room.
제 이름은 리차드 오언이고, 객실 하나를 예약했습니다.

W: Just a minute, please. I will check it for you. [pause] There must be a mistake. You are not in our

database.
잠시만 기다리세요. 제가 확인해 볼게요. [잠시 후] 착오가 있는 것 같군요. 손님은 저희 데이터베이스에 없습니다.

M: That can't be. I'm sure I made a reservation. Could you please check it again? 그럴 리가 없어요. 저는 분명히 예약했습니다. 다시 확인해 주시겠어요?

W: I'm sorry, sir. Are you sure you reserved a room at Paradise Hotel? 죄송합니다, 손님. 파라다이스 호텔에 객실을 예약하신 게 맞으세요?

M: Oh, this isn't Paradise Falls Hotel? 아, 여기가 파라다이스 폴스 호텔 아닌가요?

W: No sir, that hotel is across the street. 아니에요, 손님, 그 호텔은 길 건너편에 있습니다.

M: Oh, dear. I'm so sorry! 아 이런. 정말 죄송합니다!

해설 예약한 호텔과 찾아간 호텔이 다르다면, 당황스러울 것이다.

어휘 make a reservation 예약하다 database 데이터베이스 reserve 예약하다 across the street 길 건너에 indifferent 무관심한 regretful 후회하는 disappointed 실망한 embarrassed 당황스러운

07 ④

① W: How do you like your new job? 너의 새로운 직장은 어때?
  M: It's good. I'm still getting used to it. 좋아. 난 여전히 적응하고 있어.

② W: I hope it doesn't rain today. 오늘 비가 안 오면 좋겠어.
  M: Me too. I didn't bring an umbrella. 나도. 난 우산을 가져오지 않았거든.

③ W: Do you want something to drink? 너 마실 걸 원하니?
  M: Yeah, orange juice please. 응, 오렌지 주스를 부탁해.

④ W: Wow, look at all the sea turtles! 와, 바다거북들을 봐!
  M: I've been fishing with my dad many times. 난 아빠랑 여러 번 낚시를 하러 갔어.

⑤ W: Did you lock the car? 넌 차를 잠갔니?
  M: Oh, I forgot. I'll be right back. 이런, 깜박했어. 금방 갔다 올게

해설 ④의 대답으로는 바다거북들을 본 소감이 와야 자연스럽다.

어휘 get used to ~에 익숙해지다 many times 여러 번

08 ③

[Telephone rings.] [전화벨이 울린다.]
M: Hello? This is Steve. 여보세요? 스티브입니다.
W: Steve! It's me, Lauren. 스티브! 나, 로렌이야.
M: Hey, what's up? 야, 어쩐 일이야?
W: I was wondering if you could come over and fix my printer. 난 네가 여기서 내 프린터를 고쳐 줄 수 있을까 해서.
M: Is it broken again? What's wrong with it? 그게 또 고장 났니? 뭐가 잘못된 거야?
W: I have no idea. I tried printing my report but the paper keeps getting jammed. 나도 모르겠어. 내 보고서를

인쇄하려고 했는데, 종이가 계속 걸리더라고.
M: I see. Did you try calling the customer service center? 알았어. 넌 고객 서비스 센터에 전화해 봤어?
W: Yeah, but the line is busy. My call isn't going through. 응, 그런데 통화 중이야. 내 전화가 연결되지 않아.
M: Okay then. I'll be over in a few minutes. 그럼 알았어. 내가 몇 분 후에 거기로 갈게.

해설 여자의 대사인 'I was wondering if ~'에 부탁하는 내용이 나온다.

어휘 wonder if ~인지 궁금하다 come over 들르다 get jammed 걸리다, 끼다 call 전화; 전화하다 customer service center 고객 서비스 센터 go through (전기 등이) 통하다, ~을 겪다

09 ②

M: Janice, how are you preparing for the triathlon? 재니스, 넌 철인 3종 경기를 어떻게 준비하고 있니?
W: I run, swim, and cycle at the fitness center every day. 난 매일 피트니스 센터에서 달리고, 수영하고, 자전거를 타.
M: Do you think you're ready? 넌 네가 준비되었다고 생각하니?
W: Who knows? I'm doing my best, so hopefully there'll be good results. How about you? 누가 알아? 난 최선을 다하고 있기 때문에, 바라건대 좋은 결과가 있을 거야. 넌 어때?
M: I can't say. I haven't been able to exercise a lot lately. I've been so busy with work. 말할 수 없어. 난 최근에 많이 운동을 못했어. 일 때문에 무척 바빴거든.
W: I understand, but try to set up a daily routine. It'll keep you on track. 이해하지만, 하루 일과를 세우려고 해봐. 그것들이 너를 순조롭게 진행하도록 만들 거야.
M: I'll try that out, thanks! 노력해 볼게, 고마워!
W: Anytime. I'm sure you'll do great. Stay strong! You can do it! 천만에. 난 네가 잘해낼 거라고 믿어. 강해져! 넌 할 수 있어!

어휘 triathlon 철인 3종 경기 Who knows? 아무도 모른다, 누가 알아? hopefully 바라건대 result 결과 set up 세우다 daily routine 일과 keep ~ on track 순조롭게 진행되다

10 ②

W: Good evening. May I help you with something? 안녕하세요. 뭘 도와드릴까요?
M: How much are these puzzles? 이 퍼즐들은 얼마예요?
W: It depends on how many pieces they have. 퍼즐의 조각이 몇 개인지에 따라 달라요.
M: How much are the fifty-piece and one hundred-piece puzzles? 50 조각이랑 100 조각 퍼즐은 얼마인가요?
W: The fifty-piece puzzles are ten dollars each, and the one hundred-piece puzzles are twenty dollars each. 50 조각 퍼즐은 개당 10달러이고, 100 조각 퍼즐은 개당 20달러입니다.
M: Okay, can you give me a discount?

알겠어요, 할인해 주실 수 있나요?

W: I'm afraid not. 죄송하지만 안 됩니다.

M: All right, I will take two fifty-piece puzzles and a one hundred-piece puzzle. 알겠어요, 저는 50 조각 퍼즐 두 개랑 100 조각 퍼즐 하나를 살게요.

해설 50 조각 퍼즐($10×2) + 100조각 퍼즐 ($20×1) = $40

어휘 depend on ~에 달려 있다 piece 조각

11 ①

W: May I see your lift ticket, please?
리프트 티켓을 보여주시겠어요?

M: Here it is. Oh, is this the lift to the beginner's slope? 여기 있어요. 아, 이게 초보자용 슬로프에 가는 리프트죠?

W: No, this lift takes you to the advanced slope.
아닙니다, 이 리프트는 상급 슬로프로 갑니다.

M: Good thing I asked, because I'm a beginner. By the way, what time does the ski lesson start?
물어보기 잘했네요. 제가 초보자라서요. 그나저나 스키 수업은 몇 시에 시작하나요?

W: Normally, lessons start at four P.M. in front of the ski rental shop.
보통, 수업은 스키용품 대여점 앞에서 오후 4시에 시작해요.

M: Thank you! I should head there soon.
감사합니다! 빨리 그곳에 가야겠군요.

해설 lift, slope, ski lesson, ski rental shop을 들었다면 스키 리조트라는 것을 알 수 있다.

어휘 lift (스키장의) 리프트 beginner's slope 초보자용 슬로프 advanced 고급의, 상급의 rental shop 대여점

12 ②

W: Welcome to Fantasy Adventure, the land of imagination! We would like to announce our new special parade, *Witches and Princesses*. The parade will run three times a day, at one P.M., three P.M., and five P.M. every day, including holidays. The parade will start at the West entrance, and end at the South entrance. Each parade will last for about twenty minutes. There is no extra fee to watch the parade. Come and enjoy our new show! Thank you and have a great time!

상상의 나라, 판타지 어드벤처에 오신 걸 환영합니다! 저희는 새로운 특별 퍼레이드인 '마녀들과 공주들'에 대해 안내 말씀을 드리려고 합니다. 퍼레이드는 공휴일을 포함하여 매일 오후 1시, 3시, 5시, 이렇게 하루에 3번 진행될 겁니다. 퍼레이드는 서쪽 입구에서 시작해서 남쪽 입구에서 끝납니다. 각각의 퍼레이드는 약 20분 동안 진행될 겁니다. 퍼레이드를 보는 데 추가 비용은 없습니다. 오셔서 저희의 새로운 공연을 즐기세요! 감사합니다. 즐거운 시간을 보내세요!

어휘 fantasy 공상, 상상 adventure 모험 imagination 상상 announce 알리다, 발표하다 witch 마녀 princess

공주 including ~을 포함하여 entrance 입구 last 지속하다, 계속되다

13 ⑤

시간	8/31	9/1
오후 9시	① 드래곤 워리어	③ 매지션스 퓨리
오후 10시	맨 인 화이트	④ 드래곤 워리어
오후 11시	② 매지션스 퓨리	⑤ 맨 인 화이트

M: Sandra, let's go watch a movie.
산드라, 우리 영화 보러 가자.

W: Good idea. Let me look up the movie times. [pause] There is *Dragon Warrior*, *The Man in White*, and *Magician's Fury*.
좋은 생각이야. 내가 영화 시간을 찾아 볼게. [잠시 후] '드래곤 워리어', '맨 인 화이트', 그리고 '매지션스 퓨리'가 있어.

M: What are the times for *Dragon Warrior*?
'드래곤 워리어'는 몇 시에 있어?

W: Today is August thirty first, so... nine P.M.
오늘이 8월 31일이니까, 오후 9시에 있어.

M: How about *Magician's Fury*? '매지션스 퓨리'는?

W: Eleven P.M. 오후 11시에.

M: What times do they play tomorrow?
그 영화들은 내일 몇 시에 상영해?

W: *Magician's Fury* at nine P.M. and *Dragon Warrior* at ten and eleven P.M. 오후 9시에 '매지션스 퓨리', 그리고 오후 10시와 11시에 '드래곤 워리어'가 있어.

해설 여자의 마지막 대사에 '드래곤 워리어'는 9월 1일 10시와 11에 상영된다고 했으므로 표의 ⑤가 틀린 내용이다.

어휘 look something up ~을 찾아보다 warrior 전사 magician 마술사 fury 분노

14 ⑤

M: This is one of the biggest holidays. This holiday is celebrated in December, and people normally celebrate for two days. People buy trees to decorate with lights, and purchase gifts for their friends and family. Some children take pictures with Santa Claus and sing carols together. Most of the time, family members gather together and enjoy a delicious meal. This holiday is even more beautiful when it snows.

이것은 가장 큰 공휴일 중 하나입니다. 이 공휴일은 12월에 기념되며, 사람들은 보통 이틀 동안 기념합니다. 사람들은 전구로 장식할 나무를 사고, 친구들과 가족들을 위해 선물을 사지요. 어떤 아이들은 산타클로스와 사진을 찍고 함께 캐럴을 부릅니다. 대부분의 시간 동안, 가족들은 함께 모여서 맛있는 식사를 즐깁니다. 이 공휴일은 눈이 오면 더욱 더 아름답지요.

어휘 celebrate 기념하다, 축하하다 normally 보통은 decorate 장식하다 light 전깃불, 빛 purchase 구매하다 carol 크리스마스 캐럴

15 ③

[*Cellphone rings.*] [휴대폰이 울린다.]

W: Honey, are you almost home?
여보, 당신은 집에 거의 도착했어요?

M: Yes, I am. Do you need something?
네, 그래요. 당신 뭐 필요한 게 있어요?

W: Yeah, the light in the bathroom isn't turning on.
네, 화장실에 있는 불이 켜지지 않아요.

M: I think you should check the light bulb.
내 생각에는 당신이 전구를 확인해 봐야 할 것 같은데요.

W: I just did. I think we need to change it.
이미 했죠. 내 생각엔 전구를 갈아야 할 것 같아요.

M: Are there any extra ones in the cabinet?
보관함에 여분의 전구가 있나요?

W: Let me see. [*pause*] No, can you buy some before you come home? 내가 한번 볼게요. [잠시 후] 없어요, 당신이 집에 오기 전에 몇 개 사올 수 있어요?

M: Okay. 알겠어요.

해설 여자의 대사인 'Can you ~?'에 부탁 내용이 나오고 남자는 그것을 할 것이다.

어휘 light bulb 백열 전구　extra 여분의　cabinet 보관함, 캐비닛

16 ③

M: We need to leave the house right now.
우리는 지금 바로 집에서 출발해야 해요.

W: Why are you in such a hurry? There's still an hour left before the concert starts. 당신 왜 그렇게 서둘러요? 콘서트가 시작하기까지 아직 1시간이 남았어요.

M: I want to get there early so we can buy some snacks. 난 거기에 일찍 가서 간식을 좀 사고 싶어요.

W: Don't worry, it's only five P.M.! It only takes thirty minutes to get there. 걱정 마세요, 겨우 오후 다섯 시예요! 거기에 가는 데 30분밖에 걸리지 않아요.

M: But there's heavy traffic at this time. Can we just leave now? 하지만, 이 시간엔 교통체증이 심해요. 그냥 지금 출발할까요?

W: I'm not ready to go yet. If you're so worried, we can take Highway ninety. There's never traffic there. 난 아직 갈 준비가 되지 않았어요. 당신이 그렇게 걱정되면, 우리 90번 고속도로를 탈 수도 있어요. 거긴 절대 교통체증이 없거든요.

M: Fine, then let's leave in ten minutes.
좋아요, 그럼 10분 후에 떠납시다.

해설 현재 오후 5시이고, 콘서트가 시작하기 한 시간 전이라고 한 것으로 보아 콘서트는 6시에 시작할 것이다.

어휘 heavy traffic 교통체증, 극심한 교통량

17 ①

W: Ted and Helen drive to school every day. In class,

Ted learned about the Earth. His teacher explained how cars are bad for the environment. All the students talked about ways to reduce air pollution. Ted decided to talk to Helen about it. Since Helen lives next door to Ted, Ted asks Helen if they should drive to school together. In this situation, what would Ted most likely say to Helen?

테드와 헬렌은 매일 학교에 운전해서 간다. 수업 시간에 테드는 지구에 대해서 배웠다. 그의 선생님은 차들이 환경에 얼마나 나쁜지 설명했다. 모든 학생들은 대기 오염을 줄이는 방법에 대해 이야기했다. 테드는 헬렌에게 그것에 대해 이야기하기로 결심했다. 헬렌이 테드 옆집에 살고 있기 때문에, 테드는 헬렌에게 학교에 같이 운전해서 갈지 묻는다. 이 상황에서 테드는 헬렌에게 뭐라고 말하겠는가?

Ted: I think we should take one car to school and go together.
내 생각에는 우리가 차 한 대로 학교에 같이 가야 할 것 같아.

① I think we should take one car to school and go together.
내 생각에는 우리가 차 한 대로 학교에 같이 가야 할 것 같아.

② I can't drive to school today, my car is in the repair shop. 난 오늘 차를 운전해서 학교에 갈 수 없어. 내 차는 수리점에 있거든.

③ The water is so polluted here. Let's go to another beach. 여기는 물이 너무 오염됐어. 다른 해변으로 가자.

④ When you take out the trash, make sure you recycle. 네가 쓰레기를 버릴 때 반드시 재활용을 하도록 해.

⑤ Shall we walk to class together?
우리 같이 걸어서 학교에 갈래?

어휘 drive to school 차를 운전해서 학교에 가다　bad for ~에 나쁜　environment 환경　reduce 줄이다　air pollution 대기 오염　next door to ~의 옆집에, ~의 이웃에

18 ②

M: I didn't know baking cookies was this hard.
난 쿠키를 굽는 것이 이렇게 어려운 줄 몰랐어.

W: What do you mean? It's easy! 무슨 소리야? 그건 쉬워!

M: Could you walk me through it?
나한테 하는 법을 보여줄래?

W: First, turn on the oven and turn the temperature up. 먼저, 오븐을 켜고 온도를 높여.

M: I just did. 방금 했어.

W: Then, take the cookie mix, water, and eggs and mix them all together.
다음에 쿠키 믹스, 물, 그리고 계란을 꺼내서 모두 함께 섞어.

M: Mix all of those ingredients together? Alright, I'm done. 그 모든 재료를 함께 섞으라고? 알았어, 했어.

W: Next, put the mix onto a cookie sheet.
그 다음으로 섞은 것을 쿠키판 위에 놓도록 해.

M: Okay, is there anything else I need to do?
알았어. 내가 해야 하는 일이 또 있니?

W: Lastly, put it in the oven.

마지막으로 그걸 오븐 안에 넣어.

[해설] 여자의 마지막 지시사항이 남자가 할 일이다.

[어휘] walk somebody through something (어떤 것을 배우거나 익힐 수 있도록) ~에게 ...을 보여 주다 temperature 온도 ingredient 재료

19 ③

W: I'm so upset Leslie is leaving to New York next week.
난 레슬리가 다음 주에 뉴욕으로 떠나게 되어 너무 속상해.

M: I feel the same way you do. 나도 너랑 똑같은 기분이야.

W: Do you think she will keep in touch?
넌 그 애가 계속해서 연락할 거라고 생각하니?

M: I'm not sure. She's going to be busy getting used to a new city. 확실히 모르겠어. 그 애는 새로운 도시에 적응하기 위해 바쁠 거야.

W: You're right. She'll have new friends in no time.
네 말이 맞아. 그 애는 당장 새로운 친구를 갖게 될 거야.

M: Probably. We can't blame her though.
아마도. 하지만 그 애를 비난할 수는 없잖아.

W: Why do you say that? 왜 그런 말을 하는 거니?

M: Because, we're so far away from her. We can't see her often. 왜냐하면 우리는 그 애랑 너무 멀리 떨어져 있잖아. 우리는 그 애를 자주 못 볼 거고.

W: That's sad, but true. 슬프지만 사실이네.

① Like father, like son. 그 아버지에 그 아들.
② The more, the better. 많으면 많을수록 좋다.
③ Out of sight, out of mind.
   눈에서 멀어지면 마음에서도 멀어진다.
④ Honesty is the best policy. 정직이 최선의 방책이다.
⑤ Two heads are better than one. 백지장도 맞들면 낫다.

[해설] 'Out of sight, out of mind.'는 아무리 친한 사이라도 자주 못 보면 사이가 멀어진다는 의미로 자주 쓰이는 속담이다.

[어휘] upset 속상한 keep in touch 연락하고 지내다 get used to ~에 익숙해지다 in no time 당장에, 즉시 blame 비난하다, 탓하다 far away from ~에서 멀리 떨어진

20 ⑤

M: What do you do in your free time?
너는 여가 시간에 뭘 하니?

W: Nothing much. I read or listen to music.
별거 없어. 나는 책을 읽거나 음악을 들어.

M: Would you like to go volunteer with me?
나랑 같이 자원 봉사를 하러 갈래?

W: That sounds interesting. Where?
재미있겠는데. 어디로?

M: At the homeless shelter on Merry Road.
메리 로드에 있는 노숙자 보호시설로.

W: That's wonderful! What do you do there?
굉장한데! 넌 거기에서 뭘 하니?

M: I give out food, water, and blankets.
나는 음식과 물, 그리고 담요를 나눠 줘.

W: I'd love to help out. When do you go?
나도 돕고 싶어. 넌 언제 가니?

M: I volunteer every weekend from 2 P.M. to 4 P.M. 나는 주말마다 오후 2시부터 오후 4시까지 자원 봉사를 해.

① Can you turn on some music? 음악을 틀어 줄래?
② The bus stop is too far from here.
   버스 정류장은 여기서 너무 멀어.
③ Sorry, we are all out of food today.
   미안하지만, 오늘은 음식이 다 떨어졌어.
④ Have you done volunteer work before?
   전에 자원봉사를 해본 적이 있어?
⑤ I volunteer every weekend from 2 P.M. to 4 P.M.
   나는 주말마다 오후 2시부터 오후 4시까지 자원 봉사를 해.

[해설] 여자가 when으로 자원 봉사를 언제 하는지 물었으므로 때로 답해야 한다.

[어휘] free time 여가 시간, 자유 시간 volunteer 자원 봉사를 하다; 자원 봉사자 homeless shelter 노숙자 보호시설 give something out ~을 나눠 주다 blanket 담요 help out 돕다

08회 실전모의고사
본문 p.90-91

01	④	02	②	03	③	04	①	05	⑤
06	②	07	②	08	①	09	④	10	④
11	②	12	②	13	①	14	③	15	④
16	②	17	①	18	①	19	⑤	20	③

01 ④

W: Welcome to Pet's Mart. Which fish are you interested in? '펫츠 마트'에 오신 걸 환영합니다. 어떤 물고기에 관심이 있으신가요?

M: I saw a fish in a book yesterday that I really liked.
제가 어제 책에서 무척 마음에 드는 물고기를 봤어요.

W: Can you tell me about it?
그것에 대해 저에게 설명해 주시겠어요?

M: I remember it had spots on its fins.
지느러미에 점이 있던 게 기억나요.

W: Maybe this flat one is what you're looking for.
아마 이 납작한 물고기가 손님이 찾고 있는 걸 거예요.

M: Not quite. The fish I want was round.
그다지 아니네요. 제가 원하는 물고기는 볼록했어요.

W: Then, how about this one with large eyes?
그렇다면 커다란 눈이 있는 이 물고기는요?

M: Nope, the fish had small eyes. I think it's this one over here. 아니요, 그 물고기는 눈이 작았어요. 이쪽에 있는 이 물고기 같아요.

어휘 spot 점   fin 지느러미   flat 납작한, 평평한

02 ②

[*Telephone rings.*] [전화벨이 울린다.]

W: Hello, this is Lane Housing. 여보세요, 레인 하우징입니다.

M: Hi, my name is Jonathan. I'm calling to ask about how to get a new apartment key.
안녕하세요, 제 이름은 조나단이에요. 아파트의 새 열쇠를 구하는 방법을 물어보려고 전화했어요.

W: Okay, what exactly is the problem?
네, 정확히 무엇이 문제인가요?

M: Well, I lost the key to my apartment and I was hoping you could send someone to help me.
아, 제 아파트 열쇠를 잃어버려서 저를 도와줄 누군가를 보내주시길 바라고 있어요.

W: Alright, what is your apartment number?
알겠어요, 아파트 몇 호인가요?

M: Three one two B. 312B호입니다.

W: Do you have an ID card with you? I need to check your records and match them with your ID card information. 신분증 가지고 계신가요? 고객님의 기록을 확인하고 신분증 정보와 대조해봐야 해서요.

M: Yes, I do. 네, 갖고 있어요.

W: Okay, I'll be there soon. Please show it to me when I get there. 알겠어요, 제가 그곳으로 곧 갈게요. 제가 거기에 가면 신분증을 제게 보여주세요.

해설 남자의 첫 대사 'I'm calling to ask about ~'에 정답이 정확히 드러난다.

어휘 ID card 신분증(= identification card)   record 기록   match with ~와 대조해 보다

03 ③

① W: The neighbors are coming over today.
이웃들이 오늘 놀러 올 거야.

　 M: That's awesome! I can't wait. 멋지다! 정말 기대 돼.

② W: I ordered pizza and breadsticks.
내가 피자와 막대 빵을 주문했어.

　 M: Sounds like a perfect dinner. 완벽한 식사처럼 들리는구나.

③ W: There's someone on the telephone for you.
어떤 사람이 전화로 널 찾고 있어.

　 M: Thanks, I've been waiting for that call.
고마워, 난 그 전화를 기다리고 있었어.

④ W: I'm on my way to the gym. 나는 체육관에 가는 길이야.

　 M: Don't forget to bring your water bottle!
네 물병 가져가는 거 잊지마!

⑤ W: Do you have any discount coupons?
할인 쿠폰 갖고 있어?

　 M: No, I don't. 아니, 없어.

어휘 come over (집에) 들르다   on the telephone 전화로, 통화 중

04 ①

M: I'm looking for something to wear during the winter season. 저는 겨울철에 착용할 것을 찾고 있어요.

W: We have these scarves. They are our newest items.
저흰 이 목도리가 있어요. 그것들은 저희의 최신 상품입니다.

M: I already have a lot of scarves. Is there anything else? 저는 이미 목도리를 많이 갖고 있어요. 다른 것도 있나요?

W: Okay then, would you like to purchase some gloves? 그렇다면 좋아요, 장갑을 구매하시겠어요?

M: Let me take a look. What styles of gloves do you have? 한 번 볼게요. 어떤 스타일의 장갑이 있나요?

W: There are these leather ones, and these polka dot ones. 가죽 장갑과 물방울 무늬 장갑이 있어요.

M: Hmm, neither of them are my type. I don't think I'll be buying gloves today. I like that jacket over there.
음, 어느 것도 제 취향은 아니네요. 오늘은 장갑을 사지 않을 것 같아요. 저기 있는 재킷이 마음에 들어요.

W: Yes, this jacket is very popular nowadays. You can choose between the checked one and the plain one with no pattern on it.
네, 이 재킷은 요즘 아주 인기 있어요. 체크무늬 재킷과 아무런 모양이 없는 무지 재킷 중에서 선택할 수 있어요.

M: I'll take the one with the checked pattern.
체크무늬가 있는 것을 살게요.

해설 'I'll take ~' 혹은 'I'll buy ~'처럼 구매 의사를 밝히는 표현을 확인한다.

어휘 scarf 스카프, 목도리(복 scarves)   purchase 구매하다   leather 가죽   polka dot 물방울 무늬   neither of ~의 어느 쪽도 아닌   checked 체크 무늬의   plain 무늬가 없는, 명료한, 단순한

05 ⑤

M: Please take a seat on this chair. What seems to be the problem? 이 의자에 앉아보세요. 어떤 문제가 있는 거죠?

W: Every time I try to eat something, my teeth hurt.
제가 뭘 먹으려고 할 때마다 이가 아파요.

M: Okay, I'm going to take a look. I need you to open your mouth wide.
그렇군요, 제가 한 번 볼게요. 입을 크게 벌려보세요.

W: Alright, will this be painful? 네, 이거 아플까요?

M: No, not really. I'm just going to look at the inside of your mouth. I promise it will be over before you know it. 아니, 그다지요. 제가 당신의 입 안을 보는 것뿐이에요. 당신이 눈치도 채기 전에 끝날 거라고 약속해요.

W: Well, that's a relief. [*pause*] So, what's wrong with my teeth? 뭐, 그건 안심이네요. [잠시 후] 그래서, 제 치아에 무슨 문제가 있어요?

M: I'm afraid you have some cavities near the back of your mouth.
유감이지만 당신의 입 안쪽 주변에 충치가 좀 있어요.

W: Cavities? That's terrible! How many decayed teeth do I have?

충치요? 끔찍해라! 저에게 썩은 이가 몇 개나 있는 거죠?

M: You have three, and they need to <u>get</u> <u>pulled</u> <u>out</u> as soon as possible.
세 개 있네요, 그리고 충치는 가능한 빨리 뽑아야 해요.

해설 cavities, decayed 등의 단어를 몰라도, teeth와 mouth를 통해 정답을 찾을 수 있다.

어휘 relief 안심, 안도   cavity 충치, 구멍(복 cavities) decayed 썩은   pull out 빼다, 빠져나가다   vet 수의사 (= veterinarian)   lawyer 변호사   mechanic 정비공

06 ②

W: Owen, it's getting late. These woods are <u>getting</u> <u>darker</u> and darker.
오언, 시간이 늦었어. 숲이 점점 어두워지고 있어.

M: I know. I think I just <u>heard</u> something <u>behind</u> those trees.
나도 알아. 나 방금 저 나무 뒤에서 무슨 소리를 들은 것 같아.

W: What? What do you think it is?
뭐라고? 그게 뭐인 것 같아?

M: I have <u>no</u> <u>idea</u>. Maybe a <u>wolf</u>? Or a <u>ghost</u>?
전혀 모르겠어. 아마도 늑대? 아니면 유령?

W: Don't say that! You're <u>scaring</u> me.
그런 말 하지마! 나 무섭단 말이야.

M: Is it just me, or is it getting cold out here?
단지 내 느낌인가, 아니면 여기가 점점 추워지는 건가?

W: I'm getting cold too. Let's <u>get</u> <u>out</u> of here. Do you know <u>which</u> <u>way</u> to go? 나도 추워지는 것 같아. 여기에서 나가자. 어느 쪽으로 가야 하는지 넌 알아?

M: No, it's so dark. I <u>can't</u> <u>see</u> what's in front of me.
아니, 너무 어두워. 내 앞에 뭐가 있는지도 안 보여.

해설 dark, wolf, ghost, scaring, cold 등의 단어들로 인해, 여자의 심정을 포함한 대화 전체에서 두려움이 느껴진다.

어휘 get darker and darker 점점 어두워지다   scare 겁주다 satisfied 만족하는   frightened 겁먹은   relaxed 느긋한 disappointed 실망한   joyful 기뻐하는

07 ②

① W: I wonder if <u>anybody</u> is <u>home</u>.
누가 집에 있을지 궁금하네.

M: I don't think so. The lights are <u>turned</u> <u>off</u>.
있을 거라 생각하지 않아. 불이 꺼져 있잖아.

② W: <u>Make</u> <u>sure</u> you're not late for the recital.
발표회에 늦지 않도록 하렴.

M: I've learned ballet <u>for</u> <u>four</u> <u>years</u>.
저는 발레를 4년 동안 배웠어요.

③ W: What is your home <u>address</u>?
너의 집 주소가 뭐야?

M: I <u>live</u> <u>on</u> ninety-one thirty-eight Wicker Lane.
나는 위커레인 9138번지에 살아.

④ W: What are you doing for <u>Halloween</u>?

너는 핼러윈 때 뭐 할 거야?

M: I'm going to a <u>costume</u> <u>party</u>. 나는 변장 파티에 갈 거야.

⑤ W: Did you <u>pick</u> a lot of <u>apples</u>? 너는 사과를 많이 땄니?

M: Yeah, the trees were <u>full</u> <u>of</u> them!
응, 나무에 사과가 가득했어!

해설 조언 혹은 당부를 나타내는 ②의 질문에 어울리지 않는 대답이 왔다. 발레를 4년 배웠다는 대답은 'How long ~?'으로 시작하는 질문과 어울린다.

어휘 recital 발표회, 연주회   costume 의상, 변장   full of ~로 가득 찬

08 ①

[*Cellphone rings.*] [휴대폰이 울린다.]

M: Hey, Heather. 얘, 헤더.

W: Hi, Daniel, what are you up to?
안녕, 대니얼, 너 뭐 하고 지내?

M: Nothing much. I was just <u>wondering</u> if you could <u>help</u> me. 별거 없어. 난 네가 날 도와줄 수 있는지 궁금했어.

W: Sure, what is it? 물론이지, 뭔데?

M: Well, I'm <u>expecting</u> a package in the mail today, but I won't get home <u>until</u> late. 그게, 오늘 소포가 올 예정인데 내가 늦게까지 집에 가지 못할 것 같아.

W: Okay, so what do you want me to do?
알겠어, 그러니까 내가 무엇을 하길 원하는 거야?

M: Can you <u>keep</u> the <u>package</u> for me until I get there?
내가 집에 가기 전까지 나 대신 소포를 갖고 있을래?

W: That's <u>not</u> a <u>problem</u>. Call me when you get home and I'll <u>bring</u> the package <u>to</u> you. 그거야 문제 없지. 집에 도착하면 전화해, 그럼 내가 소포를 가져가 줄게.

해설 여자의 질문 'What do you want me to do?'에 이어지는 대답에 부탁의 내용이 있다.

어휘 nothing much 별로 없는   wonder 궁금하다; 놀라다 expect 기다리다, 기대하다   package 소포, 짐, 포장물

09 ④

M: I heard there is a new restaurant in town.
시내에 새로운 식당이 생겼다고 들었어.

W: <u>Do</u> <u>you</u> <u>mean</u> the Italian restaurant on Main Street?
메인 가에 있는 이탈리아 식당 말하는 거야?

M: Yes, that's the one. Have you <u>been</u> <u>there</u> <u>before</u>?
응, 바로 거기야. 너 거기에 전에 가본 적 있어?

W: No, but it's already <u>famous</u> <u>for</u> its steak and salad.
아니, 그런데 그곳은 벌써 스테이크와 샐러드로 유명해.

M: I see. I <u>wonder</u> <u>if</u> it's <u>better</u> <u>than</u> Sir Jack's Bistro's steak.
그렇구나. '잭 선생 비스트로'의 스테이크보다 더 좋은지 궁금하네.

W: Yeah, they have delicious steak. But, <u>in</u> <u>my</u> <u>opinion</u>, nothing can beat Sir Jack's Bistro's seafood pasta.
응, 그 집도 맛있는 스테이크가 있어. 그런데 내 의견으로는 어떤 것도 '잭 선생 비스트로'의 해산물 파스타를 능가할 수 없어.

M: Oh, yeah. I feel exactly the same way.
어, 그래. 나도 완전히 공감해.

해설 공감을 표할 때 'feel the same way,' 'couldn't agree with you more' 등이 자주 쓰인다.

어휘 Do you mean ~? ~ 의미하는 거야? ~ 말하는 거야? wonder if ~인지 궁금해 하다 bistro 작은 음식점 in my opinion 내 의견으로는 beat 이기다 exactly 정확히, 꼭

10 ④

M: Excuse me, how much does it cost to go bowling?
실례합니다만, 볼링을 치는 데 얼마가 들죠?

W: It is ten dollars per game.
경기 당 10달러입니다.

M: I see. I would like to play three games.
그렇군요. 저는 세 경기를 하고 싶어요.

W: Very well. Do you need to rent shoes?
아주 좋아요. 신발을 빌리실 건가요?

M: I would like that. My size is nine.
그러는 게 좋겠네요. 제 사이즈는 9예요.

W: That will cost you an extra five dollars.
그건 5달러의 추가 요금이 들어요.

M: That's fine. 좋아요.

해설 3경기는 30달러, 신발을 빌리는 데 5달러이므로 합은 35달러이다.

어휘 per ~마다 rent 빌리다 extra 추가의; 여분의

11 ②

W: Hello, how can I help you?
안녕하세요, 무엇을 도와드릴까요?

M: I would like to dry-clean some clothes.
저는 옷을 드라이클리닝 하고 싶습니다.

W: How many items of clothing need to be done?
몇 벌의 옷이 드라이클리닝 되어야 하죠?

M: Two shirts and a pair of pants.
셔츠 두 장과 바지 하나요.

W: Alright. They'll be done by tomorrow morning.
알겠습니다. 그것들은 내일 아침까지 완료될 거예요.

M: Can I have them delivered to my house?
저희 집까지 배달시킬 수 있나요?

W: Yes, it is possible if you pay an extra fee.
네, 추가 요금을 지불하시면 가능해요.

해설 clean, clothes만 들어도 세탁소에서 이루어지는 대화임을 짐작할 수 있다.

어휘 have something delivered ~을 배달시키다 possible 가능한, 있을 수 있는 extra fee 추가 요금 dry cleaner's 세탁소

12 ②

M: Ladies and gentlemen, boys and girls! We invite you to Trudy's Fruit Farm! We recently opened in twenty fourteen and we have a variety of fruits you can choose from. There are apples, strawberries, peaches, and watermelon. Admission is three dollars for children and five dollars for adults. We are located on forty-five Middletown Street. We are open only on weekends from ten A.M. to six P.M. One more thing! Until September seventh, you can enjoy our farm for free. Call us at nine three one, two one nine two for more questions.

신사 숙녀, 소년 소녀 여러분! 저희가 여러분을 '트루디의 과일농장'으로 초대합니다! 저희는 최근 2014년에 열었고 여러분이 선택할 수 있는 여러 가지 과일을 갖고 있답니다. 사과, 딸기, 복숭아, 그리고 수박이 있지요. 입장료는 어린이 3달러, 성인 5달러입니다. 저희는 미들타운 거리 45번지에 위치해 있습니다. 저희는 주말 오전 10시부터 오후 6시까지만 개장합니다. 한 가지 더! 9월 7일까지는 농장을 무료로 즐길 수 있답니다. 문의사항은 931-2192로 전화 주세요.

어휘 recently 최근에 a variety of 여러 가지의 choose from ~에서 선택하다 admission 입장료, 입장 located ~에 위치한

13 ①

| 최고 밴드 경연대회 |

	밴드 이름	장소
①	크레이지 페퍼스	멀린 스트리트
②	라우드 앤 프라우드	크레이들 로드
③	헝그리 파이터스	크레이들 로드
④	위핑 스크림	요크셔 레인
⑤	울트라 사운드	요크셔 레인

W: I'm so excited for this year's Ultimate Band Contest!
나는 올해의 최고밴드 경연대회 때문에 무척 흥분 돼!

M: Who are you looking forward to seeing the most?
너는 누구를 보는 게 가장 기대 돼?

W: I like Crazy Peppers and Loud and Proud. I'm glad that they will be playing on Cradle Road. I can walk there. 나는 '크레이지 페퍼스'와 '라우드 앤 프라우드'를 좋아해. 그들이 크레이들 로드에서 공연한다니 기뻐. 나는 거기까지 걸어갈 수 있거든.

M: The Hungry Fighters will be performing there too. I personally don't really like their music, though.
'헝그리 파이터스'도 그곳에서 공연할 거야. 난 개인적으로 그들의 음악을 좋아하진 않지만.

W: Yeah, me neither. Which teams are your favorites?
응, 나도 안 좋아해. 어느 팀이 네가 좋아하는 팀이야?

M: Well, I really like Whipping Scream and Ultra Sound.
음, 나는 '위핑 스크림'과 '울트라 사운드'를 아주 좋아해.

W: Oh, I've heard of them before. Where are they playing?
아, 나도 그들을 들어본 적이 있어. 그들은 어디에서 공연하니?

W: They'll be at Yorkshire Lane, which is <u>amazing</u> because I live <u>on</u> the <u>same street</u>. 그들은 요크셔 레인에서 할 건데, 굉장하지, 나는 같은 거리에 살거든.

M: I see. I'm glad we will be able to enjoy this event. 그렇구나. 나는 우리가 이 행사를 즐길 수 있게 되어서 기뻐.

해설 여자가 Crazy Peppers는 Cradle Road에서 공연한다고 말했다.

어휘 ultimate 최고의, 최대의, 궁극의 look forward to ~을 기대하다 personally 개인적으로; 직접

14 ③

M: Almost <u>everyone</u> <u>owns</u> this item and <u>carries</u> it around with them <u>every</u> <u>day</u>. It is an electronic <u>device</u> and people use it for a variety of reasons. People can use it to <u>make</u> phone <u>calls</u> or <u>send</u> <u>text</u> messages to their friends and family. Also, they can <u>take</u> <u>pictures</u> and browse the <u>Internet</u> with this item. People can also <u>download</u> <u>games</u> and <u>play</u> them on this device. What is this item?

거의 모든 사람들이 이 물건을 갖고 있으며 매일 가지고 다닙니다. 이것은 전자장치이고, 사람들은 다양한 이유로 그것을 이용합니다. 사람들은 이것을 이용하여 친구와 가족에게 전화를 하거나 문자메시지를 보냅니다. 게다가, 그들은 이 물건으로 사진을 찍고 인터넷을 검색할 수 있습니다. 사람들은 게임을 다운로드 하여 이 장치로 게임을 할 수 있습니다. 이것은 무엇일까요?

해설 통화, 메시지 전송, 사진 촬영, 인터넷 서핑, 게임 등이 모두 가능한 것은 휴대폰이다.

어휘 electronic 전자의 device 장치, 기구 for a variety of reasons 여러 가지 이유로 browse 둘러보다, 돌아다니다

15 ④

W: Honey, I think you need to go buy a new pair of shoes. 여보, 당신은 새 신발을 사야 할 것 같아요.

M: I only <u>bought</u> them <u>a month ago</u>! 난 신발을 불과 한 달 전에 샀는데요!

W: They look like you've <u>worn</u> them <u>for years</u>. 그 신발은 마치 몇 년 동안 신은 것처럼 보여요.

M: But, I don't want to <u>get rid of</u> them yet. They are the <u>most</u> <u>comfortable</u> pair I own. 하지만, 난 아직 이걸 버리고 싶지 않아요. 내가 가진 가장 편한 신발이거든요.

W: Then <u>take</u> them to the shoe <u>repair</u> shop. 그러면 신발 수선 가게에 맡기세요.

M: Where is the <u>nearest</u> one from here? 여기에서 가장 가까운 게 어디에 있나요?

W: There should be one in Brick Square Mall. 브릭스퀘어몰에 하나 있을 거예요.

M: Okay, I should go there now. 알겠어요, 내가 지금 그리로 가야겠군요.

해설 여자가 신발을 수선 가게에 맡기라고 제안하자 남자는 가까운 수선 가게가 어디인지 묻는 말로 수긍했고, 즉시 행동에 옮기기로 결심했다.

어휘 wear (신발을) 신다(wear-wore-worn) get rid of ~을 없애다, 처리하다 repair 수리; 수리하다 comfortable 편한(comfortable-more comfortable-most comfortable)

16 ②

W: Wesley, I'm going to a <u>conference</u> next week. 웨슬리, 나는 다음 주에 학회에 가.

M: <u>What kind of</u> conference are you talking about? 무슨 종류의 학회를 말하는 거야?

W: It's for <u>future leaders</u> in business. You should go too. 기업의 미래 지도자에 대한 거야. 너도 가야 해.

M: It sounds interesting. When is it? 그거 재미있겠는데. 언제야?

W: They <u>have lectures</u> on July <u>fourteenth</u>, July sixteenth, and July seventeenth. 강의가 7월 14일, 7월 16일, 그리고 7월 17일에 있어.

M: I can't go on the sixteenth and seventeenth. I'm going on a trip. 난 16일과 17일에는 못 가. 여행을 가거든.

W: That's fine. Then let's go the <u>first</u> <u>day</u>. 괜찮아. 그럼 우리 첫 날에 가자.

해설 학회는 14일, 16일, 17일에 열리는데, 첫째 날에 가기로 했으므로 14일이 정답이다.

어휘 conference 학회, 회의 leader 지도자, 대표 lecture 강의, 강연

17 ①

M: Judy and her brother <u>both received</u> ten pieces of candy for helping their mom clean the house. Judy <u>ate all</u> of her candy <u>as soon as</u> she <u>got</u> them. <u>On the other hand</u>, her brother put them in a jar to <u>eat later</u>. Judy went into his room and ate all of his candy. Judy <u>regrets</u> doing this, and she is <u>scared</u> to tell her brother what happened. So, Judy calls her friend, Joseph. After listening to her story, Joseph tells Judy to <u>tell</u> her brother the <u>truth</u>, and then offer to <u>buy</u> him a new <u>bag of</u> <u>candy</u>. In this situation, what would Joseph most likely say to Judy?

주디와 그녀의 오빠는 둘 다 엄마를 도와 집을 청소하고 사탕 10개를 받았다. 주디는 받자마자 그녀의 사탕을 전부 먹었다. 반면에 그녀의 오빠는 나중에 먹으려고 사탕을 병 안에 넣었다. 주디는 오빠 방에 가서 그의 사탕도 전부 먹었다. 주디는 이 일을 후회하고 있으며, 무슨 일이 있었는지 오빠에게 말하기 겁이 나 있다. 그래서 주디는 그녀의 친구 조셉에게 전화를 한다. 주디의 이야기를 들은 뒤 조셉은 사실대로 털어놓고 사탕 한 봉지를 오빠에게 사줄 것을 제안하라고 주디에게 말한다. 이 상황에서 조셉은 주디에게 뭐라고 말할 것 같은가?

Joseph: <u>Tell him you'll buy him some more.</u> 네가 오빠에게 좀 더 사주겠다고 말해.

① Tell him you'll buy him some more. 네가 오빠에게 좀 더 사주겠다고 말해.

② What's your favorite type of candy?
네가 좋아하는 종류의 사탕은 뭐야?

③ How could you do something like that?
넌 어떻게 그런 일을 할 수가 있어?

④ I'm busy right now. Can I call you back?
나 지금 바빠. 나중에 내가 다시 전화해도 돼?

⑤ I would prefer chocolate over candy any day.
난 언제든 사탕보다는 초콜릿을 좋아해.

해설 조셉이 주디에게 해준 조언은 사실을 털어놓은 뒤 사탕을 사준다고 제안하는 것이다. 이 내용에 해당하는 말은 ①이다.

어휘 receive 받다 on the other hand 반면에, 다른 한편으로 regret 후회하다 scared 겁먹은 offer 제안하다 a bag of candy 사탕 한 봉지

18 ①

M: You look upset. What's wrong, Hillary?
너 화가 나 보인다. 무슨 일이야, 힐러리?

W: I got into a big argument with my boyfriend.
나 남자친구와 크게 다퉜어.

M: Oh, that's too bad. What happened?
아, 그건 안 됐다. 무슨 일 있었어?

W: We were supposed to meet, but he cancelled on me. 우리가 만나기로 했는데, 남자친구가 취소했어.

M: I see. What was the reason for cancelling on you?
그렇구나. 취소한 이유가 뭔데?

W: He said his company suddenly called him in to work. 갑자기 그의 회사에서 들어와서 일하라고 전화가 왔대.

M: Well, in that situation, he probably didn't have a choice.
뭐, 그런 상황이라면, 그는 분명 선택의 여지가 없었을 거야.

W: Do you really think so? I'll call him to talk about it right now. 너 정말 그렇게 생각해? 난 지금 당장 그것에 대해 말하기 위해 그에게 전화해야겠어.

해설 여자의 마지막 대사에 'I'll call him~'이라고 할 일이 명확히 언급된다.

어휘 get into an argument with ~와 말다툼하다 be supposed to ~하기로 되어 있다 cancel on ~와 약속을 취소하다 suddenly 갑자기 have a choice 선택의 여지가 있다

19 ⑤

W: Josh, may I ask what you're doing?
조쉬, 네가 뭘 하고 있는지 물어봐도 돼?

M: I'm working on a script for the school play.
나는 학교 연극을 위해 대본을 쓰고 있어.

W: That's wonderful! Are you a good writer?
멋지다! 너는 글을 잘 쓰니?

M: Actually, I'm not. I try, but I'm not getting any better. I don't know what to do.
사실은, 그렇지 않아. 난 노력은 하지만 더는 좋아지지가 않네. 무엇을 해야 하는지 모르겠어.

W: Then why don't you take a beginner's writing class? There are two classes every week in Room three three one. 그러면 초급 작문수업을 듣는 게 어때?
331호 강의실에서 매주 두 번씩 수업이 있어.

M: Do you think that will help? 그게 도움이 된다고 생각해?

W: Of course! You just have to take it one step at a time. 당연하지! 넌 그저 한 번에 한 걸음씩 나아가면 돼.

M: You're right. Thanks for the advice!
맞아. 조언 고마워!

① Like father, like son. 그 아버지에 그 아들.

② Two heads are better than one. 백지장도 맞들면 낫다.

③ Even if the sky falls down, there is a way out.
하늘이 무너져도 솟아날 구멍은 있다.

④ One man's medicine is another man's poison. 어떤 이의 약이 다른 이에겐 독이 된다.

⑤ A journey of a thousand miles begins with a single step. 천리 길도 한 걸음부터.

해설 '천리 길도 한 걸음부터'라는 속담은 무슨 일이든 그 일의 시작이 중요하며 작은 일이 쌓여서 큰 성과를 이루게 되는 것임을 의미한다.

어휘 script 대본, 원고 get better 더 나아지다 beginner 초보자 one step at a time 한 번에 한 걸음씩 fall down 무너지다 way out (곤란한 상황의) 탈출구 poison 독

20 ③

W: Do you know how to play any instruments?
너는 연주할 수 있는 악기가 있어?

M: Hmm, just a few. I can play piano, guitar, and the drums.
음, 그냥 몇 개. 나는 피아노, 기타, 그리고 드럼을 연주할 수 있어.

W: Wow! You're so talented.
우와! 너 아주 재능이 있구나.

M: I just play for fun. How about you?
나는 그냥 재미로 하는 정도야. 너는?

W: I want to learn, but I don't have the time.
난 배우고 싶지만 시간이 없어.

M: Really? When you're not busy, I can teach you.
그래? 네가 바쁘지 않을 때 내가 가르쳐 줄 수 있어.

W: That's terrific! You are so generous.
그거 아주 좋은데! 넌 정말 마음이 넓구나.

① I ordered a new electric guitar.
나는 새로운 전자기타를 주문했어.

② How do I audition for the band?
내가 그 밴드에 어떻게 오디션을 볼 수 있어?

③ That's terrific! You are so generous.
그거 아주 좋은데! 넌 정말 마음이 넓구나.

④ There's a music store down the street.
길 아래에 악기점이 있어.

⑤ The band will perform on Sunday at noon.
그 밴드는 일요일 정오에 공연할 거야.

해설 악기 연주하는 법을 배우고 싶은데 친구가 가르쳐 주겠다고 제안하면 환영의 의사를 표할 것이다.

어휘 instrument 악기; 기구   just a few   아주 조금   talented 재능이 있는   for fun 재미로   electric guitar 전자[전기] 기타   audition 오디션에 참가하다   terrific 굉장한   generous 마음이 넓은, 너그러운   music store 악기점; 음반 가게

M: Yes, I'll be <u>leaving</u> the house <u>pretty</u> <u>soon</u>. I'll be back in about two hours.
응, 난 금방 집을 나설 거야. 약 두 시간 있다가 돌아올게.

W: Alright! I'll be there soon. 좋아! 금방 갈게.

해설 미국에서는 어린 아이를 집에 혼자 두는 것은 불법이기 때문에 외출할 때 babysitter(아이를 봐 주는 사람)를 반드시 고용한다.

어휘 get ready to ~할 준비를 하다   babysit (부모가 없는 동안) 아이를 돌보다   pretty soon 이내, 곧   be back 돌아오다

09회 실전모의고사
본문 p.102-103

01 ②	02 ⑤	03 ③	04 ⑤	05 ②
06 ④	07 ④	08 ④	09 ①	10 ①
11 ②	12 ④	13 ③	14 ①	15 ⑤
16 ④	17 ⑤	18 ④	19 ①	20 ②

01 ②

W: Hey, Mark. <u>What</u> are you going to <u>buy</u>?
얘, 마크. 넌 뭘 살 거니?

M: I need a new <u>pencil</u> <u>case</u> for school.
난 학교에서 쓸 새 필통이 필요해.

W: Here's one with <u>hippos</u> on it. Would you want this one? 여기 하마가 있는 필통이 있어. 이걸 원하니?

M: No, I <u>prefer</u> these ones with the <u>frogs</u> or <u>monkeys</u>.
아니, 나는 개구리나 원숭이들이 그려진 이런 것들이 더 좋아.

W: I see. Are those your <u>favorite</u> animals?
알았어. 그게 네가 좋아하는 동물들이니?

M: <u>Not really</u>, but there isn't much to <u>choose from</u> here. 딱히 그렇지는 않은데, 여기서는 고를 수 있는 게 많지 않네.

W: You're right. Do you want to go to a <u>different</u> <u>store</u>?
네 말이 맞아. 다른 가게로 갈까?

M: That's okay. I think I'll just <u>buy</u> the <u>one</u> with frogs.
괜찮아. 난 그냥 개구리가 있는 필통을 살 생각이야.

W: Alright, if that's what you want.
네가 원하는 것이 그거라면, 좋아

어휘 hippo 하마   frog 개구리   choose from ~에서 고르다

02 ⑤

[Cellphone rings.] [휴대폰이 울린다.]

M: Hello, Donna? This is Frank. 여보세요, 도나? 나 프랭크야.

W: Hey, what are you <u>up to</u>? 얘, 무슨 일이니?

M: I'm <u>getting</u> <u>ready</u> to go to a party with my friend. Can you <u>do</u> something <u>for me</u>? 난 내 친구와 함께 파티에 갈 준비를 하고 있어. 날 위해 뭐 좀 해줄래?

W: Yeah, what is it? 그래, 뭔데?

M: If you're not busy, I need you to <u>babysit</u> my younger <u>sister</u> <u>while</u> I'm <u>gone</u>. 네가 바쁘지 않으면 내가 없는 동안 네가 내 여동생을 돌봐주면 좋겠어.

W: Okay, I can do that. Do you need me to go <u>over</u> <u>there</u> now?
그래, 그건 해줄 수 있어. 내가 지금 그리로 가야 하니?

---

03 ③

① W: <u>Where</u> is the nearest <u>train</u> <u>station</u>?
가장 가까운 기차역이 어디 있죠?

M: It's a ten minute walk <u>from here</u>.
여기서 걸어서 10분 거리에 있어요.

② W: There are so many people <u>on</u> the <u>train</u>.
기차에 사람들이 정말 많네.

M: Yeah, it's <u>like this</u> every day during <u>rush</u> <u>hour</u>.
응, 러시아워 동안에는 매일 이래.

③ W: Is this the <u>train to</u> Lincoln Lane?
이 기차가 링컨 레인으로 가는 건가요?

M: Yes. It is three <u>stops</u> <u>away</u>. 네, 세 정거장 뒤입니다.

④ W: Thank you for <u>giving</u> me your <u>seat</u>.
당신의 자리를 제게 양보해 주셔서 감사합니다.

M: No problem. I'm <u>getting off</u> the train soon anyway.
별말씀을요. 저는 어차피 기차에서 곧 내려요.

⑤ W: I hope there are <u>seats</u> <u>left</u> on the train.
기차에 자리가 남아 있으면 좋겠어.

M: Me too. I'm <u>tired of</u> <u>standing</u> on the way home.
나도 그래. 나는 집까지 서서 가는 게 힘들어.

어휘 rush hour 러시아워, 출퇴근 혼잡 시간대   stop 정거장   get off 내리다   anyway 하여간, 어쨌든   be tired of 싫증이 나다, 지치다   on the way home 집으로 가는 길에

04 ⑤

M: Do you like my <u>pumpkin</u>? I'm going to <u>carve</u> it for Halloween and put it on my front porch.
내 호박이 마음에 드니? 나는 핼러윈을 위해 이걸 조각해서 우리 집 현관에 놓을 거야.

W: Yeah, it <u>looks</u> <u>great</u>. Do you know how you're going to carve it? 응, 멋지네. 넌 그걸 어떻게 조각할지 알아봤어?

M: I'm thinking of giving it a <u>triangular</u> <u>nose</u> and <u>scary</u> <u>eyes</u>.
나는 호박에 삼각형 코와 무시무시한 눈을 넣을 생각이야.

W: Hmm, I think it'll <u>look</u> <u>better</u> with an <u>upside</u> <u>down</u> triangular nose and a <u>smile</u>. 음, 내 생각에는 거꾸로 된 삼각형 코와 미소를 넣는 것이 더 좋을 것 같은데.

M: <u>Thanks</u> for the idea, <u>but</u> I think I <u>prefer</u> the triangular nose and scary eyes. I'm going to <u>put</u> a <u>hat</u> on it too. 의견은 고맙지만, 내 생각에는 삼각형 코와 무시무시한 눈이 더 좋을 것 같아. 난 호박에 모자도 씌울 생각이야.

W: Well, it's your pumpkin, so it's <u>up to</u> you. Maybe I

---

should carve my own pumpkin. 뭐, 이건 네 호박이니까 너한테 달린 거지. 나도 내 호박을 조각해야 할 것 같아.

M: Yes, you definitely should. It'll be a lot of fun.
그래, 넌 반드시 그래야 해. 정말로 재미있을 거야.

W: Okay, I should go to the pumpkin patch and buy one right now. 알았어, 지금 호박밭에 가서 하나를 사야겠어.

해설 삼각형 코, 무서운 눈, 모자가 있는 호박이 정답이다.

어휘 pumpkin 호박 carve 조각하다 Halloween 핼러윈(10월 31일 밤) front porch 집 앞 현관 triangular 삼각형의 scary 무서운 upside down 거꾸로의, 뒤집힌 definitely 확실히, 분명히 patch (채소를 기르는) 작은 땅

05 ②

M: Next customer in line, please. 다음 손님 오세요.

W: Hello. I would like to cash these checks.
안녕하세요. 이 수표를 현금으로 바꾸려고 하는데요.

M: Sure, how would you like the cash? Also, I need to see your ID card. 물론이죠, 현금은 어떻게 드릴까요? 그리고 손님의 신분증을 봐야 합니다.

W: Okay, here you are. I would like it in twenty-dollar bills, please. 네, 여기 있어요. 20달러 지폐로 부탁해요.

M: Alright. Please fill out this form and sign at the bottom of the page.
알겠습니다. 이 양식을 작성하시고, 페이지의 하단에 서명하세요.

W: All done. Is there anything else I need to do?
다 됐어요. 제가 또 해야 하는 게 있나요?

M: No, you're all set. Here's your two thousand dollars in cash. Thank you for visiting our bank today.
아니요, 다 됐습니다. 여기 손님의 현금 2천 달러예요. 오늘 저희 은행을 찾아 주셔서 감사합니다.

해설 돈에 관한 내용이 이어지다가 마지막에 bank라는 결정적인 힌트가 나온다.

어휘 customer 고객, 손님 in line 줄을 선 cash 수표를 현금으로 바꾸다; 현금 check 수표 ID card 신분증 bill 지폐 fill out 작성하다 form 양식 bottom 맨 아래 be all set 준비가 되어 있다 bank teller 은행 직원 sales clerk 점원, 판매원 flight attendant 항공기 승무원

06 ④

M: You look so worried, Kristin.
넌 무척 걱정이 있는 것 같구나, 크리스틴.

W: I couldn't sleep at all last night!
난 어젯밤에 한숨도 못 잤어.

M: Why, what's the matter? 왜, 무슨 일이야?

W: I have a job interview today for a company I really want to work for. I spent all night practicing for it.
난 오늘 내가 정말로 일하고 싶은 회사에서 취업 면접이 있어. 난 밤새도록 면접 연습을 했어.

M: I see. What kind of work does the company do?
그랬구나. 그 회사는 어떤 일을 하니?

W: It's an advertising company, and I applied for the team manager position. I hope I can stay calm and say everything I prepared.
광고 회사고, 난 팀장 자리에 지원했어. 난 내가 침착함을 유지하면서 준비한 모든 것을 말할 수 있으면 좋겠어.

M: That sounds like a great opportunity. I'm sure you'll do fine, since you practiced a lot for it.
대단한 기회인 것처럼 들린다. 네가 그것을 위해 많은 연습을 했으니까 잘할 수 있을 거라고 확신해.

W: I hope so. Well, I'd better head over to the company now.
나도 그러면 좋겠어. 음, 난 이제 그 회사로 가보는 게 좋겠어.

M: Okay. Be confident and do your best.
알았어. 자신감을 갖고 최선을 다해 봐.

해설 여자는 중요한 면접을 앞두고 무척 긴장한 상태이다.

어휘 look worried 걱정스러운 얼굴을 하다 not ~ at all 전혀 ~ 아닌 job interview (취업) 면접 advertising 광고 apply for ~에 지원하다 team manager 팀장 position 자리, 직위 stay calm 침착함을 유지하다 opportunity 기회 head 가다, 향하다 confident 자신감 있는 annoyed 짜증난

07 ④

① M: I can't get this stain out of my pants.
내 바지에서 이 얼룩을 지울 수가 없네.
W: Take them to the dry cleaner's.
바지를 세탁소로 가져 가.

② M: What do you want for dessert? 디저트로 뭘 먹을래?
W: A piece of red velvet cake. 레드 벨벳 케이크 한 조각.

③ M: My pen ran out of ink. 내 펜은 잉크가 떨어졌어.
W: You can use mine for the day. 오늘은 내 펜을 써도 돼.

④ M: I can't believe we won the game!
우리가 경기에서 이겼다니 믿어지지가 않아!
W: The game starts in ten minutes.
경기는 10분 후에 시작해.

⑤ M: The weather is getting colder and colder.
날씨가 점점 추워지고 있어.
W: I know. Make sure you bring a jacket!
나도 알아. 넌 반드시 재킷을 가져오도록 해!

해설 'I can't believe ~'로 놀라움을 나타낼 경우, 보통은 맞장구를 치는 내용이 이어진다.

어휘 get something out of ~에서 ...을 없애다 stain 얼룩 dry cleaner's 세탁소 dessert 디저트 a piece of 한 조각 run out of ~이 떨어지다, 다 써버리다 for the day 오늘은, 그날은 win the game 시합에 이기다

08 ④

W: Oh my goodness, I'm freaking out! The time is nearing.
맙소사, 눈앞이 캄캄해지고 있어! 그 시간이 다가오고 있어.

M: What's wrong? I've never seen you this nervous

before. Are you okay? 무슨 문제 있어? 난 전에는 네가 이렇
게 초조해하는 걸 못 봤어. 너 괜찮아?

W: No, I'm about to go get my ears pierced.
아니, 난 내 귀를 뚫으려고 하는 참이거든.

M: Don't worry! I got mine pierced last month and it
didn't hurt at all.
걱정하지 마! 나도 지난달에 내 귀를 뚫었는데, 하나도 안 아팠어.

W: If you have time, please come with me.
너 시간 있으면 나랑 같이 가자.

M: Actually, I'm free until seven P.M. but my mom asked
me to pick up her jacket from the dry cleaner's.
사실 난 오후 7시까지 한가해. 하지만 우리 엄마가 나더러 세탁소
에 가서 엄마의 재킷을 찾아오라고 하셨어.

W: We'll be back before then, I'm sure. The ear
piercing shop is close by. 우리는 그때까지 돌아올 거야, 확
실해. 귀 뚫어주는 가게가 근처에 있거든.

M: Okay then, let's go. 알았어, 그럼 가자.

> **해설** 여자의 대사 'If you have time, please ~'에 부탁 내용이
> 나온다.

> **어휘** my goodness 맙소사, 세상에 freak out 질겁하다 near
> 가까워지다; 가까운 nervous 초조한 be about to 막 ~하려는
> 참이다 get one's ears pierced ~의 귀를 뚫다 pick up
> 찾아오다 close by 가까운

09 ①

M: Are you studying well for your test?
너는 시험 공부를 잘 하고 있니?

W: Yes, professor. But I think I need more time to
prepare.
네, 교수님. 하지만 전 준비할 시간이 더 필요할 것 같아요.

M: There was a lot to learn this semester, right?
이번 학기에는 배울 것이 많았지, 그렇지?

W: Seriously, there is too much material to memorize
and so little time! 진심으로 말씀 드리면, 외워야 할 자료는 아
주 많고 시간은 너무 없네요!

M: Sorry. I wish I could do something about it.
미안하다. 나도 그것에 관해 뭔가를 할 수 있었으면 좋겠구나.

W: Can you change the test date to next Monday?
시험 날짜를 다음 주 월요일로 변경하실 수 있나요?

M: No, I can't. How about I post some hints online? It
may help you. 아니, 그렇게 못해. 내가 몇 가지 힌트를 인터
넷에 게시하는 건 어떨까? 그게 널 도울 수 있을 거야.

> **해설** 'How about ~?'은 제안할 때 자주 쓰이는 표현이다.

> **어휘** professor 교수 prepare 준비하다 semester 학기
> seriously 진심으로 말하자면 material 자료 memorize
> 암기하다 post 게시하다 online 온라인에, 인터넷에

10 ①

W: Good afternoon, what can I help you with?
안녕하세요, 어떤 걸 도와드릴까요?

M: I would like some pizza and breadsticks.

피자하고 브레드스틱을 먹고 싶어요.

W: We have pepperoni, cheese, and vegetable pizza.
저희는 페퍼로니, 치즈, 그리고 채소 피자가 있어요.

M: How much is it for one slice? 한 조각은 얼마죠?

W: It's five dollars each for pepperoni, three dollars
each for cheese, and three dollars each for
vegetable. 페퍼로니는 각각 5달러고요, 치즈는 각각 3달러, 그
리고 채소는 각각 3달러입니다.

M: And how about the breadsticks? 그럼 브레드스틱은요?

W: Two dollars, but if you buy two pieces of pizza, you
can get the breadsticks for free. 2달러지만, 피자 두 조
각을 구매하면 브레드스틱은 공짜로 얻을 수 있어요.

M: Okay then, I'll have one pepperoni and one cheese
pizza with breadsticks. 그럼 좋아요, 페퍼로니 피자 한 조각
하고, 치즈 피자 한 조각, 그리고 브레드스틱을 살게요.

> **해설** 페퍼로니 피자는 5달러이고, 치즈 피자는 3달러, 그리고 브레드
> 스틱은 무료로 받게 된다.

> **어휘** breadstick 브레드스틱, 막대 모양의 빵 pepperoni
> 페퍼로니(소시지의 일종) slice (얇게 썬) 조각 each 각각 for
> free 공짜로, 무료로

11 ②

M: Hello, ma'am. What brings you here?
안녕하세요, 부인. 무슨 일로 오셨습니까?

W: I would like to file a missing person report.
저는 실종자를 신고하려고 해요.

M: Who is missing? 누가 실종되었습니까?

W: My son. He didn't come home last night.
제 아들이요. 그 애가 어젯밤에 집에 오지 않았어요.

M: Oh no! When and where did you last see him?
아, 저런! 언제 어디서 아드님을 마지막으로 보셨나요?

W: I saw him yesterday morning, at home. He left
saying he was going to school. Please find him,
Officer.
저는 그 애를 어제 아침에 집에서 마지막으로 봤어요. 그 애는 학교
에 간다고 하면서 떠났어요. 제발 그 애를 찾아 주세요, 경찰관님.

M: I'll do my best. Please leave your phone number
and your son's name. Do you have a picture of
him? 최선을 다하겠습니다. 부인의 전화번호와 아드님의 이름을
남겨 놓으세요. 아드님의 사진을 갖고 계십니까?

W: Yes, here you go. I hope to hear from you soon.
네, 여기 있어요. 빨리 소식을 들을 수 있으면 좋겠네요.

> **해설** 경찰관을 부를 때 officer라는 용어를 쓴다.

> **어휘** What brings you here? 무슨 일로 오셨나요? file
> a report 신고하다, 보고서를 제출하다 missing 실종된, 없어진
> officer 경찰관; 장교, 공무원

12 ④

M: Leyman's Factory burnt down due to a fire. The
fire started around one P.M. and lasted for about
two hours. A person living nearby discovered the

fire and called nine one one. The police say that four people have been injured and are currently at the hospital. The property has also been badly damaged. The cause of the incident is still unknown. Please be aware that there is heavy traffic in the area. This is Miley Kent, live for GSC eight o'clock news.

레이만 공장이 화재로 인해 소실되었습니다. 화재는 오후 1시경 시작되었으며, 두 시간 가량 계속되었습니다. 화재 현장 근처에 살고 있는 사람이 그것을 발견하고 911에 전화했습니다. 경찰에 따르면 네 명이 부상을 입었고 현재 병원에 있다고 합니다. 건물도 심각한 피해를 입었습니다. 사고의 원인은 아직 밝혀지지 않았습니다. 그 지역의 교통이 무척 복잡하다는 것을 명심하시기 바랍니다. 저는 생방송으로 GSC 8시 뉴스를 전해 드린 마일리 켄트입니다.

어휘 factory 공장 burn down 불에 타다, 소실되다(burn-burned[burnt]-burned[burnt]) due to ~으로 인해 last 계속되다, 지속되다 discover 발견하다 injured 다친, 부상을 입은 currently 현재, 지금 property 건물, 재산, 부동산 badly damaged 심각한 피해를 입은 cause 원인 incident 사건 unknown 알려지지 않은 be aware ~을 알다 heavy traffic 극심한 교통량 area 지역

13 ③

| 롤리 헬스클럽의 운동 프로그램 |

	프로그램	장소/시간
①	요가	101호 오후 12시
②	자전거 타기	102호 오후 12시 30분
③	에어로빅	103호 오후 1시 30분
④	발레	103호 오후 12시
⑤	농구	105호 오후 4시

M: What program do you want to participate in? 넌 어떤 프로그램에 참가하고 싶니?
W: They all seem like a good workout. How about yoga or ballet? 모두 좋은 운동처럼 보여. 요가나 발레는 어떨까?
M: I'm not flexible enough. Plus, I won't get to the gym until one P.M. 나는 별로 유연성이 없어. 게다가 나는 오후 1시까지는 헬스클럽에 가지 못할 거야.
W: Oh. Then, that only leaves us two options. 아. 그러면 우리에게는 두 가지 선택권만 남는 거네.
M: Hmm, should we go play some basketball? 음, 우리 농구를 할까?
W: No, I've played basketball too often the past few weeks. I want to try something new. 아니, 난 지난 몇 주 동안 농구를 너무 자주 했어. 난 새로운 뭔가를 해보고 싶어.
M: Then let's do the fitness program in Room one oh three. 그럼 103호에서 운동 프로그램을 하자.
W: Okay! That works for me. 좋았어! 그건 나에게 맞아.

해설 남자는 오후 1시까지는 헬스클럽에 올 수 없으므로 가능한 정답은 ③과 ⑤이다. 둘 중 103호에서 열리는 운동은 에어로빅이다.

어휘 participate in ~에 참여하다 workout 운동 flexible 유연한 enough 충분히; 충분한 plus 게다가, 더욱이 gym 헬스클럽, 체육관 leave (어떤 결과를) 남기다 option 선택권 try something new 새로운 뭔가를 해보다 work 작동하다, 효과가 있다

14 ①

W: Most people have probably enjoyed flying one of these at least once. People fly this on beaches, rivers, and parks. They come in many shapes, sizes, and colors. They are made of paper or cloth. Normally, they have a wooden frame and are connected to a long string. All you need is some wind to fly it.

아마도 대부분의 사람들이 적어도 한 번은 이것을 날려 본 적이 있을 것이다. 사람들은 바닷가, 강가, 그리고 공원에서 이것을 날린다. 이것은 여러 가지 모양, 크기, 그리고 색상으로 나온다. 이것은 종이나 천으로 만들어진다. 보통 이것은 나무로 된 뼈대를 가지고 있으며, 긴 줄에 연결되어 있다. 당신이 필요한 것은 이것을 날릴 수 있는 바람뿐이다.

해설 나무 뼈대가 있고, 긴 끈에 연결되어 있는 모양에서 힌트를 얻을 수 있다.

어휘 probably 아마도 at least once 적어도 한 번 fly 날리다; 날다 come in (상품이) 나오다 shape 모양 cloth 천, 옷감 normally 보통, 일반적으로 wooden 나무의 frame 뼈대, 틀 be connected to ~에 연결되어 있다 string 끈, 줄

15 ⑤

W: Ken, where's your locker? 켄, 네 사물함은 어디 있니?
M: It's right down the hall from here. How about you? 여기서 복도를 따라 가면 있어. 넌?
W: Mine is in front of the computer lab. I just got finished changing my password. 내 것은 컴퓨터실 앞에 있어. 난 방금 비밀번호를 바꿨어.
M: Why did you do that? 왜 그렇게 했는데?
W: Well, it's just to be safe. If someone already knows my password, they might steal my things. 음, 그냥 안전하기 위해서지. 어떤 사람이 이미 내 비밀번호를 알고 있다면 사람들이 내 물건을 훔칠 수도 있잖아.
M: Good point. I never thought of that. I should go change my password too. 좋은 지적이야. 나는 그걸 전혀 생각 못 했네. 나도 가서 비밀번호를 바꿔야겠어.
W: Yeah. It's best to change it at least once every semester. Let me know if you need any help. 그래. 학기마다 적어도 한 번씩 바꾸는 게 최선인 것 같아. 도움이 필요하면 내게 알려 줘.

어휘 locker 사물함, 로커 down ~을 따라 hall 복도 in front of ~앞에 computer lab 컴퓨터실 password 비밀번호 safe 안전한 steal 훔치다 at least 적어도 once 한 번 semester 학기

16 ④

M: Beth, this plate is awesome. I really like the design on it.
베스, 이 접시 멋지다. 난 접시에 있는 디자인이 정말 마음에 들어.

W: Thanks! I actually made it myself at a pottery class. I've been going to the class for over a year now.
고마워! 사실 내가 도예 교실에서 그걸 직접 만들었어. 난 지금 일 년 넘게 그 수업에 다니고 있어.

M: Pottery class? That sounds like so much fun! Can I join you next time? 도예 교실? 정말 재미있게 들리는데! 다음에는 나도 같이할 수 있을까?

W: Of course! There are two classes a week, one on Monday and the other on Wednesday.
물론이지! 일주일에 두 번 수업이 있는데, 한 번은 월요일이고, 다른 한 번은 수요일에 있어.

M: I can't go to the Monday class because I do volunteer work that day. What time is the class on Wednesday? 나는 월요일에는 자원 봉사를 가기 때문에 그날은 수업에 갈 수 없어. 수요일 수업은 몇 시지?

W: That class starts at three thirty P.M. Let's meet thirty minutes earlier and go together.
그 수업은 오후 3시 30분에 시작해. 30분 전에 만나서 같이 가자.

M: That sounds perfect. I'll see you then.
완벽해. 그때 보자.

어휘 plate 접시, 그릇 awesome 기막히게 좋은, 경탄할 만한 actually 사실은, 실제로 pottery 도예, 도자기 join 함께하다; 가입하다 next time 다음번에 volunteer work 자원봉사

17 ⑤

W: Beatrice and Justin are partners for a team presentation. They were supposed to work on the project together. However, Justin is not helping Beatrice at all. He doesn't answer her phone calls or read her emails. Beatrice is tired of doing all the work by herself. So, she went to her teacher for some advice. Her teacher told her to be direct and talk to Justin about the problem. In this situation, what would Beatrice most likely say to Justin?

베아트리스와 저스틴은 팀 발표의 파트너이다. 그들은 과제를 함께 작업하기로 되어 있었다. 하지만 저스틴은 베아트리스를 전혀 돕지 않고 있다. 그는 그녀의 전화를 받지 않고, 이메일도 읽지 않는다. 베아트리스는 모든 일을 혼자서 하는 것에 지쳐 있다. 그래서 그녀는 선생님에게 가서 조언을 청했다. 그녀의 선생님은 그녀에게 직접적으로 저스틴에게 문제를 이야기하라고 말했다. 이런 상황에서 베아트리스는 저스틴에게 무슨 말을 하겠는가?

Beatrice: I'm upset with you. You need to help me with this assignment!
나는 너한테 화가 났어. 넌 나를 도와서 이 과제를 해야 해!

① Can I borrow your library card?
네 도서 대출 카드를 빌릴 수 있을까?

② I'm so excited that we are partners!
난 우리가 파트너라는 게 정말 신나.

③ The books at the library are all checked out.
도서관에 있는 책들이 모두 대출되었어.

④ The boxes need to be moved to the storage room.
상자들을 창고로 옮겨야 해.

⑤ I'm upset with you. You need to help me with this assignment!
나는 너한테 화가 났어. 넌 나를 도와서 이 과제를 해야 해!

어휘 partner 파트너, 동반자 team presentation 팀 발표 be supposed to ~하기로 되어 있다 work on ~을 작업하다 not ~ at all 전혀 ~ 아닌 answer one's phone call ~의 전화를 받다 by oneself 혼자서 direct 직접적인, 직설적인 check out (책을) 대출하다 storage room 창고, 저장소 upset 속상한, 화가 난 assignment 과제

18 ④

W: What are your plans for the weekend?
네 주말 계획은 뭐니?

M: I don't have any yet. I'm still thinking about it. What about you?
난 아직 계획이 없어. 아직 그것에 관해 생각 중이야. 넌?

W: You should go to the beach! It's near here, plus the weather is really nice. I'm going to the mountains behind the school.
넌 바닷가에 가야 해! 바닷가는 이 근처에 있고, 게다가 날씨도 정말 좋아. 난 학교 뒤쪽에 있는 산에 갈 거야.

M: I was actually thinking about going to the beach. My sister likes it there too. Maybe I should bring her along. 난 사실 바닷가에 가는 것에 관해 생각 중이었어. 내 여동생도 거길 좋아하거든. 아마도 그 애를 데려가야 할 것 같아.

W: Yeah, you should do that. I went last month and had a lot of fun. 그래, 넌 그렇게 해야 해. 난 지난달에 거기 가서 아주 즐거운 시간을 보냈어.

M: Cool! Then I'll go this weekend to swim and build a sand castle. 멋지다! 그럼 나도 이번 주말에 가서 수영도 하고, 모래성도 만들어야겠어.

W: Alright, have a good time! 그래, 좋은 시간 보내!

어휘 bring somebody along ~을 데리고 가다 build a sand castle 모래성을 만들다

19 ①

M: Grandma, what was Dad like when he was my age? 할머니, 아빠는 제 나이였을 때 어땠어요?

W: Hmm… That was a long time ago.
음, 그건 오래 전 일이구나.

M: Was he funny? I bet he liked telling jokes just like me. 아빠는 재미있었나요? 아빠도 저처럼 우스갯소리를 하는 것을 좋아했을 것 같아요.

W: Yeah, he told a lot of jokes. He also danced in front of people and imitated animals.

그래, 네 아빠는 농담을 많이 했지. 사람들 앞에서 춤도 추고 동물 흉내도 냈단다.

M: Haha, I do all of those things with my friends too! I think we have similar taste in music as well.
하하, 저도 제 친구들과 그런 것을 하거든요. 제 생각엔 우리는 음악에 관한 취향도 비슷한 것 같아요.

W: That's right. You are like a smaller version of him.
맞아. 넌 네 아빠의 보다 작은 버전 같구나.

M: I'll take that as a compliment.
그 말씀은 칭찬으로 받아들일게요.

① Like father, like son. 그 아버지에 그 아들.
② The more, the better. 많으면 많을수록 좋다.
③ All's well that ends well. 끝이 좋으면 모두 좋다.
④ As you sow, so you reap. 뿌린 대로 거둘 것이다.
⑤ Out of sight, out of mind.
눈에서 멀어지면, 마음에서도 멀어진다.

해설 'Like father, like son.'은 '부전자전', '그 아버지에 그 아들'이라는 의미의 속담이다.

어휘 a long time ago 오래 전에   funny 재미있는, 웃기는 bet 틀림없다, 분명하다   tell jokes 농담하다   imitate 흉내 내다 similar 비슷한   taste 취향   as well 또한, ~도   version 판, 버전   compliment 칭찬, 찬사   sow 씨를 뿌리다   reap 거두다, 수확하다

20 ②

M: You look so down today. Is there something wrong? 넌 오늘 무척 우울해 보여. 무슨 문제라도 있니?

W: I went to the hospital. My baby might be sick.
난 병원에 갔었어. 내 아기가 아플 수도 있어.

M: That's terrible! How long have you been pregnant?
큰일이구나! 넌 임신한지 얼마나 됐지?

W: It has been twenty weeks. I'm so worried. What if something bad happens to him? 이제 20주째야. 난 너무 걱정돼. 아기에게 나쁜 일이라도 생기면 어쩌지?

M: That's not going to happen. Think positively.
그런 일은 일어나지 않을 거야. 긍정적으로 생각해.

W: I'm trying. The test results come out tomorrow.
노력 중이야. 검사 결과는 내일 나올 거야.

M: I'll keep my fingers crossed for you.
너에게 행운을 빌어줄게.

① I'll be on the lookout for your keys.
내가 네 열쇠를 지키고 있을게.
② I'll keep my fingers crossed for you.
너에게 행운을 빌어줄게.
③ There's a vending machine over there.
저쪽에 자동판매기가 있어.
④ There's a hospital across the street from here.
여기서 길 건너편에 병원이 있어.
⑤ Check out the clothing store on West Boulevard.
웨스트 대로에 있는 옷 가게를 확인해 봐.

해설 'I'll keep my fingers crossed for you.'라고 말할 때는

자신의 검지와 중지를 겹쳐서 십자가 모양으로 만드는 제스처를 취하기도 한다.

어휘 down 우울한   pregnant 임신한   positively 긍정적으로 test result 테스트 결과   come out 나오다   keep one's fingers crossed 행운을 빌다, 기도하다   be on the lookout ~을 망보다, 지켜보다   vending machine 자동판매기   over there 저쪽에

<table>
<tr><td colspan="6">**10회 실전모의고사** 본문 p.114-115</td></tr>
<tr><td>01 ⑤</td><td>02 ③</td><td>03 ①</td><td>04 ④</td><td>05 ②</td></tr>
<tr><td>06 ④</td><td>07 ③</td><td>08 ④</td><td>09 ①</td><td>10 ③</td></tr>
<tr><td>11 ⑤</td><td>12 ②</td><td>13 ③</td><td>14 ⑤</td><td>15 ④</td></tr>
<tr><td>16 ③</td><td>17 ⑤</td><td>18 ③</td><td>19 ①</td><td>20 ⑤</td></tr>
</table>

01 ⑤

M: Do you know what's for lunch today?
넌 오늘 점심이 뭔지 아니?

W: No, let's look at the cafeteria menu on the bulletin board. 아니, 게시판에 붙은 카페테리아 메뉴를 한번 보자.

M: Let's see. We can choose from five different sandwiches.
어디 보자. 우리는 다섯 가지의 다른 샌드위치 중에서 고를 수 있네.

W: Hmm, I think I'm going to get the tuna sandwich. How about you? 음, 난 참치 샌드위치를 먹을 생각이야. 넌?

M: I can't choose between the salad and the French fries. 난 샐러드와 감자튀김 사이에서 고를 수가 없어.

W: I thought fried chicken was your favorite. Why don't you just get that one? 난 프라이드 치킨이 네가 가장 좋아하는 건 줄 알았는데. 너는 그걸 먹는 게 어때?

M: It is, but I ate fried chicken for dinner yesterday. I think I'll go with the salad with French dressing.
그렇긴 한데, 난 어제 저녁으로 프라이드 치킨을 먹었어. 프렌치 드레싱이 들어간 샐러드로 가야겠다.

W: Okay, if that's what you want!
그래, 그게 네가 원하는 거라면!

어휘 cafeteria 구내식당, 카페테리아   bulletin board 게시판 tuna 참치   go with (제안 등을) 받아들이다

02 ③

[Cellphone rings.] [휴대폰이 울린다.]

M: Honey, did you call? Sorry I missed it. I was in the middle of a meeting. 여보, 당신이 전화했어요? 전화를 못 받아서 미안해요. 회의 도중이었거든요.

W: Yeah. Do you remember I told you we're having guests over for dinner today?
네. 내가 당신한테 오늘 저녁에 손님이 온다고 말한 거 기억해요?

M: Oh, I almost forgot. Thanks for reminding me. What about it?
아, 하마터면 잊을 뻔했네요. 알려 줘서 고마워요. 뭔데 그래요?

W: I'm setting the table, but I can't find the new tablecloth we bought.
제가 식탁을 차리고 있는데, 우리가 산 새 식탁보를 못 찾겠어요.

M: Hmm, did you check the storage room?
음, 창고를 확인해 봤어요?

W: Yes. I just did, but no luck. I need you to come find it for me. 네, 방금 확인했는데, 없네요. 당신이 와서 나 대신 그걸 찾아 주면 좋겠어요.

M: Alright. If I leave now, I'll get home in about half an hour. 알았어요. 내가 지금 출발하면 약 30분 후에 집에 도착할 거예요.

W: Okay. Drive safely. 네. 운전 조심하세요.

[해설] 대화의 초, 중반까지는 상황 설명이 이어지고, 후반 여자의 대사 'I need you to ~'에 직접적인 목적이 나온다.

[어휘] miss 놓치다　in the middle of ~의 도중에　meeting 회의　guest 손님　remind 다시 알려주다　set the table 식탁을 차리다　tablecloth 식탁보　storage room 창고　no luck 운이 없는, 뜻한 바를 이루지 못한　safely 안전하게

03 ①

① W: How long has it been since you started to skateboard? 너는 스케이트보드를 탄 지 얼마나 됐어?
　M: I started learning about three months ago.
　난 3개월 전부터 배우기 시작했어.

② W: Wow, look at that skateboard! It has a unique design on it. 우와, 저 스케이트보드를 좀 봐. 디자인이 독특해.
　M: Yeah, it's probably really expensive.
　그래, 아마도 정말 비쌀 거야.

③ W: Can I borrow your ice skates? Mine are at the repair shop.
　내가 너의 스케이트화를 빌려도 될까? 내 것은 수리점에 있거든.
　M: Sure, but I need them back by tomorrow morning.
　물론, 하지만 내일 아침까지는 내가 그걸 돌려받아야 해.

④ W: Excuse me, where is the line for the roller coaster?
　실례합니다만, 롤러코스터를 타는 줄이 어디죠?
　M: It's over there by the vending machine.
　저쪽 자동판매기 옆이요.

⑤ W: Could you tell me how to get to the skateboard shop? 스케이트보드 가게에 가는 방법을 알려 주실래요?
　M: Sure. Walk straight for two blocks and take a right.
　물론이죠. 두 블록을 곧장 가서 우회전하세요.

[해설] skateboard와 ice skates를 구분하자.

[어휘] skateboard 스케이트보드　unique 독특한　probably 아마도　ice skates 스케이트화　roller coaster 롤러코스터　by ~옆에　vending machine 자동판매기　take a right 우회전하다

04 ④

M: Why did you want to meet me at the mall?
넌 왜 쇼핑몰에서 나를 만나고 싶어한 거야?

W: I need advice on which pair of sandals to get.
어떤 샌들을 사야 할지 조언이 필요하거든.

M: Okay, these sandals with zippers and no heels look good on you.
그래. 지퍼가 달리고 굽이 없는 이 샌들이 너한테 어울려.

W: Do you think so? But I prefer shoes with high heels.
그렇게 생각해? 하지만 난 높은 굽이 있는 신발을 좋아하는데.

M: Then go with the high heels with zippers or buckles. 그럼 지퍼나 버클이 있고 굽이 높은 것으로 해.

W: Which one do you think is better for the summer season? 여름철에는 어떤 게 더 좋다고 생각하니?

M: I would say the one with buckles. They seem to be a better fit for you. 난 버클이 있는 거라고 말하고 싶어. 그게 너한테 더 잘 어울리는 것 같아.

W: Then, I'll buy those. Thanks a lot!
그럼 난 그걸 살게. 정말 고마워.

[해설] 여자는 굽이 높은 신발을 좋아하며, 남자에게 추천받은 버클이 달린 샌들을 구입할 것이다.

[어휘] mall 쇼핑몰　a pair of sandals 샌들 한 켤레　zipper 지퍼　heel 뒷굽　look good on ~에게 어울리다　buckle 버클　fit for ~에게 적합한

05 ②

W: Sir, what's going on here? Why are there so many people? 저기요, 여기서 무슨 일이 있는 거죠? 사람들이 왜 이렇게 많은 거예요?

M: I'm going to put on a show. I'll be performing on this stage in five minutes. 제가 공연을 할 거라서요. 저는 이 무대에서 5분 후에 공연을 할 겁니다.

W: Wow! No wonder there's a crowd. What kind of performance is it?
우와! 사람들이 많은 게 당연하군요. 어떤 종류의 공연이에요?

M: I'll be doing a few tricks with this deck of cards.
이 카드 한 벌로 몇 가지 마술을 할 겁니다.

W: That sounds awesome. What else will you do?
아주 근사하겠는데요. 그 밖에는 뭘 하실 거예요?

M: Well, I'm going to pull a rabbit out of my hat and do some coin tricks. 음, 저는 제 모자에서 토끼를 꺼내고, 몇 가지 동전 마술을 할 겁니다.

W: Really? I'm going to have to see that to believe it.
정말요? 그걸 믿기 위해서는 제가 공연을 봐야겠네요.

M: You'll be impressed. Please take a seat, the magic show will start now. 당신은 감명을 받게 될 겁니다. 마술쇼가 지금 시작하니까 자리에 앉으세요.

[해설] 마지막에 나오는 magic show를 놓치지 않았다면 정답을 맞힐 수 있다.

[어휘] put on a show 공연하다(= perform)　stage 무대

no wonder 당연하다, 놀라운 일이 아니다   crowd 군중, 사람들
performance 공연   do a trick 마술을 부리다, 속임수를 쓰다
a deck of cards 카드 한 벌   coin 동전   impressed 감명을
받은   take a seat 자리에 앉다   magician 마술사

06 ④

W: We're finally college students! I can't wait for
school to start.
우리가 드디어 대학생이 됐어! 학교가 빨리 시작하면 좋겠다.

M: You're so happy to be here, aren't you?
여기 오게 되니 정말 기쁘지, 그렇지 않니?

W: Are you kidding me? This is the best day of my life.
농담하니? 오늘은 내 인생 최고의 날이야.

M: Why? This is the start of a lot of studying and
endless classes.
왜? 이건 많은 공부와 끝없는 수업의 시작일 뿐이지.

W: But there's so much more that college has to offer!
하지만 대학생활이 우리에게 주는 건 훨씬 더 많거든!

M: Give me an example. 나한테 예를 들어 봐.

W: You can meet a lot of new people, join a club, and
stay out late. 많은 새로운 사람들을 만날 수 있고, 동아리에 가
입하고, 그리고 늦게까지 밖에 있을 수 있잖아.

M: We'll see if you think the same way next month.
네가 다음 달에도 같은 생각을 하는지 두고 보자고.

해설 첫 문장의 'I can't wait ~'에서부터 여자의 들뜬 심정을 짐작할
수 있다.

어휘 finally 마침내, 드디어   I can't wait 어서 빨리 ~하고 싶다
kid 농담하다   endless 끝없는   offer 제공하다
give somebody an example ~에게 예를 들다
stay out late 늦게까지 외출하다   see if ~인지 확인하다
think the same way 같은 생각을 하다

07 ③

① W: Is your dog in the backyard? 뒷마당에 있는 개가 네 개니?
M: No, I gave him away because my mom was
allergic. 아니, 우리 엄마가 알레르기가 있어서 다른 사람에게 개
를 줘버렸어.

② W: Where is the art exhibition going to be held?
미술 전시회는 어디서 열리게 되나요?
M: Probably on Loft Street. 아마도 로프트 가에서요.

③ W: What time does your plane take off?
네 비행기는 언제 이륙하니?
M: I arrive at the airport on Tuesday at nine P.M.
난 화요일 오후 9시에 공항에 도착해.

④ W: The bread looks really fresh. 빵이 정말로 신선해 보이네요.
M: It just came out of the oven five minutes ago.
5분 전에 오븐에서 갓 나왔답니다.

⑤ W: Are you going to the orientation tomorrow?
넌 내일 오리엔테이션에 갈 거니?
M: I don't think so. I have other plans.
아니. 난 다른 계획이 있어.

해설 ③은 비행기 이륙 시간을 물었는데, 도착 시간을 말했기 때문에
어색하다.

어휘 backyard 뒷마당   give something away ~을 공짜로
주다   allergic 알레르기가 있는   art exhibition 미술 전시회   be
held 열리다   take off (비행기가) 뜨다, 이륙하다   fresh 신선한
orientation 오리엔테이션, 예비 교육

08 ④

M: You are probably the messiest person I know.
넌 아마도 내가 아는 가장 지저분한 사람일 거야.

W: I admit that. I can't help it! I'm a busy person.
나도 그걸 인정해. 나도 어쩔 수 없어! 난 바쁜 사람이거든.

M: Buy some cabinets and shelves to store everything.
모든 것을 보관할 수 있는 보관함과 선반을 구입해 봐.

W: I've tried that, but my desk just gets messy all over
again. 나도 그걸 해봤는데, 내 책상은 금방 다시 지저분해져.

M: Hmm, why don't I give you some tips to keep your
desk tidy?
음, 네 책상을 깔끔하게 유지할 수 있는 몇 가지 조언을 해줄까?

W: Can't you just come to my home someday and
help me organize it? 그냥 네가 언젠가 우리 집에 와서 책상
정리하는 걸 도와주면 안 되니?

M: Fine. I'll go over next week when I have time.
좋아. 시간이 나면 다음 주에 갈게.

W: Perfect. Thanks so much! 좋았어. 정말 고마워!

어휘 messiest 가장 지저분한(messy-messier-messiest)
admit 인정하다   can't help it 어쩔 수 없다   cabinet 보관함,
캐비닛   shelf 선반 (복 shelves)   store 보관하다, 저장하다
all over again 처음부터 다시   tip 조언, 팁   keep something
tidy ~을 깔끔하게 유지하다   organize 정리하다
go over 건너가다

09 ①

M: Honey, I can't sleep because of all the noise that is
coming from next door. 여보, 옆집에서 들려오는 온갖 소음
때문에 나는 잠을 잘 수가 없어요.

W: You can say that again. What do you think they're
doing this late at night? 맞는 말이에요. 저 사람들이 이 늦
은 밤에 뭘 하고 있다고 생각해요?

M: Who knows? I think they're having a party. I see a
lot of cars parked in their driveway.
누가 알겠어요? 내 생각에는 저 사람들이 파티를 하는 것 같아요.
저 집의 진입로에 많은 차들이 주차되어 있는 것을 봤거든요.

W: Another party? This is the third time this week! I've
had enough. We need to do something about it.
또 파티요? 이번 주만 해도 벌써 세 번째네요! 난 참을 만큼 참았어
요. 이 문제에 대해 뭔가를 해야만 해요.

M: What do you suggest we do? 우리가 뭘 하면 될까요?

W: Should we go talk to them about it?
저 사람들한테 가서 이 문제에 대해 이야기를 해야 할까요?

M: That would be a waste of time. I would prefer

calling the police and filing a complaint.
그건 시간 낭비가 될 거예요. 경찰을 불러서 민원을 넣는 것이 좋겠어요.

W: You're right. Hopefully they'll quiet down after that.
당신 말이 맞아요. 저 사람들이 이후로는 조용해지면 좋겠네요.

해설 'You're right.'라고 맞장구를 쳤으므로 동의의 표현이다.

어휘 noise 소음 next door 옆집 사람; 옆집에 You can say that again. 정말 그렇다. late at night 밤늦게 have a party 파티를 열다 driveway (도로에서 차고로 들어가는) 진입로 have had enough 진절머리가 나다, 더 이상 못 참다 a waste of time 시간 낭비 file a complaint 민원을 넣다, 항의를 제기하다 hopefully 바라건대 quiet down 조용해지다

10 ③

W: Hi, what are you looking for?
안녕하세요, 무엇을 찾고 계신가요?

M: I need to buy some writing materials and a notepad. 저는 필기구 몇 개랑 뜯어 쓰는 메모지가 필요해요.

W: The pens, pencils, and highlighters are in this section, and the notepads are in the back of the store. 펜, 연필, 그리고 형광펜은 이쪽 코너에 있고요, 메모지는 가게 안쪽에 있습니다.

M: How much does everything cost?
물건들은 모두 가격이 얼마죠?

W: The pens and pencils are two dollars each, the highlighters are four dollars each, and the notepad is six dollars. 펜하고 연필은 개당 2달러고, 형광펜은 개당 4달러, 그리고 메모지는 6달러입니다.

M: Okay. I'll buy a pencil, a pen, a highlighter, and a notepad. 알겠습니다. 연필 하나, 펜 하나, 형광펜 하나, 그리고 메모지 하나를 살게요.

어휘 look for ~을 찾다 highlighter 형광펜 notepad (뜯어 쓰는) 메모지 section 구역 in the back of ~의 안쪽에

11 ⑤

M: Laura, which team are you cheering for?
로라, 넌 어떤 팀을 응원하니?

W: The Hawks, of course! They're the best football team ever!
물론 '호크스'지. 그들은 역사상 최고의 미식축구 팀이야.

M: Oh please. No team will ever be better than The Bears.
아, 제발. 어떤 팀도 '베어스'보다 잘하지는 못할 거야.

W: Nonsense! Let's make a bet. If your team loses, you have to buy me coffee. If my team loses, I'll buy you coffee.
말도 안 돼! 우리 내기하자. 너네 팀이 지면 넌 나한테 커피를 사야 해. 우리 팀이 지면 내가 너한테 커피를 살게.

M: That's fine with me! I'm confident that The Bears will win this game. 그 조건이면 난 좋아! 난 '베어스'가 이번 경기를 이길 거라고 자신해.

W: Oh, look! The Hawks just scored a touchdown.
아, 저것 봐! '호크스'가 방금 터치다운으로 득점을 올렸어.

M: No! That means the score is already thirty-six to eighteen! 안돼! 그렇다면 벌써 점수가 36대 18이라는 거잖아!

W: That's right. I'm pretty sure you're going to end up buying me coffee.
맞아. 난 결국 네가 커피를 사게 될 거라는 확신이 드는 걸.

해설 football은 미국영어로는 미식축구, 영국영어로는 축구를 가리킨다. touchdown, 36 to 18과 같은 힌트로 정답을 알 수 있다.

어휘 cheer for ~을 응원하다 football 미식축구; 축구 best ~ ever 역대 최고의 nonsense 말도 안 되는 소리 make a bet 내기하다 confident 자신 있는, 확신하는 score 득점하다; 점수 touchdown (미식축구의) 터치다운 pretty 매우, 꽤 end up -ing 결국 ~하게 되다

12 ②

W: To all visitors: First of all, we would like to welcome you all to our zoo. This announcement is to introduce our bus tour through The Lost Safari. You can enjoy this tour starting on November thirtieth. You will be able to see tigers, lions, bears, zebras, and many more animals up close! You will also have the opportunity to feed the animals while on the bus. For your safety, we ask that you stay on the bus, and please keep your hands and feet inside the metal railings. Admission is free for children and twenty dollars for adults.

모든 방문객들께 알립니다: 먼저 저희 동물원을 찾아 주신 모든 분들을 환영합니다. 이 안내방송은 '더 로스트 사파리'를 통과하는 저희의 버스 투어를 소개하는 내용입니다. 여러분은 11월 30일부터 이 투어를 즐길 수 있습니다. 여러분은 호랑이, 사자, 곰, 얼룩말, 그리고 더 많은 동물을 가까이에서 볼 수 있을 것입니다. 여러분은 또한 버스를 탄 상태로 동물들에게 먹이를 줄 수 있는 기회를 갖게 됩니다. 여러분의 안전을 위해, 버스 안에만 머무를 것과 손과 발이 금속 철책을 벗어나지 않을 것을 요청 드립니다. 입장료는 어린이는 무료이고, 성인은 20달러입니다.

어휘 first of all 먼저, 우선 announcement 안내방송, 발표 tour 여행, 관광 through ~을 통해 starting ~부터 zebra 얼룩말 up close 바로 가까이에서 have the opportunity 기회를 갖다 feed 먹이를 주다 while ~하는 동안에 safety 안전 metal railing 금속 철조망 admission 입장(료)

13 ③

| 유진의 수업 일정 |

수업 번호	요일/시간
생물학 101	월요일, 수요일 / 오후 12시
독서 201	월요일, 화요일 / 오후 1시 30분
역사 201	목요일 / 오후 1시
수학 401	금요일 / 오전 11시
작문 302	금요일 / 오후 12시 30분

① Biology one oh one is Eugene's only class on Wednesday. 생물학 101은 유진의 유일한 수요일 수업이다.

② After the Reading two oh one class, Eugene is done with classes on Tuesday.
독서 201 수업이 끝난 후에 유진은 화요일 수업을 마치게 된다.

③ Eugene's one P.M. class on Thursday is the Math four oh one class.
목요일 오후 1시에 있는 유진의 수업은 수학 401 수업이다.

④ Eugene has to go to the History two oh one class every Thursday.
유진은 매주 목요일에 역사 201 수업에 가야 한다.

⑤ On Friday, Eugene will learn how to write essays and research papers.
금요일에 유진은 리포트와 연구 논문을 쓰는 방법을 배울 것이다.

[해설] 미국의 학교에서는 과목명 뒤에 숫자를 붙여 단계를 표시한다. ③은 History 수업에 대한 것이다. ⑤는 Writing 수업을 'write essays and research papers'와 같이 설명으로 대신했다.

[어휘] biology 생물학 be done with ~을 다 하다
essay 에세이, 리포트 research paper 연구 보고서, 논문

14 ⑤

M: To play this sport, you need at least two people. It is played on a court with a net secured in the middle of it. The net is fixed on the ground and is about waist high. One person stands on one side of the court, and the other person stands on the opposite side. You use a racket to hit a small green ball. One person serves the ball, and the other person receives the ball. If the ball hits the net and doesn't make it over, the other player gets the point.

이 스포츠를 하려면 적어도 두 사람이 필요하다. 이 스포츠는 코트 중앙에 네트를 고정시킨 상태에서 하게 된다. 네트는 지면에 고정되어 있고, 대략 허리 높이이다. 한 사람이 코트의 한쪽에 서고, 다른 사람은 반대쪽에 선다. 당신은 라켓을 이용해 작은 초록색 공을 친다. 한 사람이 서브를 넣고, 다른 사람은 공을 받는다. 공이 네트를 맞고 넘어가지 못하면 상대 선수가 점수를 얻는다.

[해설] 적어도 두 사람 이상이 필요하다고 했으므로, 육상, 권투, 테니스 등으로 정답을 압축할 수 있다. 초록색 공, 서브와 리시브는 테니스와 관련이 있다.

[어휘] at least 적어도 court 코트 secure 단단히 고정시키다
in the middle of ~의 중앙에 fixed 고정된 waist 허리
opposite 반대편의, 맞은편의 racket 라켓 serve 서브를 넣다

15 ④

M: I'm so exhausted. All this construction work is wearing me out.
난 너무 지쳤어. 이 모든 건축 공사가 나를 지치게 만들고 있어.

W: Are you getting muscle aches in your back again?
너 등에 다시 근육통이 도진 거니?

M: I sure am. I get cramps in my legs during the day, too. 확실히 그런 것 같아. 낮에는 다리에 쥐도 난다니까.

W: There's a spa in the neighborhood. I think you should go. 이 근처에 스파가 있어. 넌 거기 가야 할 것 같아.

M: Oh, really? Have you been there before?
아, 정말? 너 전에 거기 가본 적 있어?

W: Yeah, I go once a month to get a foot and shoulder massage.
응, 난 발하고 어깨 마사지를 받으러 한 달에 한 번 그곳에 가.

M: It's relaxing just thinking about it. I'll go later today to get one. 생각만 해도 몸이 나른해지는 것 같다. 마사지를 받으러 오늘 이따가 가봐야겠어.

W: Great. But make sure you call and make a reservation. They're usually fully booked.
좋아. 하지만 꼭 전화를 하고 예약을 하도록 해. 보통은 예약이 꽉 차 있거든.

M: Yes, I will. Thanks. 응, 그럴게. 고마워.

[어휘] exhausted 지친 construction work 건축 공사 wear somebody out ~을 지치게 하다 muscle ache 근육통 get cramps 쥐가 나다 spa 스파, 온천 in the neighborhood 근처에, 이웃에 once a month 한 달에 한 번 relaxing 편안한, 나른한 make sure 확실히 ~하다 make a reservation 예약하다 fully booked 예약이 꽉 찬

16 ③

M: What are you doing for Independence Day?
넌 독립기념일에 뭘 할 거니?

W: I have no idea, yet. Do you have any suggestions?
아직은 계획이 없어. 제안할 만한 게 있니?

M: I heard there's going to be fireworks by the lake on Wednesday and Saturday.
수요일하고 토요일에 호숫가에서 불꽃놀이가 있을 거라고 들었어.

W: Oh, really? The last time I saw fireworks was three years ago! What time do they start? 아, 정말? 내가 마지막으로 불꽃놀이를 본 게 3년 전이야! 몇 시에 시작한대?

M: It starts at seven P.M. on Wednesday and eight P.M. on Saturday.
수요일은 오후 7시에 시작하고, 토요일은 오후 8시에 시작해.

W: Hmm, I'm going on a family trip over the weekend, so I can't go on Saturday.
음, 난 주말에는 가족여행을 가기 때문에 토요일에는 못 가.

M: That's fine. I'll see you at the first fireworks show then. 좋아. 그럼 첫 번째 불꽃놀이를 할 때 보자.

W: Alright! I'll look forward to it. 알았어! 난 그걸 기대할게.

[어휘] Independence Day (미국의) 독립기념일 have no idea 하나도 모르다 suggestion 제안 fireworks 불꽃놀이 go on a family trip 가족여행을 가다 over the weekend 주말에 look forward to -ing ~을 고대하다

17 ⑤

M: Sarah bought a purse from a department store last

Tuesday. The zipper on her purse broke a week later. Today, she took it to the store to ask them to exchange the item for a new one. But Sarah didn't have her receipt, so the store could not help her. Sarah did not know what to do. So she decided to ask the store worker if there is a purse repair shop in the area. In this situation, what would Sarah most likely say to the worker?

사라는 지난 화요일에 백화점에서 지갑을 샀다. 지갑에 달린 지퍼가 일주일 후에 망가졌다. 오늘 그녀는 지갑을 상점으로 들고 가서 새 지갑으로 교환해 달라고 요구했다. 하지만 사라는 영수증을 가지고 있지 않았기 때문에 상점은 그녀를 도울 수 없었다. 사라는 어떻게 해야 할지 몰랐다. 그래서 그녀는 상점 직원에게 그 지역에 지갑 수리점이 있는지 묻기로 결심했다. 이 상황에서 사라는 직원에게 무슨 말을 하겠는가?

Sarah: Can I get my purse fixed somewhere around here? 이 근처에서 제 지갑을 고칠 수 있나요?

① The zipper on my jacket is broken.
제 재킷의 지퍼가 망가졌어요.

② I would like to buy a new one.
새 것을 하나 사고 싶어요.

③ I would like the receipt in the bag, please.
영수증은 봉투에 넣어 주세요.

④ Is there a car repair shop in this neighborhood?
이 근처에 자동차 수리점이 있나요?

⑤ Can I get my purse fixed somewhere around here?
이 근처에서 제 지갑을 고칠 수 있나요?

어휘 purse 지갑 department store 백화점 break 망가지다(break-broke-broken) item 물건, 품목 receipt 영수증 repair shop 수리점 area 지역 neighborhood 근처, 인근 get something fixed ~을 고치다 around here 이 근처에

18 ③

M: I'm going to Turkey with my sister for vacation. Can you recommend any tourist sites? 난 방학을 맞아서 여동생과 함께 터키에 갈 거야. 관광지를 추천해 줄래?

W: If I were you, I would definitely check out the mosques. 내가 너라면 난 반드시 모스크를 살펴볼 거야.

M: I already have that on my list. Is there anywhere else I should go?
그건 이미 내 리스트에 있어. 내가 가야만 하는 다른 곳이 있을까?

W: Hmm, when I was there, I personally enjoyed riding a hot air balloon.
음, 내가 거기 있었을 때 난 개인적으로 열기구를 타는 것을 즐겼어.

M: Hot air balloon? That sounds scary to me. How was it? 열기구? 나한테는 무섭게 들리는데. 어땠어?

W: It wasn't scary at all. I rode it, and it was the best time of my life! 그건 전혀 무섭지 않았어. 내가 그것을 탔을 때가 내 인생 최고의 시간이었어!

M: In that case, I'll have to ride it while I'm there.

그렇다면 내가 거기에 있는 동안 그걸 타야겠구나.

W: Good thinking. You're going to have a blast!
좋은 생각이야! 넌 정말 즐거운 시간을 보낼 거야!

어휘 recommend 추천하다 tourist site 관광지 if I were you 내가 너라면 definitely 반드시, 확실히 check out 살펴보다; 점검하다 mosque 이슬람 사원, 모스크 on one's list ~의 목록에 personally 개인적으로 ride a hot air balloon 열기구를 타다 not ~ at all 전혀 ~ 아닌 in that case 그렇다면, 그런 경우에 have a blast 아주 즐거운 시간을 보내다

19 ①

W: My children drew all over the white wallpaper in the dining room.
우리 애들이 주방의 흰색 벽지에 온통 그림을 그렸어.

M: Oh my goodness. What are you going to do about it? 아, 맙소사. 그걸 어떻게 할 거야?

W: As of now, I'm not sure. Has this happened to you before? 지금으로서는 잘 모르겠어. 너한테도 이런 일이 전에 일어난 적이 있니?

M: No, but I have an idea on what you should do.
아니, 하지만 네가 뭘 해야 할지 나한테 생각이 있어.

W: What's your idea? 네 생각은 뭐야?

M: Why don't you change your wallpaper? That way you can remodel the house and clean up the mess at the same time. 너네 벽지를 바꾸는 게 어때? 그렇게 하면 집안을 리모델링도 하고 동시에 엉망이 된 것도 깨끗하게 치울 수 있잖아.

W: Hmm, now that I think about it, the wallpaper was a bit dirty. Plus, new wallpaper will make the house look cleaner, too! I think there will be a lot of benefits from changing it. Thanks for the idea!
음, 이제 와서 생각해 보니까 벽지는 약간 더러웠어. 게다가 새 벽지가 집안을 보다 깨끗하게 만들 수도 있잖아! 벽지를 바꾸면 좋은 점이 많을 것 같아. 아이디어 고마워!

M: I'm glad I could help you out.
나도 너를 도울 수 있어서 기뻐.

① Kill two birds with one stone. 일석이조.

② Two heads are better than one. 백지장도 맞들면 낫다.

③ All roads lead to Rome. 모든 길은 로마로 통한다.

④ Strike while the iron is hot. 쇠뿔도 단김에 빼라.

⑤ Where there is a will, there is a way.
뜻이 있는 곳에 길이 있다.

해설 아이들이 그림을 그린 오래된 벽지를 바꾸면, 낙서가 없어지고 리모델링을 한 것처럼 집안도 화사해지는 두 가지 효과를 얻게 된다.

어휘 all over 온통, 곳곳에 wallpaper 벽지 dining room (밥을 먹는) 주방, 부엌 my goodness 어머나, 맙소사 as of now 현재로서는 that way 그렇게 하면, 그와 같이 remodel 리모델링하다, 개조하다 clean up 치우다 mess 엉망인 상태 at the same time 동시에 a bit 약간 plus 게다가 benefit 이점, 혜택

20 ⑤

W: Dad, I have to practice driving before my driver's license test on Saturday. 아빠, 저는 토요일에 있을 운전면허 시험을 보기 전에 연습을 해야 해요.

M: Would you like me to help you? We can use my car if you want. 아빠가 널 도와 줄까? 네가 원하면 우리는 내 차를 이용할 수 있어.

W: That would be great. Where should we go to practice? 그거 좋은데요. 우리는 어디로 연습하러 가야 해요?

M: I think the empty parking lot on Grover Lane will be a good place to start. 내 생각에는 그로버 레인에 있는 빈 주차장이 연습을 시작하기에 좋은 장소 같구나.

W: Yeah, I agree. After I try parking a few times, can we go out on the highway? 네, 저도 같은 생각이에요. 제가 몇 번 주차해본 후에 고속도로로 나갈 수 있는 거예요?

M: I don't think you're ready to do that yet. 내 생각에 넌 아직 그렇게 할 준비는 안된 것 같다.

① What time is your driver's license test? 네 운전면허 시험이 몇 시에 있니?

② Don't be upset. You'll pass the test next time. 속상해하지 마. 다음에는 시험을 통과할 거다.

③ Good luck on your test! You'll pass, don't worry. 시험 잘 보렴! 넌 합격할 거니까, 걱정하지 마.

④ Look at all this traffic. Let's take a different route. 이 차들 좀 봐. 다른 길로 가자꾸나.

⑤ I don't think you're ready to do that yet. 내 생각에 넌 아직 그렇게 할 준비는 안된 것 같다.

해설 미국에서는 16살이 되면 운전면허증을 딸 수 있으며, 필기시험을 합격하면 동승자가 있는 상태에서 주행 연습을 하고 그 후에 실기시험을 본다.

어휘 practice 연습하다 driver's license test 운전면허 시험 empty 빈 parking lot 주차장 park 주차하다 highway 고속도로 traffic 차량, 교통량 route 길, 경로 pass (시험을) 통과하다, 합격하다

11회 실전모의고사
본문 p.126-127

01 ②	02 ③	03 ①	04 ④	05 ①
06 ②	07 ⑤	08 ②	09 ①	10 ①
11 ⑤	12 ②	13 ④	14 ③	15 ①
16 ③	17 ⑤	18 ②	19 ②	20 ⑤

01 ②

M: Good morning, welcome to Bloom's Clothing. Can I help you? 안녕하세요, 블룸스 클로딩에 어서 오세요. 무엇을 도와 드릴까요?

W: I'm looking for a blouse to wear to my piano recital. 저는 제 피아노 연주회 때 입을 블라우스를 찾고 있어요.

M: Okay. We have this one with ribbons, and we also have this one with lace on it. 네. 저희는 리본이 달린 이 블라우스와 레이스가 달린 이 블라우스도 있어요.

W: They look too fancy. I would like a simple design better. 둘 다 너무 화려해 보이네요. 저는 단순한 디자인이 더 좋아요.

M: Well then, how about this one with buttons on the front? 그럼, 앞에 단추가 달린 이 블라우스는 어떠세요?

W: I'd prefer a blouse without buttons. Are there any with pockets? 저는 단추가 없는 블라우스를 선호해요. 주머니가 달린 게 있나요?

M: Yes, there are. This one has a pocket on the front. Would you like to try it on? 네, 있습니다. 이 블라우스는 앞에 주머니가 있어요. 입어 보시겠어요?

W: Okay. I will try on this blouse in size small. Where are the fitting rooms? 네. 작은 사이즈의 이 블라우스를 입어 볼게요. 탈의실이 어디에 있죠?

M: They are over there at the back of the store. 탈의실은 매장 저쪽 뒤편에 있어요.

해설 여자는 리본, 레이스, 단추 등이 없고 주머니가 있는 블라우스를 골랐다.

어휘 recital 연주회 lace 레이스 fancy 화려한, 장식이 많은 try on 입어 보다 fitting room 탈의실 at the back of ~의 뒤쪽에

02 ③

[Telephone rings.] [전화벨이 울린다.]

M: Hey, Danielle, this is Jared calling. 안녕, 다니엘, 나 재러드야.

W: Hi! It's been a long time since we've talked. How have you been? 안녕! 우리가 통화한지 정말 오랜만이구나. 잘 지냈니?

M: I've been terrific, thanks for asking. I'm calling to ask you about Mr. Rogers' chemistry class. 아주 잘 지냈어, 물어봐 주어서 고마워. 너한테 로저스 선생님의 화학 수업에 대해서 물어보려고 전화했어.

W: Sure! What would you like to know about it? 좋지! 그 수업의 무엇에 관해 알고 싶니?

M: Well, I'm planning on taking it this semester. But I wanted to know how hard the class is. 음, 내가 이번 학기에 그 수업을 들으려고 계획 중이야. 그런데 그 수업이 얼마나 힘든지 알고 싶었어.

W: Hmm... It depends on how hard you study. You have to take three tests and do a lot of assignments, too. 음, 그건 네가 얼마나 열심히 공부하느냐에 달려 있지. 너는 세 번의 시험을 봐야 하고, 숙제도 많이 해야 해.

M: Wow! That sounds like a lot of work. I'm not sure I can handle it. 와! 할 일이 정말 많은 것 같구나. 내가 해낼 수 있을지 모르겠어.

W: You should definitely think about it before signing up. 너는 신청하기 전에 반드시 그것에 대해 생각해야 해.

M: Alright, thanks for the advice! 알겠어, 충고 고마워!

어휘 terrific 아주 좋은　chemistry 화학　semester 학기　depend on ~에 달려 있다　assignment 숙제, 과제　handle 다루다, 처리하다　definitely 분명히, 확실히

03 ①

① M: I would like a cup of tea, please. 차 한 잔 부탁해요.

W: Here you are. Be careful not to spill it. It's very hot. 여기 있습니다. 쏟지 않도록 조심하세요. 무척 뜨겁습니다.

② M: Can I get you something to drink? 마실 것 좀 드릴까요?

W: No, that's okay. Thank you for the thought. 아니요, 괜찮습니다. 생각해 주셔서 감사합니다.

③ M: The weather is so hot! My drink is melting. 날씨가 정말 덥네요! 제 음료수가 녹고 있어요.

W: Here, you should put some ice cubes in it. 여기요, 음료 안에 얼음 조각을 좀 넣으세요.

④ M: Are you ready to go running? 달리기하러 갈 준비가 됐나요?

W: Just a minute. Let me fill my water bottle. 잠시만요. 물병에 물을 채울게요.

⑤ M: What do you want to eat? 무엇을 먹고 싶나요?

W: Let's order pizza for dinner today. 오늘은 저녁으로 피자를 주문하죠.

어휘 spill 엎지르다, 쏟다　melt 녹다　ice cube (네모난) 얼음　water bottle 물병

04 ④

M: Hello, ma'am. Are you looking for anything in particular? 안녕하세요, 손님. 특별히 찾으시는 게 있나요?

W: Yes, I need to buy a new flower vase. My husband dropped my old one and it broke into pieces. 네, 새로운 꽃병을 사야 하거든요. 제 남편이 오래된 제 꽃병을 떨어뜨리는 바람에 산산조각이 났어요.

M: I'm sorry to hear that. Would you be interested in this tall, skinny vase? 안타깝게 됐군요. 길고 폭이 좁은 이 꽃병은 어떠신가요?

W: No, I won't be able to fit a lot of flowers in it. I normally put an entire bouquet in the vase at one time. 아니요, 그 꽃병에는 많은 꽃을 넣을 수가 없을 거예요. 저는 보통 한 번에 꽃 한 다발을 꽃병에 넣거든요.

M: I see. This round, wide vase may be better for you. 알겠습니다. 둥글고 넓은 이 꽃병이 손님에게 더 좋겠네요.

W: It seems nice, but I think this tall, wide one with the flower print is the one I want. 멋지게 보이는데, 제 생각에는 꽃무늬가 있는 이 길고 넓은 꽃병이 제가 찾던 것 같네요.

M: Sure, this vase is one of our best selling items. Would you like me to wrap it up for you?

그렇군요, 이 꽃병은 저희 집에서 가장 잘 팔리는 상품 중 하나예요. 포장해 드릴까요?

W: Yes, that would be wonderful. I wouldn't want it to break on the way back home. 네, 그럼 정말 좋겠네요. 집으로 가져가는 길에 깨지지 않았으면 좋겠거든요.

M: Here you go. Have a nice day! 여기 있습니다. 좋은 하루 보내세요!

해설 여자는 'It seems nice, but'이라고 말하며 남자의 제안을 거절한 후 'I think ~'로 자신의 의견을 말하고 있다.

어휘 break into pieces 산산조각이 나다　skinny 폭이 좁은; 깡마른　fit (모양, 크기가) 맞다　bouquet 꽃다발　flower print 꽃무늬　best selling 가장 많이 팔리는　wrap up 포장하다

05 ①

M: Michelle, you need to work on passing the ball to other players on the team. 미셸, 너는 팀의 다른 선수들에게 공을 패스하는 연습을 할 필요가 있어.

W: I'm trying, but I don't seem to improve. For me, passing the ball is the hardest part of playing soccer.
노력하고 있는데, 하지만 실력이 향상되는 것 같지 않아요. 저에겐, 공을 패스하는 것이 축구를 할 때 가장 어려운 부분이에요.

M: I understand. Every player has a weak point. 이해해. 모든 선수들은 약점을 가지고 있지.

W: I'll practice every day for a few hours. Hopefully I'll get better at it. 저는 매일 몇 시간씩 연습할 거예요. 점점 잘할 수 있으면 좋겠어요.

M: If you want, I can help you. We can pass the ball to each other. 네가 원한다면 내가 너를 도와줄 수 있어. 우리는 서로 공을 패스할 수 있어.

W: That would be great! Can we use the field right now? 그럼 정말 좋겠네요! 우리가 지금 경기장을 사용할 수 있나요?

M: I think there are other teams who will be using the field today. 내 생각에 오늘은 경기장을 사용하는 다른 팀이 있을 것 같구나.

W: I'll meet you here tomorrow night. 내일 밤에 여기서 만나요.

M: Alright, I'll see you then. 알았어, 그때 보자.

해설 여자는 soccer(축구)에 관해 말하고, 남자는 여자의 약점을 알려주면서 같이 연습을 하자고 했으므로 여자는 축구선수, 남자는 감독이다.

어휘 pass the ball 공을 패스하다　improve 향상되다　the hardest part 가장 어려운 부분　weak point 약점　hopefully 바라건대　field 경기장

06 ②

M: Oh my goodness, this is terrible! 맙소사, 이건 정말 끔찍하군!

W: What's the matter? Did something happen to your car? 무슨 일이야? 네 차에 무슨 일 생겼니?

M: Yeah, look at this! I have a flat tire, and I need to be at an appointment in an hour. 응, 이것 좀 봐! 타이어에 펑크가 났는데, 난 한 시간 후에 약속 장소에 가야 하거든.

W: Is there anything I can do to help?
내가 도와줄 수 있는 게 있니?

M: Yes. Can you call the car repair shop and ask if they can send a mechanic over here?
응. 자동사 정비소에 전화해서 이곳으로 정비공을 보내줄 수 있는지 물어봐 줄래?

W: Sure, I'll do that. Do you think they can replace your tire in time? 그럼, 그렇게 할게. 그들이 시간 내에 타이어를 교체할 수 있을 것 같니?

M: I hope they can. I'm so stressed out. Why are all these bad things happening to me? Last week my side mirror broke, and now I have a flat tire.
그들이 할 수 있으면 좋겠어. 난 너무 스트레스를 받아. 나한테 왜 이런 모든 나쁜 일들이 생기는 거지? 지난주에는 내 사이드 미러가 부러졌고, 지금은 타이어에 펑크가 났잖아.

W: Cheer up! 기운 내!

어휘 flat tire 펑크 난 타이어 appointment 약속, 예약 car repair shop 자동차정비소 mechanic 정비사 over here 이쪽으로 replace 교체하다 side mirror (자동차의) 사이드 미러

07 ⑤

① M: I would like to check out this book.
이 책을 대출하고 싶어요.

W: Sure. May I see your library card?
네. 도서관 카드를 볼 수 있을까요?

② M: There are so many toys here.
여기엔 장난감이 정말 많이 있어.

W: Yeah, how are we going to choose one?
응, 우리가 어떻게 하나를 고르지?

③ M: What are you watching on TV?
TV에서 무엇을 보고 있니?

W: I'm watching a cooking show.
요리 프로그램을 보고 있어.

④ M: When is our homework assignment due?
우리 숙제 제출 기한이 언제까지니?

W: We have to turn it in by Monday.
우리는 그걸 월요일까지 제출해야 해.

⑤ M: Can you plug in the vacuum cleaner for me?
진공청소기의 전원을 연결해 줄래?

W: The lamp is already turned on.
램프는 이미 켜져 있어.

해설 ⑤는 vacuum cleaner에 관해 말했는데, lamp로 답했으므로 어색하다.

어휘 check out (도서관에서) 대출하다 show (방송) 프로그램, 쇼 turn something in ~을 제출하다 plug in 플러그를 꽂다 (↔ unplug 플러그를 뽑다) vacuum cleaner 진공청소기 lamp 램프, 등

08 ②

W: Honey, what are you doing? 여보, 뭐하고 있어요?

M: I'm reading a book in the bedroom. What's up?
침실에서 책을 읽고 있어요. 무슨 일이에요?

W: Can you come to the living room for a second?
잠깐 거실로 와줄 수 있어요?

M: Yeah, sure. [pause] Do you need something?
물론이죠. [잠시 후] 뭐가 필요해요?

W: Yes. I can't reach the top of the windows because I'm too short. Can you replace the curtains with these new ones? 네. 내 키가 너무 작아서 창문 위까지 닿질 않네요. 커튼을 새것으로 교체해 줄 수 있어요?

M: Of course. But I think the windows need to be cleaned first. They're so dirty! 물론이죠. 그런데 창문을 먼저 닦을 필요가 있는 것 같아요. 너무 더럽네요!

W: You're right. I'll clean the windows before you change the curtains. 당신 말이 맞아요. 당신이 커튼을 교체하기 전에 제가 창문을 닦을게요.

M: Okay, that sounds like a good plan. What should I do with the old curtains?
알겠어요, 좋은 계획 같아요. 그럼 오래된 커튼은 어떻게 하죠?

W: You can give them to me. I'll put them in the washing machine.
그건 나한테 주면 돼요. 내가 세탁기에 넣을게요.

해설 누가 누구에게 부탁하는 일인지 확인해야 오답을 피할 수 있다. 여자의 대사 'Can you ~?'에 부탁 내용이 나온다.

어휘 for a second 잠시 동안 reach (손이) 닿다 short 키가 작은 replace A with B A를 B로 교체하다 washing machine 세탁기

09 ①

M: Hey, Linda. I didn't think I'd see you at the hair salon. What a nice surprise!
야, 린다. 미용실에서 널 만날 줄은 생각도 못했어. 정말 놀랍네!

W: I know! Are you here to get a haircut?
나도! 넌 머리 자르러 왔니?

M: Yes, I am. How about you? What are you going to do with your hair? 응, 그래. 너는? 네 머리를 어떻게 하려고?

W: I haven't decided yet. Maybe I'll get a perm and dye it. What do you think? 난 아직 결정을 못했어. 아마 파마를 하고 염색을 할 것 같아. 어떻게 생각해?

M: Well, I can't picture you with curly hair. You look good with straight hair. 음, 네가 파마머리 한 것은 상상이 안돼. 넌 생머리를 했을 때 예뻐 보여.

W: Really? Then maybe I should get it cut and dye it.
그래? 그럼 머리를 자르고 염색을 해야 할까 봐.

M: That seems like a good idea. Do you have any colors in mind?
그게 좋은 생각 같아. 생각하고 있는 색깔은 있니?

W: I was thinking either light brown or dark brown.
연한 갈색 아니면 짙은 갈색을 생각하고 있었어.

M: Hmm… <u>Why don't you</u> try dying your hair <u>red</u>?
음, 머리를 빨간색으로 염색해 보는 건 어때?

해설 'Why don't you ~?'는 제안을 할 때 자주 나오는 표현이다.

어휘 hair salon 미용실   get a haircut 머리를 자르다   get a perm 파마를 하다   dye 염색하다   picture 상상하다, 떠올리다   curly (머리가) 곱슬곱슬한   straight (머리가) 곧은   have something in mind ~을 염두에 두다   light brown 연한 갈색

10 ①

M: Ma'am, may I help you find something?
손님, 제가 좀 도와드릴까요?

W: Yes, please. <u>Where</u> are Vitamin Ultra and Vitamin Plus? 네, 도와주세요. 비타민 울트라와 비타민 플러스는 어디 있나요?

M: They are <u>right</u> <u>over</u> <u>here</u>. Would you like a bottle of each? 바로 여기에 있어요. 각각 한 병씩 원하시나요?

W: Yeah. <u>How much</u> is it for each <u>bottle</u>?
네. 한 병당 얼마죠?

M: Vitamin Ultra costs <u>fifty</u> dollars each, and Vitamin Plus costs <u>seventy</u> dollars each. 비타민 울트라는 하나에 50달러이고 비타민 플러스는 하나에 70달러입니다.

W: Okay. I have this buy-one-get-one-free <u>coupon</u>. Can I use it? 알겠어요. 저한테 하나를 사면 하나를 무료로 받을 수 있는 쿠폰이 있어요. 그걸 사용할 수 있을까요?

M: Of course. But in that case, you have to <u>pay</u> for the <u>product</u> that <u>costs</u> <u>more</u>. 물론이죠. 하지만 그런 경우에 손님께서는 더 비싼 상품에 대한 값을 지불하셔야 해요.

W: So, if I buy Vitamin Plus, I get Vitamin Ultra <u>for free</u>, correct? 그럼, 제가 비타민 플러스를 사면 비타민 울트라를 무료로 받는 거죠, 맞이요?

M: Yes, ma'am. Your <u>total</u> is seventy dollars.
네, 손님. 합계는 70달러입니다.

W: Wait a minute. I <u>changed</u> my <u>mind</u>. I would just like to purchase Vitamin Ultra today. I'll come back next time to buy Vitamin Plus.
잠시만요. 생각이 바뀌었어요. 오늘은 그냥 비타민 울트라만 살게요. 다음에 비타민 플러스를 사러 다시 올게요.

해설 여자는 70달러짜리 제품을 사고 50달러짜리 제품을 무료로 받으려고 했다가, 마음을 바꿔서 50달러짜리 제품만 샀다.

어휘 bottle 병   cost (값·비용이) ~이다   buy-one-get-one-free 하나를 사면 하나를 무료로 받는   change one's mind 생각을 바꾸다   purchase 구매하다

11 ⑤

W: Sir, I would like to <u>talk</u> to you <u>about</u> your <u>daughter</u>.
아버님, 따님에 대해 이야기를 좀 나누고 싶어요.

M: Sure. Should I be <u>concerned</u> <u>about</u> her?
네. 제가 그 애에 대해 걱정을 해야 하는 건가요?

W: Well, she's <u>having</u> a <u>hard</u> <u>time</u> getting used to the people here. She cries every time you leave her

here. 사실, 따님은 여기 있는 사람들과 친해지는 데 어려움을 겪고 있어요. 아버님이 따님을 여기 두고 가실 때마다 울거든요.

M: Oh, I <u>had</u> <u>no</u> <u>idea</u>. Does she <u>get</u> <u>along</u> <u>with</u> the other children?
아, 저는 전혀 몰랐어요. 제 딸이 다른 아이들과 잘 지내나요?

W: She normally <u>plays</u> <u>by</u> <u>herself</u>. We're starting to think that this isn't the best place for her to stay.
보통은 혼자 놀아요. 저희는 이곳이 따님에게 최적의 장소가 아니라고 생각하기 시작했어요.

M: I see, but there is <u>nothing</u> <u>I</u> <u>can</u> <u>do</u>. My wife and I both work during the day, and there's <u>nobody</u> to <u>look</u> <u>after</u> her.
알겠습니다. 하지만 제가 할 수 있는 게 없네요. 제 아내와 저는 둘 다 낮에 일을 하고, 아이를 돌봐줄 사람이 없어요.

W: Okay. Let's talk about this more when you come to <u>pick</u> her <u>up</u>.
네. 따님을 데리러 오실 때 좀 더 이야기를 나누도록 하죠.

M: Alright. I'll be here around six P.M.
알겠습니다. 저는 오후 6시쯤 이곳에 도착할 겁니다.

어휘 be concerned about ~에 관심을 가지다, 걱정하다   have a hard time 힘든 시간을 보내다   get used to ~에 익숙해지다   have no idea 전혀 모르다   get along with ~와 잘 지내다   normally 보통은   by oneself 혼자, 다른 사람 없이   look after 돌보다   pick somebody up ~을 찾으러 오다, 차에 태우다   daycare center 어린이집, 탁아소

12 ②

W: To all of you who signed up to <u>participate in</u> the Spring Mint <u>Singing</u> <u>Contest</u> on <u>September</u> <u>twentieth</u>, we would like to <u>make</u> an <u>announcement</u>. There have been over one <u>thousand</u> people who <u>signed</u> <u>up</u> for our contest. However, we only have <u>time</u> <u>for</u> <u>ten</u> people. In order to choose our final <u>performers</u>, we will be <u>having</u> <u>auditions</u> on September <u>seventh</u> and September <u>eighth</u>. In order to <u>set</u> <u>up</u> an audition <u>time</u>, please <u>call</u> or <u>text</u> <u>message</u> two one oh, two three nine one.

9월 20일에 있을 스프링 민트 노래자랑 대회에 등록해 주신 모든 참가자 분들께 발표해드릴 사항이 있습니다. 이번 대회에는 천 명이 넘는 분들이 등록해 주셨습니다. 하지만 저희는 열 명을 위한 시간이 있을 뿐입니다. 최종 공연자를 선정하기 위해, 저희는 9월 7일과 8일에 오디션을 개최하려고 합니다. 오디션 시간을 정하기 위해 210-2391로 전화나 문자 메시지를 보내 주시기 바랍니다.

어휘 sign up 등록하다   participate in ~에 참가하다   singing contest 노래자랑 대회   make an announcement 발표하다   final 최종의   performer 공연자   have an audition 오디션을 갖다   in order to ~하기 위해   set up 정하다   text message 문자 메시지를 보내다

13 ④

	모비스 스키 리조트 요금	
①	스키 대여	시간당 10달러
②	스노보드 대여	시간당 20달러
③	썰매 대여	시간당 15달러
④	리프트권	종일권 10달러
⑤	장갑 대여	종일권 5달러

① At Moby's Ski Resort, you can <u>rent skis</u> for <u>ten</u> dollars an <u>hour</u>. 모비 스키 리조트에서 당신은 시간당 10달러 에 스키를 대여할 수 있습니다.

② It costs <u>twenty</u> dollars per hour to rent a <u>snowboard</u>. 스노보드를 대여하는 데 시간당 20달러가 듭니다.

③ Do you want to ride a <u>sled</u>? Rent one for <u>fifteen</u> dollars an hour.
당신은 썰매를 타고 싶나요? 시간당 15달러에 하나를 빌리세요.

④ You can purchase a <u>lift ticket</u> at the resort for <u>ten</u> dollars per hour.
리프트권은 리조트에서 시간당 10달러에 구매할 수 있습니다.

⑤ If you forgot to bring your <u>gloves</u>, don't worry. You can rent some for <u>five</u> dollars and use them <u>all day</u>.
만약에 장갑을 챙기는 것을 잊었다면, 걱정할 것 없습니다. 5달러에 대여해서 하루 종일 쓰실 수 있습니다.

해설 리프트권은 시간당이 아니라 종일 사용하는 데에 10달러이다.

어휘 rental 대여   per ~당   sled 썰매   lift (스키) 리프트
glove 장갑   rent 대여하다, 빌리다   all day 하루 종일

14 ③

M: People with this job <u>work</u> at <u>swimming pools</u>, <u>water parks</u>, <u>lakes</u>, and <u>oceans</u>. They are trained to help people who can't swim or are in <u>danger of drowning</u>. If you're in trouble, they will <u>jump into</u> the <u>water</u> to save you. They are great <u>swimmers</u>. Most of the time, they have a <u>whistle</u> around their <u>neck</u>, and <u>make sure</u> people are <u>safe</u> in the water.

이 직업을 가진 사람들은 수영장, 워터파크, 호수, 그리고 바다에서 일합니다. 그들은 수영을 못 하거나 익사할 위험에 빠진 사람들을 돕도록 훈련되었습니다. 만약 당신이 곤란에 처한다면, 그들은 당신을 구하기 위해 물에 뛰어들 것입니다. 그들은 수영을 아주 잘합니다. 대개 그들은 목에 호루라기를 걸고 다니며, 사람들이 물속에서 안전한지를 확인합니다.

어휘 swimming pool 수영장   lake 호수   be in danger 위험에 처하다   drown 익사하다   be in trouble 곤경에 빠지다
save 구하다, 구조하다   swimmer 수영할 줄 아는 사람   whistle 호루라기   around one's neck ~의 목에   make sure 확인하다, 확실히 하다

15 ①

M: Mom, my <u>head</u> <u>hurts</u>. I think I have a <u>fever</u>, too.
엄마, 제 머리가 아파요. 열도 있는 것 같아요.

W: Oh no! <u>How long</u> has this been going on?
아 이런! 얼마나 오래 이런 증상이 있었니?

M: I'm not sure, maybe a few hours. Now I'm starting to <u>cough</u>.
잘 모르겠어요, 아마 몇 시간 정도요. 이제 기침도 하기 시작했어요.

W: Why didn't you <u>tell</u> me <u>sooner</u>?
왜 더 일찍 얘기하지 않았니?

M: I didn't want you to worry. Plus, I'm <u>scared of getting</u> shots. 엄마를 걱정시켜 드리고 싶지 않았어요. 게다가, 주사를 맞는 것도 무서워요.

W: Still, you should have <u>let</u> me <u>know</u>. Let me <u>get</u> you some <u>medicine</u>.
그래도, 넌 나한테 알렸어야 해. 엄마가 약을 좀 줄게.

M: I already <u>took</u> some, but it's not <u>getting</u> any <u>better</u>.
약은 벌써 먹었는데, 나아지지가 않아요.

W: Well then, I need to <u>take</u> you to a <u>doctor</u>. I'll get my car keys.
자, 그럼, 널 병원에 데리고 가야겠구나. 자동차 열쇠를 가져올게.

어휘 have a fever 열이 나다   cough 기침하다   sooner 더 일찍   plus 게다가   be scared of ~을 두려워하다   get a shot 주사를 맞다   medicine 약   get better 나아지다, 호전되다

16 ③

M: Sandy, are you <u>going</u> on the mountain <u>bike trip</u> on November fourteenth?
샌디, 너 11월 14일에 있을 산악 자전거 여행을 갈 거니?

W: Yeah, I am. Didn't you say you were going, too?
응, 갈 거야. 너도 간다고 말하지 않았니?

M: You're right, but I haven't <u>signed up</u> yet.
맞아, 하지만 난 아직 등록을 안 했어.

W: Why haven't you? You <u>won't</u> be <u>able</u> to go if all the <u>spots</u> are <u>taken</u>. Only twenty people can go this year. 왜 안 했어? 모든 자리가 채워지면 너는 갈 수 없어. 올해는 겨우 20명만 갈 수 있어.

M: Oh, I didn't know that! Do you know <u>when</u> the <u>deadline</u> to sign up is?
아, 그건 몰랐어! 신청 마감일이 언제인지 아니?

W: Wait a minute. I <u>wrote</u> it <u>down</u> on my <u>calendar</u>. [pause] You have to sign up <u>by</u> November <u>twelfth</u>.
잠깐만 기다려. 내가 달력에 적어 뒀어. [잠시 후] 넌 11월 12일까지 신청해야 해.

M: November twelfth? That's <u>tomorrow</u>! I should <u>hurry</u> and sign up now.
11월 12일? 그건 내일이잖아! 지금 서둘러서 등록해야겠어.

W: Good idea. I hope there's a spot left for you.
잘 생각했어. 네 자리가 남아 있으면 좋겠다.

해설 11월 11일은 오늘, 12일은 신청 마감일, 그리고 14일은 산악 자전거 여행을 가는 날이다.

어휘 bike trip 자전거 여행   sign up 등록하다, 신청하다   yet 아직   spot 자리   deadline 마감일   write something down ~을 적다   calendar 달력   hurry 서두르다   left 남은

17 ⑤

M: Joe rides his bicycle everywhere he goes. But on his way home from school, the pedals broke. So, Joe asked Samantha if he could borrow her bicycle until his gets fixed. She let him use it right away. However, while he was riding it, the brakes stopped working. He was scared of what Samantha would say. He decided to tell her what happened and apologize. In this situation, what would Joe most likely say to Samantha?

조는 어딜 가던지 그의 자전거를 타고 다닌다. 하지만 학교에서 집으로 돌아가는 길에 페달이 부러졌다. 그래서 조는 사만다에게 그의 자전거를 수리할 때까지 그녀의 자전거를 빌릴 수 있는지 물어보았다. 그녀는 조가 자전거를 바로 사용할 수 있게 해주었다. 하지만 조가 자전거를 타는 동안에, 브레이크가 작동을 멈추었다. 그는 사만다가 무슨 말을 할지 두려웠다. 그는 사만다에게 무슨 일이 있었는지 이야기하고 사과하기로 결심했다. 이런 상황에서 조가 사만다에게 할 말로 가장 적절한 것은 무엇인가?

Joe: I'm so sorry about what happened. Can you forgive me?
이번 일은 정말 미안해. 나를 용서해 주겠니?

① My bike will be fixed by next Monday.
내 자전거는 다음 주 월요일까지 수리될 거야.
② Thank you for letting me borrow your bike.
네 자전거를 빌려 줘서 고마워.
③ How much does it cost to get my bike fixed?
내 자전거를 수리하는 데 비용이 얼마나 드니?
④ How much is the bicycle in the display window?
진열창에 있는 자전거는 얼마니?
⑤ I'm so sorry about what happened. Can you forgive me? 이번 일은 정말 미안해. 나를 용서해 주겠니?

어휘 ride one's bicycle 자전거를 타다   on one's way ~으로 가는 길에, 도중에   fix 수리하다, 고치다   be scared of ~을 두려워하다   apologize 사과하다   forgive 용서하다   display window 진열창

18 ②

M: Hannah, do you have plans for the weekend?
해나, 주말에 계획 있니?
W: No. I was supposed to go shopping with my friend, but that got cancelled.
없어. 친구랑 쇼핑 가기로 되어 있었는데, 취소됐어.
M: Oh, I see. Then will you go fishing with me on Sunday? My dad is taking me out on his boat, and he said I could bring a friend.
아, 알았어. 그럼 일요일에 나랑 낚시하러 갈래? 우리 아빠가 보트를 태워 주실 건데, 친구를 데려와도 된다고 하셨어.
W: I've never been fishing before, but that sounds exciting!
나는 전에 낚시를 해본 적이 없지만, 재미있을 것 같아!
M: I can teach you how to fish. It's actually really

simple.
내가 낚시하는 방법을 알려 줄 수 있어. 사실 정말 간단해.
W: Alright! I'll look forward to it. I like learning new things. 좋아! 기대되네. 난 새로운 것을 배우는 걸 좋아하거든.
M: Okay, I'll see you on Sunday. 알겠어, 일요일에 보자.

어휘 be supposed to ~하기로 되어 있다   cancel 취소하다   take somebody out ~을 외출시켜 주다   simple 간단한, 단순한   look forward to ~을 기대하다

19 ②

M: You've been working on that math problem for over two hours. 너는 두 시간 넘게 그 수학 문제를 풀고 있구나.
W: I know. I'm sick and tired of it. I'm about to give up. 나도 알아. 지겨워 죽겠어. 거의 포기하기 직전이야.
M: Let me take a look. I might be able to help you.
내가 한번 볼게. 내가 도울 수 있을 것 같아.
W: Here you are. I'm telling you, this problem is impossible to solve!
여기 있어. 내가 장담하지만, 이 문제를 푸는 건 불가능해!
M: Hmm… Give me a minute. [pause] You're right, this is really hard. I think I can solve the last part of the problem, but I don't know the first part.
음, 잠깐만 시간을 줘. [잠시 후] 네 말이 맞아, 이건 정말 어렵다. 내 생각에 내가 문제의 마지막 부분은 풀 수 있을 것 같은데, 첫 번째 부분을 모르겠어.
W: Oh, really? I can solve the first part. I was having trouble with the last part. 아, 정말? 난 첫 번째 부분을 풀 수 있어. 난 마지막 부분이 문제였어.
M: Then let's try solving it together. If we help each other, I'm sure we can do it.
그럼 같이 풀어 보자. 우리가 서로 도우면 반드시 풀 수 있을 거야.
W: That's a great idea. [pause] 좋은 생각이야. [잠시 후]
M: Yes! We finally solved it! It wouldn't have been possible without you.
좋아! 우리가 결국 풀었어! 네가 없었다면 불가능한 일이었을 거야.

① Like father, like son. 부전자전.
② Two heads are better than one. 백지장도 맞들면 낫다.
③ Kill two birds with one stone. 일석이조.
④ Even if the sky falls, there is a way out.
하늘이 무너져도 솟아날 구멍은 있다.
⑤ All work and no play makes Jack a dull boy.
공부만 하고 놀지 않으면 바보가 된다.

어휘 work on ~에 애를 쓰다   sick and tired of 아주 싫어진, 넌더리가 난   be about to 막 ~하려고 하다   give up 포기하다   take a look at ~을 한번 보다   impossible 불가능한(↔ possible 가능한)   solve (문제를) 풀다   have trouble with ~에 어려움을 겪다

20 ⑤

W: Hey, Peter. Did you feed the dog before we left home? 얘, 피터. 집에서 나오기 전에 개에게 먹이를 줬니?

M: Oh no. I completely forgot. What should we do?
아, 아니요. 완전히 까먹었네요. 우리가 뭘 해야 하죠?

W: How could you forget? I asked you three times!
넌 어떻게 잊을 수가 있니? 내가 너한테 세 번이나 부탁했잖아!

M: I'm sorry. Should we go back home?
죄송해요. 우리가 집으로 돌아가야 하나요?

W: It's too late now. We'll be late for the graduation ceremony. 지금은 너무 늦었어. 우리는 졸업식에 늦을 거야.

M: Okay then. Let's drive home as soon as it's over.
그럼 알겠어요. 끝나는 대로 차 타고 집으로 가요.

W: Our dog will probably be starving by the time we get back.
우리 개는 우리가 도착할 때까지는 굶주리게 될 거야.

① I'm hungry. Let's grab something to eat.
난 배고파. 뭐 좀 먹으러 가자.

② I need to buy some dog food before we leave.
우리가 떠나기 전에 개밥을 좀 사야 해.

③ The graduation ceremony will take place at 12 P.M.
졸업식은 오후 12시에 열릴 거야.

④ How long will it take to get to the graduation ceremony? 졸업식에 가는 데 얼마나 오래 걸리니?

⑤ Our dog will probably be starving by the time we get back. 우리 개는 우리가 도착할 때까지는 굶주리게 될 거야.

어휘 feed 먹이를 주다 completely 완전하게 three times 세 번 be late for ~에 늦다 graduation ceremony 졸업식 grab something to eat 간단히 뭔가를 먹다 take place 열리다 probably 아마도 starve 굶주리다 by the time ~할 때까지

12회 실전모의고사
본문 p.138-139

01	④	02	①	03	②	04	④	05	③
06	①	07	②	08	③	09	③	10	①
11	③	12	⑤	13	⑤	14	⑤	15	①
16	⑤	17	⑤	18	④	19	⑤	20	⑤

---

01 ④

M: Welcome to Wicked Costumes! May I help you?
위키드 의상에 오신 걸 환영합니다. 무엇을 도와드릴까요?

W: Yes. I need to buy a costume to wear to my friend's party. 네. 제 친구의 파티에서 입을 의상을 사야 해요.

M: That sounds like fun! Would you be interested in this rabbit costume? Or this witch costume?
재미있겠군요! 이 토끼 의상은 어떠세요? 아니면 이 마녀 의상은요?

W: They are great, but I would prefer the bumble bee or princess costumes.
모두 멋지네요, 하지만 저는 호박벌 또는 공주 의상이 더 좋아요.

M: Okay. There is only one more princess costume left, and it's on sale for twenty dollars.
알겠습니다. 공주 의상은 딱 한 벌이 남아 있고, 20달러에 판매되고 있습니다.

W: Really? That's a good price for a costume. I'll take it. 정말요? 의상 가격이 마음에 드네요. 그걸 살게요.

M: Alright. Would you like to buy a crown for an extra five dollars?
알겠습니다. 추가로 5달러를 내고 왕관을 구매하시겠어요?

W: Hmm… Yes, please. 음, 네, 주세요.

어휘 costume 의상, 복장 be interested in ~에 관심이 있다 witch 마녀 prefer 선호하다 bumble bee 호박벌 crown 왕관 extra 추가적인

---

02 ①

[Cellphone rings.] [휴대폰이 울린다.]

M: Hello, Megan? It's me, George. 안녕, 메건? 나, 조지야.

W: Hey, George! What's up? 아, 조지! 무슨 일이야?

M: I'm calling to ask about our science report.
우리 과학 보고서에 대해서 물어보려고 전화했어.

W: Sure. What do you need to know?
그래. 무엇을 알고 싶니?

M: Well, I wasn't listening in class when the teacher told us what to include in the report. Could you tell me what she said? 사실, 수업 시간에 선생님께서 보고서에 무엇을 포함시켜야 할지를 말씀하실 때 듣고 있지 않았거든. 선생님께서 뭐라고 하셨는지 말해 줄래?

W: Yeah, no problem. We have to write about the planets in the solar system.
그래, 물론이지. 우리는 태양계에 있는 행성들에 관해 써야 해.

M: I see. Thanks a lot. Have you finished your report?
그렇구나. 정말 고마워. 넌 보고서 작성을 끝냈니?

W: No, I'm actually in the middle of writing it right now.
아니, 사실 지금 보고서를 작성하고 있는 중이야.

어휘 report 보고서 include 포함하다 planet 행성 the solar system 태양계 actually 실은, 사실은 in the middle of ~하는 도중인

---

03 ②

① M: Would you like to go to the aquarium with me?
나랑 같이 수족관에 갈래?

W: Sure, when is a good time for you?
물론, 언제 가는 게 좋을까?

② M: Hey, look! Do you see those dolphins in the water?
얘, 저기 좀 봐! 물 속에 있는 저 돌고래들이 보이니?

W: Oh, wow! I've never seen dolphins this close before! 오, 우와! 난 이렇게 가까이서 돌고래를 본 적이 없어!

③ M: Which way is it to the dolphin show?
돌고래 쇼는 어느 쪽이죠?

W: It's that way. If you keep walking straight, you'll see it on your left.
저쪽이요. 직진해서 계속 걸어가시면, 왼쪽에 그것이 보일 거예요.

저쪽 길이에요. 계속 직진하시면, 왼쪽에 보일 거예요.

④ M: I'm going to the aquarium to see dolphins tomorrow. 난 내일 돌고래를 보러 수족관에 갈 거야.

W: Sounds like fun! I wish I could go, too.
재미있겠다! 나도 같이 갈 수 있으면 좋겠다.

⑤ M: Be careful not to fall in the water.
물에 빠지지 않도록 조심해.

W: It's okay. I'm a good swimmer. 괜찮아. 나는 수영을 잘해.

> **어휘** aquarium 수족관 dolphin 돌고래 close 가까이
> on one's left ~의 왼쪽에 fall in the water 물에 빠지다

04 ④

M: Good afternoon, ma'am. I am Officer Samuels. Could I speak with you for a moment?
안녕하세요, 부인. 저는 새뮤얼스 경관입니다. 잠시 이야기를 나눌 수 있을까요?

W: Yes, sir. Is there a problem?
네, 경관님. 무슨 문제가 있나요?

M: Well, I'm trying to catch a woman who lives around here. She robbed a bank and ran away.
음, 제가 이 근처에 살고 있는 여자 한 명을 잡으려고 합니다. 그 여자는 은행을 털고 달아났거든요.

W: Oh, that's terrible! What can I do to help?
아, 그건 끔찍하네요! 제가 무엇을 도와드릴 수 있을까요?

M: I'm going to describe her to you. Can you tell me if you've seen her in this café?
제가 그 여자를 묘사해 드릴게요. 이 카페에서 그 여자를 보신 적이 있는지 제게 말씀해 주실 수 있나요?

W: Alright, I'll do my best to help you. What does she look like?
그럼요, 최선을 다해 도와드릴게요. 그 여자는 어떻게 생겼죠?

M: She has short, curly hair and wears glasses. She was last seen wearing a short-sleeved T-shirt.
그 여자는 짧고 곱슬거리는 머리에 안경을 쓰고 있어요. 그 여자는 마지막 목격 당시에 반팔 티셔츠를 입고 있었습니다.

W: Hmm… I'm sorry. I haven't seen anyone like that.
음, 죄송해요. 그렇게 생긴 사람은 본 적이 없네요.

> **어휘** officer 경찰관, 장교, 공무원 for a moment 잠시 동안
> around here 이 근처에 rob a bank 은행을 털다, 은행 강도 짓을 하다 run away 달아나다 describe 설명하다, 묘사하다 curly 곱슬거리는 short-sleeved 반소매의

05 ③

M: You're doing great, Helen! You have five more push-ups left. 아주 잘하고 있어요, 헬렌! 이제 팔굽혀펴기 다섯 번만 하면 돼요.

W: Don't you think I've done enough? I'm so exhausted already. 제가 충분히 했다고 생각하지 않아요? 저는 이미 너무나 지쳤다고요.

M: Come on, you can do it! After push-ups you have to do some sit-ups, too. 힘내요, 당신은 할 수 있어요! 팔굽혀펴기를 한 다음에는 윗몸일으키기도 해야 해요.

W: Are you kidding me? This is the hardest day of exercise ever.
농담하는 거죠? 오늘이 가장 힘들게 운동한 날이에요.

M: I know, but this is the only way you're going to lose weight.
저도 알지만, 이게 당신이 살을 뺄 수 있는 유일한 방법이에요.

W: Alright, fine. What do you have planned for me after sit-ups?
그래, 좋아요. 윗몸일으키기 다음에는 무엇을 할 계획이죠?

M: I'm going to teach you how to use this fitness machine. 여기 있는 운동 기구의 사용법을 알려줄게요.

> **해설** 남자는 헬스클럽 트레이너, 여자는 살을 빼려고 하는 헬스클럽 회원이다.

> **어휘** push-up 팔굽혀펴기 enough 충분한; 충분히
> exhausted 지친, 기진맥진한 sit-up 윗몸일으키기 exercise
> 운동 lose weight 체중을 줄이다, 살을 빼다 fitness 운동, 건강

06 ①

M: I've only gotten three hours of sleep during the past two days. 나 지난 이틀 동안 세 시간밖에 못 잤어.

W: What? That's crazy. Why couldn't you sleep?
뭐? 그건 미친 짓이야. 왜 잠을 못 잤니?

M: I have to finish this history project by the end of this week. But it's taking me forever.
이번 주가 끝날 때까지 이 역사 프로젝트를 끝내야 하거든. 그런데 시간이 너무 오래 걸리네.

W: Hmm… How much do you have left to do?
음, 얼마나 많이 남았니?

M: I still have to make a poster, do some research, and prepare for a presentation. 나는 포스터를 만들어야 하고, 연구도 좀 해야 하고, 발표 준비도 해야 해.

W: Oh, my goodness! That sounds like a lot of work. How long is that going to take?
어머니! 할 일이 정말 많은 것 같다. 그게 시간이 얼마나 걸릴까?

M: I have no idea, but I feel like I'm never going to get this done.
모르겠어, 그런데 평생 못 끝낼 것 같다는 느낌이 들어.

> **해설** 남자뿐만 아니라 여자의 'That's crazy', 'Oh, my goodness!' 등의 말을 통해 남자의 절망적인 심정을 알 수 있다.

> **어휘** during ~동안 crazy 미친 by the end of ~의 끝까지
> take forever 시간이 엄청나게 오래 걸리다 do research
> 연구하다 presentation 발표 my goodness 맙소사, 어머나
> get something done ~을 끝마치다 hopeless 절망적인
> nervous 초조한 satisfied 만족한 disappointed 실망한

07 ②

① M: How many people are coming over for dinner?
저녁 식사에 얼마나 많은 사람들이 오나요?

W: I'm expecting about ten guests.
저는 열 명 정도 예상하고 있어요.

② M: I really like your new computer. When did you get

it? 네 새 컴퓨터가 정말 마음에 들어. 그걸 언제 샀니?

W: I bought it at the <u>electronics store downtown</u>.
난 그걸 시내에 있는 전자제품 매장에서 샀어.

③ M: Our <u>principal</u> is not <u>in</u> her <u>office</u> right now.
교장 선생님께서는 지금 교장실에 안 계십니다.

W: Okay, do you know <u>when</u> she'll be <u>here</u>?
알겠어요, 언제 여기 오시는지 아시나요?

④ M: I can't believe it's <u>snowing outside</u>!
밖에 눈이 내리는 걸 믿을 수가 없군!

W: I know! Let's go <u>make</u> a <u>snowman</u>.
맞아! 눈사람을 만들러 가자.

⑤ M: I'm at the <u>grocery</u> store. Do you need anything?
저는 지금 식료품점에 있어요. 뭐 필요한 게 있어요?

W: Yes, could you buy some ice cream?
네, 아이스크림 좀 사줄래요?

해설 ②의 질문에서 when으로 물었으므로 시기나 날짜로 답해야 한다.

어휘 come over for dinner 저녁 먹으러 오다   expect 예상하다, 기대하다   guest 손님   electronics store 전자제품 매장   downtown 시내에   principal 교장   snowman 눈사람 grocery store 식료품점

08 ③

W: Honey, the <u>remote control</u> is <u>broken</u>. The buttons aren't working.
여보, 리모컨이 고장 났어요. 버튼이 작동하지 않아요.

M: Are you sure? It was <u>working</u> a <u>second ago</u>. Let me see it.
확실해요? 방금 전까지만 해도 작동했거든요. 내가 한번 볼게요.

W: Here you go. 여기 있어요.

M: Hmm… I think the <u>batteries ran out</u>. We need to <u>replace</u> them.
음, 내 생각에는 건전지가 다된 것 같아요. 교체할 필요가 있겠어요.

W: Well, I don't think we have any <u>extra</u> ones at home.
그런데, 집에는 여분의 건전지가 없는 것 같아요.

M: You're right. <u>There</u> are <u>none</u> in the <u>drawer</u>. What should we do?
맞아요. 서랍에 하나도 없네요. 어떻게 할까요?

W: Why don't you <u>go</u> to the <u>store</u> and <u>get some</u>?
당신이 상점에 가서 좀 사오는 게 어때요?

M: Okay, I'll go right now. 좋아요, 내가 지금 바로 갈게요.

어휘 remote control 리모컨   broken 고장 난, 망가진   work 작동하다   sure 확실한   a second ago 방금 전에   battery 배터리, 건전지   run out 다 떨어지다, 고갈되다   replace 교체하다 extra 여분의, 추가의   drawer 서랍   right now 지금 바로

09 ③

[*Telephone rings.*] [전화벨이 울린다.]
W: Hello, <u>this is</u> Amanda. 여보세요, 아만다입니다.
M: Hey, Amanda! It's me, Josh. 야, 아만다! 나야, 조시.
W: Hi, Josh! How's it going? 안녕, 조시! 어떻게 지냈어?

M: Everything is fine with me, thanks for asking! I was just <u>wondering if</u> you could pick me up from the train station. 아무 일 없이 잘 지내, 물어봐 줘서 고마워! 네가 혹시 기차역으로 나를 차로 데리러 올 수 있는지 궁금해서.

W: Of course. <u>When</u> does your <u>train arrive</u>?
물론이지. 네가 탄 기차가 언제 도착하니?

M: I get there at <u>eight</u> P.M. this <u>Saturday</u>. Are you busy that day?
난 이번 주 토요일 오후 8시에 거기에 도착해. 그날 바쁘니?

W: Saturday? <u>I'm afraid</u> I can't <u>pick</u> you <u>up</u> that day because I have <u>dinner plans</u> with my parents.
토요일? 미안하지만 그날은 부모님과 저녁식사를 할 계획이라 너를 데리러 갈 수 없어.

M: Oh, <u>I see</u>. Then you can't meet me at the train station, right? 아, 알았어. 그럼 넌 기차역으로 날 보러 올 수 없다는 거지, 그렇지?

W: Yeah, I'm so sorry. <u>Why don't</u> we meet on Sunday or Monday?
응, 정말 미안해. 우리 일요일이나 월요일에 만나는 게 어때?

해설 'Why don't we ~?'는 제안하는 표현이다.

어휘 wonder if ~인지 궁금하다   pick somebody up ~을 차로 태우러 가다   train station 기차역

10 ①

M: Excuse me, ma'am. Can I help you find something? 실례합니다, 부인. 제가 부인이 찾는 것을 도와드릴까요?

W: Yeah, that would be great. I'm looking for a <u>candle</u> for my mother.
네, 그럼 좋겠네요. 저희 어머니께 드릴 양초를 찾고 있어요.

M: Okay. <u>Over here</u> we have the <u>fruit-scented</u> candles. And on this shelf we have some <u>flower</u>-scented candles. 알겠습니다. 이쪽에 과일 향이 나는 양초가 있습니다. 그리고 이 선반 위에는 꽃 향기가 나는 양초가 있어요.

W: <u>How much</u> are the orange and rose candles?
오렌지 양초와 장미 양초는 얼마죠?

M: The fruit-scented candles are <u>thirty</u> dollars each, and the flower-scented candles are <u>forty</u> dollars each. 과일 향 양초는 각각 30달러이고, 꽃 향기가 나는 양초는 각각 40달러입니다.

W: I see. I'll take one <u>orange</u>-scented candle and one <u>rose</u>-scented candle, please. Also, I would like to <u>use</u> this <u>fifty</u>-dollar <u>coupon</u> on my purchase.
알겠어요. 오렌지 향 양초 한 개와 장미 향 양초 한 개를 살게요. 그리고 구매 시 이 50달러짜리 쿠폰을 사용하고 싶어요.

M: Alright. Then you just have to <u>pay for</u> the <u>remaining twenty</u> dollars. Do you need anything else today?
알겠습니다. 그럼 부인께서는 남은 20달러만 지불하시면 됩니다. 오늘 또 필요하신 것이 있나요?

W: Yes. I would like to get the candles <u>gift-wrapped</u>.
네. 그 양초들을 선물 포장해 주세요.

M: I can do that, but it will <u>cost</u> you an <u>extra five</u> dollars. 가능합니다만, 추가로 5달러가 들 겁니다.

W: That's fine. Thank you so much.
　괜찮아요. 정말 감사합니다.

어휘 orange-scented candle은 하나에 30달러, rose-scented candle은 하나에 40달러이다. 합계가 70달러인데, 50달러짜리 쿠폰으로 할인을 받아서 잔액은 20달러이다. 여기에 선물 포장 비용으로 5달러가 들기 때문에 여자는 25달러를 지불할 것이다.

어휘 candle 양초　scented 향기가 나는　shelf 선반 (복 shelves)　purchase 구입　remaining 남은　gift-wrap 선물용으로 포장하다　extra 추가의

11 ③

W: Sir, can I help you with something?
　손님, 제가 도와드릴까요?

M: Yes, please. Where are the boxes? I need to send a package to my friend in Australia.
　네, 도와주세요. 상자는 어디에 있죠? 호주에 있는 친구에게 소포를 보내야 하거든요.

W: The boxes are on the third shelf over there.
　상자는 저쪽에 있는 세 번째 선반에 있습니다.

M: Oh, thank you. Also, where can I find the packaging tape?
　아, 감사합니다. 그리고, 포장 테이프는 어디에서 찾을 수 있죠?

W: The tape is on the table to your right. Please make sure you write your address and the address of the receiver clearly on top of the box.
　테이프는 손님 오른편 테이블 위에 있습니다. 상자 위에 손님의 주소와 받는 분의 주소를 명확하게 적어 주세요.

M: Alright. What do I do after that?
　알겠습니다. 그 다음엔 무엇을 해야 하죠?

W: You have to wait in line and pay the delivery fee.
　줄을 서서 기다리신 다음에 배달료를 지불하시면 됩니다.

M: Okay. I appreciate your help!
　알겠어요. 도와주셔서 감사합니다!

어휘 package 소포, 꾸러미　shelf 선반　over there 저쪽에　packaging 포장(재)　make sure ~을 확실히 하다　receiver 받는 사람, 수신인　clearly 또렷하게, 분명히　on top of ~의 위에　wait in line 줄을 서서 기다리다　delivery fee 배송비　appreciate 고마워하다　post office 우체국

12 ⑤

M: Have you heard of Stevie Wonder? He is probably one of the most famous musicians alive. Some people say that he is a legend. He was born on May thirteenth, nineteen fifty, and became blind when he was young. Even though he is blind, his love for music is very strong. He won over twenty-five awards and sold over one hundred million albums. He has many hit songs, such as "Isn't She Lovely," "I Just Called to Say I Love You," and "You Are the Sunshine of My Life."

스티비 원더를 들어보셨나요? 그는 아마도 현존하는 가장 유명한 음악가 중 한 명일 것입니다. 어떤 사람들은 그가 전설이라고 말합니다. 그는 1950년 5월 13일에 태어났고, 어렸을 때 시력을 잃었습니다. 앞이 안 보이지만, 음악에 대한 그의 사랑은 아주 강렬합니다. 그는 25개 이상의 상을 받았고, 1억 장 이상의 앨범을 팔았습니다. 그는 "Isn't She Lovely", "I just Called to Say I Love You", 그리고 "You Are the Sunshine of My Life"와 같은 많은 히트곡을 갖고 있습니다.

어휘 have you heard of ~? ~을 들어봤나요?　musician 음악가　alive 살아 있는　legend 전설(적인 인물)　become blind 눈이 멀다　even though 비록 ~일지라도　win awards 상을 받다　million 백만

13 ⑤

| 리버사이드 레스토랑의 라이브 음악 |

	연주자	요일
①	재즈 트리오	화요일
②	클래시컬 브리즈	수요일
③	록 스타즈	월요일
④	발라드 킹즈	목요일
⑤	댄스 피버	금요일

M: Nora, Riverside Restaurant has live music performances during dinner time this week.
　노라, 리버사이드 레스토랑에서 이번 주 저녁 시간에 라이브 음악 공연을 한대.

W: Yeah, I know. Jazz Trio will be performing on Tuesday night. I would like to see them. Do you like jazz music? 응, 나도 알아. 재즈 트리오가 화요일 저녁에 공연할 거야. 난 그들을 보고 싶어. 넌 재즈 음악을 좋아하니?

M: No, not really. I enjoy classical and rock music more, so I would rather go on Wednesday to see Classical Breeze or on Monday to see the Rock Stars. 아니, 딱히 그렇지는 않아. 나는 클래식이나 록 음악을 더 좋아하기 때문에 클래시컬 브리즈를 보러 수요일에 가거나, 록 스타즈를 보러 월요일에 가고 싶어.

W: Hmm… Listening to Classical Breeze puts me to sleep and the Rock Stars are too loud for me. What do you think of the Ballad Kings?
　음, 나는 클래시컬 브리즈의 음악을 들으면 잠이 오고, 록 스타즈는 나에게는 너무 시끄러워. 발라드 킹즈는 어떻게 생각해?

M: I like their music, but I'm going on a business trip on Thursday.
　그들의 음악을 좋아하지만, 난 목요일에 출장을 가.

W: I guess we can't go this week, then. Both the Ballad Kings and Dance Fever are performing on Thursday. 그럼 우리는 이번 주에는 못 갈 것 같구나. 발라드 킹즈와 댄스 피버 모두 목요일에 공연을 해.

해설 여자가 Dance Fever는 목요일에 공연한다고 했으므로 ⑤는 틀린 내용이다.

어휘 live music 라이브 음악　performance 공연　perform

공연하다 classical music 클래식, 고전 음악 would rather
(~하기 보다는 차라리) ~하겠다 put somebody to sleep ~을
잠들게 하다 loud 시끄러운 go on a business trip 출장을
가다

14 ⑤

W: This item can be found on the necks of most house
pets. It has the pet's name on it. Sometimes it has
the owner's phone number and address on it, too.
Even if you lose your pet, someone will be able to
contact you by looking at the information on this.
You can attach a leash to this item when you take
your pet for a walk.

이것은 집에서 기르는 대부분의 애완동물의 목에서 발견할 수 있습니
다. 이것은 그 위에 애완동물의 이름이 있습니다. 가끔은 애완동
물의 주인의 전화번호나 주소도 적혀 있습니다. 당신이 애완동물을
잃어버리더라도, 누군가가 이것의 위에 있는 정보를 보고 당신에게
연락할 수 있을 것입니다. 당신은 애완동물을 산책시킬 때 이것에
끈을 부착시킬 수 있습니다.

어휘 item 물품 neck 목 pet 애완동물 owner 주인
address 주소 contact 연락하다 attach 부착하다, 붙이다
leash (개)끈, 사슬 take somebody for a walk ~을 산책하러
데리고 가다

15 ①

M: Hey, Jenna. Are you doing anything special this
winter? 이봐, 제나. 넌 이번 겨울에 특별한 뭔가를 할 거니?

W: Yes, I am. I'm going to knit a scarf since the
weather is going to be cold.
응, 할 거야. 날씨가 추워질 테니까 목도리를 뜰 거야.

M: That's so cool! I didn't know you knew how to knit.
멋있다! 네가 뜨개질을 할 수 있는지 몰랐어.

W: Yeah, I've been knitting for about five months now.
What are you going to do during the winter? 응, 지금
5개월째 뜨개질을 하고 있어. 넌 겨울 동안 무엇을 할 계획이니?

M: I'm going to learn how to ski and visit my
grandparents' house. I haven't seen them in a
while. 나는 스키 타는 법을 배우고, 조부모님 댁을 방문할 거야.
난 그분들을 한동안 뵙지 못했어.

W: It sounds like you'll have a great time. I'll see you
after vacation.
넌 즐거운 시간을 보낼 것 같구나. 방학 끝나고 나서 보자.

M: Okay, I hope you enjoy making your scarf.
알았어. 목도리 만드는 것을 즐기길 바라.

W: Thank you! 고마워!

어휘 knit (실로 옷을) 뜨다, 짜다 scarf 목도리, 스카프 cool
멋진 in a while 한동안

16 ⑤

M: What are you doing tomorrow after school?
넌 내일 학교 끝나고 뭐 할 거니?

W: I have to go to my violin lesson at four.
나는 4시에 바이올린 레슨에 가야 해.

M: What time does your lesson end? I was hoping to
go eat ice cream with you.
레슨은 언제 끝나니? 너랑 같이 아이스크림 먹으러 가고 싶었거든.

W: It's normally over by five, but it might end later.
What time did you want to meet? 보통은 5시에 끝나지
만, 더 늦게 끝날 수도 있어. 몇 시에 만나고 싶었니?

M: I was thinking around five thirty. Is that okay with
you? 5시 30분쯤을 생각하고 있었어. 그 시간이 괜찮니?

W: Hmm… Can we meet thirty minutes later? I don't
want you to wait for me if my lesson ends later
than usual. 음, 우리 30분 늦게 만날 수 있을까? 내 레슨이 평
소보다 늦게 끝날 경우 널 기다리게 하고 싶지 않아.

M: Okay, that's fine. I'll see you then. 그래, 좋아. 그때 보자.

해설 남자가 5시 30분에 만나고 싶다고 했는데, 여자가 30분 늦게
보자고 했으므로, 둘은 6시에 만날 것이다.

어휘 after school 방과 후에 normally 보통은 later than
usual 평소보다 늦게

17 ⑤

W: Jessica is going to visit her best friend in Taiwan.
She checks in her bags and passes the security
checkpoint. After a while, she gets on the plane
and heads to her seat. When she gets there, she
realizes that she booked a window seat instead of
an aisle seat by mistake. When she looks around
her, she sees a woman sitting in an aisle seat.
Jessica wants to ask her if they can change seats.
In this situation, what would Jessica most likely
say to the woman?

제시카는 대만에 있는 친한 친구를 방문할 예정이다. 그녀는 가방을
부치고, 보안 검색대를 통과한다. 잠시 후에 그녀는 비행기에 올라
타고 그녀의 자리로 향한다. 그녀가 자리에 도착했을 때, 그녀는 실
수로 통로 자리 대신에 창가 자리를 예약했다는 것을 깨닫는다. 그
녀가 주변을 둘러봤을 때, 그녀는 통로 자리에 앉아 있는 한 여자를
본다. 제시카는 그 여자에게 자리를 바꿀 수 있는지 물어보고 싶다.
이런 상황에서 제시카는 여자에게 무슨 말을 하겠는가?

Jessica: Excuse me, ma'am. Would you please change
seats with me?
실례합니다, 부인. 저와 자리를 바꿔 주실 수 있나요?

① Where do I go to check in my bags?
제 가방을 부치려면 어디로 가야 하죠?

② Hello, ma'am. May I help you find your seat?
안녕하세요, 부인. 자리를 찾는 것을 도와드릴까요?

③ Excuse me. Could I book an aisle seat please?
실례합니다. 제가 통로 자리를 예약할 수 있을까요?

④ The flight will take off shortly. Please stay in your
seats. 비행기가 곧 이륙합니다. 자리에 앉아 계시기 바랍니다.

⑤ Excuse me, ma'am. Would you please change
seats with me?

실례합니다, 부인. 저와 자리를 바꿔 주실 수 있나요?

어휘 check in (공항에서) 짐을 부치다   pass the security checkpoint 보안 검색대를 통과하다   after a while 잠시 후에 get on the plane 비행기에 오르다   head 향하다   realize 깨닫다   book 예약하다   window seat 창가 자리   instead of 대신에   aisle seat 통로 자리   by mistake 실수로   flight 항공기, 항공편   take off 이륙하다   shortly 곧

18 ④

M: Honey, we have one <u>hundred miles</u> to go until we <u>get to</u> Las Vegas.
여보, 라스베이거스에 도착하려면 100마일을 가야 해요.

W: One hundred miles? That seems like a <u>long way from</u> <u>here</u>. 100마일이요? 여기서 무척 먼 것 같네요.

M: We'll get there <u>sooner than</u> you <u>think</u>. Oh, look. We're almost <u>out of gas</u>.
당신이 생각한 것보다 더 빨리 도착할 거예요. 아, 이거 봐요. 기름이 거의 떨어졌어요.

W: You're right. <u>I wonder</u> if there's a <u>gas station</u> around here. 맞아요. 이 근처에 주유소가 있는지 궁금하네요.

M: Yeah, the roads <u>look</u> so <u>deserted</u>.
네, 도로에 사람이 너무 없군요.

W: That <u>sign says</u> the next gas station is ten miles away. Do we have <u>enough</u> gas to get there?
저 표지판에 따르면 다음 주유소는 10마일 떨어진 곳에 있네요. 저기까지 갈 만큼 기름이 충분해요?

M: Yes, I'm <u>pretty sure</u> we do. 네, 확실히 있어요.

W: Okay, let's <u>hurry up</u> and get there.
그래요, 서둘러서 거기에 가요.

어휘 get to ~에 닿다, 도착하다   a long way from ~에서 멀리 떨어진 거리   out of gas 연료가 떨어진   gas station 주유소 around here 이 근처에   deserted 사람이 없는, 버림 받은   sign 표지판, 간판   hurry up 서두르다

19 ⑤

W: Did you see the <u>weather forecast</u> for <u>tomorrow</u>? There's a chance of <u>thunderstorms</u>.
넌 내일 일기예보를 봤니? 천둥을 동반한 폭우가 올 가능성이 있어.

M: Yeah, I saw it this morning. But look at <u>how sunny</u> it is <u>outside</u>! I don't think it's going to rain.
응, 오늘 아침에 봤어. 그런데 바깥이 얼마나 화창한지 봐! 내 생각에는 비가 올 것 같지 않아.

W: But <u>what if</u> it does? That means our <u>plans</u> to go camping will be <u>cancelled</u>. 하지만 만약 비가 온다면 어떡해? 그건 캠핑을 가기로 한 우리의 계획이 취소될 거라는 의미야.

M: If you're that <u>worried</u>, we can think of <u>something</u> <u>else</u> to do, <u>just in case</u>. 네가 만약 그렇게 걱정이 된다면, 우리는 만일의 경우에 대비해서 다른 할 일을 생각할 수 있어.

W: Okay. If there are thunderstorms, we should go <u>watch</u> a <u>movie</u>. 그래. 만약 폭풍우가 온다면, 영화를 보러 가자.

M: Alright, we can do that. I really hope the weather stays nice.
좋아, 그렇게 할 수 있지. 난 정말 날씨가 계속 좋았으면 좋겠어.

W: Me too. 나도 그래.

① Better late than never.
늦게라도 하는 것이 아예 안 하는 것보다 낫다.

② Bad news travels quickly. 나쁜 소문은 빨리 퍼진다.

③ Out of sight, out of mind.
눈에서 멀어지면 마음에서도 멀어진다.

④ Kill two birds with one stone. 일석이조.

⑤ Hope for the best, but prepare for the worst.
최상의 결과에 대해 희망을 갖되, 최악의 상황에도 대비해야 한다.

어휘 weather forecast 일기예보   chance 가능성 thunderstorm 뇌우   What if ~? ~면 어쩌지?   go camping 캠핑을 가다   just in case 만일을 대비해서

20 ⑤

M: I <u>ordered</u> some running <u>shoes</u> from an online <u>shopping mall</u> two weeks ago, but I still haven't gotten them. 내가 2주 전에 한 온라인 쇼핑몰에서 운동화를 주문했는데, 아직도 물건을 받지 못했어.

W: Hmm… Did you <u>call</u> the <u>Customer Service</u> Center? 음, 고객서비스센터에 전화해 봤니?

M: Yeah. I called them, but <u>nobody picked up</u>.
응. 전화했는데, 아무도 전화를 받지 않더라.

W: Maybe something <u>went wrong</u> with your <u>order</u>.
아마 네 주문에 문제가 생겼겠지.

M: I have <u>no idea</u>. I'll try calling them again tomorrow morning.
나도 모르겠어. 내일 오전에 다시 한 번 전화해 볼 거야.

W: Okay. Do you know their <u>operating hours</u>?
그래. 그쪽 영업 시간은 알고 있니?

M: No. I'm going to check the website to see when <u>they open</u>.
아니. 그들이 언제 여는지 내가 웹사이트에서 확인해 볼 거야.

① Yes. I paid for the running shoes already.
응. 이미 운동화 값을 지불했어.

② How much are the white running shoes?
흰색 운동화는 얼마니?

③ The phone number is on the back of the card.
전화번호는 카드 뒤편에 있어.

④ What is the name of the online shopping mall?
그 온라인 쇼핑몰 이름이 뭐니?

⑤ No. I'm going to check the website to see when they open.
아니. 그들이 언제 여는지 내가 웹사이트에서 확인해 볼 거야.

어휘 order 주문하다; 주문(품)   running shoes 운동화 Customer Service Center 고객서비스센터   pick up (전화를) 받다   go wrong 잘못되다   operating hours 영업 시간, 운영 시간   check 확인하다

01 ④	02 ①	03 ③	04 ②	05 ②
06 ③	07 ②	08 ⑤	09 ④	10 ⑤
11 ②	12 ①	13 ⑤	14 ③	15 ④
16 ⑤	17 ⑤	18 ⑤	19 ④	20 ③

01 ④

M: Mom, look at all these ladybugs! There are five of them on this leaf. 엄마, 이 무당벌레들 좀 보세요! 이 나뭇잎 위에 다섯 마리가 있어요.

W: Wow, that's so cool! They all have a different number of spots on them. 와, 멋있구나! 모두 각각 다른 개수의 반점을 가지고 있네.

M: Yeah, except for this one. This one doesn't have any spots on it. I can see its wings, though. 네, 이 한 마리만 예외에요. 이 무당벌레는 반점을 갖고 있지 않아요. 하지만 날개는 보이네요.

W: You're right. I've never seen a ladybug without spots before. Hey, there are ladybugs with two spots and four spots as well. 맞아. 엄마도 반점이 없는 무당벌레는 본 적이 없어. 얘, 여기에 두 개와 네 개의 반점을 가진 무당벌레들도 있구나.

M: Hmm… I can't see their wings. I think they're hidden. I like this one with five spots the best. I can see its wings, too! 음, 날개가 안 보이는데요. 날개가 숨어 있는 것 같아요. 저는 다섯 개의 반점을 가진 이 무당벌레가 가장 좋아요. 날개도 볼 수 있어요!

W: Well, I think I like this one with three spots the best. 글쎄, 나는 반점이 세 개 있는 이게 제일 좋구나.

M: You can see the wings on this one, too. But it's not better than the one with five spots. 이것도 역시 날개가 보여요. 하지만 반점이 다섯 개 있는 것보다 좋지는 않네요.

해설 남자는 반점이 다섯 개 있고, 날개가 보이는 무당벌레를 가장 마음에 들어 한다.

어휘 ladybug 무당벌레   spot 반점   except for ~을 제외하고   wing 날개   as well ~도, 또한   hidden 숨은

02 ①

[Cellphone rings.] [휴대폰이 울린다.]

M: Hello, this is Bob. 여보세요, 밥입니다.

W: Bob! It's me, Nora. 밥! 나야, 노라.

M: Oh, hey! What's up? I heard you've been really busy recently. 아, 노라! 무슨 일이야? 너 요새 정말 바쁘다고 들었어.

W: Yeah, I've been spending a lot of time preparing for my presentation. I'm actually calling to ask if you could help me with it. 응, 발표를 준비하는 데 많은 시간을 보내고 있었어. 사실은 네가 날

좀 도와줄 수 있는지 물어보려고 전화했어.

M: Sure, what do you need me to do? 그래. 무슨 도움이 필요하니?

W: Well, my presentation is about global warming, but I'm having trouble finding information on it. 음, 사실은 내 발표가 지구온난화에 대한 내용인데, 그것에 대한 정보를 찾는 게 어려워.

M: So, do you want me to do some research on global warming? 그럼, 내가 지구온난화에 대해 조사해주길 원하는 거야?

W: Yes, please. I really appreciate your help! 응, 부탁해. 네가 도와주면 정말 고맙겠어!

M: It's not a problem. I'll let you know what I find on the topic. 어렵지 않아. 내가 그 주제에 관해 알아낸 것을 너에게 알려줄게.

어휘 recently 최근에, 요즘에   prepare for ~을 준비하다   presentation 발표   actually 사실은   global warming 지구온난화   have trouble -ing ~하는 데 어려움을 겪다   do research 조사하다   appreciate 감사하다, 고마워하다   topic 주제

03 ③

① W: Where can I find the lemons? 레몬은 어디서 찾을 수 있죠?

M: They are over here in the fruit section. 과일 코너의 바로 이쪽에 있어요.

② W: How do I get to the marketplace? 제가 시장에 어떻게 가야 해요?

M: Walk straight for two blocks and then turn left. 두 블록을 쭉 걸어간 다음에 좌회전하세요.

③ W: What fruit do you recommend for the summer? 여름에는 어떤 과일을 추천하시나요?

M: Hmm… I think watermelons are best fit for hot weather. 음, 더운 날씨에는 수박이 제격이죠.

④ W: Would you like some watermelon? 수박 좀 드시겠어요?

M: No thanks. I prefer strawberries. 괜찮아요. 저는 딸기가 좋아요.

⑤ W: Is there something to eat in the refrigerator? 냉장고에 먹을 것 좀 있나요?

M: I'm not sure. There should be a watermelon in there somewhere. 모르겠어요. 냉장고 안 어딘가에 수박은 있을 거예요.

어휘 over here 이쪽에   section 부문, 코너   marketplace 시장   straight 직진의, 곧장   recommend 추천하다   watermelon 수박   prefer 선호하다   strawberry 딸기   refrigerator 냉장고   somewhere 어딘가에

04 ②

M: Welcome to Stevie's Pet Shop. What can I help you with today? 스티비 애완동물 상점에 오신 걸 환영합니다. 무엇을 도와드릴까요?

W: Hello. I'm <u>interested</u> <u>in</u> buying a <u>dog</u>. Can you help me choose one?
안녕하세요. 저는 개를 한 마리 사고 싶어요. 개를 고르는 걸 도와주실 수 있나요?

M: Sure, no problem. <u>What</u> <u>kind</u> of dog are you <u>looking</u> <u>for</u>? 물론이죠. 어떤 종류의 강아지를 찾고 계세요?

W: Well, I would <u>prefer</u> a <u>small</u> dog with <u>long</u> <u>fur</u>.
음, 저는 긴 털을 가진 작은 개를 원해요.

M: Okay. Here is one that you might like. What do you think? 알겠습니다. 손님이 좋아하실 만한 개가 여기 있습니다. 어떠신가요?

W: It's alright, but its <u>tail</u> is <u>too</u> <u>long</u>. I <u>want</u> a dog with a <u>short</u> tail.
좋긴 한데 꼬리가 너무 길어요. 저는 꼬리가 짧은 개를 원해요.

M: I'm sorry, but we don't have any small, long furred dogs with short tails.
죄송합니다만, 저희는 짧은 꼬리를 가진 크기가 작고 털이 긴 개는 없어요.

W: Oh, then I'll just take the one with a long tail. Thank you. 아, 그럼 그냥 꼬리가 긴 개로 할게요. 감사합니다.

해설 여자는 크기가 작고, 털이 길고, 꼬리가 긴 개를 선택했다.

어휘 pet 애완동물 be interested in ~에 관심이 있다 choose 고르다, 선택하다 prefer 선호하다 fur 털 tail 꼬리

05 ②

M: Hello, this is <u>Station</u> four five one on Linden Street. What is your <u>emergency</u>? 안녕하세요, 린든 스트리트 451서입니다. 어떤 응급 상황이신가요?

W: I <u>see</u> <u>smoke</u> coming <u>from</u> my neighbor's house. I think it's <u>on</u> <u>fire</u>! 저희 이웃집에서 연기가 나오는 게 보이네요. 제 생각에는 불이 난 것 같아요!

M: Ma'am, please stay calm. What is your neighbor's <u>address</u>? 부인, 진정하세요. 이웃집 주소가 어떻게 되죠?

W: Okay, it is thirty-nine ten Heathen Lane. How long will it take you to get here?
네, 히든 레인 3910번지예요. 여기 도착하는 데 얼마나 걸리나요?

M: We will get there <u>as</u> <u>fast</u> <u>as</u> we can.
최대한 빨리 가도록 하겠습니다.

W: Alright, is there anything I can do <u>until</u> you get here? 알겠어요, 도착하실 때까지 제가 할 수 있는 일이 있을까요?

M: No, ma'am, it is <u>dangerous</u>. Please <u>stay</u> <u>away</u> <u>from</u> the fire.
아닙니다, 부인, 위험합니다. 화재 현장에서 멀리 떨어져 계세요.

W: Yes, sir. 알겠습니다.

어휘 station 서, 본부(소방서, 경찰서, 방송국 등의 건물) emergency 긴급 상황, 비상 be on fire 불타고 있다 stay calm 침착함을 유지하다 address 주소 dangerous 위험한 stay away from ~에서 멀리 떨어져 있다 news reporter 기자 firefighter 소방관 lawyer 변호사

06 ③

M: Hey, Ashley! What are you up to?
야, 애슐리! 너 뭐 하고 있니?

W: I'm <u>getting</u> <u>ready</u> to go to the <u>beach</u> with my friends. I've been <u>looking</u> <u>forward</u> <u>to</u> it for days!
내 친구들과 함께 해변에 가려고 준비 중이야. 며칠 동안이나 그걸 기대해 왔어!

M: Hmm… It's kind of <u>windy</u> outside. Look at the trees swaying! I <u>heard</u> that there's a <u>storm</u> <u>coming</u> soon.
음, 밖에 바람이 좀 부는데. 나무들이 흔들리는 것 좀 봐! 곧 폭풍이 온다고 들었어.

W: Are you <u>serious</u>? I can't believe it! The <u>weather</u> <u>forecast</u> said that the storm wouldn't be coming <u>until</u> tomorrow. 정말이야? 말도 안돼! 일기예보에서는 내일까지 폭풍이 오지 않을 거라고 했어.

M: Look! It's <u>starting</u> to <u>rain</u> right now. I don't think you can go to the beach. 저것 봐! 지금 비가 오기 시작했어. 내 생각에 넌 해변에 갈 수 없을 것 같아.

W: Oh, my goodness. This is <u>terrible</u>! I thought we were going to <u>have</u> so much <u>fun</u> today! 아, 이런. 정말 최악이군! 오늘 정말 재미있게 놀려고 생각했단 말이야!

M: I'm sorry to hear that. <u>Cheer</u> <u>up</u>! You can always go <u>some</u> <u>other</u> <u>time</u>.
안됐구나. 기운 내! 너는 다음에 갈 수 있잖아.

W: You're right, but I'm just upset that things <u>turned</u> <u>out</u> <u>this</u> <u>way</u>.
맞아, 하지만 일이 이런 식으로 꼬여서 속상할 뿐이야.

해설 여자는 해변에 갈 마음에 들떠 있다가 비가 내리는 바람에 실망했다.

어휘 get ready 준비하다 look forward to ~을 기대하다, 학수고대하다 for days 여러 날 동안 sway 흔들리다 storm 폭풍우 weather forecast 일기예보 terrible 끔찍한 cheer up 힘내 some other time 언젠가 turn out (결과 등이 특정 방식으로) 되다 relieved 안도하는 embarrassed 당황스러운 disappointed 실망한 nervous 초조해하는 upset 속상한

07 ②

① M: Do you know <u>where</u> the coffee mugs are?
커피잔이 어디 있는지 아니?

W: Yeah, they are in the <u>second</u> <u>cabinet</u>.
응, 두 번째 보관함에 있어.

② M: What are the bank's <u>operating</u> <u>hours</u>?
은행의 영업시간이 어떻게 되죠?

W: You can <u>open</u> a <u>bank</u> <u>account</u> today.
오늘 계좌를 개설하실 수 있습니다.

③ M: I think I'll be <u>late</u> <u>for</u> <u>dinner</u>. I'm sorry.
오늘 저녁식사에 늦을 것 같아요. 죄송합니다.

W: It's okay. <u>How</u> <u>long</u> will it take you to get here?
괜찮아요. 도착하는 데 얼마나 걸리나요?

④ M: <u>What</u> are you doing this <u>weekend</u>?
이번 주말에 뭐 하세요?

W: I'm going bowling with my family.
가족들이랑 볼링을 치러 가요.

⑤ M: Can you help me write my book report?
제가 독후감 쓰는 것을 도와주실래요?

W: Sure. I'll be over to help you in thirty minutes.
물론이죠. 30분 후에 도와주러 갈게요.

어휘 mug 잔, 머그잔　cabinet 보관함, 캐비닛　operating hours 운영시간, 영업시간　open a bank account 은행 계좌를 개설하다　go bowling 볼링 치러 가다　book report 독후감

08 ⑤

W: Honey, I think we should plant some trees in the backyard. 여보, 뒷마당에 나무를 좀 심어야 할 것 같아요.

M: Yeah, I was thinking the same thing. Our backyard looks so empty. 맞아요, 나도 같은 걸 생각하고 있었어요. 우리 뒷마당은 너무 허전해 보여요.

W: What types of trees should we plant? I think flowers would look pretty, too. 어떤 종류의 나무를 심어야 할까요? 내 생각에는 꽃도 예쁠 것 같아요.

M: I agree. Should we go buy some now? There's a plant store on Sherry Road. 같은 생각이에요. 지금 좀 사러 갈까요? 셰리 가에 식물 가게가 있어요.

W: Hmm… I would love to. But I'm busy cleaning the house right now. Can you go and buy some for me? 음, 나도 그러고 싶어요. 하지만 지금은 집을 청소하느라 바쁘거든요. 당신이 가서 좀 사올 수 있겠어요?

M: Sure, no problem. 알았어요, 문제 없어요.

해설 plant는 tree(나무), flower(꽃) 등을 포함하는 단어이다.

어휘 plant 식물을 심다; 식물　backyard 뒷마당, 뒤뜰　empty 비어 있는

09 ④

M: Helen, what is your favorite class so far?
헬렌, 지금까지 어떤 수업이 가장 좋아?

W: Well, I like all of them, but I like Mr. Clark's gym class the most! How about you? 글쎄, 모두 괜찮지만, 클락 선생님의 체육 수업이 가장 좋아! 너는 어때?

M: Mr. Clark's class is my favorite, too! He is such a fun teacher.
나도 클락 선생님 수업이 가장 좋아! 정말 유쾌한 선생님이셔.

W: You're right. I always have a great time in his class. Oh, did you hear? He promised to buy us pizza after class tomorrow!
맞아. 나는 그 선생님 수업에서 항상 즐거운 시간을 보내. 아, 너 혹시 들었니? 선생님께서 내일 수업 후에 우리에게 피자를 사주기로 약속했어!

M: Really? That's awesome! It's no surprise that everyone likes him. 정말? 끝내주네! 모든 사람들이 그 선생님을 좋아하는 건 당연한 일이야.

W: Yeah, it is the best class ever! 응, 최고의 수업이야!

M: You can say that again. 나도 정말 그렇게 생각해.

해설 'You can say that again.'은 상대방의 말에 전적인 동의를 나타낼 때 쓰는 표현이다.

어휘 favorite 매우 좋아하는　gym class 체육 수업　promise 약속하다　awesome 멋진　You can say that again. 정말 그렇다, 전적으로 동의한다.

10 ⑤

M: Hey, Julia. Are you almost done making the sandwiches? 저, 줄리아. 샌드위치 만드는 건 거의 끝났어요?

W: No, not quite. I'm not sure if I made enough. Do you know how many people are coming to the picnic? 완전히는 아니에요. 내가 충분히 만들었는지 잘 모르겠어요. 얼마나 많은 사람들이 소풍에 오는지 알고 있나요?

M: I think about twenty people will be there. How many have you made so far?
내 생각에 대략 20명이 올 거예요. 지금까지 몇 개나 만들었죠?

W: Well, I've made five egg sandwiches, and five ham sandwiches.
음, 계란 샌드위치 5개와, 햄 샌드위치 5개를 만들었어요.

M: Oh, you're halfway done! Should I help you make the rest?
아, 반 정도 했군요! 내가 나머지를 만드는 것을 도와줄까요?

W: Yes, please. What type of sandwich should we make? 네, 도와줘요. 우린 어떤 종류의 샌드위치를 만들어야 할까요?

M: Hmm… How about four turkey sandwiches and six chicken sandwiches?
음, 칠면조 샌드위치 4개와 치킨 샌드위치 6개 어때요?

W: That sounds great. 그거 좋은 생각이에요.

해설 소풍에 필요한 샌드위치의 총 개수와 지금까지 만든 개수를 헷갈리지 말자.

어휘 not quite 완전히 ~하지 않은　so far 지금까지　halfway done 절반이 끝난　the rest 나머지　turkey 칠면조

11 ②

M: Excuse me, ma'am. 실례합니다, 부인.

W: Hello, may I help you with something?
안녕하세요, 제가 도와드릴 일이 있나요?

M: Yes. Which one of these has cream inside it?
네. 이것들 중에 어떤 것에 크림이 들어 있죠?

W: All of the bread on this table has cream in it.
이 탁자 위에 있는 모든 빵에는 크림이 들어 있어요.

M: Oh, okay. They look really fresh! Did they just come out of the oven? 아, 알겠습니다. 빵이 정말 신선해 보이네요! 오븐에서 갓 구워져 나온 것들인가요?

W: Yes, they did. We bake new bread every thirty minutes.
네, 그렇습니다. 저희는 30분마다 새로운 빵을 굽거든요.

M: I see. Could I also get a loaf of plain white bread and a piece of cheesecake? 알겠어요. 식빵 한 덩어리랑 치즈 케이크 한 조각도 살 수 있을까요?

W: Alright. Would you like the loaf of bread sliced?
알겠습니다. 식빵은 잘라 드릴까요?

M: That would be great. Thank you so much.
그럼 좋겠네요. 감사합니다.

어휘 inside ~의 안에 bake 굽다 loaf (빵) 한 덩어리 plain white bread (하얀) 식빵 slice 얇게 썰다

12 ①

W: Good morning, students. I would like to make an announcement about the field trip we will be going on next week. As you all know, we will be going to the Lawrence National Art Museum on February tenth. Before we go, you must fill out a form and ask your parents to sign it. You must turn in this form by February eighth. Also, make sure to bring ten dollars to enter the museum. Lastly, please remember that the bus will leave from school at eight A.M., so do not be late.

안녕하세요, 학생 여러분. 다음 주에 갈 현장 학습에 관한 공지 사항이 있습니다. 모두 아시다피시, 우리는 2월 10일에 로렌스 국립미술관으로 현장 학습을 갈 겁니다. 가기 전에, 여러분들은 신청서를 작성해서 부모님의 서명을 받아야 합니다. 이 신청서는 2월 8일까지 제출해야 합니다. 또한, 박물관 입장료로 10달러를 반드시 가져오시기 바랍니다. 마지막으로, 버스가 학교에서 오전 8시에 출발하므로, 늦지 않기를 바랍니다.

해설 마지막 문장에 ③, ④, ⑤의 내용이 모두 언급되었다.

어휘 make an announcement 안내 사항을 말하다, 공지하다 field trip 현장 학습 art museum 미술관 fill out 작성하다 make sure 확실히 ~하다 enter 입장하다

13 ⑤

| 바비의 주중 일정 |

	요일	해야 할 일
①	월요일	가족 여행
②	화요일	가족 여행
③	수요일	병원 예약
④	목요일	피아노 레슨
⑤	금요일	피아노 레슨

W: Good afternoon, Bobby. Can I do something for you? 안녕, 바비. 내가 도와줄 일이 있니?

M: Ms. Jackson, I have to reschedule my piano lesson for another day this week. I'm going on a family trip on Monday. 잭슨 선생님, 제가 이번 주에는 피아노 레슨을 다른 날로 옮겨야 해요. 월요일에 가족 여행을 가거든요.

W: Okay, that's fine. Can you come on Tuesday or Wednesday? 그래, 그렇게 하자. 넌 화요일이나 수요일에 올 수 있니?

M: I get back from the trip on Tuesday night, and I have a doctor's appointment on Wednesday. 저는 화

요일 밤에 여행에서 돌아오고, 수요일에는 병원 예약이 있어요.

W: Hmm… Do you have anything planned on Thursday and Friday? 음, 그럼 목요일이나 금요일에 무슨 계획이 있니?

M: No, I don't have any plans. I can come on either of those days.
아니요, 아무 계획도 없어요. 그 두 날 중 언제든 올 수 있어요.

W: Oh, actually, I have another student coming on Friday. I think we will have to have our lesson on Thursday. 오, 사실은 금요일에는 다른 학생이 오기로 되어 있어. 우리 레슨은 목요일에 해야 할 것 같구나.

M: Okay, that works for me. When will we start preparing for the piano recital?
알겠습니다, 저도 좋아요. 피아노 연주회 준비는 언제 시작하죠?

W: If you want, we can begin on Thursday when you come for your lesson. 네가 원한다면, 우리는 네가 레슨을 받으러 오는 목요일에 시작할 수 있어.

M: Alright, that sounds great. I'll see you then!
네, 좋네요. 그때 봬요!

해설 남자는 금요일이 아니라 목요일에 피아노 레슨을 받을 것이다.

어휘 doctor's appointment 병원 예약 reschedule 일정을 변경하다 get back 돌아오다 prepare 준비하다 recital 연주회

14 ③

M: This is a type of transportation. Sometimes, news reporters ride this to get a view of the city, and police ride this to quickly go from one place to another. It can also be used to enjoy the view of a beautiful landscape. Unlike an airplane, you can only fit a few people in this. This can be found in the sky, and it makes a loud noise as it flies by. On the top floor of some tall buildings and hospitals, there is room made especially for this to land.

이것은 교통수단의 일종이다. 때로는 뉴스 기자들이 도시의 모습을 담기 위해 이것을 타고, 경찰들이 한 곳에서 다른 곳으로 빠르게 이동하기 위해 이것을 탄다. 이것은 또한 아름다운 경치를 즐기기 위해 이용될 수 있다. 비행기와는 달리, 이것에는 오직 몇 명의 사람들만이 들어갈 자리가 있다. 이것은 하늘에서 볼 수 있으며, 이것은 날아갈 때 큰 소음을 낸다. 일부 고층 건물이나 병원의 옥상에는 특별히 이것이 착륙할 수 있도록 공간이 만들어져 있다.

해설 'Unlike an airplane', 'flies by' 등의 표현에서 비행기의 일종이라는 것을 알 수 있고, 적은 수의 사람만 타는 점이 힌트이다.

어휘 transportation 교통수단 news reporter 기자 view 경관, 모습 landscape 풍경 unlike ~와는 달리 airplane 비행기 fit 맞다, 들어맞게 하다 loud (소리가) 큰, 시끄러운 make a noise 소음을 내다 top floor 꼭대기층 especially 특별히 land 착륙하다

15 ④

M: Karen, you've already missed three days of school.

캐런, 넌 벌써 3일이나 학교에 결석했어.

W: I know, Dad. But I'm still not feeling well.
저도 알아요, 아빠. 하지만 여전히 몸이 좋지 않아요.

M: Okay. But I'm starting to worry about your schoolwork.
그래. 하지만 난 네 학교 공부가 걱정되기 시작하는구나.

W: Yeah, I don't know what to do. I don't even know what we learned in class. 네, 무엇을 해야 할지 모르겠어요. 저는 심지어 우리가 수업시간에 무엇을 배웠는지도 모르겠어요.

M: Hmm... Why don't you call your classmates and ask them what you missed? 음, 너희 반 친구한테 전화해서 네가 무엇을 놓쳤는지 물어보는 게 어떨까?

W: That's a good idea, Dad. I'll try calling them now.
좋은 생각이에요, 아빠. 그 애들한테 지금 전화해 볼게요.

M: Alright. I also hope your teacher will let you turn in your homework late. 좋아. 그리고 너희 선생님이 네가 숙제를 늦게 제출하는 것을 허락해 주셨으면 좋겠구나.

W: Me too. I just want to get better soon. Being sick is really not helping. 저도 그래요. 저는 그저 몸이 빨리 좋아지고 싶어요. 아픈 건 정말 도움이 안 돼요.

어휘 miss school 학교를 빠지다 feel well 건강 상태가 좋다 schoolwork 학업 classmate 급우, 반 친구 miss 놓치다 turn in 제출하다 get better (몸이) 나아지다

16 ⑤

M: Kristy, when should we meet to plan our trip to Busan?
크리스티, 우리는 언제 만나서 부산 여행 계획을 세울까?

W: I'm free every week on Tuesdays, Wednesdays, and Thursdays. How about you? 난 매주 화요일, 수요일, 그리고 목요일에는 시간이 비어. 너는 어때?

M: Okay, during the week I have time on Mondays, Thursdays, and Saturdays.
그래, 나는 주중에 월요일, 목요일, 그리고 토요일에 시간이 있어.

W: Well then, I guess there's only one day that we can meet. 그럼, 우리가 만날 수 있는 날은 하루뿐인 것 같아.

M: Yeah, you're right. What time works for you? I'm free all day, so it's up to you. 응, 맞아. 넌 몇 시가 괜찮니? 나는 하루 종일 시간이 있으니까 네가 결정해.

W: Hmm... I have lunch plans at twelve P.M., but that will be over around one thirty P.M. Should we meet around two P.M.? 음, 오후 12시에는 점심 약속이 있는데, 그건 오후 1시 30분쯤 끝날 거야. 우리 2시쯤 만날까?

M: Sure, I'll see you then! 그래. 그때 보자!

해설 두 사람이 공통적으로 시간이 있는 날은 목요일이다.

어휘 trip 여행 free 한가한 up to ~에게 달린

17 ⑤

W: Every month, Min's father gives Min fifty dollars for allowance. However, Min spent all of his money in a week and asked his father for more. Min's father

was upset with Min, but decided to give him an extra twenty dollars. But Min used all of this money in two days. Min's father asked Min where he was spending all of his money. Min's father found out that Min was buying things that he didn't need. Min's father decided that it was time to teach Min a lesson. In this situation, what would his father most likely say to Min?

매달, 민의 아버지는 민에게 용돈으로 50달러를 준다. 그러나 민은 일주일 만에 그의 모든 용돈을 써버리고, 그의 아버지에게 용돈을 더 달라고 부탁했다. 민의 아버지는 민에게 화가 났지만 추가로 20달러를 더 주기로 결정했다. 하지만 민은 이틀 만에 이 돈을 다 써버렸다. 민의 아버지는 민에게 그 돈을 다 어디에 사용했는지 물었다. 민의 아버지는 민이 필요하지 않은 물건들을 샀다는 것을 알게 되었다. 민의 아버지는 그때가 민에게 교훈을 가르쳐야 할 때라고 결심했다. 이런 상황에서, 민의 아버지가 민에게 할 말로 가장 적절한 것은 무엇이겠는가?

Father: Don't waste your money. You need to learn how to save it.
돈을 낭비하지 마라. 너는 돈을 아끼는 법을 배울 필요가 있어.

① Keep up the good work! 지금처럼 계속 잘하렴!

② I found a $5 bill on the street.
길에서 5달러짜리 지폐를 주웠어.

③ How much do you get for allowance every month? 매달 용돈으로 얼마를 받니?

④ There is a $20 admission fee to go to the amusement park. 놀이동산에 가려면 입장료 20달러가 필요해.

⑤ Don't waste your money. You need to learn how to save it.
돈을 낭비하지 마라. 너는 돈을 아끼는 법을 배울 필요가 있어.

어휘 allowance 용돈 upset with ~에게 화가 난 extra 추가의 find out 알아내다 teach somebody a lesson ~에게 교훈을 가르치다 keep up the good work 계속해서 열심히 하다 bill 지폐 admission fee 입장료 waste 낭비하다 save 아끼다; 저축하다; 구하다

18 ⑤

W: Harry, is that you? 해리, 너 맞니?

M: Martha! Wow, long time no see! How have you been? 마사! 우와, 정말 오랜만이다! 어떻게 지냈어?

W: I've been wonderful, thanks for asking! You look great!
아주 잘 지냈어, 물어봐 줘서 고마워! 넌 무척 좋아 보인다!

M: Thank you! What brings you here? I thought you moved to the west side of town. 고마워! 여기는 무슨 일로 왔어? 난 네가 도시의 서쪽으로 이사 갔다고 생각했어.

W: I did, but I had plans to meet a friend who lives in this neighborhood. I was about to go home when I saw you. 이사 갔어, 그런데 이 근처에 사는 친구를 만날 약속이 있었거든. 너를 봤을 때 난 막 집에 가려던 참이었어.

M: I see. Would you like to come over to my place for

some <u>tea</u>? 그렇구나. 우리 집에 가서 차 좀 마실래?

W: Yes, that'd be great! 그래, 좋지!

M: Oh, actually, I just remembered I <u>ran</u> <u>out</u> <u>of</u> tea bags. Can we <u>stop</u> <u>by</u> the <u>store</u> to buy some? 아, 사실은 티백이 다 떨어진 게 방금 생각났어. 상점에 잠깐 들려서 좀 사도 될까?

W: Yeah, of course! 그럼, 물론이지!

어휘 long time no see 오랜만이야 What brings you here? 무슨 일로 여기에 왔니? in this neighborhood 이 근처에 be about to ~ 막 ~하려고 하다 come over to ~에 오다 run out of ~을 다 쓰다, 소진하다

19 ④

M: Hey, look at this <u>photo</u>. What do you think it means? 여기, 이 사진 좀 봐. 이제 무엇을 의미하는 것 같니?

W: Hmm… I don't know. I wonder <u>what</u> the <u>photographer</u> was <u>thinking</u> when he took it. 음, 모르겠어. 사진 작가가 이 사진을 찍었을 때 무슨 생각을 했는지 궁금해.

M: Maybe he was trying to <u>express</u> his <u>emotions</u> through it. 그는 아마도 사진을 통해서 그의 감정을 표현하려고 했을 거야.

W: Yeah, I think the photographer was trying to express <u>loneliness</u> or <u>sadness</u>. 응, 사진 작가가 외로움 혹은 슬픔을 표현하려고 했던 것 같아.

M: I agree, since the man in the photo is <u>walking</u> on the <u>road</u> <u>by</u> <u>himself</u>. 나도 그렇게 생각해, 왜냐하면 사진 속의 남자는 홀로 길을 걷고 있기 때문이야.

W: You're right. I guess there are <u>some</u> <u>things</u> that <u>words</u> <u>can't</u> <u>describe</u>. 맞아, 내 생각에는 말로는 설명할 수 없는 것들이 좀 있는 것 같아.

① Look before you leap. 돌다리도 두들겨 보고 건너라.
② There's no place like home. 집만큼 편한 곳이 없다.
③ You can't always get what you want. 원하는 것을 항상 얻을 수는 없다.
④ A picture is worth a thousand words. 천 마디의 말보다 한 번 보는 것이 낫다.
⑤ A journey of a thousand miles begins with one step. 천 리 길도 한 걸음부터.

해설 어떤 말도 써 있지 않은 사진에서 여자와 남자는 작가의 감정을 읽고 있는 상황이다. 이 상황을 가장 잘 보여주는 표현은 ④이다.

어휘 photographer 사진 작가 express 표현하다 emotion 감정 through ~을 통해서 loneliness 외로움 sadness 슬픔 by oneself 혼자서(=alone) describe 묘사하다, 설명하다 leap 뛰어오르다 worth ~의 가치가 있는 journey 여행, 여정

20 ③

M: <u>What</u> <u>types</u> of <u>movies</u> do you enjoy watching? 넌 어떤 종류의 영화를 즐겨 보니?

W: I normally watch <u>comedy</u> or <u>romance</u> movies. How about you? 난 보통은 코미디나 로맨스 영화를 봐. 너는 어때?

M: I like <u>action</u> movies and <u>thriller</u> movies. 나는 액션 영화와 스릴러 영화를 좋아해.

W: I see. Have you heard of the new action movie called *Hawk Fighter*? 그렇구나. 새로 나온 '호크 파이터'라는 액션 영화를 들어 봤니?

M: Yeah! All my friends <u>recommended</u> it. It must be a good movie. 그럼! 내 친구들이 모두 그 영화를 추천했어. 좋은 영화인 게 분명해.

W: Well, I actually have <u>tickets</u> to go see it <u>tonight</u> at Regal Movies. Do you want to <u>go</u> <u>with</u> <u>me</u>? 사실, 나한테 오늘 밤에 리걸 무비스에서 그걸 볼 수 있는 티켓이 있어. 나랑 같이 갈래?

M: Of course I do! But do you know <u>how far</u> away Regal Movies is? <u>I wonder</u> how long it'll take to get there. 물론 가야지! 그런데 넌 리걸 무비스가 얼마나 먼지 알고 있니? 거기까지 가는 데 얼마나 걸리는지 궁금해.

W: The movie theater is walking distance from here. 영화관은 여기서 걸어갈 수 있는 거리야.

① Sorry, but I can't go with you. 미안하지만, 너와 같이 갈 수 없어.
② The TV show starts at 9:00 P.M. 그 TV 프로그램은 저녁 9시에 시작해.
③ The movie theater is walking distance from here. 영화관은 여기서 걸어갈 수 있는 거리야.
④ It starts at 7:00 P.M. I'll see you in front of the theater. 그건 오후 7시에 시작해. 영화관 앞에서 만나자.
⑤ I don't think there will be tickets left. It's a popular movie. 남아 있는 티켓이 없을 거야. 그건 인기 있는 영화야.

해설 남자가 'how far ~?'로 영화관까지의 거리를 물었으므로, 여자는 영화관까지의 거리를 설명해야 한다.

어휘 thriller 스릴러물 recommend 추천하다 far (거리가) 먼 walking distance 걸어갈 수 있는 거리

14회 실전모의고사 본문 p.162~163

01 ③	02 ②	03 ④	04 ②	05 ③
06 ①	07 ③	08 ④	09 ④	10 ④
11 ③	12 ①	13 ④	14 ②	15 ④
16 ⑤	17 ⑤	18 ③	19 ④	20 ③

01 ③

W: Honey, there are so many <u>keys</u> here. Do you know <u>which</u> <u>one</u> opens the <u>jewelry</u> box? 여보, 여기 정말 많은 열쇠가 있네요. 어느 것이 보석상자를 여는 열쇠인지 알아요?

M: I don't know. Let's try this <u>long</u>, <u>circular</u> key. It might open the box. 몰라요. 이 길고 둥근 열쇠로 해봅시다. 이게 상자를 열 지도 몰라요.

W: I already tried that one and this short, diamond-shaped key. But, both don't work.
제가 이미 그 열쇠하고 이 작은 마름모꼴의 열쇠로 해봤어요. 하지만 둘 다 안 돼요.

M: Well, then how about this long, triangular key?
음, 그럼 이 긴 삼각형 열쇠는 어떨까요?

W: No, that's the key to the storage room. Hey, isn't this short, circular one the key to your office drawer? 아니요, 그건 창고 열쇠예요. 여보, 이 짧고 둥근 것이 당신 사무실 서랍 열쇠 아니에요?

M: Oh, you're right. Then this long, diamond-shaped key must be the one that opens the jewelry box.
아, 당신 말이 맞아요. 그럼 이 긴 마름모꼴의 열쇠가 보석상자를 여는 열쇠가 틀림없겠네요.

W: Yes! It's finally opened. Thanks for your help.
네! 마침내 열렸어요. 도와 줘서 고마워요.

M: Sure, no problem. 천만에요.

어휘 jewelry box 보석 상자 try 시도하다 circular 둥근
diamond-shaped 마름모꼴의 work (원하는) 효과가 나다[있다]
triangular 삼각형의 storage room 창고 drawer 서랍

02 ②

[Telephone rings.] [전화벨이 울린다.]

W: Hello, this is Amanda. 여보세요, 아만다입니다.

M: My name is Jason, calling from Hickory Library.
제 이름은 제이슨이고 히커리 도서관에서 전화 드립니다.

W: Yes, may I ask why you're calling?
네, 무슨 일로 전화하셨어요?

M: I'm calling to tell you that you have to pay a late fee for two books, *The Fortune Teller* and *The Black Cat*. 당신이 '점쟁이'와 '검은 고양이', 이 두 권의 책에 대해 연체료를 내셔야 한다는 것을 말씀 드리려고 전화했습니다.

W: A late fee? I borrowed those books from the library last week.
연체료요? 저는 지난주에 도서관에서 그 책들을 빌렸는데요.

M: Actually, you were supposed to return them two weeks ago.
실은, 당신은 2주 전에 그 책들을 반납하기로 되어 있었어요.

W: Oh my goodness! Has it been that long already?
아, 맙소사! 벌써 그렇게 오래됐나요?

M: I'm afraid so. Please come by to return the books and pay the fee. 죄송하지만, 그렇습니다. 잠깐 들르셔서 책을 반납하시고 연체료를 내주세요.

W: Alright, I will. Thank you for letting me know.
알았어요, 그렇게 할게요. 알려주셔서 고맙습니다.

해설 남자는 please의 뒤에서 여자에게 요청하는 내용을 말하고 있다.

어휘 pay a late fee 연체료를 내다 fortune teller 점쟁이
borrow 빌리다 actually 사실은, 실제로는 be supposed to
~하기로 되어 있다 already 벌써, 이미

03 ④

① W: What happened to your arm?
네 팔은 왜 그래?

M: I broke it while playing soccer.
축구를 하다가 팔이 부러졌어.

② W: Dad, I think my arm is broken.
아빠, 제 팔이 부러진 것 같아요.

M: Oh, no! Let's go to the hospital.
이런! 병원에 가자.

③ W: Dad, what is that woman doing?
아빠, 저 여자분은 뭐 하는 거예요?

M: She's waiting in line to buy ice cream.
저 여자분은 아이스크림을 사려고 줄을 서 있구나.

④ W: Dad, what is that woman riding?
아빠, 저 여자분이 타고 있는 게 뭐예요?

M: Oh, she's in a wheelchair. She must have broken her leg. 아, 저 여자분은 휠체어를 타고 있구나. 다리가 부러졌나 보네.

⑤ W: Look! The people in the park are skateboarding.
저걸 봐! 공원의 사람들이 스케이트보드를 타고 있어.

M: That looks like fun. Do you want to try?
재미있어 보이네. 너도 해볼래?

어휘 arm 팔 broken 부러진 wait in line 줄을 서서 기다리다
break one's leg 다리가 부러지다 skateboard 스케이트보드(를
타다) try 시도하다, 해보다

04 ②

W: I like all of Sarah Mitchell's paintings. She is such a talented artist. 나는 사라 미첼의 모든 그림이 마음에 들어. 그녀는 정말 재능 있는 예술가야.

M: I agree. I like this painting in particular. Look at how she drew the clouds in the sky.
나도 그렇게 생각해. 난 특히 이 그림이 좋아. 그녀가 하늘에 구름을 어떻게 그렸는지 한번 봐.

W: They're beautiful! I like the butterflies, too. They look so real.
아름다워! 나는 나비도 마음에 들어. 정말 진짜 같아.

M: I know. Do you see how she painted the sunflowers? This painting must have taken her forever to finish. 나도 알아. 그녀가 어떻게 해바라기를 그렸는지 보여? 그녀는 이 그림을 끝내는 데 무척 오래 걸렸을 거야.

W: Yeah, you're right. 그래, 맞아.

M: Well, thank you for bringing me to this art exhibition. I think I'm a fan of Sarah Mitchell now.
음, 이 미술 전시회에 나를 데려와 줘서 고마워. 난 이제 사라 미첼의 팬이 된 것 같아.

W: I'm glad to hear that! I had a great time, too.
그 말을 들으니 기쁘네! 나도 아주 즐거운 시간을 보냈어.

M: Let's come back next time! 다음 번에 다시 오자고!

해설 두 사람은 clouds(구름), butterflies(나비), sunflowers(해바라기)가 있는 그림에 관해 이야기하고 있다.

어휘 painting 그림 talented 재능 있는 artist 예술가
in particular 특히 draw 그리다(draw-drew-drawn) take
forever 엄청나게 오랜 시간이 걸리다 art exhibition 미술 전시회

05 ③

W: Mr. Joseph Lance? 조지프 랜스 씨?

M: Yes, ma'am. 네.

W: Here's your medicine for today. Take one pill after
you eat lunch and dinner. Also, I will be back later
to give you some shots.
여기 오늘 드실 약이요. 점심과 저녁을 드신 후에 알약 하나를 복용
하세요. 그리고 제가 이따가 다시 와서 주사를 놓아 드릴게요.

M: Okay. I was told this morning that I might be able
to leave the hospital today. Is that true?
네. 제가 오늘 아침에 들었는데, 저 오늘 퇴원할 수 있을 거라고 하
던데요. 그게 사실인가요?

W: Well, the doctor has to come see if you're healthy
enough to go home.
글쎄요, 의사 선생님이 오셔서 환자분이 귀가할 수 있을 정도로 충
분히 건강해지셨는지를 보셔야 해요.

M: Okay, when will the doctor be here to see me?
네, 의사 선생님이 언제 저를 보러 오시죠?

W: He'll be here around noon. Let me know if there's
anything else you need. 정오쯤에 여기 오실 거예요. 필요하
신 것이 더 있으면 제게 알려주세요.

M: I will. Thank you, ma'am.
그럴게요. 고맙습니다.

해설 여자는 남자에게 알약을 주고 주사를 놓는 사람인데, 다른 의사
를 언급했으므로 의사가 아니라 간호사이다.

어휘 ma'am (여성에 대한 존칭) 부인 medicine 약 pill
알약 give somebody a shot ~에게 주사를 놓다 leave the
hospital 퇴원하다 healthy 건강한 around noon 정오쯤에
vet 수의사 pharmacist 약사

06 ①

M: You look unhappy. Is there something wrong?
너 기분이 안 좋아 보여. 무슨 일이라도 있어?

W: Yeah, I did really badly on my math test. This is the
worst grade I've ever gotten! 응, 나 수학 시험을 정말 못
쳤거든. 내가 받아 본 것 중에 최악의 성적이야!

M: Oh no, did you not study for the test?
아, 이런. 시험 공부를 안 한 거니?

W: I studied all night for it! That's why I'm so
disappointed.
밤새도록 시험 공부를 했지! 그게 내가 이렇게 실망하는 이유야.

M: It's okay. I'm sure you'll do better next time.
괜찮아. 넌 다음번 시험에서는 분명히 잘할 거야.

W: Yeah, I hope so. This grade just ruined my day.
I guess I'll just have to study even harder for the
next test. 그래, 나도 그러길 바라. 이 성적은 내 하루를 망쳐 버
렸어. 그냥 다음 시험을 위해 더 열심히 공부해야 할 것 같아.

해설 unhappy(기분이 안 좋은), disappointed(실망한) 등과 관
련이 있는 심정은 upset(속상한)이다.

어휘 do badly on the test 시험을 못 보다 worst 가장
나쁜, 최악의(bad-worse-worst) grade 성적 do better 더
잘하다 next time 다음에 ruin 망치다 thankful 고마워하는
satisfied 만족하는

07 ③

① M: What are we having for dinner?
우리는 저녁으로 뭘 먹죠?

W: I'm making chicken noodle soup.
내가 치킨누들수프를 만들고 있어요.

② M: Where is the meeting taking place?
회의는 어디서 열려요?

W: It's going to be in Room three ou five.
305호실에서 있을 겁니다.

③ M: Are you ready for the first day of school?
너 학교 첫날 준비는 됐니?

W: The first day of school is August thirty first.
학교 첫날은 8월 31일이에요.

④ M: What do you do in your free time?
넌 여가 시간에 뭘 하니?

W: I usually ride my bike or take naps.
난 주로 자전거를 타거나 낮잠을 자.

⑤ M: Listen! My favorite song is on the radio.
들어봐! 내가 좋아하는 노래가 라디오에서 나오고 있어.

W: I really like this song, too.
나도 이 노래를 정말 좋아해.

어휘 noodle 국수 meeting 회의 take place (회의가) 열리다
free time 여가 시간, 자유 시간 usually 주로 take a nap
낮잠을 자다 on the radio 라디오에서

08 ④

M: Grace, what's the matter with your car?
그레이스, 네 차에 무슨 문제가 있니?

W: Well, I ran over some nails on the side of the road,
and now I have a flat tire! I don't know what to do.
글쎄, 도로변에 있던 못 위로 달렸더니 타이어가 펑크가 났어. 어떻
게 해야 할지 모르겠어.

M: Oh no, that's terrible! Do you have an extra one in
your car? 아, 이런. 안됐구나! 네 차에 여분의 타이어가 있니?

W: Yeah, there should be one in the trunk. Do you
know how to replace tires?
응, 트렁크에 하나 있을 거야. 넌 타이어를 교체할 줄 아니?

M: Yes. I learned last year when I worked at a car
repair shop.
응. 내가 작년에 자동차 정비소에서 일했을 때 배웠어.

W: That's great! Then could you help me change it?
대단한데! 그럼 너 내가 타이어 바꾸는 것을 도와줄래?

M: Of course, I can do that. Do you have any tools
with you? 물론 할 수 있지. 공구를 좀 갖고 있니?

W: I sure do. They're in the trunk, too.
물론 있어. 그것도 트렁크에 있어.

M: Okay then, let's get started.
그럼 좋아, 시작해 보자.

해설 여자의 대사 'could you ~?'에 부탁 내용이 나온다.

어휘 nail 못 on the side of the road 도로변에 have a flat tire 타이어가 펑크 나다 extra 추가의, 여분의 trunk (자동차) 트렁크 replace 교체하다, 대체하다 car repair shop 자동차 정비소 tool 공구 get started (일을) 시작하다

09 ④

W: Hey, Victor, where are you going?
얘, 빅터, 너 어디 가고 있니?

M: I'm on my way to get my phone fixed. This is the third time this month. 난 내 휴대폰을 고치러 가는 중이야. 이번 달 들어서 벌써 세 번째야.

W: Why? What's wrong with it? 왜? 무슨 문제가 있어?

M: Well, I dropped it and the screen cracked. I have to get it replaced. 음, 내가 휴대폰을 떨어뜨려서 화면에 금이 갔어. 화면을 교체해야 해.

W: I'm sorry to hear that. It must be expensive to get it fixed. 안됐구나. 그걸 고치려면 비쌀 텐데 말이야.

M: Yeah, it is. I've wasted so much money on my phone recently.
응, 맞아. 난 요즘 들어서 휴대폰에 정말 많은 돈을 낭비했어.

W: Hmm… Why don't you buy a case for your phone and sign up for phone insurance?
음, 휴대폰 케이스를 하나 사고, 휴대폰 보험에 가입하는 건 어때?

M: Oh, those are really good ideas!
아, 그거 정말 좋은 생각이다!

해설 여자는 전화기 케이스를 살 것과 보험에 가입할 것을 제안하고 있다.

어휘 on one's way to ~으로 가는 길에 get something fixed ~을 고치다 drop 떨어뜨리다 crack 금이 가다 replace 교환하다, 교체하다 waste 낭비하다 recently 최근에 sign up for ~을 신청하다, ~에 가입하다 insurance 보험

10 ④

W: Good morning, welcome to Splash Water Park. What can I do for you? 안녕하세요. 스플래시 워터파크에 잘 오셨습니다. 무엇을 도와드릴까요?

M: I would like to purchase four tickets, please.
티켓 네 장을 사고 싶어요.

W: Okay, how many adults and children are you buying tickets for?
네. 성인 몇 명과 어린이 몇 명의 티켓을 사실 건가요?

M: I need tickets for two adults and two children.
성인 두 명과 어린이 두 명의 티켓을 주세요.

W: Alright, your total is sixty dollars.
알겠습니다. 합계는 60달러입니다.

M: Oh, can I use this thirty-dollar discount coupon? I would also like to use the locker room.
아, 제가 이 30달러짜리 할인권을 쓸 수 있나요? 그리고 라커룸도 이용하고 싶은데요.

W: Yes, you can use it. With the coupon your total is thirty dollars, and to use the locker room, you have to pay an extra ten dollars. 네, 할인권을 쓰실 수 있습니다. 쿠폰이 있으면 손님의 합계 금액은 30달러이고, 라커룸을 이용하시려면 추가로 10달러를 지불하셔야 해요.

M: That's fine. Here's the money. 좋습니다. 돈 여기 있어요.

해설 할인 받은 티켓 가격 30달러＋라커룸 이용료 10달러＝40달러

어휘 purchase 구매하다 adult 성인, 어른 total 합계 discount coupon 할인권 locker room 라커룸, 탈의실 extra 추가의

11 ③

W: Hello, sir. Can I help you?
안녕하세요, 손님. 무엇을 도와드릴까요?

M: Yes, I bought this shirt two days ago, and I would like to get a refund because the zipper is broken.
네, 제가 이틀 전에 이 셔츠를 샀는데요, 지퍼가 고장 나서 환불을 받고 싶어요.

W: Okay, do you have the receipt?
네, 영수증을 갖고 계신가요?

M: Yes, here you are. 네, 여기 있어요.

W: Please wait a minute while I take a look at the shirt. [pause] Sir, I'm afraid you can't get a refund on this item. 제가 셔츠를 살펴보는 동안 잠시만 기다리세요. [잠시 후] 손님, 죄송하지만 이 물건에 대해서는 환불을 받으실 수 없습니다.

M: Why not? 왜 안 되죠?

W: Because the price tag is not on it, and it has a stain on the front.
가격표가 붙어 있지 않고, 앞쪽에 얼룩이 묻어 있기 때문이에요.

M: I thought I just needed to bring the receipt.
저는 영수증만 가져오면 된다고 생각했는데요.

W: I'm sorry, sir. That's our store policy. If the item is damaged, you can't get a refund.
죄송합니다, 손님. 그건 저희 매장의 방침입니다. 물품이 손상되면 환불을 받으실 수 없어요.

M: Oh, okay. 아, 알았어요.

해설 shirt, zipper, price tag 등의 단어가 나오고 환불에 관한 내용이 나오므로 옷 가게에서 일어나는 대화이다.

어휘 sir (남자에 대한 존칭) 손님, 선생님 get a refund 환불을 받다 zipper 지퍼 broken 망가진 receipt 영수증 wait a minute 잠시 기다리다 while ~하는 동안 take a look at ~을 보다 I'm afraid 유감이지만 ~이다 item 물품, 품목 price tag 가격표 stain 얼룩 policy 방침, 정책 damaged 하자가 생긴; 피해를 입은 dry cleaner's 드라이클리닝점, 세탁소 stationery store 문구점

12 ①

W: It's that time of the year again! Are you ready for the Annual Puppet Festival? We invite you to come enjoy our new puppet show, *Puppets and Kings,* which opens on January second. There will be four shows a day, at twelve P.M., two P.M., three P.M., and five P.M. To see the show, you must pay a five-dollar fee. Also, you can make your own puppet at the Create-A-Puppet booth near the entrance. Lastly, there will be a display window full of puppets from all over the world. Don't forget to take a picture in the photo zone!

해마다 돌아오는 그 시기가 다시 찾아왔습니다! 연례 꼭두각시 축제를 위한 준비가 됐나요? 1월 2일에 막을 올리는 저희의 새로운 꼭두각시 공연인 '꼭두각시와 임금들'에 여러분을 초대하오니 와서 즐기세요. 하루에 네 번, 오후 12시, 2시, 3시, 그리고 5시 공연이 있을 예정입니다. 공연을 관람하시려면 5달러의 요금을 지불하셔야 합니다. 그리고 입구 근처에 있는 '꼭두각시 만들기' 부스에서 당신만의 꼭두각시를 만들 수도 있습니다. 마지막으로, 세계 각국의 꼭두각시들로 가득한 진열창도 마련될 것입니다. 포토존에서 사진을 찍는 것도 잊지 마세요.

어휘 ready for ~에 대한 준비가 된 annual 연례의, 매년의 puppet 꼭두각시 show 공연, 쇼 fee 요금 one's own ~만의 entrance 입구 lastly 마지막으로 display window 진열창 all over the world 세계 각국의 take a picture 사진을 찍다 photo zone 포토존(사진을 찍을 수 있도록 마련된 지점)

13 ④

① Take a left turn at Wicker Street, and go straight until you see a fence.
위커 스트리트에서 왼쪽으로 돌고, 담장이 보일 때까지 직진해.
② When you see the fence, take a right turn onto Franklin Road. 울타리가 보이면 프랭클린 로드로 우회전해.
③ Stay on Franklin Road until you pass the school.
학교를 지날 때까지 프랭클린 로드를 벗어나지 마.
④ As soon as you pass the school, take a left turn onto Merry Lane.
학교를 지나자마자 왼쪽으로 돌아서 메리 레인으로 들어가.
⑤ Keep going straight, and you will see Jean's house.
계속해서 직진하면 진의 집이 보일 거야.

해설 ④는 'take a left turn'이 아니라 'take a right turn'으로 수정되어야 한다.

어휘 directions 길 안내 take a left turn 왼쪽으로 돌다, 좌회전하다 go straight 곧장 가다, 직진하다 fence 울타리, 펜스 stay on 계속 머무르다 pass 지나가다

14 ②

M: This is used to transport people to the hospital quickly during emergency situations. It is normally a white vehicle, and it has a siren on top of it. The siren rings to let drivers know that there is a sick person in it. When drivers hear the siren, they move to the side of the road so that it can pass by. Inside this vehicle, there is medical equipment. Paramedics, people who take care of the patient inside the vehicle, also ride in the vehicle.

이것은 응급 상황에서 사람들을 병원으로 빠르게 수송하기 위해 이용됩니다. 이것은 보통 흰색 차량이고, 위에 사이렌이 달려 있습니다. 차량 안에 아픈 사람이 있다는 것을 운전자들에게 알리기 위해 사이렌이 울립니다. 운전자들은 사이렌을 듣게 되면 그것이 지나갈 수 있도록 하기 위해 도로변으로 이동합니다. 차량 안에는 의료 장비들이 있습니다. 차량에는 차량 안에서 환자들을 돌보는 응급 의료원들도 함께 탑니다.

어휘 transport 수송하다, 나르다 emergency situation 응급 상황, 비상 사태 normally 보통은, 일반적으로 vehicle 차량 on top of ~의 위에 ring (벨이) 울리다 so that ~할 수 있도록 pass by 지나가다 medical equipment 의료 장비 paramedic 긴급 의료원 take care of ~을 돌보다

15 ④

W: Hello, may I help you with something?
안녕하세요, 제가 뭘 도와드릴까요?
M: Yes, please. I'm looking for Ms. Williams, my guidance counselor. 네, 도와주세요. 저는 제 상담 교사이신 윌리엄스 씨를 찾고 있습니다.
W: She went abroad to attend a conference two days ago. 그분은 이틀 전에 학회에 참석하러 외국에 나가셨어요.
M: Oh, I need to speak with her as soon as possible. Do you know when she will be back?
아, 저는 가능한 한 빨리 그분하고 이야기를 해야 하는데요. 그분이 언제 돌아오는지 아세요?
W: Yes, she will be in her office starting next Wednesday. Is there anything I can help you with until she comes back?
네, 그분은 다음 주 수요일부터 사무실에 나오실 겁니다. 그분이 돌아오기 전까지 제가 도와드릴 일이 있나요?
M: Hmm… Is there any way I can contact her while she's abroad? 음, 그분이 외국에 계신 동안 제가 연락할 수 있는 방법이 있을까요?
W: Actually, I can give you her email address. Maybe you can send her an email.
사실 제가 당신에게 그분의 이메일 주소를 드릴 수 있어요. 당신이 그분에게 이메일을 보낼 수 있어요.
M: That would be wonderful! Thank you very much.
그러면 아주 좋겠네요! 정말 고맙습니다.
W: No problem. 별말씀을요.

어휘 guidance counselor (학습 지도) 상담 교사 go abroad 외국에 가다 attend a conference 학회에 참석하다 as soon as possible 가능한 한 빨리 be back 돌아오다(=come back) starting ~부터 contact 연락하다 email address 이메일 주소

16 ⑤

M: This is Queen Wedding Hall. May I help you?
퀸 예식장입니다. 무엇을 도와드릴까요?

W: Yes, I would like to reserve a date for my wedding this month. 네, 이달에 있을 제 결혼식 날짜를 예약하려고요.

M: Okay, we have April fourteenth, April twenty first, and April twenty eighth open. Will you be interested in any of those dates? 네. 저희는 4월 14일, 4월 21일, 그리고 4월 28일이 비어 있습니다. 저 날짜 중에 관심이 있으신가요?

W: Well, I have to go look at wedding dresses on April fourteenth.
글쎄요, 제가 4월 14일에는 웨딩드레스를 보러 가야 하거든요.

M: Oh, then how about the twenty first and twenty eighth? 아, 그러면 21일이나 28일은 어떠세요?

W: Hmm… The wedding cake I ordered won't be finished until April twenty second, so April twenty first won't work either.
음, 제가 주문한 웨딩 케이크가 4월 22일까지는 마련되지 않을 거니까, 4월 21일도 안 되겠네요.

M: Alright. Then should I reserve the wedding hall for you on the twenty eighth?
알겠습니다. 그럼 제가 28일에 예식장을 예약해 드려야 하나요?

W: Yes, please, I think that will be the best date.
네, 그렇게 해주세요. 그게 가장 좋은 날짜 같네요.

어휘 wedding hall 예식장 reserve 예약하다 wedding 결혼식 open 이용할 수 있는 be interested in ~에 관심이 있다 how about ~? ~는 어때? order 주문하다 work (원하는) 효과가 나다[있다] either (부정문의 끝 부분에서) 또한

17 ⑤

M: James drinks five cups of coffee every day. On days that he doesn't drink coffee, he drinks tea or soda. James' mother knows that too much caffeine is bad for James' health. She tried talking to him about it, but he wouldn't listen. One day, James suffers from a headache and can't sleep. He ends up staying up all night. The next morning, he tells his mother what happened. She tells him that it's because of all the caffeine he drinks. James decides to stop drinking coffee, tea, and soda, and start taking care of his body. In this situation, what would James most likely say to his mother?

제임스는 매일 5잔의 커피를 마신다. 커피를 마시지 않는 날에 그는 차 또는 탄산음료를 마신다. 제임스의 엄마는 너무 많은 카페인이 제임스의 건강에 좋지 않다는 것을 알고 있다. 그녀는 그에게 이 문제에 대해 말해봤지만, 그는 들으려고 하지 않는다. 하루는 제임스가 두통이 심해서 잠을 잘 수 없다. 그는 밤을 꼬박 새우고야 만다. 다음 날 아침 그는 엄마에게 무슨 일이 있었는지 말한다. 그녀는 그 일이 그가 마시는 카페인 때문이라고 말한다. 제임스는 커피, 차, 그리고 탄산음료를 그만 마시고, 그의 몸을 돌보기로 결심한다. 이런 상황에서 제임스는 엄마에게 뭐라고 말하겠는가?

James: I'm going to drink water instead of coffee from now on. 저는 지금부터 커피 대신 물을 마실 거예요.

① I'm going to keep drinking coffee.
저는 계속 커피를 마실 거예요.

② I need some medicine for my headache.
저는 두통약이 필요해요.

③ There's no more soda in the refrigerator.
냉장고에 탄산음료가 떨어졌어요.

④ I can't sleep early today. I have a lot of homework to do.
오늘은 일찍 잠을 잘 수가 없어요. 해야 할 숙제가 아주 많아요.

⑤ I'm going to drink water instead of coffee from now on. 저는 지금부터 커피 대신 물을 마실 거예요.

해설 'James decides to ~'에 나오는 결심 내용을 엄마에게 말할 것이다.

어휘 soda 탄산음료, 소다수 caffeine 카페인 suffer from ~에 시달리다 headache 두통 stay up all night 밤을 새우다 take care of ~을 돌보다, 보살피다 refrigerator 냉장고 from now on 지금부터, 앞으로

18 ③

W: What should we do after school today?
우리는 오늘 방과 후에 뭘 할까?

M: I haven't thought about it yet. Do you want to go play video games?
난 아직 그것에 관해 생각해보지 않았어. 비디오 게임을 하러 갈까?

W: Aren't you tired of video games? You play with your friends every day! 넌 비디오 게임이 지겹지도 않니? 넌 매일 네 친구들과 게임을 하잖아!

M: You're right. Then let's do something new. Do you have any ideas?
맞아. 그럼 뭔가 새로운 것을 하자. 좋은 생각이 있어?

W: Hmm… I haven't been bowling in a long time.
음, 난 오랫동안 볼링장에 못 갔어.

M: Bowling? I've never gone bowling before.
볼링? 난 전에 한 번도 볼링 치러 간 적이 없어.

W: It's easy! All you have to do is roll the ball and knock down the pins.
쉬워! 넌 그저 공을 굴려서 핀을 쓰러뜨리기만 하면 돼.

M: Alright. You can teach me when we get to the bowling alley.
좋아. 우리가 볼링장에 가면 네가 나를 가르쳐 주면 되겠네.

W: Okay! I'm excited. This should be fun!
좋아! 신나는 걸. 이건 재미있을 거야!

어휘 play video games 비디오게임을 하다 be tired of ~에 싫증나다 go bowling 볼링 치러 가다 roll the ball 공을 굴리다 knock down 쓰러뜨리다 pin (볼링)핀 bowling alley 볼링장

19 ④

W: Dad, can we please go to the clothing section?
아빠, 우리는 의류 코너에 가도 돼요?

M: Sure, Nina. 물론이지, 나나.

W: Wow! There are so many blouses here. Isn't this one pretty?
와! 여기에는 정말 많은 블라우스가 있네요. 이거 예쁘지 않아요?

M: It looks really similar to the one I bought you last week. 이건 내가 지난주에 너한테 샀던 거랑 정말 비슷하구나.

W: But, Dad! I really like this one! Can you buy it for me? 하지만, 아빠! 난 이게 정말 마음에 들어요! 저에게 이걸 사주실 수 있어요?

M: No, Nina. You already have a lot of clothes at home. You don't even wear all of them.
안 된다, 나나. 너는 이미 집에 아주 많은 옷들이 있잖니. 너는 그 옷들을 다 입지도 않잖아.

W: Dad, if you buy me this blouse, I promise I'll never ask for one again.
아빠, 이 블라우스를 사주시면, 다시는 다른 것을 사달라고 부탁하지 않을 거라고 약속해요.

M: That's what you said the last time I bought you one. My answer is no, Nina.
그건 내가 지난번에 옷을 샀을 때도 네가 했던 말이잖아. 내 대답은 '안 된다'야, 나나.

W: Okay, Dad. I'll just wear the ones I have at home.
알았어요, 아빠. 저는 그냥 집에 있는 옷들을 입을게요.

① Bad news travels quickly. 나쁜 소문은 빨리 퍼진다.
② Two heads are better than one. 백지장도 맞들면 낫다.
③ The early bird catches the worm.
일찍 일어나는 새가 벌레를 잡는다.
④ You can't always get what you want.
원하는 것을 항상 얻을 수는 없다.
⑤ Heaven helps those who help themselves.
하늘은 스스로 돕는 자를 돕는다.

어휘 clothing 옷, 의류 section 부분, 코너 similar to ~와 비슷한 ask for ~을 요구하다 worm 벌레

20 ③

W: Why do you look so sad, Jim?
넌 왜 그렇게 슬픈 표정이니, 짐?

M: My baseball team lost the game last night and I think it's my fault.
우리 야구팀이 어젯밤 경기에서 졌는데, 내 탓인 것 같아.

W: Why do you say that? I'm sure you did your best.
왜 그런 말을 하는 거야? 난 분명히 네가 최선을 다했다고 보는데.

M: Well, my teammate threw the ball to me, but I missed it. So the opposite team won the game.
글쎄, 내 팀원이 나한테 공을 던졌는데, 내가 그걸 놓쳤어. 그래서 상대팀이 경기를 이겼어.

W: I see. But everyone makes mistakes. Even famous players make mistakes sometimes. You can win

your next game.
그렇구나. 하지만 모든 사람은 실수하기 마련이잖아. 유명한 선수들도 가끔은 실수를 해. 넌 다음 경기에서는 이길 거야.

M: Do you really think so? 정말로 그렇게 생각해?

W: Yes, I sure do. I'll be at your next game to cheer for you. 응, 정말 그래. 내가 너의 다음 경기에 너를 응원하러 갈게.

M: Thanks for saying that. I feel a lot better now.
그렇게 말해 줘서 고마워. 이제 기분이 한결 나아졌어.

① Do you want to play baseball with me?
나와 함께 야구 경기를 할래?
② I'm already at the baseball stadium.
난 벌써 야구 경기장에 있어.
③ Thanks for saying that. I feel a lot better now.
그렇게 말해 줘서 고마워. 이제 기분이 한결 나아졌어.
④ I can't go to the baseball game today. I have other plans. 난 오늘은 야구 경기에 갈 수 없어. 다른 계획이 있거든.
⑤ I'm going to be late for lunch. Would you mind waiting for me?
난 점심식사에 늦을 거야. 나를 기다려 줄 수 있겠니?

어휘 lose the game 경기에 지다(↔ win the game) fault 잘못, 책임 do one's best 최선을 다하다 teammate 팀원 throw 던지다(throw-threw-thrown) miss 놓치다 opposite team 상대팀 make mistakes 실수를 하다 famous 유명한 player 선수 sometimes 가끔 cheer for ~을 응원하다 baseball stadium 야구장 feel better 기분이 나아지다

15회 실전모의고사 본문 p.174-175

01 ③	02 ④	03 ③	04 ④	05 ④
06 ①	07 ②	08 ④	09 ③	10 ③
11 ④	12 ②	13 ③	14 ②	15 ①
16 ⑤	17 ④	18 ④	19 ④	20 ⑤

01 ③

W: Hey, Michael. Did you hear that Betty gave birth to a baby girl?
야, 마이클. 너는 베티가 딸을 낳았다는 소식을 들었니?

M: Yes! I bet she's the cutest baby ever! We should go visit her and the baby. 응! 분명 최고로 귀여운 아기일 거야! 우리는 베티와 아기를 방문해야 해.

W: Yeah, but let's buy a gift for the baby before we go.
응, 그런데 우리 가기 전에 아기를 위한 선물을 사자.

M: Okay. Should we buy a bottle? Betty can use it to feed the baby. 알겠어. 우리는 젖병을 사야 할까? 베티가 그것을 사용해서 아기를 먹일 수 있잖아.

W: No, she probably already has one. How about a doll? 아니, 베티는 아마도 이미 하나 갖고 있겠지. 인형은 어때?

M: The baby is too young to play with a doll. Let's get

diapers instead.

그 아기는 인형을 가지고 놀기엔 너무 어려. 대신 기저귀를 사자.

W: Hmm… I don't think diapers would make a good gift. We should buy a blanket. It'll keep the baby warm. 음, 나는 기저귀가 좋은 선물이 될 거라 생각하지 않아. 우린 담요를 사야 해. 그것이 아기를 따뜻하게 해줄 거야.

M: Alright, that sounds like a good idea.

그래, 그거 좋은 생각 같다.

어휘 give birth to a baby 아기를 낳다   bottle 젖병, 병   feed (밥을) 먹이다   diaper 기저귀   blanket 담요   keep somebody warm ~의 몸을 따뜻하게 하다

02 ④

[Telephone rings.] [전화벨이 울린다.]

W: This is Eugene, at Bolt Electricity. What can I help you with today?

저는 볼트 전기의 유진입니다. 오늘 제가 무엇을 도와드릴까요?

M: Hi. My name is Patrick Ford. I'm calling to ask about my electricity bill for this month.

안녕하세요. 제 이름은 패트릭 포드입니다. 저는 이번 달 전기요금에 대해 여쭤보려고 전화 드렸어요.

W: Yes, sir. What seems to be the problem?

네, 고객님. 문제가 무엇이죠?

M: Well, I was charged two hundred dollars, and I would like to know why. My bill is normally one hundred dollars. 그게, 제가 200달러를 청구 받았는데, 그 이유를 알고 싶네요. 제 요금은 보통 100달러거든요.

W: Please wait a minute. I will check that for you. [pause] I see what the problem is. We charged you twice on accident.

잠시만 기다려 주세요. 제가 확인해 보겠습니다. [잠시 후] 문제가 뭔지 알겠네요. 저희가 실수로 고객님께 두 배로 청구했어요.

M: Oh, okay. So my bill is one hundred dollars, correct?

아, 알겠습니다. 그러니까 제 요금은 100달러인 거죠, 맞죠?

W: Yes, sir. 네, 고객님.

해설 남자의 첫 대사 중 'I'm calling to ~'에 전화를 건 목적이 바로 언급된다.

어휘 electricity bill 전기 요금   charge (요금, 비용을) 청구하다   twice 두 배로; 두 번   on accident 잘못하여, 의도치 않게

03 ③

① M: Honey, did you see my car keys?

여보, 내 자동차 키 봤어요?

W: Yes, they are on the kitchen table.

네, 주방 식탁 위에 있어요.

② M: You look so busy, honey.

당신은 아주 바빠 보여요, 여보.

W: I am. There are a lot of dishes to wash.

그래요. 설거지할 그릇이 아주 많거든요.

③ M: What are you doing in the kitchen?

당신, 주방에서 뭘 하고 있어요?

W: I'm cleaning the table. It's so dirty.

식탁을 닦는 중이에요. 너무 더럽네요.

④ M: When will you be done doing the laundry?

빨래하는 걸 언제 끝낼 건가요?

W: I'm not sure. Maybe around noon.

모르겠네요. 아마 정오쯤에요.

⑤ M: Honey, I smell something burning.

여보, 뭔가 타는 냄새가 나요.

W: Oh my goodness! I burnt all the cookies!

아, 맙소사! 내가 쿠키를 전부 태웠군요!

어휘 do the laundry 빨래하다   smell 냄새(를 맡다)   burn 타다(burn-burnt-burnt)

04 ④

M: Welcome to Rita's Jewels. Are you looking for something in particular?

리타 보석가게에 오신 걸 환영합니다. 특별히 찾는 물건이 있나요?

W: Yes, I want to buy some earrings that would look good with the necklace I am wearing right now.

네, 제가 지금 하고 있는 목걸이와 어울리는 귀걸이를 사고 싶어요.

M: Alright. I think these long, star-shaped earrings would look good on you. 알겠습니다. 여기 별 모양의 긴 귀걸이가 손님에게 잘 어울린다는 생각이 드네요.

W: They look nice, but I prefer short earrings. How much are these cat-shaped ones? 예쁘긴 한데, 저는 짧은 귀걸이를 선호해요. 이 고양이 모양의 귀걸이는 얼마예요?

M: Those are one hundred dollars. 100달러입니다.

W: That's too expensive for me. How about these leaf-shaped earrings? And these cross-shaped earrings? 제겐 너무 비싸네요. 이 나뭇잎 모양의 귀걸이는요? 그리고 이 십자 모양의 귀걸이는요?

M: The leaf-shaped earrings are fifty dollars and the cross-shaped ones are forty-five dollars.

나뭇잎 모양의 귀걸이는 50달러이고 십자 모양의 귀걸이는 45달러입니다.

W: Hmm… I think the leaf-shaped earrings will look best with my necklace. 음, 제 생각에 나뭇잎 모양의 귀걸이가 제 목걸이와 가장 잘 어울리겠네요.

어휘 jewel 보석   in particular 특별히   earrings 귀걸이   look good with ~와 어울리다   necklace 목걸이   shaped 모양의   look good on ~에게 어울리다   cross 십자, 십자가

05 ④

[Telephone rings.] [전화벨이 울린다.]

W: Hello, this is Susan, at Sunray Pots & Pans. What can I do for you? 여보세요, 저는 '선레이 팟츠 앤 팬즈'의 수잔입니다. 무엇을 도와드릴까요?

M: Well, I bought two sets of pots from the store last week, and I was told I would get a frying pan in the mail for free because I bought two sets. But I

haven't gotten it yet.
저기, 제가 지난주에 그 가게에서 냄비 두 세트를 샀는데, 두 세트를 샀기 때문에 프라이팬 하나를 무료로 우편으로 받게 될 거라고 들었어요. 그런데 아직 받지 못했거든요.

W: Alright, please <u>hold while</u> I <u>check</u> it for you. [*pause*] Okay, I see what's wrong. I'm sorry, but we are all <u>out of</u> frying pans.
알겠습니다, 제가 확인할 동안 기다려 주세요. [잠시 후] 네, 뭐가 잘못됐는지 알겠네요. 죄송하지만 프라이팬이 모두 나갔어요.

M: So, does that <u>mean</u> I won't be <u>receiving</u> one?
그래서, 저는 그걸 받지 못할 거라는 뜻인가요?

W: I'm <u>afraid so</u>. Would you like us to send you a <u>set of cups</u> instead? 유감이지만 그렇네요. 대신에 저희가 컵 한 세트를 보내드려도 될까요?

M: <u>Sure</u>, that'll be fine. Thank you.
물론이죠, 그러면 좋겠어요. 고맙습니다.

해설 여자가 가게 이름을 말하며 전화를 받은 점, 손님의 문의사항에 답해준 점 등을 통해 여자는 고객센터 직원임을 알 수 있다.

어휘 pot 냄비   hold (통화 도중에) 기다리다   while ~하는 동안
all out of ~이 전부 없는, 모두 떨어진   I'm afraid 유감이지만
~이다   mailman 집배원   customer service 고객 서비스
furniture 가구

06 ①

W: Dad, I've <u>made</u> a huge <u>mistake</u>. What do I do?
아빠, 제가 큰 실수를 저질렀어요. 어쩌면 좋죠?

M: Why, Gina? What's the <u>matter</u>?   왜, 지나? 뭐가 문제야?

W: Well, I <u>got off</u> the <u>train</u> and was walking home, and then I <u>realized</u> that I <u>left</u> my bag on the train! This is the <u>worst day</u> of my life. 있잖아요, 제가 기차에서 내려서 집으로 걸어오고 있었는데, 기차에 제 가방을 두고 온 걸 깨달은 거예요! 오늘은 제 인생 최악의 날이에요.

M: Oh, no! You should have been <u>more careful</u>. What was in the bag?
아, 저런! 네가 더욱 조심했어야지. 가방 안에 뭐가 있었어?

W: I <u>had</u> my jacket, my sunglasses, my camera, and my laptop computer <u>in it</u>!
제 재킷, 선글라스, 카메라, 그리고 노트북 컴퓨터가 안에 있었어요.

M: Oh my goodness, that is a lot of things you lost. Let's try <u>calling</u> the train <u>station</u>.
세상에, 네가 잃어버린 물건이 많구나. 기차역에 전화해 보자꾸나.

W: Okay, do you think they can help?
알겠어요, 그 사람들이 도와줄 수 있을 거라 생각하세요?

M: I hope they can. If there's a <u>Lost</u> and <u>Found</u> Center in the station, then you might be able to find your bag. 할 수 있다고 희망해 봐야지. 역에 분실물 센터가 있다면 네 가방을 찾을 수도 있을 거야.

해설 가방을 잃어버리고 아직 찾지 못한 상태에서 여자는 불안한 심정일 것이다.

어휘 make a huge mistake 큰 실수를 저지르다   get off the train 기차에서 내리다   realize 깨닫다   Lost and Found

Center 분실물 취급소   anxious 불안해하는   jealous 질투하는

07 ②

① M: Do you know <u>when</u> the train will <u>arrive</u>?
   넌 기차가 언제 도착하는지 알고 있어?
   W: It'll be here <u>in twenty</u> minutes.
   20분 뒤에 여기로 올 거야.

② M: <u>Where</u> can I <u>find</u> the salad dressing?
   어디에서 샐러드 드레싱을 찾을 수 있죠?
   W: I don't like <u>putting</u> dressing <u>on</u> my salad.
   저는 샐러드에 드레싱을 넣는 걸 좋아하지 않아요.

③ M: <u>How long</u> have you been <u>playing</u> the piano?
   너는 피아노를 친 지 얼마나 오래 됐니?
   W: It's been about <u>ten years</u>. 10년 정도 됐어.

④ M: Is the café <u>open</u> today?
   그 카페는 오늘 문을 열었니?
   W: No, they don't open <u>on holidays</u>.
   아니, 그 카페는 휴일에 열지 않아.

⑤ M: What <u>book</u> are you <u>reading</u>?
   너는 무슨 책을 읽고 있어?
   W: I'm reading *Under the Sea.* You <u>should read</u> it, too.
   난 '바닷속에서'를 읽고 있어. 너도 그걸 읽어야 해.

해설 ②에서는 위치를 묻는 'Where ~'로 질문했으므로 장소나 위치를 포함한 답변이 와야 한다.

어휘 holiday 휴일, 휴가, 방학

08 ④

W: Hello, my name is Anna. I just <u>moved</u> in <u>next door</u>.
안녕하세요, 제 이름은 애나예요. 저는 방금 옆집에 이사 왔어요.

M: It's nice to meet you, Anna. My name is Hank. You look like you <u>need</u> a <u>hand moving</u> the <u>furniture</u>.
만나서 반가워요, 애나. 제 이름은 행크예요. 당신은 가구를 옮길 때 도움이 필요해 보이는군요.

W: Yeah, you're right. I can't move my <u>table</u> and <u>shelf</u> because they're too <u>heavy</u>. Could you help me?
네, 맞아요. 제 탁자와 선반이 너무 무거워서 옮길 수가 없어요. 저를 도와주실 수 있나요?

M: Sure. <u>Where</u> do you need me to <u>put</u> this table?
물론이죠. 이 탁자를 어디에 두기를 원하시나요?

W: I would like it <u>in the kitchen</u>, please.
주방 안에 부탁드려요.

M: Alright. <u>How about</u> the shelf? Should I put it in the <u>bedroom</u>? 알겠어요. 선반은요? 그것을 침실에 놓을까요?

W: Yes, that would be great. Thank you so much for your help! 네, 그거 좋겠네요. 도와주셔서 정말 감사합니다.

M: No problem. <u>Let</u> me <u>know</u> if you need help with anything else.
문제 없어요. 다른 어떤 것이든 도움이 필요하면 알려 주세요.

해설 여자는 가구가 너무 무겁다고 상황을 설명한 뒤 'Could you help me?'라고 도움을 요청했다. table과 shelf를 포괄하는 단어는 furniture이다.

어휘 next door 옆집에 need a hand 도움이 필요하다
furniture 가구(목 furniture) shelf 선반, 책꽂이 let
somebody know ~에게 알리다

09 ③

[*Cellphone rings.*] [휴대폰이 울린다.]

W: Hey, Robert. Can I ask you a favor?
얘, 로버트. 내가 너에게 부탁 하나 해도 될까?

M: Sure, anything for you, Melanie. What is it?
물론, 널 위해서라면 뭐든지, 멜라니. 뭔데?

W: I'm flying in to West End Airport this Thursday, and
I was hoping you could come pick me up.
내가 이번 주 목요일에 비행기로 웨스트엔드 공항에 갈 건데, 네가
날 데리러 와 주길 바라고 있었어.

M: Yeah, I can do that. What time does your plane
land?
응, 내가 그렇게 할 수 있지. 네 비행기는 몇 시에 착륙해?

W: It's supposed to arrive at five P.M., but I need to go
to the baggage claim. You can come by five thirty.
오후 5시에 도착하기로 돼 있는데, 나는 수하물 찾는 곳으로 가야
해. 너는 5시 30분까지 오면 돼.

M: Okay, and let me know if your plane gets delayed.
응, 그리고 만약에 네 비행기가 연착하게 되면 내게 알려줘.

W: I will. Don't worry. 그렇게 할게. 걱정 마.

M: Alright. So just to be sure, you're arriving on
Thursday, right? 알겠어. 그러니까 확실히 하자면, 너는 목요
일에 도착하는 거지, 맞지?

해설 남자의 마지막 말에서 'just to be sure'는 서로 알고 있는 내
용을 재차 확인할 때 쓸 수 있는 표현이다. 문장 끝에 붙은 'right' 역시
확인하기 위해 쓰였다.

어휘 ask somebody a favor ~에게 도움을 청하다 fly in
비행기로 도착하다 pick somebody up ~을 차에 태우러 오다
land 착륙하다 be supposed to ~하기로 되어 있다 baggage
claim (공항에서) 수하물 찾는 곳 get delayed 지연되다 just to
be sure 확실히 하기 위해, 혹시나 해서

10 ③

| 졸리 매점 가격표 |

햄버거	5달러
핫도그	4달러(치즈 소스는 2달러 추가)
감자튀김	3달러
탄산음료	2달러

W: Hello, sir! What can I get for you?
안녕하세요, 손님! 무엇을 드릴까요?

M: I would like one hamburger and one hot dog with
cheese sauce, please.
햄버거 한 개와 치즈 소스를 넣은 핫도그 한 개 주세요.

W: Okay. Is there anything else you would like to
order? 네. 그 밖에 주문하고 싶은 게 있나요?

M: Yes. I would also like some French fries.
네. 감자튀김도 좀 주세요.

W: Alright. Can I get you something to drink with that?
알겠어요. 거기에 함께 마실 것도 드릴까요?

M: No, I already have a bottle of water with me.
아니요, 저는 이미 물을 한 병 갖고 있어서요.

W: Okay. Do you have any coupons with you today?
네. 오늘 어떤 쿠폰을 갖고 계신가요?

M: Yes, I have this five-dollar-off coupon. Can I use it
now? 네, 5달러 할인 쿠폰이 있어요. 이걸 지금 쓸 수 있나요?

W: Yes, of course you can. 네, 당연히 가능하죠.

해설 $5(햄버거)＋$4(핫도그)＋$2(치즈 소스)＋$3(감자튀김)
－$5(쿠폰)＝$9

어휘 food stand 매점, 간이식당 French fries 감자튀김,
프렌치프라이

11 ④

M: Excuse me, ma'am. 실례합니다, 부인.

W: Yes, can I help you? 네, 제가 도와드릴까요?

M: I need to get to Huckleberry Station, but I don't
know how to get there from here. Could you help
me out? 제가 허클베리 역까지 가야 하는데, 여기에서 거기까지
가는 방법을 모르겠어요. 저를 도와주시겠어요?

W: Sure, I can do that. The trains here only go to
stations on line nine, and Huckleberry Station is on
line seven. So you have to take the train to Crane
Station first, and then transfer to line seven.
물론, 도와드릴 수 있죠. 이곳의 열차는 9호선 역에만 가고, 허클베
리 역은 7호선에 있어요. 그러니까 열차를 타고 먼저 크레인 역까지
간 다음에 7호선으로 갈아타셔야 해요.

M: Oh, okay. How many stops is Crane Station from
here? 아, 네. 여기에서 크레인 역까지 몇 정거장이죠?

W: I'm not sure, but I think it is about four or five stops
away. 확실하진 않지만, 네다섯 정거장 뒤인 것 같군요.

M: Hmm… Alright. Once I transfer to line seven, how
many stops do I have to go to get to Huckleberry
Station? 음, 알겠습니다. 제가 7호선으로 갈아타고 나면 허클베
리 역까지는 몇 정거장을 가야 하나요?

W: There are only two stops between Crane Station
and Huckleberry Station.
크레인 역과 허클베리 역 사이에는 두 정거장만 있어요.

M: Okay, that's great! Thank you so much.
네, 좋네요! 정말 감사합니다.

해설 특정 역까지 가는 방법, 9호선에서 7호선으로 갈아타는 내용 등
을 통해 대화 장소가 지하철역임을 알 수 있다. 지하철 체계에 관해 말
할 때는 subway를 쓰지만, 운행하는 열차를 가리킬 때는 train이라
고 말한다.

어휘 help somebody out ~을 도와주다 line 노선 transfer
갈아타다, 이동하다 stop 정거장, 정류장 once 일단 ~하면; 한 번

12 ②

W: John, are you going to Cary's birthday party on

Tuesday? 존, 너는 화요일에 있을 케리의 생일 파티에 갈 거니?

M: Yes, I am. How about you? I heard it's going to be a lot of fun.
응, 갈 거야. 너는? 그 파티가 아주 재미있을 거라고 들었어.

W: I'm going, too. What time does it start again? I lost the invitation. 나도 갈 거야. 몇 시에 시작한다고 했더라? 나는 초대장을 잃어버렸어.

M: The party starts at six P.M. 파티는 오후 6시에 시작해.

W: Oh, okay. Where is she having her party?
아, 알겠어. 그 애는 어디에서 파티를 여니?

M: I think it's at a swimming pool. The invitation said to bring a swimsuit. 내 생각에 수영장에서 하는 것 같아. 초대장에 수영복을 가져오라고 했거든.

W: That sounds like fun! I wonder if there's going to be music and balloons.
재미있겠는걸! 음악이랑 풍선도 있을지 궁금하다.

M: I'm sure there will be. She said there's going to be a lot of food, too.
당연히 있을 거야. 케리가 거기엔 음식도 많을 거라고 했어.

W: That's great! I'm looking forward to going to her party. 잘됐다! 난 그 애의 파티에 가는 게 기대돼.

M: Me too! I'll see you on Tuesday then.
나도! 그럼 화요일에 보자.

어휘 invitation 초대장 swimsuit 수영복 wonder if ~인지 궁금하다 balloon 풍선 look forward to ~을 기대하다

13 ③

M: Good morning, everyone. My research team and I did a study on cellphone use. We asked a thousand people what they do with their cellphone, and here are the results. Thirteen percent of them said they make phone calls and twenty-five percent said they use the Internet the most. Also, twenty-five percent replied that they use phone applications the most, and thirty percent said they use their phone to send text messages. The last twelve percent like to take pictures with their cellphone. Thank you all for listening. I will be happy to answer any questions.

안녕하세요, 여러분. 제 연구팀과 저는 휴대폰 사용에 관한 조사를 실시했습니다. 저희는 천 명의 사람들에게 휴대폰으로 무엇을 하는지 질문했고, 여기 그 결과가 있습니다. 13퍼센트의 사람들이 통화를 한다고 말했고, 25퍼센트는 인터넷을 가장 많이 사용한다고 말했습니다. 또한 25퍼센트는 휴대폰 어플리케이션을 가장 많이 사용한다고 대답했고, 30퍼센트는 휴대폰을 이용하여 문자메시지를 보낸다고 말했습니다. 마지막 12퍼센트는 휴대폰으로 사진 찍기를 좋아한다고 했습니다. 들어주셔서 감사합니다. 어떤 질문엔든 기꺼이 답해 드리겠습니다.

해설 선택지에 나열된 순서대로 담화가 진행되므로 조사 항목에 따른 수치가 일치하는지 확인하며 듣는다.

어휘 do a study on ~에 관해 연구하다, 조사하다 result 결과 reply 대답하다(reply-replied-replied) application 휴대폰

응용 프로그램(= app)

14 ②

W: This is an animal that lives in the ocean. It can be very small in size, and it can also be very big in size, depending on what species it is. It is normally grey, and has a big fin on its back. When people see its fin in the water, they get scared. Because unlike a dolphin, this animal can attack people. It eats other fish and has very sharp teeth.

이것은 바다에 사는 동물이에요. 종류에 따라서 크기가 아주 작을 수도 있고 아주 클 수도 있지요. 이것은 보통 회색이며 등에 커다란 지느러미를 갖고 있어요. 사람들이 물 속에서 이것의 지느러미를 보면 그들은 겁을 먹어요. 왜냐하면 돌고래와는 달리 이 동물은 사람을 공격할 수 있기 때문이에요. 이것은 다른 물고기를 잡아 먹으며 매우 날카로운 이빨을 갖고 있어요.

어휘 depending on ~에 따라 species (생물 분류상의) 종 normally 보통, 일반적으로 fin 지느러미 unlike ~와 다르게 attack 공격하다 seal 물개 shrimp 새우 sea turtle 바다거북

15 ①

W: Hey, Dan. What are we doing after lunch?
이봐, 댄. 우린 점심 후에 뭘 할까?

M: I don't know. Did you want to do something special? 모르겠어. 너는 뭔가 특별한 거라도 하고 싶었어?

W: Well, I haven't exercised in a long time, and I was wondering if we could go hiking.
글쎄, 나는 한참 동안 운동을 못해서, 우리가 하이킹을 갈 수 있을까 궁금했어.

M: Hiking sounds great, but I would rather go to the gym. 하이킹도 좋지만 나는 차라리 헬스클럽에 가고 싶어.

W: Hmm… You exercise at the gym on Thompson Street, right?
음, 너는 톰슨 가에 있는 헬스클럽에서 운동을 하지, 그렇지?

M: Yes, that's the one. 응, 바로 거기야.

W: They close on the first and third Sundays of every month, so I don't think you can go today.
거기는 매달 첫 번째와 세 번째 일요일에 문을 닫아서 넌 오늘 갈 수 없을 것 같은데.

M: Oh, really? I didn't know that. Thanks for telling me. 아, 정말이야? 난 그걸 몰랐어. 말해줘서 고마워.

W: Yeah, no problem. So, do you want to go to the mountains with me?
응, 별말씀을. 그러면 나랑 같이 산에 가겠니?

M: Sure, let's go. 물론이지, 가자.

해설 여자가 처음에 제안한 하이킹에서 벗어나는 듯하다가 결국에는 산에 가는 것으로 결론이 났다.

어휘 in a long time 한참 동안, 오랫동안 hiking 하이킹, 도보 여행 would rather (차라리) ~하고 싶다 every month 매달

16 ⑤

W: Honey, what TV program do you want to watch tonight? 여보, 오늘 밤에 어떤 TV 프로그램을 보고 싶어요?

M: Hmm… How about a cooking show or a sports game? 음, 요리 프로그램 아니면 스포츠 경기 어때요?

W: I've watched too many cooking shows recently, and I'm not interested in sports. How about we watch a comedy show or a news program instead? 난 최근에 요리 프로그램을 너무 많이 봤고, 스포츠에는 관심이 없네요. 우리 대신에 코미디 쇼나 뉴스 프로그램을 보는 게 어때요?

M: Well, I don't feel like watching the news today. Let's watch the comedy show. Do you know what time and channel it's supposed to come on? 글쎄요, 오늘은 뉴스를 볼 기분이 아니에요. 코미디 쇼를 봅시다. 그것이 나오는 시간과 채널을 알고 있어요?

W: Actually, I'm not sure. Why don't you check the TV program schedule? 사실, 확실치 않아요. 당신이 TV 프로그램 편성표를 확인하는 게 어때요?

M: Okay, let's see. [pause] It says comedian Ted Baker will be doing a comedy show at six P.M. 그래요, 봅시다. [잠시 후] 코미디언 테드 베이커가 오후 6시에 코미디 쇼를 할 거라고 나와 있군요.

W: Oh, we can't watch it if it starts at that time. We won't be home from work until seven P.M. 아, 그게 그 시각에 시작한다면 우린 볼 수가 없어요. 우린 직장에서 오후 7시가 지나야 집에 올 거잖아요.

M: Yeah, you're right. Then do you want to watch a movie tonight? 네, 맞아요. 그렇다면 오늘 밤에는 영화를 볼래요?

W: That works for me. We can watch the comedy show next time. 전 그게 좋겠어요. 코미디 쇼는 다음에 봐도 돼요.

해설 두 사람은 마지막 대사 전까지는 TV 프로그램에 대해 말했으나 결국 영화를 보기로 결정했다.

어휘 show (방송) 프로그램, 쇼   recently 최근에   instead 대신에   feel like ~하고 싶다   be supposed to ~하기로 되어 있다   come on 시작하다, 등장하다   at that time 그때에   work (원하는) 효과가 나다

17 ④

M: Peter enjoys playing video games with his friends. But recently, he's been spending way too much time playing games. He doesn't do his homework, and he doesn't want to go to school. Peter's mom tells him that if he doesn't do his schoolwork, she's going to throw away all of his video games. After hearing this, Peter decides to study hard and just play video games during his free time. In this situation, what would Peter most likely say to his mom?

피터는 친구들과 비디오 게임을 즐겨 한다. 그러나 최근에 그는 게임을 하는 데 너무 많은 시간을 썼다. 그는 숙제를 하지 않고, 학교에 가기도 싫어한다. 피터의 엄마는 만약 그가 숙제를 하지 않으면 그의 비디오 게임을 전부 버리겠다고 말한다. 이 말을 들은 뒤 피터는 열심히 공부하면서 비디오 게임은 쉬는 시간에만 하겠다고 다짐한다. 이 상황에서 피터는 그의 엄마에게 뭐라고 말할 것 같은가?

Peter: I'll do my homework and play less video games. 저는 숙제를 할 거고 비디오 게임은 적게 할 거예요.

① But Mom, I don't want to study! 하지만 엄마, 저는 공부하고 싶지 않아요!

② How much are these video games? 이 비디오 게임들은 얼마예요?

③ I'm going to do my homework with my friend. 저는 제 친구와 함께 숙제를 할 거예요.

④ I'll do my homework and play less video games. 저는 숙제를 할 거고 비디오 게임은 적게 할 거예요.

⑤ I'm going to play video games after school today. 저는 오늘 방과 후에 비디오 게임을 할 거예요.

해설 공부는 열심히 하고 게임은 남는 시간에만 하겠다는 피터의 결심을 전부 포함하는 내용이 정답으로 어울린다.

어휘 recently 최근에   spend time 시간을 보내다   way 아주, 훨씬   throw something away ~을 버리다, 없애다   less 더 적게; 더 적은

18 ④

W: Excuse me, sir. Could you tell me where I can ride bus number two seven three? 실례합니다, 선생님. 273번 버스를 어디에서 탈 수 있는지 알려주시겠어요?

M: Yeah, sure. There's a bus station right down the street. But there are no buses running at this time. The last bus was at eleven P.M. 네, 물론이죠. 길을 따라가면 버스 정류장이 있어요. 그런데 이 시간에는 운행하는 버스가 없어요. 마지막 버스는 밤 11시에 있었거든요.

W: Oh, no! Then where is the nearest subway station? 아, 이런! 그러면 가장 가까운 지하철역은 어딘가요?

M: I'm afraid you can't take the subway this late at night, either. 유감스럽게도 이렇게 늦은 밤에는 지하철 역시 탈 수 없어요.

W: I'm in big trouble, then. How am I supposed to get home? 그럼 전 정말 곤란하게 됐네요. 집에 어떻게 가란 말인가요?

M: Well, the only way you can go home now is to call a taxi. 글쎄요, 지금 집에 갈 수 있는 유일한 방법은 택시를 부르는 거예요.

W: I see. Do you know the phone number for the taxi service? 그렇군요. 택시 서비스의 전화번호를 알고 계신가요?

M: Yes, it's three nine one, two nine three oh. 네, 391-2930입니다.

W: Thank you so much! You are a lifesaver. 정말 감사합니다! 절 구해 주셨어요.

해설 버스와 지하철이 모두 끊긴 상태에서 여자가 할 수 있는 일은 택시를 타는 것이다.

지도 않고 너무 춥지도 않지. 야외 활동을 하기에 완벽한 날씨거든.

M: Okay, what else do you like about it?
그렇구나, 봄에 관해 또 어떤 게 좋아?

W: It's the time of the year when all the flowers bloom and the grass is green. It makes me feel happy.
봄은 온갖 꽃들이 피고 잔디가 초록빛으로 물드는 때잖아. 그건 날 행복하게 만들어.

M: I see. I like spring too, but my favorite season is fall. 알겠다. 나도 봄이 좋긴 한데 내가 좋아하는 계절은 가을이야.

W: Oh, I don't really like fall. What do you like the most about it? 아, 나는 가을을 그다지 좋아하지 않아. 너는 가을의 어떤 점이 가장 좋아?

① What's your favorite holiday? 네가 좋아하는 휴일은 뭐야?
② It is too cold to go outside these days.
요즘엔 밖에 나가기 너무 추워.
③ The flowers in the park haven't bloomed yet.
공원의 꽃들이 아직 피지 않았어.
④ What kinds of outdoor activities do you do in your free time? 너는 자유 시간에 어떤 종류의 야외 활동을 하니?
⑤ Oh, I don't really like fall. What do you like the most about it? 아, 나는 가을을 그다지 좋아하지 않아. 너는 가을의 어떤 점이 가장 좋아?

해설 좋아하는 계절에 관한 질문과 대답이 오가는 가운데, 이번에는 남자가 좋아하는 계절에 대해 여자가 질문할 차례이다.

어휘 first of all 우선, 무엇보다 먼저 outdoor activity 야외 활동 bloom 꽃이 피다 grass 풀, 잔디

16회 실전모의고사 본문 p.186-187

01 ④	02 ②	03 ③	04 ③	05 ⑤
06 ④	07 ①	08 ③	09 ②	10 ②
11 ②	12 ⑤	13 ⑤	14 ①	15 ③
16 ⑤	17 ③	18 ⑤	19 ⑤	20 ②

01 ④

M: Good morning! Welcome to Green Spoon! What would you like in your salad today? We have tomatoes, olives, cucumbers, eggs, and onions.
안녕하세요! 그린 스푼에 오신 걸 환영합니다! 오늘은 손님의 샐러드에 어떤 것을 넣어드릴까요? 저희는 토마토, 올리브, 오이, 달걀, 그리고 양파가 있습니다.

W: I would like some tomatoes and olives in it, please.
토마토와 올리브를 조금 넣어주세요.

M: Okay. Do you want any cucumbers or eggs with that? 좋아요, 거기에다가 오이나 달걀도 넣을까요?

W: Hmm… Yes, just some cucumber. I really don't like eggs in my food. 음, 네, 오이만 조금요. 저는 음식에 달걀을

어휘 down the street 길을 따라, 길 아래로 run (버스, 기차 등이) 운행하다, 다니다 late at night 밤 늦게 be supposed to ~해야 한다 lifesaver 곤경에서 구해주는 사람

19 ④

W: There are so many people running in the marathon today. 오늘은 마라톤에서 달리고 있는 사람이 아주 많네.

M: Yeah, I know! Look at that man over there. He looks so weak! How is he going to finish the race?
응, 그러게 말이야! 저기 있는 남자를 봐. 너무 약해 보여! 저 사람이 어떻게 경주를 끝까지 할 수 있을까?

W: Yeah, he's really skinny, with no muscles. But you never know. He could be a good runner.
그러게, 저 사람은 정말 깡마른 데다가 근육도 없어. 하지만 누가 알아? 저 사람이 훌륭한 주자일 수도 있어.

M: I don't think so. He'll probably quit in the middle of the race.
난 그렇게 생각하지 않아. 그는 아마도 경주 중간에 포기할 거야.

W: I guess we'll find out when the race is over. [pause] I think the race is over. I wonder who won the race. Let's go find out.
그건 경주가 끝나면 알 수 있을 거야. [잠시 후] 경주가 끝난 것 같아. 누가 우승했는지 궁금하다. 가서 알아보자.

M: I can't believe it! The man we saw earlier won first place! He definitely didn't look like someone who could win.
믿을 수가 없어! 우리가 아까 봤던 남자가 1등을 했어! 그는 분명히 우승할 수 있는 사람처럼 보이지 않았는데.

① The walls have ears. 낮말은 새가 듣고 밤말은 쥐가 듣는다.
② Look before you leap. 돌다리도 두들겨 보고 건너라.
③ Kill two birds with one stone. 일석이조.
④ Don't judge a book by its cover.
겉을 보고 속을 판단하지 마라.
⑤ Even if the sky falls, there is a way out.
하늘이 무너져도 솟아날 구멍이 있다.

해설 'Don't judge a book by its cover.'는 우리말의 '뚝배기보다 장맛이 좋다'와 그 의미가 통하는데, 이는 비록 겉모양이 보잘것없더라도 그 내용만큼은 아주 훌륭함을 이른다.

어휘 marathon 마라톤 muscle 근육 quit 그만두다 in the middle of ~의 중간에, 도중에 find out ~을 알아내다 definitely 분명히, 확실히 leap 뛰다 way out 출구

20 ⑤

M: Linda, what's your favorite season of the year?
린다, 일 년 중 네가 좋아하는 계절은 뭐야?

W: Hmm… That's a hard question. I think I like spring the best. 음, 그거 어려운 질문이네. 난 봄이 가장 좋은 것 같아.

M: Can you tell me why? 왜 그런지 말해 줄래?

W: Well, first of all, the weather is really nice. It's not too hot and it's not too cold. It's perfect weather to do outdoor activities. 글쎄, 우선 날씨가 아주 좋잖아. 너무 덥

넣는 것을 좋아하지 않아요.

M: Alright, here is your salad.
알겠어요, 여기 손님의 샐러드가 나왔습니다.

W: Oh, I should have told you earlier, but could you add some onions in my salad too? 아, 좀 더 일찍 말했어야 했는데, 제 샐러드에 양파도 좀 넣어주시겠어요?

M: Sure, that's not a problem. But if you add onions to your salad, you will have to pay more. Is that okay? 물론이죠, 문제 없어요. 하지만 샐러드에 양파를 넣으면, 비용을 더 지불하셔야 합니다. 괜찮으신가요?

W: Okay, here's the money. Thank you!
네, 여기 돈이요. 감사합니다!

해설 여자는 tomato(토마토), olive(올리브), cucumber(오이), onion(양파)이 들어간 샐러드를 원한다.

어휘 earlier 더 일찍(early-earlier-earliest) add 추가하다

02 ②

[*Telephone rings.*] [전화벨이 울린다.]

M: Hello, this is Octagon Seafood Buffet.
여보세요. 옥타곤 씨푸드 뷔페입니다.

W: Yes, hello. My name is Tiffany Kings, and I made a reservation for two people at six P.M.
네, 안녕하세요. 저는 티파니 킹스라고 하는데요, 오후 6시에 두 사람을 예약했거든요.

M: That's right. You are on our list. What can I help you with?
맞습니다. 손님은 저희 명단에 있네요. 무엇을 도와드릴까요?

W: I would like to make some changes to my reservation. Will that be possible?
제 예약에서 몇 가지를 변경하고 싶은데요. 그게 가능할까요?

M: Well, it depends on what changes you would like to make.
음, 손님이 어떤 변경을 하고 싶으신지에 따라 다릅니다.

W: Okay. Four people will be there instead of two, and I would like to go at seven P.M. instead of six P.M.
네. 두 명이 아니라 네 명이 거기 갈 거고요, 오후 6시 대신 7시에 가려고 합니다.

M: I'm sorry, but our reservations for seven are all full. But there is one table left for seven thirty. Would you like to come then?
죄송하지만 7시 예약은 꽉 찼어요. 하지만 7시 30분에 테이블이 하나 남았네요. 그때 오시겠습니까?

W: Yes, that will work. Thank you so much!
네, 그럼 됐네요. 정말 고맙습니다!

해설 여자의 대사인 'I would like to ~'에 전화를 건 목적이 나온다.

어휘 seafood 해산물 make a reservation 예약하다 be on one's list ~의 명단에 있다 make some changes to ~의 일부를 바꾸다 depend on ~에 따라 다르다 instead of ~대신에

03 ③

① W: Did you pack all the boxes?

상자를 전부 다 포장했니?

M: Yeah. They're already in the car.
응. 상자는 이미 차 안에 있어.

② W: How many boxes do we need?
우리는 상자가 몇 개 필요하죠?

M: We'll probably need at least ten of them.
우린 아마 적어도 상자 열 개가 필요할 거예요.

③ W: Do you need a hand with that?
그걸 하는 데 도움이 필요하세요?

M: Yes, please. Can you help me take this box down?
네, 부탁해요. 이 상자를 내리는 것을 도와주시겠어요?

④ W: Where did you put my wallet?
넌 내 지갑을 어디에 두었니?

M: It should be on top of the box.
그건 상자 위에 있을 거야.

⑤ W: Why did you open the package without asking me?
왜 나에게 물어보지도 않고 소포를 열었니?

M: I'm sorry. I thought it was addressed to me.
미안해. 난 나한테 온 것인 줄 알았어.

어휘 pack 포장하다 probably 아마도 at least 적어도 need a hand 도움이 필요하다 take something down ~을 내리다 wallet 지갑 without ~을 하지 않고, ~ 없이 addressed to ~앞으로 보내진

04 ③

M: Molly, do you like our new house? You get to use this room all by yourself. 몰리, 넌 우리의 새 집이 마음에 드니? 넌 이 방을 너 혼자서 쓰게 될 거란다.

W: I'm happy that I have my own room, but I liked the old room better. It was bigger and had pretty wallpaper. 제 방을 갖게 돼서 기쁘지만, 저는 옛날 방이 더 좋았어요. 더 크고 벽지가 더 예뻤거든요.

M: We can decorate your new room with wallpaper, too! Do you want some with ballerinas? Or how about cars? 우린 네 새 방도 벽지로 꾸밀 거란다! 발레리나가 있는 벽지를 원하니? 아니면 자동차가 있는 것은 어때?

W: Hmm... I don't really like cars. And since I had ballerinas in the old room, I want something different this time. 음, 자동차는 정말 싫어요. 그리고 옛날 방이 발레리나 벽지였기 때문에 이번에는 다른 걸로 하고 싶어요.

M: Alright. Do you have anything in mind?
좋아. 생각해 둔 것이 있니?

W: Well, how about wallpaper with butterflies or flowers on it? 음, 나비나 꽃이 있는 벽지는 어때요?

M: Those all sound great. I think butterflies would be the best choice.
모두 괜찮게 들리네. 내 생각엔 나비가 최고의 선택이 될 것 같구나.

W: Yeah, I agree. 네, 저도 그래요.

어휘 get to ~하게 되다 (all) by oneself 혼자서 own 자신의 wallpaper 벽지 decorate 장식하다, 꾸미다 ballerina 발레리나 have something in mind ~을 염두에 두다 butterfly 나비

83

응, 나도 빨리 너처럼 멋진 컴퓨터를 갖고 싶어.

해설 남자의 마지막 말 'I can't wait ~'에 여자의 새 컴퓨터를 부러워하는 심정이 드러난다.

어휘 graduation present 졸업 선물   awesome 굉장한, 엄청난   be made of ~로 만들어지다   leather 가죽   be in bad condition 나쁜 상태이다   at least 적어도, 최소한   disappointed 실망한   jealous 부러워하는   relieved 안도하는

05 ⑤

M: Oh, my goodness! I can't believe I'm finally getting to meet you! Could you sign this poster for me?
오, 맙소사! 제가 드디어 당신을 만나게 되다니 믿을 수가 없군요! 저를 위해 이 포스터에 사인해 주시겠어요?

W: Sure, I can do that. What's your name?
물론이죠, 그럴게요. 이름이 어떻게 되세요?

M: My name is Jason Hurley. Wow, this is so exciting!
제 이름은 제이슨 헐리예요. 와우, 이거 정말 신나네요!

W: Here you go, Jason. 여기 있어요. 제이슨.

M: Thank you so much! I admire you a lot. I really like your songs "Love Melody" and "Dance Tonight."
정말 고맙습니다! 전 당신을 많이 존경해요. 저는 당신의 노래인 "러브 멜로디"랑 "댄스 투나잇"을 정말 좋아해요.

W: I appreciate that very much. 정말 감사해요.

M: Oh, one last thing. When is your next album coming out? I've been waiting for it for months!
아, 한 가지만 더요. 당신의 다음 앨범은 언제 나오죠? 몇 달간 그걸 기다려 왔거든요.

W: I'm working on it now. It should be out by next month. 지금 작업 중이에요. 다음 달까지 나올 거예요.

해설 song, album 등을 통해 여자가 가수라는 것을 알 수 있다.

어휘 my goodness 맙소사, 어머나   finally 마침내, 드디어   sign 사인하다; 사인   admire 존경하다   appreciate 감사하다, 고마워하다   come out (책, 앨범 등이) 나오다

06 ④

M: Wow, Susie. What a nice computer! When did you get it? 와, 수지야. 컴퓨터 멋진데! 이걸 언제 샀니?

W: Thank you! My dad bought it for me last week for a graduation present.
고마워! 우리 아빠가 내 졸업 선물로 지난주에 사주셨어.

M: That's so awesome! Did you get a case and keyboard cover for it, too?
굉장한데! 케이스랑 키보드 커버도 받았니?

W: Yeah. The case is made of leather and the keyboard cover is white.
응. 케이스는 가죽으로 되어 있고 키보드 커버는 흰색이야.

M: Cool! You're so lucky. I wish I had a computer like this! I've used my computer for over five years so it's in bad condition.
멋져! 넌 정말 운이 좋구나. 나도 이런 컴퓨터가 있었으면 좋겠어! 내 컴퓨터는 5년 넘게 썼기 때문에 상태가 안 좋거든.

W: Why don't you ask your parents to buy you one?
부모님께 하나 사달라고 부탁하는 게 어때?

M: I already tried asking them, but they said to use it for at least one more year.
이미 부모님께 부탁해 봤지만 최소한 1년은 더 쓰라고 하셨어.

W: Oh, I see. Then I guess you just have to wait until next year. 아, 그렇구나. 그럼 넌 내년까지 기다려야겠네.

M: Yeah, I can't wait to get a nice computer like you.

07 ①

① W: Let me see your report card for this semester.
내게 이번 학기 네 성적표를 보여 주렴.

M: The package hasn't come in the mail yet.
소포가 아직 우편으로 오지 않았어요.

② W: Can you tell me your email account password?
네 이메일 계정 비밀번호를 말해줄 수 있니?

M: No, that's personal information.
안돼, 그건 개인 정보잖아.

③ W: Do you want to grab a bite to eat?
뭘 좀 먹으러 갈래?

M: No, I'm not that hungry.
아니, 난 그렇게 배고프지는 않아.

④ W: Why were you late to school today?
왜 오늘 학교에 늦었니?

M: I forgot to set an alarm last night.
제가 어젯밤에 알람을 맞추는 것을 깜박했어요.

⑤ W: Are you saving this seat for somebody?
누군가를 위해 이 자리를 맡아 놓으신 건가요?

M: Yes, my friend will be sitting here.
네, 제 친구가 여기에 앉을 거예요.

해설 ①의 질문에서는 성적표를 보여 달라고 했는데, 성적표와 무관한 소포 이야기로 답했다.

어휘 report card 성적표   semester 학기   package 소포   email account 이메일 계정   personal information 개인 정보   grab a bite 간단히 먹다   set an alarm 알람을 맞추다   save a seat 자리를 맡다

08 ③

M: Honey, have you seen my white shirt? I can't find it anywhere.
여보, 내 흰색 셔츠 봤어요? 어디에서도 찾을 수가 없네요.

W: Hmm… It should be in the third drawer. I put it there this morning. 음, 그건 세 번째 서랍 안에 있을 거예요. 내가 오늘 아침에 거기에 넣었거든요.

M: Oh, you're right. I found it. But it has a lot of wrinkles on it. Can you iron it for me? 아, 당신이 맞아요. 찾았어요. 하지만 주름이 아주 많네요. 셔츠를 다려 줄래요?

W: I'm busy washing the dishes right now. Can't you wear something else?
난 지금 설거지하느라 바빠요. 다른 걸 입을 수는 없나요?

M: No, this is the only shirt I can wear today.
아뇨, 이건 내가 오늘 입을 수 있는 유일한 거예요.

W: Why is that? Where did you put all of your other shirts? 왜 그렇죠? 당신은 다른 셔츠들을 어디에 뒀어요?

M: They're all at the dry cleaner's and they won't be cleaned until this weekend. 다른 건 모두 세탁소에 있는데, 이번 주말까지는 세탁되지 않을 거예요.

W: Alright then. Put the shirt on the chair. I'll iron it after I finish washing the dishes. 그럼 알겠네요. 의자 위에 셔츠를 두세요. 설거지를 다한 다음에 셔츠를 다릴게요.

M: Thank you so much! You're the best! 정말 고마워요! 당신이 최고예요!

어휘 anywhere 어디에서도　drawer 서랍　wrinkle 주름　iron 다리미질을 하다; 다리미　wash the dishes 설거지하다　dry cleaner's 세탁소

09 ②

M: Hey, Rebecca! You look different today. Did you do something to your hair? 얘, 레베카! 넌 오늘 달라 보여. 머리에 뭘 했어?

W: Yeah, I got my bangs cut yesterday. What do you think? 응, 어제 앞머리를 잘랐어. 어떻게 생각해?

M: Well, it's definitely a change from your old hair. 음, 너의 옛날 머리랑 완전히 달라졌어.

W: So, does that mean you don't like my new hairstyle? 그래서, 그 말은 내 새 헤어스타일이 마음에 들지 않는다는 거니?

M: No, I think it looks wonderful on you! I see you bought a new hairpin, too. 아니, 너에게 정말 잘 어울린다고 생각해! 난 네가 새 머리핀을 산 것도 알겠다.

W: Yes. I'm glad you noticed! It was on sale at the department store, and I couldn't resist. 응, 알아봐 주니 기쁘네! 백화점에서 할인 중이어서 참을 수가 없었어.

M: It's beautiful! I like how it sparkles. 예뻐! 난 그게 반짝이는 게 마음에 들어.

W: Thank you for saying that! 그렇게 말해줘서 고마워!

M: Plus, it fits your bangs really well. 게다가, 너의 앞머리랑 정말 잘 어울린다.

어휘 bangs (단발의) 앞머리　definitely 분명히, 틀림없이　hairpin 머리핀　notice 알아차리다　on sale 할인 중인, 판매되는　resist 참다　sparkle 반짝이다　plus 게다가

10 ②

M: Hello, ma'am! Welcome to Bath & Body Mart. Are you looking for anything in particular? 안녕하세요, 손님! 배스앤바디 마트에 어서 오세요. 특별히 찾고 있는 것이 있으세요?

W: Yes, actually. I need to buy some shampoo, body wash, and soap. Can you tell me how much they are? 네, 실은 있어요. 저는 샴푸, 바디워시, 그리고 비누를 좀 사야 해요. 그것들이 얼마인지 말씀 주시겠어요?

M: Well, all of our shampoo and body wash products are normally ten dollars each, but they are on sale

this week for fifty percent off. Our soaps are five dollars each. 음, 저희의 모든 샴푸와 바디워시 제품은 보통은 개당 10달러인데, 이번 주에 50% 할인을 하고 있어요. 저희 비누는 개당 5달러입니다.

W: Oh, I see. Then I would like one bottle of shampoo, one bottle of body wash, and one bar of soap. 아, 알겠어요. 그럼 샴푸 한 병, 바디워시 한 병 그리고 비누 한 개 주세요.

M: Alright, ma'am. Do you have any coupons that you would like to use? 알겠습니다. 사용하고 싶은 쿠폰을 갖고 있으신가요?

W: Yes, I have this five-dollar discount coupon. 네, 여기 5달러짜리 할인권이 있어요.

M: Okay. Do you need anything else today? 네. 오늘 더 필요한 게 있으세요?

W: No, that will be all. Thank you. 아니요, 그게 다입니다. 감사합니다.

해설 $5(shampoo) + $5(body wash) + $5(soap) – $5(할인권) = $10

어휘 in particular 특별히　soap 비누　normally 보통은　bottle 병　discount coupon 할인권

11 ②

M: Mrs. Albright, can you tell me what the homework assignment is? I was absent yesterday. 올브라이트 선생님, 과제가 뭔지 말씀해 주시겠어요? 제가 어제 결석해서요.

W: Sure. You have to write a report on bones and muscles. 그래. 넌 뼈와 근육에 관한 보고서를 써야 한단다.

M: I see. What exactly do I have to include in the paper? 알겠어요. 보고서에 정확히 어떤 내용을 담으면 돼요?

W: Well, do some research on the human body, and write about the different types of bones and muscles. 음, 인간의 신체에 관해 조사를 하고, 다양한 종류의 뼈와 근육에 대해 글을 쓰도록 해.

M: Hmm… Okay. Where can I find information about the topic? 음, 알겠어요. 그 주제에 관한 정보는 어디서 찾을 수 있을까요?

W: I'm sure there are plenty of books in the library you can use. Also, you can use our class textbook. 도서관에 네가 이용할 수 있는 책이 많을 거야. 그리고 우리 교과서를 이용할 수도 있지.

M: Oh, alright. When is the deadline for the assignment? 아, 알겠어요. 그 과제의 마감일은 언제예요?

W: You have to turn it in before our next class, so October first. 우리의 다음 수업 전까지 제출해야 하니까, 10월 1일이지.

M: Okay! Thanks a lot! 알겠어요! 정말 감사합니다!

어휘 homework assignment 과제　absent 결석한, 결근한　report 보고서(= paper)　bone 뼈　muscle 근육　exactly 정확히　include 포함하다　research on ~에 관한 조사

different types of 다양한 종류의 information 정보 plenty of 많은 class textbook 과목 교과서 deadline 마감 날짜 turn in 제출하다 classroom 교실 museum 박물관 electronics store 전자제품 매장

12 ⑤

M: Ladies and gentlemen! Are you <u>ready for</u> the biggest <u>match</u> of the year? That's right! Anderson and Hartfield will be <u>boxing</u> against each other this <u>Sunday</u>, <u>May seventeenth</u> at Horizon <u>Stadium</u>! The match will <u>start</u> at <u>seven</u> P.M. so make sure you're here <u>on time</u>! Front row seats are <u>one hundred dollars</u> and all other seats are <u>seventy-five</u> dollars. Please remember that children <u>under fifteen</u> years old will <u>not</u> be <u>allowed</u> to enter. Come out and have a great time!

신사 숙녀 여러분! 올해 최고의 경기를 위한 준비가 되셨나요? 맞습니다! 앤더슨과 하트필드가 이번 주 일요일 5월 17일에 호라이즌 경기장에서 맞붙어 권투 경기를 합니다! 시합은 오후 7시에 시작하니, 반드시 정시에 도착해 주세요! 앞 좌석은 100달러이고, 나머지 모든 좌석은 75달러입니다. 15세 미만의 어린이들은 입장이 허용되지 않는다는 것을 기억해 주십시오. 오셔서 즐거운 시간을 보내세요!

어휘 match 경기, 시합 box 권투를 하다 stadium 경기장 on time 정시에 front row 앞줄 be allowed to ~하는 것이 허용되다

13 ⑤

| 주간 일기예보 |

요일	날씨
월요일	흐림, 미풍
화요일	화창
수요일	흐림, 비
목요일	폭우, 강풍
금요일	눈보라
토요일	눈보라
일요일	눈보라

① On <u>Monday</u>, there will be a gentle <u>breeze</u>, and it may be a little <u>cloudy</u>, but it will not rain.
월요일에는 미풍이 불겠으며, 약간 흐릴 수 있지만 비는 내리지 않겠습니다.
② On <u>Tuesday</u>, the clouds will clear, and the <u>sun</u> will <u>come out</u>. Enjoy a day outdoors!
화요일에는, 구름이 개고 해가 나올 겁니다. 야외에서 하루를 즐기세요!
③ <u>Starting</u> on <u>Wednesday</u>, the clouds will <u>come back</u>, and it will <u>rain</u>. Make sure to <u>bring</u> your <u>umbrella</u>.
수요일부터 구름이 다시 끼고 비가 내리겠습니다. 우산을 꼭 챙기세요.
④ On <u>Thursday</u>, there will be a lot of <u>rainfall</u>, with

<u>strong winds</u>, so be prepared before you go outside. 목요일에는, 강한 바람과 함께 강수량이 많겠습니다. 그러니 바깥에 나가기 전에 준비하세요.
⑤ We advise you to <u>stay indoors</u> over the <u>weekend</u>, because there will be <u>rainstorms</u> on <u>Friday</u>, <u>Saturday</u>, and <u>Sunday</u>. 금요일, 토요일, 일요일에는 폭풍우가 있을 예정이니, 주말 동안에는 실내에 계시기를 권합니다.

해설 금요일, 토요일, 일요일에는 폭풍우가 아니라 눈보라가 칠 예정이다.

어휘 weather forecast 일기예보 gentle breeze 미풍, 산들바람 heavy rain 폭우 snowstorm 눈보라 come out 나오다 outdoors 실외에서, 야외에서 rainfall 강수량 be prepared 준비하다, 대비하다 advise 조언하다, 권하다 indoors 실내에서 rainstorm 폭풍우, 비바람

14 ①

W: This is a very commonly used item. You can see people <u>wearing</u> this everywhere you go. People who <u>can't see very well</u> wear these on their nose and ears. The <u>lens</u> is normally <u>circular</u> or <u>rectangular</u> and it helps people see <u>things</u> that are <u>far away</u>. It is hard for people to see once they <u>take</u> this <u>off</u> their face. When the lens gets dirty, people <u>clean</u> it with a soft <u>cloth</u>. Also, there are many different <u>styles</u> and <u>sizes</u> of this item, so you can <u>choose</u> one that fits you the best.

이것은 매우 흔히 쓰이는 물건입니다. 당신은 어디서나 이것을 착용한 사람들을 볼 수 있지요. 눈이 잘 보이지 않는 사람들은 그들의 코와 귀 위에 이것을 씁니다. 렌즈는 보통 둥글거나 직사각형이며, 이것은 사람들이 멀리 있는 물체를 보도록 도와줍니다. 이것을 벗게 되면, 사람들은 보기가 힘듭니다. 렌즈가 더러워지면, 사람들은 부드러운 천으로 그것을 닦습니다. 또한 이 물건은 많은 다양한 스타일과 사이즈가 있어서, 당신에게 가장 잘 어울리는 것을 선택할 수 있습니다.

어휘 commonly used 흔히 사용되는 item 물품 everywhere 어디서나 normally 보통은 circular 원형의 rectangular 직사각형의 once 일단 ~하면 take something off ~을 벗다 cloth 천 fit 어울리다, (크기, 모양 등이) 맞다

15 ③

M: Honey, I think I <u>lost</u> my <u>wallet</u>. My <u>credit card</u> was in it, too. 여보, 나 내 지갑을 잃어버린 거 같아요. 내 신용카드도 거기에 있었는데.
W: What? <u>How</u> did you lose it?
뭐라고요? 어떻게 그걸 잃어버렸어요?
M: I don't know. I <u>normally keep</u> it in my <u>pocket</u>, but when I checked, it wasn't there. What should I do?
모르겠어요. 난 보통은 그걸 내 주머니에 넣고 다니는데, 내가 확인했을 때 주머니에 없더라고요. 어떻게 해야 하죠?
W: I'm not sure. <u>What if</u> somebody finds your wallet

and uses your credit card? 모르겠어요. 누군가 당신 지갑을 발견해서 당신 신용카드를 쓰면 어쩌죠?

M: That would be terrible! Do you know how I can cancel my credit card? 그럼 끔찍하겠네요! 어떻게 내 신용 카드를 해지할 수 있는지 알아요?

W: No, I've never had this problem before. Should we try calling the bank? 아뇨, 난 이런 문제를 전에 겪어보질 않아서요. 은행에 전화를 해봐야 할까요?

M: Hmm… Would the bank be able to help? 음, 은행이 도와줄 수 있을까요?

W: I think so. If they can cancel your card, nobody will be able to use it. 그럴 것 같아요. 은행이 당신의 신용카드를 해지할 수 있으면, 아무도 그걸 사용하지 못 할 거예요.

M: Oh, you're right! That's a really good idea. I'll call them now. 아, 당신 말이 맞아요! 그거 정말 좋은 생각이에요. 바로 은행에 전화할게요.

어휘 lose 잃어버리다(lose-lost-lost) wallet 지갑 pocket 주머니 what if ~? ~라면 어쩌죠? cancel 해지하다

16 ⑤

W: Wesley, where do you want to meet to prepare for our presentation? 웨슬리, 어디에서 만나서 우리의 발표를 준비하고 싶니?

M: How about the coffee shop on Rose Street? It's a new place that opened recently. 로즈 가에 있는 커피숍 어때? 최근에 새로 문을 연 곳이거든.

W: I don't think we should meet at the coffee shop. There are too many people there, and it's hard to concentrate. The library might be better. 우리는 커피숍에서 만나면 안 될 것 같아. 거기엔 사람들이 너무 많고 집중하기 힘들잖아. 도서관이 더 좋을 것 같은데.

M: Well, we have to be very quiet in the library. It'll be uncomfortable to talk to each other. 글쎄, 우린 도서관에서 매우 조용히 해야 하잖아. 서로 이야기하기 불편할 거야.

W: Yeah, I guess you're right. Then where should we meet? 응, 네 말이 맞다고 생각해. 그럼 어디에서 만날까?

M: Let's see… Do you want to come over to my house? 어디 보자… 너 우리 집으로 올래?

W: Okay, I don't mind. Are you sure that'll be okay with you? 좋아, 난 상관없어. 너한테 괜찮겠니?

M: I'm sure. Nobody is home during the day and we can talk as loud as we want. 응. 그날은 낮에 아무도 없어서 우리가 원하는 대로 큰소리로 말할 수 있어.

W: Alright, that sounds perfect. I'll see you later! 좋아, 완벽하게 들리네. 이따 보자!

어휘 prepare for ~을 준비하다 presentation 발표 recently 최근에 concentrate 집중하다 uncomfortable 불편한 come over to ~에 오다 loud 크게, 시끄럽게

17 ③

M: Kate and George have been best friends since elementary school. They do everything together and even live next door to each other. One day, George meets a new friend. George starts to spend more and more time with his new friend instead of Kate. Over the weekend, Kate sees George and his new friend going to the movies together. Kate thinks that George no longer wants to play with her. She decides to tell him how she feels. In this situation, what would Kate most likely say to George?

케이트와 조지는 초등학교 이래로 친한 친구다. 그들은 모든 것을 같이하고, 심지어 서로 옆집에 산다. 어느 날, 조지는 새 친구를 만난다. 조지는 케이트 대신에 새 친구와 점점 더 많은 시간을 보내기 시작한다. 주말 동안에, 케이트는 조지와 그의 새 친구가 함께 영화를 보러 가는 것을 본다. 케이트는 조지가 더 이상 자기와 놀고 싶지 않아 한다고 생각한다. 그녀는 자기가 어떻게 느끼는지 그에게 말하려고 결심한다. 이런 상황에서, 케이트는 조지에게 뭐라고 말하겠는가?

Kate: I don't like how you left me for a new friend. 난 네가 새 친구 때문에 날 떠난 게 싫어.

① I'm so happy that you're my friend. 난 네가 내 친구라서 정말 행복해.

② I'm so disappointed with the movie. 난 그 영화에 정말 실망했어.

③ I don't like how you left me for a new friend. 난 네가 새 친구 때문에 나를 떠난 게 싫어.

④ Can you tell me the name of your new friend? 네 새 친구의 이름을 알려줄래?

⑤ I would like to go see a movie with you this weekend. 난 이번 주말에 너랑 영화를 보러 가고 싶어.

어휘 elementary school 초등학교 next door ~의 옆집에 instead of ~대신에 no longer 더 이상 ~ 아닌 disappointed 실망한

18 ⑤

M: Hi, Hannah. How did you do on the history test? 안녕, 해나. 역사 시험은 어떻게 봤니?

W: I got a D on it. But there must be something wrong. I knew every problem on the test. 난 그거 D 받았어. 그런데 틀림없이 뭔가 잘못된 것 같아. 난 시험에 나온 모든 문제를 알았거든.

M: That's strange. Are you sure you wrote down the right answers? 그거 이상하다. 맞는 답을 적은 게 확실해?

W: Yes, I'm sure. I even checked the right answers in my textbook. 응, 확실해. 난 심지어 교과서에서 정답을 확인해 봤다고.

M: Then maybe Mr. Owen made a mistake when he was grading your test. 그럼 아마 오웬 선생님이 네 시험지를 채점했을 때 실수하신 것 같은데.

87

W: Yeah, you might be right. <u>What</u> do you think I <u>should</u> do? 응, 네 말이 맞을 거야. 내가 어떻게 해야 한다고 생각해?

M: Well, <u>send</u> him an <u>email</u> and ask him about your grade. 음, 선생님께 이메일을 보내서 너의 성적에 관해 여쭤어 봐.

W: <u>Alright</u>, I'll do that now. Do you know his email <u>address</u>? 좋아. 지금 그렇게 할게. 그 분의 이메일 주소를 아니?

M: It's o-w-e-n at bmail dot com. owen@bmail.com이야.

W: Thank you so much! I hope this works out well. 정말 고마워! 난 이 일이 잘됐으면 좋겠어.

어휘 write down 적다 check 확인하다 textbook 교과서 make a mistake 실수하다 grade 성적을 매기다, 채점하다; 성적

19 ⑤

M: Nancy, are you eating ice cream again? I thought you were <u>on a diet</u>! 낸시, 너 또 아이스크림 먹고 있니? 난 네가 다이어트 중인 줄 알았는데!

W: I was going to start today, but these ice cream cones were <u>on sale</u>! I had to buy some. I'll <u>start</u> my diet <u>tomorrow</u>. 오늘 시작하려고 했는데, 이 아이스크림 콘이 할인 중이더라고! 난 몇 개 사지 않을 수 없었어. 난 내일부터 다이어트를 시작할 거야.

M: You've been saying that for the past few months, Nancy. 넌 지난 몇 달 동안 그렇게 말했거든, 낸시.

W: I know, but I <u>hate exercising</u>, and it's <u>hard</u> for me to <u>eat less</u>. 나도 알지만, 난 운동하는 게 싫고, 적게 먹는 것도 힘들어.

M: Well, you'll never <u>lose weight</u> if you <u>eat</u> the same <u>amount</u> and don't exercise. 음, 네가 같은 양을 먹고 운동을 하지 않으면 결코 살을 뺄 수 없을 거야.

W: Yeah, you're right. Will you <u>help</u> me <u>get started</u>? 응, 네 말이 맞아. 내가 시작하는 것을 도와줄래?

M: Yes, I can help you. But <u>don't</u> just <u>say</u> that you'll go on a diet. You <u>have to show me</u> that you're trying. 응, 도와줄게. 하지만 다이어트할 거라고 말만 하지 마. 네가 노력하는 것을 내게 보여줘야 해.

W: I'll start tomorrow, I promise! I'll show you <u>through</u> my <u>actions</u>. 난 내일 시작할게, 약속해! 내 행동으로 보여줄게.

① Like father, like son. 그 아버지에 그 아들.
② Every rule has its exception. 예외 없는 규칙은 없다.
③ If it's not broken, don't fix it. 긁어 부스럼 만들지 마라.
④ Even Homer sometimes nods. 원숭이도 나무에서 떨어진다.
⑤ Actions speak louder than words. 말보다 행동이 중요하다.

어휘 be on a diet 다이어트 중이다, 식이요법 중이다 on sale 할인 중인, 판매되는 for the past few months 지난 몇 달간 less 더 적게 lose weight 살이 빠지다 amount 양, 분량 exercise 운동하다 get started 시작하다 through ~을 통해 rule 규칙, 법칙 exception 예외 fix 고치다 nod 고개를 끄덕이다, 꾸벅꾸벅 졸다 action 행동

20 ②

W: David, do you have any <u>plans</u> for the <u>weekend</u>? 데이비드, 넌 주말 계획이 있니?

M: Yes, I do. I'm <u>going camping</u> with my friends <u>on Saturday</u>. Why do you ask, Mom? 네, 있어요. 저는 토요일에 친구들과 함께 캠핑을 갈 거예요. 왜 물어 보세요, 엄마?

W: Well, I <u>invited</u> your grandparents, aunts, uncles, and cousins over <u>for dinner</u> on Saturday. That's the only day everyone can come. 음, 내가 네 할아버지 할머니와 이모들, 삼촌들, 그리고 사촌들을 토요일 저녁 식사에 초대했거든. 그 날이 모두가 올 수 있는 유일한 날이란다.

M: You invited them on Saturday? Hmm… Then I'll <u>talk to</u> my <u>friends</u> and go camping on <u>Sunday instead</u>. 그분들을 토요일에 초대했다고요? 음, 그럼 전 친구들에게 얘기해서 대신 일요일에 캠핑을 가자고 말할게요.

W: Oh, that'll be perfect! Thank you so much for doing that. 아, 그럼 되겠다! 그렇게 해줘서 정말 고마워.

M: It's <u>not</u> a <u>problem</u>. <u>When</u> are they going to <u>be here</u>? 괜찮아요. 그분들이 언제 우리 집에 오죠?

W: Your grandparents will <u>get here around seven</u>, and everyone else will be here by seven thirty. 네 할아버지 할머니는 7시쯤 오실 거고, 나머지 사람들은 모두 7시 반까지 여기 올 거다.

M: Okay. I can't wait to see everyone! 알았어요. 모두 빨리 보고 싶어요!

① I don't have any plans for Sunday.
  저는 일요일에는 아무 계획도 없어요.
② Okay. I can't wait to see everyone!
  알았어요. 모두 빨리 보고 싶어요!
③ I don't want to eat anything right now.
  저는 지금 아무것도 먹고 싶지 않아요.
④ I'm a busy person. I always have plans over the weekend. 저는 바쁜 사람이에요. 항상 주말에 계획이 있다고요.
⑤ I'm going to be late. I'll meet you guys at the camping grounds.
  나는 늦을 거야. 캠핑장에서 너희들을 만날게.

어휘 go camping 캠핑을 가다 cousin 사촌 instead 대신에 over the weekend 주말에 camping ground 캠핑장

17회 실전모의고사   본문 p.198-199

01 ⑤	02 ③	03 ②	04 ③	05 ④
06 ③	07 ①	08 ⑤	09 ①	10 ④
11 ③	12 ④	13 ④	14 ④	15 ③
16 ④	17 ④	18 ③	19 ④	20 ④

01 ⑤

M: Ruth, do you know which <u>princess doll</u> you want yet? 루스, 네가 어떤 공주 인형을 원하는지 이제 알겠니?

W: No, I like all of them, Dad! It's <u>hard to choose</u> one.
아니요, 모든 인형이 다 좋아요, 아빠! 하나만 고르는 건 너무 어려워요.

M: Okay, then let me help you. How do you like this <u>long-haired</u> doll wearing a long <u>dress</u>?
알았다, 그럼 내가 도와주마. 이 긴 머리에 긴 드레스를 입고 있는 인형은 어떠니?

W: It's alright, but I <u>prefer</u> a doll with a <u>crown</u> on <u>her head</u> like this one with the short dress and short hair. 좋긴 한데, 저는 이 짧은 드레스에 짧은 머리를 한 인형처럼 머리에 왕관을 쓴 인형이 좋아요.

M: Hmm… <u>Here's one</u> with long hair and a short dress. She has a crown on her head, too. Do you want this one? 음, 여기 긴 머리와 짧은 드레스를 한 인형이 있구나. 머리에 왕관도 쓰고 있어. 이걸 원하니?

W: No. I like this one with the <u>short hair</u> and <u>long dress</u> <u>the best</u>. 아니요. 저는 이 짧은 머리에 긴 드레스를 입은 인형이 제일 마음에 들어요.

M: Alright, then. <u>Are you sure</u> this is the one you want? 좋아, 그럼. 이게 정말 네가 원하는 거 맞지?

W: Yes, Dad. I'm <u>sure</u>! 네, 아빠. 확실해요!

어휘 princess 공주 long-haired 머리가 긴 prefer 선호하다 crown 왕관

02 ③

[Telephone rings.] [전화벨이 울린다.]

W: Hello, Time-Warp Cable here. How can I help you?
안녕하세요, 저희는 타임와프 케이블입니다. 무엇을 도와드릴까요?

M: I would like to get <u>cable on</u> my <u>TV</u>, please.
제 TV에 케이블을 달고 싶어요.

W: Okay. You can <u>choose from</u> three <u>packages</u>. Package A gives you one hundred <u>channels</u>. If you sign up for Package B, you get one hundred fifty channels. And Package C provides two hundred channels. 알겠습니다. 3개의 패키지 상품 중에서 선택하실 수 있어요. A 패키지는 100개의 채널을 제공합니다. 만약 B 패키지를 신청하시면 150개의 채널을 제공 받으실 수 있습니다. 그리고 C 패키지는 200개의 채널을 제공합니다.

M: Hmm… I think I will <u>sign up for</u> Package B. Can you <u>send someone</u> to my house to <u>set it up</u> for me? 음, 저는 B 패키지를 신청할게요. 케이블을 설치할 사람을 저희 집으로 보내주실 수 있나요?

W: Yes, sir. If you tell me <u>your address</u>, I will <u>send</u> a <u>technician</u> over by ten o'clock tomorrow morning. 네, 손님. 주소를 말씀해 주시면 내일 오전 10시까지 기사를 보내드리겠습니다.

M: Alright, forty-four thirty-one Allenwood Road. Oh, and how do I <u>pay for</u> the <u>monthly</u> cable <u>fee</u>? 알겠습니다. 앨렌우드 로드 4431번지입니다. 아, 그리고 매월 케이블 요금을 내는 방법은 어떻게 되죠?

W: A <u>bill</u> will be <u>mailed</u> to your home address at the end of each month.
매월 말에 청구서가 우편으로 고객님의 주소지로 갈 겁니다.

M: Okay, that sounds good. Thank you!
네, 좋네요. 감사합니다!

어휘 channel (TV) 채널 sign up for 신청하다, 등록하다 address 주소 technician 기술자 pay for (비용을) 지불하다 mail 우편 배송하다

03 ②

① W: <u>Take a look</u> at all those flowers in the park!
공원에 있는 저 꽃들을 좀 보세요!

M: Wow! They're so beautiful! 와! 정말 아름답군요!

② W: <u>What flowers</u> would you like today?
오늘은 어떤 꽃을 원하세요?

M: I would like a <u>bouquet of roses</u>, please.
장미꽃 한 다발 주세요.

③ W: I need to buy a <u>present</u> for my <u>sister</u>.
제 여동생에게 줄 선물을 사야 합니다.

M: <u>Why don't you</u> buy her a necklace?
그녀에게 목걸이를 사주는 건 어때요?

④ W: You <u>look</u> really <u>tired</u> today.
당신 오늘은 정말 피곤해 보여요.

M: I know. I only <u>slept</u> for <u>two hours</u> last night.
나도 알아요. 어젯밤에 두 시간밖에 못 잤어요.

⑤ W: <u>Would you like</u> some flowers for your mother's birthday? 당신 어머니의 생신을 위해 꽃을 살래요?

M: <u>No thanks</u>. She doesn't really like flowers.
아니요, 괜찮아요. 어머니가 꽃을 그다지 좋아하지 않으세요.

어휘 take a look at ~을 한번 보다 bouquet 꽃다발 present 선물 necklace 목걸이 look tired 피곤해 보이다

04 ③

W: Jeff, what food do you <u>like</u> eating <u>the most</u>?
제프, 넌 어떤 음식을 가장 좋아하니?

M: <u>Guess</u> what it is. If you <u>get it right</u>, I'll <u>buy you dinner</u>. 뭔지 맞혀 봐. 만약 네가 맞힌다면, 내가 저녁을 사줄게.

W: Okay! Is it a type of <u>Italian food</u>, like pasta?
알겠어! 파스타 같은 이탈리아 음식이니?

M: No. I don't really like Italian food. I'll <u>give</u> you a <u>hint</u>. You normally <u>eat</u> this <u>with</u> a type of <u>fried</u> food and <u>soda</u>. 아니, 난 이탈리아 음식을 그렇게 좋아하지는 않아. 내가 힌트를 하나 줄게. 넌 보통은 튀긴 음식과 탄산음료와 함께 이 음식을 먹어.

W: Oh! I think I'm starting to <u>figure it out</u>. The fried food is <u>French fries</u>, right? 아! 나에게 감이 오는 것 같아. 그 튀긴 음식은 감자튀김이지, 그렇지?

M: Yes! You <u>got</u> that part <u>right</u>. So what do you eat with French fries and soda? 응! 그 부분은 맞았어. 그럼 감자튀김이랑 탄산음료랑 같이 무엇을 먹니?

W: Hmm… I'm <u>pretty sure</u> this is it. It has <u>bread</u>, <u>vegetables</u>, and <u>meat</u> in it, right? And you use your hands to eat it.

음, 난 이거라고 확신해. 그건 빵, 채소, 그리고 고기가 안에 들어 있지? 그리고 그걸 먹으려고 손을 사용하지.

M: Yeah! You figured it out! Let's go eat dinner now.
맞아! 알아냈구나! 이제 저녁 먹으러 가자.

어휘 guess 짐작하다, 추측하다 get something right ~을 바르게 이해하다 normally 보통은, 일반적으로 soda 탄산음료 figure out 알아내다 French fries 감자튀김 pretty 꽤 sure 확신하는 meat 고기

05 ④

W: Welcome aboard flight three oh one, sir. May I help you? 301편 항공기에 탑승하신 것을 환영합니다, 손님. 무엇을 도와드릴까요?

M: Yes, could you help me find my seat? It's thirty-two A. 네, 제 좌석을 찾는 걸 도와주시겠어요? 32A이거든요.

W: Of course, it's right this way. Is there anything else I can do for you?
물론이죠, 이쪽으로 가시면 됩니다. 제가 도와드릴 일이 더 있나요?

M: Actually, yes. I would like an extra blanket, please. It gets cold during the flight. 실은 있어요. 추가 담요를 받고 싶네요. 비행 도중에는 추워지거든요.

W: Okay, I will get it for you right away.
알겠습니다. 바로 가져다 드리겠습니다.

M: Alright. One last thing, what is this seatbelt sign for? 네. 마지막으로, 이 좌석벨트 표시는 뭐죠?

W: When the sign is turned on, you must put on your seatbelt and stay in your seat. When the sign is turned off, you can get up and walk around.
표시가 켜지면 좌석벨트를 착용하시고 좌석에 앉아 계셔야 합니다. 표시가 꺼지면, 일어나셔서 걸어 다니셔도 좋습니다.

M: Oh, I see. Thank you for your help!
아, 알겠습니다. 도와주셔서 고맙습니다!

해설 여자의 첫 번째 대사인 'Welcome aboard flight ~'에서 바로 정답을 짐작할 수 있어야 한다.

어휘 aboard 탑승한 flight 항공편, 비행 extra 추가의 blanket 담요 right away 즉시, 바로 one last thing 마지막으로 한 가지 seatbelt 좌석 벨트 sign 표시, 표지판 turn on 켜다 turn off 끄다

06 ③

W: Steve, you look so down today. Are you okay?
스티브, 넌 오늘 무척 우울해 보이는구나. 괜찮니?

M: No, not really. I really miss my family. I haven't seen them in over two months. 아니, 별로야. 난 가족이 무척 보고 싶어. 두 달 넘게 가족을 못 봤어.

W: I understand. I felt the same way when I first started my semester here as an international student. 이해해. 나도 유학생으로 이곳에 온 첫 학기 때 같은 기분을 느꼈거든.

M: I want to go back to my hometown right now. I feel so alone living in a different country.

지금 당장 내 고향으로 돌아가고 싶어. 다른 나라에서 사는 건 정말 외로워.

W: I'm sure you'll be okay. Have you met any new friends yet?
넌 분명히 괜찮아질 거야. 새로운 친구들을 만나봤니?

M: No, nobody wants to talk to me. I feel like I don't belong here. I miss my friends back home.
아니, 아무도 나에게 말하려고 하지 않아. 나는 여기에 속하지 않는 느낌이야. 고향에 있는 친구들이 그리워.

W: Well, there are only four weeks left until the semester is over. Hang in there!
글쎄, 이번 학기가 끝나려면 4주밖에 안 남았어. 조금만 견뎌!

M: Okay, I'll try. Thank you! 알겠어, 노력해 볼게. 고마워!

해설 남자의 'miss my family', 'feel so alone', 'don't belong here', 'miss my friends' 등의 말은 남자의 외로운 심정을 나타낸다.

어휘 down 우울한 miss 그리워하다 feel the same way 똑같이 느끼다, 같은 생각을 하다 semester 학기 international student 유학생 hometown 고향(나고 자란 곳) alone 외로운 belong ~에 속하다 hang in 견디다, 버티다

07 ①

① M: How many people are going to the volleyball game? 배구 경기에 얼마나 많은 사람들이 가나요?

W: The game is supposed to start at six thirty P.M.
경기는 오후 6시 30분에 시작하기로 되어 있어요.

② M: What do you want to eat for breakfast?
아침으로 무엇을 먹고 싶어요?

W: I would like toast or a ham sandwich.
토스트나 햄 샌드위치가 먹고 싶어요.

③ M: Is meeting room A available today?
오늘 A 회의실을 이용할 수 있나요?

W: No, the marketing team will be using it.
아니요, 마케팅 팀이 거길 사용할 거예요.

④ M: Are you on your way home yet?
아직 집으로 오는 중인가요?

W: Yes. I'll be there in ten minutes.
네. 십 분 후에 거기 도착해요.

⑤ M: Where is the parking lot?
주차장이 어디에 있나요?

W: It's behind the building across the street.
길 건너편 건물의 뒤편에 있어요.

어휘 volleyball 배구 be supposed to ~하기로 되어 있다 available 이용 가능한 on one's way ~가는 중 parking lot 주차장 across ~건너편의

08 ⑤

M: Hey, Sophie. Why were you late to class today?
소피. 오늘 수업에 왜 늦었니?

W: I forgot to set an alarm before going to sleep. This isn't the first time I've been late.
잠들기 전에 알람을 맞춰 놓는 것을 깜박했어. 내가 지각한 건 이번

이 처음이 아니야.

M: If you keep coming to class late, Mr. Hoover is going to take points off your attendance grade.
네가 계속 수업에 지각하면, 후버 선생님께서 네 출석 성적에서 감점을 하실 거야.

W: Yeah, I know. But I have a bad memory. What should I do?
응, 알아. 하지만 난 기억력이 안 좋아. 어떻게 하면 좋을까?

M: Hmm… I don't know. I never have trouble getting up in the morning.
음, 모르겠어. 나는 아침에 일어나는 것에 전혀 문제가 없거든.

W: I see. Then could you call me every morning? That way even if I forget to set an alarm, I can wake up on time. 그렇구나. 그러면 네가 아침마다 나한테 전화해 줄 수 있니? 그러면 내가 알람을 맞춰 놓는 걸 잊어버려도, 제시간에 일어날 수 있을 텐데.

M: Sure, I can do that for you. I normally get up at seven. Is that a good time?
물론, 내가 해줄 수 있어. 난 보통 7시에 일어나. 그 시간이 괜찮니?

W: Yes! That works for me. Thank you!
그럼! 나한테 좋아. 고마워!

해설 여자의 대사 'Could you ~?'에 부탁 내용이 나온다.

어휘 set an alarm 알람을 맞추다   keep -ing 계속 ~하다 take points off 점수를 깎다   attendance grade 출석 성적 bad memory 안 좋은 기억력(↔ good memory)   on time 제시간에   normally 보통, 평소에

09 ①

W: What's up, Brad? You look excited for something.
무슨 일이야, 브래드? 뭔가 신나 보이는구나.

M: Well, I'm excited and nervous at the same time. I'm going on a date with this girl that I really like.
음, 신나기도 하고 동시에 긴장되기도 해. 내가 진짜 좋아하는 여자애랑 데이트하기로 했어.

W: Good for you! Have you decided what you're going to wear? It's important to make a good impression.
잘됐네! 뭘 입을지 결정했니? 그건 좋은 인상을 주기 위해서 중요해.

M: Yeah, I know. I have an outfit planned out, but I don't know if I should wear it. Can you tell me how it looks? 응, 나도 알아. 입을 옷을 계획해 놨는데, 그걸 입어야 할지 잘 모르겠어. 어떤지 좀 봐줄래?

W: Sure, I can do that. 물론, 내가 봐줄게.

M: Okay, I was going to wear these black pants and denim shirt.
그래, 난 이 검은 바지와 데님 셔츠를 입으려고 했어.

W: Hmm… Why don't you wear this white shirt instead? It looks better on you.
음, 대신 이 흰색 셔츠를 입는 게 어때? 그게 너한테 더 잘 어울려.

해설 여자의 마지막 대사의 'Why don't ~?'는 제안할 때 사용되는 표현이다.

어휘 excited 신이 난   nervous 긴장한   at the same time 동시에   go on a date 데이트하러 가다   make a good impression 좋은 인상을 주다   outfit 의상, 복장   plan out 계획하다   denim 데님(청바지를 만드는 푸른 면직물)

10 ④

커피/차	디저트
아이스 라떼 5달러	초콜릿 케이크 3달러
아이스 모카 6달러	치즈 케이크 4달러
핫 초콜릿 4달러	블루베리 머핀 3달러
녹차 4달러	도넛 3달러

W: Thanks so much for helping me on my project!
내 프로젝트를 도와줘서 정말 고마워!

M: It's no problem. I can help you anytime you need.
천만에. 네가 필요할 때면 언제든 도와줄 수 있어.

W: To thank you, I would like to buy you some coffee and dessert. What would you like?
고마움에 대한 보답으로, 내가 너에게 커피랑 디저트를 사주고 싶어. 뭘 먹고 싶니?

M: Oh, that's so thoughtful of you. I'll have the ice mocha and chocolate cake. 아, 넌 정말 속이 깊구나. 나는 아이스 모카와 초콜릿 케이크를 먹을게.

W: Okay. Are you sure that's all you want? You can order more dessert if you'd like. 알겠어. 원하는 게 그게 다야? 네가 원하면 디저트를 더 주문해도 돼.

M: Really? Well then, I'll have the blueberry muffin, too. What are you going to order?
정말? 그럼, 블루베리 머핀도 시킬게. 너는 뭘 주문할 거니?

W: I think I'll get a cup of green tea and cheesecake.
나는 녹차 한 잔이랑 치즈 케이크를 시킬 거야.

M: Okay! I appreciate you doing this.
알겠어! 이렇게 사줘서 고마워.

해설 주문한 내용을 듣고 바로 표에 체크하는 것이 좋다. 남자가 주문한 것은 ice mocha($6)+chocolate cake($3)+blueberry muffin($3)으로 $12이고, 여자가 주문한 것은 green tea($4)+cheesecake($4)이므로 $8이다. 합계는 $20이다.

어휘 thoughtful 사려 깊은, 배려심 있는   order 주문하다 appreciate 감사하다

11 ③

W: Good afternoon, welcome to Speedy Bicycles. Can I help you? 안녕하세요, 스피디 자전거에 오신 걸 환영합니다. 제가 도와드릴까요?

M: Yes, I bought this bicycle a few months ago, and the brake doesn't seem to work. 네, 제가 몇 달 전에 이 자전거를 샀는데, 브레이크가 작동하지 않는 것 같아요.

W: Okay, but there isn't anything we can do for you here. You'll have to take your bicycle to the repair shop down the street. 알겠습니다, 하지만 여기서는 저희가 해드릴 수 있는 게 없어요. 길을 따라가시면 나오는 수리점으로 자

전거를 가지고 가셔야 할 거예요.

M: Oh, alright. Would you happen to know how much it will cost to fix my brakes? 아, 알겠습니다. 혹시 제 브레이크를 수리하는 데 비용이 얼마나 들지 아시나요?

W: It will cost you about one hundred dollars. 100달러 정도 나올 겁니다.

M: What? That's so expensive! I might as well buy a new one. 네? 너무 비싸네요! 새로운 자전거를 사는 게 낫겠어요.

W: I know, it does cost a lot. Would you be interested in buying a new bicycle? 맞아요, 비용이 많이 들죠. 새로운 자전거를 구매하실 생각이 있으신가요?

M: Yes. I'll take a look around. Thank you. 네, 구경 좀 할게요. 감사합니다.

해설 여자의 인사말인 'welcome to Speedy Bicycles'에서 단서를 얻을 수 있다.

어휘 bicycle 자전거   work 작동하다   repair shop 수리점 down the street 길을 따라, 길 아래로   cost 비용이 들다   fix 고치다   might as well ~하는 편이 낫겠다   be interested in ~에 관심이 있다   take a look around 둘러보다, 구경하다

12 ④

M: Ladies and Gentlemen! We are pleased to announce the grand opening of Peabody Circus! We will open our gates on Wednesday, March nineteenth at ten A.M. We are located on Seventh Avenue. There will be elephants that draw pictures, lions that jump through fire, magicians doing tricks, and so much more! There will be three shows every day, at one P.M., two thirty P.M., and five P.M. Admission is free for children and five dollars for adults. Come out and have the time of your life!

신사 숙녀 여러분! 피바디 서커스의 개장을 알리게 되어 정말 기쁩니다! 저희는 3월 19일 수요일 오전 10시에 문을 엽니다. 저희는 7번가에 위치해 있습니다. 그림 그리는 코끼리, 불을 통과하는 사자, 마술을 선보이는 마술사, 그리고 더 많은 것들이 있습니다! 매일 오후 1시, 2시 30분, 그리고 5시, 이렇게 세 번의 공연이 있을 것입니다. 입장료는 어린이는 무료이고 성인은 5달러입니다. 오셔서 더할 수 없이 즐거운 한때를 보내시기 바랍니다!

해설 개장일은 나와 있지만 폐장일은 나오지 않았다.

어휘 pleased 기쁜   grand opening 개장, 개막   gate 출입구 be located 위치하다   through ~을 통과하여, ~을 통해 magician 마술사   do tricks 마술을 하다, 속임수를 쓰다 admission 입장료   have the time of one's life 아주 재미있는 시간을 보내다

13 ④

| 기숙사 셔틀버스 시간 |

오후 12:00,	오후 12:20,	오후 12:40
오후 1:00,	오후 1:15,	오후 1:30
오후 2:00,	오후 2:20,	오후 2:40
오후 4:00,	오후 4:15,	오후 4:35
오후 5:00,	오후 5:15,	오후 5:30

① Students who want to go to the dormitory can ride the shuttle bus at noon.
기숙사에 가고 싶은 학생들은 정오에 셔틀버스를 탈 수 있다.

② The shuttle bus runs every fifteen minutes from one P.M. to one thirty P.M.
셔틀버스는 오후 1시부터 1시 30분까지 15분 간격으로 운행된다.

③ Students who wait for the shuttle bus at three thirty P.M. will have to wait for thirty minutes until it comes. 오후 3시 30분에 셔틀버스를 기다리는 학생들은 버스가 올 때까지 30분을 기다려야 한다.

④ The shuttle bus runs at four ten P.M., four fifteen P.M., and four twenty-five P.M. 셔틀버스는 오후 4시 10분, 4시 15분, 그리고 4시 25분에 운행된다.

⑤ If you do not ride the shuttle bus by five thirty P.M., you will have to walk to the dormitory.
오후 5시 30분까지 셔틀버스를 타지 않는다면, 기숙사까지 걸어가야 한다.

어휘 dormitory 기숙사   ride 탑승하다   shuttle bus 셔틀버스 run 운행되다, 운행하다

14 ③

W: This is a type of fruit that grows on trees. It is yellow with green leaves. The skin of this fruit has many spikes on it, so you must be careful not to poke yourself. You have to remove the skin before eating it. This fruit is sweet and sour at the same time. This fruit grows in places where there is hot weather. You can buy it at a market or grocery store.

이것은 나무에서 자라는 과일의 일종입니다. 이것은 노란색이며 초록색 잎을 가지고 있습니다. 이 과일의 껍질에는 뾰족한 것이 많이 있어서 당신은 찔리지 않도록 조심해야 합니다. 먹기 전에는 껍질을 제거해야 합니다. 이 과일은 달고, 동시에 신맛이 납니다. 이 과일은 더운 날씨의 지역에서 자랍니다. 당신은 이것을 시장이나 식료품점에서 구입할 수 있습니다.

해설 껍질에 뾰족한 것이 많은 노란색 과일은 파인애플이다.

어휘 leaf 잎(복 leaves)   spike 뾰족한 것; 못   poke 찌르다 remove 제거하다   sweet 달콤한   sour 신, 신맛이 나는   at the same time 동시에   grocery store 식료품점

15 ③

W: Aaron, have you finished your math homework?
애런, 네 수학 숙제 끝냈니?

M: No, Mom. I don't think I can do it today.
아니요, 엄마. 오늘은 못 끝낼 것 같아요.

W: Why not? 왜 못 끝내?

M: I can't solve any of the problems because there's something wrong with my calculator.
제 계산기에 뭔가 문제가 있어서 어떤 문제도 풀 수가 없어요.

W: Let me see it. [pause] I see what the problem is. The addition and multiplication buttons on your calculator aren't working.
어디 한 번 보자. [잠시 후] 문제가 뭔지 알겠구나. 계산기의 더하기와 곱하기 버튼이 작동하지 않네.

M: Oh, I see. How am I going to finish my assignment with a broken calculator? 아, 그렇네요. 고장 난 계산기를 갖고 제가 어떻게 과제를 끝내야 하죠?

W: Hmm… Can you borrow one from a friend tomorrow? 음, 내일 친구에게 계산기를 빌릴 수 있니?

M: I think so. I'll ask someone from my math class if I can use theirs. 그럴 수 있을 거예요. 제가 그들의 계산기를 사용할 수 있는지 수학 시간에 누군가에게 물어볼게요.

> 어휘 calculator 계산기 addition 더하기 multiplication 곱하기 working 작동하는 assignment 과제 borrow 빌리다

16 ④

W: Wow, John! I didn't know you could swim so well! How long have you been swimming? 우와, 존! 네가 수영을 그렇게 잘하는지 몰랐어! 넌 얼마나 오랫동안 수영을 했니?

M: Thanks for the compliment. I've been swimming for about two years.
칭찬해 줘서 고마워. 난 약 2년 동안 수영을 했어.

W: That's a long time. No wonder you're so good! I wish I could swim well, too.
오래됐구나. 네가 잘하는 게 당연해! 나도 수영을 잘했으면 좋겠어.

M: If you want, I can teach you how to swim. It's easier than it looks, I promise. 네가 원하면, 내가 수영하는 법을 가르쳐줄 수 있어. 약속하는데, 보기보다 쉬워.

W: I would love that! When do you want to meet? I'm free every day this week except for Tuesday and Wednesday. 나야 좋지! 언제 만날래? 나는 화요일과 수요일을 빼면 이번 주에는 매일 한가해.

M: Okay, I can do Monday and Friday. You can choose between those two days. 알겠어. 난 월요일과 금요일에 할 수 있어. 네가 두 요일 중에 골라봐.

W: Hmm… I think Friday would be best. That way I can rest over the weekend.
음, 금요일이 제일 좋겠다. 그러면 내가 주말에 쉴 수 있잖아.

M: Alright, I'll see you then! 좋아, 그때 보자!

> 해설 두 사람이 정하는 것이므로 의견 조율 과정이 나온 후에 마지막 부분에 정답이 나오는 경우가 많다.

> 어휘 compliment 칭찬 no wonder ~은 놀라운 일이 아니다, ~하는 것도 당연하다 promise 약속하다 except for ~을 제외하고 rest 휴식을 취하다, 쉬다 over the weekend 주말에

17 ④

W: Danielle and Jane made plans to meet each other for lunch on Thursday. Danielle got to the restaurant first, so she waited for Jane to come. However, Jane never showed up. She didn't even call Danielle to tell her that she wouldn't be coming. Danielle got very angry with Jane and decided to call her. But Jane did not answer her cellphone. The next day, when Danielle sees Jane at school, what would Danielle most likely say to Jane?

대니엘과 제인은 목요일에 만나 점심을 같이 하기로 약속했다. 대니엘이 먼저 식당에 도착해서 제인이 오기를 기다렸다. 하지만 제인은 끝내 오지 않았다. 심지어 대니엘에게 전화해서 자신이 못 온다는 말도 하지 않았다. 대니엘은 제인에게 매우 화가 났고 그녀에게 전화하기로 결심했다. 하지만 제인은 휴대폰을 받지 않았다. 다음 날 대니엘이 학교에서 제인을 본다면 대니엘이 제인에게 할 말로 가장 적절한 것은 무엇인가?

Danielle: I waited 3 hours for you! Why didn't you come to meet me?
내가 널 세 시간 기다렸어! 왜 날 만나러 오지 않았니?

① I couldn't find my cellphone. 내 휴대폰을 못 찾았어.

② Let's grab lunch on Thursday. 목요일에 점심을 먹자.

③ The restaurant doesn't open on weekends.
그 식당은 주말에는 열지 않아.

④ I waited 3 hours for you! Why didn't you come to meet me? 내가 널 세 시간 기다렸어! 왜 날 만나러 오지 않았니?

⑤ I'll call you back in 30 minutes. I'm in the middle of eating lunch.
내가 30분 후에 다시 전화할게. 지금 점심을 먹는 중이야.

> 어휘 get to ~에 도착하다 show up 등장하다, 나타나다 grab lunch (간단히) 점심을 먹다 in the middle of ~하는 도중인

18 ③

M: Are you looking forward to going on your trip to Hong Kong? 넌 홍콩으로 떠나는 여행을 기대하고 있니?

W: Yes, I am. By this time tomorrow, I'll be touring the city streets! 응, 기대하고 있어. 내일 이 시간이면 나는 도시의 거리를 여행하고 있을 거야!

M: Did you double check to see if you packed everything? 모든 짐을 다 챙겼는지 다시 한 번 확인했니?

W: Of course I did! My bags are all ready to go. I just need to go to the bank.
물론 했지! 내 가방들은 모두 준비되었어. 난 은행만 가면 돼.

M: You didn't exchange your money, yet?
아직 환전을 하지 않았니?

W: No, I was going to go later today. Is there a problem? 안 했어, 오늘 이따가 가려고 했어. 무슨 문제가 있니?

M: Well, the bank closes early today because it's a national holiday tomorrow. 음, 내일이 공휴일이어서 은행이 오늘 일찍 문을 닫아.

W: Oh, my goodness! I almost forgot! I'd better go now. 아 이런! 하마터면 잊을 뻔했어! 지금 가야겠다.

어휘 look forward to ~을 기대하다, 학수고대하다　by this time 이맘때면　double check 다시 확인하다　exchange money 환전하다　national holiday 공휴일　had better ~하는 게 좋겠다

19 ④

W: Robert, what did you do over summer vacation? 로버트, 여름 방학 동안 뭐 했니?

M: I read a few books, went backpacking in the mountains, and visited my cousins. What did you do? 난 책을 몇 권 읽었고, 산으로 배낭여행도 갔고, 내 사촌 집도 방문했어. 너는 뭐 했니?

W: That's awesome! I went to the beach with my friends and learned how to bake a cake. 멋지다! 나는 친구랑 해변에 갔고, 케이크를 굽는 법을 배웠어.

M: It seems like you had a great summer! Can you believe that we start school again tomorrow? 넌 아주 멋진 여름을 보낸 것 같구나! 내일 다시 개학하는 것이 믿겨지니?

W: No, I can't! It feels like summer vacation just started, but it's already over! 아니, 믿기지 않아! 이제 막 여름방학이 시작한 것 같은데, 이미 끝났어!

M: I couldn't agree with you more. I'm not ready for the first day of school. 나도 정말 그렇게 생각해. 난 아직 학교 첫날에 대한 준비가 안 됐어.

W: I'm not ready, either. I wish we could turn back time and go on vacation again. 나도 준비가 안 됐어. 우리가 시간을 돌려서 다시 휴가를 갔으면 좋겠어.

M: I guess we'll just have to look forward to the last day of school. 우리 그냥 학기의 마지막 날을 기다려야 할 것 같아.

① Better late than never. 하지 않는 것보다 늦더라도 하는 것이 낫다.

② Too many cooks spoil the broth. 사공이 많으면 배가 산으로 간다.

③ The early bird catches the worm. 일찍 일어나는 새가 벌레를 잡는다.

④ All good things must come to an end. 모든 좋은 일에는 끝이 찾아온다.

⑤ Heaven helps those who help themselves. 하늘은 스스로 돕는 자를 돕는다.

어휘 go backpacking 배낭여행을 가다　awesome 엄청난, 어마어마한　feel like ~인 것처럼 느끼다　I couldn't agree with you more. 전적으로 동의해.

20 ④

W: Hello, would you like to try out for our school dance team? 안녕, 우리 학교의 댄스팀에 지원해 볼래?

M: Hmm… I'm not sure. What kind of dance team is it? 음, 난 잘 모르겠어. 어떤 종류의 댄스팀이니?

W: Well, we do all types of dance, from ballet and jazz to tap dancing and hip-hop! Are you interested in any of those genres? 사실, 우리는 발레와 재즈에서부터 탭 댄스 그리고 힙합까지, 모든 종류의 춤을 춰! 이 장르들 중에서 관심 있는 것이 있니?

M: Yes, I really like hip-hop dance. When do you have auditions? 응, 난 힙합 댄스를 정말 좋아해. 넌 언제 오디션을 갖니?

W: Auditions are this Wednesday and Thursday in the student hall. 오디션은 이번 주 수요일과 목요일에 학생회관에서 있어.

M: Okay. What do I need to prepare for the audition? 알았어. 내가 어떻게 오디션 준비를 해야 할까?

W: You have to dance to two songs. One of the songs we will decide for you, and the other song is your choice. 넌 두 곡의 노래에 맞춰 춤을 춰야 해. 한 곡은 우리가 너를 위해 정하고, 다른 곡은 네가 직접 정할 수 있어.

M: Alright. Can you write my name down on the list? I want to try out. 알았어. 목록에 내 이름을 적어 줄 수 있니? 난 지원해 보고 싶어.

① How long have you been dancing? 넌 얼마나 오래 춤을 췄어?

② I'll meet you in front of the student hall on Thursday. 목요일에 학생회관 앞에서 만나자.

③ What's your favorite type of dance? Mine is ballet and jazz. 가장 좋아하는 댄스 종류가 뭐야? 나는 발레와 재즈를 가장 좋아해.

④ Alright. Can you write my name down on the list? I want to try out. 알았어. 목록에 내 이름을 적어 줄 수 있니? 난 지원해 보고 싶어.

⑤ There is a dance performance in the student hall on Wednesday. 수요일에 학생회관에서 댄스 공연이 있어.

해설 여자가 남자에게 댄스팀 지원에 대해 제안을 했고, 오디션에서 해야 할 것에 대해 말해주었으니, 남자는 지원할지 말지에 대해서 결정할 것이다.

어휘 try out for 지원하다, 도전하다　tap dancing 탭 댄스　be interested in ~에 관심이 있다　genre 장르　have an audition 오디션을 실시하다　student hall 학생회관　write down ~을 적다　list 목록, 명단　performance 공연, 행사

01 ⑤		**02** ②		**03** ③		**04** ③		**05** ④	
06 ①		**07** ②		**08** ②		**09** ①		**10** ③	
11 ②		**12** ③		**13** ⑤		**14** ②		**15** ④	
16 ③		**17** ④		**18** ②		**19** ④		**20** ④	

01 ⑤

W: Hey, Mark. If you could travel to anywhere in the world, where would you go?
얘, 마크. 네가 세계 어디로든 여행할 수 있다면, 어디로 갈 거야?

M: Hmm… There are a lot of places I would like to go to, but there is one special place I really want to visit. 음, 가고 싶은 곳은 아주 많은데, 내가 정말로 방문하고 싶은 특별한 장소가 하나 있어.

W: Oh, and where is that? 아, 그게 어딘데?

M: You should try guessing it! I'll give you a hint. It's located in Egypt.
네가 알아맞혀 봐! 힌트를 줄게. 그것은 이집트에 위치해 있어.

W: Are you kidding me? There are probably hundreds of things to see in Egypt. Can you give me another hint? 장난하니? 이집트에는 볼거리가 아마 수백 가지는 있을 텐데. 다른 힌트를 주겠니?

M: Okay. It is shaped like a triangle, and it has a big lion statue in front of it.
알겠어. 그곳은 삼각형 모양이고 그 앞에 커다란 사자상이 있어.

W: I think I can guess it right if you give me one last hint.
네가 마지막으로 힌트를 하나 준다면 내가 맞힐 수 있을 것 같아.

M: Alright. The purpose of this place was to store mummies. Plus, it is a symbol of Egypt.
좋아. 이곳의 목적은 미라를 보관하기 위한 거야. 그리고, 이집트의 상징이기도 해.

W: Oh! I think I know exactly where you're talking about. I would like to go there sometime, too!
아! 네가 말하고 있는 곳을 정확히 알겠다. 나도 언젠가 거기에 가고 싶거든!

어휘 be located in ~에 위치하다   shaped like ~모양의
statue 조각상   purpose 목적, 용도   mummy 미라   symbol
상징(물)   exactly 정확히, 틀림없이

02 ②

[Cellphone rings.] [휴대폰이 울린다.]

M: Hey, Anna! This is Brad from your Writing one oh one class. 애나! 난 작문 101 수업을 같이 듣는 브래드야.

W: Oh, hey Brad! What's up? 아, 브래드! 무슨 일이니?

M: Well, I have to write a research paper, but my laptop suddenly stopped working. I was wondering if I could borrow yours.

사실은 내가 연구 보고서를 써야 하는데, 갑자기 내 노트북이 작동하지 않아. 그래서 네 노트북을 빌릴 수 있는지 궁금했어.

W: Sure, you can. But I need it back by tomorrow night. I have to use it for an assignment as well.
물론, 사용해도 좋아. 하지만 내일 밤까지는 돌려 줘야 해. 나도 과제 때문에 그걸 써야 하거든.

M: Yeah, that's not a problem. I'll be finished writing my paper tonight.
응, 문제없어. 난 오늘 밤에 보고서 작성을 마칠 거야.

W: Okay then. Where do you want to meet me?
그럼 좋아. 어디서 만나는 게 좋을까?

M: I'm in the Central Library right now. Are you nearby? 난 지금 중앙 도서관에 있어. 넌 근처에 있니?

W: Actually, yes. Plus, I have my laptop with me so I can give it to you right now. 실은 그래. 그리고 지금 노트북을 가지고 있어서 너한테 바로 줄 수 있어.

M: Alright! I'll meet you in front of the entrance in a few minutes. 좋아! 몇 분 후에 입구 앞에서 만나자.

어휘 research 연구, 조사   paper 보고서   suddenly 갑자기
stop working 작동을 멈추다   assignment 과제   nearby
근처의   entrance 입구   in a few minutes 몇 분 후에

03 ③

① M: Do you want to go make a snowman?
눈사람을 만들러 가고 싶니?

W: No, I would rather have a snowball fight.
아니, 난 차라리 눈싸움을 하고 싶어.

② M: What did you do over the weekend?
주말 동안에 뭐 했니?

W: I went skiing with my family.
난 가족들이랑 스키를 타러 갔었어.

③ M: Wow, that's a really cool snowman. I like its black hat.
우와, 정말 멋진 눈사람이네. 눈사람의 검은 모자가 맘에 들어.

W: Thanks! Your igloo is amazing, too!
고마워! 네 이글루도 놀라워!

④ M: Look at the snowflakes! They're so pretty!
눈송이들 좀 봐! 정말 예쁘다!

W: Wow! They all look different. 와! 모두 다르게 생겼어.

⑤ M: How many snowmen did you make?
눈사람을 몇 개나 만들었니?

W: I made three yesterday and two today.
어제 세 개, 그리고 오늘 두 개를 만들었어.

어휘 snowman 눈사람   have a snowball fight 눈싸움을 하다
go skiing 스키 타러 가다   igloo 이글루   snowflake 눈송이

04 ③

W: Justin, did you hear about the Rock Festival this Saturday?
저스틴, 이번 주 토요일에 하는 록 페스티벌에 대해 들었니?

M: Yes, of course. Everybody's been talking about

it. I'm glad it's going to be at the <u>park</u> in front of Harrison <u>Station</u>. I <u>live</u> right <u>next to</u> it.
물론, 들었지. 모든 사람들이 그것에 대해 이야기하고 있어. 나는 페스티벌이 해리슨 역 앞에 있는 공원에서 열리게 되어 기뻐. 내가 바로 옆에 살고 있거든.

W: Oh, really? Well then, do you want to <u>go together</u>? I can meet you <u>in front of</u> the <u>subway</u> station.
아, 정말? 그럼 같이 갈래? 내가 널 지하철역 앞에서 만나면 되잖아.

M: I would love to go with you. <u>What time</u> do you think you'll <u>get to</u> Harrison Station?
나야 너랑 같이 가면 좋지. 넌 해리슨 역에 몇 시쯤 도착할 것 같니?

W: Well, I'm not sure yet. I can ride the <u>five</u> P.M., <u>six</u> P.M., or <u>seven</u> P.M. train, and it will <u>take</u> me <u>an hour</u> to get there.
음, 아직 확실히 모르겠어. 나는 오후 5시, 6시, 그리고 7시 열차를 탈 수 있는데, 거기까지 가는 데 1시간이 걸릴 거야.

M: Hmm… Then you should <u>take</u> the <u>six</u> P.M. <u>train</u> since the festival <u>starts</u> at <u>seven thirty</u> P.M. 음, 그럼 페스티벌이 오후 7시 30분에 시작하니까 넌 6시 열차를 타야겠다.

W: Okay, that <u>sounds perfect</u>! I'll call you when I get on the six P.M. train.
알겠어, 딱 좋네! 오후 6시 열차를 타면 네게 전화할게.

M: Alright. I'll see you when you get to Harrison Station! 좋아. 네가 해리슨 역에 도착하면 보자!

해설 여자는 6시 열차를 탈 것이고, 1시간이 걸리므로 열차는 7시에 해리슨 역에 도착할 것이다. 페스티벌이 시작하는 시각과 헷갈리지 말자.

어휘 next to 바로 옆에   take (시간이) 걸리다   get on (열차에) 올라타다

05 ④

W: Good afternoon! Welcome to Bruner's! Are you looking for something <u>in particular</u>?
안녕하세요! 브루너스에 오신 걸 환영합니다! 특별히 찾고 계신 것이 있나요?

M: Yes, I'm <u>looking for</u> the model, Starlight Z. Do you have it here?
네. 저는 스타라이트 제트 모델을 찾고 있어요. 그게 여기 있나요?

W: Of course, it's <u>on</u> this <u>shelf</u>. It must be a <u>popular model</u>. There have been a lot of people here asking for it. Would you like to <u>try</u> some <u>on</u>?
물론이죠, 이 진열대 위에 있어요. 인기 있는 모델이 틀림없나 봐요. 여기서 이 모델을 찾는 사람들이 많았거든요. 한번 신어보시겠어요?

M: I would like that, thank you. My <u>size</u> is two seventy.
그러고 싶네요, 감사합니다. 제 사이즈는 270이에요.

W: Please wait a minute while I go to the <u>storage room</u> to get it for you. [pause] Here you go. How does it <u>fit</u>? 그걸 제가 창고에서 가져오는 동안 잠시만 기다려 주세요. [잠시 후] 여기 있습니다. 크기가 맞나요?

M: Hmm… I think it's <u>too big</u>. That's strange because I always wear size two seventy. 음, 너무 큰 것 같아요. 이상하네요, 왜냐하면 저는 항상 270 사이즈를 신거든요.

W: Actually, this model <u>came out bigger</u> than normal <u>soccer shoes</u>. You may need to try it on in a <u>smaller</u> size.
사실 이 모델은 일반 축구화보다 조금 크게 나왔어요. 좀 더 작은 사이즈로 신어 보셔야 할 것 같네요.

M: I see. Then, could you bring me a smaller size?
그렇군요. 그럼, 더 작은 사이즈로 가져다 주실래요?

W: Sure, I can do that. I'll <u>be right back</u>.
네, 가져다 드릴게요. 금방 돌아올게요.

해설 270 사이즈, 축구화 등을 통해 신발 가게가 배경임을 알 수 있으며 여자는 신발을 판매하는 사람이다.

어휘 in particular 특별히   shelf 선반   popular 인기 있는   try something on ~을 착용해 보다   storage room 창고   fit (크기가) 맞다   strange 이상한   come out (제품이) 생산되다, 나오다   soccer shoes 축구화

06 ①

M: Brittany, you <u>look</u> so <u>tired</u>. Is something the matter?
브리트니, 넌 정말 피곤해 보이는구나. 무슨 문제가 있니?

W: Today has been such a long day! I had to go to so <u>many places</u> and <u>get</u> a lot of <u>things done</u>.
오늘은 정말로 긴 날이었어! 정말로 많은 곳에 가서 많은 일을 해야 했거든.

M: Why? <u>What</u> have you been <u>doing</u> all day?
왜? 하루 종일 뭘 했던 거야?

W: Well, in the <u>morning</u> I had to <u>pick up</u> some <u>laundry</u> at the dry cleaner's. Then, I <u>met with</u> some <u>classmates</u> at the coffee shop to prepare for a presentation. And now, I just <u>got back from</u> finishing a ten page research paper for my history class. 음, 난 아침에 세탁소에서 세탁물 몇 개를 찾아와야 했어. 그리고 나서 발표 준비를 하기 위해 커피숍에서 반 친구들을 만났어. 그리고 역사 수업을 위한 10페이지 분량의 연구 보고서를 마치고 방금 온 거야.

M: Wow, you did all that <u>in one day</u>? <u>No wonder</u> you look so tired. 와, 넌 그 모든 걸 하루 만에 다 했니? 네가 피곤해 보일 수밖에 없구나.

W: Yeah, but I'm so glad that I got everything done. Now I can <u>go home</u> and <u>get</u> some <u>rest</u>. 응, 하지만 모든 걸 끝내서 정말 기뻐. 난 이제 집에 돌아가서 쉴 수 있어.

M: That's a good idea. Will you be <u>busy tomorrow</u>, too? 좋은 생각이야. 넌 내일도 바쁘니?

W: No, thank goodness. I didn't make any plans because I wanted to <u>stay home</u> and <u>relax</u>.
아니, 다행이지. 집에 있으면서 쉬고 싶어서 아무런 계획도 세우지 않았어.

해설 여자는 'thank goodness(고마워라, 다행이야)'라는 말로 안도하는 심정을 드러냈다.

어휘 pick up 찾아오다   laundry 세탁물   dry cleaner's 세탁소   classmate 학급 친구   prepare for a presentation

발표를 준비하다   no wonder ~은 놀라운 일이 아니다   get rest 휴식을 취하다   relax 느긋하게 쉬다   relieved 안도하는

07 ②

① M: When's the last time you cleaned the house?
언제 마지막으로 집을 청소했나요?

W: I cleaned it a few days ago. 며칠 전에 청소했어요.

② M: Can you put this book back on the bookshelf over there? 이 책을 저기 있는 책꽂이에 다시 꽂아 주실래요?

W: You have to fill out this form to make a library card.
도서관 카드를 만들기 위해서는 이 양식을 작성하셔야 합니다.

③ M: Excuse me, ma'am. The line starts back there.
실례합니다, 부인. 줄은 저쪽 뒤에서부터 시작됩니다.

W: Oh, I'm sorry. I didn't see the line.
아, 죄송해요. 줄을 못 봤네요.

④ M: When was this picture taken?
언제 이 사진을 찍었나요?

W: Hmm… I'm not sure. Probably a few years ago.
음, 잘 모르겠어요. 아마도 몇 년 전일 거예요.

⑤ M: Why are there so many people here?
여기에는 왜 이렇게 많은 사람이 있는 거죠?

W: They're here to see the street performers.
거리 공연자들을 보러 이곳에 온 사람들이에요.

어휘 a few days ago 며칠 전에   bookshelf 책꽂이   over there 저쪽에   fill out 작성하다   form 양식   probably 아마도   performer 공연자, 연주자

08 ②

W: Hey, Kurt. Are you going to be in class tomorrow?
얘, 커트. 넌 내일 수업 들으러 올 거니?

M: Yeah, I'll be here. How about you?
응, 여기 올 거야. 너는?

W: I'm going to be absent because I have a doctor's appointment. 난 내일 병원 예약이 있어서 결석할 거야.

M: Oh, tomorrow isn't a good day to miss class. Ms. Levine said that we will be learning important material that will be on the test.
아, 내일은 수업을 빠지면 좋지 않을 텐데. 레빈 선생님께서 우리가 시험에 나오게 될 중요한 내용을 배우게 될 거라고 하셨거든.

W: Yes, I know. I'm worried because I'm going to miss everything she will be teaching during class.
응, 나도 알아. 난 선생님이 수업 시간에 가르치는 모든 내용을 놓치게 될 테니 걱정돼.

M: Yeah, I would be worried too if I were you. Is there anything I can do to help?
응, 내가 너였어도 걱정되었을 거야. 내가 도와줄 일이 있을까?

W: Would you mind taking notes during class for me? I'll make a copy and give them back to you.
네가 수업 시간에 나 대신 노트 필기를 해줄 수 있을까? 내가 복사를 하고 다시 너에게 줄게.

M: Sure, I can do that. I'll give them to you after school. 물론, 해줄 수 있지. 방과 후에 너에게 줄게.

W: Thank you so much! You're a lifesaver!
정말 고마워! 네가 날 살렸어!

어휘 absent 결석한, 부재의   doctor's appointment 병원 예약   miss class 수업에 빠지다   material 자료, 내용, 재료   take notes 필기를 하다, 기록하다   make a copy 복사하다, 사본을 만들다   lifesaver 궁지에서 구해주는 사람

09 ①

W: Steve, can I ask your opinion about something?
스티브, 뭔가에 대한 네 의견을 구해도 될까?

M: Yes, of course you can. What's on your mind?
그럼 물론이지. 무슨 생각을 하는데?

W: Well, I applied for a job at two companies and had an interview with both of them. I found out today that both of the companies want me to work for them. 음, 내가 두 군데의 회사에 지원을 해서 두 곳 모두 면접을 봤어. 두 회사 모두 내가 그 회사에서 일하길 원한다는 것을 오늘 알게 되었거든.

M: Wow, that's great! So, what's the problem?
우와, 대단하구나! 그런데, 뭐가 문제야?

W: I can't decide which company to work for! Both have good things and bad things about them.
어느 회사에서 일해야 할지 결정을 못 하겠어! 두 회사 모두 장점과 단점을 갖고 있거든.

M: Well, you should think about a few things. First, which one is closer to your house?
그럼, 몇 가지에 대해서 생각을 해봐야 해. 첫째, 어느 회사가 너네 집에서 더 가깝니?

W: One company is an hour away from my house, and the second company is ten minutes away.
한 회사는 우리 집에서 한 시간 거리에 있고, 두 번째 회사는 10분 거리에 있어.

M: Alright. Then which one pays you more?
좋아. 그럼 어느 회사가 급여를 더 많이 주니?

W: I think both companies are willing to pay me the same amount.
내 생각에는 두 회사 모두 나에게 똑같은 돈을 줄 것 같아.

M: Okay. Then think about which company you'll enjoy working for more.
그래. 그럼 어느 회사가 네가 일할 때 더 즐거울지 생각해 봐.

어휘 opinion 의견   What's on your mind? 무슨 일이니?   apply for ~에 지원하다, 신청하다   company 회사   have an interview 면접을 보다   both of ~의 양쪽 모두   pay (보수를) 지급하다   be willing to 기꺼이 ~하다   amount 금액, 양

10 ③

M: Welcome to Seven Flags Amusement Park! May I help you? 세븐 플래그 놀이공원에 오신 것을 환영합니다! 제가 도와드릴까요?

W: Yes, I would like to buy tickets for three people. One adult, one senior, and one child. How much is the admission fee? 네, 3명에 대한 티켓을 구입하고 싶어요. 어른 1명, 노인 1명, 그리고 어린이 1명이요. 입장료가 얼마죠?

M: Well, admission is normally thirty dollars for adults, twenty dollars for seniors, and ten dollars for children. But for this week only, you can get a fifty percent discount on admission fees.
네, 입장료는 보통은 어른은 30달러, 노인은 20달러, 그리고 어린이는 10달러입니다. 하지만 이번 주에 한해 입장료의 50%를 할인 받으실 수 있어요.

W: Wow, that's great! I also have this ten percent off coupon. Can I use it today? 우와, 좋네요! 제게 10% 할인 쿠폰도 있거든요. 제가 오늘 이것을 사용할 수 있나요?

M: I'm sorry, but we are not letting people use other coupons because we are already giving them a discount. 죄송합니다만, 저희가 이미 할인을 해드리고 있기 때문에, 다른 쿠폰은 사용하실 수 없어요.

W: Oh, alright. I guess I'll use it the next time I come. 아, 알겠어요. 다음에 올 때 사용해야겠네요.

M: Yes, but remember that you can't use the coupon during this week.
네, 하지만 이번 주에는 사용하실 수 없다는 점을 기억해 주세요.

W: Okay. How much is my total?
알겠습니다. 제가 내야 할 총 금액이 얼마죠?

[해설] 어른($30) + 노인($20) + 어린이($10) = $60. 50% 할인하면 $30.

[어휘] amusement park 놀이공원   senior 노인   admission fee 입장료   normally 보통은, 일반적으로   get a discount 할인을 받다   give somebody a discount ~에게 할인을 해주다   total 총액, 합계

11 ②

W: Excuse me, sir. I'm visiting the Elite Department Store. Should I go this way? 실례합니다. 저는 엘리트 백화점에 갈 겁니다. 이쪽으로 가면 되나요?

M: Hello, ma'am. I'm not sure if there are any spots left. Let me check for you. [pause] Actually, there is one spot left, but I don't think your car will be able to fit because the space is very small.
안녕하세요. 자리가 남아 있을지 모르겠네요. 제가 한번 확인해 보겠습니다. [잠시 후] 한 자리가 남아 있는데, 공간이 무척 작아서 손님 차는 들어갈 수 없을 것 같아요.

W: Hmm… Okay. Are there any other parking lots in this area? 음, 알겠어요. 이 지역에 다른 주차장이 있나요?

M: Yes, there's one on Bridget Lane and one on Georgetown Street. But the one on Bridget Lane is pretty far from the department store, so you'll have to walk for a while.
네, 브리짓 레인에 하나가 있고, 조지타운 스트리트에 하나가 있습니다. 하지만 브리짓 레인에 있는 주차장은 백화점에서 아주 멀리 떨어져 있어서 한참을 걸으셔야 할 겁니다.

W: Alright. So do you recommend that I park on Georgetown Street? 알겠어요. 그럼 제가 조지타운 스트리트

에 주차하는 걸 권하시는 거죠?

M: Yes. That one is only a five minute walk from the department store.
네. 그곳은 백화점에서 5분만 걸으시면 됩니다.

W: Oh, that's great! I guess I'll park there, then. Thanks for your help! 아, 그거 좋네요! 그럼 그곳에 주차해야겠어요. 도와주셔서 감사합니다!

M: No problem. Have a great day!
천만에요. 좋은 하루 보내세요!

[해설] 여자가 차를 몰고 백화점 주차장에 들어온 상황이다.

[어휘] spot 자리, 공간   fit 맞다, 알맞다   parking lot 주차장   pretty 꽤, 아주   far from ~에서 먼   for a while 한동안, 잠시   recommend 추천하다, 권고하다   car repair shop 자동차 수리점   travel agency 여행사   used-car market 중고차 시장

12 ③

M: Are you interested in photography exhibits? Would you like to see the works of famous photographers? Then Flash Gallery is the perfect place for you! Starting on May sixteenth, our gallery will be opening an exhibit of Jane Truman and Michael Stewart's photos! As you may already know, both of these photographers are known for taking beautiful scenery photos. There is no admission fee, and you may come any time between ten A.M. and five P.M. Please hurry and take advantage of this great opportunity! The exhibit will only be open until May twenty first.

사진 전시회에 관심이 있으신가요? 유명 사진 작가들의 작품을 보고 싶으신가요? 그렇다면 플래시 갤러리가 당신에게 딱 맞는 곳입니다! 5월 16일부터 저희 갤러리에서는 제인 트루먼과 마이클 스튜어트의 사진 전시회를 열게 됩니다! 이미 아시겠지만, 이 두 명의 사진 작가는 모두 아름다운 풍경 사진을 찍는 것으로 잘 알려져 있습니다. 입장료는 무료이며, 오전 10시와 오후 5시 사이에 언제든지 방문하실 수 있습니다. 서둘러 이 놀라운 기회를 이용하세요! 전시회는 5월 21일까지만 문을 엽니다.

[어휘] photography 사진(술), 사진 기법   exhibit 전시회, 전시품   photographer 사진작가   known for ~로 알려진   scenery 풍경, 경치   admission fee 입장료   take advantage of ~을 이용하다, 활용하다   opportunity 기회

13 ⑤

| 라이트 야구 경기장 |

	구역	요금	
		성인	어린이
①	A 구역	50달러	30달러
②	B 구역	40달러	25달러
③	C 구역	30달러	15달러
④	D 구역	20달러	5달러

⑤	E 구역	10달러	무료

W: Good evening, sir. Would you like to purchase tickets for tonight's game?
안녕하세요, 손님. 오늘 밤 경기 티켓을 구매하시겠어요?

M: Yes, I would like to buy some for myself and my son. How much are seats in Sections B and C?
네, 저와 제 아들의 표를 사고 싶어요. B구역과 C구역의 좌석 티켓은 얼마죠?

W: The seats in Section B are forty dollars for adults and twenty-five dollars for children, and those in Section C cost ten dollars less than Section B for both adults and children.
B구역 좌석은 성인은 40달러, 어린이는 25달러이고, C구역은 성인과 어린이 모두 B구역보다 10달러 저렴합니다.

M: Hmm… Okay. What's the difference between Sections A and E?
음, 알겠어요. A구역과 E구역은 무슨 차이가 있죠?

W: Well, Section A is the area closest to the baseball field, and it is fifty dollars for adults and thirty dollars for children. Section E is the area farthest from the field, and it is ten dollars for adults and five dollars for children.
음, A구역은 야구 경기장에서 가장 가까운 구역이고, 성인은 50달러, 어린이는 30달러입니다. E구역은 경기장에서 가장 먼 구역으로, 성인은 10달러, 어린이는 5달러입니다.

M: Oh, alright. Which section would you recommend?
아, 그렇군요. 어떤 구역을 추천하시나요?

W: I think you should sit in D.
손님께서는 D구역에 앉으시면 될 것 같습니다.

M: Why do you say that? 왜 그렇게 말씀하시죠?

W: Well, Sections C and D are the same distance from the field. But Section D costs ten dollars less than Section C. Plus, you might be able to catch a homerun ball in Section D. 음, C구역과 D구역은 경기장으로부터 동일한 거리에 있어요. 하지만 D구역이 C구역 보다 10달러 저렴하거든요. 게다가 D구역에서는 홈런 공을 잡으실 수도 있어요.

M: My son would love that! I'll get two tickets for Section D, please.
제 아들이 정말 좋아하겠네요! D구역으로 2장 주세요.

해설 E구역의 어린이 입장료는 무료가 아니라 5달러이다.

어휘 section 구역   difference 차이점   closest 가장 가까운 (close-closer-closest)   field 경기장   farthest 가장 먼(far-farther-farthest)   recommend 추천하다   distance 거리   less than ~보다 적은

14 ②

M: This is a type of sport that is played on ice. You have to wear ice skates in order to play. Players are mostly men, and they tend to be rough and push each other. They wear big, heavy uniforms and helmets so they don't get hurt. You play the game by hitting and passing a black puck with a wooden stick. The team that hits the puck past the goal keeper and into the net gets a point.
이것은 얼음 위에서 경기하는 스포츠의 일종입니다. 당신은 경기를 하기 위해 스케이트를 신어야 합니다. 선수들은 대부분 남자들이고, 그들은 거칠게 굴며, 서로를 밀쳐 내는 경향이 있습니다. 그들은 다치지 않기 위해 크고 무거운 유니폼과 헬멧을 착용합니다. 경기는 나무 막대기로 검은 고무원반을 치고 패스하면서 진행됩니다. 고무원반을 쳐서 골키퍼를 지나 네트 안으로 넣는 팀이 득점합니다.

어휘 ice skates 스케이트   mostly 대부분   tend to ~하는 경향이 있다   rough 거친   get hurt 다치다   puck 고무원반; 퍽   wooden 나무로 된   stick 막대기, 스틱   get a point 득점하다

15 ④

W: Greg! Look at all those grocery bags! Why did you buy so much?
그레그! 저 모든 식료품 봉지들을 좀 봐! 왜 이렇게 많이 샀니?

M: There is a sale going on at Horizon Foods right now! I went to buy a box of cereal, and ended up buying all of this.
지금 호라이즌 푸드에서 세일을 하고 있어! 나는 시리얼 한 박스를 사러 갔다가, 이 모든 걸 사고 말았어.

W: What? I didn't know that there was a sale! What did you buy? 뭐라고? 나는 세일이 있는지 몰랐어! 넌 뭘 샀니?

M: Well, everything in the store is thirty percent off, so I basically bought everything I could find.
음, 상점 안에 있는 모든 상품이 30% 할인 중이라서, 기본적으로 내가 찾을 수 있는 건 다 샀어.

W: Everything in the store is thirty percent off? That's a huge sale! There must be nothing left on the shelves by now.
상점에 있는 모든 게 30% 할인이라고? 정말 엄청난 세일이네! 지금쯤이면 분명히 진열대에 남아 있는 상품이 없겠다.

M: Actually, the sale started a few hours ago. If you go now, there'll probably be a lot of items left.
사실, 세일은 몇 시간 전에 시작했어. 만약 네가 지금 가면 아마도 남아 있는 상품이 많을 거야.

W: Hmm… Then I should head over there now. I needed to go grocery shopping anyway. Thanks for letting me know! 음, 그럼 지금 그곳으로 가 봐야겠다. 어쨌든 식료품을 사야 했거든. 알려줘서 고마워!

M: Don't mention it. 별말씀을.

해설 여자의 마지막 말인 'I needed to ~'에 여자가 할 일이 나온다. 시리얼 한 박스를 살지는 알 수 없으므로 ⑤는 오답이다.

어휘 grocery bag 식료품 봉투   sale 세일, 할인판매, 판매   cereal 시리얼, 곡물   end up –ing 결국 ~하게 되다   basically 기본적으로   shelf 진열대, 선반(복 shelves)   probably 아마도   head ~로 가다

16 ③

99

W: Hi, Ted. Are you busy tomorrow after school?
안녕, 테드. 내일 방과 후에 바쁘니?

M: No, I don't have anything planned. Why do you ask? 아니, 난 잡힌 계획이 없는데. 왜 묻니?

W: Well, I have movie tickets for *True Mystery*, but I can't find anyone to go with. Would you be interested? 음, 내가 '트루 미스터리' 영화 티켓이 있는데, 같이 갈 사람을 못 찾았어. 혹시 관심 있니?

M: How did you know I wanted to watch that? I'd love to go with you! 넌 내가 그 영화를 보고 싶어 하는 걸 어떻게 알았니? 너랑 같이 가고 싶어!

W: I'm so glad to hear that! We can use the tickets for any of the show times, so you can pick one. There are showings at five P.M., six thirty P.M., and ten P.M. 그 얘기를 들으니 반갑네! 우리는 상영 시간에 상관 없이 티켓을 사용할 수 있기 때문에, 네가 하나를 골라도 좋아. 상영 시간은 오후 5시, 6시 30분, 그리고 10시야.

M: Hmm… Would you mind going to the last showing? 음, 마지막 상영 시간에 봐도 괜찮겠니?

W: Actually, my parents told me to be home by nine thirty, so I think we should watch the movie at five or six thirty.
사실은 우리 부모님께서 9시 30분까지 집에 오라고 하셨기 때문에 5시나 6시 30분 영화를 봐야 할 것 같아.

M: Hmm… Okay then. Let's watch the second showing of the movie. 음, 그럼 알겠어. 영화의 두 번째 상영을 보자.

해설 오후 5시와 6시 30분 상영 중에서 두 번째 것은 6시 30분이다.

어휘 interested 관심 있는   would love to ~하고 싶다   show time 상영 시간   showing 상영

17 ④

W: Sarah likes talking to her friends on the phone. Ever since school started, she has been using her phone more than usual. Her phone plan includes four hundred text messages and one hundred minutes of phone calls, but she sent over one thousand text messages and talked on the phone for three hundred minutes. When the phone bill came in the mail, her dad was shocked because the total was two hundred dollars. He couldn't understand why the bill came out to be so much. So he decided to talk to Sarah about it and ask her what she's been using her phone for. In this situation, what would Sarah's Dad most likely say to Sarah?

사라는 전화로 친구들과 이야기하는 것을 좋아한다. 학교가 시작된 이후로 사라는 평소보다 더 많이 전화기를 사용하고 있다. 사라의 요금제에는 400개의 문자 메시지와 100분의 통화가 포함되어 있지만, 사라는 1000개가 넘는 메시지를 보냈고, 300분의 통화를 했다. 전화 요금 청구서가 우편으로 왔을 때, 사라의 아버지는 합계 금액이 200달러인 것을 보고 충격을 받았다. 그는 요금이 왜 그렇게 많이 나왔는지 이해할 수 없었다. 그래서 그는 사라에게 그 문제

에 관해 얘기하고, 그녀가 어디에 전화기를 사용했는지 물어보기로 결심했다. 이런 상황에서 사라의 아버지가 사라에게 할 말로 가장 적절한 것은 무엇인가?

Dad: What have you been doing on your phone? The bill is so expensive!
네 전화기로 뭘 해온 거니? 요금이 너무 비싸잖아!

① Call me when you have time. 시간 있을 때 내게 전화해.

② I want to change my phone plan.
내 휴대폰의 요금제를 바꾸고 싶구나.

③ If you don't get a text message from me by 2, give me a call. 2시까지 나에게서 문자 메시지를 받지 못하면 전화하렴.

④ What have you been doing on your phone? The bill is so expensive!
네 전화기로 뭘 해온 거니? 요금이 너무 비싸잖아!

⑤ How much is the phone plan for 400 texts and 100 minutes of phone calls? 400개의 문자 메시지와 100분간 통화할 수 있는 요금제는 얼마니?

어휘 on the phone 전화로   than usual 평소보다   phone plan 요금제   include 포함하다, 들어 있다   text message 문자 메시지   phone call 전화 통화   phone bill 전화 요금 고지서   shocked 충격을 받은, 놀란   give somebody a call ~에게 전화하다

18 ②

W: Ricky, I think I'm going to start learning Taekwondo. What do you think?
리키, 난 태권도를 배우려고 생각하고 있어. 넌 어떻게 생각하니?

M: Why all of a sudden? You were never interested in that sport before.
왜 이렇게 갑자기? 넌 전에는 그 스포츠에 전혀 관심이 없었잖아.

W: Well, there are a lot of crimes going on lately. I just want to learn how to protect myself.
음, 최근에 범죄가 너무 많이 일어나고 있어. 난 단지 나 자신을 보호하는 방법을 배우고 싶을 뿐이야.

M: That's actually a really good idea. Maybe I should learn with you. It sounds like fun.
그건 정말 좋은 생각이구나. 아마 나도 너와 함께 배워야 할 것 같아. 재미있겠다.

W: Yes, you definitely should! We'll learn how to punch, kick, and break wooden boards! Doesn't that sound exciting?
응, 너도 반드시 그래야 해! 우리는 주먹으로 치고, 발로 차고, 나무 판자를 격파하는 법을 배울 거야. 흥미로울 것 같지 않니?

M: Now that you mention it, I'm looking forward to it more and more. Once we master the sport, we'll be able to protect ourselves against criminals.
네가 그 말을 하니까 말인데, 난 점점 더 그걸 기대하고 있어. 일단 우리가 태권도를 익히고 나면, 우리는 범죄자들에 맞서서 자신을 보호할 수 있을 거야.

W: Yeah, you're right. Thanks for offering to go with me. I appreciate your support. 응, 네 말이 맞아. 나랑 함께 하자고 제안해 줘서 고마워. 너의 지지가 고맙게 느껴져.

M: It's no problem. Let's go sign up for our first class.
천만에. 같이 첫 수업을 등록하러 가자.

해설 그들은 태권도에 대한 이야기를 나누고 있고, 남자가 마지막에 'Let's go sign up for our first class.'라고 말했으므로, 태권도 수업에 등록하러 갈 것이다.

어휘 all of a sudden 갑자기　interested in ~에 관심이 있는　crime 범죄　lately 최근에　protect oneself 스스로를 보호하다　definitely 반드시, 분명히　punch 주먹으로 치다　wooden board 나무 판자　now that ~이므로, ~이기 때문에　once 일단 ~하면　master 숙달하다, 익히다　criminal 범죄자　offer 제안하다　support 응원, 지지

19 ④

W: Jason, have you gotten used to living in Korea, yet? 제이슨, 한국 생활에 적응하고 있니?

M: No, not yet. Korea's culture is so different from the culture in the United States.
아니, 아직이야. 한국 문화는 미국 문화와 너무 달라.

W: Really? Can you give me an example?
정말? 나에게 예를 들어 줄 수 있니?

M: Well, I saw someone from my class and I wanted to say hello, so I waved my hand at her. But instead of waving back, she bowed her head at me.
음, 우리 반에 있는 누군가를 보고 인사를 하고 싶었거든. 그래서 그 친구에게 손을 흔들었어. 하지만 그녀는 같이 손을 흔들어 주는 대신 나에게 고개를 숙여 인사했어.

W: Oh, okay. In Korea, you bow heads to each other until you become friends. Once you become friends, then you wave to each other.
아, 그래. 한국에서는 서로 친구가 되기 전까지 서로 고개를 숙여 인사를 해. 친구가 되고 나면, 그때는 서로에게 손을 흔들어.

M: I see. It's so hard for me because the culture is so different.
알겠어. 문화가 너무 달라서 그런 게 나에게 너무 어려워.

W: I understand. But since you live here now, you have to get used to it. 이해해. 하지만 너는 지금 여기서 살고 있으니까, 그것에 익숙해져야 해.

M: Yeah, you're right. 응, 네 말이 맞아.

① All roads lead to Rome. 모든 길은 로마로 통한다.
② A stitch in time saves nine.
제때의 바늘 한 번이 아홉 바느질을 던다.
③ All that glitters is not gold. 빛나는 것이 모두 금은 아니다.
④ When in Rome, do as the Romans do.
로마에 가면 로마법에 따르라.
⑤ A journey of a thousand miles starts with a single step. 천 리 길도 한 걸음부터.

어휘 get used to ~에 익숙해지다, 적응하다　culture 문화　different from ~과 다른　give somebody an example ~에게 예를 들다　wave 흔들다　instead of ~대신에　bow one's head 고개를 숙이다　since ~이기 때문에

20 ④

M: Hey, Mom. I'm going to start working at Café Rose starting tomorrow.
엄마. 저 내일부터 카페 로즈에서 일을 시작하기로 했어요.

W: Oh, really? I hope you know it's going to be harder than you think. I know because I used to work at a café too when I was your age. 아, 정말이요? 네가 생각하는 것보다 더 어려울 거란 걸 알아 두었으면 좋겠구나. 엄마도 네 나이 때 카페에서 일을 했었기 때문에 그걸 안단다.

M: What is so hard about it? Don't you just ask people what they want to order and give them their drinks?
어떤 게 그렇게 어려운 거죠? 그냥 사람들에게 뭘 주문하고 싶은지 물어보고, 음료수를 갖다 주면 되는 거 아닌가요?

W: No, it's not that simple. You have to do other work too, like washing the cups, cleaning tables, and taking out the garbage. You also have to learn how to make coffee.
아니, 그렇게 단순하지만은 않아. 넌 컵 닦기, 테이블 치우기, 그리고 쓰레기를 내다 버리는 것과 같은 다른 일들도 해야 해. 그리고 커피 만드는 법도 배워야 한단다.

M: Wow, I had no idea I had to do all of that! Maybe I should think about this again.
우와, 제가 그 모든 걸 해야 하는지 몰랐어요! 아마도 이 일에 대해 다시 한 번 생각해 봐야겠네요.

W: Well, didn't you already tell the café that you would start working tomorrow?
음, 넌 이미 카페에 내일부터 일을 시작하겠다고 말하지 않았니?

M: Yes, I did. But I don't know if I can handle it.
네, 그랬어요. 하지만 제가 일을 처리할 수 있을지 모르겠어요.

W: I'm sure you'll be fine. Be a responsible person and work hard. 난 네가 잘할 거라고 확신해. 책임감 있는 사람이 되어서 열심히 일하렴.

① Can you clean the tables, please?
테이블들을 정리해 주겠니?
② Why don't you call the café and ask them what time they open?
카페에 전화해서 몇 시에 문을 여는지 물어보는 게 어때?
③ I'm driving to the café now, but I think I'll be about 5 minutes late.
지금 카페로 운전해서 가고 있는데, 5분 정도 늦을 것 같아.
④ I'm sure you'll be fine. Be a responsible person and work hard. 난 네가 잘할 거라고 확신해. 책임감 있는 사람이 되어서 열심히 일하렴.
⑤ Do you see the traffic light in front of Café Rose? Take a left turn there.
카페 로즈 앞에 있는 신호등이 보이니? 거기서 좌회전해.

어휘 starting tomorrow 내일부터　harder 더 어려운(hard-harder-hardest)　used to (과거에) ~하곤 했다　simple 간단한, 단순한　take out the garbage 쓰레기를 내다 버리다　handle 다루다, 처리하다　responsible 책임감 있는　traffic light 신호등　take a left turn 좌회전하다

01 ②	02 ③	03 ①	04 ③	05 ⑤
06 ③	07 ②	08 ①	09 ③	10 ②
11 ③	12 ②	13 ③	14 ②	15 ④
16 ③	17 ⑤	18 ③	19 ①	20 ⑤

01 ②

M: Good morning, ma'am. Can I help you find something? 안녕하세요, 손님. 제가 찾는 것을 도와드릴까요?

W: Yes, please. I'm going on vacation, and I need to buy a hat to wear. Do you have any recommendations? 네, 도와주세요. 제가 휴가를 떠나는데, 쓸 모자가 필요해요. 추천하실 것이 있나요?

M: I would recommend this baseball hat. It's casual and you can wear it with anything. 이 야구 모자를 추천하고 싶습니다. 격식이 없고, 아무 옷에나 함께 쓰실 수 있거든요.

W: Well, I already own a lot of baseball hats. Plus, I would like a hat with a wider brim to protect my face from the sunlight. 음, 저는 이미 야구 모자를 많이 갖고 있어요. 게다가 저는 햇빛으로부터 얼굴을 가릴 수 있도록 챙이 더 넓은 모자를 사고 싶어요.

M: Okay, how about this hat with stripes on it? Or this one with ribbons on it? Both of them have wide brims. 알겠습니다. 위에 줄무늬가 들어간 이 모자는 어떠세요? 아니면 위에 리본이 달린 이 모자는요? 둘 다 챙이 넓어요.

W: I think both are great! But I think this hat with the polka dots is better. It has a wide brim, too. 둘 다 좋네요! 하지만 물방울 무늬가 있는 이 모자가 더 좋네요. 챙도 넓고요.

M: Yes, this hat is very popular among women during the summer season. Would you like to purchase this one? 네, 이 모자는 여름철에 여성분들 사이에서 무척 인기가 많죠. 이걸로 사시겠어요?

W: Yes please, that would be great. Thank you! 네, 그게 좋겠어요. 감사합니다!

어휘 go on vacation 휴가를 가다 hat (사방으로 챙이 있는) 모자 recommendation 추천 (사항) recommend 추천하다 baseball hat 야구 모자(= baseball cap) casual 격식을 차리지 않은 own 소유하다 brim (모자의) 챙 sunlight 햇빛 stripe 줄무늬 polka dots 물방울 무늬 purchase 구매하다

02 ③

[Cellphone rings.] [휴대폰이 울린다.]

M: Hello, this is Steven. 여보세요. 스티븐입니다.

W: Hey, Steven, It's me, Sarah. I'm calling to ask you if we can change our meeting time from four P.M. to five P.M. I'm so sorry for the sudden request. 스티븐, 나야 사라. 우리 약속 시간을 오후 4시에서 5시로 변경할 수 있는지 물어보려고 전화했어. 갑작스럽게 부탁해서 정말 미안해.

M: Hmm… Moving the time isn't a problem, but may I ask why? 음, 시간을 바꾸는 건 문제가 되지 않는데, 이유를 물어봐도 될까?

W: I'm at the doctor's office, and my appointment was at three, but there are still a lot of people in line in front of me. I think they're behind schedule. 난 지금 병원에 있고, 내 예약 시간은 3시였는데 내 앞에 여전히 많은 사람들이 줄을 서 있어. 그들도 예정보다 늦어진 것 같아.

M: Oh, alright. Are we still meeting at Garden Grove? If you want, I can meet you closer to the doctor's office. 아, 알겠어. 우리는 여전히 가든 그로브에서 만나는 거지? 네가 원하면 병원 가까이에서 너를 볼 수도 있어.

W: Thanks for the offer, but I can't ask you to do that. Let's just meet at Garden Grove. I'll get there as soon as I can. 제안은 고맙지만, 너한테 그런 부탁을 할 수는 없지. 그냥 가든 그로브에서 만나자. 최대한 빨리 갈게.

M: Okay, then. Can you give me a call when you leave the doctor's office? 알겠어, 그럼. 병원에서 출발할 때 전화해 줄래?

W: Yes, of course I can. I'll see you soon! Thanks for understanding. 물론이지. 금방 보자! 이해해 줘서 고마워.

어휘 sudden 갑작스러운 request 요청, 부탁 ask why 이유를 묻다 doctor's office 병원 in line 줄을 선 behind schedule 예정보다 늦은 offer 제안 give somebody a call ~에게 전화하다 understanding 이해, 양해

03 ①

① W: I'm getting water on my clothes from washing these dishes. 설거지를 하면서 옷에 물이 튀고 있어요.

M: Here, let me help you put this apron on. 여기, 내가 앞치마를 입는 것을 도와줄게요.

② W: Where did you put the clean plates and cups? 깨끗한 접시와 컵들은 어디에 두었죠?

M: The plates are in the second cabinet and the cups are in the third cabinet. 접시는 두 번째 보관함에 있고, 컵은 세 번째 보관함에 있어요.

③ M: How do you like the dress I got you? 제가 준 원피스가 마음에 드나요?

W: It's beautiful! I'm going to wear it every day. 아름다워요! 매일매일 입을 거예요.

④ W: Can you help me lower these plates? They're too high up. 이 접시들을 내리는 걸 도와주실 수 있나요? 너무 높이 있어요.

M: Sure, how many plates do you need? 물론이죠, 접시 몇 개가 필요해요?

⑤ W: I'm too tired to cook today. Let's go out for dinner. 오늘은 너무 피곤해서 요리를 못하겠어요. 나가서 저녁을 먹기로 해요.

M: Okay, that's fine with me. What do you want to eat? 알겠어요. 그건 나도 좋아요. 뭘 먹고 싶어요?

어휘 wash the dishes 설거지하다　put on ~을 입다, 착용하다, 걸치다　apron 앞치마　plate 접시　cabinet 보관함, 캐비닛　lower 내리다, 낮추다　go out for dinner 나가서 저녁을 먹다

04 ③

M: Janice, are you going to the conference on Sunday? 재니스, 당신은 일요일에 학회에 가나요?

W: Yes, I am. But it's really far from my house. I need to figure out the fastest way to get there. 네, 가요. 하지만 거긴 우리 집에서 정말 멀어요. 그곳에 가는 가장 빠른 방법을 찾아야 해요.

M: I see. We live near each other, so I can help you find the quickest route. 그렇군요. 우리가 서로 근처에 사니까, 제가 가장 빠른 길을 찾는 걸 도와 줄게요.

W: Okay! I wonder if we can drive there. You have a car, right? 좋아요! 우리가 거기까지 운전해서 갈 수 있는지 궁금해요. 당신은 차가 있죠, 그렇죠?

M: Yeah, I do. But there's probably going to be a lot of traffic during that time. Let's check the subway times. 네, 있어요. 하지만 그 시간 동안에는 아마 교통량이 엄청나게 많을 거예요. 지하철 시간을 확인해 보죠.

W: Alright. If we take the six P.M. train, we can get to Newbury Station in one hour. Do you know how far Newbury Station is from the conference center? 알겠어요. 우리가 오후 6시 열차를 타면, 우리는 뉴베리 역에 1시간 후에 도착할 수 있어요. 회의장에서 뉴베리 역까지 얼마나 먼지 알고 있나요?

M: I think it's a ten minute walk from the station. 역에서 걸어서 10분일 거예요.

W: So it'll probably take us a little over an hour. I think that's the fastest way to get to the conference. 그럼, 우리는 아마도 한 시간 좀 넘게 걸리겠군요. 그게 학회에 가는 가장 빠른 방법인 것 같아요.

M: Yeah, I agree. 네. 저도 그렇게 생각해요.

해설 두 사람은 오후 6시 열차를 타고 Newbury Station(뉴베리 역)에 7시에 도착한 후, 10분 동안 걸어서 conference center(회의장)에 도착할 것이다.

어휘 conference 학회, 회의　far from ~에서 먼　figure out 생각해 내다　fastest 가장 빠른(fast-faster-fastest)　quickest 가장 빠른(quick-quicker-quickest)　route 길, 경로　traffic 교통(량)

05 ⑤

M: Good afternoon, ma'am. How may I help you today? 안녕하세요, 손님. 제가 무엇을 도와드릴까요?

W: Yes, hello. I want to buy some shrimp, tuna, squid, and salmon. 네, 안녕하세요. 새우, 참치, 오징어, 그리고 연어를 좀 사고 싶어요.

M: Alright. The tuna and salmon are in the tanks to your right. The shrimp are lined up in these ice boxes, and the squid are in the tank to your left. 알겠습니다. 참치와 연어는 오른쪽에 있는 수조에 있습니다. 새우는 이 아이스 박스 안에 진열되어 있고, 오징어는 손님의 왼편 수조에 있습니다.

W: I see. I would like a box of shrimp, fifteen of both the tuna and salmon, and five squid. 알겠어요. 저는 새우 한 상자, 참치와 연어 둘 다 열다섯 마리, 그리고 오징어 다섯 마리를 살게요.

M: Okay! Are you cooking for a lot of people today? I'm asking because people normally don't buy so much seafood at one time. 알겠습니다! 오늘 많은 사람들을 위한 요리를 하시나요? 일반적으로 한 번에 그렇게 많은 해산물을 사는 사람이 없어서 여쭤봤어요.

W: Actually, I work at the restaurant down the street. Our customers have been satisfied with our special seafood menu, so we decided to make it a main dish. 사실은, 저는 길 아래에 있는 음식점에서 일해요. 고객들이 우리의 특별 해산물 메뉴에 만족스러워해서 그것을 주 요리로 만들기로 결정했거든요.

M: Oh, that's great! I'll get everything ready for you now. 아, 정말 좋네요! 지금 모든 것을 준비해 드리겠습니다.

W: Thank you! I'll be back next week for more. 고마워요! 다음 주에 더 사러 올게요.

어휘 shrimp 새우(복 shrimp/shrimps)　tuna 참치　squid 오징어(복 squid/squids)　salmon 연어　to one's right ~의 오른쪽에(↔ to one's left ~의 왼쪽에)　line something up 줄지어 진열하다　tank 수조, 물탱크　normally 보통, 일반적으로　seafood 해산물　satisfied with ~에 만족하는　main dish 주요리

06 ③

M: Mom, what is that animal hanging upside down from the branch? 엄마, 저 나뭇가지에 거꾸로 매달려 있는 동물은 뭐예요?

W: Tommy, that animal is called a bat. It hangs upside down when it's sleeping. 토미, 저 동물은 박쥐라고 해. 박쥐는 잘 때 거꾸로 매달려 있어.

M: Oh, that's so cool! Why does it hang upside down? What does a bat eat? And why do bats live in dark places? I have so many questions! 아, 정말 멋지네요! 왜 거꾸로 매달려 있죠? 박쥐는 무엇을 먹나요? 그리고 왜 어두운 장소에서 살죠? 궁금한 게 아주 많아요!

W: Wow, there's so much that you want to know! Well, I don't know why they hang upside down or why they live in dark places. But I know that they eat sweet fruit like apples and oranges. 우와, 넌 알고 싶은 게 정말 많구나! 사실, 엄마도 박쥐가 왜 거꾸로 매달리는지, 혹은 왜 어두운 곳에서 지내는지 모른단다. 하지만 박쥐가 사과나 오렌지 같은 달콤한 과일을 먹는다는 건 알고 있단다.

M: I see. Can we go ask the zoo keeper some questions? I want to know more about bats. 그렇군요. 동물원 사육사에게 물어보러 갈 수 있을까요? 박쥐에 대

W: Yeah, we can do that. Are there any other animals that you're interested in?
그래, 그렇게 하자꾸나. 또 관심 있는 동물이 있니?

M: I want to know about all of them, the polar bears, the giraffes, the alligators, and the elephants!
저는 북극곰, 기린, 악어, 그리고 코끼리, 이 모든 동물들에 대해 알고 싶어요!

W: Okay then, let's go explore and learn about all those animals.
그래, 그럼 그 동물들에 대해서 자세히 알아보고 배우러 가보자.

어휘 hang 매달리다 upside down 거꾸로, 뒤집혀 branch 나뭇가지 bat 박쥐 zoo keeper 동물원 사육사 polar bear 북극곰 giraffe 기린 alligator (북미산) 악어, 앨리게이터 explore 탐험하다, 탐구하다 scared 겁에 질린 curious 호기심이 많은 jealous 질투하는 relieved 안도하는

07 ②

① W: Dad, where's the new bottle of shampoo we just bought? 아빠, 우리가 방금 사온 새 샴푸 통은 어디에 있죠?
   M: I already put it in the bathroom for you.
   이미 욕실에 놓아 두었단다.

② W: Can you tell me how many jars are in the kitchen cabinets? 부엌 찬장에 병이 몇 개나 있는지 말해줄 수 있나요?
   M: The jars are all different shapes and sizes.
   병은 모두 모양과 크기가 달라요.

③ W: What are you doing on Monday night?
   월요일 밤에 뭘 할 건가요?
   M: I don't have plans yet, but I want to go bowling.
   아직 아무런 계획이 없는데, 볼링을 치러 가고 싶어요.

④ W: Are you sure you locked the car doors?
   차 문은 확실히 잠그셨나요?
   M: Yes, I'm sure. I double checked, so don't worry.
   네, 확실해요. 재차 확인했으니 걱정 마세요.

⑤ W: Are you going to the basketball game next Friday?
   다음 주 금요일에 농구 경기하러 갈 건가요?
   M: No, I'm spending some time with my family that day. 아니요, 그날은 가족들과 시간을 보낼 거예요.

어휘 bottle 병, 통 bathroom 욕실 jar 병; 단지 go bowling 볼링 치러 가다 double check 다시 확인하다

08 ①

M: Molly, what's wrong? You look so sick.
몰리, 무슨 일 있니? 넌 많이 아파 보여.

W: I feel terrible! Every time the season changes, I get these allergies. It's driving me crazy. 나 몸이 안 좋아! 계절이 바뀔 때마다, 이 알레르기가 생겨. 이것 때문에 너무 짜증 나.

M: Oh, no! What happens when you get allergies? Do you get a fever or a stuffy nose? 아, 저런! 알레르기가 생기면 무슨 증상이 있니? 열이 나거나 코가 막히니?

W: I don't get a fever. My nose itches and then it gets

really stuffy. Plus, my eyes get itchy and tired, too. I hate allergies so much!
열은 나지 않아. 코가 간지럽고 그 다음엔 코가 심하게 막혀. 게다가 눈까지 가렵고 피로해져. 난 알레르기가 너무 싫어!

M: Is there anything I can do to help you? Maybe you should go to the hospital.
내가 도와줄 수 있는 게 있니? 넌 병원에 가봐야 할 것 같아.

W: Well, I've been to the hospital many times, but it doesn't really help. I'd rather just take medicine from the pharmacy. Would you mind getting me some? 음, 병원에는 많이 갔었는데, 별 도움은 되지 않아. 차라리 약국에서 약을 먹는 게 좋겠어. 약 좀 사다 줄 수 있겠니?

M: Okay, I'll go to the pharmacy right now. Sit down and rest until I get back. 알겠어. 지금 바로 약국에 다녀 올게. 내가 올 때까지 앉아서 쉬고 있어.

W: Thanks a lot. I appreciate it.
정말 고마워. 잊지 않을게.

어휘 season 계절 allergy 알레르기 drive somebody crazy ~을 미치게 하다 get a fever 열이 나다 get a stuffy nose 코가 막히다 itch 가렵다, 가렵게 하다 stuffy (코가) 막힌; 답답한 itchy 가려운 would rather 차라리 ~하겠다 pharmacy 약국

09 ③

M: Hey, Sophia. You look worried. What's the matter?
안녕, 소피아. 걱정이 있어 보이는구나. 무슨 일 있니?

W: It's my grandmother's eightieth birthday on the weekend before our final exam week. All of my relatives are going to be there, and we will be spending the whole weekend together.
우리 기말고사 전 주말이 우리 할머니의 여든 번째 생신이야. 친척들이 모두 거기로 가서 주말 내내 함께 시간을 보낼 거야.

M: Okay, what seems to be the problem?
그래, 뭐가 문제가 되는 거니?

W: If I go to her birthday celebration, I won't have enough time to prepare for my exams. If I don't go, I feel like my grandmother would be upset.
만약 할머니의 생신 축하연에 가면, 시험을 준비할 시간이 충분하지 않을 거야. 만약 가지 않으면 할머니께서 속상하실 것 같다는 생각이 들어.

M: Hmm… That does sound like a big decision to make. Did you talk to your parents and grandmother about the situation?
음, 그건 정말 중요한 결정처럼 들리네. 이 상황에 대해서 부모님이랑 할머니랑 얘기해 봤니?

W: I told my parents, and they think I should go since it's a big family event. I haven't talked to my grandmother about it yet.
부모님께는 말씀 드렸더니, 큰 가족 행사이니 가야 한다고 하셨어. 아직 할머니께는 말씀 드리지 못했어.

M: Well then, I think you should call your grandmother and explain your situation. Maybe you can visit her after final exams. I think she'll understand even if you can't be there.

음, 그럼, 할머니께 전화를 드려서 너의 상황을 설명하는 게 좋을 것 같아. 넌 아마도 기말고사 후에 찾아뵐 수 있을 거야. 네가 가지 않더라도 할머니께서는 이해해 주실 거라고 생각해.

해설 제안을 할 때는 'I think ~', 'Why don't you ~?' 등의 표현을 사용한다.

어휘 on the weekend 주말에   final exam 기말고사   relative 친척   whole 모든, 전체의   celebration 축하연   enough 충분한   prepare for ~을 준비하다   upset 속상한, 화가 난   big decision 중요한 결정   situation 상황   event 행사   compliment 칭찬   gratitude 감사, 고마움   denial 거절

10 ②

M: Hello, ma'am. Welcome to Sunnyside Museum. What can I do for you today?

안녕하세요, 손님. 써니사이드 박물관에 오신 걸 환영합니다. 무엇을 도와드릴까요?

W: I would like to purchase tickets for myself and my two children. 저와 제 아이들 두 명의 표를 사고 싶어요.

M: Okay. How old are your children? The admission fee may differ depending on their age. 네. 아이들이 몇 살인가요? 입장료는 나이에 따라 달라질 수 있습니다.

W: My son is three years old and my daughter is eight years old. How much would the admission fee be? 제 아들은 3살, 그리고 딸은 8살입니다. 입장료가 얼마나 될까요?

M: Admission is free for children under the age of five, and the fee for children between the ages of five and twelve is five dollars. Anyone over twelve, including adults, must pay ten dollars to enter.

5살 미만의 아이들은 무료 입장이고, 5살에서 12살 사이의 아이들의 요금은 5달러입니다. 어른을 포함해서 12살 이상은 입장하려면 10달러를 내야 합니다.

W: Oh, alright. Can I use this free entrance coupon for my daughter's admission? 아, 알겠습니다. 제 딸의 입장료로 이 무료 입장 쿠폰을 쓸 수 있을까요?

M: Yes, you can. Is there anything else I can do for you?

네, 사용하실 수 있습니다. 제가 도와드릴 것이 또 있을까요?

W: No, that will be all. Thank you. How much do I owe you? 아니요. 그게 전부인 것 같네요. 감사합니다. 제가 얼마를 드려야 할까요?

해설 여자($10) + 딸(무료쿠폰) + 아들(무료) = $10.

어휘 museum 박물관   purchase 구매하다   admission fee 입장료   differ 다르다, 달라지다   depending on ~에 따라   including ~을 포함하여   owe 지불할 의무가 있다, 빚을 지다

11 ③

M: Excuse me, ma'am. Is there anything I can help you with? 실례합니다, 부인. 제가 도와드릴 것이 있나요?

W: Actually, yes. I need to put more money into my subway card, but I don't know how. Could you give me a hand? 실은 있어요. 지하철 카드에 돈을 더 넣어야 하는데, 어떻게 하는지 모르겠어요. 좀 도와주시겠어요?

M: Absolutely! Do you see those machines over there against the wall? Those are the subway card charging machines. 물론이죠! 저쪽 벽에 있는 기계들이 보이시죠? 저것들이 지하철 카드 충전기입니다.

W: Oh, I see. How do I use it?
아, 그렇군요. 어떻게 사용해야 하죠?

M: First, place your subway card on the scanner. Then, choose the amount of money you want to put in the card. Once you do that, insert the dollar bills into the machine. Wait a few seconds until the card finishes charging, and then you can take your card and go.

처음에는 스캐너 위에 지하철 카드를 올려 주세요. 그리고 나서 카드에 넣고 싶은 금액을 선택하세요. 거기까지 하시고 나면, 기계에 지폐를 삽입해 주세요. 카드가 충전이 끝날 때까지 기다리신 다음에 카드를 갖고 가시면 됩니다..

W: Alright! I thought it would be a lot harder than that. Oh, one more thing. Can I use a twenty-dollar bill with the machines?

알겠어요! 그보다 훨씬 더 어려울 거라고 생각했었어요. 아, 한 가지만 더요. 기계에 20달러 지폐도 사용할 수 있나요?

M: No, I'm afraid not. The machine only takes one-dollar, five-dollar, and ten-dollar bills. 아니요, 안됩니다. 저 기계는 1달러, 5달러, 그리고 10달러 지폐만 받아요.

W: Okay. Thank you so much for all of your help! 알겠어요. 도와주셔서 정말 감사합니다!

어휘 put something into ~을 …의 안으로 넣다   give a hand 도움을 주다   absolutely 물론이지   against the wall 벽에 기대어   charge 충전하다   scanner 스캐너   amount of money 금액   insert 삽입하다   bill 지폐   electronics store 전자제품 매장

12 ②

W: All residents of Spring View Apartments, we would like to make an important announcement. There have been some problems with our apartment elevators, and they need to be fixed. The repair work will begin on April fourteenth at eight A.M. and end on April sixteenth around six P.M. Please remember that during this time, the elevators will not be operating. Please use the stairs until the elevators are ready to be used. We apologize for the inconvenience. If you have any further questions, please contact our office at four three two, two one nine three.

스프링 뷰 아파트의 모든 거주자 분들께 중요한 안내 사항을 말씀 드리겠습니다. 저희 아파트 엘리베이터에 문제가 있어서 수리를 해야 합니다. 수리 작업은 4월 14일 오전 8시에 시작해서 4월 16일

오후 6시경에 끝날 예정입니다. 이 기간 동안은 엘리베이터가 운행되지 않는다는 것을 기억하시기 바랍니다. 엘리베이터가 다시 운행할 준비가 될 때까지는 계단을 이용해 주십시오. 불편을 끼쳐 드려 죄송합니다. 더 질문이 있으시면 432-2193번으로 사무실로 연락 주시기 바랍니다.

어휘 resident 주민, 거주자   make an announcement 발표하다, 공지하다   fix 고치다, 수리하다   repair 수리(하다)   operate 운행하다; 운영하다   stairs 계단   apologize 사과하다   inconvenience 불편

13 ③

| 케이크를 구울 때 무엇이 필요한가요? |

	재료	양
①	물	한 컵
②	밀가루	반 컵
③	설탕	세 큰술
④	계란	두 개
⑤	버터	두 큰술

W: Welcome to Anne's Cooking Class! Before we get started on baking the cake, we will prepare the ingredients. Take a cup and fill it completely with water. Now, pour some flour into another cup, but only fill it halfway. Next, you will need five tablespoons of sugar. After that, take out two eggs from the refrigerator and set them aside. Lastly, you will need to prepare two tablespoons of butter. Once you have gotten all of the ingredients ready, we will be able to start baking the cake!

앤의 요리 교실에 오신 것을 환영합니다. 케이크 굽기를 시작하기에 앞서, 재료를 준비하겠습니다. 컵을 들어서 물을 가득 채워 주세요. 이제, 다른 컵에 밀가루를 붓는데, 절반만 채워 주세요. 다음으로 설탕 다섯 큰술이 필요합니다. 그 다음에는, 냉장고에서 달걀 두 개를 꺼내서 한쪽에 두세요. 마지막으로, 버터 두 큰술을 준비하셔야 합니다. 모든 재료가 준비되었으면, 이제 우리는 케이크 굽기를 시작할 수 있습니다!

해설 'five tablespoons of sugar'라고 했으므로 설탕은 다섯 큰술이 필요하다.

어휘 cooking 요리   get started 시작하다   ingredient 재료   completely 완전히   pour 붓다, 따르다   flour 밀가루   halfway 중간에, 가운데쯤   tablespoon 큰술   refrigerator 냉장고   set aside 한쪽에 두다   lastly 마지막으로   get something ready ~을 준비하다

14 ②

M: This can be found in an amusement park. To ride this, you have to be a certain height. Once you put on a seatbelt, a safety bar is lowered to protect you from getting hurt. At the beginning, you are taken up a huge hill, and then all of a sudden, it

goes down the hill at a very fast speed. There are many of these hills, and sometimes there are even spirals, where you go upside down and sideways. Some people enjoy riding this, and some people are afraid of riding it.

이것은 놀이동산에서 찾을 수 있다. 이것을 타려면 특정한 키가 되어야 한다. 일단 안전벨트를 착용하면, 부상 방지를 위해 안전바가 내려온다. 처음에는, 거대한 언덕으로 올라가게 되고, 이것은 그 다음에 갑자기 그 언덕을 매우 빠른 속도로 내려간다. 이런 언덕들이 매우 많이 있고, 가끔은 나선형도 있는데, 여기에서는 거꾸로 가고 옆으로 가게 된다. 어떤 사람들은 이것을 타는 것을 즐기고, 또 어떤 사람들은 이것을 타는 것을 무서워한다.

어휘 amusement park 놀이공원   certain 특정한   height 키   put on a seatbelt 안전벨트를 하다   safety bar 안전바   get hurt 다치다   huge 거대한   hill 언덕   all of a sudden 갑자기   spiral 나선(형), 소용돌이   upside down 거꾸로   sideways 옆으로   be afraid of ~을 무서워 하다   roller coaster 롤러코스터   haunted house 유령의 집   merry-go-round 회전목마

15 ④

M: The weather is so weird lately. Don't you think so?
요즘은 날씨가 정말 이상해. 그렇게 생각하지 않아?

W: Yeah, you're right. I can't tell if it's still summer or if it's fall. The temperature changes so much during the day. 응, 맞아. 지금이 여전히 여름인지 아니면 가을인지 알 수가 없어. 낮 동안에 기온이 너무 많이 바뀌어.

M: You can say that again. When I leave the house in the morning, it is super cold, and during the day it's really hot. But then at night, it gets cold again! 맞는 말이야. 내가 아침에 집을 나설 때는 정말 추운데, 낮 동안에는 정말 더워. 그렇지만 밤이 되면 또 다시 추워져.

W: I know what you mean. I don't know how to dress nowadays. Oh, by the way, are you going to the fireworks festival this weekend?
네 말이 무슨 말인지 알아. 요즘은 옷을 어떻게 입어야 할지 모르겠어. 아 그런데 말이야, 이번 주말에 불꽃놀이 축제에 갈 거니?

M: Yes, I'm planning on going. How about you?
응, 가려고 계획 중이야. 너는?

W: I'll be there, too. The festival is near the lake, so it'll probably be even colder at night, right?
나도 갈 거야. 축제가 호숫가에서 하기 때문에 밤에는 아마도 더 추울 거야, 맞지?

M: I think so. You have to be careful not to catch a cold during times like this. You should wear long pants and bring a jacket just in case it gets cold.
내 생각에도 그래. 이럴 때에는 감기에 걸리지 않도록 조심해야 해. 추울 경우를 대비해서 긴 바지를 입고 재킷을 챙겨야 해.

W: That's a good idea. I'll look for a jacket when I get home. I'll see you this weekend then!
좋은 생각이야. 집에 가면 재킷을 찾아 봐야겠어. 그럼 주말에 보자!

M: Alright, see you! 알았어, 그때 봐!

어휘 weird 이상한   tell 구별하다   fall 가을   temperature 온도

during the day 낮 동안에   super 아주, 굉장히   nowadays 요즘에   fireworks 불꽃놀이   catch a cold 감기에 걸리다   just in case 만약의 경우에 대비하여

16 ③

M: Julie, when is your birthday? I'm writing all my friends' birthdays in my calendar. 줄리, 넌 생일이 언제니? 난 지금 달력에 모든 친구들의 생일을 적고 있어.

W: Try to guess it! When do you think I was born? 한번 맞혀 봐! 내가 언제 태어났을 것 같니?

M: Hmm… Were you born during the spring, summer, fall, or winter? 음, 봄, 여름, 가을, 겨울 중에서 언제 태어났어?

W: I was born during the winter. It normally snows a lot on my birthday.
나는 겨울에 태어났어. 내 생일에는 보통은 눈이 많이 와.

M: So, that means your birthday is in December, January, or February, right? Give me some more hints! 그럼, 네 말은 네 생일이 12월, 1월, 아니면 2월 중에 있다는 말이지? 조금 더 힌트를 줘.

W: Well, an important holiday is in the same month as my birthday. People celebrate it with their friends and family, give gifts to each other, and decorate a tree. 음, 중요한 공휴일이 내 생일과 같은 달에 있어. 사람들은 가족, 친구들과 그날을 같이 기념하고, 서로에게 선물을 주고, 나무를 장식해.

M: Oh, okay! How many days before or after this holiday is your birthday?
아, 알겠어! 네 생일이 그 공휴일의 앞 또는 뒤로 며칠이나 있어?

W: My birthday is ten days before this holiday. Do you know when my birthday is now? 내 생일은 이 공휴일의 열흘 전이야. 이제 내 생일이 언제인지 알겠니?

해설 두 사람이 말하는 holiday는 크리스마스(December 25)를 가리키며 여자의 생일은 이보다 열흘 전이다.

어휘 calendar 달력   guess 짐작하다, 추측하다   be born 태어나다   normally 보통은   holiday 공휴일   celebrate 축하하다, 기념하다   decorate 장식하다

17 ⑤

W: Martha wants to go talk to her guidance counselor about college applications. She has a list of colleges that she's interested in, but she can't decide which colleges to apply for and which ones may want to accept her. Her grades are pretty good and she has participated in a lot of volunteer work. The next day, Martha and her guidance counselor have a meeting. Martha asks her counselor to recommend some colleges that would fit her the best. Her counselor says that she should go to the college's websites first and look at the programs and the campuses. That way, it will be easier to decide which one to go to. In this situation, what would her guidance counselor most likely say to Martha?

마사는 지도 교사에게 가서 대학 지원에 대해 이야기를 하고 싶다. 그녀는 가고 싶은 대학의 목록을 갖고 있지만, 어느 학교에 지원해야 할지, 어느 학교가 자신을 받아줄지 결정할 수 없다. 그녀의 성적은 꽤 좋고, 봉사 활동에도 많이 참여했다. 다음 날 마사와 그녀의 지도 교사는 회의를 한다. 마사는 지도 교사에게 그녀에게 가장 적절한 대학을 추천해 달라고 부탁한다. 그녀의 지도 교사는 그녀가 먼저 대학교의 홈페이지에 들어가서 프로그램과 캠퍼스를 봐야 한다고 말한다. 그렇게 하면 어떤 학교를 갈지 결정하기 쉬워질 것이다. 이런 상황에서 그녀의 지도 교사가 마사에게 할 말로 가장 적절한 것은 무엇인가?

Counselor: I think you should check out the different colleges online before deciding.
내 생각에는 네가 결정하기 전에 온라인으로 먼저 다른 대학들을 확인해 보는 것이 좋을 것 같구나.

① Can we reschedule our meeting?
우리 회의 일정을 조정할 수 있을까?

② I'll make sure I go to your graduation.
난 네 졸업식에 꼭 갈 거야.

③ How many school clubs have you participated in?
넌 얼마나 많은 학교 동아리에 참여했니?

④ 100 hours of volunteer service are required to apply to any college. 어느 대학이든지 지원하기 위해서는 100시간의 봉사 활동이 요구된단다.

⑤ I think you should check out the different colleges online before deciding.
내 생각에는 네가 결정하기 전에 온라인으로 먼저 다른 대학들을 확인해 보는 것이 좋을 것 같구나.

어휘 guidance counselor 진로 지도 교사; 지도 상담사   application 지원   apply for ~에 지원하다, 신청하다   accept 받아들이다   grade 성적   volunteer work 자원봉사   have a meeting 회의하다   recommend 추천하다   fit 맞다, 적절하다   graduation 졸업식, 졸업   require 요구하다

18 ③

M: Megan, your bracelet is so unique. Where did you get it? 메건, 네 팔찌는 정말 독특해. 어디서 그걸 샀니?

W: Thanks! It's actually a charity bracelet. I ordered it online a few days ago.
고마워! 사실 이건 자선 팔찌야. 며칠 전에 인터넷으로 주문했어.

M: A charity bracelet? What is that? I've never heard of it before.
자선 팔찌? 그게 뭐야? 난 한 번도 들어본 적이 없어.

W: Well, if you buy a bracelet, then that money goes to help people around the world. For example, countries that suffered through a tsunami or an earthquake. Or it could go to help feed people or cure diseases in places like Africa.
음, 만약 네가 팔찌 한 개를 사면, 그 돈이 세계에 있는 사람들을 도와주는 데 쓰이게 돼. 예를 들면, 쓰나미 혹은 지진으로 피해를 입은

국가들이지. 아니면 아프리카와 같은 곳의 사람들에게 먹을 것을 주거나 질병을 치료하는 데 쓰일 수도 있어.

M: Wow! That is such a wonderful thing to do! Can you tell me the website where I can order one too?
우와! 정말 멋진 일이구나! 나에게 주문을 할 수 있는 웹사이트를 알려줄 수 있니?

W: Sure! It is www dot betweenworlds dot org. The color of the bracelet changes depending on which country you want to help, so make sure you check that out. 물론이지! www.betweenworlds.org야. 팔찌의 색상은 어떤 나라를 도와 주고 싶은지에 따라 바뀌니까, 그걸 확인해야 해.

M: Alright, I'll be sure to do that. I'm so glad you told me about this! I think I'm going to tell my friends about it too. 알겠어, 꼭 그렇게 할게. 네가 이것을 말해줘서 정말 기뻐! 내 친구들에게도 말해줘야겠어.

W: I'm glad to hear that! It's nice to know that people are so willing to help each other.
정말 반가운 소리구나! 사람들이 기꺼이 서로를 돕고 싶어한다는 것을 아는 건 정말 멋지잖아.

어휘 bracelet 팔찌 unique 독특한 actually 사실은 charity 자선(단체) order 주문하다 suffer 고통을 겪다 tsunami 쓰나미, 지진해일 earthquake 지진 feed ~에게 먹을 것을 주다 cure diseases 질병을 치료하다 check out 확인하다 be willing to 기꺼이 ~하다

19 ①

M: Hey, Cassandra, what are you doing? You look so busy. 얘, 카산드라, 너 뭐 하고 있니? 굉장히 바빠 보인다.

W: I'm writing my research paper for history class. Why aren't you working on yours? Have you finished already? 난 역사 수업을 위한 연구 보고서를 쓰고 있어. 넌 왜 네 보고서를 쓰지 않는 거니? 벌써 다 끝냈어?

M: No, I haven't even started yet. It's due next week, so I still have a lot of time to do it. 아니, 나는 아직 시작도 안 했어. 다음 주가 마감이라서 그걸 할 시간이 아직 많이 있어.

W: What are you talking about? The assignment is due tomorrow! We have to turn it in before class starts.
무슨 소리를 하는 거야? 과제 마감일은 내일이야! 우리는 수업 시작 전에 그걸 제출해야 해.

M: What? Please tell me you're joking! I thought it was due next week. 뭐라고? 제발 농담하는 거라고 말해줘! 난 다음 주가 마감이라고 생각했어.

W: Well, it was. But Mr. Groves changed the due date. He sent everyone an email. Didn't you get it?
음, 그랬지. 하지만 그로브 선생님께서 마감일을 바꾸셨어. 모든 학생들에게 이메일을 보내셨어. 넌 그걸 못 받았니?

M: I don't check my email that often! Oh my goodness, what should I do? Even if I start on it now, I won't be able to finish it by tomorrow.
난 이메일을 그렇게 자주 확인하지 않아. 아, 안돼! 내가 어떻게 해야 하지? 지금 시작한다 하더라도, 내일까지 끝낼 수는 없을 거야.

W: Well, you'd better start working on it now! Even if you turn it in late, that's a lot better than not turning it in at all. 음, 그래도 지금 시작하는 것이 좋겠어! 늦게 제출하더라도, 아예 제출하지 않는 것보다 훨씬 나을 거야.

① Better late than never.
하지 않는 것보다는 늦더라도 하는 것이 낫다.
② No smoke without fire. 아니 땐 굴뚝에 연기 나랴.
③ Many hands make light work. 백지장도 맞들면 낫다.
④ Make hay while the sun shines.
해가 비추는 동안에 건초를 말려라.
⑤ Actions speak louder than words.
말보다 행동이 중요하다.

어휘 research paper 연구 보고서 work on ~에 대한 작업을 하다 due 마감인, ~하기로 되어 있는 assignment 과제 turn in 제출하다 joke 농담하다 due date 마감일 check one's email ~의 이메일을 확인하다

20 ⑤

M: Jane! Why didn't you pick up your phone yesterday? Do you have any idea how worried I was?
제인! 어제 왜 전화를 안 받았어? 내가 얼마나 걱정했는지 알아?

W: I'm so sorry, Ben. I left my cellphone on the bus ride home. By the time I got off the bus and realized that I didn't have my phone, it was too late. 정말 미안해, 벤. 집에 오는 버스에 휴대폰을 두고 내렸어. 버스에서 내리고 휴대폰이 없다는 걸 깨달았을 때는 너무 늦었지.

M: I see. I'm relieved that you're safe. What are you going to do about your phone?
그랬구나. 네가 안전하니 다행이다. 네 휴대폰은 어떻게 할 거야?

W: I don't know. I called the bus company, but they said it would be impossible to find since there are so many buses in the city.
나도 모르겠어. 버스 회사에 전화해 봤지만, 시내에 너무 많은 버스가 있어서 찾는 건 불가능할 거라고 하더라고.

M: Oh, I'm sorry to hear that. Then what do you plan on doing? 아, 그 말을 들으니 정말 안됐다. 그래서 어떻게 할 계획이야?

W: I guess I'll just have to buy a new phone. There's nothing I can do about my old cellphone now.
그냥 새 휴대폰을 사야 할 것 같아. 지금은 예전 휴대폰에 대해 내가 할 수 있는 게 없어.

M: Okay, call me when you get your new phone so I can save your new phone number.
알았어. 휴대폰을 새로 구입하면 내가 네 새 전화번호를 저장할 수 있도록 나한테 전화해.

W: Okay! I'll call you as soon as I get it. Sorry for worrying you yesterday. 알았어! 내가 사자마자 너한테 바로 전화할게. 어제 걱정시켜서 미안해.

① I'll meet you at the bus company. 버스 회사에서 만나자.
② Thanks for coming with me to get my new phone.

새 휴대폰을 사러 같이 와주어서 고마워.

③ I can never thank you enough for finding my phone for me. 내 휴대폰을 찾아준 것에 대해 어떻게 고마움의 표시를 해야 할지 모르겠어.

④ Why didn't you tell me that you changed your phone number? 왜 네 전화번호를 바꿨다고 말하지 않았니?

⑤ Okay! I'll call you as soon as I get it. Sorry for worrying you yesterday. 알았어! 내가 사자마자 너한테 바로 전화할게. 어제 걱정시켜서 미안해.

어휘 pick up the phone 전화를 받다 bus ride 버스 탑승 by the time ~할 때쯤에 realize 깨닫다 relieved 안도하는 as soon as ~하자마자

20회 고난도 실전모의고사 본문 p.244-245

01 ③	02 ④	03 ②	04 ④	05 ④
06 ②	07 ①	08 ③	09 ①	10 ⑤
11 ④	12 ④	13 ③	14 ③	15 ⑤
16 ②	17 ⑤	18 ④	19 ④	20 ⑤

01 ③

W: Hey, Mark! What are you up to these days? I haven't seen you in a long time. I heard you got a girlfriend! 얘, 마크! 요즘 뭐하고 지내니? 널 정말 오랜만에 본다. 너한테 여자친구가 생겼다고 들었어!

M: Hi, Susie! Yeah, we've been dating for six months now. How have you been? 안녕, 수지! 응, 지금 6개월째 사귀고 있어. 너는 어떻게 지냈니?

W: I've been great! It's nice to hear that you're dating! Can you tell me about her? How did you meet? 난 잘 지냈어! 네가 데이트를 하고 있다니 좋네! 그녀에 대해서 말해 줄 수 있니? 어떻게 만났니?

M: Well, she has a great personality and we have a lot in common. I met her at a book club last year. 음, 내 여자친구는 성격도 아주 좋고, 우리는 서로 공통점이 많아. 난 그녀를 작년에 독서 동아리에서 만났어.

W: Oh, I see. That's great! What does she look like? 오, 그렇구나. 잘됐네! 그녀는 어떻게 생겼니?

M: She has long, curly hair and she doesn't wear glasses. She likes wearing skirts, and she likes hats. Here, let me show you a picture. 음, 머리는 길면서 곱슬이고, 안경은 쓰지 않아. 그리고 치마 입는 것을 좋아하고, 모자를 좋아해. 여기, 너한테 사진을 보여 줄게.

W: She looks just like your description! Except she's not wearing a hat in this picture. I think you guys make a great couple! 네가 묘사한 그대로구나! 하지만 이 사진에서는 모자를 쓰고 있지 않네. 너희들은 잘 어울리는 커플인 것 같아!

M: Thanks for saying that! 그렇게 말해주니 고마워!

해설 여자의 말인 'Except she's not wearing a hat ~'이 중요한 최종 힌트이다.

어휘 in a long time 오랜만에 date 데이트하다 personality 성격 have in common 공통점이 있다 curly 곱슬곱슬한 wear glasses 안경을 쓰다 description 설명, 묘사 except ~을 제외하고

02 ④

[Telephone rings.] [전화벨이 울린다.]

W: Hello? Ross, this is Mom calling. 여보세요? 로스야, 엄마다.

M: Hey, Mom. What's up? 아, 엄마. 무슨 일이세요?

W: I'm calling to ask if you can order some dinner before your dad and I get home from work. I was supposed to make dinner tonight, but I'm so exhausted. 혹시 엄마랑 아빠가 퇴근하기 전에 저녁을 좀 주문해 줄 수 있는지 물어보려고 전화했어. 내가 오늘 밤에 저녁을 만들려고 했는데, 너무 지쳤거든.

M: Yeah, I can do that for you. What do you want me to order? 네. 제가 해드릴게요. 어떤 음식을 주문하면 될까요?

W: Well, we had pizza last night, so how about some fried chicken? Is there anything that you'd like to eat? 음, 우리가 어젯밤에 피자를 먹었으니, 프라이드치킨은 어떠니? 네가 먹고 싶은 것이 있니?

M: Fried chicken sounds good to me. I'll order some from Ultra Chicken. Didn't we get a free drink coupon the last time we ordered? 프라이드치킨은 좋아요. 울트라 치킨에서 제가 주문할게요. 우리가 지난번에 주문했을 때 무료 음료 쿠폰을 받지 않았나요?

W: Yeah, it should be in the drawer next to the kitchen sink. Oh, and can you ask them for some extra sauce? 그래, 그건 부엌 싱크대 옆 서랍에 있을 거야. 아, 그리고 소스를 추가로 가져다 달라고 말할래?

M: Alright. I'll make sure to ask them when I order. 알겠어요. 주문할 때 꼭 말할게요.

어휘 order 주문하다 be supposed to ~하기로 되어 있다 exhausted 지친 drawer 서랍 extra 여분의, 추가의 sauce 소스, 양념 make sure to 확실히 ~하다

03 ②

① W: Here's your coffee, sir. Please be careful not to spill it. 여기 커피 나왔습니다, 손님. 쏟지 않도록 조심하세요.

M: Thank you, I'll be careful. 감사합니다, 조심할게요.

② W: Excuse me, sir. There is a spill on the floor. 실례합니다. 바닥에 뭔가 쏟아졌네요.

M: I'm sorry about that, ma'am. I'll get it cleaned up right away. 죄송합니다, 부인. 바로 치워 드리겠습니다.

③ W: The flowers are all dried up. What should we do? 꽃들이 모두 시들었어요. 우리가 어떻게 해야 하죠?

M: I'm sure they'll come back to life once we water

them. 우리가 물을 주면 분명히 다시 살아날 거예요.

④ W: Can you get me a cup of water? I'm so thirsty.
물 한 잔 주시겠어요? 목이 너무 마르네요.

M: Yeah, sure. Do you want ice with it?
네, 물론이죠. 얼음도 함께 넣어 드릴까요?

⑤ W: Are you done vacuuming the floor? There was dust everywhere. 바닥에 진공청소기를 돌리는 게 끝났나요? 바닥에 온통 먼지가 있었어요.

M: Yes, I just got finished. Everything's clean now.
네, 방금 끝났어요. 이제 모든 것이 깨끗해요.

어휘 careful 조심하는, 신중한 spill 흘린 액체; 쏟다 floor 바닥 clean up 치우다, 청소하다 dried up 바싹 마른 come back to life 다시 살아나다 once 일단 ~ 하면 water 물을 주다 thirsty 목이 마른 vacuum 진공청소기로 청소하다 dust 먼지

04 ④

W: Are you ready for our trip to the mountains? I hope the weather isn't too hot or cold during the weekend. 산으로 여행을 떠날 준비가 됐어? 주말 동안에 날씨가 너무 춥거나 덥지 않으면 좋겠어.

M: Yeah, I'm so excited! I'm sure the weather will be fine. I think we should check the traffic report before leaving tomorrow morning.
응, 난 아주 신나! 날씨는 분명 좋을 거야. 우리는 내일 아침에 떠나기 전에 교통방송을 확인해야 할 것 같아.

W: Okay, let me look it up. [pause] Oh, no! It says there's going to be heavy traffic over the weekend!
알겠어, 내가 알아볼게. [잠시 후] 아, 안돼! 주말 동안에 교통량이 많을 거라고 나와 있어.

M: It must be because it's vacation season for everybody. Wait, but it says that there will be heavy traffic on Saturday morning and Sunday night.
모두 휴가철이라 그런 게 분명해. 잠깐만, 그런데 토요일 오전과 일요일 밤에 교통량이 많을 거라고 나와 있어.

W: Oh, then that means we won't be stuck in traffic since we're leaving on Friday morning and coming back on Sunday morning!
아, 그럼 우리는 금요일 오전에 출발해서 일요일 오전에 돌아오니까 차 막히는 일은 없다는 말이네!

M: That's such a relief! I was so worried we wouldn't be able to go on our hiking trip. 정말 다행이다! 우리의 하이킹 여행을 갈 수 없을까 봐 정말 걱정했어.

W: Me too! Now all we have to do is pack our hiking equipment and put everything in the car.
나도 그래! 이제 우리가 해야 할 일은 하이킹 장비를 챙기고 모든 것을 차에 실어 놓는 거야.

M: Alright! I already packed our hiking clothes, shoes, backpacks, tent, two flashlights, and two water bottles. What else should we bring?
좋아! 난 이미 하이킹 복장, 등산화, 배낭, 텐트, 손전등 두 개, 그리고 물병 두 개를 챙겼어. 또 무엇을 가져가야 하지?

W: I think we should bring some snacks to eat on the

way up the mountain.
산에 올라가면서 먹을 간식을 조금 가져가야 할 것 같아.

M: Oh, yeah! That's a good idea.
아, 그래! 그거 좋은 생각이야.

어휘 traffic report 교통방송 look something up ~을 찾아보다 heavy traffic 교통 체증 vacation season 휴가철 stuck in traffic 교통체증 때문에 움직일 수 없는 relief 안도, 안심 pack (짐을) 싸다 equipment 장비 flashlight 손전등 water bottle 물병 snack 간식

05 ④

W: Richard, please take a seat. I need to speak with you. 리처드, 자리에 앉으세요. 당신에게 할 말이 있어요.

M: Yes, ma'am. Is there a problem? 네, 문제가 있나요?

W: I'm afraid so. You have been late to work every day for the past week. If you can't come to the café on time, I'm going to have to fire you.
안타깝지만 그래요. 당신은 지난주에 매일 지각을 했어요. 만약 제시간에 카페에 출근하지 않는다면, 당신을 해고할 수밖에 없어요.

M: I'm sorry about that, ma'am. I'll make sure to get here on time from now on. 그 점은 정말 죄송합니다. 이제부터는 항상 제시간에 이곳에 오겠습니다.

W: There are still a few more things I need to talk to you about. First, customers have been complaining about your bad attitude when taking drink orders. You need to smile and treat them with respect.
제가 이야기하고 싶은 사항이 아직 몇 가지 더 있어요. 첫째, 손님들이 당신이 음료를 주문받을 때 태도가 좋지 않다고 불평을 하고 있어요. 당신은 웃으면서 손님들을 정중하게 대해야 해요.

M: I apologize. I'll be careful next time. What else did you want to speak to me about?
제가 사과하겠습니다. 다음에는 조심하도록 할게요. 또 제게 하실 얘기가 무엇이었나요?

W: When you're working during closing hours, you have to take out the garbage every day. If you don't, it starts to rot and smell.
마감 시간에 근무할 때는, 매일 쓰레기를 내다버려야 해요. 만약 그렇게 하지 않으면 쓰레기가 썩어서 냄새가 나기 시작해요.

M: Alright. I promise that I'll get here on time, be nice to customers, and take out the garbage every day. Thank you for letting me know.
알겠습니다. 제시간에 이곳에 오고, 손님들을 친절히 대하고, 매일 쓰레기를 버리겠다고 약속할게요. 알려주셔서 감사합니다.

어휘 take a seat 자리에 앉다 late to work 회사에 지각하다 on time 제시간에 fire 해고하다 complain 불평하다 attitude 태도 take orders 주문을 받다 treat 다루다, 대접하다 respect 존중(하다) apologize 사과하다 closing hours 폐점 시간 take out the garbage 쓰레기를 내다버리다 rot 썩다

06 ②

W: Hey dad, did anything come for me in the mail

M: No, <u>not that I know of</u>. Why? Are you <u>expecting</u> a <u>package</u>? 아니, 내가 아는 한 없어. 왜? 소포를 기다리고 있니?

W: Yes, I ordered a <u>dress</u> for my <u>graduation ceremony</u> on Friday, and I was supposed to <u>get</u> it <u>in</u> the <u>mail</u> yesterday. But it's still not here.
네, 저는 금요일 졸업식에서 입을 드레스를 주문했고, 어제 우편으로 받았어야 했어요. 하지만 아직 여기로 오지 않았어요.

M: Did you <u>call</u> the clothing <u>store</u>? Maybe there was an <u>unexpected delay</u> with the <u>delivery</u>.
옷 가게에 전화해 봤니? 아마 배송에 예상치 못한 지연이 생겼을 수 있어.

W: Yeah, I called this morning, but <u>nobody answered</u> the <u>phone</u>. <u>What if</u> the dress doesn't come before Friday? I won't have anything to wear to my graduation! 네, 오늘 아침에 전화했는데, 아무도 전화를 받지 않았어요. 만약 드레스가 금요일 전에 오지 않으면 어쩌죠? 저는 졸업식에 입고 갈 옷이 없을 거예요!

M: I'm sure it'll get here by then. There are still <u>two days left</u>, so don't worry too much. 분명히 그때까지는 올 거다. 아직 이틀이나 남았으니 너무 걱정하지 말거라.

W: I hope you're right. I just want it to <u>get here soon</u> so I can stop thinking about it.
아빠 말씀이 맞았으면 좋겠어요. 그것에 대해 생각하지 않을 수 있도록 옷이 빨리 여기 도착했으면 좋겠어요.

M: I understand. I'll <u>let you know</u> if the package gets here tomorrow. 이해한다. 내일 소포가 여기 오면 알려줄게.

해설 여자는 주문한 옷이 졸업식 전날까지 오지 않을까 봐 걱정하고 있다. 또한 남자의 말 'don't worry'에서 여자의 심정을 알 수 있다.

어휘 expect 기대하다, 예상하다 package 소포 graduation ceremony 졸업식 unexpected 예상치 못한 delay 지연 delivery 배달, 배송 answer the phone 전화를 받다 anxious 걱정하는 embarrassed 당황한

07 ①

① W: When are you going to <u>mail</u> the <u>documents</u> to me? 언제 제게 서류를 우편으로 보내실 거죠?

M: The <u>post office</u> is open every day from ten A.M. to five P.M.
우체국은 매일 오전 10시부터 오후 5시까지 운영합니다.

② W: Have you been to the <u>Chinese restaurant</u> down the street? 길 아래에 있는 중국 음식점에 가 봤나요?

M: Yes, but it <u>wasn't that great</u>. I <u>prefer</u> the one on Central Avenue.
네, 하지만 별로였어요. 저는 센트럴 가에 있는 식당이 더 좋아요.

③ W: <u>How many people</u> are you inviting to your birthday party? 당신의 생일 파티에 얼마나 많은 사람을 초대할 건가요?

M: I'm not sure yet, but I'm thinking <u>about twenty</u> people.
아직 확실하지 않지만, 20명 정도 생각하고 있어요.

④ W: <u>How</u> much <u>longer</u> do we have to <u>wait in line</u>? 우리가 얼마나 더 오래 줄을 서서 기다려야 하죠?

M: There are three people in front of you, so it'll be about twenty minutes.
당신 앞에 세 사람이 있으니, 약 20분 정도가 될 겁니다.

⑤ W: Can I <u>call</u> you <u>after school</u> today? I have to talk to you. 오늘 방과 후에 전화해도 될까? 너랑 이야기를 해야 해.

M: Of course, but <u>make sure</u> you call <u>before six</u> P.M.
물론이야, 하지만 반드시 오후 6시 전에 전화해.

어휘 document 서류, 문서 prefer 선호하다 invite 초대하다 wait in line 줄을 서서 기다리다

08 ③

W: Jonathan, are you busy right now?
조너선, 당신 지금 바빠요?

M: No, not really. Do you need something?
아니요, 괜찮아요. 필요한 것이 있나요?

W: Yeah, I need you to <u>do me a favor</u>. I have to go to my <u>dentist appointment</u> at one P.M., but my <u>car broke down</u> yesterday and it's in the repair shop. So, I was wondering if you could <u>give</u> me <u>a ride</u> there.
네. 제가 당신에게 부탁할 것이 있어요. 제가 오후 1시까지 치과 예약에 가야 하는데, 어제 제 차가 고장 나서 정비소에 있어요. 그래서, 당신이 거기까지 저를 데려다 줄 수 있는지 궁금하네요.

M: I would <u>love to</u>, <u>but</u> my sister is using my car for the day. She's not getting back until three P.M. Can you <u>reschedule</u> your appointment?
저도 그러고 싶은데, 오늘은 제 여동생이 제 차를 사용하고 있어요. 그 애는 오후 3시까지는 돌아오지 않을 거예요. 당신의 예약 시간을 변경할 수 있나요?

W: Oh, I see. Let me <u>call</u> them and <u>ask if</u> I can go at a later time. [*pause*] Okay, they said that I could come <u>at four</u> P.M. <u>instead of one</u> P.M.
아, 알겠어요. 제가 전화해서 좀 늦은 시간에 갈 수 있는지 물어볼게요. [잠시 후] 됐어요. 오후 1시 대신 4시에 와도 좋다고 하네요.

M: That's great! Then I can give you a ride there after my sister gets home.
잘됐네요! 그럼 제 여동생이 집에 오면 제가 거기까지 태워 줄게요.

W: Alright, that <u>sounds perfect</u>! Thank you so much, Jonathan. 좋아요, 정말 딱이네요! 정말 고마워요, 조너선.

M: It's not a problem. I'll <u>give</u> you <u>a call</u> once my sister gets back.
천만에요. 제 여동생이 돌아오면 당신한테 전화할게요.

해설 여자의 대사 'I was wondering if you could ~'에 부탁 내용이 나온다.

어휘 do a favor 부탁을 들어주다 dentist appointment 치과 예약 break down 망가지다, 고장 나다 repair shop 수리점 give somebody a ride ~을 차로 태워주다 get back 돌아오다 reschedule 일정을 변경하다 instead of ~대신에

09 ①

[*The answering machine beeps.*]

[자동응답기가 삐 소리를 낸다.]

W: Hi Elizabeth! This is Jessica. I wanted to talk to you in person, but I guess you're busy preparing for the wedding. I just got your invitation in the mail today and I plan on taking the day off of work to be there. I just want to tell you how happy I am for you! I can't believe you and John are finally getting married! I've known you two for over seven years now, and I knew you guys would get married someday. I wish the best for you and I hope your life will be filled with happiness. I'll see you at the wedding ceremony!

안녕, 엘리자베스! 나야, 제시카. 너랑 직접 얘기하고 싶었지만 아마 너는 결혼 준비로 바쁠 것 같다. 오늘 우편으로 네 청첩장을 받았고, 그날은 거기 가기 위해 일을 쉴 계획이야. 난 그저 내가 얼마나 기쁜지 너에게 말해주고 싶어. 너와 존이 마침내 결혼을 한다는 게 믿기지가 않아! 내가 너희 둘을 7년 넘게 알고 지냈는데, 언젠가는 너희 둘이 결혼할 거란 걸 알았어. 네가 잘되기를 바라고, 네 삶이 행복으로 가득하길 바랄게. 결혼식에서 보자!

어휘 in person 직접   invitation 초대장   take a day off 일을 하루 쉬다   get married 결혼하다   someday 언젠가는   be filled with ~로 가득 차다   wedding ceremony 결혼식

10 ⑤

M: Good afternoon, welcome to Gretchen Hair & Spa. What can I do for you today? 안녕하세요, 그레첸 헤어 앤 스파에 오신 것을 환영합니다. 무엇을 도와드릴까요?

W: Hello, I would like to get my hair done. Also, I would like to get a massage, please.
안녕하세요, 제 머리를 하고 싶어요. 그리고 마사지도 받고 싶네요.

M: Alright, what would you like to do to your hair? And what kind of massage would you like?
알겠습니다. 머리를 어떻게 해드릴까요? 그리고 어떤 종류의 마사지를 원하시나요?

W: I want to get it cut, permed, and dyed. After doing my hair, I would like to get a foot massage. How much would it cost me to do all of that?
머리를 커트하고 파마한 다음에 염색을 하고 싶어요. 머리를 다 하고 나면, 발 마사지를 받고 싶어요. 이 모든 걸 다 하면 얼마죠?

M: Getting a cut costs ten dollars, and a foot massage costs twenty dollars. Depending on how much hair you want to get cut off, the price for getting a perm and dyeing your hair changes.
커트를 받는 비용은 10달러, 발 마사지는 20달러가 됩니다. 머리를 얼마나 자르기를 원하는지에 따라서 파마와 염색을 받는 비용이 달라져요.

W: Oh, what if I get my hair cut to shoulder length? How much would that be? 아, 어깨 길이까지 머리를 자르면 어떤가요? 그 비용이 얼마나 되죠?

M: Shoulder length hair costs seventy dollars to perm and fifty dollars to dye. If that's okay with you, we will get started.

어깨 길이의 머리는 파마하는 데 70달러, 그리고 염색하는 데 50달러입니다. 손님께서 괜찮다고 하시면 시작하겠습니다.

W: Okay, that sounds great. 그래요, 좋네요.

해설 커트($10) + 파마($70) + 염색($50) + 발 마사지($20) = $150

어휘 get one's hair done ~의 머리를 하다   get a massage 마사지를 받다   perm 파마를 하다   dye 염색하다   depending on ~에 따라   length 길이   get started 시작하다

11 ④

W: Good morning, sir. What may I do for you today? 안녕하세요, 선생님. 무엇을 도와드릴까요?

M: I bought a plane ticket online, and I would like to confirm my flight and check in.
제가 온라인으로 항공권을 구매했는데, 항공권을 확인하고 탑승수속을 밟으려고요.

W: Okay, could I see your passport and reservation number, please?
네, 제가 여권과 예약 번호를 볼 수 있을까요?

M: Here you go. I would also like to check in these two suitcases. 여기요. 이 여행가방 두 개도 부치고 싶어요.

W: Alright. We have to weigh them first. [pause] Both of your suitcases weigh sixty pounds each. You can only check in bags that are lighter than fifty pounds. 알겠습니다. 먼저 무게를 재야 합니다. [잠시 후] 여행가방 두 개가 각각 60파운드네요. 50파운드보다 가벼운 가방만 부칠 수 있거든요.

M: Oh no! Is there anything I can do?
아, 이런! 제가 할 수 있는 게 있나요?

W: Well, I think it'll be a good idea to take some things out of the suitcases to make them lighter. After you do that, we can weigh the suitcases again.
음, 제 생각에는 가방에서 짐을 좀 꺼내셔서 가볍게 만드시는 게 좋을 것 같아요. 그렇게 하신 다음에 여행가방의 무게를 다시 재 드릴 수 있어요.

M: Alright then, I'll try to do that right now. Thank you.
알겠어요, 지금 바로 그렇게 할게요. 감사합니다.

어휘 buy something online ~을 인터넷으로 사다   passport 여권   reservation 예약   check in (짐을) 부치다; 탑승 수속을 하다   suitcase 여행가방   weigh 무게를 재다

12 ④

W: Hello, ladies and gentlemen, boys and girls! Today, April fourteenth, is the grand opening of our new dolphin show! There will be four shows every day at one P.M., three P.M., four thirty P.M., and six P.M. The shows will take place in Splash Theater, which is in Section A of the aquarium. For people who paid the admission fee to enter the aquarium, there is no extra fee for the show. However, for people who only want to watch the dolphin show, there is a fee of fifteen dollars. Come and watch dolphins jump, flip in the air, dance, and do other cool tricks!

안녕하세요 신사 숙녀, 그리고 꼬마 여러분! 오늘 4월 14일은 저희의 새로운 돌고래 공연의 개막일입니다. 매일 오후 1시, 3시, 4시 30분, 그리고 6시, 이렇게 4번의 공연이 열릴 예정입니다. 공연은 아쿠아리움의 A구역 내에 있는 스플래시 극장에서 열릴 것입니다. 아쿠아리움의 입장료를 지불하신 분들은 공연을 보는 데 추가 요금이 들지 않습니다. 하지만 돌고래 쇼만 관람하고 싶은 분들에게는 15달러의 요금이 있습니다. 오셔서 돌고래가 점프하고, 공중에서 회전하고, 춤추고, 다른 멋진 재주를 부리는 것을 보시기 바랍니다!

어휘 grand opening 개막, 개장 take place 열리다, 일어나다 aquarium 아쿠아리움, 수족관 admission fee 입장료 extra 추가의 flip 홱 뒤집다 do tricks 재주를 부리다

13 ③

| 원저 주택의 아파트 가격 |

	침실 & 욕실	월세
①	침실 1, 욕실 1	100달러
②	침실 2, 욕실 1	175달러
③	침실 3, 욕실 2	250달러
④	침실 4, 욕실 3	325달러
⑤	침실 4, 욕실 4	375달러

W: Hello, sir. May I help you look for an apartment?
안녕하세요, 손님. 제가 아파트를 찾으시는 것을 도와드릴까요?

M: Yes, that would be great! Could you tell me about my options? How much is it for each apartment type? 네, 그러면 좋겠네요! 제가 선택할 수 있는 것들에 대해서 말해 주실 수 있나요? 각 아파트 유형마다 가격은 어떻게 되죠?

W: Alright. We have apartments with one bedroom and one bathroom at one hundred dollars per month. We also have some with two bedrooms and one bathroom for one hundred seventy-five dollars a month. Also, there are apartments with three bedrooms and two bathrooms at two hundred twenty-five dollars a month or four bedrooms and three bathrooms at three hundred twenty-five dollars a month. The apartments that are three hundred seventy-five dollars a month have four bedrooms and four bathrooms.
네. 저희는 침실 1개, 욕실 1개에 월세가 100달러인 아파트가 있고, 침실 2개, 욕실 1개에 월세가 175달러인 아파트도 있습니다. 또한, 침실 3개, 욕실 2개에 월세 225달러, 혹은 침실 4개, 욕실 3개에 월세가 325달러인 아파트도 있습니다. 월세가 375달러인 아파트는 침실 4개와 욕실 4개가 있습니다.

M: I see. Then which apartment would you recommend for me?
알겠어요. 그럼 저에게 어떤 아파트를 추천해 주실 수 있나요?

W: Will you be living by yourself, or will you be living with a roommate or a family member? 혼자 사실 계획 이신가요, 아니면 룸메이트나 가족과 함께 사실 건가요?

M: I plan on living here with my younger sister, but my parents will be visiting often. 저는 여기서 제 여동생이랑 둘이 지낼 건데, 부모님이 자주 방문하실 것 같아요.

W: Okay, then. How about an apartment with two bedrooms and one bathroom?
알겠습니다. 그럼 침실 2개와 욕실 1개인 아파트는 어떤가요?

M: That sounds okay, but I would prefer the apartment with three bedrooms and two bathrooms. That way my parents can use the extra room when they visit.
괜찮은 것 같지만 저는 침실 3개와 욕실 2개의 아파트가 좋을 것 같아요. 그래야 부모님이 오셨을 때 남은 방을 쓰실 수 있으니까요.

W: Sure, if that's what you want. That'll be two hundred twenty-five dollars a month. Would you like to sign a contract now?
그걸 원하신다면 물론이죠. 그건 한 달에 225달러입니다. 지금 계약하시겠어요?

M: Yes, please. That would be great!
네, 할게요. 아주 좋네요!

해설 남자의 질문 'How much is it for each apartment type?' 이후에 표를 보면서 맞지 않은 부분을 체크한다. ③의 가격이 $225로 수정되어야 한다.

어휘 option 선택권, 옵션 per ~당 recommend 추천하다 by oneself 혼자서 visit 방문하다 sign a contract 계약서에 서명하다

14 ③

M: This can be found on all roads. It is used to keep traffic flowing and allows people to take turns while driving. It has three colors on it; green means to go, yellow means to slow down, and red means to stop. There are also signals to make left and right turns. People who drive must be alert of these colors at all times. Normally, this is located high above the ground and hangs from a metal pole. Sometimes there are cameras set up next to it to catch people who do not follow traffic rules.

이것은 모든 도로에서 찾을 수 있다. 이것은 교통의 흐름을 유지하기 위해 사용되고, 운전 중에 사람들이 순서를 지킬 수 있도록 해준다. 이것은 세 가지 색깔을 갖고 있는데, 녹색은 주행을 의미하고, 노란색은 서행을, 마지막으로 빨간색은 정지를 의미한다. 또 좌회전과 우회전 신호도 있다. 운전하는 사람들은 이 색깔들을 항상 예의 주시해야 한다. 이것은 보통 땅으로부터 높은 곳에 위치해 있고, 철제 기둥에 매달려 있다. 때로는 교통 규칙을 어기는 사람들을 잡기 위해 이것의 옆에 카메라가 설치되어 있다.

어휘 traffic 교통 take turns 순서를 지키다; 교대로 하다 slow down 속도를 줄이다 signal 신호 make left turns 좌회전하다 alert 경계하는 at all times 항상 be located 위치하다, 있다 pole 기둥 set up 설치하다 follow rules 규칙을 따르다

15 ⑤

W: Honey! What is that on the side of the street?

113

여보! 길가에 있는 저게 뭐예요?

M: I think it's a dog! I wonder what it's doing there. It's not safe with all these cars driving by.
개인 것 같아요! 저 녀석이 저기에서 뭘 하고 있는지 모르겠어요. 모든 차들이 옆을 지나가기 때문에 안전하지 않을 텐데요.

W: I think it might be lost! It has a collar on its neck. Do you think we can find the owner's phone number or address on it?
제 생각에는 길을 잃은 것 같아요. 목에 목걸이를 하고 있어요. 목걸이에서 주인의 연락처나 주소를 찾을 수 있을까요?

M: I think so. [pause] Seventy-three eighty-one West Lane, three eight one, one nine two one. I'll try calling now, let's hope that someone answers. Nobody's picking up the phone. What should we do? 그럴 거예요. [잠시 후] 웨스트 레인 7381번지, 381-1921. 지금 전화해 볼게요, 누군가 받았으면 좋겠네요. [잠시 후] 아무도 전화를 받지 않아요. 우리가 어떻게 해야 할까요?

W: Well, West Lane is really close to our house, isn't it? Why don't we just take the dog to its owner?
음, 웨스트 레인은 우리 집에서 정말 가깝죠, 그렇지 않나요? 그냥 우리가 저 개를 주인에게 데려가는 게 어때요?

M: We can do that, if that's what you want to do. West Lane is just a ten minute drive from our house.
그게 당신이 원하는 거라면 그렇게 해요. 웨스트 레인은 우리 집에서 차로 10분밖에 안 걸려요.

W: Then let's head over there as soon as we can. Its owner must be so worried about it! 그럼 최대한 빨리 거기로 가요. 주인이 개를 엄청 걱정하고 있을 거예요!

M: Okay. We can try calling again on our way there.
알겠어요. 그쪽으로 가면서 다시 전화를 해볼 수 있겠네요.

어휘 on the side of the street 도로변에 lost 길을 잃은 collar 개 목걸이 owner 주인 address 주소 pick up the phone 전화를 받다 head over ~로 향하다

16 ②

W: Dad, you haven't forgotten about my piano recital on Friday, right? 아빠, 금요일에 있는 제 피아노 연주회를 잊지는 않으셨겠죠, 그렇죠?

M: Of course not! I'll get there as soon as I can.
물론 안 잊었지! 최대한 빨리 갈 거야.

W: Well, do you know what time you will be arriving to the recital hall?
그럼, 연주회장에 몇 시에 도착하실지 아세요?

M: I plan on leaving my office at seven P.M., so I'll probably get there by seven thirty at the latest. 내가 사무실에서 오후 7시에 출발할 예정이니까, 아마 늦어도 7시 30분까지는 거기에 도착할 거야.

W: Seven thirty? That's thirty minutes after the recital starts! What if you miss my performance?
7시 30분이요? 그건 연주회가 시작하고 30분 후예요! 아빠가 제 공연을 놓치면 어떻게 하죠?

M: Don't worry! You'll be the fifteenth person to

perform, so I'm sure I'll get there in time to watch you play. 걱정 말거라! 너는 15번째 연주자니, 아빠가 시간 맞춰 도착해서 네 연주를 볼 거란다.

W: Okay. I'll be looking for you in the audience, Dad. I'll be really disappointed if you're not there.
알겠어요. 저는 청중들 사이에서 아빠를 찾을 거예요. 만약 아빠가 없으면 정말 실망할 거예요.

M: Okay, sweetheart. I'll be there, I promise!
알았다, 귀염둥이야. 아빠는 거기 있을 거야, 약속해!

해설 아빠의 도착 예정 시간인 7시 30분은 연주회 시작 시각에서 30분 후라고 했으므로 연주회 시작 시각은 7시이다.

어휘 recital 연주회 at the latest (아무리) 늦어도 miss 놓치다 performance 공연 in time 시간 맞춰, 제시간에 audience 청중 disappointed 실망한

17 ⑤

M: Anna's friend Jenna lost her phone charger while using it in the library last week. So, Jenna asked Anna if she could borrow her phone charger because they use the same type of cellphone. Anna let Jenna use it, thinking that she would get it back the next day. However, Jenna didn't give it back. Anna couldn't charge her own phone for a whole week. Jenna kept using Anna's charger as if it was her own. She didn't even think of buying a new one for herself. Anna wanted to talk to Jenna about this situation. In this situation, what would Anna most likely have said to Jenna?

애나의 친구인 제나는 지난주에 도서관에서 휴대폰 충전기를 사용하다가 그것을 잃어버렸다. 그래서, 제나는 애나에게 그들이 똑같은 휴대폰을 사용하기 때문에 충전기를 빌릴 수 있는지 물어보았다. 애나는 제나에게 그것을 사용하게 해주었고, 다음 날 그것을 돌려 받을 생각을 했다. 그러나 제나는 그것을 돌려주지 않았다. 애나는 일주일 내내 본인의 휴대폰을 충전할 수 없었다. 제나는 애나의 충전기가 마치 자신의 것처럼 계속 사용했다. 그녀는 본인의 것을 새로 살 생각조차 하지 않았다. 애나는 제나에게 이런 상황에 대해서 얘기하고 싶었다. 이런 상황에서 애나가 제나에게 했을 말로 가장 적절한 것은 무엇인가?

Anna: Could I have my charger back now? I need to use it, too.
지금 내 휴대폰 충전기를 돌려줄 수 있니? 나도 그걸 사용해야 해.

① I think I lost my phone charger.
내 휴대폰 충전기를 잃어버린 것 같아.

② Is there an electrical outlet here?
여기에 전기 콘센트가 있니?

③ Did you break my phone charger?
네가 내 휴대폰 충전기를 고장 냈니?

④ You should buy me a new charger since you broke mine.
네가 내 것을 망가뜨렸으니 내게 새 충전기를 사줘야 해.

⑤ Could I have my charger back now? I need to use

it, too.
지금 내 휴대폰 충전기를 돌려줄 수 있니? 나도 그걸 사용해야 해.

어휘 charger 충전기 borrow 빌리다 cellphone 휴대폰 give something back ~을 돌려주다 charge 충전하다 whole 전체의 as if 마치 ~인 것처럼 electrical outlet 전기 콘센트 since ~이므로

18 ④

M: Good evening, ma'am. May I help you?
안녕하세요, 부인. 제가 도와드릴까요?

W: Yes. I got a text message earlier today saying that my fitness center membership has ended. I would like to sign up for another month, please.
네, 오늘 아침에 제 피트니스 회원권이 만료되었다는 문자 메시지를 받았어요. 한 달간 더 등록하고 싶어요.

M: Of course. I need your full name, phone number, and your identification card.
물론이죠. 전체 성함과 전화번호, 그리고 신분증이 필요합니다.

W: Alright, my name is Heather Morris, my phone number is two nine one, three four eight eight, and here is my ID card.
네, 제 이름은 헤더 모리스이고, 제 전화번호는 291-3488입니다. 그리고 여기 제 신분증이요.

M: Please wait a moment while I search for you in our database. [pause] Okay, I see that you have signed up for our monthly membership plan for the past few months. Would you be interested in signing up for three months instead of one?
제가 저희 데이터베이스에서 손님의 정보를 찾는 동안 잠시만 기다려 주세요. [잠시 후] 네, 지난 몇 개월 동안 저희 월 회원으로 등록해 주셨었네요. 혹시 1개월 말고 3개월 등록에 관심이 있으신가요?

W: Hmm… How much is the price difference between a one-month and a three-month membership?
음, 1개월과 3개월 회원권은 가격 차이가 얼마나 되죠?

M: Well, a three-month membership is only ten dollars more. So in my opinion, it would be a better choice. 음, 3개월 회원권은 10달러가 더 추가될 뿐이에요. 그래서 제 생각에는 그게 더 나은 선택인 것 같아요.

W: Oh! I didn't know that! Then I would like to sign up for the three-month membership, please.
아! 그건 몰랐네요! 그럼 3개월 회원권으로 등록할게요.

어휘 text message 문자 메시지 fitness center 피트니스 센터, 헬스클럽 membership 회원권 sign up for ~을 신청하다 full name 성과 이름을 합친 이름 identification card 신분증 (=ID card) database (정보)자료 monthly 매월의, 월별의 instead of ~대신에 difference 차이 in my opinion 내 의견으로는

19 ④

W: Greg, thanks so much for inviting me to your house! It looks like you spent a lot of time decorating it. It looks so nice!
그레그, 너희 집에 초대해 줘서 아주 고마워! 집을 꾸미느라 시간이 많이 들었겠구나. 무척 멋있어!

M: Thanks for the compliment! Yeah, it took me about two months to decorate all of the rooms. I even made a small library in my bedroom!
칭찬해 줘서 고마워! 맞아, 모든 방을 꾸미는 데 약 두 달이 걸렸어. 나는 심지어 내 침실에 작은 서재까지 만들었다니까.

W: Wow! That sounds amazing! Can you show it to me? I'd love to see your library.
우와! 놀라운데! 보여줄 수 있니? 네 서재가 보고 싶어.

M: Yes, of course! Follow me. [pause] Here it is! I organized all the books by genre. All the fiction books are on the top shelf, the science fiction books are on the second shelf, the mystery books are on the third shelf, and so on.
응, 물론이지! 따라와. [잠시 후] 여기야! 모든 책은 장르별로 정리했어. 모든 소설책은 제일 위 칸에, 공상과학소설은 두 번째 칸에, 그리고 미스터리 책은 세 번째 칸에, 이렇게 말이야.

W: Oh, my goodness! You have so many books here! It makes me want to sit down and start reading.
어머나! 넌 여기에 책이 정말 많이 있구나! 내가 여기 앉아서 책을 읽고 싶게 만들어.

M: Well, you're welcome to borrow them at any time! Just remember to return them after you're done reading them.
음, 언제든지 책을 빌리러 와! 다 읽고 돌려주는 것만 기억하면 돼.

W: That would be awesome! Then, can you recommend a book for me?
그럼 정말 멋지겠는데! 그럼 책 한 권을 나한테 추천해 줄래?

M: I think you would enjoy reading this fantasy book, *Wings of Fire*. 넌 이 판타지 소설 '윙즈 오브 파이어'를 재밌게 읽을 것 같아.

① Do you know how I can make a library card?
내가 어떻게 도서관 카드를 만들 수 있는지 아니?

② If you check out books today, they will be due in 2 weeks. 네가 만약 오늘 책을 빌려가면, 2주 후에 반납해야 해.

③ Well, you can always go to the library to check out a book. 음, 넌 도서관에 가면 항상 책을 대여할 수 있어.

④ I think you would enjoy reading this fantasy book, *Wings of Fire*.
넌 아 판타지 소설 '윙즈 오브 파이어'를 재밌게 읽을 것 같아.

⑤ The science fiction and mystery books are on the 3rd floor of the library.
공상과학소설과 추리소설은 도서관 3층에 있어.

어휘 decorate 꾸미다, 장식하다 compliment 칭찬, 찬사 library 도서관; 서재 organize 정리하다 genre 장르 fiction 소설 science fiction 공상과학소설 and so on 기타 등등 at any time 언제든지 awesome 엄청난, 끝내주는 check out (책을) 대출하다 due ~하기로 되어 있는, 예정된 floor 층; 바닥

20 ⑤

W: Henry, did you put on sunblock before coming out to the beach?
헨리, 넌 해변에 나오기 전에 자외선 차단제를 발랐니?

M: No, I completely forgot! What should I do?
아니, 난 까맣게 잊어버렸어! 어떻게 해야 하지?

W: I knew you'd forget. Here, I brought some in my backpack just in case. 네가 잊을 거란 걸 알고 있었어. 여기, 이럴 경우를 대비해서 내 배낭에 몇 개 챙겨 왔어.

M: What would I do without you? Thanks so much!
네가 없었으면 난 어떻게 했을까? 정말 고마워!

W: No problem. Did you bring the bucket and shovel to make sand castles? How about the beach towels?
천만에. 모래성을 만들 양동이랑 삽은 가져왔니? 비치 타월은?

M: Oh, my goodness! I forgot about those too! I don't know what's wrong with me today. Should we go to the store and buy some?
아, 이런! 난 그것도 잊어버렸어! 오늘 내가 왜 이러는지 모르겠어. 가게에 가서 좀 사와야 할까?

W: I thought you'd forget that, too. Don't worry, I bought some already before you got here.
난 네가 그것도 잊을 거라고 생각했어. 걱정 마, 네가 오기 전에 내가 좀 사뒀어.

M: You are amazing. I would be so lost without you. How do you remember everything so well?
넌 정말 대단하다. 네가 없었으면 난 정말 큰일 났을 거야. 모든 걸 다 어떻게 기억하니?

W: I make a list of things to do so I don't forget. You should try it, too. 나는 해야 할 일의 목록을 만들기 때문에 잊어버리지 않아. 너도 그렇게 해봐.

① Why didn't you pick up your phone? I called you 5 times.
왜 전화를 받지 않았니? 난 다섯 번이나 전화했어.

② I drove here early so I could see the sunrise in the morning.
나 아침에 해가 뜨는 것을 보기 위해 차를 타고 이곳에 일찍 왔어.

③ I think I'm going to be late to the beach. I'll be there in 20 minutes.
난 해변에 늦을 것 같아. 20분 후에 도착할 거야.

④ The store is down the street. You have to walk for about 10 minutes.
가게는 길 아래에 있어. 넌 10분 정도 걸어가야 할 거야.

⑤ I make a list of things to do so I don't forget. You should try it, too. 나는 해야 할 일의 목록을 만들기 때문에 잊어버리지 않아. 너도 그렇게 해봐.

어휘 sunblock 자외선 차단제 completely 완전히
backpack 배낭 just in case 만약을 위해 bucket 양동이
shovel 삽 sand castle 모래성 lost 어찌할 바를 모르는, 길을 잃은 sunrise 일출, 해돋이

01 ⑤	02 ②	03 ④	04 ③	05 ①
06 ①	07 ②	08 ⑤	09 ③	10 ②
11 ⑤	12 ②	13 ④	14 ①	15 ③
16 ④	17 ④	18 ⑤	19 ①	20 ⑤

01 ⑤

W: Joe, look! This is the poster I made for my favorite baseball player.
조, 여기를 봐! 이건 내가 좋아하는 야구 선수를 위해 만든 포스터야.

M: It looks cool! You used his uniform number, eighty-eight. 멋진데! 넌 그의 등번호인 88번을 활용했구나.

W: Yeah. I also added his last name, KIM, on the poster. 응. 그리고 난 그의 성인 '김'을 포스터에 추가했어.

M: Not bad. Then, why did you use a baseball bat icon?
나쁘지 않네. 그럼 넌 왜 야구 방망이 아이콘을 사용한 거니?

W: You know, he's known as a great hitter.
그러니까, 그는 대단한 타자로 알려져 있거든.

M: I see. And you put a heart shape under the last name, KIM.
알겠어. 그리고 넌 '김'이라는 성 밑에 하트 모양을 넣었구나.

W: Yes. I'm a big fan. 응. 난 열성적인 팬이거든.

어휘 favorite 좋아하는 cool 멋진 uniform number 등번호
add 추가하다, 더하다 last name (이름의) 성 icon 아이콘
hitter 타자 shape 모양 big fan 열성팬

02 ②

[Cellphone rings.] [휴대폰이 울린다.]

W: Hello. This is ABC Insurance Company. May I help you? 여보세요. ABC 보험사입니다. 무엇을 도와드릴까요?

M: Hello. This is Ray Wilson. My car suddenly stopped at seven oh two Main Street. Could you send somebody to help?
여보세요. 저는 레이 윌슨이라고 합니다. 제 차가 메인 가 702번지에서 갑자기 서 버렸어요. 사람을 보내서 도와주실 수 있나요?

W: Okay, but have you tried restarting your car?
네, 하지만 차의 시동을 다시 걸어 보셨나요?

M: Yes, I did. But it didn't work.
네, 해봤죠. 하지만 시동이 안 걸리네요.

W: I see. Someone should be there in about half an hour. 알겠습니다. 대략 30분 후에 사람이 그쪽으로 갈 겁니다.

M: Thank you so much. 정말 고맙습니다.

해설 'Could you send somebody to help?'에서 전화를 건 목적이 나온다.

어휘 insurance company 보험사 suddenly 갑자기
restart one's car ~의 차를 다시 시동을 걸다 work 작동하다 in half an hour 30분 후에

03 ④

① M: The escalator is <u>out of order</u>. 에스컬레이터가 고장 났어.
W: Let's <u>take</u> the <u>elevator</u>. 엘리베이터를 타자.

② M: Sorry. This elevator is <u>full</u>.
죄송합니다. 이 엘리베이터는 꽉 찼습니다.
W: Okay. I'll take the <u>next one</u>.
알겠어요. 다음 것을 탈게요.

③ M: Excuse me. Where is the elevator?
실례합니다. 엘리베이터가 어디 있나요?
W: Go <u>around the corner</u>. You'll see it.
모퉁이를 돌아서 가세요. 엘리베이터가 보일 겁니다.

④ M: <u>Which floor</u> are you going to? 몇 층에 가세요?
W: I'm <u>getting off</u> on the tenth floor. Thank you.
저는 10층에서 내려요. 고맙습니다.

⑤ M: <u>How</u> may I <u>help</u> you? 어떻게 도와드릴까요?
W: Hi. Can I <u>get</u> a <u>refund</u> on these?
안녕하세요. 이것들을 환불 받을 수 있을까요?

해설 손에 짐을 든 여자에게 남자가 층수를 묻고 엘리베이터 버튼을 대신 눌러주는 상황이다.

어휘 escalator 에스컬레이터 out of order 고장 난 take the elevator 엘리베이터를 타다 floor 층, 바닥 get off 내리다, 하차하다 get a refund 환불받다

04 ③

M: Hi, Sarah. <u>How's</u> your video project <u>going</u>?
안녕, 사라. 네 비디오 프로젝트는 어떻게 되어가고 있니?
W: Well, I'm <u>having</u> a <u>problem with</u> the movie software program. <u>I don't know how</u> to add music to my video clip. 음, 난 영화 소프트웨어 프로그램에 문제를 겪고 있어. 내 비디오 클립에 어떻게 음악을 덧붙이는지 모르겠어.
M: Oh, I can <u>help</u> you <u>with that</u>.
아, 그건 내가 도와줄 수 있어.
W: Great! If you're <u>free</u> this afternoon, can we <u>meet</u> at the <u>computer lab</u> and work on it?
좋아! 네가 오늘 오후에 시간이 나면 우리가 컴퓨터실에서 만나서 그것을 작업할 수 있을까?
M: <u>No problem</u>. Let's meet there at two o'clock!
문제 없어. 2시에 거기서 만나자.
W: Thanks! See you then. 고마워! 그때 봐.

어휘 video 비디오, 동영상 have a problem with ~에 문제가 있다 add 더하다, 덧붙이다 video clip 비디오 클립, 판촉용의 짧은 동영상 free 한가한, 시간이 있는 computer lab 컴퓨터실 work on ~을 작업하다

05 ①

M: How can I help you? 무엇을 도와드릴까요?
W: My <u>dog</u> got away from me and was <u>hit by</u> a <u>car</u>. I should have been holding her more tightly.
제 개가 저한테서 도망치다 차에 치었어요. 개를 더 꽉 잡고 있어야 했는데 말이죠.

M: All right. <u>Let me see</u>. [*pause*] Oh, it doesn't seem <u>that bad</u>, but she needs to get an X-ray.
좋습니다. 제가 한번 볼게요. [잠시 후] 아, 그렇게 심해 보이지는 않지만, 엑스레이를 찍어볼 필요는 있습니다.
W: Okay. Do you think she'll <u>recover quickly</u>?
네. 제 개가 빠르게 회복될 수 있을 거라고 생각하세요?
M: Well, I have to see her X-ray first and then I can tell you about it. 글쎄요, 개의 엑스레이를 먼저 봐야 하고, 그 다음에 그 문제에 관해 말씀 드릴 수 있을 것 같네요.
W: Oh, I see. 아, 알겠어요.

해설 dog, X-ray 등을 들었다면 정답을 고를 수 있다.

어휘 get away from ~에서 도망치다 be hit by a car 차에 치이다 hold 잡다, 쥐다 tightly 꽉, 단단히 get an X-ray 엑스레이를 찍다 recover 회복하다, 낫다

06 ①

W: Minsu, I have some <u>big news</u> for you.
민수야, 너한테 굉장한 소식이 있어.
M: Big news? Can I ask you what it is?
굉장한 소식? 그게 뭔지 물어봐도 되니?
W: You've been <u>accepted</u> to the <u>overseas volunteer</u> program you <u>applied</u> for last month. This is really good for you, Minsu! 네가 지난달에 신청했던 해외 자원봉사 프로그램에 합격했어. 이건 정말로 너한테 잘된 일이야, 민수야!
M: Really? I <u>can't believe</u> it! 정말이야? 믿을 수가 없네!
W: In addition, they <u>provide</u> a lot of interesting <u>field trips</u> for the volunteers. 덧붙이자면, 그들은 자원 봉사자들에게 많은 흥미로운 현장 학습을 제공한대.
M: That's wonderful. I <u>can't wait</u>! Thank you so much!
정말 굉장하네! 난 어서 빨리 가고 싶어! 정말 고마워!

해설 여자와 남자 모두 남자의 합격 사실에 들떠 있다.

어휘 big news 중대한 소식 be accepted 합격하다, 채택되다 overseas 해외의 volunteer 자원 봉사자 apply for ~에 지원하다 in addition 게다가, 덧붙여 provide 제공하다, 주다

07 ②

① M: What would you like to <u>eat for lunch</u>?
점심으로 뭘 먹고 싶나요?
W: I'm <u>not</u> that <u>hungry</u>. I'm going to <u>skip</u> lunch today.
저는 그렇게 배고프지 않아요. 오늘은 점심을 거를 거예요.

② M: Could you <u>give</u> me a <u>ride</u> to school?
저를 학교까지 차로 태워다 줄래요?
W: Yes. I can <u>walk</u> to school <u>by myself</u>.
네. 저는 혼자서 학교까지 걸어갈 수 있어요.

③ M: Eating breakfast is <u>important for</u> good health.
아침식사를 하는 것은 좋은 건강을 위해 중요해.
W: You can say that <u>again</u>. 맞는 말이야.

④ M: <u>What</u> is your <u>hobby</u>? 네 취미는 뭐니?
W: I like <u>singing</u> and <u>dancing</u>.
나는 노래 부르기와 춤 추기를 좋아해.

⑤ M: How long will it take to get my order?
　　제 주문품을 받는 데 얼마나 오래 걸릴까요?

W: It should be delivered within about three days.
　　약 3일 이내에 배달될 겁니다.

해설 'You can say that again.'은 '정말 그래', '전적으로 동의해'라는 의미로, 상대방에게 맞장구를 칠 때 사용하는 표현이다.

어휘 skip 거르다, 건너뛰다　give somebody a ride ~을 차로 태워 주다　by oneself 혼자서, 스스로　hobby 취미　get one's order 주문한 것을 받다　deliver 배달하다, 배송하다　within ~이내에

08 ⑤

[Cellphone rings.] [휴대폰이 울린다.]

W: Hello, Kevin. 여보세요, 케빈.

M: Hi, Tiffany. I think I left my English book in your kitchen when I came over to study.
　　안녕, 티파니. 내 생각에는 내가 공부하러 들렀을 때 너희 집 부엌에 영어책을 놓고 온 것 같아.

W: You did. I was just about to call you. Should I bring it to your house later? 맞아. 나도 너한테 전화를 하려는 참이었어. 내가 나중에 그걸 너네 집으로 가지고 갈까?

M: You don't have to do that. Could you just bring it to school tomorrow?
　　넌 그럴 필요는 없어. 그냥 내일 학교로 그것을 가지고 올래?

W: No problem. See you tomorrow. 문제 없어. 내일 보자.

어휘 come over ~의 집에 들르다　be about to 막 ~하려는 참이다　later 나중에　don't have to ~할 필요가 없다

09 ③

W: Michael, what are you doing? 마이클, 너 뭐 하니?

M: Hey, Kate. I'm searching online for the cheapest round-trip ticket to the Grand Canyon.
　　얘, 케이트. 나는 그랜드 캐니언으로 가는 가장 저렴한 왕복 티켓을 인터넷으로 찾고 있었어.

W: Wow! When are you planning to go?
　　와! 언제 가려고 계획하고 있는데?

M: During the second week of March. My spring break starts then. 3월 둘째 주 동안에. 내 봄방학이 그때 시작하거든.

W: Oh, I envy you. I wish I could go, too.
　　아, 네가 부러워. 나도 갈 수 있으면 좋겠다.

M: Really? If you want to go, we can go together.
　　정말? 네가 가고 싶으면 우리는 함께 갈 수 있어.

W: I'd like to, but I have to work part-time at the school library during the break. 나도 가고 싶지만, 방학 동안에 학교 도서관에서 아르바이트를 해야 해.

해설 'I'd like to, but ~', 'I'd love to, but ~'과 같은 표현 뒤에는 거절의 내용이 이어진다.

어휘 search online 온라인으로 검색하다, 인터넷에서 찾다　cheapest 가장 저렴한(cheap-cheaper-cheapest)　round-trip ticket 왕복 티켓　spring break 봄방학　then 그때;

그러면　envy 부러워하다　work part-time 파트타임으로 일하다, 아르바이트를 하다

10 ②

W: Excuse me, I'd like to buy a sports uniform.
　　실례합니다만, 운동복을 사고 싶어요.

M: How about this one? It's fifty dollars.
　　이건 어떤가요? 50달러입니다.

W: Yes, I like it. I also need a pair of running shoes. Do you have any?
　　네, 마음에 드네요. 운동화 한 켤레도 필요해요. 운동화가 있나요?

M: Over here. These are our best sellers. They're forty dollars. 이쪽으로요. 이게 우리 가게에서 가장 잘 팔리는 물건입니다. 40달러예요.

W: I like the design, but I'm afraid I can't afford them both. I'll just take the sports uniform for now.
　　디자인은 마음에 드는데, 두 개를 전부 살 여유가 없네요. 우선은 운동복만 살게요.

M: Okay. Here you are. 네, 여기 있습니다.

해설 운동복과 운동화의 가격을 묻고 나서 결국 운동복만 구입했다.

어휘 sports uniform 운동복, 스포츠 유니폼　a pair of 한 켤레의, 한 쌍의　running shoes 운동화　over here 이쪽으로　best seller 잘 나가는 상품　afford (살 수 있는) 여유가 되다　both 둘 다　for now 우선은, 현재로서는

11 ⑤

M: Hello, may I help you? 안녕하세요, 제가 도와드릴까요?

W: Yes. I dropped my cellphone on the floor, and its screen got broken.
　　네, 제가 휴대폰을 바닥에 떨어뜨렸는데, 화면이 깨졌어요.

M: That's too bad. You have to replace it with a new one. It'll cost about one hundred dollars.
　　정말 안됐군요. 화면을 새것으로 교체하셔야 합니다. 약 100달러가 들 거예요.

W: Okay. How long does it take to get it fixed?
　　좋아요. 그걸 고치는 데 얼마나 걸릴까요?

M: It usually takes about two hours. Why don't you have a coffee in the lobby and read a magazine or something? 보통은 두 시간 정도가 걸려요. 로비에서 커피 한 잔 드시고 잡지를 읽거나 다른 뭔가를 하시는 게 어때요?

W: Thanks, but I think I'll go shopping and come back later. 고맙지만, 쇼핑을 갔다가 이따가 돌아오려고 해요.

어휘 drop 떨어뜨리다　cellphone 휴대폰　floor 바닥　screen 화면　broken 깨진, 고장 난　replace A with B A를 B로 교체하다　cost 비용이 들다　get something fixed ~을 고치다　lobby 로비　magazine 잡지　later 나중에, 이따가

12 ②

M: Good morning. This is your English teacher, Mr. Han speaking. Are you interested in showing off your spelling skills? I'm inviting you to attend this year's Spelling Genius Contest! It'll be held on May fifth. The winner will get a trophy and a fifty-dollar gift card. To sign up, please download the application form from our school website, and hand it in to my office by Friday, April twentieth. Thank you!

안녕하세요. 저는 여러분의 영어 교사인 한 선생님입니다. 여러분의 철자법 실력을 뽐내는 데 관심이 있나요? 여러분을 올해의 스펠링 지니어스 콘테스트에 초대합니다! 콘테스트는 5월 5일에 열립니다. 우승자는 트로피와 50달러의 상품권을 받게 됩니다. 신청을 하려면 우리 학교 웹사이트에서 신청 양식을 다운로드해서 4월 20일 금요일까지 제 사무실로 제출해 주세요. 고맙습니다!

어휘 This is ~ speaking 저는 ~입니다 be interested in ~에 관심이 있다 show off 자랑하다, 뽐내다 spelling 철자법, 맞춤법 skill 능력, 기술 invite 초대하다 attend 참가하다 genius 천재 contest 대회, 콘테스트 be held 열리다 winner 우승자 trophy 트로피 gift card 상품권 sign up 등록하다, 신청하다 download 다운로드하다, 내려받다 application form 신청 양식 hand in 제출하다

13 ④

W: Look, Jason. There are five sections left for the monthly flea market. Which section would be best for us? 얘, 제이슨. 월례 벼룩시장에 다섯 개의 구역이 남았어. 어떤 구역이 우리에게 가장 좋을까?

M: The sections next to the restroom are not good. I don't like the smell.
화장실 옆에 있는 구역은 안 좋아. 난 그 냄새를 싫어해.

W: You're right. Then, what about section C?
네 말이 맞아. 그럼 C구역은 어때?

M: It's too far from the entrance.
거긴 입구에서 너무 멀리 떨어져 있어.

W: Well, we have two options now. Which section do you think is better? 음, 우리에게는 이제 두 개의 선택권이 있어. 네 생각에는 어떤 구역이 더 좋은 것 같아?

M: I think the section right next to the information booth is better because there'll be more people walking by. 내 생각에는 더 많은 사람들이 지나다닐 것이기 때문에, 안내소 바로 옆에 있는 구역이 더 좋은 것 같아.

W: Good! Let's take that section then.
좋아! 그럼 그 구역을 차지하자.

해설 화장실 옆에 있는 구역은 A, B 구역이고, C구역도 입구에서 멀다는 이유로 선택하지 않았다. Information 바로 옆에 있는 구역은 D 구역이다.

어휘 section 구역 left 남은 monthly 월례의 flea market 벼룩시장 next to ~의 옆에 restroom 화장실 smell 냄새

far from ~로부터 먼 entrance 입구 option 선택권 information booth 안내소 walk by ~을 지나가다

14 ①

W: This is a device that is used in many different places. For example, you can see it in bakeries, grocery stores, seafood markets, or even in factories. It is a machine for measuring the weight of an object. To do so, you usually put an object on top of it. It was made of two balanced dishes in the old days, but electronic ones are more popular now.

이것은 많은 다른 장소에서 사용되는 기기입니다. 예를 들어, 당신은 제과점, 식료품점, 해산물 시장, 또는 심지어 공장에서도 이것을 볼 수 있습니다. 이것은 물건의 무게를 재는 기계입니다. 그렇게 하려면 당신은 보통 물건을 이것의 위에 올려 놓습니다. 이것은 옛날에는 두 개의 균형이 잡힌 접시로 만들어졌지만, 지금은 전자 방식이 더 인기 있습니다.

어휘 device 기기, 장치 grocery store 식료품점 seafood 해산물 factory 공장 measure 측정하다, 재다 weight 무게 object 물건, 물체 on top of ~의 위에 be made of ~으로 만들어지다 balanced 균형 잡힌 in the old days 예전에는 electronic 전자의

15 ③

W: Thomas, it's raining really hard outside! Did you bring an umbrella?
토머스, 밖에 비가 엄청나게 세게 내리고 있어! 넌 우산을 가져왔니?

M: No, I didn't. I hope it stops before our class finishes.
아니, 안 가져왔어. 우리 수업이 끝나기 전에 비가 그치면 좋을 텐데.

W: It looks like it's not going to stop anytime soon, but don't worry. I have an extra.
비는 금방 그칠 것 같지는 않지만 걱정 마. 나한테 또 하나가 있어.

M: Really? May I borrow it? 정말? 내가 그걸 빌려도 돼?

W: Sure. It's in my locker. I'll go get it for you.
물론이지. 그건 내 사물함 안에 있어. 내가 가서 가져올게.

M: Thank you, Rachel. 고마워, 레이첼.

어휘 rain hard 비가 세차게 내리다 outside 밖에 umbrella 우산 look like ~인 것 같다 anytime soon (부정문, 의문문에서) 곧 extra 여분의 것 borrow 빌리다 locker 사물함

16 ④

M: Mom, you look so busy. Is there anything I can help you with? 엄마, 바쁘신 것 같아요. 제가 도와드릴 일이 있어요?

W: Sure. I'm making a pizza. I need tomato sauce and two red peppers. 물론. 내가 피자를 만들고 있거든. 토마토 소스와 빨간 피망 두 개가 필요하단다.

M: I can get them for you. Are they in the fridge?
제가 갖다 드릴 수 있어요. 그게 냉장고 안에 있나요?

W: Yes, next to the cheese. Oh, I forgot to get some

mushrooms for the topping.
응, 치즈 옆에. 아, 토핑으로 쓸 버섯 몇 개를 사오는 걸 잊어버렸네.

M: Don't worry. I can go to the supermarket to get some. 걱정 마세요. 제가 슈퍼마켓에 가서 몇 개 사올 수 있어요.

W: Thank you. 고맙다.

어휘 red pepper 붉은 피망, 붉은 고추 fridge 냉장고 mushroom 버섯 topping 토핑, 고명

17 ④

M: Jenny works for a family restaurant. Since today is Saturday, there're so many customers, and she's very busy serving them. Jenny notices that a customer has left his sunglasses on the table where he was eating. He's about to pay his bill and leave the restaurant. Jenny runs to the customer with the sunglasses. In this situation, what would Jenny most likely say to the customer?

제니는 패밀리 레스토랑에서 일한다. 오늘이 토요일이기 때문에 손님들이 아주 많고, 그녀는 손님들에게 음식을 내오느라 무척 바쁘다. 제니는 한 손님이 식사를 했던 테이블 위에 선글라스를 놓고 간 것을 알아차린다. 손님은 돈을 계산하고 음식점을 나가려고 하는 참이다. 제니는 선글라스를 가지고 손님에게 달려간다. 이런 상황에서 제니는 손님에게 어떤 말을 하겠는가?

Jenny: I'm afraid you forgot your sunglasses.
손님이 선글라스를 잊으신 것 같아요.

① Did you enjoy your meal?
음식은 맛있게 드셨나요?
② I apologize for my mistake.
제 실수를 사과 드립니다.
③ I'll give you a refund if you want.
원하신다면 환불을 해드리겠습니다.
④ I'm afraid you forgot your sunglasses.
손님이 선글라스를 잊으신 것 같아요.
⑤ The restaurant is fully booked on Saturdays.
음식점은 토요일마다 예약이 꽉 찹니다.

어휘 work for ~에서 일하다 since ~이므로 customer 손님, 고객 serve 음식을 제공하다 notice 알아차리다 be about to 막 ~하려는 참이다 pay one's bill 돈을 계산하다 I'm afraid 유감이지만 ~이다 enjoy one's meal ~의 식사를 즐기다 apologize for ~에 대해 사과하다 mistake 실수 give a refund 환불해 주다 fully booked 예약이 꽉 찬

18 ⑤

[Cellphone rings.] [휴대폰이 울린다.]

W: Hello, John. Where are you? 여보세요, 존. 너 어디 있니?

M: I'm working on my science project at Billy's house. What are you doing? 저는 빌리네 집에서 과학 과제를 하고 있어요. 뭐 하고 계세요?

W: I just finished grocery shopping. If you want, I can drop by Tom's Bakery and get something for you.

방금 장을 봤지. 네가 원하면 톰스 베이커리에 들러서 뭘 좀 사다 줄게.

M: No thanks, Mom. I don't need anything. Are you going home?
괜찮아요, 엄마. 아무것도 필요 없어요. 집에 가시는 거예요?

W: Yes. I'll be leaving here in a few minutes.
응. 몇 분 후에 여길 떠날 거다.

M: That's great. I'm almost done with my school work. Could you pick me up on your way home?
좋네요. 제 학교 과제가 거의 끝났거든요. 집으로 가는 길에 저를 태워 가실 수 있어요?

W: No problem! I'll be there in about twenty minutes.
문제 없지! 한 20분 후에 거기로 가마.

어휘 work on ~을 작업하다 project 과제, 프로젝트 grocery shopping 장보기 drop by 잠깐 들르다 pick somebody up ~을 차에 태우다 on one's way home 집으로 가는 길에

19 ①

M: Have you done your assignment on the green house effect? 넌 온실 효과에 관한 과제를 끝냈니?

W: Almost. How about you? 거의. 너는 어때?

M: I haven't even started yet. I don't know how to get the information.
난 아직 시작도 안 했어. 어떻게 정보를 얻어야 할지 모르겠어.

W: Did you check the school library?
학교 도서관은 확인해 봤니?

M: Yeah. I went there yesterday, but people had already checked out all the books on that topic.
응. 어제 거기 갔었는데, 사람들이 이미 그 주제에 대한 모든 책을 대출해 갔더라고.

W: Actually, I checked out two books on Monday, but I returned them this afternoon. 사실은 내가 월요일에 두 권의 책을 대출했는데, 오늘 오후에 반납했어.

M: Great. Then, I should go to the library right now.
좋은데. 그럼 난 지금 바로 도서관에 가야겠어.

① Great. Then, I should go to the library right now.
좋은데. 그럼 난 지금 바로 도서관에 가야겠어.
② You need a library card to borrow a book.
넌 책을 빌리려면 도서관 카드가 필요해.
③ Well, the book is too difficult to read.
음, 그 책은 너무 읽기 어려워.
④ Right. We should protect our planet.
맞아. 우리는 우리의 행성을 보호해야 해.
⑤ I couldn't return the book earlier.
나는 더 일찍 책을 반납할 수 없었어.

해설 여자가 오늘 오후에 책을 반납했으므로 도서관에는 남자가 찾는 책이 있을 것이다.

어휘 assignment 과제 green house effect 온실 효과 information 정보 check 확인하다, 점검하다 check out (책을) 대출하다 topic 주제 library card 도서관 카드 protect 보호하다 planet 행성 earlier 더 일찍(early-earlier-earliest)

20 ⑤

W: Hey, Mike. What's wrong? Are you okay?
얘, 마이크. 무슨 문제 있니? 너 괜찮아?

M: Yeah. I just didn't do well on the math test.
응. 난 그저 수학 시험을 잘 못 봤을 뿐이야.

W: I can't believe it. You always get perfect scores in math. 믿을 수가 없는데. 넌 항상 수학에서 만점을 받잖아.

M: Maybe before, but this time I made so many foolish mistakes. 아마도 전에는 그랬겠지만, 이번에는 바보 같은 실수를 너무 많이 했어.

W: Don't feel bad. This kind of thing happens to everyone. 속상해하지 마. 이런 종류의 일은 누구에게나 일어나.

M: Well, I don't know. I don't feel confident any more.
글쎄, 난 모르겠어. 난 더 이상 자신감이 없어.

W: Don't worry about it. You'll do better next time.
그건 걱정하지 마. 다음에는 더 잘할 거야.

① Okay. I'll go to the hospital later.
알았어. 나중에 병원에 갈게.

② Oh, no. I should have studied harder.
아, 안돼. 난 좀 더 열심히 공부를 했어야 해.

③ Right. I have a math exam tomorrow.
맞아. 난 내일 수학 시험이 있어.

④ Never mind. I can take care of myself.
신경 쓰지 마. 난 나 자신을 돌볼 수 있어.

⑤ Don't worry about it. You'll do better next time.
그건 걱정하지 마. 다음에는 더 잘할 거야.

어휘 do well 잘하다   get perfect scores 만점을 받다
make mistakes 실수를 저지르다   foolish 바보 같은
feel bad 속이 상하다   confident 자신감 있는   harder 더 열심히
never mind 신경 쓰지 마   take care of 돌보다, 보살피다

02회 기출 듣기평가

본문 p.274-275

01 ④	02 ③	03 ⑤	04 ②	05 ②
06 ⑤	07 ④	08 ④	09 ①	10 ②
11 ④	12 ⑤	13 ③	14 ①	15 ③
16 ③	17 ⑤	18 ①	19 ③	20 ①

01 ④

W: Let's take a break. We've been sitting too long.
좀 쉬자. 우리는 너무 오래 앉아 있었어.

M: Hey, I learned some stretches. This will help. First, put your right hand behind your head like this.
있잖아, 내가 스트레칭을 몇 가지 배웠거든. 이게 도움이 될 거야.
먼저 네 오른손을 이렇게 네 머리 뒤에 대.

W: Okay. Now what? 알았어. 그리고 이제는?

M: Then, hold your right elbow with your left hand.

And gently pull your elbow to the left.
그리고 나서 네 왼손으로 네 오른쪽 팔꿈치를 잡아. 그리고 네 팔꿈치를 왼쪽으로 부드럽게 당겨.

W: Oh, I feel the stretch in my muscles.
아, 내 근육들이 땅겨지는 게 느껴져.

M: Hold it for ten seconds and then do it again.
10초 동안 그대로 있다가 그 동작을 다시 해 봐.

어휘 take a break 휴식을 취하다, 쉬다   stretch 스트레칭,
(근육의) 당김; 늘이다   behind ~뒤에   hold 유지하다, 잡다
elbow 팔꿈치   gently 부드럽게   pull 당기다   muscle 근육

02 ③

[Cellphone rings.] [휴대폰이 울린다.]

M: Hello, Mary. This is Brian. Where are you?
여보세요, 메리. 나 브라이언이야. 너 어디 있니?

W: Hi, Brian. I'm about to leave the school library.
안녕, 브라이언. 난 막 학교 도서관을 떠나려던 참이야.

M: Good. Can you do me a favor?
잘됐다. 내 부탁 좀 들어 줄래?

W: Sure. What is it? 응. 뭔데?

M: I'm going to Jeju Island with my family next week.
Can you check out a Jeju guidebook for me?
내가 다음 주에 우리 가족과 함께 제주도에 가거든. 나 대신 제주도 안내서를 대출해 줄래?

W: No problem. I'd be glad to. 문제 없어. 그렇게 할게.

어휘 do somebody a favor ~의 부탁을 들어주다   check out
(책을) 대출하다   guidebook 안내서

03 ⑤

① W: How long will it take to get my bag fixed?
제 가방을 고치는 데 얼마나 걸릴까요?

M: It'll take about a week. 일주일 정도 걸릴 겁니다.

② W: I bought you a new pair of shoes for your birthday.
내가 네 생일 선물로 새 신발 한 켤레를 샀어.

M: Really? Thank you so much. 그래? 정말 고마워.

③ W: I lost my bag. What should I do?
제 가방을 잃어버렸어요. 저는 어떻게 해야 하죠?

M: You should fill out this form first.
먼저 이 양식을 작성해 주십시오.

④ W: When does the shoe-making class start?
신발 만들기 수업은 언제 시작하죠?

M: It begins next Monday. 다음 주 월요일에 시작합니다.

⑤ W: These shoes feel so loose. Could you show me another pair?
이 신발은 너무 헐겁게 느껴지네요. 다른 것을 보여주실 수 있나요?

M: Sure. Let me go get them for you.
물론이죠. 제가 가져다 드릴게요.

어휘 get one's bag fixed ~의 가방을 고치다   take (시간이)
걸리다   a pair of shoes 신발 한 켤레   fill out a form 양식을
작성하다, 서류를 기재하다   loose 헐거운, 느슨한   pair 켤레, 쌍

04 ②

W: Hello, Justin! What's up? 안녕, 저스틴! 무슨 일이야?

M: Hi, Linda. I heard you're <u>transferring to</u> a new school next <u>Friday</u>. 안녕, 린다. 네가 다음 주 금요일에 새로운 학교로 전학 간다는 소리를 들었어.

W: Yeah, that's true. I'll <u>miss you</u>. 응, 사실이야. 난 네가 그리울 거야.

M: Me, too. Why don't we <u>have lunch</u> together this <u>Saturday</u>? 나도 그래. 우리 이번 주 토요일에 점심을 같이 먹는 게 어떨까?

W: <u>Sorry</u>, <u>but</u> I have to help my parents pack stuff during the weekend. <u>What about</u> on <u>Monday</u>? 미안하지만 난 주말 동안에는 우리 부모님이 물건을 싸는 걸 도와야 해. 월요일은 어때?

M: <u>Okay</u>. I'll <u>see you</u> at the school cafeteria <u>at noon</u>. 좋아. 정오에 학교 식당에서 보자.

해설 처음에 제시된 요일은 거부당하고 'What about~?'에 정답이 되는 요일이 등장한다.

어휘 transfer to a new school 새로운 학교로 옮기다   next Friday 다음 주 금요일   miss 그리워하다; 놓치다   pack (짐을) 싸다, 꾸리다   stuff 물건   cafeteria 구내식당, 카페테리아

05 ②

W: Dad, look! There's a <u>parrot</u>. 아빠, 저것 봐요! 앵무새가 있어요.

M: Oh, it <u>looks</u> so <u>real</u>. 아, 진짜같이 보이는구나.

W: Yeah. It even <u>sounds like</u> a parrot. That's great. 네. 심지어 소리도 앵무새 같아요. 굉장해요.

M: It also has colorful <u>feathers</u> though they're <u>made of plastic</u>. 그건 플라스틱으로 만들어졌지만 다양한 색깔의 깃털도 가지고 있네.

W: Dad, can you <u>buy</u> me this one? 아빠, 저 이거 사주실 수 있어요?

M: Okay. It's your birthday. If that's what you want, I'll buy it for you. 그래. 네 생일이잖아. 그게 네가 원하는 거라면 사줄게.

W: Thanks, Dad. 고마워요, 아빠.

어휘 parrot 앵무새   look real 진짜같이 보이다   colorful 형형색색의, 다채로운 색깔의   feather 깃털   be made of ~으로 만들어지다

06 ⑤

M: Sumi, why didn't you <u>hand in</u> your <u>homework</u>? 수미야, 넌 왜 숙제를 제출하지 않았니?

W: What? I <u>emailed</u> it last Friday. 네? 전 지난 금요일에 숙제를 이메일로 보냈는데요.

M: You just wrote your name and student number with <u>no attached file</u>. 넌 첨부 파일 없이 네 이름하고 학생 번호만 적었더구나.

W: Oh, I'm so <u>sorry</u>. I didn't know that. Can I send the file this afternoon? 아, 정말 죄송해요. 제가 그걸 몰랐어요. 제가 오늘 오후에 파일을 보내도 되나요?

M: <u>I'm afraid</u> that's not possible. The deadline was last Friday. 미안하지만 그건 안 될 것 같다. 마감일은 지난 금요일이었어.

W: Oh, no! I <u>can't believe</u> that I <u>made</u> such a big <u>mistake</u>. 아, 안돼. 제가 그렇게 큰 실수를 저질렀다니 믿을 수가 없네요.

어휘 hand in 제출하다, 내다   attached file 첨부파일   deadline 마감일, 데드라인   make a mistake 실수를 저지르다   bored 지루한   satisfied 만족한   thankful 고마운   frustrated 좌절한

07 ④

① M: <u>How</u> would you like to <u>pay</u>? 어떻게 지불하시겠습니까?
   W: By <u>credit card</u>. 신용카드로요.

② M: I was <u>disappointed</u> with the film. 난 그 영화에 실망했어.
   W: You were? I <u>felt</u> the <u>same</u> way. 너 그랬어? 나도 똑같이 느꼈어.

③ M: This <u>jacket</u> is too <u>big</u> for me. 이 재킷은 저한테 너무 크네요.
   W: Would you like to <u>exchange</u> it for a <u>smaller</u> one? 더 작은 것으로 교환하시겠습니까?

④ M: <u>When</u> do you think we can <u>finish</u> the <u>project</u>? 넌 우리가 언제 프로젝트를 끝낼 수 있을 거라고 생각해?
   W: I <u>don't know whether</u> you like it or not. 난 네가 그걸 좋아하는지 안 좋아하는지 모르겠어.

⑤ M: You look so <u>pretty</u>! Is that a new <u>dress</u>? 넌 정말 예쁘구나! 그거 새 옷이야?
   W: Yes. It's a <u>birthday</u> gift from my mom. 응. 우리 엄마가 주신 생일 선물이야.

해설 ④에서 when으로 질문했으므로 날짜나 시간 등의 때를 포함하여 답변해야 한다.

어휘 pay 지불하다   be disappointed with ~에 실망하다   film 영화   feel the same way 똑같이 느끼다   whether ~ or not ~인지 아닌지

08 ④

M: Helen, I've heard the <u>movie</u>, *The Man from Somewhere*, is a box-office <u>hit</u>. Have you seen it? 헬렌, 난 '어딘가에서 온 사람'이라는 영화가 흥행하고 있다고 들었어. 넌 그 영화를 봤니?

W: No, not yet. 아니, 아직이야.

M: Why don't we go <u>see</u> it <u>Friday</u> night? 우리 금요일 밤에 그걸 보러 가지 않을래?

W: I'd love to, <u>but</u> I <u>wonder</u> if there are <u>tickets available</u>. 나도 그러고 싶은데 표를 구할 수 있을지 모르겠네.

M: I can <u>check</u> for tickets with my <u>cellphone</u> right now. [pause] Oh, there are <u>still</u> a few <u>left</u>. 내가 지금 휴대폰으로 티켓을 확인할 수 있어. [잠시 후] 아, 아직 몇 장 남아 있어.

W: That's good. Can you book them for us? Then, I'll buy some popcorn.
좋은데. 네가 우리 표를 예매해 줄래? 그러면 내가 팝콘을 살게.

M: That sounds perfect. 아주 좋은 생각이야.

해설 여자의 대사 'Can you ~?'에 부탁의 내용이 있다.

어휘 somewhere 어딘가에 box-office hit 흥행 영화 available 구할 수 있는, 이용할 수 있는 check 확인하다, 점검하다 cellphone 휴대폰 right now 지금, 당장 book 예약하다

09 ①

M: Honey, I have a special present for you. Please close your eyes.
여보, 당신한테 줄 특별한 선물이 있어요. 눈을 감아 봐요.

W: Okay. What is it? 알았어요. 그게 뭔데요?

M: Now open your eyes and look at this.
이제 눈을 뜨고 이걸 봐요.

W: Wow! It's a new bookshelf. Did you make it yourself?
와! 새 책꽂이잖아요. 당신이 직접 만들었어요?

M: Of course! You're such a bookworm. I hope you like it. 물론이죠! 당신은 대단한 책벌레잖아요. 당신 마음에 들었으면 좋겠어요.

W: Yeah, I love it. There couldn't be a better present for me. 아주 마음에 들어요. 저에게 이보다 더 좋은 선물은 없을 거예요.

해설 'There couldn't be a better present.' 더 좋은 선물은 없을 거라고 말함으로써 감사하는 마음을 표현했다.

어휘 close one's eyes 눈을 감다 open one's eyes 눈을 뜨다 bookshelf 책꽂이 bookworm 책벌레

10 ②

M: Did you enjoy your meal? 식사는 즐거우셨어요?

W: Yes, very much. Thank you. How much do I owe you? 네, 대단히요. 고맙습니다. 제가 얼마를 드리면 되죠?

M: You had the T-bone steak, French fries, and a salad. So your total is thirty dollars. 손님은 티본 스테이크, 감자튀김, 그리고 샐러드를 드셨네요. 그래서 합계 금액은 30달러입니다.

W: That's with a fifty percent discount, right?
그게 50% 할인이 적용된 거죠, 그렇죠?

M: Yes, the regular price for the same meal is sixty dollars. This is the price of the discounted lunch special. 네, 같은 음식에 대한 정가는 60달러입니다. 이건 할인된 점심 특선 메뉴 가격이고요.

W: Thank you. It was delicious. Here's my credit card.
고맙습니다. 맛있었어요. 여기 제 신용카드요.

해설 지불할 금액은 'total is ~'와 함께 나올 수 있다.

어휘 enjoy meal 식사를 즐기다 owe 빚지고 있다 French fries 감자 튀김 total 합계 discount 할인 regular price 정가 lunch special 점심 특선 메뉴

11 ④

M: Excuse me. Can you give me a wake-up call for seven A.M.? I have a plane to catch tomorrow morning. 실례합니다. 오전 7시에 제게 모닝콜을 해주시겠어요? 내일 아침에 비행기를 타야 하거든요.

W: Sure. What's your room number?
물론입니다. 객실 번호가 무엇인가요?

M: It's room nine oh two. 902호예요.

W: Okay! Is there anything else I can help you with?
네! 제가 더 도와드릴 건 없을까요?

M: I'll need a taxi to the airport at eight A.M.
저는 오전 8시에 공항으로 가는 택시가 필요해요.

W: No problem. I'll have one ready for you.
문제 없습니다. 손님을 위해 한 대 준비해 놓겠습니다.

해설 대화 장소를 먼저 추측해 본다. wake-up call 서비스를 해주는 곳은 호텔이다.

어휘 give a wake-up call 모닝콜을 해주다 catch a plane 비행기를 잡아타다 have something ready ~을 준비하다

12 ⑤

M: Are you looking for an English camp? Our Angel English Camp was founded in two thousand. We provide modern dormitory facilities as well as high-tech computer labs to promote a quality learning environment. The camp is located in Ottawa. Our program includes English conversation in the morning and sports activities in the afternoon. For more information, visit our website, www dot angelenglishcamp dot com.

영어 캠프를 찾고 계세요? 저희 앤젤 영어 캠프는 2000년에 설립되었습니다. 저희는 양질의 학습 환경을 촉진하기 위해 첨단 컴퓨터 실험실뿐만 아니라 현대적인 기술사 시설을 제공합니다. 캠프는 오타와에 위치해 있습니다. 저희 프로그램은 오전에는 영어 회화, 그리고 오후에는 스포츠 활동을 포함합니다. 보다 자세한 정보를 얻으려면 저희 웹사이트인 www.angelenglishcamp.com을 방문하세요.

어휘 English camp 영어 캠프 found 설립하다 provide 주다, 제공하다 modern 현대적인 dormitory 기숙사 facility 시설 as well as ~뿐만 아니라 high-tech 첨단 기술의 lab 실험실 promote 촉진하다 quality 양질의; 품질 be located in ~에 위치해 있다 include 포함하다 activity 활동 for more information 더 자세한 정보를 얻으려면

13 ③

W: Honey, where should we park at the airport?
여보, 우리가 공항에서 어디에 주차해야 할까요?

M: Hmm, the long-term parking is cheaper, isn't it?
음, 장기 주차가 저렴하죠, 그렇지 않아요?

W: Right, but it's too far from the entrances.
맞아요, 하지만 입구에서 너무 멀리 떨어져 있어요.

M: Then, we can park in the short-term parking lot.
그렇다면 우리는 단기 주차장에 주차할 수 있겠네요.

W: What about section A or B? We can exchange some money at the bank before boarding. A구역이나 B구역은 어때요? 우리는 탑승 전에 은행에서 돈을 좀 환전할 수 있어요.

M: But section C is closest to our airline's entrance. It would be convenient to check in first because we have a lot of baggage. 하지만 C구역이 우리가 비행기를 타는 입구에서 가장 가까워요. 우리가 짐이 많기 때문에 먼저 탑승 수속을 밟는 것이 편리할 거예요.

W: I agree. Then let's park there. 당신 말이 맞아요. 그럼 거기에 주차해요.

해설 한 번 언급한 위치나 내용을 'it,' 'there' 등으로 받아서 대화를 이어가기 때문에 앞서 언급된 내용을 잘 기억하면서 들어야 한다.

어휘 park 주차하다 long-term 장기간의 cheaper 더 저렴한(cheap-cheaper-cheapest) far from ~에서부터 먼 entrance 입구 short-term 단기간의 parking lot 주차장 section 구역 boarding 탑승 convenient 편리한 check in 탑승 수속을 밟다, 체크인하다 baggage 수하물, 짐

14 ①

W: This is a team sport using a ball. You can play it both indoors and outdoors. The goal is high above the ground. A net is attached to a metal ring on a board, and the bottom of the net is open. People score by throwing the ball into the net. You don't need any other equipment to play. You can dribble the ball with your hands, but not with your feet.

이것은 공을 사용하는 단체 경기예요. 당신은 이것을 실내와 야외 모두에서 할 수 있어요. 골문은 지상으로부터 높은 곳에 있어요. 판자에 붙은 금속 고리에 그물이 부착되어 있고, 그물의 아랫부분은 개방되어 있어요. 사람들은 그물 안으로 공을 던져서 득점해요. 당신은 경기를 하기 위해 다른 장비가 필요하지 않아요. 당신은 손으로 공을 드리블할 수 있지만, 발로는 할 수 없어요.

어휘 team sport 단체 경기, 팀 스포츠 indoors 실내에서; 실내로 outdoors 야외에서; 야외로 goal 골문 high above 높은 ground 땅, 지면 net 그물, 네트 attach 붙이다, 부착하다 ring 고리 board 판자, 널빤지 bottom 맨 아래 score 득점하다 equipment 장비 dribble 몰다, 드리블하다

15 ③

M: Hey, Vicky. What are you doing here?
얘, 비키. 너 여기서 뭐하고 있니?

W: I'm handing out pictures of my puppy to people.
난 사람들에게 내 강아지 사진을 나눠주고 있어.

M: Why are you doing that? 왜 그런 일을 하는데?

W: I was walking him in the park yesterday, but he ran away while I was doing my exercises. 내가 어제 공원에서 강아지를 산책시키고 있었는데, 내가 운동을 하는 사이 강아지가 달아났어.

M: That's strange. Have you checked at any of the animal shelters? 그거 이상하네. 동물 보호소들은 확인해 봤니?

W: Yes, but he's nowhere to be found. Could you help me find my puppy? 응, 하지만 어디에서도 강아지를 찾을 수 없어. 내가 강아지를 찾는 것을 네가 도와주겠니?

M: Sure. No problem. Give me some of the pictures, and I'll pass them out to people. 물론이지. 나한테 사진을 좀 주면 내가 사람들에게 나눠 줄게.

해설 여자의 부탁 'Could you ~?'와 남자의 대답 'Sure.'를 확인한다.

어휘 hand out 나눠주다(= pass out) puppy 강아지 walk 산책시키다, 걷게 하다 run away 도망치다(run-ran-run) while ~하는 동안 do exercise 운동하다 strange 이상한 animal shelter 동물 보호소 nowhere to be found 어디에서도 발견되지 않는

16 ③

W: James, the front tire of my bicycle keeps going flat. I took the tube out of the tire, but I couldn't find the hole. 제임스, 내 자전거의 앞 바퀴가 계속 바람이 빠져. 내가 타이어에서 튜브를 꺼내 봤는데, 구멍을 못 찾겠어.

M: Don't worry. Just put the tube in some water and you'll find it. 걱정하지 마. 튜브를 물에 담그면 구멍을 찾을 수 있을 거야.

W: Like this? [pause] Wow! Now I can see the air bubbles coming from the holes. 이렇게? [잠시 후] 우와! 이제 구멍에서 기포가 나오는 것을 볼 수 있어.

M: Let me see. Hmm, there are several holes, so you need to put in a new tube. 내가 한번 볼게. 음, 구멍이 여러 개 있어서 새 튜브를 끼워야 할 것 같아.

W: But I don't have an extra one.
하지만 난 여분의 튜브가 없어.

M: Then we need to go out and buy a new one.
그럼 우리가 나가서 새 튜브를 사야겠다.

W: Okay, let's go. 알았어. 나가자.

해설 남자가 말한 'new tube'가 대화 후반에서는 그저 'one'으로 대체되어 언급되는 점에 유의한다.

어휘 front tire 앞 바퀴 go flat 바람이 빠지다 take A out of B B에서 A를 꺼내다 tube 튜브 hole 구멍 air bubble 기포, 공기방울 extra 추가의, 여분의 screwdriver 드라이버 glue 접착제 air pump 공기 펌프 water bottle 물병

17 ⑤

M: Sean bought a new suit for his job interview tomorrow. He wants to look nice for the interview, but he's not sure if he looks okay in his new clothes. So he decides to ask his mom how he looks in his new suit. In this situation, what would Sean most likely say to his mom?

숀은 내일 있을 취업 면접을 위해 새 정장을 샀다. 그는 면접에서 멋

있게 보이기를 원하지만, 새 옷을 입은 자신의 모습이 괜찮은지 확신이 안 선다. 그래서 그는 그의 엄마에게 새 정장을 입은 자신이 어떻게 보이는지 물어보기로 결심한다. 이 상황에서 숀은 그의 엄마에게 무슨 말을 할 것 같은가?

Sean: Mom, does this suit look good on me?
엄마, 이 정장이 저한테 잘 어울려요?

① when is the job interview? 취업 면접이 언제예요?
② how much did you pay for it? 그거 얼마나 주고 샀어요?
③ could you buy me a new suit?
저한테 새 정장을 사주실 수 있어요?
④ where is the department store? 백화점이 어디예요?
⑤ does this suit look good on me?
이 정장이 저한테 잘 어울려요?

어휘 suit (상하의 한 벌의) 정장 job interview 취업 면접 look okay 괜찮게 보이다 look good on somebody ~에게 어울리다

18 ①

W: Honey, I'm busy cooking. Can you take the garbage out for me? 여보, 난 요리하느라 바빠요. 나 대신 쓰레기 좀 가지고 나갈래요?

M: But isn't it Wednesday today? We're supposed to take it out on Thursdays! 하지만 오늘은 수요일이잖아요? 우리는 목요일마다 쓰레기를 배출하도록 되어 있잖아요!

W: Oh, I forgot. You're right. I wish we could do that every day. 아, 깜박했어요. 당신 말이 맞아요. 쓰레기 버리는 걸 매일 할 수 있으면 좋겠어요.

M: Is there anything else I can do for you?
내가 또 도와줄 수 있는 게 있어요?

W: As a matter of fact, there is. We need to change the light bulb in the bathroom. It's out. 사실은 있어요. 우리는 욕실의 전구를 교체해야 해요. 전구가 나갔어요.

M: Okay. I'll do it right now. 알았어요. 지금 바로 할게요.

어휘 take something out ~을 가지고 나가다, 제거하다 garbage 쓰레기 be supposed to ~하기로 되어 있다 as a matter of fact 사실 change the light bulb 전구를 갈다 out (불이) 나간, 꺼진

19 ③

W: Hey, Tommy. You told me your mom's birthday is this coming Sunday. Did you buy a present for her? 토미야. 너희 엄마 생신이 이번 일요일이라고 했잖아? 엄마를 위한 선물은 샀니?

M: Not yet. I wanted to get her a hat, but they were all so expensive at the department store. 아직이야. 나는 엄마에게 모자를 사드리고 싶었는데, 백화점에 있는 모자는 죄다 너무 비싸.

W: Oh, the problem is money, huh?
아, 문제는 돈이네, 그렇지?

M: Yeah. I saved some money while doing my part-time job, but it's not enough. 응. 내가 아르바이트를 하면서 돈을 좀 모았는데 그걸로는 충분하지가 않아.

W: Then, why don't you shop for a hat online?
그럼, 인터넷으로 모자를 사는 건 어때?

M: Why is it better to do that? 그렇게 하는 게 왜 더 좋은데?

W: Online prices are usually lower than offline prices.
보통 온라인 가격이 오프라인 가격보다 낮거든.

① I'd like to buy a birthday present for you.
난 너에게 생일 선물을 사주고 싶어.
② Online stores are available 24 hours a day.
인터넷 상점은 하루 24시간 이용할 수 있거든.
③ Online prices are usually lower than offline prices.
보통 온라인 가격이 오프라인 가격보다 낮거든.
④ It's easy to find part-time jobs on the Internet.
인터넷에서는 아르바이트를 찾기 쉽거든.
⑤ You should make sure the website is safe first.
넌 그 웹사이트가 안전한지부터 확인해야 해.

어휘 department store 백화점 save some money 돈을 모으다 do part-time job 아르바이트를 하다 enough 충분한 shop 사다, 쇼핑하다 online 온라인으로; 온라인의 offline 오프라인의 available 이용할 수 있는 24 hours a day 언제라도 항상, 하루 24시간 on the Internet 인터넷에서 make sure 확인하다, 확실히 하다

20 ①

W: Hey, Jin-su. What's the matter? 진수야, 무슨 문제 있어?

M: Hi, Susan. I'm worried about my English presentation tomorrow. 안녕, 수잔. 난 내일 있을 내 영어 발표가 걱정돼.

W: Have you written down what you're going to say?
넌 네가 말할 내용을 적어 두었니?

M: Yes, I have. But I'm having trouble memorizing it.
응, 적어 놨어. 하지만 그걸 외우기가 어려워.

W: You don't have to memorize every word. Just think about the key words. 넌 모든 단어를 외울 필요가 없어. 키워드만 생각하도록 해.

M: What do you mean? 무슨 말이니?

W: Just write down the key words on a small note card. Then, you can look at them during the presentation. 작은 메모지에 키워드들을 적어 놔. 그러면 발표 도중에 그것들을 볼 수 있잖아.

M: That's a good idea! I'll give it a try.
좋은 생각인 걸! 한번 해봐야겠다.

① That's a good idea! I'll give it a try.
좋은 생각인 걸! 한번 해봐야겠다.
② Sure, I'll try to memorize the whole script.
물론이야. 모든 원고를 외우려고 노력해야겠어.
③ Okay. I'll take notes during the presentation.
응. 내가 발표 도중에 메모를 할게.
④ So, do you mean I should check the grammar?
그럼 넌 내가 문법을 확인해야 한다는 거니?
⑤ Then, you need to practice English conversation.
그럼 넌 영어 회화를 연습할 필요가 있어.

어휘 presentation 발표 write down 적다, 쓰다 have trouble –ing ~하는 데 어려움을 겪다 memorize 암기하다 key word 핵심어, 키워드 note card 메모지 give it a try 시도하다, 한번 해보다 whole 전체의, 모든 script 대본, 원고 take notes 메모하다, 노트하다 grammar 문법

01 ①	02 ⑤	03 ⑤	04 ⑤	05 ②
06 ③	07 ②	08 ④	09 ③	10 ③
11 ①	12 ①	13 ⑤	14 ⑤	15 ③
16 ④	17 ③	18 ④	19 ②	20 ①

01 ①

M: Mom, this is the city flag I designed for the Richmond Flag Contest. 엄마, 이건 제가 리치먼드 깃발 대회를 위해 디자인한 도시 깃발이에요.

W: It looks great! You used trees as a symbol for the city. 아주 멋지구나! 넌 나무들을 도시의 상징으로 이용했구나.

M: Yeah, because the city planted many trees this year. 네, 시에서 올해 많은 나무들을 심었기 때문이에요.

W: That's true, but why didn't you include any sunflowers? A lot of those were planted, too. 그건 맞지만 왜 해바라기는 하나도 포함시키지 않았니? 해바라기도 많이 심었는데.

M: I know, but I wanted to make my flag unique. 알아요, 하지만 저는 제 깃발을 독특하게 만들고 싶었어요.

W: I see. I like your idea to put the city name above the trees. 알겠다. 나무 위에 도시 이름을 넣은 네 아이디어가 마음에 드는구나.

M: Thanks, Mom. 고맙습니다, 엄마.

어휘 design for ~을 목적으로 그리다, 계획하다 symbol 상징 plant (나무, 씨앗 등을) 심다; 식물 include 포함하다 unique 독특한 above ~위에

02 ⑤

[Cellphone rings.] [휴대폰이 울린다.]

M: Honey, I'm at the bakery. I have bad news for you. 여보, 난 제과점에 있어요. 당신에게 안 좋은 소식이 있어요.

W: Don't tell me there are no tuna sandwiches left! 참치 샌드위치가 남지 않았다는 말은 하지 말아요!

M: Sorry. They're sold out. 미안하지만, 그건 모두 팔렸어요.

W: Wow, they're really popular. 와, 그게 정말 인기가 많군요.

M: I should have come earlier. 내가 좀 더 일찍 왔어야 했어요.

W: It's okay. Please get me a cheeseburger at the Burger World next to the bakery. 괜찮아요. 제과점 옆에 있는 버거월드에서 치즈버거를 하나 사다 주세요.

M: Okay. I will. 알았어요. 그럴게요.

해설 남자의 첫 대사에 'bad news(안 좋은 소식)'을 알리려는 목적이 드러난다. 그 구체적인 내용은 그 다음 대사에 나타난다.

어휘 leave 남다(leave-left-left) sold out 품절의, 매진된 earlier 더 일찍(early-earlier-earliest)

03 ⑤

① M: Would you like to take a picture? 사진을 찍으시겠어요?

W: Not now. After I ride the bumper car. 지금은 말고요. 제가 범퍼카를 타고 난 다음에요.

② M: Look at that monster car over there. 저기 있는 괴물 같은 차를 좀 봐.

W: Oh, it looks so scary. 와, 정말 무섭게 생겼다.

③ M: How long have you been waiting? 당신은 얼마나 오래 기다렸나요?

W: About half an hour. 약 30분이요.

④ M: Can I see your ticket, please? 티켓을 볼 수 있을까요?

W: Here you are. 여기 있어요.

⑤ M: I'm sorry, but you're not tall enough to ride this. 미안하지만, 넌 이걸 탈 만큼 키가 충분히 크지 않구나.

W: Oh, no! I'm so sad. 아, 안 돼! 정말 슬프네요.

어휘 scary 무서운 half an hour 30분 tall enough 충분히 키가 큰

04 ⑤

W: Wow, there are so many clocks here. It's difficult to choose one for Annie's birthday. 와, 여기에는 정말 시계가 많네. 애니의 생일 선물로 하나를 고르기가 어려워.

M: How about this round one? 이 둥근 시계는 어때?

W: Round clocks are so common. I think she'd like a square-shaped one. 둥근 시계는 너무 흔해. 그 애는 네모난 것을 좋아할 것 같아.

M: Okay, then how about this square one with a cute monkey? 알았어, 그럼 귀여운 원숭이가 있는 이 네모난 건 어때?

W: Well, that's nice, but she'd prefer one with a bear. Oh, look at this square one with two bears. 음, 귀엽지만 그 애는 곰이 있는 것을 좋아할 거야. 아, 곰 두 마리가 있는 이 네모난 시계를 봐.

M: I think she'd really like that. Let's buy this one. 그녀가 정말로 좋아하겠어. 이걸 사자.

어휘 common 흔한, 평범한 square-shaped 정사각형 모양의 prefer 선호하다

05 ②

W: Sam, how are you feeling today? 샘, 너는 오늘 몸이 어떠니?

M: I feel great. Thank you. 아주 좋아요. 고마워요.

W: I'm really happy that your ankle is better. 네 발목이 나아졌다니 정말 기쁘다.

M: Me too. I'm so excited to finally leave the hospital.
저도 그래요. 마침내 퇴원하게 되어 정말 신나요.

W: Please make sure you visit me next Friday to check your ankle again. 다음 주 금요일에 발목을 다시 확인하러 병원에 꼭 오거라.

M: Okay. I will. 알았어요. 그렇게 할게요.

W: My nurse will help you get your medicine before you leave. 내 간호사가 네가 가기 전에 약을 챙겨줄 거야.

M: Thank you. 고맙습니다.

어휘 ankle 발목   better 더 좋은(good-better-best)   finally 마침내   leave the hospital 퇴원하다   make sure 반드시 ~하다, ~을 확실히 하다

06 ③

M: Mom, have you seen my backpack?
엄마, 제 책가방 보셨어요?

W: Yes, it's getting washed in the washing machine. You asked me to wash it. 그래, 그건 세탁기로 세탁 중이야. 네가 세탁해 달라고 했잖니.

M: Oh, no! I should have taken my stuff out of my backpack.
오, 이런! 제가 책가방에서 제 물건을 꺼내 놨어야 했는데요.

W: What was inside? 안에 뭐가 있었는데?

M: There was a picture of me and my friends in the pocket. 주머니에 저랑 제 친구가 나온 사진이 있었어요.

W: That's too bad. Sorry to hear that.
정말 안됐구나. 그 얘기를 듣게 돼서 유감이다.

M: Yeah. I should have been more careful.
네. 제가 좀 더 조심했어야죠.

해설 'should have done'과 'shouldn't have done'의 형태는 과거에 하지 않은 일이나 한 일에 대한 후회를 나타낼 때 쓰인다.

어휘 see 보다(see-saw-seen)   take something out ~을 꺼내다(take-took-taken)   stuff 물건   picture of ~가 나온 사진   careful 조심하는(careful-more careful-most careful)   regretful 후회하는   indifferent 무관심한

07 ②

① M: Have you seen my bag? 제 가방을 보셨나요?
   W: Yes. It's right over there. 네. 그건 저기 있어요.

② M: How long will it take to get there by taxi?
   거기까지 택시로 가는 데 얼마나 걸릴까?
   W: I haven't seen it for a long time.
   난 오랫동안 그걸 못 봤어.

③ M: I'm getting married next month. 난 다음 달에 결혼해.
   W: Congratulations! What is the exact date?
   축하해! 정확한 날짜가 언제야?

④ M: I'm wondering if you could send me the file again.
   당신이 제게 파일을 다시 보내주실 수 있는지 알고 싶어요.
   W: Sure. I will send it as soon as possible.
   물론이죠. 가급적 빨리 보내드릴게요.

⑤ M: Would you have dinner with me this evening?
   오늘 저녁에 저와 함께 저녁식사 하실래요?
   W: That sounds great! 좋아요!

해설 ②에서 'How long ~?'으로 질문했으므로 'It will take ~'로 소요시간을 포함하여 답변해야 한다.

어휘 for a long time 오랫동안   get married 결혼하다   as soon as possible 가능한 빨리

08 ④

W: Excuse me, Sir. 실례합니다, 선생님.

M: Yes? 네?

W: My son and I aren't seated next to each other on the train. 제 아들하고 제가 기차에서 나란히 앉아 있지 않거든요.

M: So do you want me to change seats with you?
그러니까 저와 자리를 바꾸고 싶으시다는 거죠?

W: Yes, please. My son isn't comfortable not sitting next to me. 네, 부탁 드려요. 제 아들은 제 옆에 앉아 있지 못해서 불편해 하거든요.

M: Okay. No problem. I know what young kids are like.
네, 문제 없죠. 저도 어린 아이들이 어떤지 알거든요.

W: Thank you very much. I really appreciate it.
정말 고맙습니다. 정말 감사 드려요.

해설 여자의 부탁을 남자가 대신 'Do you want me to ~?'로 말해줬다.

어휘 be seated 앉다, 앉아 있다   next to each other 나란히   comfortable 편한   appreciate 감사하다

09 ③

M: Julie, the Halloween party is next week.
줄리, 핼러윈 파티가 다음 주야.

W: I know. I need to go shopping for my costume.
나도 알아. 내 의상을 사러 가야겠어.

M: Me too. Why don't we go to the shopping mall some time? 나도야. 우리 언제 쇼핑몰에 가는 게 어때?

W: Great idea. How about now? Do you have time?
좋은 생각이야. 지금은 어때? 너 시간 있니?

M: I'd love to, but I have to take my mother to the hospital now.
나도 그러고 싶은데, 지금 어머니를 병원에 모셔다 드려야 해.

해설 'I'd love to, but ~'은 거절할 때 자주 쓰이는 표현이다.

어휘 Halloween 핼러윈(10월 31일 밤)   costume 의상, 복장   some time 언젠가

10 ③

M: Did you enjoy your meal? 식사는 즐거우셨습니까?

W: Yes. It was great. 네, 훌륭했어요.

M: Thank you. So you had two dishes of spaghetti and one chicken salad. Your total is forty dollars.
감사합니다. 스파게티 두 접시와 치킨 샐러드 한 접시를 드셨네요.

총 40달러입니다.

W: Oh, we didn't order a chicken salad.
아, 저희는 치킨 샐러드를 주문하지 않았어요.

M: Let me see. [pause] Oh, I'm sorry. I made a mistake.
확인해 볼게요. [잠시 후] 아, 죄송합니다. 제가 실수를 했네요.

W: That's okay. 괜찮아요.

M: So you don't have to pay for the chicken salad, which is ten dollars. 그럼 10달러인 치킨 샐러드는 계산하실 필요가 없습니다.

W: All right. Here's my credit card.
알겠어요. 여기 제 신용카드요.

해설 금액 문제에는 반드시 둘 이상의 숫자 정보가 등장하거나 계산을 요구한다.

어휘 meal 식사   dish 요리   make a mistake 실수하다   pay for 지불하다   credit card 신용카드

11 ①

W: Hello, how may I help you?
안녕하세요, 제가 도와드릴까요?

M: I'm looking for the book *The American Tourist*. Can you help me find it? 저는 '아메리칸 투어리스트'라는 책을 찾고 있거든요. 책을 찾는 것을 도와주실래요?

W: Sure. That's a popular book these days.
네. 그거 요즘 인기 있는 책이거든요.

M: Yeah. I'm buying it as a gift for my friend who loves traveling. 네. 저는 그 책을 여행을 좋아하는 제 친구에게 주는 선물로 사는 거예요.

W: How nice! It's on that bookshelf over there. Right next to the education section. 멋지네요! 그 책은 저쪽 책장에 있어요. 교육 코너 바로 옆에요.

M: Thank you for your help. 도와주셔서 감사합니다.

해설 책을 찾는 대화는 bookstore(서점)와 library(도서관)에서 가능하다. 남자의 대사 'I'm buying it ~'을 통해 서점을 정답으로 고를 수 있다.

어휘 popular 인기 있는   these days 요즘에   as a gift 선물로   right next to 바로 옆에

12 ①

W: Do you like steak? Then come down to Cowboy Steak House. We're located on second Avenue. We're open every day from eleven a.m. to ten p.m., except Mondays. Customers with a Cowboy Steak House membership will get a ten percent discount for every meal they order. To sign up to become a member, please visit our website and fill out a registration form.

스테이크를 좋아하세요? 그렇다면 카우보이 스테이크하우스로 오세요. 우리는 2번가에 위치해 있습니다. 우리는 월요일을 제외한 매일 오전 11시부터 오후 10시까지 문을 엽니다. 카우보이 스테이크하우스 회원권이 있는 고객은 주문하는 모든 음식에 대해 10% 할

인을 받게 됩니다. 회원 신청을 하려면 저희 웹사이트를 방문하여 등록 양식을 작성해 주세요.

어휘 come down 오다, 내려오다   be located on ~에 위치하다   except 제외하고   get a discount 할인을 받다   sign up 등록하다   fill out a form 서식을 작성하다

13 ⑤

M: Ms. White, here's a map of the sections for the school festival. Which section do you think would be good for the photography club? 화이트 선생님, 여기 학교 축제 구역이 표시된 지도가 있습니다. 사진 동아리에게는 어느 구역이 좋은 것 같으세요?

W: What about section B? B구역은 어때요?

M: The science club has already been given that section. 그 구역은 이미 과학 동아리에게 배정됐어요.

W: Hmm... How about putting the photography club in a section next to the lounge? 음, 사진 동아리를 라운지 옆의 구역에 배정하는 건 어때요?

M: Good idea! The lounge is always crowded, which can help them sell more postcards. Which is better, section D or E? 좋은 생각이네요! 라운지는 항상 붐비는데, 그건 사진 동아리가 더 많은 엽서를 판매하는 것을 도울 수 있을 겁니다. D구역과 E구역 중에서 어디가 더 괜찮은가요?

W: Why don't we give them the section near the entrance? 그들에게 입구 근처에 있는 구역을 주는 건 어때요?

M: Okay. Great. 네. 좋습니다.

어휘 map 지도   section 구역   already 이미, 벌써   next to ~옆에   lounge 라운지, 휴게실   crowded 붐비는, 복잡한   Which is better, A or B? A와 B 중 무엇이 더 좋은가?   entrance 입구

14 ⑤

M: This is a vehicle which you ride by sitting on it. Usually, it has two wheels attached to a frame, one behind the other. To move forward, you have to keep pushing two pedals with your feet. To change directions, you turn a bar that is connected to the front wheel. It is used for recreation, general fitness, or racing.

이것은 앉아서 탈 수 있는 운송수단입니다. 보통 이것은 프레임에 부착된 두 개의 바퀴를 가지고 있는데, 하나는 다른 하나의 뒤쪽에 있습니다. 앞으로 나아가기 위해 당신은 발로 두 개의 페달을 밟아야 합니다. 방향을 바꾸기 위해 당신은 앞 바퀴에 연결된 막대를 돌립니다. 이것은 기분전환과 일반적인 운동, 혹은 경주에 사용됩니다.

어휘 vehicle 탈것, 차량   ride 타다   attached to ~에 붙은   move forward 전진하다   keep pushing 계속 밀다   pedal 페달   be connected to ~에 연결되다   recreation 오락, 기분전환, 레크리에이션   general 일반적인, 보편적인   fitness 신체단련

15 ③

W: Ted, wake up! 테드, 일어나.

M: Oh, Jina. Is lunch time over?
아, 지나야. 점심시간이 지났니?

W: Not yet. Let's go for a walk.
아직 안 지났어. 산책하러 가자.

M: Well, okay. [pause] Wait. What time is it?
음, 알았어. [잠시 후] 잠깐. 지금 몇 시지?

W: It's one ten. Why? 1시 10분이야. 왜?

M: Oh, no! My English teacher told me to come to the teachers' office by one o'clock. 아, 안돼! 우리 영어 선생님이 나한테 1시까지 교무실로 오라고 하셨거든.

W: Really? Then, hurry up. 정말? 그럼 서둘러.

M: Okay. See you later. 알았어. 이따 보자.

어휘 be over 끝나다   teachers' office 교무실

16 ④

W: Dad, when are we going on our summer vacation trip? 아빠, 우리는 언제 여름방학 여행을 떠나요?

M: Well, I haven't decided yet. When does your summer school end? 글쎄, 아빠가 아직 결정을 못했다. 네 여름학교가 언제 끝나지?

W: July twelfth. 7월 12일이요.

M: Hmm… I have a three-day business trip from July fourteenth. 음, 내가 7월 14일부터 3일간 출장이 있거든.

W: Then we can leave after July seventeenth, right?
그럼 우린 7월 17일 이후에 떠날 수 있겠네요, 그렇죠?

M: Yes, so let's leave on July twentieth and come back on July twenty third. 그래, 그럼 7월 20일에 떠나서 7월 23일에 돌아오자꾸나.

W: That's perfect. I'm so excited.
완벽하네요. 전 무척 신나요.

해설 다섯 개의 날짜가 언급되므로 각 의미를 정확히 파악해야 한다.

어휘 decide 결정하다   business trip 출장

17 ③

W: Ms. Brown manages a fast food restaurant. She needs to hire one more weekend part-time worker. One day Susan comes to the restaurant to apply for the part-time job. Ms. Brown wants to make sure that Susan can work on the weekends. In this situation, what would Ms. Brown most likely say to Susan?

브라운 씨는 패스트푸드 음식점을 운영하고 있어요. 그녀는 또 한 사람의 주말 아르바이트생을 고용해야 해요. 하루는 수잔이 아르바이트를 지원하러 음식점에 와요. 브라운 씨는 수잔이 주말에 근무할 수 있는지를 확실히 하고 싶어요. 이런 상황에서 브라운 씨는 수잔에게 무슨 말을 할까요?

Ms. Brown: I can hire you if you can work on the weekends.
당신이 주말에 일할 수 있다면 제가 당신을 고용할 수 있습니다.

① Right now our onion rings are on sale.
지금 현재 저희 어니언링이 할인 중입니다.

② We start serving dinner at six thirty on weekends.
우리는 주말에는 6시 30분부터 저녁식사를 제공합니다.

③ I can hire you if you can work on the weekends.
당신이 주말에 일할 수 있다면 제가 당신을 고용할 수 있습니다.

④ For your hard work, I'll give you a raise next week.
당신의 노고를 인정해서 다음 주에 급여를 인상해 드리겠습니다.

⑤ After you clean the tables, please take out the trash. 테이블을 치운 다음에는 쓰레기를 버리세요.

어휘 manage 운영하다   hire 고용하다   part-time worker 단시간 근로자   apply for a job 취직 신청하다   on sale 할인중인; 판매되는   serve dinner 식사를 제공하다   give a raise 급여를 올려주다

18 ④

M: Honey, please hurry up or we're going to be late for the concert.
여보, 서두르지 않으면 우리는 콘서트에 늦을 거예요.

W: Just a minute! I can't find my scarf.
잠시만요. 제 스카프를 못 찾겠어요.

M: Scarf? I saw it in the car. 스카프? 내가 차에서 그걸 봤어요.

W: Ah, right. Let's go. Wait! My gloves! I need them. It's freezing outside. 아, 맞다. 가요. 기다려요! 내 장갑! 장갑이 필요해요. 밖은 몹시 춥다고요.

M: I'll get them for you. Where are they?
내가 당신에게 그걸 가져다 줄게요. 그게 어디 있어요?

W: They're on the sofa. Thanks, Honey.
그건 소파 위에 있어요. 고마워요, 여보.

M: No problem. 별 말씀을.

어휘 freezing 꽁꽁 얼게 추운

19 ②

M: Judy, did you finish packing your bag for your trip?
주디, 여행을 가기 위해 가방은 다 쌌니?

W: Yes, I did. 네, 다 쌌어요.

M: Did you put your passport in your bag?
가방에 네 여권을 넣었니?

W: Of course, I did. I even made a copy of it. 물론이죠. 넣었어요. 저는 심지어 여권 사본도 만들었다고요.

M: Good. Make sure you take your flight ticket with you, too. 좋아. 비행기표를 가지고 가는지 확인해 봐라.

W: Come on, Dad. I already double-checked everything.
아빠도 참. 저는 이미 모든 걸 두 번씩 확인했어요.

M: Well, you can never be too careful about whatever you do. 음, 무슨 일을 하던 간에 아무리 조심해도 부족하단다.

어휘 pack (짐을) 싸다   make a copy of ~의 복사본을

만들다 take something with ~을 가져가다 double-check
재확인하다

20 ①

M: Bella, you're going to be late for your piano lesson.
벨라, 넌 피아노 교습에 늦겠다.

W: Dad, can I skip today's lesson?
아빠, 저 오늘 교습을 안 가도 돼요?

M: Why? You really enjoy playing the piano.
왜? 넌 피아노 치는 걸 아주 좋아하잖아.

W: I really hate playing the same pieces over and over.
저는 같은 곡을 계속 반복해서 치는 걸 정말로 싫어해요.

M: I thought your dream is to become a professional pianist.
나는 네 꿈이 전문 피아니스트가 되는 거라고 생각했는데.

W: That's true, but I don't think I need to spend this much time practicing. 그건 맞지만 저는 이렇게 많은 시간을 연습하는 데 쓸 필요는 없다고 생각해요.

M: Little by little, that's how great things get done.
조금씩 천천히, 그게 위대한 일들이 이루어지는 방식이란다.

① Little by little, that's how great things get done.
조금씩 천천히, 그게 위대한 일들이 이루어지는 방식이란다.

② All right. I'll give you a ride to the piano concert.
알았다. 내가 피아노 콘서트가 열리는 곳까지 차로 데려다 줄게.

③ Let's go to a shop for other musical instruments.
다른 악기를 사러 상점에 가자.

④ Above all, let's buy a brand-new grand piano first.
무엇보다도 먼저 최신 그랜드피아노를 사자.

⑤ Your teacher will start organizing an orchestra.
네 선생님은 오케스트라를 조직하는 걸 시작할 거야.

어휘 skip lesson 수업을 빼먹다 hate 싫어하다 over and over 반복해서 professional 전문적인 spend time -ing ~하는 데 시간을 보내다 little by little 조금씩, 천천히 give a ride ~을 태워주다 musical instrument 악기 brand-new 아주 새로운 organize 조직하다

04회 기출 듣기평가
본문 p.298-299

01 ⑤	02 ⑤	03 ②	04 ③	05 ①
06 ②	07 ④	08 ②	09 ④	10 ⑤
11 ⑤	12 ⑤	13 ③	14 ①	15 ④
16 ③	17 ⑤	18 ②	19 ③	20 ①

01 ⑤

M: Hello. How may I help you?
안녕하세요. 무엇을 도와드릴까요?

W: Hi, I'd like to buy a face mask for my son. 안녕하세요,

저는 제 아들에게 줄 얼굴 마스크를 사고 싶어요.

M: Okay. What about this one with cars on it? It's popular among boys. 그렇군요. 자동차가 있는 이것은 어떤가요? 남자아이들 사이에서 인기가 많은 거예요.

W: It's nice, but do you have any with animals?
좋긴 한데 동물이 있는 것도 있나요?

M: Yes, we do. How about this one with rabbits?
네, 있습니다. 토끼가 있는 이건 어떤가요?

W: Not bad, but do you have any with more than one animal on it?
나쁘지 않지만 한 마리 이상의 동물이 있는 것도 있나요?

M: Yes. How about this one with rabbits and monkeys? 네. 토끼와 원숭이가 있는 이것은 어떤가요?

W: Great! I'll take it! 좋네요. 그걸 살게요.

어휘 popular among ~사이에서 인기 있는 more than one 하나 이상, 많은

02 ⑤

[Cellphone rings.] [휴대폰이 울린다.]

W: Hello, Dad. 안녕하세요, 아빠.

M: Alice, I'm still waiting for your decision.
앨리스, 난 너의 결정을 아직 기다리고 있단다.

W: Sorry it took so long. My answer is "Yes."
너무 오래 걸려서 죄송해요. 제 대답은 "네"예요.

M: Great. I'm glad we'll be able to join the Grandma's birthday party together. 잘됐구나. 우리가 할머니 생신 잔치에 함께 갈 수 있어서 기쁘구나.

W: Me too. I told my friends that I can't go to the concert with them that day. 저도 그래요. 친구들에게 저는 그날 콘서트에 갈 수 없다고 말했어요.

M: Good. Grandma will be so happy to see you. I'll book our train tickets to Busan. 좋아. 할머니께서 널 봐서 아주 기뻐하실 거야. 내가 부산행 기차표를 예매하마.

어휘 wait for ~을 기다리다 decision 결정 be able to ~할 수 있다 tell 말하다, 전하다 book 예약하다; 책

03 ②

① W: James, the curtain is so dirty. 제임스, 커튼이 너무 더러워요.
M: Okay. Let's wash it then. 알겠어요. 그럼 그걸 세탁합시다.

② W: Honey, would you close the curtain?
여보, 커튼 좀 닫아줄래요?
M: Sure, I'll do that for you. 당연하죠, 당신을 위해서 해줄게요.

③ W: Oh, it's raining outside! 오, 밖에 비가 내려요!
M: I'll go get an umbrella for you.
제가 당신을 위해 우산을 가져올게요.

④ W: This is such a lovely curtain. 이거 아주 예쁜 커튼이군요.
M: Thank you. I bought it last month.
고마워요. 제가 지난 달에 그걸 샀어요.

⑤ W: Do you know how to hang a curtain?
당신은 커튼 다는 방법을 알아요?

M: I'm afraid I've never done that before.
미안하지만 저는 전에 그걸 해 본 적이 없군요.

04 ③

W: Honey, look at this cake. Isn't the star beautiful?
여보, 이 케이크 봐요. 별이 아름답지 않아요?

M: It's nice, but I'm not sure if Mark will like it.
좋긴 한데, 마크가 그걸 좋아할 지는 확실치 않네요.

W: Then, how about this one with a snowman?
그러면 눈사람이 있는 이건 어때요?

M: It's good too, but I think Mark would like one with animals more. 그것도 좋은데, 마크는 동물이 있는 것을 더 좋아할 것 같아요.

W: Okay. Then we should choose either the one with a polar bear or a penguin. 알겠어요. 그러면 우린 북극곰이 있는 것과 펭귄이 있는 것 중에서 선택해야 해요.

M: I think Mark would prefer the polar bear to the penguin. 마크는 펭귄보다 북극곰을 더 좋아할 것 같군요.

W: I agree. Let's buy it. 저도 동의해요. 그걸로 사죠.

해설 별, 눈사람, 펭귄은 결국 오답 함정이다. 마지막에 언급되는 내용을 잘 들어야 한다.

어휘 not sure if ~일지 확실하지 않은   either A or B A와 B 중 하나   prefer A to B B보다 A를 좋아하다

05 ①

W: Hello. 안녕하세요.

M: Hi. May I help you? 안녕하세요. 도와드릴까요?

W: Yes. A week ago, I checked out this book, and I'd like to keep it one more week. Is that possible?
네. 일주일 전에 제가 이 책을 빌렸는데 전 이것을 일주일 더 갖고 있으면 좋겠어요. 가능할까요?

M: Let me check. [pause] Yes, you can. There is no one on the waiting list. 제가 확인해 볼게요. [잠시 후] 네, 가능하네요. 대기자 명단에 아무도 없거든요.

W: Great. And can you tell me where the earth science books are? 잘됐군요. 그리고 지구과학책이 어디에 있는지 제게 알려주시겠어요?

M: They're in section D, on the second floor.
2층 D구역에 있어요.

W: Thank you. 감사합니다.

어휘 ago ~전에   check out (책을) 대출하다   possible 가능한   waiting list 대기자 명단   earth science 지구과학

06 ②

M: Hi, Nancy. Looks like you're in a hurry.
안녕, 낸시. 너 바쁜 것처럼 보인다.

W: Yeah. I'm on my way to get my phone back.
응. 나는 내 전화기를 되찾으러 가는 길이야.

M: Did you leave it somewhere?
네가 그걸 어딘가에 두고 왔어?

W: Yes, I did. I left it in a taxi last night.

응, 그랬어. 내가 어젯밤에 택시에 놓고 왔어.

M: Oh, my! Did you call your phone after you realized that?
오, 저런! 네가 그 사실을 깨달은 뒤에 네 휴대폰에 전화를 한 거야?

W: Yeah. The taxi driver answered and said he'd return it to me. He's at the school gate now.
응. 그 택시 기사님이 전화를 받았고 내게 돌려주겠다고 말했어. 그분은 지금 학교 정문에 있어.

M: How nice! You're very lucky to get it back.
잘됐다! 그걸 돌려받다니 넌 아주 운이 좋은 거야.

해설 잃어버린 물건을 찾았을 때의 심정을 떠올리면 정답을 쉽게 찾을 수 있다.

어휘 in a hurry 바쁜; 급히   on one's way to ~로 가는 길에   get something back (잃었던 것을) 되찾다   realize 깨닫다   return 돌려주다

07 ④

① M: Would you like something to drink? 마실 것을 드릴까요?
   W: Just water, please. Thank you. 물만 주세요. 감사합니다.

② M: I lost my watch yesterday. 나는 어제 시계를 잃어버렸어.
   W: Oh, sorry to hear that. 아, 그거 안됐다.

③ M: What did you do last Monday? 너는 지난 월요일에 뭐 했어?
   W: I watched a movie with my friend. 난 친구와 영화를 봤어.

④ M: Ron is absent today because he is sick.
   론은 아파서 오늘 결석했어.
   W: Right. He wants to be a doctor. 맞아. 그 애는 의사가 되고 싶어 해.

⑤ M: Do you mind if I sit here? 제가 여기 앉아도 될까요?
   W: Sorry. This seat is already taken.
   죄송해요. 이 자리는 이미 주인이 있어요.

어휘 something to drink 마실 것   lose 잃어버리다(lose-lost-lost)   absent 결석한

08 ②

[Cellphone rings.] [휴대폰이 울린다.]

W: Hello. 여보세요.

M: Hi, Sue. Are you on your way to the baseball park?
안녕, 수. 너는 야구장으로 오는 길이야?

W: Yes, I'm on the bus. Where are you?
응, 난 버스에 있어. 넌 어디야?

M: I'm standing in line to buy tickets.
나는 표를 사려고 줄을 서 있어.

W: Oh, really? I'll be there in ten minutes.
아, 정말이야? 나는 10분 뒤에 그곳에 갈게.

M: Okay. Can you buy some snacks? I skipped lunch. I'm really hungry. 알았어. 네가 간식 좀 사올래? 난 점심을 걸렀어. 정말 배가 고프다.

W: Sure, no problem. I'll buy some.
물론, 문제 없지. 내가 좀 사갈게.

어휘 on one's way to ~로 가는 길에   stand in line 줄을 서다

skip 거르다, 건너뛰다

09 ④

W: Kevin, you look so happy in this picture!
케빈, 너 이 사진에서 매우 행복해 보여!

M: Yes, I was. I had so much fun during the global camp. This French boy was my best friend there.
응, 그랬지. 나는 국제캠프 기간에 정말 재미있었거든. 이 프랑스 소년이 그곳에서 나의 가장 친한 친구였어.

W: He looks nice. 인상이 좋네.

M: He is. He helped me a lot during the team activities. I really miss him. 맞아. 그가 팀 활동 시간에 나를 많이 도와줬어. 난 그 애가 아주 그리워.

W: Why don't you send this picture to him by e-mail?
이 사진을 그에게 이메일로 보내지 그래?

해설 'Why don't you ~?'는 제안할 때 많이 쓰는 표현이다.

어휘 global 세계적인   during ~동안   miss 그리워하다; 놓치다   by e-mail 전자우편으로

10 ③

W: Hello. Welcome to King Fishing.
안녕하세요. '킹 피싱'에 오신 걸 환영합니다.

M: Hi. I'd like to fish here with my son. How much is it?
안녕하세요. 저는 제 아들과 이곳에서 낚시를 하려고 해요. 얼마죠?

W: Thirty dollars for adults. How old is your son?
성인은 30달러입니다. 아들이 몇 살인가요?

M: He's seven years old. 그는 7살입니다.

W: Then, his admission is free. Would you like to rent fishing chairs? 그러면 그의 입장료는 무료예요. 낚시 의자도 빌리실 건가요?

M: Yes. Two chairs, please. 네. 의자 두 개 주세요.

W: Okay. They're five dollars each.
알겠습니다. 의자는 각각 5달러입니다.

M: Great. Here's the money. 좋아요. 여기 돈이요.

해설 아빠의 입장료는 30달러, 아들은 무료, 거기에 의자 두 개를 빌리는 데에 10달러, 그러므로 총 40달러가 된다.

어휘 admission 입장료, 입장   rent 빌리다

11 ⑤

M: Honey, this trip is going to be so refreshing.
여보, 이 여행은 아주 기운을 북돋을 것 같아요.

W: Definitely. I'm so excited to be here.
그렇고 말고. 전 이곳에 와서 정말 신이 나요.

M: What beautiful scenery! 얼마나 아름다운 풍경이에요!

W: For sure. Well, let's set up the tent before it gets dark. 확실히 그래요. 자, 어두워지기 전에 텐트를 칩시다.

M: Okay. Let's make sure the tent is not close to the fire area. 알겠어요. 텐트가 불이 있는 곳에 너무 가까이 가지 않도록 합시다.

W: Good point. After we set up the tent, I'll prepare dinner.
좋은 지적이에요. 우리가 텐트를 친 다음에 전 식사를 준비할게요.

M: All right. Sounds great. 그래요. 좋은 생각이군요.

어휘 refreshing 기운을 돋우는, 신선한   definitely 분명히   scenery 풍경, 경치   set up a tent 텐트를 치다   get dark 어두워지다   make sure 반드시 ~하다, ~을 확실히 하다   close to ~에 가까이   prepare 준비하다

12 ⑤

W: Hello, listeners. Have you ever visited Central City Museum? The museum first opened in nineteen seventy-three. It is located next to the City Hall. It has five exhibition rooms and a gift shop. The museum is open daily from nine a.m. to six p.m. Ticket prices are thirty dollars for adults and ten dollars for children. If you have any questions, please visit the Central City Museum website.

안녕하세요, 청취자 여러분. 센트럴시티 박물관에 가본 적이 있나요? 이 박물관은 1973년에 처음 문을 열었습니다. 시청 옆에 위치해 있습니다. 그곳은 전시실 다섯 곳과 선물 가게가 있습니다. 박물관은 매일 오전 9시부터 오후 6시까지 개방됩니다. 티켓 가격은 성인은 30달러, 어린이는 10달러입니다. 궁금한 사항이 있으면 센트럴시티 박물관 웹사이트를 방문해주십시오.

어휘 be located 위치해 있다   exhibition room 전시실   gift shop 선물 가게   daily 매일

13 ③

W: Honey, I'd like to sell Ben's old bike on the Internet. Can you help me fill out the form? 여보, 제가 인터넷으로 벤의 오래된 자전거를 팔려고 해요. 이 양식 채우는 걸 도와줄래요?

M: Sure. The brand name is Apollo.
물론이죠. 상표 이름은 아폴로예요.

W: Okay. 알겠어요.

M: And the wheel size is twelve inches.
그리고 바퀴 크기는 12인치고요.

W: All right. 그렇군요.

M: And it's green. What condition do you think it's in?
그리고 초록색이에요. 그 상태가 어떻다고 생각해요?

W: I'd say excellent. Ben rarely rode it. 저는 훌륭하다고 말하겠어요. 벤이 그걸 거의 타지 않았어요.

M: Hmm… Then I think we can ask sixty dollars for it.
음, 그러면 우리가 60달러를 요청할 수 있다고 생각해요.

어휘 fill out the form 양식을 작성하다   brand name 상표 이름   condition 상태   rarely 별로 ~않는, 드물게

14 ①

M: This is used to slow down a person falling through the air. It enables a person to jump from an aircraft and land on the ground safely. It consists of a large piece of thin cloth attached to a person's body by strings. It is mostly used in emergency situations or in the military, but people also use it for leisure.

이것은 사람이 공중으로 떨어지는 속도를 늦추는 데에 사용됩니다. 그것은 사람이 항공기에서 뛰어내려 땅 위에 안전하게 착지할 수 있게 합니다. 그것은 주로 사람의 몸에 줄로 장착된 얇고 넓은 천 조각으로 이루어져 있습니다. 그것은 주로 비상사태나 군대에서 사용되지만 사람들은 그것을 여가를 위해 사용하기도 합니다.

어휘 slow down (속도, 진행을) 늦추다   fall 떨어지다   through the air 공중으로   enable ~을 가능하게 하다   consist of ~로 구성되다   attach to ~에 붙이다   string 줄, 끈   emergency situation 비상사태   military 군대; 군사의   leisure 여가

15 ④

M: Kaylee, we're going to be late for the movie.
케일리, 우리 영화에 늦겠다.

W: Sorry, Dad. I was looking for my glasses.
죄송해요, 아빠. 저는 안경을 찾고 있었어요.

M: I've told you so many times to put them in the same place.
내가 안경을 같은 장소에 놓으라고 몇 번이나 말했잖아.

W: I know, Dad. Sorry. [pause] Oh, wait. I left my cellphone on my desk. 알아요, 아빠. 죄송해요. [잠시 후] 아, 잠깐만요. 제 휴대폰을 책상 위에 놓고 왔어요.

M: Come on. Mom's waiting for us outside.
서둘러. 엄마가 밖에서 우릴 기다리고 있어.

W: Okay. I'll just quickly go get it.
네. 제가 빨리 가서 가져올게요.

어휘 many times 여러 번   in the same place 같은 장소에   quickly 빨리

16 ③

W: Jack, we should decide on a date for our company picnic. 잭, 우리는 회사 야유회 날짜를 결정해야 해.

M: Okay, Jean. How about June second or June seventh? 알았어, 진. 6월 2일이나 6월 7일 어때?

W: I think we need a couple more days than that to prepare for it. How about June ninth? 야유회 준비를 위해서 그보다 며칠 더 필요할 것 같아. 6월 9일은 어때?

M: We already have a weekly meeting planned on that day at ten o'clock.
우린 그날 10시에 주간 회의가 이미 계획되어 있잖아.

W: I'm sure we can reschedule the meeting.
우린 그 회의 일정을 변경할 수 있을 거야.

M: Okay, then let's go with your suggested date.
알았어, 그러면 네가 제안한 날짜로 하자.

해설 한 번 언급된 날짜를 반복하지 않고 남자가 마지막에 'your suggested date'라고 말했다. 여자가 제안한 날짜를 기억하고 있어야 한다.

어휘 decide on ~으로 정하다   a couple more days 며칠 더   prepare for ~을 준비하다   planned 계획된   reschedule 일정을 변경하다   go with something (계획, 제안 등을) 받아들이다

17 ⑤

W: Chris takes his friend Anna to his favorite Italian restaurant for dinner, but he didn't make a reservation. He sees many people waiting to get a table. The waiter is writing people's names on a waiting list. Chris really wants to eat with Anna at this restaurant, so he decides to ask Anna if she doesn't mind waiting. In this situation, what would Chris most likely say to Anna?

크리스는 저녁 식사를 하기 위해 그의 친구 애나를 자신이 좋아하는 이탈리아 식당으로 데려갔는데, 그는 예약을 하지 않았다. 그는 자리를 얻으려고 기다리는 많은 사람들을 본다. 웨이터는 대기자 명단에 사람들의 이름을 적고 있다. 크리스는 이 식당에서 애나와 꼭 식사를 하고 싶어서, 애나에게 기다리는 게 괜찮은지 물어보기로 결심한다. 이 상황에서 크리스는 애나에게 뭐라고 말할까?

Chris: Are you okay with waiting for a table?
자리가 날 때까지 기다리는 거 괜찮은가요?

① What's the special today? 오늘의 특별요리가 뭐죠?

② Can you recommend us a dish?
저희에게 요리를 추천해주시겠어요?

③ Do you like to cook Italian food?
이탈리아 음식을 요리하기 좋아하시나요?

④ How did you like your food here? 여기 음식 어땠어요?

⑤ Are you okay with waiting for a table?
자리가 날 때까지 기다리는 거 괜찮은가요?

어휘 make a reservation 예약하다   waiting list 대기자 명단   mind 언짢아하다   special 특별요리   recommend 추천하다   dish 요리; 접시

18 ②

M: Mom, I've decided what to get Jenny for her birthday. 엄마, 제니의 생일에 무엇을 줄 지 전 결정했어요.

W: What did you decide on? 무엇으로 결정했니?

M: I think I'll get her a wallet.
그 애에게 지갑을 사주려고 생각해요.

W: Good idea. What kind of wallet do you have in mind? 좋은 생각이구나. 어떤 종류의 지갑을 생각하고 있니?

M: I saw a nice one at the mall. I took a picture of it with my cellphone. 쇼핑몰에서 좋은 걸 봤어요. 제 휴대폰으로 그것의 사진을 찍었어요.

W: Did you? Can I see it? 그랬어? 보여줄래?

M: Sure. Wait a second. 물론이죠. 잠깐만 기다리세요.

어휘 decide on ~으로 결정하다   have in mind ~을 생각하다, 염두에 두다

19 ③

M: Jane, how was the science <u>competition</u> last weekend? 제인, 지난 주말 과학 경연대회 어땠어?

W: It was a <u>disaster</u>. My team members couldn't <u>work together</u>. 엉망이었어. 우리 팀원들은 함께 일할 수가 없었거든.

M: What do you mean? 무슨 뜻이야?

W: All of them <u>thought</u> that their ideas were <u>the best</u>, and they wouldn't <u>listen to anybody</u> else's ideas. 모두들 자신의 생각이 최고라고 생각했고 각자 다른 누구의 생각도 듣지 않으려고 했어.

M: That's too bad. So you didn't <u>do well</u> in the competition. 그거 안 좋은데. 그래서 그 대회에서 잘 하지 못했구나.

W: Actually, we didn't even <u>finish</u> our project <u>before</u> the <u>deadline</u>. 사실, 우린 마감시간 전에 프로젝트를 끝내지도 못했어.

M: That was terrible. 그거 끔찍했구나.

어휘 competition 경쟁, 대회 disaster 재난, 실패 do well 잘 하다, 성공하다 deadline 마감시간

20 ①

M: How can I help you, Ma'am? 무엇을 도와드릴까요, 손님?

W: I'd like to <u>get</u> a <u>refund</u> for this dress I bought here. Here's the <u>receipt</u>. 제가 여기에서 구매한 이 드레스에 대해 환불받고 싶어요. 영수증 여기 있어요.

M: Hmm… Your receipt shows that you bought this item <u>three weeks ago</u>. 음, 손님의 영수증에 이 제품을 3주 전에 구매하신 걸로 나오네요.

W: That's right. Is that a problem? 맞아요. 그게 문제가 되나요?

M: I'm afraid so. You can <u>only</u> get a refund for goods <u>within two weeks</u> from the <u>date of purchase</u>. It's clearly written on the receipt. 죄송하지만 그렇습니다. 제품에 대한 환불은 구매한 날로부터 2주 안에만 가능합니다. 영수증에 분명히 명시되어 있습니다.

W: I don't understand. That's nonsense. 이해가 안 되는군요. 그건 말도 안돼요.

M: I'm sorry, but that's our policy. 죄송하지만 그게 저희의 정책입니다.

① I'm sorry, but that's our policy. 죄송하지만 그게 저희의 정책입니다.

② Actually, refunding takes longer. 사실, 환불은 더 오래 걸립니다.

③ Sure. People like to save money. 물론입니다. 사람들은 돈을 절약하는 걸 좋아하지요.

④ Well, would you like a larger size? 글쎄요, 더 큰 사이즈를 원하시나요?

⑤ Right. This is a good place to shop. 맞습니다. 이곳이 쇼핑하기 좋은 장소예요.

어휘 get a refund 환불 받다 receipt 영수증 item 물품, 품목 goods 제품 within two weeks 2주 안에 date of

purchase 구매일 clearly 분명히, 또렷하게 nonsense 터무니없는 말, 허튼소리 policy 정책, 방침 save money 돈을 절약하다

01 ⑤	02 ②	03 ②	04 ④	05 ③
06 ③	07 ④	08 ①	09 ②	10 ②
11 ④	12 ④	13 ③	14 ⑤	15 ①
16 ②	17 ②	18 ⑤	19 ③	20 ①

01 ⑤

M: <u>What</u> are you doing <u>on</u> the <u>computer</u>, Julia? 컴퓨터로 무엇을 하고 있니, 줄리아?

W: I'm looking for a <u>box for</u> the <u>chocolate</u> I made for my mom's birthday. 내가 엄마 생신을 위해 만든 초콜릿을 담을 상자를 찾는 중이야.

M: Let's see… I like this <u>heart-shaped</u> box. 같이 보자… 나는 이 하트 모양 상자가 마음에 든다.

W: Hmm. Not bad, but isn't it <u>too simple</u>? 음. 나쁘진 않은데 너무 단순하지 않아?

M: Well, then how about the heart-shaped one <u>with stars</u>? It looks fancy. 글쎄, 그러면 별이 있는 하트 모양 상자는 어때? 화려해 보이잖아.

W: Oh, look! Here's a <u>bear</u>-shaped one <u>with</u> a <u>ribbon</u>. 오, 봐! 여기 리본이 있는 곰 모양 상자가 있어.

M: Wow, that's pretty! 우와, 그거 예쁘다!

W: I think so, too. I'll order that one. 나도 그렇게 생각해. 난 저걸 주문해야겠어.

어휘 heart-shaped 하트 모양의 simple 단순한 fancy 화려한

02 ②

W: What can I do for you? 무엇을 도와드릴까요?

M: I <u>bought</u> this CD yesterday for my friend. But she <u>has</u> one <u>already</u>! 제가 어제 친구를 주려고 이 CD를 샀는데요. 그런데 친구가 이미 이걸 갖고 있어요!

W: Would you like to <u>exchange it for</u> a <u>different</u> CD? 다른 CD로 교환하고 싶으신가요?

M: I'd rather just <u>get</u> a <u>refund</u>. 환불받는 게 좋겠어요.

W: Well, you can get a <u>free gift</u> if you buy the new special album of JC Band. 음, JC밴드의 새로 나온 특별 앨범을 사면 사은품을 받을 수 있는데요.

M: No, thanks. 고맙지만 됐어요.

해설 여자의 질문과 제안에 대한 남자의 반응에 주목한다. 남자는 환불을 고수하고 있다.

어휘 exchange 교환하다 get a refund 환불받다 free gift 사은품

03 ②

① W: Dad, what's for dinner? I'm starving.
아빠, 저녁은 뭐예요? 저 무척 배고파요.

M: We're having beef steak.
우리 소고기 스테이크를 먹을 거야.

② W: Excuse me. This isn't what I ordered.
실례합니다. 이건 제가 주문한 게 아니에요.

M: Oh, I'm sorry. Let me check your order.
아, 죄송합니다. 제가 손님의 주문을 확인할게요.

③ W: What's today's special?
오늘의 특별요리는 뭔가요?

M: Vegetable spaghetti with mushroom soup.
버섯 수프를 곁들인 야채 스파게티입니다.

④ W: Have you finished cleaning the table, honey?
탁자 치우는 걸 끝냈나요, 여보?

M: Of course, I have. And I'm washing the dishes now.
물론 다 했죠. 그리고 지금은 설거지를 하고 있어요.

⑤ W: Do you know where the food court is in this building? 이 건물에 푸드코트가 어디 있는지 아세요?

M: I'm afraid not. It's my first time here.
죄송하지만 모릅니다. 전 이곳이 처음이에요.

어휘 starve 굶주리다 today's special 오늘의 특선 요리

04 ④

M: I'm looking for a chair for my daughter.
저는 딸에게 줄 의자를 찾고 있어요.

W: How about this one with four wheels? It's very popular among students. 바퀴 네 개가 달린 이것은 어떤가요? 학생들 사이에 매우 인기 있습니다.

M: Oh, my daughter is only five years old. I like this square one. 오, 제 딸은 겨우 다섯 살인걸요. 저는 이 네모난 것이 좋네요.

W: But it might be dangerous for five-year-olds because it doesn't have a back. How about this one? 하지만 이건 등받이가 없기 때문에 다섯 살 아이들에겐 위험할 수 있습니다. 이건 어떤가요?

M: Good. The crown shape looks unique. How much is it? 좋아요. 왕관 모양이 독특해 보이는군요. 얼마죠?

W: It's thirty dollars. 30달러입니다.

M: Okay, I'll take it. 좋아요, 그걸 살게요.

어휘 wheel 바퀴 square 정사각형 모양의 dangerous for ~에게 위험한 back 등받이 crown shape 왕관 모양 unique 독특한

05 ③

M: How may I help you, ma'am? 무엇을 도와드릴까요, 부인?

W: I've lost my six-year-old son. Please help me,

Officer. 제가 여섯 살짜리 아들을 잃어버렸어요. 제발 도와주세요, 경찰관님.

M: When and where did you last see him?
언제 어디에서 그를 마지막으로 봤나요?

W: At the street market, not far from this police station, about thirty minutes ago. 이 경찰서에서 멀지 않은 길거리 시장에서, 약 30분 전에요.

M: What's his name? 아이의 이름이 뭐죠?

W: Kevin Anderson. He's wearing a yellow T-shirt and jeans.
케빈 앤더슨이요. 그는 노란색 티셔츠와 청바지를 입고 있어요.

M: Okay, we'll start searching right away. Write down your phone number here, please. 알겠습니다, 저희가 곧장 수색하기 시작할게요. 당신의 전화번호를 여기에 적어주세요.

W: Thank you. Please find him.
감사합니다. 제발 아이를 찾아주세요.

해설 여자가 남자를 Officer라고 부른 것이 첫 번째 힌트이다.

어휘 search 수색하다 right away 즉각 shop manager 매장 관리자, 점장

06 ③

M: You look nice in your pants.
네 바지 입은 모습이 멋지다.

W: Thanks. But they're too tight. I shouldn't have bought them.
고마워. 그런데 바지가 너무 꽉 껴. 사지 말걸 그랬어.

M: Why don't you exchange them for a larger size?
더 큰 사이즈로 교환하는 게 어때?

W: I can't. I've already washed them once.
그럴 수가 없어. 내가 이걸 벌써 한 번 세탁했거든.

M: Oh, I see. But they'll stretch if you keep wearing them.
아, 그렇구나. 하지만 네가 계속 입다 보면 늘어날 거야.

W: I doubt it. I wish I hadn't bought them.
그럴 것 같지 않아. 내가 이걸 사지 않았더라면 좋겠어.

해설 여자는 'I shouldn't have bought them.' 'I wish I hadn't bought them.' 등으로 계속해서 후회하는 말을 했다.

어휘 tight 꽉 조이는 exchange 교환하다 stretch 늘어나다 keep -ing ~을 계속하다 doubt 의문을 갖다, 믿지 않다 satisfied 만족하는 regretful 후회하는

07 ④

① M: How can I get to the city library?
시립 도서관으로 어떻게 갈 수 있나요?

W: Cross the road and take bus number two six one.
길을 건너서 261번 버스를 타세요.

② M: I'd like to buy a ticket for the next show.
저는 다음 쇼의 티켓을 사려고 해요.

W: I'm sorry, sir. They're all sold out.
죄송합니다, 손님. 그건 모두 매진됐어요.

③ M: Why are some of the seats on this bus yellow?
이 버스의 몇 개 좌석은 왜 노란색이야?

W: Oh, they're for senior citizens.
아, 그건 어르신들을 위한 거야.

④ M: Are there any good Korean restaurants around here? 이 근처에 좋은 한식당 있나요?

W: Thank you, but I don't like fast food.
고맙지만 저는 패스트푸드를 좋아하지 않아요.

⑤ M: Let's go see a movie tonight. 오늘 밤에 영화 보러 가자.

W: I can't. I have to study for my math test.
안 돼. 나는 수학 시험 공부를 해야 해.

해설 ④에서 'Are there ~?'로 물었으므로 'Yes'나 'No'를 포함하여 답변해야 한다.

어휘 sold out 매진된   senior citizen 어르신, 고령자

08 ①

W: Hi, Steve. You look busy these days.
안녕, 스티브. 너 요즘 바빠 보여.

M: I'm preparing for a presentation in my Korean class. 나는 한국어 수업에 발표를 준비하고 있거든.

W: What are you going to talk about?
너는 무엇에 대해 말할 거야?

M: I've decided to talk about cultural differences.
문화적 차이에 대해 말하기로 결정했어.

W: Did you write a script? 너는 원고를 작성했니?

M: I did, but it took me so much time to write it in Korean.
했는데, 내가 한국어로 쓰는 데 시간이 아주 많이 걸렸어.

W: Do you need any help? 너는 도움이 필요하니?

M: Yes. Would you read the script and correct any errors? 응. 네가 내 원고를 읽고 실수를 고쳐주겠니?

W: Sure, no problem. 물론, 문제 없지.

어휘 prepare for a presentation 발표를 준비하다   cultural differences 문화적 차이   write a script 원고를 쓰다, 대본을 쓰다   correct 고치다, 바로잡다   error 실수, 오류

09 ⑤

M: I finally finished my science project, Ms. Brown.
제가 드디어 과학 프로젝트를 완성했어요, 브라운 선생님.

W: Great! I'm proud of you, Tom.
잘 했구나! 난 네가 자랑스럽다, 톰.

M: I couldn't have finished it without your encouragement.
선생님의 격려가 없었다면 제가 이걸 끝내지 못했을 거예요.

W: I know how hard you've been working on the project.
난 네가 이 프로젝트에 얼마나 열심히 임했는지 알고 있어.

M: I don't know how to thank you enough for your help.
선생님의 도움에 어떻게 충분히 감사 드려야 할지 모르겠어요.

해설 남자의 마지막 대사는 큰 고마움을 표할 때 쓰는 말이다.

어휘 be proud of ~을 자랑스러워 하다   encouragement 격려

10 ②

M: Excuse me. How much is that red shirt?
실례합니다. 저 빨간 셔츠는 얼마죠?

W: It's fifty dollars. 50달러입니다.

M: Hmm. It's too expensive for me.
음. 제겐 너무 비싸네요.

W: How about this blue one? It's only thirty dollars.
이 파란 셔츠는 어떤가요? 겨우 30달러예요.

M: I like the design. Do you have the same shirt in green as well?
디자인은 마음에 드네요. 같은 셔츠로 초록색도 있나요?

W: Yes. And if you buy two in this design, you get five dollars off of the total. 네. 그리고 이 디자인으로 두 장을 사면 합계에서 5달러를 깎아드려요.

M: Great! Then I'll take one green and one blue.
잘됐네요! 그럼 저는 초록색 한 장과 파란색 한 장을 살게요.

W: Okay. 알겠습니다.

해설 30달러짜리 셔츠를 두 장 구매하면 60달러, 거기에서 5달러 할인되므로 지불할 금액은 55달러이다.

어휘 get something off ~에서 빼다

11 ④

W: How may I help you? 무엇을 도와드릴까요?

M: My car is making a funny noise.
제 차가 이상한 소리를 내요.

W: Okay. Is it your first visit here?
그렇군요. 이곳에 처음 방문하셨나요?

M: Yes, it is. 네, 그렇습니다.

W: Then, would you please fill out this form?
그렇다면 이 양식을 작성해 주시겠어요?

M: Sure. How long will it take to have it fixed?
네. 차를 고치는 데 얼마나 걸릴까요?

W: Well, we have to take a look at it first.
글쎄요, 저희가 먼저 살펴봐야 합니다.

어휘 fill out the form 양식을 작성하다   fix 고치다   take a look at ~을 보다

12 ④

M: The Max Sports Center, which opened in June, two thousand two, is the first five-star fitness facility in our city. It is open twenty-four hours a day, seven days a week for your convenience. We offer a variety of programs free of charge. Popular fitness programs like yoga, aerobics, and Taekwondo are offered throughout the year. Come and enjoy yourself!

2002년 6월에 개관한 맥스 스포츠센터는 우리 도시의 첫 번째

5성급 체력 단련 시설입니다. 그곳은 여러분의 편의를 위해 일주일 내내 하루 24시간 개방됩니다. 저희는 다양한 프로그램을 무료로 제공합니다. 요가, 에어로빅, 태권도와 같은 인기 피트니스 프로그램이 1년 내내 제공됩니다. 와서 마음껏 즐기세요!

어휘 five-star 별 다섯 개의, 오성의, 최고의 fitness facility 피트니스 시설 24 hours, 7 days a week (휴일 없이) 항상 convenience 편의, 편리 free of charge 무료로 throughout the year 1년 내내

13 ③

M: Which seats do you think are the best?
어느 좌석이 가장 좋다고 생각해?

W: The seats in Section B, of course.
당연히 B구역 좌석이지.

M: But they're really expensive. How about Section A?
하지만 그곳은 아주 비싸. A구역은 어때?

W: You can see only one side of the stage from there.
거기에서는 무대의 한쪽 면만 볼 수 있어.

M: Right, and the seats on the second floor are too far from the stage. 맞아, 그리고 2층 좌석은 무대에서 너무 멀어.

W: I agree. We have only one option left.
나도 동의해. 우리에게 남은 선택은 한 곳뿐이야.

M: That's right. I'll book two tickets in that section.
맞아. 내가 그 구역의 티켓 두 장을 예매할게.

어휘 second floor 2층 option 선택할 수 있는 것, 선택권 leave 남아있다(leave-left-left) book 예약하다; 책

14 ⑤

W: This is stretched on a frame of wood or metal and designed to cover the opening of a window. It is used to keep insects from entering. It is most useful in areas where there're large populations of insects, especially mosquitoes. It also allows fresh air to flow into a house.

이것은 나무나 금속 테두리에 펼쳐져 있고 창문 앞면을 덮기 위해 만들어진 것입니다. 이것은 벌레가 들어오는 걸 막기 위해 사용됩니다. 이것은 벌레, 특히 모기가 아주 많이 살고 있는 지역에서 매우 유용합니다. 이것은 또한 신선한 공기가 집 안으로 흘러들어올 수 있게 합니다.

어휘 stretch 뻗다, 펴다 frame 테두리; 액자 be designed to ~하도록 제작되다 cover 덮다, 가리다 keep something from –ing 무언가 ~하는 것을 막다 large populations of 다수의 mosquito 모기 flow into ~로 흘러들다

15 ①

W: Mike, are you playing computer games again?
마이크, 너는 또 컴퓨터 게임을 하는 중이니?

M: Mom, I'm just posting pictures on my blog.
엄마, 저는 단지 블로그에 사진을 포스팅하고 있어요.

W: Did you finish all of your homework already?
네 숙제는 벌써 다 한 거니?

M: Actually, I still have a little bit left to do.
사실, 아직 할 일이 약간 있어요.

W: Then I think you should finish your homework first.
그렇다면 난 네가 숙제를 먼저 끝내야 한다고 생각해.

M: Okay, I will, Mom. 네, 그럴게요, 엄마.

해설 여자의 마지막 대사에 드러난 충고의 말을 남자가 'Okay, I will'로 받아들이는 말까지 확인한다.

어휘 post pictures 사진을 게시하다 a little bit 조금

16 ②

M: Jenny, the school club festival is on May twenty fourth. 제니, 학교 동아리 축제가 5월 24일에 있어.

W: Yeah, I know. We need to have a meeting sometime this week so we can get things ready. 응, 나도 알아. 우리는 이번 주 언젠가 회의를 열어서 일을 준비해야 해.

M: Sure. Why don't we meet on May fifteenth?
좋아. 5월 15일에 만나는 게 어때?

W: I don't think that's a good idea. We have two after-school classes on that day.
난 그게 좋은 생각 같지 않아. 우린 그날 방과후 수업이 두 개 있어.

M: Right. What about May sixteenth? It's Wednesday.
맞아. 5월 16일은 어때? 그건 수요일이야.

W: That's probably the best day because we don't have any after-school classes on that day. 그 날에는 우리에게 방과후 수업이 없으니 그게 아마 가장 좋은 날일 거야.

M: Okay. Let's meet on Wednesday. 그래. 수요일에 만나자.

어휘 probably 아마도, 대체로

17 ②

W: Chris usually comes home before five p.m. Today, Chris and his friends played a soccer game. His team won, and the game finished around seven p.m. Chris didn't tell his mother that he would be late today. His mother was waiting for him and getting worried. In this situation, what would his mother most likely say to Chris when he came home?

크리스는 주로 오후 5시 전에 집으로 온다. 오늘, 크리스와 그의 친구들은 축구 경기를 했다. 그의 팀은 이겼고 게임은 오후 7시쯤 끝났다. 크리스는 오늘 늦을 거라고 엄마에게 말하지 않았다. 크리스의 엄마는 그를 기다리면서 걱정하고 있었다. 이 상황에서 크리스가 집에 왔을 때 엄마가 크리스에게 뭐라고 말하겠는가?

Mother: My goodness! Where have you been?
맙소사! 너 어디에 있었니?

① Have you ever played soccer before?
너는 전에 축구를 해본 적이 있니?

② My goodness! Where have you been?
맙소사! 너 어디에 있었니?

③ Cheer up! You can beat them next time.

④ How many times did you win the game?
경기를 몇 번이나 이겼니?

⑤ I'm sorry to have kept you waiting for me.
네가 날 기다리게 해서 정말 미안하구나.

어휘 situation 상황 My goodness! (놀라서) 맙소사!
beat 이기다

18 ⑤

M: Linda, I can't open this website. I don't know what's wrong with it. 린다, 나는 이 웹사이트를 열 수가 없어. 뭐가 잘못된 건지 모르겠다.

W: Did you check the address? 너는 주소를 확인했어?

M: Yes. And the Internet cable is okay.
응. 그리고 인터넷 선도 괜찮아.

W: Hmm. Have you checked for viruses on your computer? 음. 네 컴퓨터에 바이러스를 확인해 봤니?

M: No, I haven't. I just tried turning it off and on again.
아니, 안 해봤어. 나는 그저 컴퓨터를 껐다가 켜보기만 했어.

W: Well, you should've checked for viruses first. Let me do that for you. 글쎄, 너는 바이러스를 먼저 확인해야 했어. 내가 네 대신 해 볼게.

M: Thanks. 고마워.

어휘 cable 케이블, 전선, 줄 virus (컴퓨터) 바이러스(복 viruses)

19 ③

W: You look so tired. What's the matter?
너 아주 피곤해 보여. 무슨 일이야?

M: I've been trying to be a morning person for weeks.
나는 몇 주 동안 아침형 인간이 되려고 노력 중이야.

W: Why did you decide to do that?
왜 그렇게 하기로 결정했어?

M: I read this book called *Early Bird*. And I've been following everything in it, but it doesn't seem to work for me.
'얼리 버드'라는 책을 내가 읽었거든. 그리고 거기에 있는 모든 걸 따라 하고 있는데 내게는 그게 효과가 있는 것 같지 않아.

W: Well, then I don't think you're a morning person after all. That's why you feel tired these days.
음, 그렇다면 너는 결국 아침형 인간이 아닌 것 같아. 그게 요즘 네가 피곤함을 느끼는 이유지.

M: Right. I'd rather go back to my own style.
맞아. 나만의 스타일로 돌아가는 게 좋겠다.

어휘 follow (충고, 지시 등을) 따르다, 따라 하다 seem to ~인 것 같다 work 효과가 있다

20 ①

M: Hi. I'd like to get a library card.
안녕하세요. 저는 도서관 카드를 받고 싶어요.

W: Do you live in this area? 당신은 이 지역에 살고 있나요?

M: Yes, right across from this library.
네, 이 도서관 바로 건너편에요.

W: Then you can get a Special Membership Card.
그렇다면 당신은 특별 회원 카드를 만들 수 있어요.

M: What benefits does it have? 그것은 어떤 혜택이 있죠?

W: You can borrow up to five books at a time.
당신은 책을 한 번에 다섯 권까지 빌릴 수 있어요.

M: Good. Is that all? 좋네요. 그게 전부인가요?

W: You can also check out our DVDs free of charge.
당신은 저희의 DVD를 무료로 대출할 수도 있어요.

M: Great! That sounds like the card that I want.
좋아요! 제가 원하는 카드인 것 같네요.

① Great! That sounds like the card that I want.
좋아요! 제가 원하는 카드인 것 같네요.

② Okay. I'll bring my library card right away.
알겠어요. 제 도서관 카드를 당장 가져올게요.

③ Really? Have you already bought the DVDs?
정말이에요? 당신은 이미 DVD를 구매했나요?

④ Of course. You'll probably like this library.
물론이죠. 당신은 아마 이 도서관을 좋아할 거예요.

⑤ Yes. I want to return these books.
네. 저는 이 책들을 반납하고 싶어요.

어휘 area 지역 benefit 혜택 up to something (특정한 수, 시점)까지 at a time 한 번에 free of charge 무료로

강남인강 강의 교재

쎄듀 빠르게 중학 영어 듣기 모의고사 20회 시리즈

전국 16개 시·도 교육청 공동 주관 영어듣기평가 완벽 분석
실전 시험 난이도와 실전 시험보다 높은 난이도 모두 제공
영어권 원어민과 스크립트 공동 개발
개정 교과서 의사소통 기능 반영

독해가 안 된다고
**독해 문제집만 풀면
될까요?**

'독해가 된다' 시리즈로
**근본적인 원인을
해결하세요!**

독해가 됩니다!

1 고등 독해가 읽히는 기본 문법사항 정리

2 문법 → 구문 → 독해로 단계별 학습

3 수능형 & 내신형을 아우르는 독해 유형

1 수능 독해가 풀리는 필수 구문 정리

2 구문이해 → 문장적용 → 독해적용으로
　　단계별 학습

3 최신 수능 & 모의고사에서 출제된
　　구문으로 구성

쎄듀북닷컴(www.cedubook.com)에서 부가 자료를 무료로 다운로드할 수 있습니다.

쎄듀

쎄듀 초·중등 커리큘럼

	예비초	초1	초2	초3	초4	초5	초6
구문		천일문 365 일력 |초1-3| 교육부 지정 초등 필수 영어 문장		초등코치 천일문 SENTENCE 1001개 통문장 암기로 완성하는 초등 영어의 기초		
문법					초등코치 천일문 GRAMMAR 1001개 예문으로 배우는 초등 영문법		
			왓츠 Grammar		Start (초등 기초 영문법) / Plus (초등 영문법 마무리)		
독해				왓츠 리딩 70 / 80 / 90 / 100 A / B		쉽고 재미있게 완성되는 영어 독해력	
어휘				초등코치 천일문 VOCA&STORY 1001개의 초등 필수 어휘와 짧은 스토리			
		패턴으로 말하는 초등 필수 영단어 1 / 2		문장 패턴으로 완성하는 초등 필수 영단어			
ELT	Oh! My PHONICS 1 / 2 / 3 / 4		유·초등학생을 위한 첫 영어 파닉스				
		Oh! My SPEAKING 1 / 2 / 3 / 4 / 5 / 6		핵심 문장 패턴으로 더욱 쉬운 영어 말하기			
		Oh! My GRAMMAR 1 / 2 / 3		쓰기로 완성하는 첫 초등 영문법			

	예비중	중1	중2	중3
구문	천일문 STARTER 1 / 2			중등 필수 구문 & 문법 총정리
문법	개정 천일문 중등 GRAMMAR LEVEL 1 / 2 / 3			예문 중심 문법 기본서
	GRAMMAR Q Starter 1, 2 / Intermediate 1, 2 / Advanced 1, 2			학기별 문법 기본서
	잘 풀리는 영문법 1 / 2 / 3			문제 중심 문법 적용서
	GRAMMAR PIC 1 / 2 / 3 / 4			이해가 쉬운 도식화된 문법서
			1센치 영문법	1권으로 핵심 문법 정리
문법+어법			첫단추 BASIC 문법·어법편 1 / 2	문법·어법의 기초
문법+쓰기	EGU 영단어&품사 / 문장 형식 / 동사 써먹기 / 문법 써먹기 / 구문 써먹기			서술형 기초 세우기와 문법 다지기
				올씀 1 기본 문장 PATTERN 내신 서술형 기본 문장 학습
쓰기	개정 천일문 중등 WRITING LEVEL 1 / 2 / 3 *거침없이 Writing 개정			중등 교과서 내신 기출 서술형
	중학 영어 쓰작 1 / 2 / 3			중등 교과서 패턴 드릴 서술형
어휘	천일문 VOCA 중등 스타트 / 필수 / 마스터			2800개 중등 3개년 필수 어휘
	어휘끝 중학 필수편	중학 필수어휘 1000개	어휘끝 중학 마스터편	고난도 중학어휘 +고등기초 어휘 1000개
독해	ReadingGraphy LEVEL 1 / 2 / 3 / 4			중등 필수 구문까지 잡는 흥미로운 소재 독해
	Reading Relay Starter 1, 2 / Challenger 1, 2 / Master 1, 2			타교과 연계 배경 지식 독해
	READING Q Starter 1, 2 / Intermediate 1, 2 / Advanced 1, 2			예측/추론/요약 사고력 독해
독해전략			리딩 플랫폼 1 / 2 / 3	논픽션 지문 독해
독해유형			Reading 16 LEVEL 1 / 2 / 3	수능 유형 맛보기 + 내신 대비
			첫단추 BASIC 독해편 1 / 2	수능 유형 독해 입문
듣기	Listening Q 유형편 / 1 / 2 / 3			유형별 듣기 전략 및 실전 대비
		쎄듀 빠르게 중학영어듣기 모의고사 1 / 2 / 3		교육청 듣기평가 대비